Designing Interactive Systems

People, Activities, Contexts, Technologies

PEARSON
Education

We work with leading authors to develop the strongest educational materials in computing, bringing cutting-edge thinking and best learning practice to a global market.

Under a range of well-known imprints, including Addison-Wesley, we craft high-quality print and electronic publications which help readers to understand and apply their content, whether studying or at work.

To find out more about the complete range of our publishing, please visit us on the World Wide Web at: www.pearsoned.co.uk

Visit the *Designing Interactive Systems* Companion Website at **www.booksites.net/benyon** to find valuable **student** learning material including:

- Chapter aims identifying key learning points
- Exercise material for each chapter
- Links to relevant sites on the Web

access

Designing Interactive Systems

People, Activities, Contexts, Technologies

**David Benyon, Phil Turner
and Susan Turner**

ADDISON-WESLEY

An imprint of **Pearson Education**

Harlow, England • London • New York • Boston • San Francisco • Toronto
Sydney • Tokyo • Singapore • Hong Kong • Seoul • Taipei • New Delhi
Cape Town • Madrid • Mexico City • Amsterdam • Munich • Paris • Milan

Pearson Education Limited
Edinburgh Gate
Harlow
Essex CM20 2JE
England

and Associated Companies throughout the world

Visit us on the World Wide Web at:
www.pearsoned.co.uk

First published 2005

ISBN 0 321 11629 1

British Library Cataloguing-in-Publication Data
A catalogue record for this book is available from the British Library

Library of Congress Cataloging-in-Publication Data
A catalog record for this book is available from the Library of Congress

10 9 8 7 6 5 4 3 2 1
09 08 07 06 05

Typeset in 9.25pt Stone Serif by 30
Printed and bound by Mateu Cromo, Spain

The publisher's policy is to use paper manufactured from sustainable forests.

Brief contents

Contents

Part II

People and Technologies   96

Part III

Activities and Contexts of Interactive Systems Design

190

Part IV

Psychological Foundations for Interactive Systems Design   350

Part V

Techniques for Interactive Systems Design and Evaluation 448

Part VI

Information Spaces   564

Part VII

Computer-supported Cooperative Working   674

Companion Website resources

Visit the Companion Website at **www.booksites.net/benyon**

For students

- Chapter aims identifying key learning points
- Exercise material for each chapter
- Links to relevant sites on the Web

For lecturers

- Teaching ideas for each chapter
- Solutions to exercises
- Additional links to relevant sites on the Web
- PowerPoint slides that can be downloaded and used as OHTs

Preface

Designing Interactive Systems is aimed squarely at the next generation of interactive system designers. This book presents a coherent introduction to the practical issue of creating interactive systems and products from a human-centred perspective. It develops the principles and methods of human–computer interaction (HCI) to deal with the demands of twenty-first century computing. Interactive systems design is concerned with the design of websites, desktop applications, 'information appliances', ubiquitous computing systems and systems to support cooperation between people. This book aims to be the core text for university courses in HCI and interactive systems design from introductory to masters levels and to meet the needs of usability professionals working in industry.

Human–computer interaction established itself as an important area of study in the early 1980s and by the early 1990s there was a coherent syllabus and several textbooks. In the early 1990s the 'world wide' Web appeared, opening up website design as a new area. Information architecture and information design emerged as important areas of study and new issues of usability became important in the open and untamed world of the Web. By the late 1990s mobile phones had become a fashion statement for many people; style was as important as function. With colour displays and better screens, mobile phones became increasingly programmable. Interaction designers were needed along with software engineers to create exciting experiences. Personal digital assistants (PDAs – sometimes called 'palmtop' computers), tablet computers and other information appliances made further new demands on software developers. User interfaces became tangible, graspable and immediate and software systems had to be engaging as well as functional. Digital technologies, wireless communications and new sensing devices provided new media for a new generation of artist–designers.

All this has brought us to where we are today: a dynamic mix of ideas, approaches and technologies being used by lots of people doing very different things in different contexts. *Designing Interactive Systems* aims to focus this emerging discipline by bringing together the best practice and experience from

HCI and interaction design (ID). We present a human-centred approach to inter-action design. The strength and tradition of HCI has been in its human-centredness and usability concerns. HCI specialists would critique designs from this perspective, pointing out where people would have problems in using a particular design. HCI evolved methods, guidelines, principles and standards to ensure that systems were easy to use and easy to learn. In the 1980s computers were primarily still in the hands of software engineers. A generation later they are pervasive, ubiquitous and in the hands of everyone.

Practitioners of HCI, website designers, usability experts, user experience designers, software engineers – indeed all those concerned with the design of interactive systems in all their forms – will find much that they recognize in this book. It is concerned with how to design engaging interactions between people and technologies to support the activities that people want to do and the contexts in which they act.

Organization of the book

In compiling the text we have had many iterations around different organizational structures, trying to satisfy the needs of different readers (see below). We finally settled on a seven-part structure because it offered the flexibility we felt was required in this rapidly changing discipline.

Part I provides an essential guide to the issues of designing interactive systems – the main components of the subject, key features of the design process and how these are applied to different types of system. The unifying idea is encapsulated by the acronym PACT; designers should strive to achieve a harmony between the needs of different people who undertake activities in contexts using technologies. It is the very large amount of variation in these components that makes designing interactive systems such a fascinating challenge.

Part II provides an approachable treatment of people and technologies. People are social beings who think, reason, have feelings and act with purpose. In Part II these different characteristics of people are explored through various theories about how these processes come about and how they are undertaken. The person as a cognitive being using technology alone is the subject of the first two chapters in this part. This is followed by a chapter that explores why this view does not tell the whole story and different ways of considering interaction.

Part III provides methods and techniques for doing interactive systems design. A key concept throughout is the idea of 'scenarios'. Scenarios are stories about interactions. They provide an effective representation for reflecting on a design throughout its development. Part III also considers techniques for understanding the requirements of interactive systems, envisioning, prototyping and evaluating design ideas. A more formal approach to conceptual and physical design is included along with a detailed real-world case study of design in action.

Part IV provides a deep treatment of the psychological foundations of human–computer interaction. It deals with memory, attention, hearing, haptics (touch) and emotion and how these affect interactive systems design. This is fundamental knowledge that the professional should seek to acquire and is material aimed at the specialist student.

Part V does three things. It presents a slimmed-down version of a packaged and prescriptive method (Contextual Design) that has been widely used in industry, primarily for the design of interactive information systems to support commercial activities. Secondly it describes a key set of task analysis methods – again with the focus on a practical exposition of the techniques – that are core to human–computer interaction. Finally it provides further material on evaluation, focusing on techniques which supplement the basic set in Part III and special evaluation contexts. Pitched at much the same level as the material in Part III, it allows for designers to specialize in particular areas and to compose their own methods tuned to meet their own situations.

Part VI takes an alternative perspective on interactive systems design which may be more appropriate for the design of information spaces such as websites and situations in which many interconnected devices are distributed through an environment. These are the sorts of situations that designers are increasingly engaged with, supplementing their work in the design of more traditional interactive information systems, and the means which help us to do this successfully.

Part VII places the emphasis on connecting people and supporting cooperative work through technologies.

Whilst this organization does have a clear logic to it, we do not expect many people will start at the beginning and read the book from cover to cover. Accordingly we have provided a number of routes through the text for different people with different needs (see below). The book also contains a comprehensive index so that people can find their own ways in to topics of interest. It is an ambitious task to write a complete guide to the design of interactive systems when the area is still evolving. However, we have made an effort to mention all the currently important issues and the further reading at the end of each chapter provides directions on where to go next for more detailed coverage of specific issues.

The pedagogic style adopted by the text ensures that it meets the needs of students and teachers alike. Boxes are used to highlight significant examples of the subject under discussion and to point readers to interesting diversions. Forward and backward references help to show how topics are linked. Case studies that the authors have been involved with have been included to illustrate the issues and to provide a rich source of examples for students and teachers.

Readership

There is a wide range of people involved in the design and development of interactive systems in the twenty-first century. *Software engineers* are developing new applications for their organizations. They redesign systems to take advantage of developments in technologies and add on extra features to legacy systems. Software engineers working for software companies develop new generic software products or new releases of existing systems. *Systems analysts and designers* work with clients, end-users and other stakeholders to develop solutions to business problems. *Web designers* are increasingly in demand to organize and present content and new functionality for websites. People are developing applications for new media such as interactive television, 'third generation' (3G) mobile phones, personal digital assistants and other information appliances. *Product designers* are increasingly finding themselves working with interactive features in their products. Many other people with job titles such as *User Experience Designers*, *Information Architects* and *Interaction Designers* are involved in this rapidly changing business. All these people need education and training, and require ready access to proven methods and techniques of design and evaluation and to the key theoretical concepts.

Just as the range of people involved in the development and deployment of interactive systems is increasing, so is the range of activities. The basic components of design – establishing requirements and developing systems – are common across all these types of interactive products and systems, but detailed activities vary. For example, the analyst/designer working in an office environment would be likely to use traditional requirements generation techniques such as interviewing, whereas the developer of a new PDA application might use focus groups and 'future workshops'. A website designer would make use of navigation maps, whereas an application developer might produce a prototype in a programming language such as Visual Basic to show to potential users. An evaluation of a mobile phone might focus on aesthetics, style and 'teenage appeal', whereas an evaluation of a shared diary system in a large bank might concentrate on efficiency and time-saving and acceptance issues.

Contexts of interaction are increasingly diverse. Large organizations such as hospitals are introducing PDAs for consultants and nurses. A university has introduced a purpose-built shared intranet system to control development of course materials. Oil-rigs have three-dimensional 'virtual reality' training programs and electricity companies are using text messaging to record meter readings. A start-up software company wants to introduce quality and usability control through its software development process and a new media company is developing a Web-based service for its customers. Household environments, on-line communities, mobile computing, offices and remote 'virtual organizations' are just a few of the contexts for twenty-first century human–computer interaction design. Most importantly, we are seeing technologies bringing people into contact with people. The design of on-line communities and other systems to support the social aspects of life is a move away from the retrieval of information that characterized older systems.

Finally, technologies are changing. Software development is primarily object-oriented now with the Unified Modelling Language (UML) dominant, but languages such as C and C++ are still important. Websites often include Java programming and have to interface with databases. PDAs run under new operating systems and new network protocols are needed for voice applications through mobile phones and remote control of other devices such as heating controllers. Geographical positioning systems and complete in-car navigational systems have to be seen alongside new concepts in digital entertainment through interactive television and home information centres. Mobile phones converge with PDAs that converge with digital cameras and MP3 music systems.

So, how do educators and practitioners cross these diverse areas and combinations of people, activities, contexts and technologies? We need to train software engineers to know about and apply principles of usability, Web designers to produce creative designs that are accessible to all, and systems analysts to be sympathetic to the situated nature of work. We need product developers who design for the elderly and infirm, engineers who understand people, their capacities and limitations, and creative people who understand the constraints of software engineering. *Designing Interactive Systems* aims to meet the educational and practical needs of this diverse group by providing the variety of perspectives that is necessary.

How to use this book

Human–computer interaction and the design of interactive systems take place in a large variety of contexts, by individuals working alone or in design teams of various sizes. The systems or products to be produced vary enormously in size and complexity and utilize a range of technologies. There is no 'one size fits all' approach that can deal with this variety. In this book we provide a variety of perspectives to match the variety inherent in the design of interactive systems. A professional interactive system designer will need to achieve a competence in all the methods and techniques described in this book and will need to understand all the issues and theories that are raised. To achieve this level of competence would take three years of study for an undergraduate student. But not everyone needs to achieve this level, so we have organized the material to make different types of understanding available.

The book can be used in part or in total on a wide variety of courses, from specialist degrees in Human–Computer Interaction to a minor part of a degree in Software Engineering to specialist modules on Design or Engineering degrees, Psychology, Communication and Media degrees or other programmes where the design of interactive systems and products is important. To explain how the material might be used, we will refer to a first- or second-year undergraduate course of study as 'level 2' material, third-year as 'level 3' and fourth or masters as 'level 4'.

Part I would form the basis of a level 2 course and indeed this is what we teach to our second-year computing students. They study Flash as a prototyping language and we include a number of 'motivational' lectures on current topics in addition to delivering Part I as a series of six two-hour lectures:

1. Overview of designing interactive systems   Chapter 1
2. PACT analysis   Sections 2.1–2.5
3. The design process   Sections 2.6–2.8

4. Evaluation; case study   Chapter 4

5. Access, usability, engagement   Sections 3.1–3.4

6. Principles and contexts   Sections 3.5–3.9

Part I material is also suitable for courses on interaction design and as introductory material to a wide variety of level 3 modules. For example, with the materials from Part III it would form a user-centred design module; with more material on psychology from Part II it would make a level 3 module on human–computer interaction. Part III can be used as a course on scenario-based design. The material in Part V is pitched at this same level and so allows lecturers to mix and match techniques suitable for different contexts and for different degree programmes. We run another module based on Chapters 18 and 19, Contextual Inquiry and Contextual Design. Part II is also suitable at this level where the theoretical background for human–computer interaction is required. Part II provides a wealth of examples that students can be pointed to that illustrate design issues or to see where design principles have come from. Material in Parts IV, VI and VII is more advanced and can be used selectively to supplement material from the other parts or as the basis of one or more level 4 modules. We teach one level 4 module on computer supported cooperative work based on Part VII and another on designing information spaces based on Part VI.

Our 'rule of thumb' for a typical course or module unit is 8–10 hours of student time per week. This would be composed as follows and constitutes one 'credit'. Over the period of a year, full-time students study eight 15-credit modules or six 20-credit modules per week.

Activity	Hours
Primary exposition of material (e.g. lecture)	1-2
Secondary presentation (e.g. seminar)	1
Unmoderated, informal student discussions	1
Practical exercises and activities	2
Research and further reading	2
Revision and assessment	1-2

The following are examples of modules and courses that illustrate how the material in this book could be used. These are just a few of the many variations that are possible.

Course/module	Material, chapter numbers
Level 2 Introduction to HCI (15 credits).	
A basic-level course intended to equip computing students with an appreciation of HCI issues and a set of practical skills.	Chapters 1–4 plus basic introduction to prototyping using Flash.
Level 3 Interaction Design (15 credits).	
A more advanced module aimed at developing the issues concerned with designing useful and engaging interactions. Based around the development of paper prototypes, it encourages students to focus on design issues rather than programming issues.	Quickly revise material in Chapters 1–4, but base the module around Chapters 8–11, supplemented with chapters from Part II according to the interest of the lecturer and students. The focus here is on scenarios and developing the skills of envisionment, prototyping and the evaluation of ideas. A critical study of Chapter 14 case study is useful.
Level 3 User-Centred Design (15 credits).	
A module focusing on industrial strength, human-centred design process. Fits nicely alongside Interaction Design.	This can be based on Chapters 18 and 19 as the design method. The conceptual and physical design described in Chapter 13 would supplement this, along with task analysis methods (Chapter 20) and further evaluations (Chapters 21 and 22).
Level 4 Future and Emerging Issues in HCI (15 credits).	
This advanced course deals with more philosophical issues of website and 'information space' design.	Review of usability and cognitive foundations (Chapters 3 and 5); discuss conceptual and physical design (Chapter 13). Then a detailed discussion of Part VI.
Level 4 Advanced Interactive Systems Design (15 credits).	A masters level module that looks at concepts of wearable and tangible computing (Chapter 16), information spaces (Part VI) and CSCW (Part VII).
Level 4 Designing for Cooperation (15 credits).	Based on Part VII.
Level 2 Web Design (15 credits).	Part I material supplemented with Part II materials on individual cognition and selected techniques from Part VI on information architecture and web design methods. Evaluation (Chapter 12) and the use of heuristics (Chapter 3).
Level 3 or 4 Module on Psychological Foundations of Human–Computer Interaction (15 credits).	In-depth coverage of Part II and Part IV materials. Examples from Part VII.

Other resources

In this text we highlight other important resources where appropriate. Here we point to a few general resources. The Usability Professional Association is a good place for interested people to look for examples of good practice and links to other resources: http://www.upassoc.org. The American Institute of Graphic Arts (AIGA, http://www.aiga.com) is increasingly involved with interaction and information design. The Association of Computing Machinery (ACM, http://acm.org) has an active special interest group in computer–human interaction (SIGCHI) and the British Computer Society also has an excellent group for both academics and professionals (http://www.bcs-hci.org.uk). Both of these have extensive resource libraries and organize many relevant conferences. Other countries have their own organizations and groups. The interaction community is less well served with professional bodies, but there are several key design centres, e.g. Ivrea in Italy (http://www.interaction-ivrea.it/en/index.asp) and centres in the US such as the MIT Media Lab (http://www.media.mit.edu). There are many good websites devoted to aspects of usability, human–computer interaction and interaction design that can be found by following links from the sources above. For web design, useit.com and uie.com are both recommended. Finally, there are two international standards that deal with usability. They are ISO 9241-11 and 13407. The European resource centre, 'usability net', has details (http://www.usabilitynet.org). Finally an important resource is the website that accompanies this book. It can be found at www.booksites.net/benyon.

The authors

Between them the authors of this book have over fifty years' experience of designing and developing interactive systems. These cover traditional business applications to state-of-the-art cooperative systems, virtual reality systems and new devices for the home. They came together in 1999 when developing the undergraduate degree curriculum in Human–Computer Systems at Napier University, Edinburgh. It soon became clear that the single-thread, HCI syllabus was no longer suitable for the type of students and range of jobs that were encapsulated under the title of interaction designer, or usability professional. Accordingly the project that has resulted in this book was begun.

David Benyon is Professor of Human–Computer Systems at Napier University. He began his career as a systems analyst working for a number of 'software houses' and industrial companies. After several years he moved into academia where he developed a more formal understanding of issues of human–computer interaction. The first US conference on computer–human interaction took place in the same year that David began an MSc in Computing and Psychology at Warwick University and in 1984 he published his first paper on the subject. Since then he has continued to publish and now has over 100 published papers and 12 books. He obtained his PhD in Intelligent User Interfaces in 1994. He continues to take an active part in the HCI and ID communities, acting as chair for *ACM Designing Interactive Systems, DIS 2004* conference and programme chair for the British HCI group's conference in 2005.

Phil Turner is a Senior Lecturer in Computing at Napier University (and does not like writing about himself).

Susan Turner has worked in user-centred design and related areas since 1985 in a variety of commercial and academic environments. Some of these were more fun than others, but all contributed to her experience of putting human–centred interaction design into practice. Her doctorate concerned the study of designers and their use of cooperative technologies. She is currently a lecturer in the School of Computing at Napier University. The main strand of Susan's current research work explores concepts of 'sense of place' in relation to virtual environments.

Authorship

This book is a joint production, and we have each reviewed, edited, re-edited and argued over the contents and structure of each other's contributions. Nonetheless, the primary responsibility at part and chapter level reflects our individual interests and expertise.

The overview of the field in Part I was contributed by David Benyon, culminating in the case study from the FLEX project which forms Chapter 4. Phil Turner authored Part II, much of which reflects his background in psychology. Any scepticism which may have crept in here and in Part IV about the role of traditional cognitive psychology is entirely intentional.

David Benyon and Susan Turner shared the authorship of Part III. The accounts of scenario-based design, envisionment, conceptual and physical design and the extended FLEX case study were largely David's responsibility, while Susan contributed much of the material on requirements and evaluation, together with the DISCOVER case study which is introduced here and reappears throughout the book.

Most of the extended treatment in Part IV of the psychological bases for interactive systems design is again Phil's, while Susan was primarily responsible for the discussion of emotion and affect. All three authors contributed to the further methods in Part V. Phil and Susan co-authored the light(er) weight treatment of Contextual Design. In their tireless pursuit of material, even on weekends away, they acknowledge the Swan Hotel for inspiring the examples. David wrote the task analysis chapter, and Susan those on evaluation.

Part VI was written by David and draws on his current research interests in social navigation and information spaces. Finally, Part VII was co-authored by Phil and Susan. The material is informed by experience of a series of CSCW-related research projects.

Acknowledgements

We have been developing this text for over three years and in that time many friends and colleagues have helped with ideas, comments and evaluations of materials. Draft materials have been used with students and we would like to acknowledge their help in producing the finished text. Methods and techniques have been developed and used on a variety of research and development projects and we would like to thank all the students and researchers who helped in this respect. In particular all the people who worked on the European FLEX project helped to produce the case study in Chapters 4 and 13 and many of the examples used in Part II. These included Tom Cunningham, Lara Russell, Lynne Baillie, Jon Sykes, Stephan Crisp and Peter Barclay. Our other major case study, DISCOVER, was also a European project and we gratefully acknowledge the contribution of our colleagues, particularly friends at STATOIL, the Warsash Maritime Centre and the Danish Maritime Institute. Other past and present students who have contributed to the ideas and examples in this book include Bettina Wilmes, Jesmond Worthington, Shaleph O'Neil, Liisa Dawson, Ross Philip, Jamie Sands, Manual Imaz, Oli Mival, Martin Graham, Mike Jackson, Rod McCall, Martin Clark, Sabine Gordzielik, Philip Hunt and David Tucker.

We would like to thank all our colleagues at Napier and those who have moved on. In particular Catriona Macaulay was involved in many of the early discussions and contributed much through her innovative teaching and curriculum development. Michael Smyth, Tom McEwan, Sandra Cairncross, Alison Crerar, Alison Varey, Richard Hetherington, Ian Smith, Iain McGregor, Malcolm Rutter, Shaun Lawson, and Gregory Leplatre have all contributed through discussions, criticisms and chance remarks. The contribution of other members of the School of Computing is also acknowledged.

David Benyon
Phil Turner
Susan Turner

Napier University, Edinburgh

Publisher's acknowledgements

We are grateful to the following for permission to reproduce copyright material:

Box 1-1 Table adapted from *Things That Make Us Smart: Defending human attributes in the age of the machine*, copyright © 1994 by Donald Norman, reprinted by permission of Perseus Books PLC, a member of Perseus Books, L.L.C. (Norman, D. 1994); Figure 1-3 courtesy of Rebecca Allen; Figure 1-4 courtesy of Sony Electronics Inc.; Figures 1-5 and 2-2 (left) PA Photos; Figures 1-6 (top left), 7-9 and 17-10 Science Photo Library; Figure 1-6 (top right) courtesy of Horstmann Controls Ltd.; Figures 1-6 (bottom left), 2-2 (middle), 2-3, 2-4, 3-5, 5-24, 25-5 and 27-1 Dorling Kindersley; Figures 1-6 (bottom right) and 7-2 courtesy of Hewlett-Packard Ltd.; Figure 1-8 Design and Concept Development: IDEO; Figure 2-2 (right) Corbis; Figure 2-6 redrawn from The rich picture: a tool for reasoning about work context in *Interactions*, 5(2), © 1998 ACM, Inc., reprinted by permission (Monk, A. and Howard, S. 1998); Figure 3-1 redrawn from Individual differences and inclusive design in *User Interfaces for All: Concepts, Methods and Tools* edited by C. Stephanidis, published and reprinted by permission of Lawrence Erlbaum Associates, Inc. (Benyon, D. R., Crerar, A. and Wilkinson, S. 2001); Figure 3-4 redrawn from The gulfs of execution and evaluation in *User-Centered System Design: New Perspectives on Human-Computer Interaction*, published and reprinted by permission of Lawrence Erlbaum Associates, Inc. (Norman, D. A. and Draper, S. eds 1986); Figure 3-6 redrawn from *The Invisible Computer: Why Good Products Can Fail*, ©1998 Donald A. Norman, published and reprinted by permission of The MIT Press (Norman, D. A. 1999); Figure 3.7 game shots © Cyan Worlds, Inc. Used by permission; Figure 3-8 screen shot frame reprinted by permission from Microsoft Corporation; Figure 3-9 (top left) screen shot reprinted by permission of Pearson Education Ltd.; Figure 3-9 (bottom left) screen shot reprinted by permission of Lands' End Direct Merchants UK Ltd., www.landsend.co.uk; Figures 3-9 (bottom right) and 25-10 screen shots reprinted by permission of Google Inc., Google ™ is a trademark of Google Inc.; Figure 3-10 screen shot Copyright © European Communities, 2004. Neither the Commission of the European Communities, nor any person acting on its behalf, is responsible for the use, which might be made of the attached information. The attached information is drawn from the Community R&D Information Service (CORDIS). The CORDIS services are carried on the CORDIS Host in Luxembourg – http://www.cordis.lu. Access to CORDIS is currently available free-of-charge; Table 5-1 after *Graphic Design for Electronic Documents and User Interfaces*, © 1992 ACM, Inc., reprinted by permission (Marcus, A. 1992); Box 5-3 Figure redrawn from On the perception of incongruity: a paradigm in *Journal of Personality*, 18, reprinted by permission of Blackwell Publishing Ltd. (Bruner, J. and Postman, L. 1949); Figures 5-4, 5-5, 5-15, 5-17, 5-18, 5-19, 5-31, 5-33, 6-1, 6-3, 6-5, 6-7, 6-10, 6-12, 6-13, 6-15, 6-19, 6-26, 15-2, 15-3, 15-5, 15-9, 15-11, 15-15, 15-19, 15-25, 25-3, 28-9, 29-1, 29-2, 29-4, 30-1, 30-10, 30-11 and 30-12 reprinted by permission from Microsoft Corporation; Figure 5-30 redrawn from *Psychology: The Science of Mind and Behaviour*, © 2001 Richard Gross, published and reproduced by permission of Hodder Arnold (Gross, R. 2001); Figures 6-14, 17-9, 23-8 screen shots reprinted by permission of Microsoft Corporation; Figure 6-17 screen shot reprinted by permission of RealNetworks, Inc.; Figure 6-18 screen shot reprinted by permission of Blackwell Publishing Ltd.; Figure 6-20 courtesy of ComputerWare; Figure 6-22 © 2004 Microsoft Corporation. All rights reserved. Printed with permission from Microsoft Corporation. Microsoft and IntelliMouse are either registered trademarks or trademarks of Microsoft Corporation in the United States and/or other countries; Figure 6-23 printed by permission of Microsoft Corporation. Microsoft and SideWinder are either registered trademarks or trademarks of Microsoft Corporation in the United States and/or other countries; Figure 6-30 image courtesy: www.5DT.com; Figure 7-1 © 2004 Microsoft Corporation. All rights reserved. Printed with permission from Microsoft Corporation; Table 7-1 from Designing a non-verbal language for expressive avatars in *Proceedings of CVE '00 Conference*, © 2000 ACM, Inc., reprinted by permission (Salem, B. and Earle, N. 2000); Figure 7-4 screen shot © copyright HSBC Bank plc. All rights reserved; Figure 8-1 redrawn from *Making Use: Scenario-based Design of Human-Computer Interactions*, © 2000 Massachusetts Institute of Technology, published and reprinted by permission of The MIT Press (Carroll, J. M. 2000); Figure 9-3 from Cultural Probes in *Interactions*, 6(1), © 1999 ACM, Inc., reprinted by permission (Gaver, W. W. et al. 1999); Table 10-1 from Introduction to the MIT Press edition in M. McLuhan *Understanding Media: The Extensions of Man*, *New Edition*, © 1964, 1994 Corrine McLuhan. Introduction © 1994 Massachusetts Institute of Technology, published and reprinted by permission of The MIT Press (Lapham, L. H. 1994); Figure 12-1 image provided with kind permission of Sony Ericsson; Table 12-1 the terms and definitions taken from ISO 9241-11:1998 Ergonomic requirements for office work with visual display terminals (VDTs), extract of Table B.2, are reproduced with the permission of the International Organization for Standardization, ISO. This standard can be obtained from any ISO member and from the Web site of the ISO Central Secretariat at the following address: www.iso.org. Copyright remains with ISO; Figure 15-1 reprinted from *The Psychology of Learning and Motivation*, Vol. 2 by K. W. Spence and J. T. Spence (eds), Atkinson, R. C. and Shiffrin, R. M., Human memory: a proposed system and its control processes, Copyright 1968, with permission from Elsevier; Table 15-2 from *Engineering Psychology and Human Performance*, *3rd Edition*, reprinted by permission of Pearson Education, Inc. (Wickens, C. D. and Hollands, J. G. 2000); Figure 15-12 screen shot reprinted by permission of Xerox Ltd.; Figure 15-22 screen shot reprinted by permission of Lastminute.com; Figure 15-24 redrawn from Cognitive underspecification: its variety and consequences in *Experimental Slips and Human Error: Exploring the Architecture of Volition* edited by B. J. Baars, pub Plenum Press, reprinted by permission of Kluwer Academic/Plenum Publishers (Reason, J. 1992); Figure 15-26 screen shot courtesy of John Kerridge; Figure 16-4 redrawn from Perceptual user interfaces: haptic interfaces in *Communications of the ACM*, 43(3), © 2000 ACM, Inc., reprinted by permission (Tan, H. Z. 2000); Figure 16-5 courtesy of Sphere Research Corporation; Figure 16-9 redrawn from Bricks: laying the foundations for graspable user interfaces in *Proceedings of CHI '95 Conference*, © 1995 ACM, Inc., reprinted by permission (Fitzmaurice, G. W. *et al.* 1995); Figure 16-10 from Illuminating Clay: a 3-D tangible interface for landscape analysis in *Proceedings of CHI '02 Conference*, © 2002 ACM, Inc., reprinted by permission (Piper, B. *et al.* 2002); Figures 16-11 and 16-12 from The Actuated Workbench: Computer-controlled actuation in tabletop tangible interfaces in *Proceedings of UIST '02,* © 2002 ACM, Inc., reprinted by permission (Pangaro, G. et al. 2002); Figure 16-13 redrawn from The Actuated Workbench: Computer-controlled actuation in tabletop tangible interfaces in *Proceedings of UIST '02,* © 2002 ACM, Inc., reprinted by permission (Pangaro, G. *et al.* 2002); Figure 16-14 courtesy of Sun Microsystems, Inc.; Figure 16-15 courtesy of The Museum of HP Calculators, http://www.hpmuseum.org; Figures 16-19 and 16-20 courtesy of Eleksen Ltd.; Figure 17-1 redrawn from *Emotion. A Psychoevolutionary Synthesis*, published by Allyn and Bacon, Copyright © 1980 by Pearson Education, reprinted by permission of the publisher (Plutchik, R. 1980); Table 17-1 adapted from *Affective Computing*, © 1997 Massachusetts Institute of Technology, published and reprinted by permission of The MIT Press (Picard, R. W. 1998); Table 17-2 reprinted from *International Journal of Human Computer Studies*, Vol. 59, McNeese, M. D., New visions of human-computer interaction: making affect compute, pp. 33–53, Copyright 2003, with permission from Elsevier; Figure 17-5 from Emma Project, EU Funded Project IST-2001-39192, courtesy of Mariano Alcañiz; Figure 17-6 reprinted from *International Journal of Human Computer Studies*, Vol. 59, Lisetti, C. *et al.*, Developing multimodal intelligent affective interfaces for tele-home health care, pp.245–55, Copyright 2003, with permission from Elsevier; Figures 17-7 and 17-8 courtesy of Frank Dabek; Figure 17-11 reprinted from *International Journal of Human Computer Studies*, Vol. 59, Paiva, A. *et al.*, SenToy: an affective sympathetic interface, pp. 227–35, Copyright 2003, with permission from Elsevier; Figure 17-12 from Understanding remote presence in *Proceedings of 2nd Nordic Conference in HCI, NordiCHI '02*, © 2002 ACM, Inc., reprinted by permission (Tollmar, K. and Persson, J. 2002); Figure 17-13 from Doom as an interface for process management in *Proceedings of CHI '02 Conference*, © 2001 ACM, Inc., reprinted by permission (Chao, D. 2001); Figure 17-14 from A wheelchair can be fun: a case of emotion-driven design in *Proceedings of DPPI '03 Conference*, © 2003 ACM, Inc., reprinted by permission (Desmet, P. and Dijkhuis, E. 2003); Figure 18-8 courtesy of David Tucker; Figure 19-4 © Fiona Carroll, reproduced with kind permission; Figure 20-5 reprinted from *HCI Models, Theories and Frameworks* by J. M. Carroll (ed.), John, B., Information processing and skilled behaviour, Copyright 2003, with permission from Elsevier; Figure 20-6 reprinted from *International Journal of Human Computer Studies*, Vol. 44, No. 6, Green, T. R. G. and Benyon, D. R., The skull beneath the skin: entity-relationship modeling of information artefacts, pp.801-28, Copyright 1996, with permission from Elsevier; Figure 21-1 from *New techniques for assessing audio and video quality in real-time interactive communication*, Tutorial, HCI 2001, reprinted by permission of Jim Mullin (Mullin, J. *et al. 2001)*; Figure 21-2 reprinted from *Being There: Concepts, Effects and Measurement of User Presence in Synthetic Environments* by G. Riva *et al.* (eds), Inkso, B. E., Measuring presence: subjective, behavioral and physiological methods, Copyright 2003, with permission from IOS Press and courtesy of the Department of Computer Science, University of North Carolina at Chapel Hill; Table 21-3 adapted from A survey of user-centered design practice in *Proceedings of CHI '02 Conference*, © 2002 ACM, Inc., reprinted by permission (Vredenburg, K. *et al.* 2002); Figure 22-1 redrawn from Gestural and audio metaphors as a means of control for mobile devices in *Proceedings of CHI '02 Conference*, © 2002 ACM, Inc., reprinted by permission (Pirhonen, A. *et al.* 2002); Figure 22-2 redrawn from http://www.ejeisa.com/nectar/megataq/4.3/2.htm reprinted by permission of Delft University of Technology and Interlynx Ltd.; Figures 23-7, 23-13 and 25-12 screen shots reproduced with permission of Yahoo! Inc. © 2004 by Yahoo! Inc. YAHOO! and the YAHOO! logo are trademarks of Yahoo! Inc.; Figure 23-9 screen shot reprinted by permission of PriceGrabber.com, LLC; Figure 23-12 redrawn from *Information Architecture for the World Wide Web*, © 2002, pub O'Reilly, www.oreilly.com, used by permission of O'Reilly Media, Inc. (Rosenfeld, L. and Morville, P. 2002); Figure 24-1 redrawn from *Visual Explanations*, pub Graphics Press, reprinted by permission of Edward R. Tufte (Tufte, E. R. 1997); Figures 24-2(a), 24-2(b) and 25-6 (top left) reprinted by permission of London's Transport Museum; Figure 24-5 redrawn from *The Elements of User Experience: User-centered design for the Web*, pub New Riders Publishing, reprinted by permission of Pearson Education, Inc. (Garrett, J. J. 2003); Figure 24-6 redrawn from http://www.jjg.net/ia/visvocab/ reprinted by permission of Jesse James Garrett; Figure 24-8 from Visual information seeking: tight coupling of dynamic query filters and starfield displays in *Proceedings of CHI '94 Conference*, © 1994 ACM, Inc., reprinted by permission (Ahlberg, C. and Shneiderman, B. 1994); Figure 24-10 screen shot © SmartMoney 2004. All rights reserved. Used with permission. SmartMoney is a joint venture of Dow Jones & Company, Inc. and Hearst Communications, Inc.; Figure 24-11 screen shot *Visual Thesaurus*™ (powered by *Thinkmap*®) © 2004

Plumb Design, Inc. All rights reserved; Figure 25-4 reprinted from *The Concise Townscape* by G. Cullen, Copyright 1961, with permission from Elsevier (Cullen, G. 1961, reprinted 1994); Figure 25-7 screen shot reprinted by permission of Vincent Flanders; Figures 25-8, 25-13 and 26-5 © 2004 Amazon.com. All rights reserved. Used with permission; Figure 25-11 screen shot reprinted by permission of Fredrik Espinoza; Figure 25-14 screen shot reprinted by permission of GroupLens Research Group, University of Minnesota; Figure 25-15 from Socially translucent systems: social proxies, persistent conversation, and the design of 'babble' in *Proceedings of SIGCHI '99 Conference on Human Factors in Computing Systems*, © 1999 ACM, Inc., reprinted by permission (Erickson, T. *et al.* 1999); Figure 26-1 courtesy of iRobot Corporation; Table 26-1 from Stereotypes and user modeling in *User Models in Dialog Systems* edited by A. Kobsa and W. Wahlster, © Springer-Verlag Berlin Heidelberg 1989, reprinted by permission of Springer-Verlag GmbH & Co. KG (Rich, E. 1989); Figure 26-6 redrawn from Adaptive hypermedia in *User Modeling and User Adapted Interaction*, 11(1-2), reprinted by permission of Kluwer Academic Publishers (Brusilovsky, P. 2001); Figure 26-7 screen shot reprinted by permission of Ananova Ltd.; Figure 26-8 reprinted by permission of Justine Cassell; Figure 27-12 from *The Home Workshop: a method for investigating the home*, reprinted by permission of the author (Baillie, L. 2002); Figure 27-13 from Exploring and enhancing the home experience in *Cognition, Technology and Work*, 5(1), © Springer-Verlag London Limited 2003, reprinted by permission of Springer-Verlag GmbH & Co. KG (Eggen, B. *et al.* 2003); Figure 28-1 from Why distance matters: effects on cooperation, persuasion and deception in *Proceedings of CSCW '02 Conference*, © 2002 ACM, Inc., reprinted by permission (Bradner, E. and Mark, G. 2002); Tables 28-1 and 28-2 from Distance Matters in *Human-Computer Interaction*, 15, published and reprinted by permission of Lawrence Erlbaum Associates, Inc. and the authors (Olson, G. M. and Olson, J. S. 2000); Figure 28-2 reprinted by permission of the Smithsonian Institution; Figure 28-3 courtesy of Gavin Payne; Table 28-3 adapted from When conventions collide: the tensions of instant messaging attributed in *Proceedings of CHI '02 Conference*, © 2002 ACM, Inc., reprinted by permission (Voida, A. *et al.* 2002); Figures 28-4 and 28-10 courtesy of Nokia; Figure 28-5 courtesy of Motorola; Section 28.8 Table from *Human-Computer Interaction in the New Millennium*, p.292, Table 13.4, © 2002 ACM Press. Reprinted by permission of Pearson Education, Inc. Publishing as Pearson Addison Wesley (Turoff, M. *et al.* 2002); Figure 28-11 reprinted with permission of AT&T; Figure 28-12 from Are you looking at me? Eye contact and desktop video conferencing in *ACM Transactions on Computer-Human Interaction (TOCHI)*, 10(3), © 2003 ACM, Inc., reprinted by permission (Grayson, D. M. and Monk, A. M. 2003); Figure 28-13 from Design of Team WorkStation: a realtime shared workspace fusing desktops and computer screens in *Multi-User Interfaces and Applications* edited by S. Gibbs and A. A. Verrijn-Stuart, pub Elsevier North-Holland, reprinted by permission of Hiroshi Ishii (Ishii, H. and Ohkubo, M. 1990); Figures 28-14 and 30-9 courtesy of Bill Buxton; Figures 28-16 and 28-17 redrawn from Deixis and points of view in media spaces: an empirical gesture in

Behaviour and Information Technology, Vol.15, reprinted by permission of Taylor & Francis Ltd., http://www.tandf.co.uk/journals (Barnard, P. J. *et al.* 1996); Figure 29-5 adapted from Unpublished tutorial notes on ethnography and collaborative systems development, HCI '94 Conference, reprinted by permission of D. Randall (Randall, D. and Bentley, R. 1994); Figure 29-6 reprinted from *International Journal of Human-Computer Studies*, Vol. 53, 1, Viller, S. and Sommerville, I., Ethnographically informed analysis for software engineers, pp.169-96, Copyright 2000, with permission from Elsevier; Figures 29-7 and 29-8 from *Proceedings of ECSCW '01 Conference*, pub 2001, pp. 39–58, Finding patterns in fieldwork by Martin, D. *et al.*, Fig. 5, © 2001 Kluwer Academic Publishers, with kind permission of Kluwer Academic Publishers; Table 30-2 from The effects of workspace awareness support on the usability of real-time distributed groupware in *ACM Transactions on Computer-Human Interaction (TOCHI)*, 6(3), © 1999 ACM, Inc., reprinted by permission (Gutwin, C. and Greenberg, S. 1999); Figures 30-3 and 30-4 screen shots of Lotus Notes [Copyright 1989] IBM Corporation. Used with permission of IBM Corporation. Lotus and Lotus Notes are trademarks of IBM Corporation, in the United States, other countries, or both; Figure 30-5 screen shot reprinted by permission of FIT Fraunhofer and OrbiTeam Software GmbH; Figure 30-6 redrawn from Workflow: An Introduction in *The Workflow Handbook 2001*, reproduced with permission from Workflow Management Coalition (wfmc.org) (Allen, R. 2001); Figure 30-8 screen shot reprinted by permission of DISCOVER Laboratory, S.I.T.E., University of Ottawa; Figures 30-13 and 30-14 redrawn from *Proceedings of ECSCW '93 Conference*, pub 1993, pp. 109–24, A spatial model of interaction in large virtual environments by Benford, S. D. and Fahlén, L. E., Fig. 3, © 1993 Kluwer Acadenic Publishers, with kind permission of Kluwer Academic Publishers; Figure 30-15 screen shot reprinted by permission of Chris Greenhalgh.

North Carolina State University for an extract from *Principles of Universal Design* by B. R. Connell, M. Jones, R. Mace, J. Mueller, A. Mullick, E. Ostroff, J. Sanford, E Steinfeld, M. Story and G. Vanderheiden © Centre for Universal Design, School of Design, North Carolina State University; Lawrence Erlbaum Associates, Inc for the extracts 'surrogates and mappings: two kinds of conceptual models for interactive devices' by R.M. Young published in *Mental Models* eds D. Gentner and A.L. Stevens 1983, and 'Hierarchical task analysis' by J. Annett published in *The Handbook of Task Analysis for Human Computer Interaction* eds D. Diaper and N. Stanton 2004; Cambridge University Press for an extract from *Human Error* by J. Reason 1991; an extract from Rosalind W. Picard from *Affective Computing*, Cambridge, MA, The MIT Press for an extract from *Affective Computing* by R. W. Picard, 1997; Siemens Mobile Phones for an advertisement for the SL55 mobile phone, courtesy of Siemens Mobile Phones; Elsevier Ltd for extracts from *Contextual Design* by H. Beyer and K. Holtzblatt 1998; Blackwell Publishing Ltd for an extract from *Real World Research: A Resource for Social Scientist and Practitioner-Researchers* by C. Robson, 1983; ACM Press for extracts from, 'Participatory Heuristic Evaluation' by M.J. Muller *et al.*, 1998 and

'Grounding blue-sky research' by Y.Rogers and V.Bellotti, 1997, both published in *Interaction* 5 (5) and an extract from 'Empirical Development' by K. Baker and S. Greenberg published in the *Proceedings of CSCW'02 Conference*, November 2002; UIE for an extract from *'Strategies for Categorizing Categories'* published on www.uie.com 7th May 2003; and Guardian News Services Limited for an extract from 'Council ban emails to get staff to talk' by David Ward published in *The Guardian* 7th October 2002 © Guardian.

In some instances we have been unable to trace the owners of copyright material, and we would appreciate any information that would enable us to do so.

Guided tour

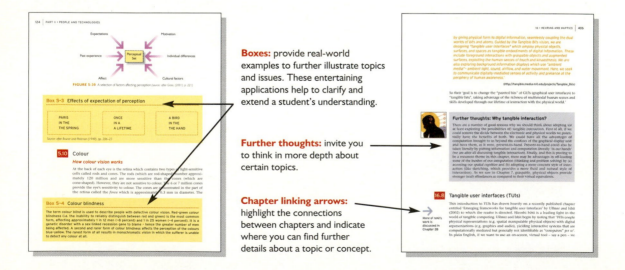

Parts: the book is split into 7 parts, each with a part opener describing the main themes and links between chapters within that part.

Chapter aims introduce topics covered and summarize what you should have learnt by the end of the chapter.

Boxes: provide real-world examples to further illustrate topics and issues. These entertaining applications help to clarify and extend a student's understanding.

Further thoughts: invite you to think in more depth about certain topics.

Chapter linking arrows: highlight the connections between chapters and indicate where you can find further details about a topic or concept.

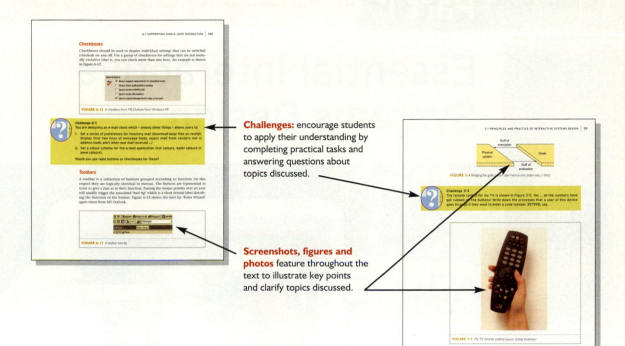

Challenges: encourage students to apply their understanding by completing practical tasks and answering questions about topics discussed.

Screenshots, figures and photos feature throughout the text to illustrate key points and clarify topics discussed.

Summary and key points: pulls together the main issues addressed in the chapter to provide a useful reminder of topics covered.

Further reading: offers sources of additional information for those who wish to explore a topic further.

Comments on challenges: provide guideline answers to chapter challenges.

Exercises: practical challenges and tasks feature at the end of every chapter to test students' understanding and encourage them to apply their knowledge.

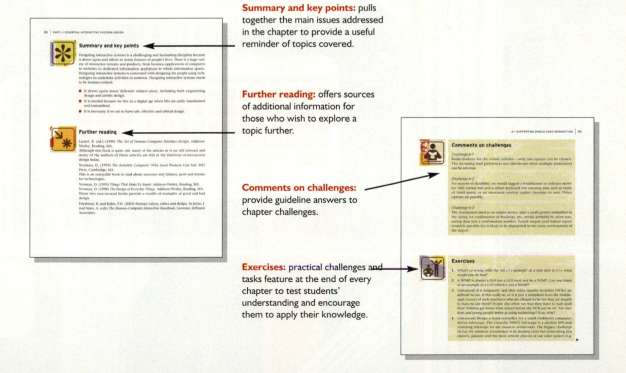

Part I:

Essential Interactive Systems Design

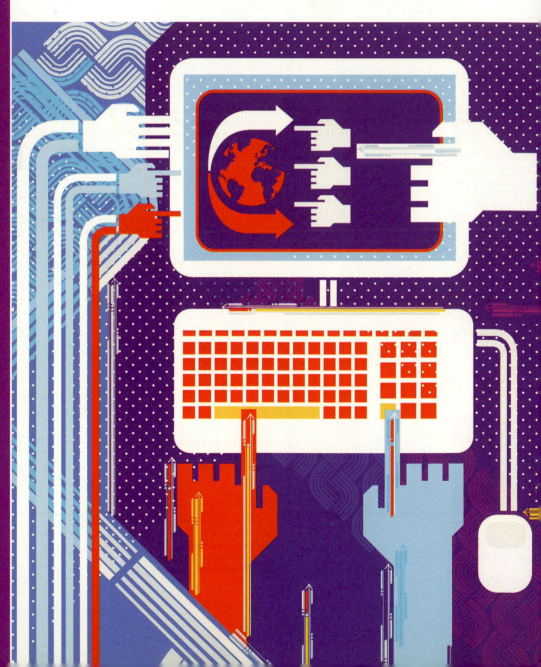

Introduction

Our goal is to design interactive systems that are enjoyable to use, that do useful things and that enhance the lives of the people who use them. We want our interactive systems to be accessible, usable and engaging. In order to achieve this we believe that the design of such systems should be human-centred. That is, designers need to put people rather than technology at the centre of their design process. Unfortunately the design of computer systems and products in the past has not always had a good record of considering the people who use them. Many systems have been designed by programmers who use computers every working day. Many designers are young males. Many designers have been playing computer games for years. This means that they forget just how difficult and obscure some of their designs can be to people who have not had these experiences.

In the days of the Web, issues of usability are critical to e-commerce. Before the immediacy of e-commerce, usability problems were discovered only after purchase. If you bought a nice-looking CD player and brought it home only to find it was difficult to use, you could not take it back! The shop would say that it delivers its functions; all you had to do was to learn how to operate it properly. On the Web, customers look at usability first. If the system is hard to use, or if they do not understand it, they will go somewhere else to make their purchase. People are learning that systems do not have to be hard to use and are becoming more critical about the design of other products, such as their CD players, too.

This first part of the book provides a guide to the essence of the human-centred design of interactive systems. Chapter 1 focuses on the main elements of interactive systems design. It considers the nature of design, the features of interactive systems and what it means to be human-centred. The chapter provides a brief history of human–computer interaction and interaction design and a glimpse of the future, before focusing on why designing interactive systems is important. Chapter 2 is about the processes involved in designing interactive systems. We see why the evaluation of ideas is central to the process. The requirements for products, early designs and prototypes of systems all need to be evaluated to ensure that they meet the needs of the people who will use them. But people will make use of technologies in many different contexts, to undertake different activities. We introduce the key components of interaction – people, activities, contexts and technologies (PACT). Alongside this view we need to consider the products we are designing: what they will do, how they will do it and what information content they will manipulate. In Chapter 3 we look at principles of design: how to ensure systems are accessible, usable and acceptable and how to design for 'user experiences'. When people use the devices we have designed, what do they feel? Do they have a sense of satisfaction, enjoyment and engagement? The chapter looks at these issues in a variety of contexts and on a variety of technological platforms. Once again this serves to illustrate the wide scope of interactive systems design. The final chapter is an extended case study of a design, showing how and why decisions were made and illustrating many of the ideas developed in the first three chapters.

After studying this part you should understand the essential features of designing interactive systems. In particular

- What interactive systems design is
- Who is involved
- What is involved
- How to develop systems that are human-centred
- Principles of interactive systems design to ensure systems are usable and engaging.

Teaching

With some supplementary material showing examples, the material in this part would make an ideal introductory course on human–computer interaction (HCI) or interaction design (ID). A schedule along the following lines is suggested which would account for about one quarter of a student's entire load:

Week 1	Overview of the course and subject	Section 1.1
Week 2	Overview of designing interactive systems	Chapter 1
Week 3	PACT analysis	Sections 2.1-2.5
Week 4	Doing a PACT analysis	Section 2.6
Week 5	The design process	Sections 2.7, 2.8
Week 6	Evaluation case study	Chapter 4
Week 7	Evaluation case study	Chapter 4
Week 8	Access	Section 3.2
Week 9	Usability and acceptability	Sections 3.3-3.4
Week 10	Engagement	Section 3.5
Week 11	Design principles	Sections 3.6-3.7
Week 12	Principles in other contexts	Sections 3.8-3.9

01

Designing interactive systems: A fusion of skills

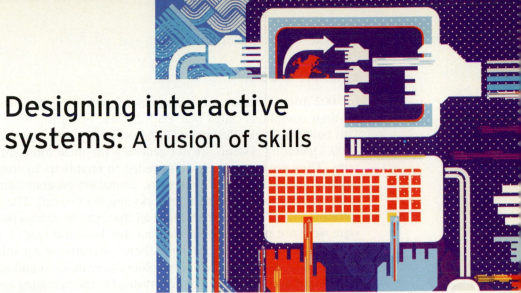

Aims

Designing interactive systems is concerned with developing high quality interactive systems and products that fit with people and their ways of living. Computing and communication devices are embedded in all sorts of everyday devices such as washing machines and televisions, ticket machines and jewellery. No self-respecting exhibition, museum or library is without its interactive component. We carry and wear technologies that are far more powerful than the computers of just a few years ago. There are websites, on-line communities, cellphone applications and all manner of other interactive devices and services that need developing. Interactive systems design is about all this.

In this chapter we explore the width and breadth of designing interactive systems. After studying this chapter you should be able to:

- Understand the concepts underlying the design of interactive systems
- Understand why being human-centred is important in design
- Understand the historical background to the subject
- Understand the skills and knowledge that the designer of interactive systems needs to draw upon.

1.1 The variety of interactive systems

Designing interactive systems is concerned with many different types of product. It is about designing software systems that will run on a computer at work. It is about designing websites, games, interactive products such as MP3 players, digital cameras and applications for personal digital assistants (PDAs). It is about designing whole environments in which phones, PDAs, laptop computers, digital projectors and other devices communicate with one another and through which people interact with one another. It is about designing interactive systems and products for the home, for work or to support communities.

Here are some examples of recent interactive products and systems.

Example 1: OS X

In 2002 Apple Computer, Inc. announced the release of a new operating system for their computers called Mac OS X.2 ('Mac operating system ten point two'). This built on the revolutionary OS X operating system that had been released in 2000. Operating systems are not generally the most interesting of software systems. They are a necessary evil needed to enable us to store files and access applications such as word processors, animation programs and spreadsheets, to print documents, connect to networks and read e-mail. They are dull pieces of software. With OS X Apple changed all that. The functions provided by the software were not particularly special, but the 'look and feel' of the new operating system was substantially different. There were interesting animations that gave the interface an exciting feel. The colours were modern and aesthetic. The icons were bright and engaging. The advertising for the operating system proclaimed a 'new user experience' and how 'Apple human interface engineers labour painstakingly over every pixel you encounter.' Although not universally loved, Apple soon had a committed group of users for their system. See Figure 1-1.

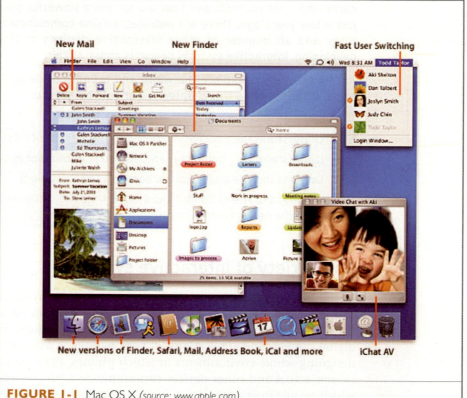

FIGURE I-I Mac OS X *(source: www.apple.com)*

Example 2: iPod

Another Apple product is the iPod (Figure 1-2), a device for storing and playing MP3 music files. Apart from the very stylish physical design, one of the reasons why this is so revolutionary is its browsing mechanism. This combines a well-structured and clear display with a central tracking wheel that makes locating a particular track by artist, title or genre simplicity itself.

FIGURE I-2 iPod *(source: www.apple.com)*

Example 3: Emergence

'Emergence' is a PC-based software system, designed for the creation of interactive art. Three-dimensional, computer-generated environments and autonomous, animated characters are displayed in real-time. People who enter this world are represented as 'avatars'. Through a programming language people can utilize techniques of Artificial Life to specify behaviours and relationships between characters and objects. Additional animation and sounds such as voice, music or background effects can be attached to objects and characters in the environment. The developers are experimenting with forms of communication that rely on symbolic gestures, movements and behaviours. The focus is on the 'life' of the virtual environment. Through the avatar a person enters a world that encourages exploration, participation and the development of relationships. See Figure 1-3.

FIGURE 1-3 The Bush soul environment using 'Emergence'
(source: http://emergence.design.ucla.edu/ Courtesy of Rebecca Allen)

Further thoughts: Artificial Life

Artificial Life (often abbreviated to 'Alife') is a branch of Artificial Intelligence (AI), the discipline that looks at whether intelligent software systems can be built and at the nature of intelligence itself. The tradition in AI has been to represent knowledge and behaviours through rules and rigid structures. Alife tries instead to represent more high-level features of the things in an environment such as the goals that a creature has and the needs that it must satisfy. The actual behaviour of the artificial creatures is then more unpredictable and evolves in the environment. Increasingly characters in computer games are using Alife techniques.

Example 4: AIBO

The AIBO is a robotic dog that has been developed by Sony Corporation. The dog walks independently around the house, recharges itself when the battery runs low and can recognize its owner. The dog can be programmed to perform various other functions. One of the features of the AIBO shown in Figure 1-4 is the engaging way in which it moves its head and limbs. Other features include the noises it makes and the way its head lights up.

Example 5: Co-Muse

Co-Muse is a collaborative museum application. Exhibits are marked with a RFID (radio-frequency identification) tag. Visitors to the museum are issued with PDAs. When the PDAs come into range of the RFID tag, information about the exhibit is displayed. Visitors can interact with others at the museum through the PDA, posing questions about exhibits for others to answer. See Figure 1-5.

FIGURE I-4 AIBO Light Off, model ERS-7 *(source: courtesy of Sony Electronics Inc.)*

FIGURE I-5 Collaborative museum *(source: PA Photos)*

Summary

These were just five of the thousands of examples of interaction design that we could have chosen. OS X shows that functional software does not have to be dull, and it was quickly followed by Microsoft's Windows XP (the user 'experience'). The iPod is an information appliance designed and optimized for a

Part VI is concerned with information spaces

certain limited set of activities. 'Emergence' is art in new media, creating experiences that were impossible only a few years ago. The AIBO is a programmable product which brings companionship and fun, but which has little functional use. Co-Muse creates a community from the museum visitors, placing people at the centre of an 'information space'.

Challenge 1-1

Find five interactive products or systems that you use – perhaps a coffee machine, a cellular phone, a fairground ride, a TV remote control, a computer game and a website. (If you do not visit websites often, type your favourite thing into the box at www.google.com and click 'I'm Feeling Lucky'.) Write down what it is that you like about each of them and what it is that you do not like. Think about the whole experience and not just the functions. Think about the content that each provides: is it what you want? Is it fun to use?

If possible find a friend or colleague to discuss the issues. Criticism and design are social activities that are best done with others. What do you agree on? What do you disagree on? Why?

1.2 The concerns of interactive systems design

The design of interactive systems covers a very wide range of activities. Sometimes designers will be working on both the hardware and the software for a system, in which case the term 'product design' seems to be most appropriate to describe what they are doing. Sometimes the designer will be producing a piece of software to run on a computer, on a programmable device or over the Internet. In these cases the term 'system design' or 'service design' seems more appropriate. We switch between these expressions as appropriate. However, the key concerns of the designer of interactive systems are

- Design – what is design and how should you do it?
- Technologies – the interactive systems, products, devices and components themselves
- People – who will use the systems and whose lives we would like to make better through our designs
- Activities and contexts – what people want to do and the contexts within which those activities take place.

Design

'What is design?... It's where you stand with a foot in two worlds – the world of technology and the world of people and human purposes – and you try to bring the two together'.

Mitch Kapor in Winograd (1996), p. 1

The term 'design' refers both to the creative process of specifying something new and to the representations that are produced during the process. So, for example, to design a website a designer will produce and evaluate various designs such as a design of the page layout, a design of the colour scheme, a design for the graphics and a design of the overall structure. In a different field of design, an architect produces sketches and outlines and discusses these with the client before formalizing a design in the form of a blueprint.

Design is rarely a straightforward process and typically involves much iteration and exploration of both requirements (what the system is meant to do and how it should do it) and design solutions. There are many definitions of 'design'. Most definitions recognize that *both* problem and solution need to *evolve* during the design process; rarely can you completely specify something before some design work has been done.

One thing that is useful is to distinguish the amount of formality associated with a design.

Chapter 9 discusses requirements in detail

- At one end of a spectrum is engineering design (such as the design of a bridge, a car or a building) where scientific principles and technical specifications are employed to produce formal models before construction starts.
- At the other end of this spectrum is creative or artistic design where innovation, imagination and conceptual ideas are the key ingredients.
- Somewhere in the middle lies 'design as craft' that draws upon both engineering and creative approaches.

Most design involves aspects of all of these. A fashion designer needs to know about people and fabrics, an interior designer also needs to know about paints, lighting and so on, and a jewellery designer needs to know about precious stones and the properties of metals such as gold and silver. The famous design commentator Donald Schön has described design as a 'conversation with materials', by which he means that in any type of design, designers must understand the nature of the materials that they are working with. Design works with and shapes a medium; in our case this medium consists of interactive systems. Others emphasize that design is a conscious, social activity and much design is often undertaken in a design team.

People and technologies

Interactive system is the term we use to describe the technologies that interactive system designers work with. This term is intended to cover components, devices, products and software systems that are primarily concerned with processing information. Interactive systems are things that deal with the transmission, display, storage or transformation of information that people can perceive. They are devices and systems that respond to people's actions.

This definition is intended to exclude things such as tables, chairs and doors (since they do not process information) but to include things such as

- telephones (since they transmit information – and increasingly store and transform it),
- websites (since they store and display information),
- washing machine controllers (the interactive component of a washing machine).

Increasingly, interactive components are being included in all manner of other products (such as clothes, buildings and jewellery).

A fundamental challenge for interactive systems designers is to deal with the fact that people and interactive systems are different (see Box 1-1). Of course we take the people-centred view, but many designers still take the machine-centred view because it is quicker and easier for them, though not for the person who finishes up using the product. Another difference between people and machines is that we speak different languages. People express their desires and feelings in terms of what they want to do or how they would like things to be (their goals). Machines need to be given strict instructions.

Box 1-1 Machine- and people-centred views

View	People are	Machines are
Machine-centred	Vague	Precise
	Disorganized	Orderly
	Distractible	Undistractible
	Emotional	Unemotional
	Illogical	Logical
People-centred	Creative	Dumb
	Compliant	Rigid
	Attentive to change	Insensitive to change
	Resourceful	Unimaginative
	Able to make flexible decisions based on context	Constrained to make consistent decisions

Source: Adapted from Norman (1993), p. 224

The user interface

What is often called the 'user interface' (or just 'interface') to an interactive system is all those parts of the system with which people come into contact physically, perceptually and conceptually.

■ Physically we might interact with a device by pressing buttons or moving levers and the interactive device might respond by providing feedback through the pressure of the button or lever.

■ Perceptually the device displays things on a screen which we can see, or makes noises which we can hear.

■ Conceptually we interact with a device by trying to work out what it does and what we should be doing. The device provides messages and other displays which are designed to help us do this.

The interface needs to provide some mechanisms so that people can provide instructions and enter data into the system: 'input'. It also needs to provide some mechanisms for the system to tell people what is happening by providing feedback and mechanisms for displaying the content: 'output'. This content might be in the form of information, pictures, movies, animations and so on. Figure 1-6 shows a variety of user interfaces.

Chapter 6 discusses input and output devices in more detail.

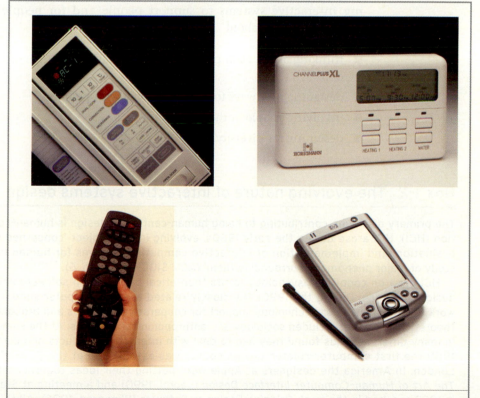

FIGURE 1-6 Various user interfaces
(sources: John Heseltine/Science Photo Library; Horstmann Controls Ltd; Dorling Kindersley; Hewlett-Packard Ltd.)

Challenge 1-2
Look at the pictures in Figure 1-6. What does the user interface to (a) the microwave, (b) the heating controller, (c) the remote control, or (d) the PDA consist of?

Designing interactive systems is not just a question of designing user interfaces, however. The whole human–computer interaction needs to be considered, as does the human–human interaction that is often enabled through the systems. Increasingly, interactive systems consist of many interconnected devices, some worn by people, some embedded in the fabric of buildings, some carried. Interactive systems designers need to consider the whole environments they are creating.

Being human-centred

Interactive systems design is ultimately about creating interactive experiences for people. Being human-centred is about putting people first; it is about designing interactive systems to support people and for people to enjoy. Being human-centred is about

- thinking about what people want to do rather than what the technology can do,
- designing new ways to connect people with people,
- involving people in the design process,
- designing for diversity.

Box 1-2   The evolving nature of interactive systems design

The primary discipline contributing to being human-centred in design is human–computer interaction (HCI). HCI arose during the early 1980s, evolving into a subject 'concerned with the design, evaluation, and implementation of interactive computing systems for human use and with the study of major phenomena surrounding them' (ACM SIGCHI, 1992, p. 6).

HCI drew on cognitive psychology for its theoretical base and on software engineering for its design approach. During the 1990s the closely related area of computer supported cooperative work (CSCW) focused on technology support for cooperative activities and brought with it another theoretical base that included sociology and anthropological methods. At the same time designers in many different fields found they had to deal with interactive products and components, and in 1989 the first computer-related design course was established at the Royal College of Art in London. In America the designers at Apple were putting their ideas together into a book called *The Art of Human-Computer Interface Design* (Laurel, 1990) and a meeting at Stanford University in 1992 resulted in the book *Bringing Design to Software* (Winograd, 1996). All this – coupled with the phenomenal changes in computing and communication technologies during the same period – has brought us to where we are today: a dynamic mix of ideas, approaches and philosophies applied to the design of interactive systems and products.

This book is about human-centred interactive systems design. It is about human–computer interaction (HCI) in the twenty-first century.

1.3 Being digital

In 1995 Nicholas Negroponte, head of the Massachusetts Institute of Technology's 'Media Lab', wrote a book called *Being Digital* in which he explored the significance of an era in which we change atoms for bits. We live in a digital age, when all manner of devices represent things using binary digits (bits). The significance of being digital is that bits are transformable, transmittable and storable using digital technologies. Consider the following scenario.

In the morning you get woken up by a digital alarm clock which automatically turns on the radio. To change the radio channel you might press a button that searches for a strong signal. You pick up your mobile, cellular phone and check for messages. You might go to your computer and download a personalized newspaper into a personal digital assistant (PDA). As you leave the house you set the security alarm. In the car you adjust the heating, use the radio and attend to the various warning and information symbols that detect whether doors are open, or seat belts are buckled. Arriving at the station, you scan your season ticket through the car parking machine, get a train ticket from the ticket machine and get money from an automated teller machine (ATM). On the train you read the newspaper on your PDA, scrolling through text using a stylus. Arriving at your office, you log onto the computer network, check e-mail, use various computer packages, browse the Web and perhaps listen to an Internet radio station broadcasting from another country. You have a video link with colleagues in other cities and perhaps work together on a shared document. During the day you use a coffee machine, make calls on the cellphone, check names and numbers in the address book, download a new ringing tone, photograph a beautiful plant that you see at lunchtime and video the swans on the river. You mail these to your home website. Arriving home, you open the garage doors automatically by keying a number on your phone and in the evening you spend an hour or so on the games machine, watch TV and program the video to record a late-night show.

This is the world we are living in and the world that designers of interactive systems are designing for. The huge range of interactions that we engage in and the interfaces that we use offer an exciting if daunting challenge. Moreover, increasingly designers are having to deal with the issue of people engaged in multiple interactions with different devices in parallel. One important commentator, Bruce 'Tog' Tognazinni, prefers the term 'interaction architect' to describe this emerging profession.

How we got here

The revolution that has brought us to where we are today started towards the end of the Second World War with the development of the first digital computers. These were huge machines housed in specially built, air-conditioned rooms. They were operated by scientists and specialist computer programmers and operators, who physically pressed switches and altered circuits so that the electronics could complete their calculations.

During the 1960s computer technology was still dominated by scientific and accounting applications. Data was stored on paper tape or cards with holes punched in them, on magnetic tapes and large magnetic disks, and there was little direct interaction with the computer. Cards were sent to the computer centre, data was processed and the results were returned a few days later. Under the guidance of 'Lick' Licklider, however, things were beginning to change. The first screens and cathode ray tubes (CRTs) were being used as interactive devices and the first vision of a computer network – an internet – was formulated by Licklider. He worked at the Advanced Research Projects Agency (ARPA) at the US Department of Defense. His work also led to the establishment of computer science at four US universities (Licklider, 2003). Licklider was followed by the pioneering work of Ivan Sutherland at MIT, Doug Englebart who is credited with inventing the computer mouse, and Ted Nelson who developed the concept of hypertext. In the UK pioneering work on computers was based at Manchester University and in 1959 Brian Shackel had published the paper 'Ergonomics for a computer'.

Box 1-3 Ergonomics

Ergonomics is the study of the 'fit' between people and the things that they use. A chair is said to be 'ergonomically designed' if it takes into consideration the shape of someone's back and provides good support for sitting. Until the late 1950s ergonomics had to consider only physical characteristics of interaction. With the arrival of computers, ergonomics was forced to take on the psychological fit between people and devices as well. The term 'cognitive ergonomics' is sometimes used to describe the study of human-computer interaction. Ergonomics is discussed in more detail in Chapter 7.

During the 1970s computing technology spread into businesses and screens linked to a central computer began to emerge. Computers were becoming networked together and indeed the first e-mail was sent over the ARPANET in 1972. The method of interaction for most people in the 1970s was still primarily 'batch'; transactions were collected together and submitted as a batch of work and computing power was shared between different people. Interest in HCI began to grow, with publications in the *International Journal of Man–Machine Studies*. As the decade ended so keyboards and screens became more common, but it was not until 1982 that the first real graphically based interfaces appeared in the form of the Xerox Star, Apple Lisa and Apple Macintosh computers. These used a bit-mapped display, allowing a graphical user interface (GUI) and interac-

Chapter 6 discusses GUIs

tion through pointing at icons and with commands grouped into menus. This style became ubiquitous when, in 1985, the Windows operating system appeared on (what were then usually IBM) personal computers (PCs). The personal computer and Windows-like operating system are attributed to another important pioneer, Alan Kay. Kay obtained his PhD, studying under Ivan Sutherland, in 1969 before moving to Xerox Palo Alto Research Center (PARC). It was here that the object-oriented language Smalltalk was developed. Many argue that it was the development of the VisiCalc spreadsheet program on the Apple II computer (the 'killer app') in 1979 that really fired the personal computer market (Pew, 2003).

The 1980s was the decade of the micro computer with the BBC micro home computer selling over 1 million units and a whole plethora of home computers being adopted worldwide. Games consoles were also gaining in popularity in the home entertainment market. In business people were getting networked and the Internet began to grow based around e-mail. It was during the 1980s that human–computer interaction (HCI) came of age as a subject. In both the USA and Europe the first big conferences on HCI were held: the CHI '83 conference on Human Factors in Computing Systems in Boston, MA, and INTERACT '84 in London. Don Norman published his famous paper 'The trouble with UNIX: the user interface is horrid' (Norman, 1981a) and Ben Shneiderman published *Software Psychology* (Shneiderman, 1980).

In the 1990s colour and multimedia arrived on the PC which had begun to dominate the computer market. In 1993 a new interface was produced that took advantage of a simple mark-up or specification 'language' (called hypertext mark-up language, HTML). Thus the 'World Wide Web' came about and revolutionized the whole process of transmitting and sharing files. Pictures, movies, music, text and even live video links were suddenly available to everyone at work and at home. The growth of personal, community and corporate websites was phenomenal and the vision of a wholly connected 'global village' community began to become a reality. Of course this growth was primarily in the West and in the USA in particular, where 'broadband' communications enabled a much more satisfying experience of the Web than the slow connections in Europe. Many parts of the world were not connected, but in the twenty-first century connections to the Web are global. Figure 1-7 summarizes the development of interactive systems.

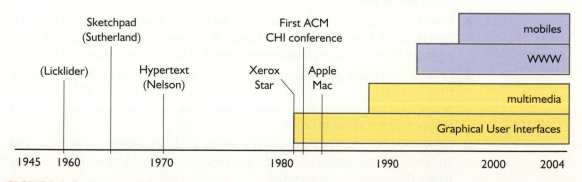

FIGURE 1-7 The interactive systems timeline

By the turn of the century the convergence of communications and computing technologies was just about complete. Anything could potentially be connected to anything, anywhere. Since all the data was digital, it could all be transmitted over the airwaves or over wired networks, and it could easily be transformed from one form into another. And so we come to 2004 and the age of 'ubiquitous computing', a term first coined by the late Mark Weiser in 1993.

Where are we heading?

It is a brave person who makes any strong prediction about where new technologies are headed as there are so many confounding factors. It is never just a technology that wins, but technology linked with a good business model linked with timing. Don Norman delivers an interesting insight into both the past and future of technologies in his book *The Invisible Computer* (1999). Discussing such things as why VHF video format succeeded over Betamax and why Edison's phonograph was not as successful as Emile Berliner's, he takes us forward to something he calls 'information appliances'. This notion has been taken up by others (Sharpe and Stenton, 2003), providing the following set of characteristics of information appliances.

- Appliances should be everyday things requiring only everyday skills to use. Think of things like a knife and fork, a pen or a wrist watch. They may take time to learn, but once mastered they slip into the background of everydayness. Text messaging on mobile phones has become like this for some people.

- Appliances have a clear, focused function that can be used in a variety of circumstances. Computers are general purpose – they can be used for many things. But often the purpose-built appliance is preferable. People like MP3 players, digital cameras and cellphones because they are more clearly focused.

- Peer-to-peer interaction. A key idea of appliances is that they work together without the need for central control or uploading and downloading. If a digital camera can effortlessly transfer pictures to a printer, then the camera does not need to know about printing and the printer does not need to know about taking pictures.

- Direct user interface. Appliances need to be simple and intuitive to use. Of course this is a goal for interface design in general. One way to do this is to organize the interaction around simple physical actions such as button presses.

- Closure. Successful appliances are those which support the notion of completion of a task. Although the notion of what is a 'task' will differ between people, appliances should focus on completion of a simple task rather than an open-ended series of tasks.

- Immediacy. Appliances represent the ability to do something on impulse and are aimed at situations where the user may be engaged in another task, or where their attention is diverted.

■ Personal. Appliances are personal and portable. This allows people to take the tool to the task rather than the task to the tool (think of a pair of scissors versus a washing machine).

The design challenges that such devices raise focus on ensuring that they can be used effectively in a wide range of circumstances and contexts, can focus the functions and access those functions on a small, portable device, and can deal with automatic peer-to-peer connectivity. A particular issue here is knowing the validity of any data when you do not know where it has come from.

Further thoughts: Whom do you trust?

Wireless connectivity between devices is now common both through the 'wi-fi' standard called IEEE 802.11 and through Bluetooth. For example, your mobile phone will connect to your laptop computer via Bluetooth, and the laptop may be connected to an internal company network via a wireless network and hence to the Internet through the company's wired connection and hence to any other device in the world. How will you know where any piece of data that you look at actually is? If you look at the address book 'in your phone', you might in reality be accessing an address book on your laptop, or on any computer on the company's network or indeed anywhere on the World Wide Web. If data is duplicated how will it be kept consistent? Across which devices will the consistency be reliable?

Companies such as IDEO are already making activity-focused devices, and we wait to see whether they will prove popular. Inevitably the personalization of these products requires either the end-users to become programmers and designers themselves, or the devices to adapt to personalized use. Neither of these trends has had any success in the past.

What we do know is that new products, business models, services and a range of other features will rapidly come into the world and the interactive systems designer has to be ready to cope. Whether information appliances is just one of many directions that the future takes, we will have to see.

Figure 1-8 illustrates some design concepts that have come from IDEO in their project looking at identity and how the business card might be developed in the future. The purpose of the project is to explore different concepts and ideas of identity rather than to simply produce new products. Follow the Web link to discover more about what the designers were investigating and how the production of these prototypes helped them.

Challenge 1-3
Visit the website of IDEO and look at the identity project. As it says on their front page, 'Talk about the ideas with a friend'.

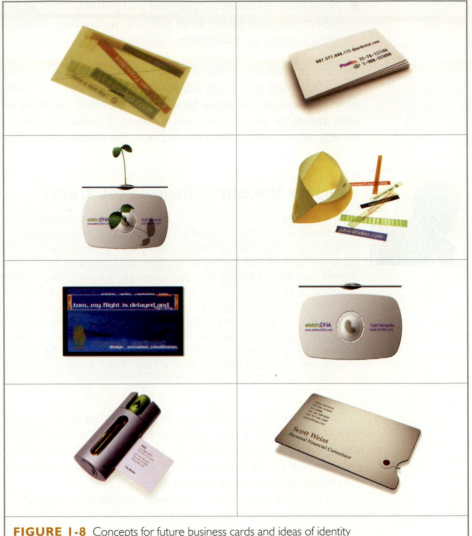

FIGURE 1-8 Concepts for future business cards and ideas of identity
(source: IDEO, 2003. Courtesy of IDEO)

1.4 The skills of the interactive systems designer

Designers of interactive systems need a variety of skills and need to understand a variety of disciplines if they are to be able to do their jobs well. They need the mixture of skills that allows them to be able to:

■ study and understand the activities of people and the contexts within which some technology might prove useful and hence generate requirements for technologies,

■ know the possibilities offered by technologies,

- research and design technological solutions that fit in with people, the activities they want to undertake and the contexts surrounding those activities,
- evaluate alternative designs and iterate until a solution is arrived at.

The range of skills and academic disciplines that will contribute to such a person is significant. Indeed it is often the case that no single person possesses all the skills needed for some design activity, which is why the design of interactive systems is often an affair for a design team. An interactive systems designer may be involved in a community information system project on one occasion, a kiosk for processing photographs on another, a database to support a firm of estate agents on another, and a children's educational game on another! Designers of interactive systems cannot be expert in all these fields, of course, but they must be aware enough to be able to take techniques from different areas, or access research in different disciplines when appropriate. We group the subjects that contribute to the design of interactive systems under the headings of knowledge of People, Technologies, Activities and contexts, and Design, and illustrate the relationships in Figure 1-9.

People

People are social beings, so it is important that the approaches and techniques adopted in the social sciences are used to understand people and technologies. Sociology is the study of the relationships between people in society, the social, political and other groups that they participate in, and the settings in which such relationships take place. Anthropology is similar but focuses also on the study of culture, biology and language and on how these have evolved and changed over time. Both use techniques such as interviews and observation to arrive at their conclusions. A key approach, particularly in anthropology, is 'ethnography' which uses qualitative methods such as observations and unstructured interviews to produce a description of a particular culture or social group and its setting. Also related is cultural studies, which looks at people and their relationship with cultural issues such as identity, but also much more prosaic cultural activities such as shopping, playing computer games or watching TV. Descriptions tend to be from a more literary criticism background, informed by experience and reflection. Psychology is the study of how people think, feel and act. In particular, cognitive psychology seeks to understand and describe how the brain functions, how language works and how we solve problems. Ergonomics is the study of the fit between people and machines. In designing interactive systems, the designer will borrow much from each of these disciplines, including methods to help understand and design for people.

Chapter 9 includes a discussion of ethnography

Chapter 5 on cognitive psychology

Technologies

The technologies that interactive systems designers need to know about include both software and hardware. Software engineering has developed methods for

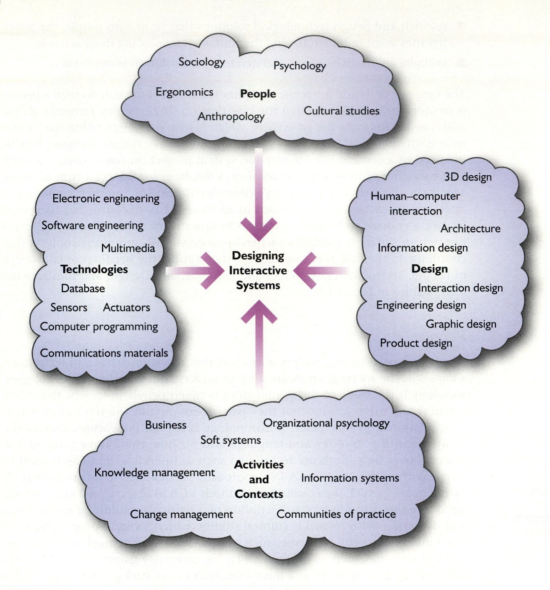

FIGURE 1-9 Disciplines contributing to interactive systems design

specifying and implementing computer programs. Programming languages are used to issue instructions to any programmable device such as a phone, computer, robot dog or, soon, earrings, shirts and chairs. Designers need to be aware of hardware for sensing different types of data (sensors) and for bringing about some change (actuators, or effectors). There are many different components available that produce many different effects and here designers will draw upon engineering knowledge, principles and methods. Communication between devices uses various communication 'protocols'. Designers need to know how different devices can communicate.

Activities and contexts

Interaction will usually take place in the context of some 'community of practice'. This term is used to denote groups of people who have shared interests and values and engage in similar activities. In business communities and organizations information systems methods have developed over the years to ensure information systems are developed that are effective and meet the needs of people who work there. In particular, soft systems theory (Checkland and Scholes, 1999) provides a very useful framework for focusing on the design of interactive systems. Social and organizational psychology are needed to look at the effects of technological change on organizations, and recently knowledge management has become an important area. Finally, new technologies offer new opportunities as business and interactive systems designers find they are sometimes creating whole new ways of working with their designs.

Design

Principles and practices of design from all manner of design disciplines are used in designing interactive systems. Ideas and philosophy from architecture, garden design, interior design, fashion and jewellery design all crop up in various ways and different forms. It is not easy to simply pick up ideas from design disciplines, as much design knowledge is specific to a genre. Designers need to know the materials they work with and it is likely that more specialist design disciplines will emerge. One such discipline is product design which is itself changing as it takes on board the nature of interactivity. Product design is an important contributing discipline to the skills of the designer of interactive systems. Graphic design and information design are particularly important for issues of information layout and the understandability and aesthetic experience of products. Human–computer interaction has itself evolved many techniques to ensure that designs are people-focused, but many people in HCI are still more engineering-focused in their work.

Chapter 24 discusses information design

Challenge 1-4
Imagine that you are put in charge of a design team that was to work on a project investigating the possibility of a new set of Web services for a large supermarket. These services would allow connection from any fixed or mobile device from any location allowing food items to be ordered and delivered. The client even wants to investigate the idea of a 'smart refrigerator' that could automatically order items when it ran out. What range of skills might you need and which subject areas would you expect to draw upon?

1.5 Why being human-centred is important

Being human-centred in design is expensive. It involves observing people, talking to people and trying ideas out with people, and all this takes time. Being human-centred is an additional cost to any project, so businesses rightly ask whether taking so much time to talk to people, produce prototype designs and so on is worthwhile. The answer is a fundamental 'yes'. Taking a human-centred approach to the design of interactive systems is advantageous for a number of reasons.

Safety

In the early 1980s there was an accident at a nuclear power plant in the USA at Three Mile Island that almost resulted in a 'meltdown'. Reportedly one of the problems was that the control panel indicated that a valve was closed when it was in fact open, and another indicator was obscured by a tag attached to another control: two fundamental design errors – one technical and one organizational – that human-centred design techniques would help to avoid. Other classic horror tales include a number of plane and train disasters that have been attributed to faulty displays or to operators not understanding or interpreting displays correctly. Systems have to be designed for people and for contexts. It is no good claiming 'human error' if the design was so bad in the first place that an accident was waiting to happen.

Effectiveness

Two key features of effectiveness are acceptability and productivity. Acceptability concerns ensuring that systems fit in with people's ways of working. They will not be effective if they are not used! Involving people closely in the design of their systems will help to ensure acceptability. Systems will be more effective if they are designed from a human-centred perspective and people will be more productive. Nowhere is the economic argument more pertinent than in Web design and e-commerce sites. Jared Spool and his company User Interface Engineering have a number of reports demonstrating the importance of good design to e-commerce and claim that sales can be increased by 225 percent by turning 'browsers' into 'buyers' (UIE, 2003). The executive summary of this paper says:

> *'Every online shopper is presented with a group of products from which he tries to select the one he wants. When he finds the one that meets his needs and expectations, he puts it in his cart. The first step along the customer's path to product evaluation is the product list. It's a make-or-break page – it's where the site introduces its product offerings to the shopper. Does it make a difference how you display lists of products? How much time and money should you invest in designing product lists?*

When we watched users shop, we saw that some of them looked at the product list, decided that one of the products listed was just what they wanted, and added it to their shopping cart. Other shoppers could not ascertain enough information from the product list, so they clicked back-and-forth between the list and multiple individual product pages before deciding whether to select a product for purchase. Pogo-sticking is the name we gave to this comparison-shopping technique of bouncing up-and-down between pages. Shoppers pogo-sticked when they did not find enough information in the product lists. On the other hand, shoppers bought more and had more satisfying experiences when they encountered product lists that provided sufficient product information so they could make a product selection right from the list without pogo-sticking.

If you see shoppers pogo-sticking on your site, it's an indication that you are losing sales. By understanding your customer expectations and needs, and designing your product lists accordingly, you can reduce the likelihood of pogo-sticking and increase your potential sales.'

Source: http://www.uie.com/whitepaperlinks.htm, E-Commerce White Paper – Are the product lists on your site reducing sales?

Ethics

Being human-centred also ensures that designers are truthful and open in their design practice. Now that it is so easy to collect data surreptitiously and to use that data for purposes other than what it was intended for, designers need to be ever more vigilant. As systems are increasingly able to connect autonomously with one another and share data it is vital that people know where the data that they give is going and how it might be used. People need to trust systems and be in a position to make choices about privacy and how they are represented.

The issue of intellectual property is another important aspect of ethical design; it is very easy to take an image from a website and use it without giving proper acknowledgement for its source. There are many issues associated with plagiarism or other dishonest uses of written materials. Privacy, security, control and honesty are all significant features of the interactive systems designer's life. Equality and attention to access are two of the 'political' issues that designers must address.

As technology changes so do traditional views and approaches to big moral and ethical questions. There are standards and legal requirements that need to be met by designs. Fundamentally, ethical design is needed because the systems that are produced should be easy and enjoyable to use, as they affect the quality of people's lives. Designers have power over other people and must exercise that power in an ethical fashion.

Summary and key points

Designing interactive systems is a challenging and fascinating discipline because it draws upon and affects so many features of people's lives. There is a huge variety of interactive systems and products, from business applications of computers to websites to dedicated information appliances to whole information spaces. Designing interactive systems is concerned with designing for people using technologies to undertake activities in contexts. Designing interactive systems needs to be human-centred.

- It draws upon many different subject areas, including both engineering design and artistic design.
- It is needed because we live in a digital age when bits are easily transformed and transmitted.
- It is necessary if we are to have safe, effective and ethical design.

Further reading

Laurel, B. (ed.) (1990) *The Art of Human–Computer Interface Design*. Addison-Wesley, Reading, MA.
Although this book is quite old, many of the articles in it are still relevant and many of the authors of those articles are still at the forefront of interaction design today.

Norman, D. (1999) *The Invisible Computer: Why Good Products Can Fail*. MIT Press, Cambridge, MA.
This is an enjoyable book to read about successes and failures, pasts and futures for technologies.

Norman, D. (1993) *Things That Make Us Smart*. Addison-Wesley, Reading, MA.
Norman, D. (1998) *The Design of Everyday Things*. Addison-Wesley, Reading, MA.
These two easy-to-read books provide a wealth of examples of good and bad design.

Friedman, B. and Kahn, P.H. (2003) Human values, ethics and design. In Jacko, J. and Sears, A. (eds) *The Human–Computer Interaction Handbook*. Lawrence Erlbaum Associates.

Comments on challenges

Challenge 1-1

Of course what you say will be dependent on the product or systems chosen. The important thing is to think in broad terms about the nature of the interaction with the device and at the activities that the device enables, and how good it is at doing them!

I could talk about the coffee machine at work which is a simple, functional device. A single button press produces a reasonable cup of coffee. It is limited, however, in the variety of coffees that I can get (four types only) so I would ideally prefer a person mixing coffee for me rather than getting it from a machine. If I stay late at work and have to use the other coffee machine, it is a nightmare. The money slots don't work properly, the cups are too thin so the drink burns your hands, and the default is coffee with sugar (which I hate) so I have to remember to press the 'no sugar' button. Which I frequently forget to do!

This simple device can be contrasted with a website. Take www.ideo.com, for example: a site for the IDEO design company. Here the opening page is nice and clean, but there is no site map or other help to get the visitor oriented. Clicking on any of the three images or on the 'enter IDEO' button takes you to the same location. Once again the screen is dominated by some nice images but this means that there is not much room for the information! A very small scrolling window on the right-hand side is difficult to read and difficult to control.

Challenge 1-2

The interface to the microwave consists of the various switches on the front that allow programming the time and temperature. There is also an audio part – the 'ping' when the timing is finished. The heating controller has a small liquid crystal display and some large buttons. The remote control just consists of buttons and the PDA uses a pen (pointer) and a touch-sensitive screen. Icons are used on the screen and there are a few buttons on the casing. The PDA accepts 'graffiti' handwriting recognition.

Challenge 1-3

The aim of this challenge is to get you to think beyond user interfaces and beyond human–computer interaction to the changes that new technologies are bringing or could bring. As we create new information appliances and new products such as business cards we, you, interactive systems designers, change the world. We change what is possible and change how people interact with other people. Reflect on (and discuss with someone else, if possible) the political, moral and ethical issues of these concepts.

▶

Challenge 1-4

This project will demand a wide range of skills. On the technology side there are networking and software engineering issues concerned with how devices can be programmed to do this and how the information about products and orders can be stored. There will be issues of authorization and authentication of payments. Product design may come in if there are to be purpose-built devices created to access the services (e.g. an in-store smart scanner that could be used to record items bought). There will be a lot of information design expertise required and some graphic design to help in the layout of information. On the people side of things, general psychological knowledge will help to inform the design, and sociology may help to understand the social setting and impact that such services would have. Business models may need to be developed and certainly the skills of information systems designers will be needed.

Exercises

1. Spend some time browsing the websites of corporations such as IDEO, Sony and Apple. Do not just look at the design of the site (though that can be useful); look at the products they are talking about and the philosophy of their design approach. Collect together your favourites and be prepared to spend time discussing them with your colleagues. Think of the whole range of issues about the site: what it looks like, how easy it is to use, how relevant the content of the site is, how clearly the content is organized, what the overall 'feel' of the site is.

2. Being human-centred is about

   ■ thinking about what people want to do rather than what the technology can do,
   ■ designing new ways to connect people with people,
   ■ involving people in the design process,
   ■ designing for diversity.

   Write down how you might approach the design of the supermarket shopping service discussed in Challenge 1–4. Don't do the design; think about how to approach the design. Are there any issues of effectiveness, safety and ethics that need to be considered?

02

People, activities, contexts and technologies:
A framework for designing interactive systems

Aims

An essential part of our approach to designing interactive systems is that it should put people first; it should be human-centred. We use the acronym PACT (People, Activities, Contexts, Technologies) as a useful framework for thinking about a design situation. Designers also need to know about the features of interactive technologies and how to approach designing interactive systems. After studying this chapter you should be able to:

- ■ Understand the relationship between activities and technologies
- ■ Understand the PACT framework
- ■ Undertake a PACT analysis
- ■ Understand the key features of interactive technologies
- ■ Understand the process of interactive systems design.

2.1 Introduction

People use technologies to undertake activities in contexts. For example, teenagers use cell (mobile) phones to send text messages to their friends whilst sitting on a bus. Secretaries use Microsoft Word to write documents in a firm of solicitors. Air traffic controllers work together to ensure the smooth operation of an airport. A septuagenarian woman presses various buttons to set the intruder alarms in her house. People use Internet-based dating services to make contact with other people when sitting in an Internet café.

In all these settings we see people using technologies to undertake activities in contexts and it is the variety of each of these elements that makes designing interactive systems such a difficult and fascinating challenge. Technologies are there to support a wide range of people undertaking various activities in

Requirements

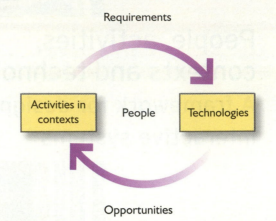

Activities in contexts

People

Technologies

Opportunities

FIGURE 2-1 Activities and technologies *(source: after Carroll (2002), Figure 3.1, p. 68)*

different contexts. If the technology is changed then the nature of the activities will also change. This issue is nicely summed up in Figure 2-1.

Figure 2-1 shows how activities (and the contexts within which they take place) establish requirements for technologies which in turn offer opportunities that change the nature of activities. And so the cycle continues as the changed activity results in new requirements for technologies and so on. Designers need to keep this cycle in mind as they attempt to understand and design for some domain. (The word 'domain' here means an area of study, a 'sphere of activity'.) For example, as personal computers have become more common so the domain of e-mail has changed. Originally e-mail was all in text only, but now it is in full colour with pictures and video embedded. Other items can be attached to e-mails easily. This has led to a need for better facilities for managing it for organizing pictures, documents and addresses. Software now keeps track of threads of e-mails and links between e-mails. Another example is illustrated in Figure 2-2.

FIGURE 2-2 The changing nature of telephoning activity as technology changes *(sources: PA Photos; Dorling Kindersley; © Royalty-Free/Corbis)*

Challenge 2-1
Think of the activity of watching a film. List some ways in which this activity has changed with the introduction of video cassette recorders (VCRs) and digital versatile discs (DVDs). How have the contexts changed since the early days of cinema?

To design interactive technologies we need to understand the variety inherent in all these four elements. We also need to understand what is involved in interactive systems design and how to undertake design.

2.2 People

There can be few less controversial observations than that people differ from one another in a variety of ways. The chapters in Parts II and IV of this book deal with these differences in detail. Here we summarize some of the most important features.

Physical differences

People differ in physical characteristics such as height and weight. People have different personalities and different cognitive skills and preferences. Variability in the five senses – sight, hearing, touch, smell and taste – has a huge effect on how accessible, how usable and how enjoyable using a technology will be for people in different contexts. For example, colour blindness (usually the inability to correctly distinguish between red and green colours) affects about 8 percent of western males, short-sightedness and long-sightedness affect many, and many people are hearing impaired. In Europe there are 2.8 million wheelchair users so designers must consider where technologies are placed, and many people have dexterity impairments involving the use of their fingers. All of us have relatively large fingers compared to the small size we can make buttons. Look at the ticket machine in Figure 2-3. What are the physical aspects of people that need to be taken into account in the design?

Ergonomics,
Chapter 7,
Section 7.1

Psychological differences

Psychologically, people differ in a variety of ways. For example, people with good spatial ability will find it much easier to find their way around and remember a website than those with poor ability. Designers should design for people with poor ability by providing good signage and clear directions. Language differences are of course crucial to understanding, and cultural differences affect how people interpret things. For example, in the Microsoft Excel spreadsheet application there are two buttons, one labelled with a cross and the other a tick.

FIGURE 2-3 Ticket machine *(source: Dorling Kindersley)*

In the US a tick is used for acceptance and a cross for rejection, but in Britain a tick or a cross can be used to show acceptance (e.g. a cross on a voting paper).

People also have different needs and abilities when it comes to attention and memory and these can change depending on factors such as stress and tiredness. No-one can remember long numbers or complicated instructions. All people are better at recognizing things than they are at remembering things. Some people can quickly grasp how something works whereas for others it can take much longer. People have had different experiences and so will have different conceptual 'models' of things. The understanding and knowledge that we possess of something is often referred to as a 'mental model' (e.g. Norman, 1998).

If people do not have a good mental model of something, they can only perform actions by rote. If something goes wrong they will not know why and will not be able to recover. This is often the case with people using software systems, but it is also the case with 'simpler' domestic systems such as central heating systems, thermostats and so on. A key design principle is to design things so that people will form correct and useful mental models of how they work and what they do.

Chapter 5, Section 5.11, on mental models

Challenge 2-2
Write down your mental model of how an e-mail gets sent from one person to another. Compare it with a colleague's and discuss.

Usage differences

Novice and expert users of a technology will typically have very differing requirements. Experts use a system regularly and learn all sorts of details, whereas a novice user of the same system will need to be guided through an interaction. An interesting type of system users are the 'discretionary' users – people who do not have to use a system and who are often quickly put off if things are difficult to do. Designers need to entice these people to use their systems.

Designing for homogeneous groups of people – groups who are broadly similar and want to do much the same things – is quite different from designing for heterogeneous groups. Websites have to cater for heterogeneous groups and have particular design concerns as a result. A company's intranet, however, can be designed to meet the particular needs of particular people. Representatives from a relatively homogeneous group – secretaries or managers or laboratory scientists, say – could be made part of the design team and so provide much more detailed input as to their particular requirements.

Challenge 2-3
Look again at the ticket machine in Figure 2-3 and consider the people who will use it. Identify the variety of characteristics of the users, physically, psychologically and in terms of usage of the system.

2.3 Activities

There are many characteristics of activities that designers need to consider. The term is used for very simple tasks as well as highly complex, lengthy activities, so designers need to be careful when considering the characteristics of activities. Below is our list of the 10 important characteristics of activities that designers need to consider. First and foremost, the designer should focus on the overall *purpose* of the activity. After that the main features are:

- Temporal aspects (items 1–4)
- Cooperation (5)
- Complexity (6)
- Safety-critical (7 and 8)
- The nature of the content (9 and 10).

1. Temporal aspects covers how regular or infrequent activities are. Something that is undertaken every day can have a very different design from something that happens only once a year. People will soon learn how to make calls using a cellphone, but may have great difficulties when it comes to changing the battery. Designers should ensure that frequent tasks are easy

to do, but they also need to ensure that infrequent tasks are easy to learn (or remember) how to do.

2. Other important features of activities include time pressures, peaks and troughs of working. A design that works well when things are quiet can be awful when things are busy.

3. Some activities will take place as a single, continuous set of actions whereas others are more likely to be interrupted. If people are interrupted when undertaking some activity, the design needs to ensure that they can 'find their place' again and pick up. It is important then to ensure that people do not make mistakes or leave important steps out of some activity.

4. The response time needed from the system must be considered. If a website takes two minutes to deliver a response when the server is busy, that may be frustrating for a normal query but it could be critical if the information is needed for some emergency. As a general rule people expect a response time of about 100 milliseconds for hand–eye coordination activities and one second for a cause–effect relationship such as clicking a button and something happening. Anything more than 5 seconds and they will feel frustrated and confused (Dix, 2003).

There are many examples of cooperative activities in Part VII

5. Another important feature of activities is whether they can be carried out alone or whether they are essentially concerned with working with others. Issues of awareness of others and communication and coordination then become important.

6. Well-defined tasks need different designs from more vague tasks. If a task or activity is well defined it can be accomplished with a simple step-by-step design. A vague activity means that people have to be able to browse around, see different types of information, move from one thing to another and so on.

7. Some activities are 'safety-critical', in which any mistake could result in an injury or a serious accident. Others are less so. Clearly where safety is involved designers must pay every attention to ensuring mistakes do not have a serious effect.

8. In general it is vital for designers to think about what happens when people make mistakes and errors and to design for such circumstances.

9. Consider the data requirements of the activity. If large amounts of alphabetic data have to be input as part of the activity (recording names and addresses, perhaps, or word processing documents) then a keyboard is almost certainly needed. In other activities there may be a need to display video or high quality colour graphic displays. Some activities, however, require very modest amounts of data, or data that does not change frequently and can make use of other technologies. A library, for example, just needs to scan in a bar code or two, so the technology can be designed to exploit this feature of the activity.

10. Just as important as data is the media that an activity requires. A simple two-tone display of numeric data demands a very different design from a full motion multimedia display.

Challenge 2-4
List the main characteristics of the activity of sending an e-mail. Use the 10 points above to guide you.

2.4 Contexts

Activities always happen in a context, so there is a need to analyse the two together. Three useful types of context are distinguishable: the organizational context, the social context and the physical circumstances under which the activity takes place. Context can be a difficult term. Sometimes it is useful to see context as surrounding an activity. At other times it can be seen as the features that glue some activities together into a coherent whole.

For the 'withdraw cash from an ATM' activity, for example, an analysis of context would include things such as the location of the device (often as a 'hole-in-the-wall'), the effect of sunshine on the readability of the display, and security considerations. Social considerations would include the time spent on a transaction or the need to queue. The organizational context for this activity would take into consideration the impact on the bank's ways of working and its relationships with its customers. It is important to consider the range of contexts and environments in which activities can take place.

Physical environment

The physical environment in which an activity happens is important. For example, the sun shining on an ATM display may make it unreadable. The environment may be very noisy, cold, wet, or dirty. The same activity – for example, logging on to a website – may be carried out in geographically remote environments where Internet access is slow, or with all the facilities of a large city and fast networks.

Social context

The social context within which the activity takes place is also important. A supportive environment will offer plenty of help for the activity. There may be training manuals available, tuition or experts to hand if people get into trouble. There may be privacy issues to consider, and an interaction can be very different if the person is alone than if they are with others. Social norms may dictate the acceptability of certain designs. For example, the use of sound output is often unacceptable in an open-plan office environment, but might be quite effective where a person is working alone.

Organizational context

Finally the organizational context (Figure 2-4) is important as changes in technology often alter communication and power structures and may have effects on jobs such as deskilling. There are many books devoted to the study of organizations and the impact of new technologies on organizations. We cannot do justice to this subject here. The circumstances under which activities happen (time, place, and so on) also vary widely and need to be taken into consideration.

FIGURE 2-4 Different working contexts *(source: Dorling Kindersley)*

2.5 Technologies

The final part of the PACT framework is the technologies. Interactive systems typically consist of hardware and software components and transform some input data into some output data. They can perform various functions and typically contain a good deal of data, or information content. People using such systems engage in interactions and physically devices have various degrees of style and aesthetics. Interactive systems constitute the medium that interactive system designers work with. Some important features of technologies are:

→

Chapter 6 on technologies

■ Input. Input devices are concerned with how people enter data and instructions into a system securely and safely. The characteristics of the data are important for choosing input methods. Bar codes, for example, are only sensible if the data does not change often. Touch screens are useful if there are only a few options to choose from. Speech input is possible if there is no noise or background interference and if there are only a few commands that need to be entered.

■ Output. Output needs to be considered, including the characteristics of different displays (e.g. video vs. photographs; speech vs. screen). 'Streamy' outputs such as video, music and speech have different characteristics from 'chunky' media such as icons, text or still photographs. Most important, perhaps, is that streamy media do not stay around for long. Instructions given as speech output, for example, have to be remembered, whereas if displayed as a piece of text, they can be read over again.

- ■ Communication. Communications between people and between devices need to be considered. Here issues such as bandwidth and speed are critical. So too is feedback to people so that they know what is going on and indeed that something is going on! In some domains the transmission and storage of large amounts of data becomes a key feature. Communication between devices is another important consideration.

- ■ Content. This concerns the data in the system and the form it takes. Good content is accurate, up-to-date, relevant and well presented. There is little point in having a sophisticated information retrieval system if the information, once retrieved, is out of date or irrelevant. In some technologies content is just about everything (e.g. websites are usually all about content). Other technologies are more concerned with function (e.g. a remote control for a TV). Most technologies have a mixture of function and content.

2.6 Scoping a problem with PACT

The aim of human-centred interactive systems design, as we discuss in the next chapter, is to harmonize the PACT elements in a particular domain. Designers want to get the right mix of technologies to support the activities being undertaken by people in different contexts. A PACT analysis is useful for both analysis and design activities: understanding the current situation, seeing where possible improvements can be made or envisioning future situations. To do a PACT analysis the designer simply scopes out the variety of Ps, As, Cs and Ts that are possible. This can be done using brainstorming and other envisionment techniques and by working with people through observations, interviews and workshops. The results can be written up as detailed concrete 'scenarios of use'. The designer should look for trade-offs between combinations of PACT and think about how these might affect design.

Scenario-based design in Chapter 7, envisionment in Chapter 9

For people, designers need to think about the physical, psychological and social differences and how those differences change in different circumstances and over time. It is most important that designers consider all the various stakeholders in a project, not simply the 'end users'. There are often groups of people who have an interest, or stake, in a project who will never use the system; managers, administrators and customers can all be affected by changed systems that other people are using. Developing 'personas' can be useful here (see Box 2-1). For activities they need to think about the complexity of the activity (focused or vague, simple or difficult, few steps or many), the temporal features (frequency, peaks and troughs, continuous or interruptible), cooperative features and the nature of the data. For contexts they think about the physical, social and organizational setting, and for technologies they concentrate on input, output, communication and content.

Box 2-1 Developing personas

Christine Perfetti of UIE writes:
'A persona is a profile of a typical user; it is a description of an archetypal user synthesized from a series of interviews with real people and includes a name, a social history, and a set of goals that drive the design of the product or web site.

By closely adhering to the goals of a specific persona, the designers satisfy the needs of the many users who have goals similar to those of the persona. The process is even more effective when designers design for several personas simultaneously, as they can satisfy an even larger number of users. Although designing for one to satisfy many may initially seem counter-intuitive, teams we've talked to who have employed it tell us it's a very effective technique.

A financial services client recently told us that they had thousands of users, each with very different goals, coming to the site every week, and the client didn't know how to approach the design. Our advice was to develop several personas, one for each major class of audience member. In talking with the client, we determined that they could get by with a couple of key personas: a seasoned investor and an infrequent investor.'

Source: http://world.std.com/~uieweb/Articles/Personas.htm, Personas: Matching a Design to the Users' Goals

As an example, let us assume that we have been asked by a university department to consider developing a system controlling access to their laboratories. A PACT analysis might include the following.

People

Students, lecturers and technicians are the main groups. These are all well educated and understand things such as swipe cards, passwords and so on. People in wheelchairs need to be considered as do other design issues such as colour blindness. There may be language differences. Both visitors and frequent users need to be considered. However, there are other stakeholders who need access to rooms, such as cleaning staff and security personnel. What are the motivations for management wanting to control access in the first place?

Activities

The overall purpose of the activity is to enter some form of security clearance and to open the door. This is a very well-defined activity that takes place in one step. It happens very frequently with peaks at the start of each laboratory session. The data to be entered is a simple numeric or alpha-numeric code. It is an activity that does not require cooperation with others (though it may be done with others, of course). It is not safety-critical, though security is an important aspect.

Contexts

Physically the activity takes place indoors, but people might be carrying books and other things that makes doing anything complicated quite difficult. Socially it may happen in a crowd, but also it may happen late at night when no-one else is about. Organizationally, the context is primarily about security and who has access to which rooms and when they can gain access. This is likely to be quite a politically charged setting.

Technologies

A small amount of data has to be entered quickly. It must be obvious how to do this to accommodate visitors and people unfamiliar with the system. It needs to be accessible by people in wheelchairs. The output from the technology needs to be clear: that the security data has been accepted or not and the door has to be opened if the process was successful. Communication with a central database may be necessary to validate any data input, but there is little other content in the application.

Challenge 2-5
Write down a quick PACT analysis for the introduction of a 'point of sale' system (i.e. where goods are priced and paid for) for a café at a motorway service station. Discuss your ideas with a colleague.

2.7 The process of human-centred interactive systems design

Design is a creative process concerned with bringing about something new. It is a social activity with social consequences. It is about conscious change and communication between designer and user. Different design disciplines have different methods and techniques for helping with this process. Approaches to and philosophies of design change over time. In mature disciplines, examples of good design are built up and people can study and reflect upon what makes a certain design great, good or awful. Different design disciplines have different constraints such as whether the designed object is 'stand alone' or whether it has to fit in and live with legacy systems or conform to standards.

Activities in design

There are many different ways of characterizing the activities involved in the design process. For David Kelley, founder of the product design company IDEO,

'Design has three activities: understand, observe and visualize.'

He says

'Remember, design is messy; designers try to understand this mess. They observe how their products will be used; design is about users and use. They visualize which is the act of deciding what it is.'

Kelley and Hartfield (1996), p. 156

For Gillian Crampton Smith and Philip Tabor (1996) there are five activities:

- Understanding – where designers observe and analyse the information or the problem
- Abstracting – where the designer focuses on the main elements of a problem and on the kind of information
- Structuring – where the designer considers the relationships between the elements and what people are interested in
- Representing – concerned with how the structure can be represented
- Detailing – concerned with what colour an item should be, how elements can move, etc.

We characterize the interactive system design process in terms of the five activities illustrated in Figure 2-5. This is a modified version of the Star Life Cycle (Hix and Hartson, 1993). Hix and Hartson developed this model for the software design process after studying real designers at work. The activities are discussed in more detail below, but the key features of this representation are as follows:

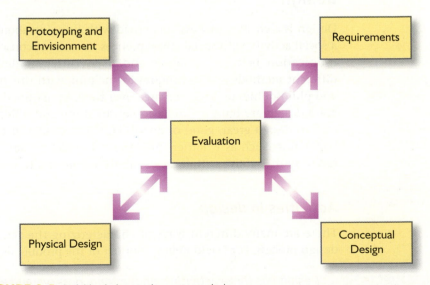

FIGURE 2-5 Activities in interactive systems design

■ Evaluation is central to designing interactive systems. Everything gets evaluated at every step of the process.

■ The process can start at any point – sometimes there is a conceptual design in place, sometimes we start with a prototype, sometimes we start with requirements.

■ The activities can happen in any order, for example requirements might be evaluated and a prototype built and evaluated and some aspect of a physical design might then be identified.

Requirements

Requirements are concerned with what the system has to do, what it has to be like, how it has to fit in with other things. There are both functional and non-functional requirements to consider. Functional requirements are concerned with what the system should be able to do and with the functional constraints of a system. It is important for the designer to think about the whole human–computer system in an abstract way. Deciding who does what, when something should be displayed or the sequence in which actions are undertaken should come later in the design process. A good analysis of an activity will strive to be as independent of current practice as possible. Of course, there are always functional constraints – the realities of what is technically possible – which render certain ordering, sequencing and allocation of functions inevitable. There are also logical and organizational constraints which may make particular designs infeasible.

Chapter 9 on requirements

Requirements are generated through discussions with future clients or users of the system, and observations of existing systems and what people do. Requirements can be generated through working with people in focus groups, design workshops and so on, where different scenarios can be considered (see Box 2-2). The aim is to collect and analyse the stories people have to tell. Requirements are essentially about understanding.

Chapter 8 on scenarios

Box 2-2 Scenarios in design

Scenarios are a key feature in interactive systems design that are used throughout the processes of requirements, conceptual and physical design, envisionment, prototyping and evaluation. Scenarios are stories, or narratives. They describe people using technologies to undertake some activities in context. People often express their ideas and requirements in the form of scenarios. Designers find it useful to present design ideas in the form of scenarios and people can work through scenarios in order to evaluate specific design ideas.

Conceptual design

Conceptual design covers the same ground as abstracting and structuring in Crampton Smith and Tabor's description. It is about designing a system in the abstract, about considering what information and functions are needed for the system to achieve its purpose. It is about deciding what someone will have to know to use the system. It is about finding a clear conceptualization of a design solution and how that conceptualization will be communicated to people (so that users will quickly develop a clear mental model).

There are a number of techniques to help with conceptual design. Software engineers prefer modelling possible solutions with objects, relationships and 'use cases' (a semi-formal scenario representation). Entity–relationship models are another popular conceptual modelling tool. Flow can be represented using dataflow diagrams and structure can be shown with structure charts. The conceptual design of a website, for example, will include a site map and a navigation structure. Many different conceptual models are used in the contextual inquiry method.

Chapters 18 on contextual inquiry and 19 on design

One way to conceptualize the main features of a system is to use a 'rich picture'. Two examples are shown in Figure 2-6. A rich picture captures the main conceptual relationships between the main conceptual entities in a system – a model of the structure of a situation. Peter Checkland (Checkland, 1981;

(a)

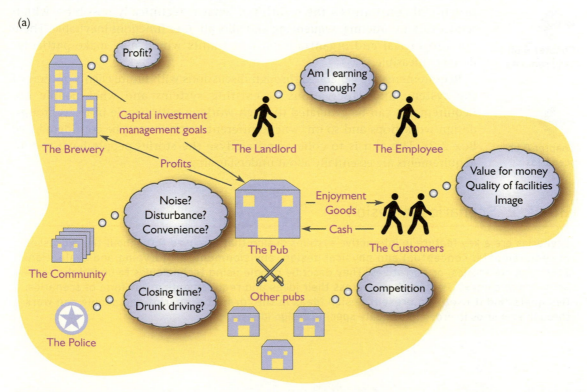

FIGURE 2-6 Rich pictures of (a) a pub and (b) a Web design company *(source: after Monk, A. and Howard, S. (1998) The rich picture: a tool for reasoning about work context, Interactions, 5(2), pp. 21–30, Fig. 1 and Fig. 2. © 1998 ACM, Inc. Reprinted by permission)*

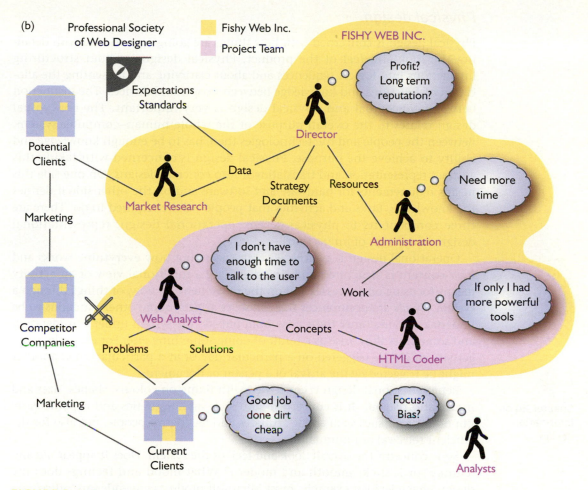

FIGURE 2-6 Continued

Checkland and Scholes, 1999), who originated the soft systems approach, also emphasizes focusing on the key transformation of a system. This is the conceptual model of processing. The principal stakeholders – customers, actors, system owners – should be identified. The designer should also consider the perspective from which an activity is being viewed as a system (the *Weltanschauung*) and the environment in which the activities take place. (Checkland proposes the acronym CATWOE – customers, actors, transformation, *Weltanschauung*, owners, environment – for these elements of a rich picture.) Most importantly the rich picture identifies the issues or concerns of the stakeholders, thus helping to focus attention on problems or potential design solutions.

The key feature of conceptual design is to keep things abstract – focus on the 'what' rather than the 'how' – and to avoid making assumptions about how functions and information will be distributed. There is no clear-cut distinction between conceptual and physical design, but rather there are degrees of conceptuality.

Physical design

Physical design is concerned with how things are going to work and with detailing the look and feel of the product. Physical design is about structuring interactions into logical sequences and about clarifying and presenting the allocation of functions and knowledge between people and devices. The distinction between conceptual and physical design is very important. The conceptual design relates to the overall purpose of the whole human–computer system. Between the people and the technologies there has to be enough knowledge and ability to achieve the purpose. Physical design is concerned with taking this abstract representation and translating it into concrete designs. On one side this means requirements for hardware and software and on the other side it defines the knowledge, tasks and activities that people will be required to do. There are three components to physical design: operational design, representational design, and design of interactions.

Operational design is concerned with specifying how everything works and how content is structured and stored. Taking a functional view of an activity means focusing on processes and on the movement, or flow, of things through a system. *Events* are occurrences that cause, or trigger, some other functions to be undertaken. Sometimes these arise from outside the system under consideration and sometimes they arise as a result of doing something else. For example, some activity might be triggered on a particular day or at a particular time; another might be triggered by the arrival of a person or document.

Chapter 24 on Information design

Representational design is concerned with fixing on colours, shapes, sizes and information layout. It is concerned with style and aesthetics and is particularly important for issues such as the attitudes and feelings of people, but also for the efficient retrieval of information.

Style concerns the overall 'look and feel' of the system. Does it appear old and 'clunky' or is slick, smooth and modern? What mood and feelings does the design engender? For example, most Microsoft products engender an 'office' and 'work' mood, serious rather than playful. Many other systems aim to make the interaction engaging, some aim to make it challenging and others entertaining. In multimedia and games applications this is particularly important.

Interaction design, in this context, is concerned with the allocation of functions to human agency or to technology and with the structuring and sequencing of the interactions. Allocation of functions has a significant impact on the usability of the system. For example, consider the activity of making a phone call. Certain functions are necessary: indicate a desire to make a phone call, connect to the network, enter the phone number, make connection. Years ago a telephone exchange was staffed by people and it was these people who made connections by physically putting wires into connectors. In the days of wired phones, picking up the receiver indicated the desire to make a call, the full number had to be dialled in and then the telephone exchange would automatically make the connections. Nowadays a person just has to press the connect button on a cellular phone, choose someone's name from the phone's address book and the technology does the rest.

Prototyping and envisionment

Designs need to be visualized both to help designers clarify their own ideas and to enable people to evaluate them. Prototyping and envisionment is concerned with finding appropriate media in which to render to design ideas. The medium needs to be appropriate for the stage of the process, the audience, the resources available and the questions that the prototype is helping to answer.

There are many techniques for prototyping and envisionment, but they include any way in which abstract ideas can be brought to life. Sketches 'on the back of an envelope', fully functioning prototypes and cardboard mock-ups are just some of the methods used. Scenarios, sometimes represented in pictorial form as storyboards, are an essential part of prototyping and envisionment. They provide a way of working through a design idea so that the key issues stand out.

More detail in Chapters 10 and 11

Evaluation

Evaluation is tightly coupled with envisionment because the nature of the representation used will affect what can be evaluated. The evaluation criteria will also depend on who is able to use the representation. Any of the other design activities will be followed by an evaluation. Sometimes this is simply the designer checking through to make sure something is complete and correct. It could be a list of requirements or a high-level design brief that is sent to a client, an abstract conceptual model that is discussed with a colleague, or a formal evaluation of a functional prototype by the future system users.

Chapters 12, 21 and 22 provide detail on evauation

Techniques for evaluation are many and various depending once again on the circumstances. Expressing the design ideas in terms of a concrete scenario that people have to work their way through can be very effective. The important thing to keep in mind is that the technique used must be appropriate for the nature of the representation, the questions being asked and the people involved in the evaluation.

Challenge 2-6
If you were to have a new room built onto your house – or have a room converted from one use to another – consider the processes that you would have to go through, starting with:

- A conceptual design
- A physical design
- Some requirements
- A prototype or other envisioned solution.

Implementation

Figure 2-5 does not include the implementation or production of the design (nor all the planning and management stages of a project). But of course ultimately things have to be engineered and software has to be written and tested. Databases have to be designed and populated and programs have to be validated. The whole system needs to be checked to ensure that it meets the requirements until finally the system can be formally 'launched' and signed off as finished. Since this book is primarily about design, we do not spend a lot of time on issues of implementation, but they can account for a significant portion of total development costs. Clients will often want extra features when they see a system nearing completion, but these will have to be costed and paid for. On the other hand the developers need to ensure that their system really does meet the specification and does not contain any 'bugs'.

Chapter 18 provides a number of semi-formal models

If interactive systems designers were architects they would have well understood methods and conventions for specifying the results of the design process. They would produce various blueprints from different elevations and engineering specifications for particular aspects of the design. In interactive systems design there are a variety of formal, semi-formal and informal methods of specification. The best known of these is the Unified Modeling Language (UML) (Pender, 2003).

Chapter 16 on specification

2.8 Doing design

To illustrate the design process, let us return to the example of the laboratory access system. We use letters to illustrate which activity is being undertaken:

R = requirements
C = conceptual design
P = prototyping and envisionment
D = physical design
E = evaluation.

Notice the iterative nature of the design and how some details get fixed that then affect other possibilities. Notice also how the problem and solution evolve together, for example through clarification of requirements.

The PACT analysis has resulted from an initial brief (R) and discussions between the clients (the university department) and our designers (R). Some requirements have been written down (P) and discussed further by clients and designers (E). As a result a discussion of some points of clarification with the university department has taken place (R). We can now speculate about possible designs; three conceptual designs have been suggested (C):

1. Each user of the laboratory could be issued with a card that is swiped through a card reader at the door.

2. Instead of having a card, people could type in a number on a key pad.

3. Other technologies such as iris recognition could be used.

These conceptual designs can now be evaluated (E) by discussing them with colleagues and the client. For example, the advantage with option 1 is that most people already have some form of card, but visitors would have to be issued with a temporary card. The activity would be quite quick if the technology works, but sometimes cards do not swipe properly. Even a total time of only 2 seconds per person might be considered too long at the start of a lab session. The card has the advantage that different laboratories can allow access to different groups, but it may be confusing for people if they cannot get into a particular lab when they want to. Good signage is needed to go with such a system. Option 2 would take longer than swiping a card, but it is easier to issue people with a number than it is to issue cards. Technologies for option 3 are still in their infancy. Besides, the same problems with visitors arise.

The case study in Chapter 4 also illustrates the iterative nature of design

As result of these discussions some further technical research would probably be undertaken so that technical opportunities and constraints can be clarified (R). In terms of physical design (D) there is not much opportunity in this case as most of the technology will be bought in, but it may be that concrete prototypes (P) would need to be developed and evaluated (E) to verify that the system would work when under time pressure.

Summary and key points

The design of interactive systems is concerned with people, the activities they are undertaking, the contexts of those activities and the technologies that are used. There is considerable variety in each of these and it is this variety – and all the different combinations that can occur – that makes the design of interactive systems so fascinating.

- The design of interactive systems requires the analyst/designer to consider the range of PACT elements.
- There are also many areas of interactive systems to consider such as the functions, interactions, content and form that the system will take.
- The process of design is highly iterative, going backwards and forwards through requirements, conceptual and physical design, prototyping and envisionment.

Further reading

Winograd, T. (ed.) (1996) *Bringing Design to Software*. ACM Press, New York.
This book contains a number of interesting articles from interactive systems designers and is essential reading for all would-be interactive systems designers.

Cooper, A. (1999) *The Inmates are Running the Asylum*. SAMS, Macmillan Computer Publishing, Indianapolis, IN.
Cooper gives an insightful and enjoyable tour through some of the worst aspects of interactive systems design and introduces his approach that focuses on developing personas and taking a goal-oriented approach to design.

Interactions is an excellent journal focusing on interactive systems design.

Comments on challenges

Challenge 2-1
With VCRs came the video hire shop and so the activity of watching a film moved from the cinema into the home. VCRs also allowed films to be recorded from the television so people could watch them whenever they wanted. With DVDs people are given more options than just watching the film, so now the activity includes watching pieces that were cut out of the original film, slightly different versions, interviews with the actors and director and so on. The activity of watching a film is now more interactive; the people watching have more control over what they see.

Challenge 2-2
How an e-mail actually gets from one place to another is surprisingly complicated! It is much more like sending a letter by post than like making a telephone call. The e-mail is sent as one or more 'packets' of data which may be routed across the world by any of a host of different routes. The e-mail travels from your computer through the computer providing the Internet connection, then to a major 'hub' where it joins a high-capacity 'backbone' cable. As it comes closer to its destination this process is reversed as it moves off the main cables into more remote areas. A sophisticated database of addresses and routing information is used to find the best way.

Challenge 2-3
Physically the siting is important so that people in wheelchairs, children, etc. can reach the buttons. Buttons must be easy to press so that the elderly are not excluded from its use. Psychologically the machine should not make undue demands on people. It is difficult to say anything certain since we do

not know the complexity of the machine. Some ticket machines are very simple – just designed to select the destination and deliver the ticket. Others try to offer the whole range of functions, different ticket types, groups, period return tickets and so on. These machines tend to become very complicated and hard to use. From the usage perspective the design needs to support both those people who are in a hurry and perhaps use the machine every day and those people who have never encountered such a machine before, perhaps speak a different language and are trying to do something quite complex. It is difficult to design optimally for both of these types of use.

Challenge 2-4

Sending e-mails is a fairly frequent activity that is often interrupted. It is a straightforward activity in itself but it can become very complex when it is interleaved with other things such as finding old e-mails, finding addresses, attaching documents and so on. It is not necessary to coordinate the activity with others. The tasks of finding and entering addresses are made much easier if the e-mail program has an embedded address book as the person only has to remember and type small amounts of data. Otherwise long e-mail addresses have to be typed in.

Challenge 2-5

There are many complex issues involved, of course. Here are just a few to start with. People – the whole range! From a coachload of football supporters or elderly people on an outing to individuals wandering around late at night. The key thing to consider is how to deal with crowds at one time and just a few people at another. The activities are simple and well defined. The items have to be identified, priced and totalled. The money has to be taken and a receipt printed. Occasionally there will be a question to be answered that goes outside this simple task structure, such as 'how much would this cost if I …?', or disputes over prices need to be settled. There are also other stakeholders involved: the serving staff, the managers and so on. They also need information from the system. As for technologies, items could have a bar code on them, but for meals this is difficult, so usually individual items need to have the price typed in. This takes time. The interface design will be quite critical – e.g. there could be specific keys for things like tea and coffee, but whether it is a good idea to have a specific key for everything is another matter. Now you have had a chance to think about this, spend some time looking at all the different solutions that different cafés use in different contexts.

Challenge 2-6

A conceptual design would focus on the idea for the room. You may think it would be nice to have a conservatory or a downstairs toilet and proceed

▶

from there. You would evaluate the idea, perhaps by looking at some physical prototypes at a large store or at a friend's house. This might help to define the requirements such as the size of the conservatory, where you would locate it and so on. Starting with a physical design, you might see something at a friend's or on television and this might trigger the idea that it would be a nice thing to have. Once you have the concept, proceed as above. Seeing a picture in a book is another example of an envisioned solution starting the process off. On other occasions the process might be started by some requirements. You may feel that you need a study, a new room for a baby, or somewhere to sit in the sun in the winter and it might be these requirements that begin the process. Notice how, wherever the process starts from, the next step will be some evaluation.

Exercises

1. You have been asked to design the information system for a new cycle path network that is to run through part of your town. The aim of the system is to provide information on directions and distances for leisure cyclists to the main points of interest in the town. It also needs to provide information on other things, such as bus and train times for those cyclists who are commuting to and from work. Undertake a PACT analysis for this application.

2. For the same application produce a project development plan. You should detail what sort of requirements work will be needed, the people or skills that will be needed in the project team, and the approach that will be taken. Identify any milestones that you would have in the project.

03 Principles and practice of interactive systems design

Aims

The aim of this chapter is to provide advice and guidance that will result in high-quality designs. When interactive systems were used almost exclusively in the workplace, good design was thought of mainly in functional terms: did the system do what it was meant to do? In the last 10–15 years, of course, computers and other interactive systems and devices have moved out of the work arena and into the wider world of home, community and personal products. Now designers have to consider not just the functionality of a system but also the whole experience of using it and owning it. In this chapter we explore how designers can create appropriate experiences for the users of their products and systems in different contexts. After studying this chapter you should be able to:

- Understand the key issues and concepts of access and usability
- Understand the key issues of acceptability and engagement
- Understand the general principles of good interactive systems design
- Understand the principles applied to different technological platforms.

3.1 Introduction

Good design cannot be summed up in a simple way and nor can the activities of the interactive systems designer, particularly one who takes a human-centred approach to design. One view might say 'The interactive systems designer aims to produce systems and products that are accessible, usable, socially and economically acceptable and engaging'. Another view might say 'The interactive systems designer aims to produce systems that are learnable, effective and accommodating'. A third view could be 'The aim of the interactive systems designer is to harmonize the PACT elements in a domain'. All of these views are valid. In this chapter we explore these complementary views of good design. We also develop some high-level design principles that can guide designers and be used to evaluate design ideas. Finally we put these ideas into practice by looking at some examples of good and bad design across different design contexts.

The first four sections are concerned with key concerns of good design. *Access* concerns removing the barriers that would otherwise exclude some people from using the system at all. *Usability* refers to the quality of the interaction in terms of parameters such as time taken to perform tasks, number of errors made and the time to become a competent user. A system may be assessed as highly usable according to some usability evaluation criteria, but may still fail to be adopted or to satisfy people. *Acceptability* refers to fitness for purpose in the context of use. It also covers personal preferences that contribute to users 'taking to' an artefact, or not. Finally we can consider designing for the 'wow' factor. *Engagement* concerns designing for great, exciting and riveting experiences.

3.2 Accessibility

Access to physical spaces for people with disabilities has long been an important legal and ethical requirement and this is now becoming increasingly so for information spaces. Legislation such as the UK's Disability Discrimination Act and Section 508 in the US now requires software to be accessible. The United Nations and the World Wide Web Consortium have declarations and guidelines on ensuring that everyone can get access to information that is delivered through software technologies. With an increasingly wide range of computer users and technologies, designers need to focus on the demands their designs make on people's abilities. Designers have to design for the elderly and for children. Newell (1995) points out that the sort of issues that face an ordinary user in an extraordinary environment (such as under stress, time pressures, etc.) are often similar to the issues that face an extraordinary user (e.g. a user with disabilities) in an ordinary environment.

People will be excluded from accessing interactive systems for any of a number of reasons:

■ Physically people can be excluded because of inappropriate siting of equipment or through input and output devices making excessive demands on their abilities. For example, an ATM may be positioned too high for a person in a wheelchair to reach, a mouse may be too big for a child's hand or a joystick may be too fiddly for someone with arthritis to use.

■ Conceptually people may be excluded because they cannot understand complicated instructions or obscure commands or they cannot form a clear mental model of the system.

■ Economically people are excluded if they cannot afford some essential technology.

■ Cultural exclusion results from designers making inappropriate assumptions about how people work and organize their lives. For example, using a metaphor based on American football would exclude those who do not understand the game.

Chapter 24, Section 24.2 on metaphors in design

■ Social exclusion can occur if equipment is unavailable at an appropriate time and place or if people are not members of a particular social group and cannot understand particular social mores or messages.

Overcoming these barriers to access is a key design consideration. Two main approaches to designing for accessibility are 'design for all' and inclusive design. Design for all (also known as universal design) goes beyond the design of interactive systems and applies to all design endeavours. It is grounded in a certain philosophical approach to design encapsulated by an international design community (see Box 3-1). Inclusive design is based on four premises:

■ Varying ability is not a special condition of the few but a common characteristic of being human and we change physically and intellectually throughout our lives.

■ If a design works well for people with disabilities, it works better for everyone.

■ At any point in our lives, personal self-esteem, identity and well-being are deeply affected by our ability to function in our physical surroundings with a sense of comfort, independence and control.

■ Usability and aesthetics are mutually compatible.

Box 3-1 Principles of universal design*

1. **Equitable Use:** The design does not disadvantage or stigmatize any group of users.
2. **Flexibility in Use:** The design accommodates a wide range of individual preferences and abilities.
3. **Simple, Intuitive Use:** Use of the design is easy to understand, regardless of the user's experience, knowledge, language skills, or current concentration level.
4. **Perceptible Information:** The design communicates necessary information effectively to the user, regardless of ambient conditions or the user's sensory abilities.
5. **Tolerance for Error:** The design minimizes hazards and the adverse consequences of accidental or unintended actions.
6. **Low Physical Effort:** The design can be used efficiently and comfortably, and with a minimum of fatigue.
7. **Size and Space for Approach and Use:** Appropriate size and space is provided for approach, reach, manipulation, and use, regardless of the user's body size, posture, or mobility.

* Compiled by advocates of universal design, listed in alphabetical order:
Bettye Rose Connell, Mike Jones, Ron Mace, Jim Mueller, Abir Mullick, Elaine Ostroff, Jon Sanford, Ed Steinfeld, Molly Story, Gregg Vanderheiden.

© Centre for Universal Design, School of Design, North Carolina State University

Inclusive design is a more pragmatic approach which argues that there will often be reasons (e.g. technical or financial) why total inclusion is unattainable. Benyon, Crerar and Wilkinson (2001) recommend undertaking an inclusivity analysis that ensures that inadvertent exclusion will be minimized and that common characteristics that cause exclusion and which are relatively cheap to fix will be identified. Distinguishing between fixed and changing user characteristics, they present a decision tree (see Figure 3-1). We all suffer from disabilities from time to time (e.g. a broken arm) that affect our abilities to use interactive systems.

As a way of ensuring an accessible system, designers should

- include people with special needs in requirements analysis and testing of existing systems;
- consider whether new features affect users with special needs (positively or negatively) and note this in the specification;
- take account of guidelines, include evaluation against guidelines;
- include special needs users in usability testing and beta tests.

There are a number of assistive technologies, such as Web browsers which read Web pages, and screen enlargers which allow people to set and move the area of focus. Voice input is increasingly available not just for text entry but also as a substitute for mouse/keyboard control, and keyboard filters can compensate for tremor, erratic motion and slow response time.

In the MS Windows XP operating system there is an Accessibility Option (under the control panel) which allows the setting of keyboard, sound, visual warnings and captions for sounds. The display can be altered including setting a

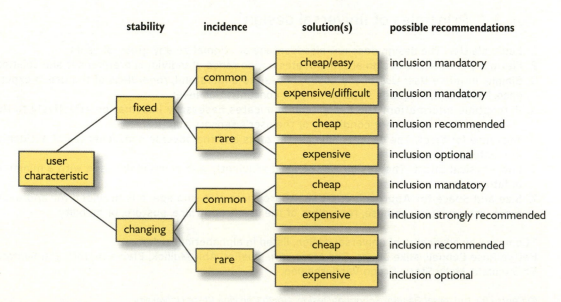

FIGURE 3-1 Decision tree for inclusivity analysis *(source: after Benyon et al. (2001), Figure 2.3, p. 38)*

high contrast, and mouse settings can be adjusted. The Universal Access control panel on the Mac offers similar options (Figure 3-2).

To a large extent design for all is just good design. The aim is to design to cater for the widest range of human abilities. By considering access issues early in the design process, the overall design will be better for everyone. Stephanidis (2001) provides a range of views on how this can be accomplished, from new computer 'architectures' that can accommodate different interfaces for different users, to better requirements generation processes, consideration of alternative input and output devices and the adoption of international standards.

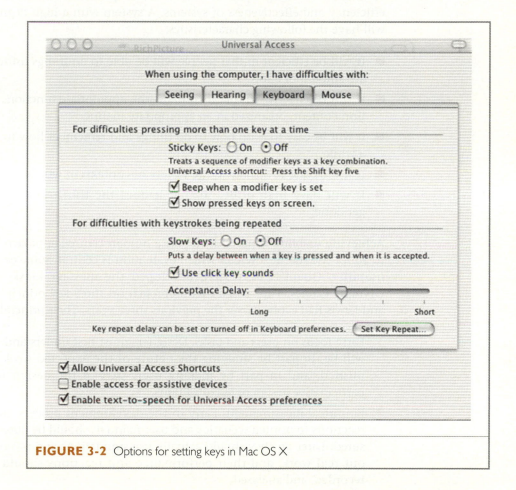

FIGURE 3-2 Options for setting keys in Mac OS X

Challenge 3-1
The UK government is considering introducing electronic access to a variety of social benefits (such as unemployment benefit, housing benefit, etc.). What are some of the access issues involved with this?

3.3 Usability

Usability has always been the central pursuit of human–computer interaction (HCI). The original definition of usability is that systems should be easy to use, easy to learn, flexible and which engender a good attitude in people (Shackel, 1990). As the variety of people, activities, contexts and technologies of interactive system design has increased so this definition, whilst still being valid, hides many important issues. For example, accessibility is now a key design aim, as is sustainability. The goals of usability are now primarily seen as concerned with efficiency and effectiveness of systems. A system with a high degree of usability will have the following characteristics.

- ■ It will be efficient in that people will be able to do things using an appropriate amount of effort.
- ■ It will be effective in that it contains the appropriate functions and information content, organized in an appropriate manner.
- ■ It will be easy to learn how to do things and remember how to do them after a while.
- ■ It will be safe to operate in the variety of contexts in which it will be used.
- ■ It will have high utility in that it does the things that people want to get done.

Achieving usability requires us to take a human-centred approach to design and to adopt the star life cycle in which evaluation is central. Some early pioneers of usability, Gould *et al.* (1987), developed the message kiosks for the 1984 Olympic Games. They based their approach on three key principles that Gould and Lewis had evolved over the previous three years. Their principles were:

1. Early focus on users and tasks. Designers must first understand who the users will be, in part by studying the nature of the expected work to be accomplished, and in part by making users part of the design team through participative design or as consultants.

2. Empirical measurement. Early in the development process, intended users' reactions to printed scenarios and user manuals should be observed and measured. Later on they should actually use simulations and prototypes to carry out real work, and their performance and reactions should be observed, recorded, and analysed.

3. Iterative design. When problems are found in user testing, as they will be, they must be fixed. This means design must be iterative: there must be a cycle of design, test and measure, and redesign, repeated as often as necessary. Empirical measurement and iterative design are necessary because designers, no matter how good they are, cannot get it right the first few times. (Gould *et al.*, 1987, p. 758)

As a result of their experiences with that project they added a fourth principle, integrated usability:

4. 'All usability factors must evolve together, and responsibility for all aspects of usability should be under one control'. (p. 766)

The development of the Olympic Message System (OMS) is described in detail in Gould *et al.* (1987) and it still makes interesting reading in terms of the different types of testing that were done, from written scenarios of use to 'try-to-destroy-it' tests!

One way to look at usability is to see it as concerned with achieving a balance between the four principal factors of human-centred interactive systems design, PACT:

- People
- Activities people want to undertake
- Contexts in which the interaction takes place
- Technologies (hardware and software).

The combinations of these elements are very different in, for example, a public kiosk, a shared diary system, an airline cockpit or a cellphone; and it is this wide variety that makes achieving a balance so difficult. Designers must constantly evaluate different combinations in order to reach this balance.

Figure 3-3 illustrates an important feature of human–computer interaction. There are two relationships that need to be optimized. On the one hand there is the interaction between people and the technologies that they are using. This focuses on the user interface. The other relationship is the interaction between

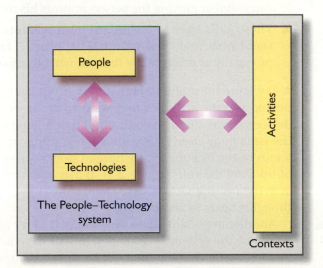

FIGURE 3-3 Usability aims to achieve a balance in the PACT elements

the people and technologies considered as a whole (the people–technology system), the activities being undertaken, and the contexts of those activities.

The idea of a people–technology system optimized for some activities is nicely illustrated with an example from Erik Hollnagel (1997). He discusses the difference between a person on a horse travelling across open countryside and a person in a car travelling along a road. The combinations of technologies are balanced for the different contexts of travelling; neither is better in all circumstances. It is important to remember that the people–technology system may consist of many people and many devices working together to undertake some activities.

Challenge 3-2
Think of the activity of writing and all the various contexts in which we undertake this activity. For example, you might be writing a report for a student assignment, writing a postcard from a poolside chair on holiday, writing down some thoughts on a train, taking notes in a lecture and so on. Now think about the different technologies that we use for writing: ballpoint pens, felt-tipped pens, computers, palmtop PDAs and so on. Which combinations are most usable in which circumstances? Why?

This is discussed further in Chapter 5, Section 5.3

Don Norman (Norman, 1988) focuses on the interface between a person and the technology and on the difficulty of people having to translate their goals into the specific actions required by a user interface. Norman's characterization is as follows.

■ People have goals – things they are trying to achieve in the world. But devices typically only deal with simple actions. This means that two 'gulfs' have to be bridged.

■ The gulf of execution is concerned with translating goals into actions, and the gulf of evaluation is concerned with deciding whether the actions were successful in moving the person towards his or her goal.

■ These gulfs have to be bridged both semantically (does the person understand what to do and what has happened?) and physically (can the person physically or perceptually find out what to do or what has happened?).

A key issue for usability is that very often the technology gets in the way of people and the activities they want to do. If we compare using an interactive device such as a remote control to using a hammer or driving a car, we can see the issue more clearly. Very often when using an interactive system we are conscious of the technology; we have to stop to press the buttons; we are conscious of bridging the gulfs (Figure 3-4). When hammering or driving we focus on the activity, not the technology. The technology is 'present to hand' (see Further thoughts boxes in Section 3.5).

Mental models are discussed further in Chapter 5, Section 5.11

Another important aspect of usability is to try to engender an accurate mental model of the system. A good design will have adopted a clear and well structured conceptual design that can be easily communicated to people. A complex design will make this process much more difficult. Striving for a clear, simple and consistent conceptual model will increase the usability of a system.

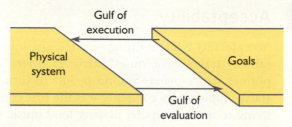

FIGURE 3-4 Bridging the gulfs (source: after Norman and Draper (eds) (1986))

Challenge 3-3
The remote control for my TV is shown in Figure 3-5. Yes ... all the numbers have got rubbed off the buttons! Write down the processes that a user of this device goes through if they want to enter a code number, 357998, say.

FIGURE 3-5 My TV remote control (source: Dorling Kindersley)

3.4 Acceptability

Acceptability is about fitting technologies into people's lives. For example, some railway trains have 'quiet' carriages where it is unacceptable to use mobile phones, and cinemas remind people to turn their phones off before the film starts. Apple's iMac computer was the first computer designed to look good in a living room. A computer playing loud music would generally be considered to be unacceptable in an office environment.

An essential difference between usability and acceptability is that acceptability can only be understood in the context of use. Usability can be evaluated in a laboratory (though such evaluations will always be limited). Acceptability cannot.

The key features of acceptability are:

Evaluation, Chapters 12, 21 and 22

- Political. Is the design politically acceptable? Do people trust it? In many organizations new technologies have been introduced for simple economic reasons, irrespective of what people may feel about them and the ways that people's jobs and lives might change. In the broader environment human rights might be threatened by changes in technologies.

- Convenience. Designs that are awkward or that force people to do things may prove unacceptable. Designs should fit effortlessly in to the situation. Many people send documents electronically nowadays, but many people find reading on-line unacceptable. They print out the document because it is more convenient to carry and read.

- Cultural and social habits. If political acceptability is concerned with power structures and principles, cultural and social habits are concerned with the way people like to live. It is rude to disturb other people, for example. 'Spam' e-mail has become such an unacceptable aspect of life that some companies have given up on e-mail altogether.

- Usefulness. This goes beyond the notions of efficiency and effectiveness and concerns usefulness in context. For example, many people have found the diary function on their PDAs perfectly usable, but not sufficiently useful in the context of everyday living.

- Economic. There are many economic issues that render some technology acceptable or not. Price is the obvious one and whether the technology offers value for money. But the economic issues go further than that as the introduction of new technologies may completely change the way businesses work and how they make money. A new 'business model' is often a part of economic acceptability. Don Norman characterizes the situation for a successful technology as a stool with three legs: user experience, marketing and technology (Figure 3-6).

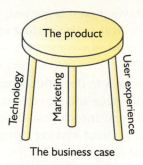

FIGURE 3-6 The three legs of product development
(source: after Norman (1999), The Invisible Computer: Why Good Products Can Fail, p. 40. Published and reprinted by permission of The MIT Press)

3.5 Engagement

Engagement is concerned with all the qualities of an experience that really pull people in – whether this is a sense of immersion that one feels when reading a good book, or a challenge one feels when playing a good game, or the fascinating unfolding of a radio drama. When we have produced an interactive system that is accessible, usable and acceptable, engagement is concerned with all the qualities of the interactive experience that make it memorable, satisfying, enjoyable and rewarding. Engagement is about ensuring that the interaction flows. If usability is concerned with optimizing the PACT elements in some domain, then engagement is when the elements are truly harmonized.

Further thoughts: Technological breakdown

When using a hammer, driving or writing with a pen we will usually focus on the activity itself: we are hammering, driving or writing. It is only when something happens to interfere with the smooth operation of these technologies that we become aware of them. If you hit your finger whilst hammering, if you have to swerve to avoid a hole in the road, or if the pen stops working, then the unconscious use of the technology turns into a conscious interaction with the technology. Winograd and Flores (1986) refer to this as a 'breakdown'. One aim of interactive systems design is to avoid such breakdowns, to provide people with a way of undertaking activities without really being aware of the technologies that enable them to do what they are doing.

There is, of course, much debate as to what the key features of engagement are and, arguably, this is really the domain of artistic creation. However, Nathan Shedroff in his book *Experience Design* (Shedroff, 2001) presents a 'manifesto' for what he sees as a new discipline. From his work we identify as the key elements:

■ Identity – a sense of authenticity is needed for identity and expression of the self. The sense of authenticity is often only noticed when it breaks down. If you are engaged in some experience and something happens that suddenly reminds you that it is not real, then the authenticity of the experience can be lost. Shedroff is also getting at the idea of identifying with something as a key element of engagement. Are you a 'Mac' or a Windows person or don't you care?

- ■ Adaptivity is to do with change and personalization with changing levels of difficulty, pace and movement. Musical instruments are often cited as examples of great interaction design. Engagement is not about making things easy; it is about making things that can be experienced at many levels of skill and enjoyment.

- ■ Narrative is to do with telling a good story, with convincing characters, plot and suspense. Narrative is not just about fiction, however. Good narrative is just as important for a company's promotional video, a lecture on interaction design, a menu structure on a mobile phone or any other design problem.

- ■ Immersion is the feeling of being wholly involved within something, with being taken over and transported somewhere else. You can get immersed in all manner of things (such as reading a book) so immersion is not about the medium; it is a quality of the design.

- ■ Flow is the sense of smooth movement, the gradual change from one state to another (see the Further thoughts box on this).

A medium is engaging if it draws the person in, if it seems to surround the activity, if it stimulates the imagination. Malcolm McCullough in his book *Abstracting Craft* (McCullough, 2002a) argues that an engaging medium allows for continuity and variety, for 'flow' and movement between many subtle differentiations of conditions. The medium can take many slightly different positions along a spectrum that are just discernible by a person. Think of the way the lights go down in a cinema just before the movie starts. The sense of anticipation, satisfaction and being drawn in is created by the just discernible change in lighting. Interactive technologies are the medium which the interactive system designer shapes.

An engaging animated computer game will allow for these differentiations of conditions. An important feature here is also the integration of media. A boring computer game relies on too little change and flow and too little depth in the media components. Computer games illustrate all the other features of engagement above – a feeling of immersion, the need for a good story line, the authenticity of the game play and identification with characters, the different levels accommodating different abilities and the gradual smooth change of scenes: the flow. One of the most engaging games was *Myst* which appeared on the Macintosh in the early 1990s and remains a best seller today. Figure 3-7 shows some of the images from the game, but the atmosphere was considerably enhanced by excellent use of sound and by character and the slow pace of the movement.

FIGURE 3-7 Pictures for the game Myst
(source: http://sirrus.cyan.com/Online/Myst/GameShots. © Cyan Worlds, Inc)

Further thoughts:
Digital ground: fixity, flow and engagement with context

'Flow needs contexts. A river, for example, needs riverbanks otherwise it spreads out in every direction until it becomes a brackish swamp. Similarly, cars need highways, capital needs markets and life's energy needs bodies through which to course.

Flows influence one another. For example, we know that telecommunication generates transportation at least as often as it substitutes for it, starting with Alexander Graham Bell whose first words on his new telephone were "Watson, please come here". Similarly, when you order a book from Amazon, the flow of data on the web has an effect outside the web, namely it causes a package to be put on an airplane. This in turn has geographic consequences: the warehouse where your order is filled is probably located near an airport.

Where regular crossovers between flows occur, places emerge. …

Here we arrive at Mihaly Csikszentmihalyi's often-cited expression: Flow is the sense of engagement that emerges, between boredom and anxiety, when practised abilities are applied to challenges that are just about manageable. This notion of engaged tacit knowledge grounds much interaction design. We tend to be familiar with psychological notions of "activity theory", "situated actions" and "persistent structures". We know how possibilities for action are perceived especially amid engaged activity (and we overuse the word "affordance" to describe this). Increasingly, we understand how that perception depends on persistent structures, both mental and physical, that surround and

Chapter 7, Section 7.6 discusses activity theory; Section 7.3 discusses affordance

give meaning to those activities. We recognize how such response to context is not necessarily deliberative. We find the phenomenology of engagement at the roots of interactivity.

So this is the heart of the matter: Flow needs fixity. Persistently embodied intentional settings, also known as architecture, provide a necessary context for Flow.'

Source: McCullough (2002b)

Challenge 3-4
Think about your favourite activity. It may be talking to a friend on your cell-phone, driving your car, riding your bike, playing a computer game, going to the cinema, shopping or attending a lecture. Using Shedroff's five features above, analyse what it is about the activity that makes it engaging. Could it be more engaging if the design were different?

3.6 Design principles

Over the years many principles of good interactive system design have been developed. Don Norman in his book *The Design of Everyday Things* (Norman, 1998) provides several, as does Jacob Nielsen in *Usability Engineering* (Nielsen, 1993). However, the level of abstraction provided by different people at different times is sometimes rather inconsistent and confusing. Design principles can be very broad, such as 'make things visible' (Norman, 1998), or they can be more specific, such as 'provide clearly marked exits' (Nielsen, 1993). There are also good design principles that derive from psychology such as 'minimize memory load' (i.e. do not expect people to remember too much). The application of design principles has led to established design guidelines and patterns of interaction in certain circumstances such as the 'undo' command in a Windows application, the 'back' button on a website or the greying-out of inappropriate options on menus.

Chapter 5 on psychology

Design principles can guide the designer during the design process and can be used to evaluate and critique prototype design ideas. Our list of high-level design principles, put together from Norman, Nielsen and others, is shown below. All the principles interact in complex ways, affecting each other, some-times conflicting with each other and sometimes enhancing each other. But they help to orientate the designer to key features of good design and sensitize the designer to important issues.

For ease of memorizing and use we have grouped them into three main cate-gories – learnability, effectiveness and accommodation – but these groupings are not rigid. Systems should be learnable, effective *and* accommodating.

■ Principles 1–4 are concerned with access, ease of learning and remembering (learnability).

■ Principles 5–7 are concerned with ease of use, and principles 8 and 9 are concerned with safety (effectiveness).

■ Principles 10–12 are concerned with accommodating differences between people and respecting those differences (accommodation).

Designing interactive systems from a human-centred perspective is concerned with the following.

Helping people access, learn and remember the system …

1. Visibility – Try to ensure that things are visible so that people can see what functions are available and what the system is currently doing. This is an important part of the psychological principle that it is easier to recognize things than to have to recall them. If it is not possible to make it visible, make it observable. Consider making things 'visible' through the use of sound and touch.

2. Consistency – Be consistent in the use of design features and be consistent with similar systems and standard ways of working. Consistency can be something of a slippery concept (see the Further thoughts box). Both conceptual and physical consistency are important.

3. Familiarity – Use language and symbols that the intended audience will be familiar with. Where this is not possible because the concepts are quite different from those people know about, provide a suitable metaphor to help them transfer similar and related knowledge from a more familiar domain.

4. Affordance – Design things so it is clear what they are for; for example, make buttons look like buttons so people will press them. Affordance refers to the properties that things have (or are perceived to have) and how these relate to how the things could be used. Buttons afford pressing, chairs afford sitting on, and Post-it notes afford writing a message on and sticking next to something else. Affordances are culturally determined.

Giving them the sense of being in control, knowing what to do and how to do it …

Chapter 25 discusses navigation

5. Navigation – Provide support to enable people to move around the parts of the system: maps, directional signs and information signs.

6. Control – Make it clear who or what is in control and allow people to take control. Control is enhanced if there is a clear, logical mapping between controls and the effect that they have. Also make clear the relationship between what the system does and what will happen in the world outside the system.

7. Feedback – Rapidly feed back information from the system to people so that they know what effect their actions have had. Constant and consistent feedback will enhance the feeling of control.

Safely and securely …

8. Recovery – Enable recovery from actions, particularly mistakes and errors, quickly and effectively.

9. Constraints – Provide constraints so that people do not try to do things that are inappropriate. In particular, people should be prevented from making serious errors through properly constraining allowable actions and seeking confirmation of dangerous operations.

In a way that suits them …

10. Flexibility – Allow multiple ways of doing things so as to accommodate users with different levels of experience and interest in the systems. Provide people with the opportunity to change the way things look or behave so that they can personalize the system.

11. Style – Designs should be stylish and attractive.

12. Conviviality – Interactive systems should be polite, friendly, and generally pleasant. Nothing ruins the experience of using an interactive system more than an aggressive message or an abrupt interruption. Design for politeness (see Box 3-2). Conviviality also suggests joining in and using interactive technologies to connect and support people.

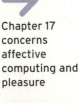

Chapter 17 concerns affective computing and pleasure

Further thoughts: Consistency

Consistency is a slippery concept because consistency is always relative. A design will be consistent with respect to some things but may be inconsistent with respect to others. There are also times when to be inconsistent is a good thing because it draws people's attention to something that is important. The difference between conceptual consistency and physical consistency is important. Conceptual consistency is about ensuring the mappings are consistent, that the conceptual model remains clear. This involves being consistent both internally to the system and externally as the system relates to things outside it. Physical consistency is ensuring consistent behaviours and consistent use of colours, names, layout and so on.

One famous example of the difficulty of maintaining conceptual consistency in a design comes from the design of the Xerox Star interface (described in Smith *et al.*, 1982). To print a document, the document was dragged onto a printer icon. This was consistent with the overall style. The question then arose as to what to do with it after it had printed. The options considered were (1) the system deletes the icon from the desktop, or (2) the system does not delete the icon, but (a) replaces it on the desktop in its previous location, (b) places it at an arbitrary location on the desktop, or (c) leaves it on the printer for the user to deal with. Discuss!

Kellogg (1989) quotes the designers as saying that in this example the trade-off was between the external consistency of not deleting the icon, as it behaved more like a real-world object (a photocopier), against the internal consistency of behaving like other actions in the interface, such as dragging the icon to the wastebasket or to a folder icon. They opted for option 2a. Whether designers would do that nowadays when more people are much more familiar with these types of interface is another matter.

Box 3-2 Polite software

Alan Cooper (1999) argues that if we want people to like our software we should design it to behave like a likeable person. Drawing on work by Reeves and Nass (1996), who found that people interacting with new media were treating the media like a person, they argue that the essentials of polite behaviour are quality, quantity, relevance and clarity. Cooper continues with his list of characteristics:

Polite software:
is interested in me   is taciturn about its personal problems
is deferential to me   is well informed
is forthcoming   is perceptive
has common sense   is self-confident
anticipates my needs   stays focused
is responsive   is fudge-able
gives instant gratification   is trustworthy

3.7 Designing for windows applications

The computer 'desktop' is likely to remain with us for some time with its familiar combination of windows, icons, menus and pointer, called a WIMP interface. This form of interaction – the graphical user interface (GUI) – is as ubiquitous as information and communication technologies are becoming and appears on PDAs and other mobile devices as well as on desktop computers.

Designing for windows applications is still dominated primarily by issues of usability. In particular the key issue is **consistency**. There are clear guidelines for issues such as menu layout, ordering, dialogue boxes and use of the other 'widgets' associated with graphical user interfaces. There are standards for providing **constraints** such as greying out items on a menu that are not relevant at a particular point. A toolkit, or a design environment such as Visual Basic, will probably be used that will help to ensure the design confirms to an overall style.

Chapter 6, Section 6.3 describes these features

Screen design is a key issue in such environments and attention needs to be paid to the layout of objects on a screen. Avoiding clutter will help to ensure **visibility**. Attention needs to be paid to the use of appropriate, non-clashing colours and the careful layout of information using tables, graphs or text as appropriate.

Often in the design of windows applications, the designer can talk to the actual future users of the system and find out what they want and how they refer to things. This will help the designer to ensure **familiar** language is used. It can be fitted in with preferred ways of working. Participatory design techniques – involving people closely in the design process – can be used, and future users can participate in the design process through workshops, meetings and evaluation of design ideas. Documentation and training can be given.

A good design will ensure that there is easy error **recovery** by providing warning signs for drastic actions such as 'are you sure you want to destroy the database?'. A good example of designing for recovery is the Undo command.

Affordances are provided by following windows design guidelines. People will expect to see a menu at the top of the screen and will expect the menu items to be displayed when the header is clicked on. Items that are not greyed out will afford selecting. The various 'widgets' such as check boxes, radio buttons and text entry boxes should afford selecting because people familiar with the standards will know what to expect. However, care needs to be taken to ensure that opportunities are easily and correctly perceived.

Menus are also the main form of **navigation** in windows applications. People move around the application by selecting items from menus and then by following dialogue structures. Many windows applications make use of 'wizards'. These provide step-by-step instructions for undertaking a sequence of operations, allowing users to go forward and backwards to ensure that all steps are completed.

Control is usually left in the hands of the users. They have to initiate actions, although some features that provide security features are undertaken automatically. Many applications, for example, automatically save people's work to help with recovery if mistakes are made. **Feedback** is provided in a variety of ways. A 'bee' symbol or an 'egg timer' symbol is used to indicate that the system is busy doing something. Counters and progress bars are used to indicate how much of an operation is complete. Feedback can be provided through sound such as a beep when a message is received on an e-mail system or a sound to indicate that a file has been safely saved.

Flexibility is provided with things such as short-cut keys, allowing more expert users to use combinations of keyboard controls in place of using menus to initiate commands and navigate through the system. Many windows applications allow the user to set their own preferences, to configure features such as the navigation bars and menu items and to disable features that are not often used.

In terms of **style** and **conviviality**, windows applications are rather limited as they should remain within the standard design guidelines. Error messages are one area where the designer can move towards a more convivial design by thinking hard about the words used on the messages. However, all too frequently messages appear very abruptly and interrupt people unnecessarily.

Challenge 3-5
Look at Figure 3-8, an example of a typical 'windows'-type application. Critique the design from the perspective of the general design principles and from design for windows in particular.

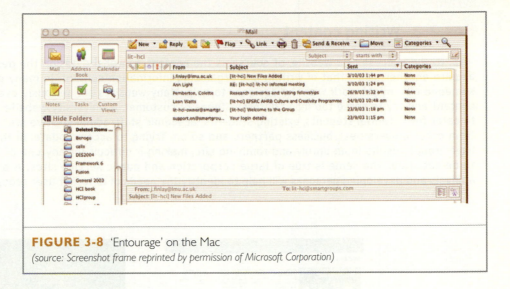

FIGURE 3-8 'Entourage' on the Mac
(source: Screenshot frame reprinted by permission of Microsoft Corporation)

3.8 Designing websites

One of the most likely things that interactive system designers will design is a website. There are dozens of books on website design all offering advice, but some are more focused on the usability and experience than others. Albert Badre (2002) identifies four main genres of websites: News, Shopping, Information and Entertainment. Each of these has several sub-genres (for example, News has Broadcast TV, Newspaper and Magazine), and within a genre certain design features are common. For example, shopping sites will have a fill-in form to collect data on delivery address and payment details; news sites must pay special attention to the presentation of text. The genres also have different ways of arranging the content. News sites will have long scrolling pages whereas shopping sites will have short pages. Combination sites are of course common. For example, a site for booking plane flights will often have a news site associated with the destination.

The development of a website involves far more than just its design. There are a lot of pre-design activities concerned with establishing the purpose of the site, who it is aimed at and how it fits into the organization's overall publicity strategy. In larger organizations there will be plenty of disagreement and arguments about all these issues and these internal politics often affect the final quality of the site. Many sites finish up as too large, trying to serve too many issues with the marketing people in charge; usability and engagement come a long way down the list of priorities. At the other end of the process the launch of the site has to be carefully managed and other infrastructure issues will need to be addressed such as how, when and by whom the content is written and updated, who deals with e-mails and site maintenance, and so forth.

In the middle of these two is the part that interests us – the design and development of a site that is effective, learnable and accommodating.

Box 3-3 Writing content

Vital to the success of a website, of course, is the content. In website design the designer has to acquire another skill – that of writing and organizing information content. In many organizations someone else might work with the designer to help. Many websites are seriously overloaded with content and try to serve too many different types of customer. A university website will often try to cater for potential students, existing students, academic staff, administrative staff (its own and from other universities), business partners and so on. Trying to accommodate all these different user groups results in an unruly and rambling site, making it difficult for any one of these groups to be satisfied. The same is true of large corporation and public service sites. A detailed PACT analysis and developing personas will help to identify the needs of different user groups.

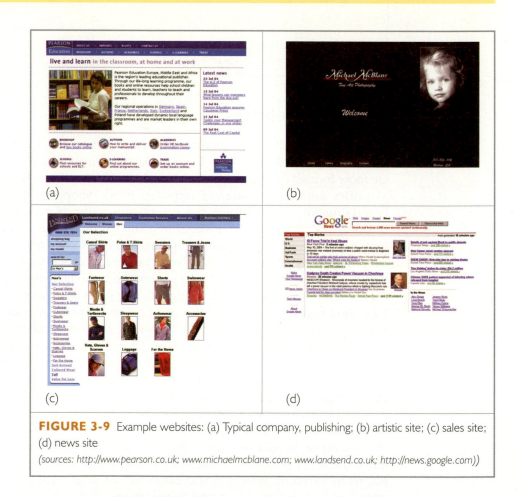

(a)

(b)

(c)

(d)

FIGURE 3-9 Example websites: (a) Typical company, publishing; (b) artistic site; (c) sales site; (d) news site

(sources: http://www.pearson.co.uk; www.michaelmcblane.com; www.landsend.co.uk; http://news.google.com))

Design principles and websites

Even if a site is well focused, it will soon get large and so issues of how to move around a website become important; **navigation** is a central concern here. Support to enable people to discover the structure and content of the site and to find their way to a particular part of the site is the key issue. Information architecture is an emerging area of study devoted to designing websites and helping users to answer questions such as: Where am I? Where can I go? Where have I been? What is nearby? An emerging standard for websites is that the **top banner** lets people know where they are, through clear and obvious labelling, and a **navigation bar** down the left-hand side tells people where they can go. It is also useful to include some form of 'path' at the bottom to let them know where they have been. The hope is that through these people will develop a clear overall 'map' of the site. In fact it has been shown that navigation of a website is very similar to navigation in the built environment. People start off by learning simple routes from one place to another, by following the signposts. They gradually build up this route knowledge, adding landmarks along the way until they are able to form survey knowledge – an overall understanding of the structure of the site.

Chapter 23 on information architecture

It is also vital to distinguish links from non-links so that people will quickly recognize a signpost when they see one. A key feature of *consistency* is the use of standard Web features such as a blue underline for showing a link. If it is not desirable to use the standard underlined links then ensure that links are consistent so people will quickly learn them. Many sites confuse people by not making links sufficiently visible and distinguishable from other text in the site.

Provide people with *feedback* on where they are in the site and clarify contexts and content. Using meaningful URLs (Uniform Resource Locators, i.e. Web addresses) and familiar titles will help people find what they are looking for and understand what other content is in the site. *Flexibility* of navigation can be enabled by providing alternatives for people. A good design guideline for websites is to minimize the need for scrolling and plan for entry at (almost) any page, as not all your visitors will go in through the front page.

In general there is a trade-off in designing pages between people who have just arrived there and people who have followed the *navigational* structure. Having a link to the 'home' (front) page of a site in a prominent position and having a site map will *afford* people getting oriented. *Consistency* is always a key design principle, but unlike windows applications there are few overall standards to be followed. The designer has to establish a consistent design 'language' – consistent use of colour, positioning, text and so on that people can quickly learn and become familiar with. Consistency can also be enhanced through the naming of links, sub-sites and other details. Style sheets help to ensure consistency.

The site's home page is particularly important and should feature a directory, a summary of important news/stories and a search facility (Nielsen, 1993). This will help people to feel in *control* rather than feeling lost. Different people have different strategies on websites. Half of all users are 'search dominant', 20 per cent 'link dominant' and the rest mixed (Nielsen, 1993). Search-focused people are task-centred and want to find what they want, whereas the others are more happy to browse around.

Issues of *recovery*, *feedback* and *control* figure most highly in shopping sites. Because the Web is primarily a publishing medium rather than one with lots of functionality, there are often long pauses when processing things such as a payment transaction. *Feedback* is critical here, but can often be difficult to provide as the site cannot be updated in real time. *Recovery* from an erroneous click can usually be provided through the 'Back' button in the browser, but again this can go wrong if the site is in the middle of a transaction.

Conviviality can be provided by allowing people to join in, to support and create communities. Unlike windows applications, websites can easily connect people with other people – though many do not. *Style* is also key to websites and offers the most opportunities for designers to demonstrate their creative flair. The use of animation, video and other design features can really develop a whole sense of engagement with the site.

The website from the EU research programme is shown in Figure 3-10. Notice the menu down the left-hand side, the path at the top and the standard underlined links for PDF (portable document format) file downloads. However, the Activity Areas is an example of a non-standard link. It looks just like a graphic until the mouse moves over it.

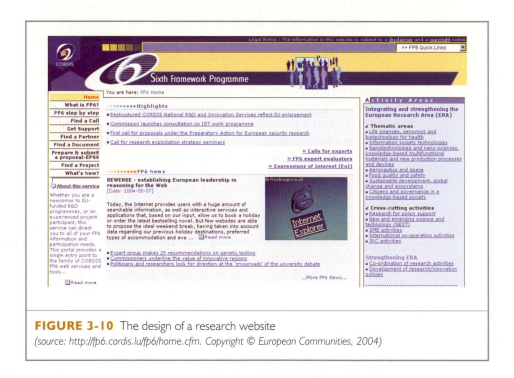

FIGURE 3-10 The design of a research website
(source: http://fp6.cordis.lu/fp6/home.cfm. Copyright © European Communities, 2004)

3.9 Designing for other technologies

Increasingly websites and other information such as e-mail, diary functions and so on are displayed on hand-held computers, PDAs and other small devices. Each of these platforms has its own usability issues. In this section we raise just a few of these and point to the main design principles that need to be considered.

Mobiles

A key design feature with mobile technology is the limited screen space. Other significant technological features include the battery life and there may be limitations on storage and memory. Many of the screens on mobiles are not 'bit-mapped', so graphical user interfaces that rely on the direct manipulation of images on the screen cannot be used. All sorts of people will be using the device and of course it will be used in all manner of physical and social contexts. This is significant as it means that designers cannot design for specific people or contexts of use.

Because of the small screen it is very difficult to achieve the design principle of *visibility*. Functions have to be tucked away and accessed by multiple levels of menu, leading to difficulties of *navigation*. Another feature is that there is not room for many buttons so each button has to do a lot of work. This results in the need for different 'modes' and this makes it difficult to have clear *control* over the functions. *Feedback* is generally poor and people have to stare into the device to see what is happening. There is no *consistency* in the interfaces – even to the point of pressing the right-hand or left-hand button to answer a call on a mobile phone. *Flexibility* is provided to a limited extent, e.g. being able to press any key to answer a call, but it is generally not possible to personalize things such as menus. Physically swapping the covers is one way to personalize mobile phones and being able to select different ring tones is another. *Style* is very important and many mobile devices concentrate on the *convivial* nature of the physical interaction (e.g. the size and weight of the device). The physical buttons *afford* pressing, but there is little in most of the graphical aspects of the interface that afford anything and the obscure symbols on many buttons do not easily convey any meaning. Although those growing up with mobiles might be familiar with much of the terminology and where to find things, this is not the case for newcomers.

Ubiquitous computing

Computers are becoming increasingly small, so much so that they are now wearable, and they are increasingly able to communicate with each other autonomously. So now people are surrounded by devices that are interacting with each other and with other devices. Households will be 'wired' for communication just as they are wired for electricity, meaning that the concept of household extends outside the home because of communications technology, and similarly community extends into the house.

Chapter 27 discusses ubiquitous computing

The major change happening as a result of pervasive, distributed and ubiquitous computing is the contexts. All HCI research and experience has been developed in a working environment and there is a paucity of design knowledge associated with home and leisure technologies. At home these devices begin to compete with the social space – particularly if the activities are primarily work-based. As with mobile devices, designers have to design for the whole range of people – from the very young to the elderly. Safety at home is a key issue, especially where children are concerned, and understandability is key particularly for older people.

Designs for these new devices and in these new contexts such as the home need to support people as social beings. Households are the site of all sorts of activities that provide us with the context for the use of household technology for recreation, communication, development, health and well-being. For example, there are toddler beds that detect movement, picture frames that respond to distant events, and fridges that have e-mail.

Visibility is critical to ensure people know what is connected to what, and *consistency* will only be achieved once certain standards have been evolved. Similarly the devices must provide good *feedback* so that people do not feel that they have lost *control*. How devices will represent suitable *affordances* is a significant design challenge. For example, if a picture frame can display the status of a baby in a cot, how will we know? The proliferation and non-standard nature of these new devices will mean that familiarity is very difficult to achieve. Security and the ability to recover from errors becomes even more important when devices are controlling other devices in the home such as heaters.

An example of an emerging concept is 'e-gadgets' (Kameas et al, 2003). An e-gadget is an autonomous everyday physical object that has communication ability, and a range of sensing, acting and processing abilities. e-Gadgets 'express' their capabilities through plugs, so that other gadgets, as well as the people using them, know what to do with them (connect them, plug them to each other, etc.). An early version of software has made about 10 different e-gadgets to test from, including desks, lamps, carpets, clocks, MP3 players, etc.

Other examples of ubiquitous computing include the InteracTable, an interactive table, and CommChair, a chair with built-in communications ability. Mixed-reality games – in which real people move around real offer while others chase them in virtual environments – offer another example of how ubiquitous computing is leading to new forms of interaction.

Summary and key points

Good design is about usability and engagement. It is about ensuring that systems are accessible to all and that designs are acceptable for the people and contexts in which they will be used. Designers need to evaluate their designs with people and involve people in the design process. Paying attention to design principles can help sensitize the designer to key aspects of good design.

■ Access to interactive systems for all people is an important right.

■ Usability is concerned with balancing the PACT elements in a domain.

■ Engagement aims to harmonize the PACT elements.

■ Interactive systems design is different in different contexts and on different technological platforms.

Further reading

Gould, J.D., Boies, S.J., Levy, S., Richards, J.T. and Schoonard, J. (1987) The 1984 Olympic Message System: a test of behavioral principles of system design. *Communications of the ACM*, **30**(9), 758–769.

Shedroff, N. (2001) *Experience Design 1*. New Riders, Indianapolis, IN.
A good book for experience designers. The text ranges over a wide number of areas and provides lots of examples of good design. Nathan Shedroff also has a chapter in Jacobson, R. (ed.) (2000) *Information Design*, MIT Press, Cambridge, MA, which includes a good collection of essays on this subject.

Stephanidis, C. (ed.) (2001) *User Interfaces for All: Concepts, Methods and Tools*. Lawrence Erlbaum Associates, Mahwah, NJ.
This book provides a good collection of papers covering issues of inclusive design and design for all. There are a number of general chapters and a large section describing the AVANTI project – an EU research project concerned with developing the software architecture for the design-for-all concept.

Kellogg, W. (1989) The dimensions of consistency. In Nielsen, J. (ed.), *Coordinating User Interfaces for Consistency*. Academic Press, San Diego, CA.

Smith, D.C., Irby, C., Kimball, R., Verplank, B. and Harslem, E. (1982) Designing the Star user interface. *BYTE*, **7**(4), 242–282.

Part VI of Carroll, J. (ed.) (2002) *Human–Computer Interaction in the New Millennium*, Addison-Wesley, includes several chapters on ubiquitous computing (Chapters 23–26, pp. 573–601).

Comments on challenges

Challenge 3-1
This, of course, is a real problem not just for the UK government but for authorities worldwide as they seek to save costs by making use of electronic methods of delivery. The potential barriers include fear of computers amongst some people (often the most vulnerable and in need of support). If this can be overcome then physical access to a computer is necessary, or via other technologies such as interactive TV. However, the interface to interactive TV is still quite poor and the functionality is also limited. Access can be provided in public buildings such as libraries and at social security offices where staff could be on hand to help people enter their details. There are also factors such as privacy where people may not want to provide the sort of detail that is required, or they may distrust the gathering of this information and may need clear reassurance on how any personal data would be used.

▶

Challenge 3-2

The postcard needs a pen to write it – a felt-tipped pen would be too big. But I like writing with felt-tipped pens when I am playing around with some ideas in a notebook – sitting on a train, perhaps. A laptop computer is quite good and saves the trouble of having to transfer things from a book to the computer, but you cannot use a laptop when taking off or landing in a plane whereas you can still write in your book. I have tried the PDAs and handwriting, but have not found it a very satisfying way of working. Perhaps it is better for people who have to write short amounts of material.

Challenge 3-3

There is a lot of bridging of gulfs! Since the display is on the TV, feedback is very poor. In my case I need to take my glasses off to see the remote and put them on again to see the TV. There is a lot of taking my glasses on and off! With no numbers on the remote, the feedback that would usually come from this source is no longer there. If this does not seem like a real problem to you, one way to program a video recorder is to use the code printed in the newspaper or TV guide. This is often six or seven digits long!

Challenge 3-4

The computer game *Myst* was a huge success when it first appeared in the mid-1990s. I spent several years playing it off and on with my son until we had finally solved all the puzzles and travelled to all the different worlds.

- Identity – the game soon developed a dedicated following of people who identified with the mysterious worlds in which the game took place.
- Adaptivity was key to the success of the game. Like many games there were levels that became harder and harder. Once the challenges of one level had been completed, the players were ready for the next. But also like many games, without the 'cheats' many players would not progress past level 1!
- Narrative was also keenly observed in *Myst*. All the game's players knew was that something terrible had happened to two brothers. The purpose of the game was to discover what had happened. Snippets of information were carefully revealed as the players progressed through the game to maintain the momentum of the narrative.
- Immersion was remarkable given the tiny screen of the early Mac computers. However, the speakers on our machine were good and the sound in *Myst* excellent and very evocative, with chilling winds blowing and the sounds of water trickling in the distance. Turn off the light on a dark winter's afternoon and you were transported into the *Myst* worlds.
- Flow was present, as the scenes shifted gently from one to another and as vistas one saw from a distance gradually came into view. It is much better in later, animated versions of the game.

Challenge 3-5

Aesthetically the display is quite pleasant. There is not much clutter, which ensures that most things are visible. Parts of the display can be made larger and smaller, allowing the sort of flexibility that is needed for different people doing different things. Of course the design is wholly consistent with the Macintosh guidelines. One interesting problem with Entourage is that it does not let people recover easily from inadvertently moving e-mails. For some reason 'Undo' does not relate to transferring e-mails into folders. The use of different font styles for read and unread messages affords focusing on the unread ones, and constraints on allowable actions are enforced – e.g. if you try to move an e-mail message to an inappropriate place it springs back.

Overall this system demonstrates the implementation of many of the design guidelines recommended in Section 3.6.

Exercises

1. Suppose that the designers of the laboratory access system described in Chapter 2 have settled on a system that uses a swipe card and a card reader to access laboratories. How would set about evaluating this design? Use the design principles to discuss the key issues.

2. Describe how design principles could be used to help in the design of the bicycle route information system described in Chapter 2. How would this be evaluated, for usability and for the whole user experience?

04 The Home Information Centre (HIC) 1: A case study in designing interactive systems

Aims

In this chapter we will use a case study to illustrate many of the features of the design and evaluation of interactive systems that you have encountered in the first three chapters. In particular we focus on discussing requirements and on the evaluation of early prototype design ideas. We will return to the case study in Chapter 14 when we look at scenarios, requirements, prototyping, envisionment, design and evaluation in more detail. The case concerns the development of a new concept for a device known as the *Home Information Centre (HIC)*. It was a real project that involved one of the authors along with a small design team. The aim of the chapter is to illustrate a quick and effective method of evaluation and to raise design issues that can be used as fuel for debate. After studying this chapter you should be able to:

- Understand how to assess requirements
- Discuss how design decisions are made
- Appreciate the trade-offs that are inherent in a design project
- Critically comment on an evaluation strategy.

4.1 Introduction

The concept for the HIC came from the observation that there are two typical situations in the home. The TV, video, DVD and music centre are in the living room. It is a 'lean-back' situation, where people are being entertained and where they relax. In the home office there is a PC (personal computer). It is a 'lean-for-ward' situation where people are actively engaged with and focused on producing things. The relatively poor uptake of devices such as WebTV (which provided Internet access through the television) suggests that neither the lean-forward situation of a PC nor the lean-back situation of a TV in a living room will be the right context or the right device for new services such as home banking, shopping and so on. Instead, a new device, the home information centre, HIC, is proposed. This should be a device where people can get at and provide information while they are occupied with other household activities. The industrial partner characterized this as 'a move-around situation for infotainment'.

Box 4-1 Infotainment

Infotainment is a term intended to convey a mixture of information and entertainment and is one example of how traditional activities and technologies are increasingly converging. Other terms such as 'edutainment' (education and entertainment) and 'infomercial' (information and commercial, or advertising) are increasingly common. Technologies similarly converge: a phone and a camera, for example, or a PDA and an MP3 player. One of the challenges for interactive systems designers is to understand when and where it is appropriate to converge technologies. Is it better – simpler, more convivial, etc. – to put technologies together or is it better to keep them apart in separate devices?

The project was established to explore the concept of a HIC to see whether full-blown manufacture of such a device was sensible. There were many parallel activities going on in the project to do with issues such as market analysis, hardware costs and so on. There were also many other aspects of the whole software system that were investigated by different partners. In this chapter we focus on the initial design of the overall concept and on the key features of the user interface and human–computer interaction. Physically the HIC was imagined to look something like a lectern with a touchscreen, wireless keyboard and pointer.

The abstract concept of a HIC as a device to deal with 'a move-around situation for infotainment' was initially translated into a number of high-level features and functions. Some of these were derived directly from the concept, whereas others were included in order to prototype the technology to evaluate its suitability.

Chapter 14 provides more detail on the case study

The HIC would need to employ software to address the problems of complexity, difficult navigation and query formulation that bedevil the Web and other large information spaces. Two key features were required: an intuitive navigation support system and a flexible query system. The software should provide the following:

- An abstract representation of the contents of information sources that should be extracted and maintained semi-automatically
- Speech, pen, touch, and keyboard as input
- Sound, images, text, and animation as output
- Speech recognition (SR)
- Natural language (NL) queries
- An intuitive user interface.

The industrial partner on the project who was most likely to subsequently build and market the device also imposed a key constraint on the project: the HIC should not look or behave like a PC. They were keen to explore alternative interface designs in the project – particularly having a design that did not include scrolling or window management. This was a tough design challenge.

A scenario for the HIC

The original project specification included the following illustrative scenario of how the HIC would operate. Read it and answer the challenges below.

Arnold is busy in the kitchen, washing up the dishes from the party he gave yesterday evening. He listens to the morning news on the loudspeakers connected to his HIC in the kitchen. He is meant to be at work within an hour, and the news reader was saying something about a roadblock on the road between his home and his work. He turns his attention to the HIC, saying 'turn on'. He could have used touch or the keyboard as well, but is occupied with his hands right now.

The screen now gives Arnold some possibilities. Arnold has earlier defined his personal profile in the HIC, very dependent on the traffic situation between his home and his work, so one of the options given is service number 5, 'traffic'. He could say 5, but he chooses to say 'traffic situation'. He is now given some more possibilities, and says 'local', number 2. The screen now shows the block on the main road, and he realizes that he has to leave 10 minutes earlier, because he has to take another road. He hurries up, leaving everything in the kitchen. He takes the pen from the pen holder attached to the HIC, and quickly writes 'Good morning dear. Have to leave early, will you finish cleaning up, and walking the dog. Love Arnold'.

He turns the HIC off (really switching to standby mode, ready for new interaction) and leaves.

Jane is woken by the sound of his car, and when she comes down to the kitchen, she sees a flashing note indicator on the HIC. She says 'turn on' and she sees the message from Arnold attached to the local traffic map, and understands why the kitchen is in such a mess. She presses the CD button on the remote and begins cleaning up while she listens to the new record by Placido Domingo.

Finished cleaning up and walking the dog, she goes to the HIC, rolls out the keyboard and writes: 'When will the road be cleared for traffic?'. The HIC, intelligent and flexible as it is, will know automatically that she is referring to the roadblock on the local road, due to Arnold's request earlier in the morning, so it displays and says '13:30'. Jane writes 'mail Arnold', and the HIC then automatically turns on the Internet connection, turns on the mail application, and has filled out the 'to:' address ready for keyboard input. Jane now writes 'Road is clear, take the easy way home. Love Jane'. She says 'send' and 'turn off', and is already on her way to her job.

Scenario analysis

This scenario contains a number of big assumptions, some of which were to cause problems during the project and most of which are no closer to being solved today. For example, consider the following: 'He turns his attention to the HIC, saying "turn on".'

Speech recognition of simple commands such as this is possible and is common, particularly in phone-based systems. The reason for this is that the background noise can be controlled in a phone-based system.

Challenge 4-1
Discuss the difficulties of having a speech recognition system that can understand any person in the household (and consider visitors), when the radio or TV is playing, or when someone is doing the washing up on the other side of the room.

Challenge 4-2
Another quotation from the scenario says 'Arnold has earlier defined his personal profile in the HIC, very dependent on the traffic situation between his home and his work …'. The slightly strange construction of this sentence hides a huge issue. How can this be done? Discuss how this requirement could be met.

Challenge 4-3
Later in the scenario, 'He takes the pen from the pen holder attached to the HIC, and quickly writes …'. Discuss the issues of handwriting recognition.

4.2   The design process

Chapter 2, Section 2.7 discusses the activities involved in design

The development approach that was adopted was based on the 'Star' model of design activities (see Figure 2-5). The development was planned to be iterative, beginning with mock-ups and 'Wizard of Oz' style[1] experimentation and finally ending with experiments in real homes. The project plan specified that the HIC would be developed as a series of prototypes, leading to a final pilot-like complete system. Four prototypes were planned:

1. *Prototype P0* should be delivered by the end of month 6, and was to be used for the very first 'discount' engineering experiments with the HIC system to aid in the design specification. P0 would not contain software.

[1] In the film *The Wizard of Oz* the wizard pretends to be much larger and more powerful than he is by hiding behind a curtain. In interactive systems design this approach to prototyping and testing refers to simulating advanced features through a person hiding and providing responses as if he or she were a computer.

Box 4.2 Discount usability engineering

Discount usability engineering is a term now applied to any 'quick and dirty' method of usability evaluation. It derives from Nielsen (1993) where he argues 'I focus on achieving "the good" with respect to having some usability engineering work performed, even though the methods needed to achieve this result may not always be the absolute "best" method ...' (p. 17). He recommends an evaluation method based on

- User and task observation
- Scenarios as prototypes of the system
- Simplified 'think aloud' method when users of a system are encouraged to undertake some activities and talk through their thoughts whilst the analyst makes notes
- Heuristic evaluation where the designer uses high-level, abstract principles of good design to critique a design. Our principles (or heuristics) were given in Section 3.6.

More details on discount evaluation in Chapter 12

Chapter 11 discusses prototyping

2. *Prototype P1* would be delivered by the end of month 13, and would be used for the first laboratory experiments collecting data on usage, including user actions and usage of the natural language query system. A feature of natural language systems is that they need to accommodate synonyms. For example, if someone were to run a query on a database of shows at an arts festival, the system would need to recognize synonyms such as 'show', 'spectacle', 'play', 'event' and so on. Which synonyms would people use? This data should be gathered through observing people using the natural language query system. The prototype would include full monitor setup in the laboratory, a PC simulating the HIC client, the content server, a first version of the display visualization, a simple interaction model, a control module and simple or dummy versions of the other modules. An operator at the PC (hidden from the user) would start computer actions requested orally by the user, but not yet handled by the software (the Wizard of Oz approach).

3. *Prototype P2* would be delivered at the end of month 19 and used for full laboratory experiments at first and then in real user homes. The prototype would be used for the final user validation of the HIC and its associated concepts. This prototype would include full monitor setup, including a PC running the client modules and connected to a second PC running the server modules. All modules should be present in full. The prototype would be improved according to the laboratory experiments and the user site experiments.

4. *Prototype P3* was to be the final official version of the HIC, usable for demonstrations and for the possible basis of further exploitation. It would correspond to P2 but with corrections and enhancements made following the experiments.

It is fair to say that this was an ambitious plan and the project did not succeed in following it in detail. With so much new technology and so many 'unknowns', there were always going to be difficulties. Indeed in the end two P3 prototypes were produced – one for the functionality of the system and one for the interface concepts. They were never robust enough to be used in people's homes.

Challenge 4-4
Discuss the development approach taken.

4.3 A PACT analysis for the HIC

Chapter 8 discusses scenarios

As we have seen (Chapter 2), a useful structure for thinking about interactive systems design is the PACT approach: people, activities, contexts and technologies. This can be used to help think about conceptual scenarios of use. Conceptual scenarios are abstract descriptions of the PACT elements in some domain. For the HIC design, we brainstormed ideas at a number of internal workshops about how the HIC might be used. We finished up with three general, highly abstract uses for the HIC – informational, communicational and entertainment. From these abstract ideas, 11 more concrete scenarios were developed that looked at the general ideas in terms of more specific terms. Examples of these are given throughout Part III and specifically in Chapter 14. The aim was to cover activities, contexts and people which explored the whole range of information content, input, output, media and communication abilities of the HIC technology. Distinguishing between the 'what' (i.e. the content) and the 'how' (the functions) was important.

Early ideas about communication centred on how the HIC might be used as a sort of 'Post-it' system as we saw in the original scenario. One member of the family might leave a message for another to buy cat food, get some milk or whatever. The HIC would also be used as a video phone, e-mail system, etc.

The informational scenarios concerned activities such as finding a recipe. This in turn leads to 'What's in the fridge? What else do we need? What can we cook?'. The HIC would be able to calculate the quantities in a recipe for one, two or three people. Other scenarios concerned activities such as going sailing, hence the need to get information on the tides, going skiing (finding out about the weather), going out (getting information about pubs, restaurants and concerts), etc.

The entertainment scenario led to ideas that users might like to play a game, find some sport, watch TV on demand or automatically record preferred programmes. It would be possible to have a chat room running alongside a TV programme and so on.

Other scenarios included integration with other devices, such as heating control, home security and so on. The children doing homework was another, investigating finding out, doing crosswords and quizzes, ordering videos, photographs and so on. Often the issue came back – how to accommodate large amounts of data, large visualizations, and the multitude of media that would be needed. Remember that the project was exploring a new device – a home information centre – which was not to be a PC. It was to be different in its look, feel and usage.

Eleven scenarios finally formed the complete 'corpus' effectively defining the functionality of the HIC, but still based around the three main uses: entertainment, information and communication and combinations of these.

Challenge 4-5

One of the scenarios we developed was known as the 'What shall we do now?' or 'Edinburgh Festival' scenario, after the large arts festival that is held in Edinburgh every August. A basic, high-level PACT analysis for this gives:

- People – young, wealthy, no children
- Activities – searching for information about events, making bookings, meeting friends
- Context – flat in Edinburgh, assume fast Internet connection
- Technology – HIC as currently specified.

Develop this scenario and the personas involved by imagining some concrete activities and interactions that could occur. Concentrate on developing a rich description of the context in which the interaction might take place. What questions does this start to raise?

4.4 Evaluating early interface prototypes

In order to evaluate some interface concepts, three prototype design solutions, each taking one of the scenarios as a starting point, were produced. These draft prototype designs (A, B and C) were developed as working solutions to some of the questions that had arisen from three of the scenarios which developed out of the work done on use analysis in the early stages of the project. This section discusses the three prototypes produced and analyses the decisions made by the three designers in response to the design of the HIC as a whole. This work then served as the basis of the development of the second interface design.

Usability principles

The usability principles introduced in Chapter 3 were used as a basis for the evaluations. The principles outline the three main categories of usability that interface design should encompass and this can provide the basis for an early high-level 'discount' evaluation (see Box 4-2).

Chapter 14 discusses the future workshop

Since we do not have a system at this point, it is difficult to undertake user and task observation, but we did hold some future workshops (Chapter 14) and look at people's information searching using current technologies such as paper and Internet entertainment guides. At this point in the design process we were still primarily concerned with concepts and with exploring alternative design solutions. For our discount usability method we used the 'heuristics' or design principles identified in Chapter 3 and critiqued the interfaces, commenting on the key issues of:

- Learnability – Can people guess easily what the system will do, based upon previous experience? This covers the usability principles of visibility, consistency, affordance and familiarity.

- Accommodation – Is the system designed to afford a multiplicity of ways in which people can accomplish their goals? Is it pleasant to use? This covers the usability principles of flexibility, style and conviviality.

- Effectiveness – Can people correct or change previous decisions, and complete their desired task easily, effectively and safely? This covers the usability principles of navigation, control, feedback, recovery and constraints.

In the next subsections we describe the evaluations that took place of three prototypes. Of course, when the evaluations were done, there were working prototypes to try out. In reporting the evaluations we have only a single static image of the interface to illustrate it.

Evaluation of Prototype A

Prototype A had explored one of the scenarios concerned with electronic books (e-books) and use of the HIC to obtain information on films and music. The prototype had been mocked up, as illustrated in Figure 4-1.

Based around the theory of successful interface design being made up of easily identifiable metaphors such as those utilized by Microsoft and Macintosh in the development of their operating systems, this interface design utilizes a metaphor based on a personal organizer type of object. Buttons allow the user to select whether they want to search for music or films with the results displayed on the right-hand side.

Analysis

A few basic problems are immediately obvious with the interface of this design, which are not consistent with the basic usability principles.

- Learnability – The basic principles would be easily understood from the user's previous knowledge, but it is also not at all obvious how to use the DEFINE button. The buttons below Music, Film and All also confuse the user and clutter the design. They have no labels, and serve no purpose, which leads us to question why they are there at all.

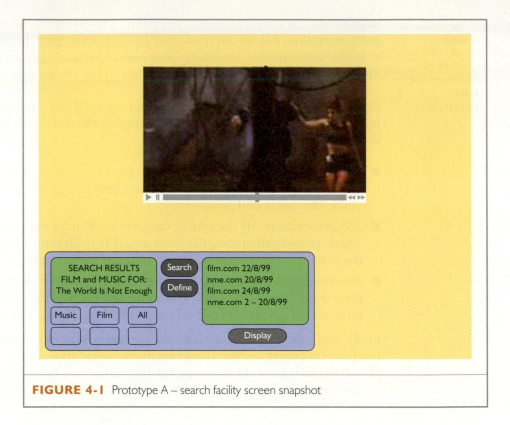

FIGURE 4-1 Prototype A – search facility screen snapshot

■ Accommodation – The interface looks as if it offers a variation on the paths that the user can follow. The user may search for any information on the text query, or narrow their search from a larger list by selecting music or film results only. However, to give greater flexibility, the HIC system should allow a more varied form of search, for example searching a particular content provider for information, or searching a particular category of information, such as local news. It could be necessary for the keypad design to display a great number of categories of information and the content providers that the user has subscribed to, and this functionality would have to be incorporated into this design. This would clutter the keypad and lose the simplicity of the design and therefore its effectiveness. The HIC interface is to eventually accommodate multi-modal input. This may take the form of touching the screen, speech input, keyboard, remote control or pen input. This design does not enable touching all of the elements with ease as the icons and text in many cases are too small.

■ Effectiveness – The interface also does not score highly in terms of effectiveness, as the user is not able to 'undo' any errors, go back or forward or display a previous search.

Conclusions

Many questions arise as to how the look and feel of this interface would develop and translate into other aspects of the HIC's operation. For example, if people wanted to utilize other areas of the system as described in other scenarios such as to watch TV, where would the TV object appear on the screen? Would the objects as they appear be of the same style of design? In one of the scenarios, the user wants to send a message to another user and attaches a picture taken with the internal camera to the message before sending it. The question arises as to how such a complex variety of actions, facilities and operations of the HIC system could be integrated into this design. Would they all fit onto the screen at one time, involving the manipulation of multiple windows? What space would each object occupy? Would this not be ineffective for a 'lean-back' situation?

This design really only provides a solution for a very limited search and does not seem to accommodate the complexity of the HIC system. With continuity of design a basic requirement of any good interface design, and the unsuitability of the design in incorporating the complete functionality of the HIC system, it would be unlikely to be developed further.

Challenge 4-6
Put yourself in the place of the industrial partner and offer a brief critique of this interface. Remember that the company was interested in high quality, novel, 'intuitive' user interfaces and escaping from the PC look and feel.

Evaluation of Prototype B

This second prototype is a solution to the presentation of huge amounts of information, which will be accessible through the HIC. Figure 4-2 shows a screenshot from this draft prototype illustrating the use of conceptual categories relevant for a 'festival' content provider. An issue at this point was who would define such categories and how many categories are appropriate. This question continued to be extremely important for the project.

The prototype defines multiple levels of information available through the use of a colour-coded history top bar. It also provides a solution for the many actions and operations to be presented on screen only when required, by means of hidden docks. It deals with the issues involved with utilizing the HIC from a distance in connection with speech input or remote control with the implementation of 'Near' and 'Far' buttons which magnify the contents on the screen.

Analysis

Evaluation of this prototype in terms of its usability provided many interesting solutions to problems that were looked at in the evaluation of Prototype A.

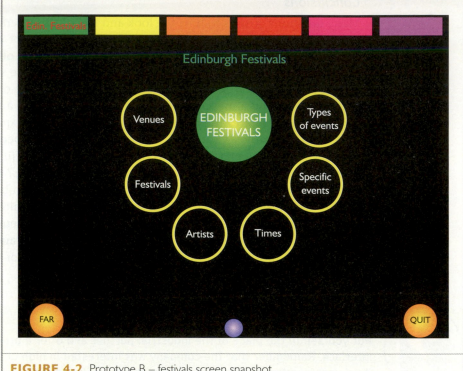

FIGURE 4-2 Prototype B – festivals screen snapshot

■ Learnability – The interface was easy to follow. The inclusion of 'hotspot' rollovers on certain areas of the interface confirms to the user that these areas are clickable buttons. The animated arrow at the bottom of the interface indicates that there is a hidden dock available at the bottom of the screen. When the user clicks on a button on the main interface and is taken to the next level, their 'route' through the information space is recorded on the history bar at the top of the screen. The separate levels have backgrounds of different colour to separate them. A problem here is that they do not correspond to the colours on the history bar, which is slightly confusing. The history bar contains a group of rainbow-coloured cells that at some points could be completely empty or contain no history, which could confuse. The question also arises as to what would happen to the history bar when the user had gone through more than six pages of information, as the bar has only six cells.

■ Accommodation – In terms of flexibility, this interface solution offers people a number of ways in which to complete the same task. For example, they could search for a particular event in the Edinburgh Festival, look through a number of events on a certain date, or look for events in a certain area of the city. People can access previous levels of information through the history bar, or through the Back button on the hidden navigation bar, but cannot then return to the level they were on without searching for it again. The Near and Far buttons also provide some kind of solution to the problem of a small 15-inch screen being viewed from the other side of the room by someone who is using voice activation or a remote control as a means of operating the HIC. The buttons on the screen were also well proportioned for using with the touch screen facility.

■ Effectiveness – The design is fairly successful concerning effectiveness. People are able to go back to previous levels easily via the history bar or Back button. The design contains a Forward button, which is non-functional, indicating that it was intended to be included in the design. However, its functionality is not clear, and what would the history bar show if people were to go back? How would it indicate that they might also go forward?

Conclusions

After evaluation this solution provided a great many ideas and questions that needed answering. Although not perfect, this design gave a good starting point for providing an effective solution to the many problems that the HIC poses.

In particular, a history bar was an effective idea, but the colour coordination, representation of the bar with no history or huge amounts of history, and representation of the bar when the user is moving backward through the information all needed to be looked at further.

Colour coordination of the different levels was also a good idea, but it was not really used to good effect and could be confusing. Used in another way, it could provide a powerful tool for navigating the HIC's huge information space. The allocation of colour to the levels of information needed to be investigated further.

The hidden navigation bar was also an effective idea, and would solve the problem of a large number of actions or facilities having to be available to the user quickly and easily without cluttering and confusing the screen. This was also an idea that would be looked at further.

Challenge 4-7
Put yourself in the place of the industrial partner and offer a brief critique of this interface. Remember that the company was interested in high quality, novel, 'intuitive' user interfaces and escaping from the PC look and feel.

Evaluation of Prototype C

This prototype also tackles some of the problems involved with a multi-level information system, by categorizing the information spaces available on the HIC. It was based on a recipe scenario, where the HIC was used to select recipes depending on various criteria. It addresses some of the issues involved with the actions that the user may make, such as to search or take notes. As with the previous prototype it makes an attempt to categorize the information by means of colour (Figure 4-3).

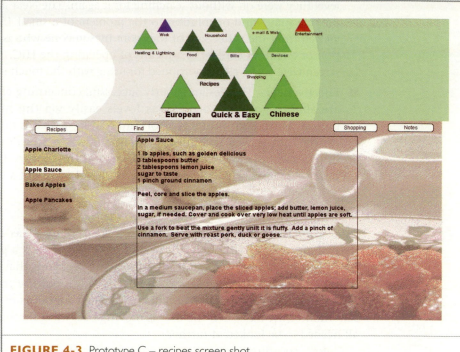

FIGURE 4-3 Prototype C – recipes screen shot

Analysis

■ Learnability – The design is fairly simple to use. Initially people are given four choices of categories to choose from; these are colour-coded triangles, which highlight when rolled over, indicating that they are clickable. When people select a category, they are presented with subsections of that category, which are shown in the same colour as the main category. This continues through further selections, which helps to keep track of the path followed. Another very effective visual is the reduction in size of the triangles as the search goes further into the information levels, the first choice of triangles being the smallest and thus the furthest away. This gives visualization of the depth and distance that has been covered in the information space. However, a problem must arise when the user has navigated through several levels of information and the bulk of the screen is taken up with the history of their actions rather than the display of information itself. Unreadable text labels on the smaller triangles, especially at a distance, and their unsuitability for touch screen input is also a problem associated with this design solution.

■ Accommodation – The interface does allow the user some flexibility, especially in relation to the search facility. People are able to search according to four different categorizations and are given the option either to scroll through text lists alphabetically to find a subject to search, or to input text in a search text field. The real problem with the search facility is that it does not add to the history above, and therefore cannot be re-accessed once the search result is displayed. People would have to search again if they wanted to have a second look at the search results. They have also been given the option of taking notes from the information presented, and adding to a shopping list if required.

- Effectiveness – In terms of effectiveness, this solution does not accommodate the need to go back or forward, or undo errors. Although the triangle history shows the path that has been taken, it does not enable the user to retrace their path and go back to a previous level.

Conclusions

As with Prototype B, this prototype gives interesting solutions to the navigational aspect of the HIC, especially the tracing of the user's actions as a type of history. Although problems are associated with this, such as unreadable labels and the potentially inappropriate utilization of space, it is a solution which would be worth looking at further.

The use of colour coordination as an attempt to simplify the wealth of information was also an effective idea. The idea of categorizing information and linking it to colour affords strong association to the user and has potential for further development.

Challenge 4-8
Put yourself in the place of the industrial partner and offer a brief critique of this interface. Remember that the company was interested in high quality, novel, 'intuitive' user interfaces and escaping from the PC look and feel.

4.5 Conclusions

The outcome of this evaluation, taking on board the industrial partner's comments and the views of the design team, is set out in Table 4-1. The activity was very beneficial in highlighting some key interface design issues. In Part III a number of design features that build upon these concepts are illustrated.

TABLE 4-1 Outcome of the evaluation

Problem or issue	Suggested solutions
History of navigation ideas need to be developed further	Use of animated triangles, utilization of partner's remote control button shapes, recording the user's path, providing a bar along the top of the screen, or recording the direction of navigation
Utilization of colour to categorize the huge amount of information stored within the HIC	Define categories and subcategories within the information space and allocate colour accordingly
Attention needs to be paid to the multi-modal element	All design decisions must accommodate multi-modal element. Text must be readable from a distance, and any selections regardless of mode of input must confirm user interactions
Separation of the various navigational aspects	Navigational elements must be organized according to definable groupings. Navigation should be available as needed; hidden docks could be used for those least utilized so as not to clutter screen
Formalization and order of the functionality of the system	The actions and activities, as well as the information which needs to be navigated, have to be ordered. Generic actions of the system must therefore be classified
Utilization of the industrial partner's design concepts where possible	Existing style and design of remote controls could be integrated into the design

Summary and key points

In this chapter we have brought some of the abstract ideas to life, by showing what happens in a small part of a real project development. The aim of the chapter is to provide experience in doing interactive systems design.

- Scenarios are a very useful representation of ideas and can be used throughout the development life cycle.
- Prototypes can be used to bring aspects of the scenarios to life and to structure a project development process.
- Evaluation can be undertaken based on the design principles. In this case we have based the evaluation on three groups of principles: effectiveness, learnability and accommodation.

Further reading

Mayhew, D. (1999) *The Usability Engineering Lifecycle: a Practitioner's Handbook for User Interface Design*. Morgan Kaufmann, San Francisco.
This is a comprehensive book on Mayhew's commercial approach to ensuring usability in systems.

Rosson, M.-B. and Carroll, J. (2002) *Usability Engineering*. Morgan Kaufmann, San Francisco.
This book provides a scenario-based approach to interactive systems design illustrated with a detailed case study.

Nielsen, J. (1993) *Usability Engineering*. Academic Press, New York.

Comments on challenges

Challenge 4-1

Every year since the early 1970s I have been hearing talks that tell us that speech recognition is nearly perfected. The old joke in this context is to say to someone 'Wreck a nice beach' and see what they think you said. Even on *Star Trek* the only place where they do not explicitly issue a command to 'wake up' the computer is in the 'turbo lift' where it is assumed that statements such as 'bridge' or 'deck ten' are instructions. Elsewhere use of the computer through speech recognition is prefaced by the word 'computer'.

During the project, the best we achieved was about 45 percent recognition and this was using a microphone. Imagine the difficulties of someone shouting across a room, perhaps with the radio playing or other background noise. If 'turn on' is the command to start the HIC, how will it distinguish this from any other use of the words such as 'turn on the television'? Many design opportunities were discussed such as having a microphone built into a remote control unit, but in terms of usability, speech recognition of this sort remains a long way away. What other technology would you tolerate using if it only worked less than 50 percent of the time?

Challenge 4-2

This can be done by specifying a route using some mapping software but this then has to be connected to the description given on the radio, or the radio station has to be linked in with the mapping company. Then there are issues of how many routes could someone have, how many people would take advantage of such a facility, who would provide the data and so on. It is a difficult requirement to implement in any clearly usable way, as so much is involved in setting up a sensible profile and the key piece of functionality –

▶

connecting a radio report with such a profile – can only be provided if the radio station works with the content provider of the mapping software.

Challenge 4-3

From the quotation it is not clear whether the HIC will recognize Arnold's handwriting or whether it will just store an image of what he writes. If it just stores the image then messages will be difficult to retrieve and store later. Handwriting recognition is available on many hand-held computers, but how effective does it have to be in order to be acceptable in this context? If training of the system to recognize different handwriting is required, is this an overhead that people will bother with?

Challenge 4-4

The approach is iterative, which is good. Prototype P0 uses scenarios of use rather than spending time building systems. In order to provide some project management and control, some milestones have been established at months 6, 13 and 19. This will help to keep the project on schedule and shows how an iterative design approach is not incompatible with the demands of project management. Evaluation is central and consistent.

Challenge 4-5

The full version of this scenario is in Chapter 14. Here is just the development of the personas and context.

Jan and Pat are a couple in their mid-thirties. Pat is a university lecturer in Cultural Studies and Jan is an accounts manager at Standard Life insurance. They live in the Stockbridge area of Edinburgh in a two-bedroom flat overlooking the river. It is 12.00 noon on 15 August. Jan and Pat are sitting in their large, airy kitchen/dining room. The remains of pizza and mixed salad mingle with a pile of newspapers on the kitchen table. Jan and Pat have recently returned from a holiday on the island of Zante and, apart from checking their e-mail, have not gone back to work. They decide that they would like to go to see one of the events that is happening as part of the Edinburgh Arts festival.

Challenge 4-6

Prototype A: the industrial partner did not like the keypad metaphor. They stated that they did not like the idea of physical entities on the screen and would prefer something simpler. They were also not keen on the need for manipulation of windows. A problem with 'ghosting' of buttons was noted as it was felt that it made the text on the buttons unreadable. The buttons were too small for a touch screen. The sequence of interaction was unclear, as was use of the 'Define' button.

Challenge 4-7

Prototype B: The menu bar or 'history' bar was thought to be a good idea, although the text on the buttons was unclear. The use of colour in the 'history' bar was ineffective, as was the presence of all of the buttons when they had no labels. Use of highlighting of the main screen buttons obscured the text. The animation included in the arrival of the hidden dock on screen was very much approved of, and was seen as a device which should be looked at further.

The organization of buttons in a semi-circle around a topic was liked as a concept for the organization of information and would interpret well for use with the touch screen. The idea of the Near and Far buttons was a good one. The interaction was felt to be too spread out all over the screen.

Challenge 4-8

Prototype C: The use of standard terminal colours was liked for the navigation. Mapping the shape of the buttons to the partner's own design of remote control buttons rather than the existing triangles was suggested. The animation of the navigation interaction was seen as a good idea, as was the 'disappearing' triangles. The idea of having the selected triangle rotate 180 degrees to point down at the next level was suggested as a way to further indicate the route the user had taken. Clarification of the colour allocated to categories and subcategories would be required in any further development of this navigational idea.

Exercises

1. Develop some scenarios for the use of the HIC as an MP3 music player. Think hard about the personas that you need to develop and try to scope the whole problem domain by covering the range of functions and facilities that would be needed.

2. Develop the Edinburgh Festival scenario. Include facilities that enable Pat and Jan to browse different shows, select which one they want to see, book tickets and arrange to meet friends. Think about who is in control of the interface at different stages of the interaction.

Part II:
People and Technologies

Introduction

This part of the book considers some of the theoretical and practical foundations of designing interactive systems. Part II comprises three chapters which are:

Chapter 5 aims at introducing cognitive psychology and human information processing (HIP) in particular. Historically, cognitive psychology has been one of the major contributors to the discipline of human–computer interaction. As cognitive psychology is an enormously large subject area, we have selected four of the most relevant aspects for discussion. These main elements of cognitive psychology are (a) memory; (b) attention; (c) visual perception, including the *Gestalt* laws of perception, depth perception, factors affecting perception and colour; and finally (d) mental models. The chapter concludes with a brief discussion of the shortcomings of the HIP approach.

Chapter 6 introduces the range of technologies available to support single user interaction. It begins with a discussion of user interfaces, and graphical user interfaces (GUI) in particular. We then pick apart the major components of a GUI and discuss the main components of form fill user interfaces which are the mainstay of many web-based applications. Then we turn to consider how we get information 'into' and 'out of' computers by means of input devices and output devices. Finally we introduce virtual reality and its corresponding input and output devices.

The final chapter of this part goes beyond the narrow cognitive treatment of interaction to consider embodiment. The chapter begins with a discussion of ergonomics which, historically, was concerned with 'fitting the machine to the man', now updated to include women. Ergonomics focuses on the strengths and limitations of our bodies when considering the design of interactive devices. From physical embodiment we turn to embodiment in collaborative virtual environments (CVE). In CVEs we assume form by way of avatars. We next turn to a brief discussion of affordance. It is argued that we can see the use to which certain artefacts and things in the world can be put without prior learning: these features are called affordances. If we could design affordances into interactive devices then many of the problems associated with their use would disappear. The chapter concludes by discussing three alternative theoretical perspectives on the use, design and evaluation of interactive systems. These are situated action, distributed cognition and activity theory.

In the teaching of interactive systems design, it is intended that the material could be used to extend the material of Part I in an introductory module, or to complement the methods-based material in Part III. For this reason, the chapters can be used individually or as a set of three.

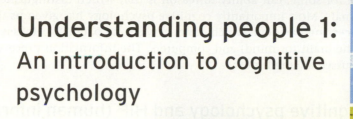

05

Understanding people 1:
An introduction to cognitive psychology

Aims

This chapter introduces the role of cognitive psychology in the design of **single-user interactive systems**. This chapter should be read in conjunction with Chapter 6. After studying this chapter you should be able to understand:

- The human information processing (HIP) view of human cognition
- The role of cognitive psychology in interactive systems design
- The importance of memory, attention, perception and mental models to the design of interactive systems
- Criticisms of the cognitive psychological approach

5.1 Introduction

If we are to design and build usable interactive systems, we must understand something about the capabilities of people – us – and psychology is the discipline which has been primarily concerned with understanding people. Consequently psychology, specifically cognitive psychology, has been a very important part of the theoretical foundations of HCI. Having decided that understanding people is important, we are then faced with the practical problem of dealing with the complexity of human beings and our behaviour – which aspects should we focus on? Historically HCI has divided this question into a number of overlapping disciplines or fields, namely cognitive psychology and other aspects of psychology such as affect (see Chapter 17) and ergonomics (usually referred to as human factors in the United States). The contribution of ergonomics is discussed in Chapter 7.

Cognitive psychology (or *cognition* – the two terms are used interchangeably) comprises those aspects of our mental life concerned with perception, reasoning, memory and attention, and language. Of course, all these mental faculties are interdependent. Attention guides both perception and memory; language and reasoning are closely connected, but what would language be without memory?

And for some, our ability to reason is that which distinguishes us from other animals. Most importantly cognitive psychology has given us the **information processing** paradigm which draws very strong parallels between the functioning of the brain (or mind) and computers. The information processing paradigm is discussed at length next.

5.2 Cognitive psychology and HIP (human information processing)

In 1983 Card, Moran and Newell published *The Psychology of Human–Computer Interaction*. In the preface to this, one of the first and certainly the most celebrated book on psychology and HCI, we find this earnest hope expressed:

The domain of concern to us, and the subject of this book, is how humans interact with computers. A scientific psychology should help us in arranging the interface so it is easy, efficient and error free – even enjoyable.

Card *et al.* (1983), p. vii

The book has at its core the *Model Human Processor* which is a simplified model of **human information processing** from the perspective of (a) the psychological knowledge at that time and (b) a task-based approach to human–computer

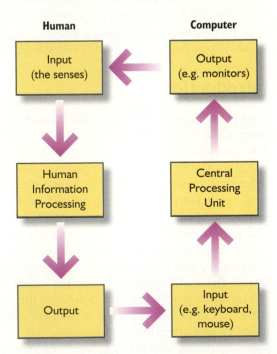

FIGURE 5-1 The information processing paradigm (in its most simple form)

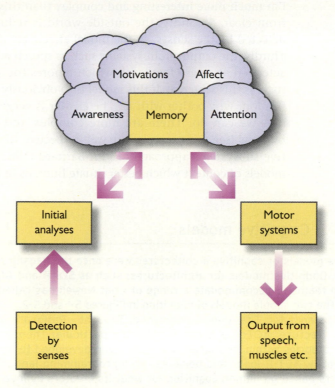

FIGURE 5-2 A more detailed information processing paradigm

interaction (again this was the state of the art in HCI at the time). Task-based approaches to HCI are discussed in Section 5.2 and Chapter 20. The human information processing paradigm characterizes or simplifies people's abilities into three 'blocks' or subsystems: (a) a sensory input subsystem, (b) a central information processing subsystem, and (c) a motor output subsystem. This is, of course, remarkably similar to how we generally partition the main elements of a computer. Figure 5-1 is an illustration of this relation between people and computers. In this view of human–computer interaction, humans and computers are functionally similar and form a closed loop.

In this model, all of our cognitive abilities have been grouped into a box labelled 'Human Information Processing'. Figure 5-2 is a redrawing of this diagram and offers a generalized example of a more detailed and up-to-date treatment of the same basic concepts. This time (starting at the bottom left) information from the senses is seen to be analysed before being stored in memory. Once stored in memory a range of other processes may act on it, before some form of action can be taken via motor systems (this might include physical movement, button pushing or some form of verbal behaviour).

Looking at this figure reveals a number of problems. Firstly, this is a massive and perhaps unjustifiable simplification of human beings (speaking for myself –

I'm much more interesting and complex than this). The role of the 'clouds' is far from clear. Secondly, the outside world is reduced to stimuli, which can be detected by the senses, so the model effectively *de-contextualizes* human beings. Thirdly, the output from systems such as speech and the muscular system is characterized at a very low level, which ignores the subtle complexities of outputs such as this sentence. If this model is so obviously incomplete and an oversimplification, why bother with it? The answer is very simple – it is, more or less, the best we can do. There are more complex and empirically tested models of humans (see, for example, the well-respected, though rather demanding, cognitive subsystems approach of Phil Barnard (1985) and Box 5-1). And there are models of context which better situate humans in the world (see Chapter 7).

Box 5-1 Cognitive models

Cognitive models or cognitive architectures were once the flagships of both cognitive psychology and HCI. Cognitive models (or architectures) such as SOAR and ACT-R have been developed by research teams to accommodate a range of what Newell has called micro-theories of cognition, such as the two simple models of cognition in Figures 5-1 and 5-2.

ACT-R stands for 'The Adaptive Control of Thought - Rational' and is strictly speaking a cognitive architecture. ACT-R is broader than any particular theory and can even accommodate multiple theories within its framework. It has been developed to model problem solving, learning and memory. ACT-R looks and behaves like a programming language except that it is based on constructs based on human cognition (or what its creators believe to be the elements of human cognition). Using ACT-R the programmer/psychologist or cognitive scientist can solve or model problems such as logic puzzles, or control an aircraft and then study the results. These results might give insights into the time to perform tasks and the kinds of errors which people might make in doing so.

Other cognitive architectures work in similar ways.

As researchers, academics and designers we are interested in understanding and predicting the use of interactive systems and, for many of us, this is best done using an underlying theory such as cognitive psychology. But human beings are very complex, so we have to simplify our view of human cognitive abilities in order to them manageable.

5.3 A seven-stage model of activity

So far in this chapter we have discussed cognition as studied by psychologists but have yet to link it closely to HCI. One celebrated psychologist who has been at the forefront of making this connection is Donald Norman. Figure 5-3 is a representation of Norman's seven-stage model of how an individual completes an activity (Norman, 1988). This is by no means the only model of activity but it is typical of such approaches (see Chapter 20 on task analysis). This model is a

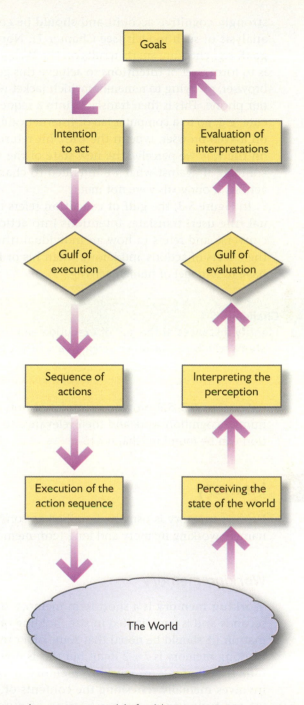

FIGURE 5-3 Norman's seven-stage model of activity *(source: after Norman, 1988)*

strongly cognitive account and should be contrasted with Suchman's critical analysis of such models (see Chapter 7). Norman argues that we begin with a **goal**, e.g. checking sports results on the Web, or phoning a friend. Our next step is to form a set of **intentions** to achieve this goal, e.g. finding a computer with a browser, or trying to remember which jacket we were wearing when we last used our phone. This is then translated into a sequence of actions which we then execute, e.g. go to a computer lab or Internet café, then log on to a PC, double-click on a Web browser, type in the URL, hit return, read sports results. At each step on the way we perceive the new state of the world, interpret what we see, and compare it against what we intended to change. We may have to repeat these actions if our goals were not met.

In Figure 5-3, the **gulf of execution** refers to the problem of how an individual (the user) translates intentions into action. The **gulf of evaluation** is the converse and refers to how an individual (the user) understands, or evaluates, the effects of actions and knows when his or her goals are satisfied. So there we have it: a model of human activity.

Challenge 5-1
Identify instances of the gulf of execution and the gulf of evaluation in devices or systems which you (or other people) have difficulty using.

Sections 5.3–5.9 provide examples of how four of the major components of human cognition work and their relevance to HCI. More on memory and attention can be found in Chapter 15.

5.4 Memory

Human memory is usually described as consisting of two major components, namely working memory and long-term memory.

Working memory

Working memory is a short-term memory store holding material for up to 30 seconds and is very limited in size, holding only three or four 'chunks' of information (it should be noted that some older textbooks claim that the capacity of working memory is 7 ± 2 items but this is now known to be incorrect). To maintain the contents of working memory it needs to be rehearsed. Rehearsal involves mentally refreshing the contents of working memory. For example, if we are trying to remember a string of numbers or words (say, a telephone number or URL) it is usual to simply repeat the words or numbers either mentally or out loud. For pictures we might revisualize them (or look at the original again) or augment the picture with a verbal label ('It's a red rose.'). If we do not refresh the contents of working memory within 30 seconds or so, it will decay, fade away and be lost. In addition to the short-lived nature of working memory, it is also very limited in capacity, its contents being easily overwritten or pushed out by new materials. The other aspect of working memory which psychologists have identified is the two different modalities it supports. Working memory can store a small amount of visual information (in what is called the visuo-spatial sketchpad) *and* a small amount of verbal information (in the articulatory loop). The visuo-spatial sketchpad is effectively the mind's eye while the articulatory loop is your inner voice. If you picture the face of someone you know, you are using the visuo-spatial sketchpad, and if you are singing to yourself you are using the articulatory loop.

Long-term memory

In sharp contrast, long-term memory is effectively the inverse of working memory. Its capacity is effectively unlimited; you will never run out of storage space. Memories can last from a few minutes to a lifetime. We also appear to have multi-modal memories – try remembering the smell of a flower, the taste of chocolate, the voice of a friend, your home address, the first few words of the song 'Happy Birthday', or the feel of a cold shower. Other memories are just as long-lived but may be harder to articulate, e.g. signing your name (and recognizing your signature), riding a bicycle, making a sandwich or typing.

Recall and recognition

Chapter 15 examines these issues more closely

A great deal is known about the structure and processes of long-term memory, too much to be discussed here, but it is worth highlighting two crucially important mechanisms, namely **recall** and **recognition**. Recall is the process whereby individuals actively search their memories to retrieve a particular piece of information. Recognition involves searching your memory and then deciding whether the piece of information matches what you have in your memory store. Recognition is generally easier and quicker than recall.

Challenge 5-2
Find instances of designing for recall and recognition in software you use regularly. Hint: websites requiring form-filling are often good sources of examples.

So, in summary:

- Memory has two major components (working memory and long-term memory).
- Memory should be thought of as a set of processes (e.g. recall, recognition, chunking, rehearsal) rather than as a 'database' in your head.

■ Memory appears to be multi-modal – we can remember colours, sounds and the feel and smell of things. Memories in the brain, of course, are not stored as colours, sounds or smells but appear so when we recall them.

So, given these abilities and limitations, what are the consequences for the design of interactive systems? The short answer is *considerable*, and they are discussed at greater length in Chapter 15. However, let's begin by analysing the user interface widget in Figure 5-4. This is an image of the formatting palette which is part of the version of Microsoft Word current at the time of writing. Microsoft have extensive usability laboratories and the design of this application will have benefited from a sound understanding of the capabilities of people. As such it is an excellent example of designing for memory and embodies a whole series of **design principles** reflecting good design practice.

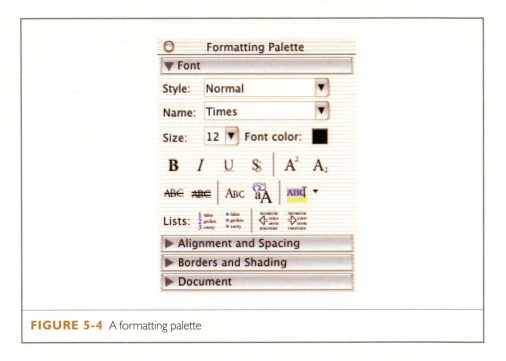

FIGURE 5-4 A formatting palette

In no particular order, we now analyse the design of the palette.

→

Direct manipulation is discussed in Chapter 6.

■ The palette has been designed to use **recognition** rather than **recall**. The drop-down menus for style, name and size remove the need to recall the names of the fonts installed and the range of styles available. Instead the main memory mechanism is recognition. In addition to this, the burden on working memory is kept to a minimum using **direct manipulation** (i.e. clicking on an item) rather than having to memorize the name of a font (e.g. Zapf Dingbats) and then having to correctly type it in a dialog box.

■ The extensive use of **chunking**. Chunking is a technique we all use, mostly without realizing it, to group items into more meaningful units. The usual quoted example is that of telephone numbers – 12344678900 becomes '123' double 4 '6789' double zero, four chunks being easier to remember than 11 individual numerals. Similarly, the palette has been organized into four chunks – font, alignment and spacing, borders and shading, and document – which are logical groups or chunks of functions.

■ The use of meaningful associations: **B** stands for bold, *I* for italic. It is good design practice to use these natural mappings.

Of course, the palette also relies on aspects of visual processing and the use of icons (discussed in Chapter 15).

Box 5-2 Shock finding! Men's and women's memories are different

Canli and fellow researchers used a brain scanner to see how 12 men and 12 women responded to a set of 100 photographs ranging from images with no emotional content (e.g. a fire hydrant) to those with highly emotional content (e.g. a mutilated body). The brain scans revealed that different parts of the brain became active, indicating the processing of this information (e.g. the creation of new memories) between men and women.

   Three weeks later the participants were given a surprise memory test. 'Women recall more emotional autobiographical events than men in timed tests, produce memories more quickly or with greater emotional intensity in response to cues, and report more vivid memories than their spouses for events related to their first date, last vacation and a recent argument.'

Source: The Independent, 23 July 2002

5.5   Attention

Attention is usually defined in terms of the focusing of mental resources at or on a particular task or object. Attention is a pivotally important human ability. In an everyday sense, as opposed to a strictly psychological interpretation, attention is central to learning, perception, operating a machine, using a computer and so forth. Failures in attention are a frequently cited reason for accidents: car accidents have been attributed to the driver using their mobile phone while driving; aircraft have crashed when the pilots have paid too much attention to the 'wrong' cockpit warning; control room operators can be overwhelmed by the range and complexity of instruments to which they must attend, and so on. So we clearly need to be able to understand the mechanism of attention, its capabilities and limitations, and how to design to make the most of these abilities while minimizing their limitations. Attention can not only be focused but also be divided between several tasks up to a certain limit. Some researchers think of attention as being a resource which can be split between several tasks until, in some sense, we have used it all up. How quickly we consume these mental resources depends upon the characteristics of the tasks we are performing. Most of us can watch TV and hold a conversation until perhaps the conversation or the TV programme becomes very diverting. So, we can perform a small number of simple tasks more or less concurrently or one demanding task alone. Of course, practice also makes perfect. When we first learn to drive a car it demands all of our attention; with practice, we can hold conversations, listen to the radio, eat a hamburger, drink a coke and drive a car (though this is not recommended). Practice reduces the amount of attention required, freeing us to perform other tasks concurrently. Attention is also closely linked with **awareness**, particularly of other people and their activities. So, in summary,

Chapter 30 has more material on awareness

- Attention can be directed at a particular task and/or divided between a number of different tasks.
- Practice reduces the amount of attention required by a particular task.
- Attention and awareness are closely linked.

These issues are closely linked to the design principles in Chapter 3

Why does this matter? We need to consider the design of interactive systems from a number of points of view, for example the design of alerts and warnings, designing for awareness, and designing for carrying out more than one task at a time.

How attention works

Historically there have been three different kinds of models (that is, accounts of how attention works) which psychologists have developed to account for attention. To make matters worse, these three different groups of models, by and large, do not agree with each other. The oldest group of models begins with the work of Broadbent who developed a single-channel theory of attention in the 1950s (Broadbent, 1958) which was subsequently modified, refined and developed by his co-workers and others (Triesman, 1960; Deutsch and Deutsch, 1963; Norman, 1968) but which remained broadly similar. Broadbent's model assumes that there is a kind of mental switch or filter which selects material either to be ignored or to which we pay attention. It may be useful to think of this switch or filter to be rather like the tuning dial on a radio. These models are not widely accepted today.

Another approach to attention has been developed by Kahneman (1973) in which it is argued that we have a limited amount of processing power at our disposal, and whether or not we are able to carry out a task depends on how much of this capacity is applied to the task. Of course, some tasks require relatively little processing power and others may require more – perhaps more than we have available. This and other similar models are referred to as **allocation** models. While Kahneman portrays attention as being more flexible and dynamic than the single-channel models, he is unable to describe how attention is channelled or focused. Similarly he is unable to define exactly what is meant by 'capacity'.

Finally, another group of models consider attention in terms of controlled and automatic processing. For example, Schneider and Shiffrin (1977) distinguish between controlled and automatic attentional processing:

- **Controlled processing** makes heavy demands on attentional resources, is slow and limited in capacity, and involves consciously directing attention towards a task.

- **Automatic processing** makes no demands on attentional resources, is fast, unaffected by capacity limitations, unavoidable and difficult to modify, and is not subject to conscious awareness.

Despite our best efforts, there is no one agreed account of attention. One reason for this is that attention has been studied in many different ways and another is that it is difficult to define what actually constitutes attention. So, at present, there are two broad types of accounts of attention which propose a limited capacity information processing system, which may or may not have general purpose or specific elements. In addition to this there is support for automatic tasks which do not require attentional resources *per se*.

Attention and vigilance

Vigilance is an aspect of attention which refers to detecting a rare event or a signal in a desert of inactivity or noise. For example, during World War II mariners were required to be on watch for enemy submarines; radar operators sat for hours before primitive VDUs watching for attacking aircraft. The study of vigilance became important because people were regularly failing to spot the enemy even under ideal conditions. However, early attempts to improve the vigilance of pilots on bombing trips were not always very successful. It was found that bombing crews who were issued with powerful stimulants such as amphetamines did succeed in staying awake and paying attention, but the drugs also made them hallucinate destructive imps (usually known as **gremlins**, which were seen to be tearing vital components off their aircraft). The extended use of amphetamines was also found to induce psychotic episodes. All in all, the use of amphetamines is not recommended.

More usually people are required to be vigilant on production lines looking for defective parts, or watching for weapons on airport X-ray machines, or monitoring temperature or pressure levels in a control room. It is important that we understand our interaction with large complex systems, particularly with respect to the monitoring of such systems.

Designing alerts and warnings

Figure 5-5 illustrates two different approaches (by the same software vendor) of alerting a user to the presence of new mail. Figure 5-5(a) is the unobtrusive display of an envelope or mailbox symbol. In this instance one would expect the user to notice the message but in their own time. The second approach, in contrast, may interrupt the user's work, so do not display this kind of alert box, which requires interaction, unless it is important, urgent or life threatening. Allow the user to configure the application to turn off such alerts. Figure 5-5(b) is an illustration of an unobtrusive alert signalling the delivery of a new email message.

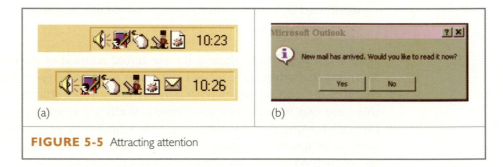

(a) (b)

FIGURE 5-5 Attracting attention

Next, consider the following two alerts which might be presented on an aircraft's flight deck: *'Number two engine is on fire'* and *'In-flight movie tape jammed'*. One is significantly more important than the other but both require attention – in due course. In this instance attention-grabbing techniques must be used cautiously. Reporting the fire may involve using a siren to alert the crew irrespective of where they are looking or what they are doing, accompanied by the use of graphical alerts and warning lights. In contrast, alerting the crew to the movie tape being jammed may be achieved though less dramatic means.

The **wording** and **presentation** of attention-getting alerts also require a little thought. For example, there is abundant evidence that phrases which contain a negative expression or are in the passive voice take longer to read and understand. For example, in an emergency situation, air traffic controllers will issue the simple, direct and positive command 'climb, climb, climb' to an aircraft in danger of colliding with another, rather than 'do not descend'.

5.6   Visual perception

Visual perception, arguably, is the best understood of all the forms of perception. Visual perception is concerned with extracting meaning (and hence recognition and understanding) from the light falling on our eyes. Visual perception allows us to recognize a room and the people and furniture therein, or to recognize the Windows XP 'start' button, or the meaning of an alert. In contrast, vision is a series of computationally simpler processes. Vision is concerned with such things as detecting colour, shapes and the edges of objects.

Normally sighted people perceive a stable, three-dimensional, full-colour world filled with objects. This is achieved by the brain extracting and making sense of the sensory data pickup by our eyes. The study of visual perception is often divided into a number of interwoven threads, namely theories of visual perception (accounts of how we perceive the world and how these can be explained) including depth perception, pattern recognition (including such things as how we recognize each other) and developmental aspects (how we learn to perceive, or how our perceptual abilities develop). For the purposes of this chapter we will concentrate on the first of these, namely accounts of how we perceive the world. We begin with a discussion of top-down visual perception, followed by an account of Gibson's direct perception theory. Moving from these theoretical positions, the so-called *Gestalt* laws of visual perception are then discussed with their application to user interface design.

Understanding visual perception

Richard Gregory has presented (e.g. in Gregory, 1973, among many related works) a good example of a **constructivist** account of visual perception. He has argued that we *construct* our perception of the world from *some* of the sensory data falling on our senses. His theory is based on the nineteenth-century thinking of Helmholtz who had concluded that we perceive the world by means of a series of **unconscious inferences**. Gregory has drawn on numerous practical examples of the constructive/interpretative processes to support his theory. Of this supporting evidence we shall consider perceptual constancies and so-called visual illusions (actually better described as perceptual illusions). A red car appears red in normal daylight because it reflects the red elements of (white) light. Yet the same car will appear red at night or parked under a yellow street light. This an example of a **perceptual constancy** – in this instance, colour constancy. Similarly a coin always appears coin-shaped (that is, disc-shaped) no matter how it is held in one's hand. This too is an example of another constancy – shape constancy. This ability to perceive an object or a scene in an unchanged fashion despite changing illumination, viewpoint and so forth affecting the information arriving at our senses is described as perceptual constancy.

Visual (perceptual) **illusions** are studied because they are thought to be very revealing of how perception works by understanding what happens when perception does not work! The argument goes like this. Perception is seamless and, as it works very well, it is almost impossible to find a way into the process unless we study it when it does not work. When perception is faulty we can, so to speak, lift a corner and peek underneath and see how it works. Figure 5-6 is an illustration of the Müller–Lyer illusion. The central shaft of the upper figure looks longer despite being exactly the same length as the one below. Gregory explains this illusion by suggesting that our knowledge of the real world causes us to infer (incorrectly) that the upper figure must have a longer shaft. Figure 5-7 is an image of the corner of a door in a corridor. A vertical Müller–Lyer 'arrow'

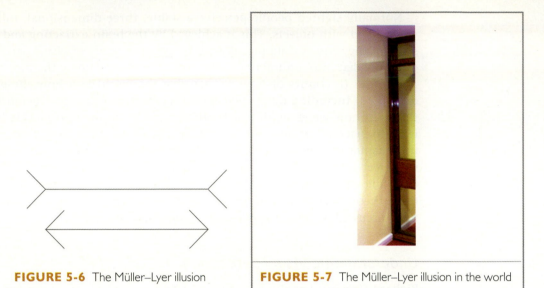

FIGURE 5-6 The Müller–Lyer illusion

FIGURE 5-7 The Müller–Lyer illusion in the world

can be seen, made up from the door frame and the wall. A vertical Müller–Lyer 'arrow' points away from the viewer and thus appears to be longer than an equivalent 'arrow' pointing towards the viewer.

Figure 5-8 illustrates a pair of Necker cubes. The Necker cube illustrates **hypothesis testing** very effectively. Gregory has argued that when we are faced with an ambiguous figure such as a Necker cube we unconsciously form a hypothesis that the cube is, say, facing to the right or left. But if we gaze for a few more seconds at the figure it appears to turn inside-out and back again as we try to make sense of the figure. This is hypothesis testing (and is a form of unconscious inference).

Gregory has produced an interesting and engaging account of visual perception which is supported by numerous examples. However, the central weakness of his argument lies with the question – how do we get started? If visual perception relies on knowledge of the world, how do we bootstrap the process? We can only acquire (visual) knowledge of the world from visual perception which relies on knowledge of the world.

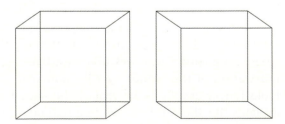

FIGURE 5-8 A pair of Necker cubes

Direct perception

In sharp contrast to Gregory's work is that of J.J. Gibson. Gibson's work on visual perception dates back to the Second World War (Gibson, 1950) and his work for the US military in improving the training of aircraft pilots, particularly during taking off and landing. He observed that a pilot sitting in the fixed point (the pilot's seat at the front of the aircraft) experiences the world apparently flowing past him. Gibson called this flow of information the **optic array**. This optic flow supplies *unambiguously* all information relevant to the position, speed and altitude of the aircraft to the pilot. So there is no need for unconscious inference or hypothesis testing. Figure 5-9 is an illustration of the flow of the optic array. As we drive down a road the environment appears to flow out and past us as we move. What is actually happening is that the **texture** of the environment is expanding.

Texture gradients provide important depth information. Examples of texture gradients include such things as pebbles on a beach or trees in a wood. As we approach a beach or a forest the texture gradient expands as individual pebbles or trees reveal themselves against the higher density of pebbles and trees of the beach or forest. Equally, as we retreat from a scene the texture gradient is seen to condense. Thus Gibson argued (e.g. Gibson, 1966, 1979) that the environment provides all of the information we required to experience it. Gibson also introduced the idea of **affordance** (Gibson, 1977) which has been a recurring concept in HCI design for many years; this is discussed in Chapter 7.

In practice, many psychologists believe that there is merit in both theories: Gibson offers an account for optimal viewing conditions, Gregory for sub-optimal (or restricted) conditions.

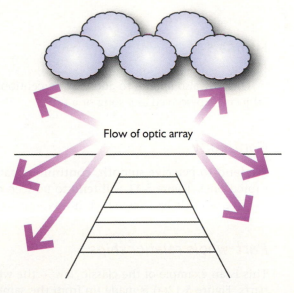

Flow of optic array

FIGURE 5-9 Flow of optic array

5.7 The *Gestalt* laws of perception

The Gestaltists were a group of psychologists working in the early years of the twentieth century who identified a number of 'laws' of perception which they regarded as being **innate** (i.e. we are born with them). While they did not create a theory of visual perception as such, their influence is still widely regarded as important. Indeed, despite their age, these laws map remarkably well onto a number of modern user interface design features.

Proximity

The law of proximity refers to the observation that objects appearing close together in space or time tend to be perceived together. For example, by the careful spacing of objects they will be perceived as being organized into either columns or rows (Figure 5.10).

FIGURE 5-10 Proximity

This law also applies to auditory perception, where the proximity of auditory 'objects' is perceived as a song or a tune.

Continuity

We tend to perceive smooth, continuous patterns rather than disjoint, interrupted ones. Figure 5-11 will tend to be seen as a continuous curve rather than the five semi-circles from which it was actually constructed.

Part-whole relationships

This is an example of the classic 'law' – the whole is greater than the sum of its parts. Figure 5-12(a) is made up from the same number of H's as Figure 5-12(b): same parts – different whole(s).

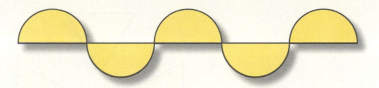

FIGURE 5-11 Continuity

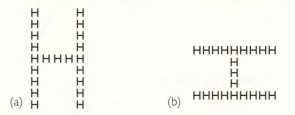

FIGURE 5-12 Part–whole relationships

Similarity

Similar figures tend to be grouped together. Figure 5-13 is seen as two rows of circles with a single row of diamonds sandwiched between them.

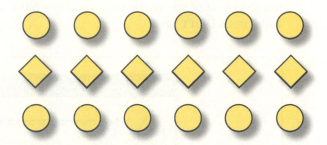

FIGURE 5-13 Similarity

Closure

Closed figures are perceived more easily than incomplete (or open) figures. This feature of perception is so strong that we even supply missing information our-selves to make a figure easier to perceive. Figure 5-14 is either four triangles or a Maltese cross.

Now we move from theory to the application of these concepts at the user inter-face. We begin with a discussion of proximity.

FIGURE 5-14 Closure

Using proximity to organize buttons

As we have seen, this law refers to the observation that objects appearing close together in space or time tend to be perceived together. The usefulness of this law can be seen by contrasting the next two figures. Figure 5-15 is a standard Microsoft Windows XP alert box with the buttons equally spaced. Figure 5-16 is the Mac OS X equivalent. The Mac version makes clear use of proximity. The **Cancel** and **Save** buttons are grouped away from the option **Don't Save**. This has the effect of seeing the pair together – **Save** or **Cancel** – from the potentially ambiguous **Don't Save**.

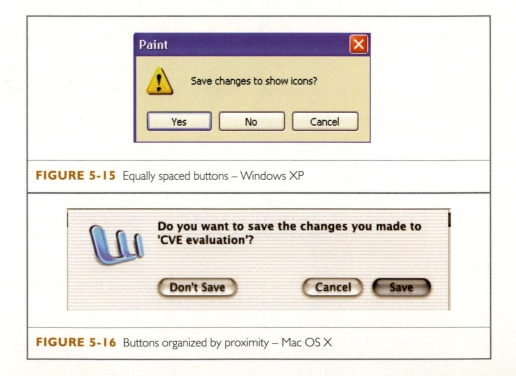

FIGURE 5-15 Equally spaced buttons – Windows XP

FIGURE 5-16 Buttons organized by proximity – Mac OS X

Using similarity to organize files

A second *Gestalt* law we consider is that of **similarity**. Figure 5-17 is a screenshot of the contents of a folder. All of the files are ordered alphabetically starting at the top left. The PowerPoint files are perceived as a contiguous block. This stands in sharp contrast to the file icons in Figure 5-18.

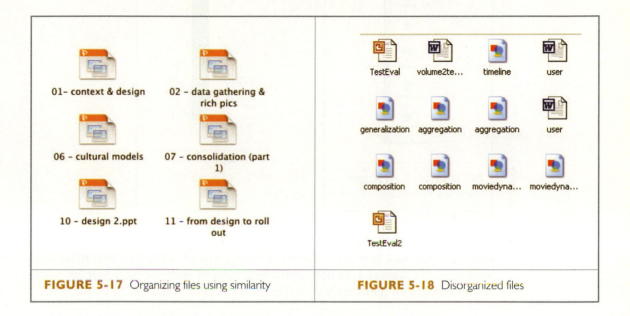

FIGURE 5-17 Organizing files using similarity

FIGURE 5-18 Disorganized files

Using continuity to connect disconnected elements

A third *Gestalt* law is **continuity**. Disconnected elements are often seen to be part of a continuous whole. Figure 5-19 illustrates part of a MS Windows scroll-bar which indicates that there is more of the document to be seen below the current windowful. The length of the slider is an indication of how much of the total document is visible. The slider indicates that about 80 percent of the document is visible. Figure 5-20 is an illustration of the Mac implementation of an scrollbar. Here an oval-shaped slider on the scrollbar provides a visual indicator of the viewpoint within the document. In this instance we are only 10–15 percent of the way from the start of the document.

Closure

This particular law refers to the fact that it has been found that closed objects are easier to perceive than those which are open. As evidence of this, we will often unconsciously add missing information to close a figure so that it is more easily perceived against its background.

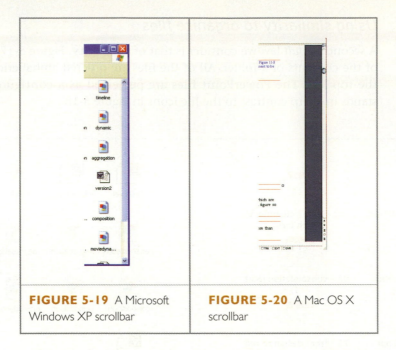

FIGURE 5-19 A Microsoft Windows XP scrollbar

FIGURE 5-20 A Mac OS X scrollbar

An example of the use of closure is the Finder application (Figure 5-21) which offers a visual track from the top level of a computer's hard disc (down) to an individual file. We perceive a connection running from *My hard disc* on the far left to the file *MS Scrollbar* on the extreme right, yet the connection is not strictly continuous.

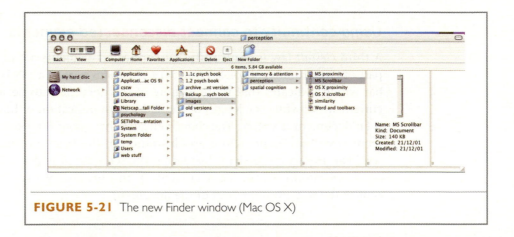

FIGURE 5-21 The new Finder window (Mac OS X)

Illustrating part-whole relationships

These are based on the principle that an object is more than the mere sum of its parts. Figure 5-22 is a schematic drawing of the layout of the lunar module (LM) ascent stage (this was the element of the LM which returned the astronauts from

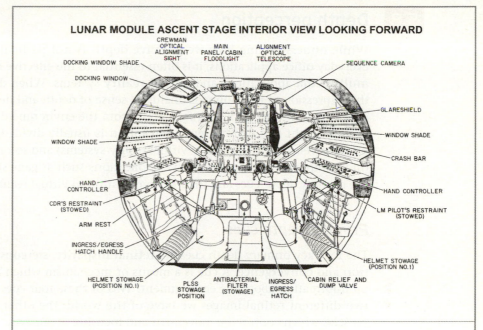

FIGURE 5-22 The lunar module (LM) ascent stage instrument panel
(Apollo Program Press Information Notebook (1972). NASA)

the moon's surface). We do not (and perhaps cannot) see it as a series of separate elements but instead we see the interior of a very cramped spacecraft. Contrast this with the detail below (Figure 5-23) which is a decontextualized detail taken from the larger image.

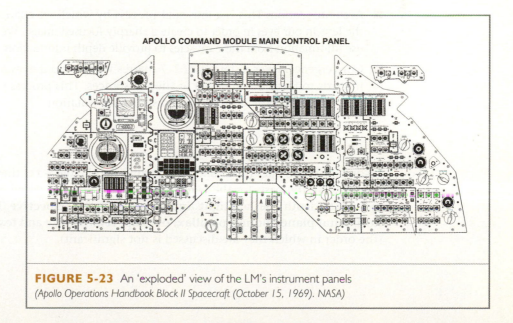

FIGURE 5-23 An 'exploded' view of the LM's instrument panels
(Apollo Operations Handbook Block II Spacecraft (October 15, 1969). NASA)

5.8 Depth perception

While understanding how we perceive depth is not particularly relevant to everyday office applications, it is often essential to the effective design of **games**, **multimedia** applications and **virtual reality** systems. When designing to give the impression of three-dimensionality (a sense of depth and height) we need to understand how we pick up information from the environment which we interpret as height and depth. Depth perception is usually divided into the role of primary (relevant to immersive virtual reality systems) and secondary depth cues (more important to non-immersive applications such as games). We begin with the primary depth cues and their key application in virtual reality systems.

Primary depth cues

The four key primary depth cues are **retinal disparity, stereopsis, accommodation** and **convergence**. A **cue** is a means or mechanism which allows us to pick up information about the environment. Two of these four cues make use of the two different retinal images we have of the world; the other two rely on the muscles which control the movement and focusing of our eyes.

- Retinal disparity. As our eyes are approximately 7 cm apart (less if you are a child, more if you have a big head) each retina receives a slightly different image of the world. This difference (the retinal disparity) is processed by the brain and interpreted as distance information.
- Stereopsis. Stereopsis is the process by which the different images of the world received by each eye are combined to produce a single three-dimensional experience.
- Accommodation. This is a muscular process by which we change the shape of the lens in our eyes in order to create a sharply focused image. We unconsciously use information from these muscles to provide depth information.
- Convergence. Over distances of 2–7 metres we move our eyes more and more inwards to focus on an object at these distances. This process of convergence is used to help provide additional distance information.

Secondary depth cues

Secondary depth cues (also called monocular depth cues – i.e. they rely on only one eye) are the basis for the perception of depth on flat visual displays. These secondary depth cues are **light and shade, linear perspective, height in the horizontal plane, motion parallax, overlap, relative size** and **texture gradient** (the order in which they are discussed is not significant).

■ Light and shade. An object with its attendant shadow (Figure 5-24) improves the sense of depth.

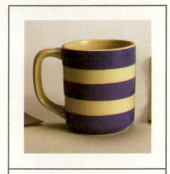

FIGURE 5-24 A three-dimensional teacup
(source: Dorling Kindersley)

■ Linear perspective. Figure 5-25 illustrates some examples of the use of linear perspective to give an impression of depth.

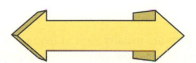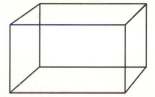

FIGURE 5-25 Examples of linear perspective, using 'shadow' and wire-frame

■ Height in horizontal plane. Distant objects appear higher (above the horizon) than nearby objects. Figure 5-26 is a screenshot of a chessboard which uses height in the horizontal plane to give the impression of the black pieces being further away than the white.

FIGURE 5-26 Use of height in the horizontal plane to give an impression of depth

■ **Motion parallax.** This cannot be demonstrated in a static image as it depends upon movement. It is perhaps best seen when looking out through a window in a fast-moving train or car. Objects such as telegraph poles which are nearby are seen to flash past very quickly while, in contrast, a distant building moves much more slowly.

■ **Overlap.** An object which obscures the sight of another is understood to be nearer. Figure 5-27 illustrates this point with an image of three overlapping windows.

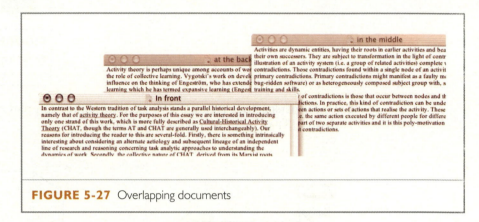

FIGURE 5-27 Overlapping documents

■ **Relative size.** Smaller objects are usually seen as being further away, particularly if the objects in the scene are of approximately the same size (Figure 5-28).

FIGURE 5-28 Relative size

■ **Texture gradient.** Textured surfaces appear closer; irregularities tend to be smoothed out over distance (Figure 5-29).

FIGURE 5-29 Texture gradient

5.9 Factors affecting perception

More on this in Chapter 15

Perceptual set refers to the effect of such things as our expectations of a situation, our state of arousal and our past experiences on how we perceive others, objects and situations. For example, as children we all interpreted every sound on our birthdays as the delivery of birthday cards and presents; to nervous fliers, every noise is the sound of engine failure or the wings falling off. The effects of these situations and other stimuli have long been studied by psychologists and a selection of these factors can be seen in Figure 5-30.

More than 50 years ago Bruner and Postman (1949) demonstrated a link between expectation and perception. They briefly presented the sentences in Box 5-3 and asked a number of people to write down what they had seen. People reliably wrote down what they had *expected* they had seen, e.g. Paris in the spring, rather than Paris in *the the* spring which is what they had seen.

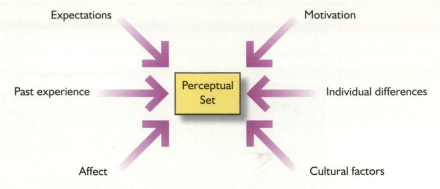

FIGURE 5-30 A selection of factors affecting perception *(source: after Gross, (2001), p. 221)*

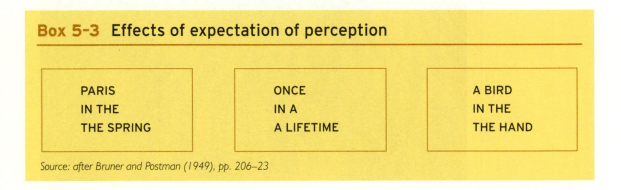

Box 5-3 Effects of expectation of perception

PARIS IN THE THE SPRING	ONCE IN A A LIFETIME	A BIRD IN THE THE HAND

Source: after Bruner and Postman (1949), pp. 206–23

5.10 Colour

How colour vision works

At the back of each eye is the retina which contains two types of light-sensitive cells called rods and cones. The rods (which are rod-shaped) number approximately 120 million and are more sensitive than the cones (which are cone-shaped). However, they are not sensitive to colour. The 6 or 7 million cones provide the eye's sensitivity to colour. The cones are concentrated in the part of the retina called the *fovea* which is approximately 0.3 mm in diameter. The

Box 5-4 Colour blindness

The term *colour blind* is used to describe people with defective colour vision. Red-green colour blindness (i.e. the inability to reliably distinguish between red and green) is the most common form, affecting approximately 1 in 12 men (~8 percent) and 1 in 25 women (~4 percent). It is a genetic disorder with a sex-linked recession gene to blame – hence the greater number of men being affected. A second and rarer form of colour blindness affects the perception of the colours blue-yellow. The rarest form of all results in monochromatic vision in which the sufferer is unable to detect any colour at all.

colour-sensitive cones are divided into 'red' cones (64 percent), 'green' cones (32 percent), and 'blue' cones (2 percent). The 'colour' of these cones reflects their particular sensitivity. The cones are also responsible for all high-resolution vision (as used in such things as reading), which is why the eye moves continually to keep the light from the object of interest falling on the fovea.

Designing with colour

Colour is very important to us. To describe someone as being colourless is to say that they are without character or interest. Designing colour into interactive systems is very difficult. If it were otherwise, why are most domestic electronic devices black? Look at the choice of default colours in software applications. Microsoft appears to be fond of greys and blues as can be seen in Figure 5-31. Apple's OS X offers a choice between blue and graphite. Figure 5-32 illustrates the choices available.

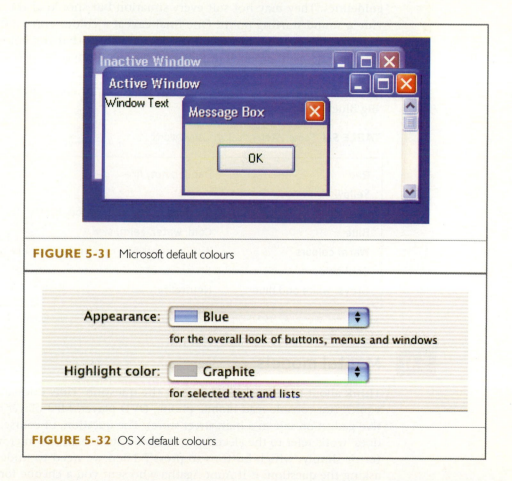

FIGURE 5-31 Microsoft default colours

FIGURE 5-32 OS X default colours

What follows draws heavily on Chapter 4 of Aaron Marcus's excellent book *Graphic Design for Electronic Documents and User Interfaces* (Marcus, 1992). The following rules have been taken directly from Marcus's book.

Rule 1. Use a maximum of 5 ± 2 colours.

Rule 2. Use foveal (central) and peripheral colours appropriately.

Rule 3. Use a colour area that exhibits a minimum shift in colour and/or size if the colour area changes in size.

Rule 4. Do not use simultaneous high-chroma, spectral colours.

Rule 5. Use familiar, consistent colour codings with appropriate references.

Colour conventions

Table 5-1 holds a number of Western (Western Europe, US and Australia) denotations as identified by Marcus. These guidelines are, of course, just that – guidelines. They may not suit every situation but should at the very least provide a sound starting point. One final caveat – colour connotations can vary dramatically even within a culture. Marcus notes that the colour blue in the United States is interpreted different by different groups – for healthcare professionals it is taken to indicate death; for movie-goers it is associated with pornography; for accountants it means reliability or corporateness (think of the 'Big Blue' – IBM).

TABLE 5-1 Some Western colour conventions

Red	Danger, hot, fire
Yellow	Caution, slow, test
Green	Go, okay, clear, vegetation, safety
Blue	Cold, water, calm, sky
Warm colours	Action, response required, proximity
Cool colours	Status, background information, distance
Greys, white and blue	Neutrality

Source: after Marcus, A. (1992) Graphic Design for Electronic Documents and User Interfaces, p. 84. © 1992 ACM, Inc. Reprinted by permission.

5.11 Mental models

Think about how you would answer the question 'How does a games console work?' (for console read mobile phone, DVD player, MP3 player or any interactive gadget on sale in a high street store). The question, of course, is ambiguous: does 'work' refer to the electronics, the solid-state laser, the microwave transmitter or simply 'which buttons to press'? Then we need to understand who is asking the question: is it Aunt Agatha who sent you a cheque for €100 for your birthday (which you used to buy the phone, player or whatever) or are you sitting in an exam hall wondering when the lecture on games consoles was? A third possibility is ourselves. We have unpacked the device, ignored the manual (of course), inserted the batteries (connected it to the mains power supply) and after randomly pressing some buttons asked ourselves 'How does this work?' or asserted 'It's broken'. Despite these difficulties, most of us could pull together some kind of an account of how the device works which might convince Aunt Agatha and we might even get it to work eventually. All of these activities are concerned with our mental models of the interactive device in question. A **mental model** is a cognitive representation of our understanding. It may have a structure; it is larger and more complex than knowing a fact.

For Norman, good design depends upon a mapping between the user's mental model and the designer's design or conceptual model. But this is not always the case.

1. The user's mental model is *developed* through *interaction* with the system.
2. The designer *expects* the user's model to be *identical* to the design model.
3. But the designer does not communicate directly with the user – all communication takes place through what Norman calls the **'system image'** and may be thought of as the physical design. If the 'system image' is not a clear and consistent reflection of the design model, then the user will end up with the wrong mental model.

There is little agreement on mental models except to recognize their importance. We now present three different perspectives on mental models from three leading psychologists.

Norman on mental models

Norman has made the following general observations about the nature of mental models of interactive systems (Norman, 1983). He concludes that:

- Mental models are incomplete.
- People's abilities to 'run' (or try out) their models are severely limited.
- Mental models are unstable – people forget details.
- Mental models do not have firm boundaries: similar devices and operations get confused with one another.
- Mental models are unscientific, exhibiting 'superstitious' behaviour.
- Mental models are parsimonious. People are willing to undertake additional physical operations to minimize mental effort, e.g. people will switch off the device and start again rather than trying to recover from an error.

Challenge 5-3
Write down your mental model of how an ATM (automated bank teller/cash machine) works, including the link between the ATM and your account. Have two or three other people do the same. Now compare your models.

Payne on mental models

The psychologist Stephen Payne (1991, pp. 4–6) describes mental models as having the following properties:

1. Beliefs predict behaviour. The claim is that, in many situations, a great deal of explanatory work can be done by a description of what people know and believe, and how this affects their behaviour. While this is undoubtedly true, this statement is not without its problems. The central question is one of the accessibility of a given mental model.

2. Inferences can be made by 'mental simulation'. Mental models can support reasoning about devices, or the physical world in general, by running simulations in the **mind's eye** (*cf.* the visuo-spatial sketchpad of working memory). Mental models of computer systems are models of the way such systems work, at some level of analysis. The mental simulation of such device models may support the inference of different kinds of knowledge, namely the procedural knowledge needed to work the device.

3. Mental representations can be analogical. Payne argues that some definitions of a mental model are essentially descriptions of an analogical representation. He supports this statement by citing a claim by Johnson-Laird (1983) that mental models are represented in such a way that their manipulation is constrained and biased by the structure of relations that exist in the represented target domain. In short, they are analogical. This is particularly easily illustrated in spatial mental models where only determinate linguistic descriptions, such as 'to the right of', can be used to create mental models (Payne, 1993), whereas indeterminate relations such as 'next to' cannot be used to create such models.

Young on mental models

A consequence of the above is that different researchers investigating the mental models of, say, an automated teller machine (e.g. Payne, 1991) could produce a whole series of different views (or conceptual models) of the same underlying mental model. Here are Young's views (Young, 1983), reproduced verbatim:

1. Strong analogy. The device is sufficiently similar to another device that a representation of the latter can serve as a mental model of the former.

2. Surrogate. The mental model is a physical or notational analogue of the mechanism of the device, and can be used to answer questions about the device's behaviour.

3. Mapping. The mental model is the core mapping between the user's actions on the device and what the device does.

4. Coherence. The mental model is the schema that provides long-term stability in memory for the user's skills and knowledge about the device.

5. Vocabulary. The mental model is the set of terms in which knowledge is encoded about the device.

6. Problem space. The mental model is the problem space in which problems about the use of the device are formulated.

7. Psychological grammar. The mental model serves the same role for behaviour concerning the device as the 'grammar in the head' does of one's own language.

8. Commonality. The mental model is constructed by the observer, and results in positing a common data structure accessed by all behaviours concerning the device.

An empirical investigation of mental models

Chapter 25 on navigation discusses a similar idea – survey vs. route knowledge

Kieras and Bovair (1984) investigated the role of a device model in learning how to operate a mock-up of the weapons control panel of the USS Enterprise from *Star Trek*. In their first experiment subjects learned how to operate the 'phasers' either by means of rote learning (*press this button, then turn that knob to the second position ...*) or by learning the underlying principles (*the energy booster takes power from the ship ...*) which required the subjects to infer the procedures. Kieras and Bovair found that learning, retention, and use of 'short-cuts' were all enhanced for the device model group, demonstrating that knowledge of how the system worked enables the users to infer how to operate it. Their second experiment was almost identical to the first except that the model group were actively instructed to infer the operation of the device. Again the results indicated that the model group learned significantly more quickly and made fewer 'nonsense' actions than the rote group. Verbal protocols were taken from both groups, which revealed the model group explaining their actions in terms of the model whereas the rote group tended to follow a systematic trial-and-error approach. Kieras and Bovair concluded by making two key points: firstly, for a device model to be useful it must support inference about exact and specific control actions, and secondly, the model need not be very complete or thorough.

However, mental models continue to be troublesome, as Rouse and Morris (1986) wrote:

> At present, this area of study is rife with terminological inconsistencies and a preponderance of conjectures rather than data. This situation arises, to a great extent, because a variety of subdisciplines have adopted the concept of mental models, and proceeded to develop their own terminology and methodology, independent of past or current work in this area in other subdisciplines.

Rouse and Morris (1986), p. 360

While this quotation is almost two decades old, the situation has not improved.

Summary and key points

- **Human information processing**. A once-popular means of characterizing human cognition which drew heavily on a simplified model of the major constituents of a computer. The HIP model mapped our senses onto a computer's input devices, our muscles and limbs (effectors) onto a computer's output devices, and our brains and cognition onto the computer's central processing unit, memory and arithmetic-logic unit. The HIP model is still *implicitly* part of the design of interactive systems.

- **Memory**. Those parts of the brain and our cognition which store our knowledge about the world, our abilities such as being able to drive a car, to speak both our native and foreign languages, and a multitude of other things which make us who we are. The truth of this is all too easily witnessed when degenerative diseases such as Parkinson's strike and effectively erase our memories and identities.

- **Attention**. The focusing of our mental abilities. Attention can be split and focused. Attention can be thought of as a mental resource which can be allocated. Extended attention is called vigilance.

- **Perception**. Perception refers to the high-level processing of sensory data to extract meaning. Visual perception is probably the most important form of perception for the HCI specialist, but auditory (sound), tactile (touch), gustatory (taste) and olfactory (smell) perception exist too. There are a number of theories of visual perception, ranging from bottom-up to top-down accounts. Visual perception has been studied in a wide variety of ways, often with a particular emphasis on visual illusions.

- **Mental models**. A mental model is a term used to cover a number of high-level cognitive structures which we use to store knowledge of, among other things, interactive devices. Our knowledge of how to operate a DVD player is not thought to be stored as a series of facts but as a mental model of how these devices work. A mental model is like having a working model of, for example, a device in the real world in our heads. We can use it to visualize how the device works. Mental models are thought to be very important in learning how to use an interactive device.

Why HIP is not enough

While the human information processing account of cognition proved to be popular both within psychology and in the early years of human–computer interaction, this popularity has diminished dramatically in recent years, for the following reasons.

- It is *too simple* – we are much more complex and cannot be represented meaningfully as a series of boxes, clouds and arrows. Human memory is not a passive receptacle; it is not analogous an SQL database. It is active, goal-directed and multi-modal. Visual perception has very little in common with a pair of binocular cameras connected to a computer. Perception exists to guide purposive action – to hunt game, to gather crops, to avoid predators, not to allow us to enjoy pretty sunsets. It has evolved to facilitate the recognition of friend and foe.

■ HIP arose from *laboratory studies*. The physical and social contexts of people are many and varied and conspicuous by their absence from these diagrams.

■ HIP models assume that *we are alone in the world*. Human behaviour is primarily social and hardly ever solitary. Work is social, travel is usually social, playing games is often social, writing a document (e-mail, assignment, book, text message, graffiti) is social as it is intended to be read by someone else. Where are these people represented in the block and arrow models of cognition?

■ These models are very clearly *incomplete* as they omit important aspects of human psychology such as affect (our emotional response); they also fail to notice that we have bodies.

Further reading

Designing interactive systems

Norman, D. (1988) *The Psychology of Everyday Things*. Basic Books, New York.
A very readable classic text. Highly recommended.

Carroll, J.M. (1990) *The Nurnberg Funnel: Designing Minimalist Instructions for Practical Computer Skill*. MIT Press, Cambridge, MA.
How to write high-impact but lightweight manuals.

Mental models and cognitive architectures

Payne, S.J. (1991) A descriptive study of mental models. *Behaviour and Information Technology*, **10**, 3–21.

Newell, A. (1990) *Unified Theories of Cognition*. Harvard University Press, Cambridge, MA.

Newell, A. and Simon, H. (1972) *Human Problem Solving*. Prentice-Hall, Englewood Cliffs, NJ.

Newell, A., Rosenbloom, P.S. and Laird, J.E. (1989) Symbolic architectures for cognition. In Posner, M.I. (ed.), *Foundations of Cognitive Science*. Bradford Books/MIT Press, Cambridge, MA.

Academic journals

The following journals are particularly strong on cognitive issues in interactive systems design.

IJHCS – *International Journal of Human–Computer Studies* (http://www.elsevier.com/)
'The International Journal of Human–Computer Studies publishes original research over the whole spectrum of work on both the theory and practice of human–computer interaction and the human–machine interface. The journal covers the boundaries between computing and artificial intelligence, psychology, linguistics, mathematics, engineering, and social organization' (quoting from the above website).

IwC – *Interacting with Computers* (http://www.elsevier.nl/locate/intcom)
IwC 'acts as an international forum for the discussion of HCI issues, fosters communication between academic researchers and practitioners, encourages the flow of information across the boundaries of its contributing disciplines and stimulates ideas and provokes widespread discussion with a forward-looking perspective' (quoting from the above website).

TOCHI – *ACM Transactions on Computer–Human Interaction* (http://www.acm.org/tochi/)
'This archival journal publishes original research that spans the field of human–computer interaction. Beginning with its first issue in March 1994, it has sought to present work of high scientific quality that contributes to practice in the present and future. The primary emphasis has been on results of broad application, but the journal considers original work focused on specific domains, on special requirements, on ethical issues – the full range of design, development, and use of interactive systems' (quoting from the above website).

HCI – *Human–Computer Interaction* (http://hci-journal.com/)
This, like *TOCHI*, is a major journal publishing very important new work in the field of HCI. It is a major resource.

Presence – *Presence: Teleoperators and Virtual Environments* (http://mitpress.mit.edu/)
This is the main journal publishing state-of-the-art research into all aspects of virtual reality, collaborative virtual environments and the experience of presence. It is an indispensable source for those interested in VR.

Comments on challenges

Challenge 5-1
There remain many examples of this, despite the best efforts of designers and books such as this one. Here are just a couple. Vending machines frequently sink users in gulfs of execution. In one local example, the sequence required is actually to insert money first, then select the desired chocolate indulgence, but no indication of this is given. The gulf of evaluation in this

case is narrowly avoided by the sight of the bar moving towards the dispenser. A very common instance of the evaluation gulf is the 'send' function on Internet inquiry or shopping pages – the confirmation message, if present at all, often appears too slowly to prevent users clicking the 'send' button several times.

Challenge 5-2
Again, instances abound. An example of design for recognition is the provision of a drop-down list of all airports for a particular city destination in a flight booking site rather than expecting customers to recall which airports exist and type in the exact name.

Challenge 5-3
The models almost certainly differ in quite important respects and illustrate several of Norman's observations. Nonetheless all their authors probably use ATMs effectively.

Exercises

1. Examine the tabbed dialogue widget shown in Figure 5-33. Which of the major components of human cognition are being addressed in the design?

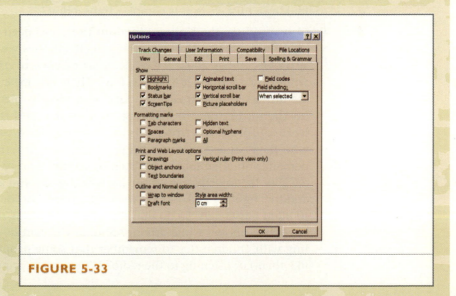

FIGURE 5-33

2. Is Norman's seven-stage model of activity (Figure 5-3) a complete account of how we behave in the world? Or a partial account which is good enough for designing interactive systems or devices? Or does it completely miss the point? Or, finally, is it useful sometimes, depending on context?

3. (Advanced) I pay my household credit card bill every month using my debit card (which is used for transferring money from my bank account). The procedure is as follows:

- I have to phone the credit card company on a 12-digit telephone number.
- Then from the spoken menu I press 2 to indicate I wish to pay my bill.
- I am instructed to enter my 16-digit credit card number followed by the hash key.
- I am then told to enter the amount I want to pay in pounds and pence (let's imagine I wish to pay £500.00 – 7 digits).
- Then I am told to enter my debit card number (16 digits) followed by the hash key.
- Then I am asked for the debit card's issue number (2 digits).
- Then the system asks me to confirm that I wish to pay £500.00, by pressing the hash key.
- This ends the transaction. The number of keystrokes totals 12 + 1 + 16 + 7 + 16 + 2 + 1 = 55 keystrokes on a handset which does not have a backspace key.

What design changes would you recommend to reduce the likelihood of making a mistake in this complex transaction?

4. (Advanced) In the United Kingdom there has been much debate concerning the safety of using mobile (cell) phones while driving. Indeed since December 2003, it has been an offence to use a mobile phone while driving unless it is 'hands free'. There is some evidence that drivers are distracted from their main task of driving by placing extra demands on their attention by speaking on a phone, and from what we have learned from this chapter this must be true. However, there are those who have argued that using a phone is no worse (i.e. places no more demands on attention) than listening to the radio or singing along with a CD or having children in the back of the car who are almost certainly arguing, fighting and asking 'Are we there yet?' or for that matter talking to adult passengers. So do you think that the UK is right to ban the use of mobile phones while driving? Should this ban be extended to travelling with children (try to remember that some people actually claim to like them) or listening to the radio? What would you recommend?

Technology 1: Supporting single user interaction

Aims

Technologies are so pervasive and are changing at such a rate that many would hesitate to write about them. Well, that is what the major vendors of such devices would have us believe. Thirty years ago (deep, remote computing history) computer users sat before a monitor and used a keyboard to enter commands or data – a situation which is still true today. Computer monitors still look like TVs with the styling removed; keyboards would be recognizable by typists from 100 years ago – right down to the bizarre QWERTYUIOP organization. While computers are unbelievably fast, with enormous storage and high-resolution graphical displays, perhaps the most important change in the last 30 years (from the perspective of HCI) in how we interact with computers has been the introduction of a pointing device – the mouse. After studying this chapter you should be able to:

- Describe the characteristics of graphical user interfaces
- Understand the range of technologies to support single user interaction.

6.1 Introduction

If we look at the science fiction TV shows of 30 years ago, writers envisioned interaction with computers in the future as being voice-based: 'Computer, search library files for ...', imagined that we would all be equipped with highly portable, personal communicators, and computers would recognize us from our 'voice prints' or finger, thumb or handprints. We would all be carrying palm-sized computers, and video-telephones would be sitting on our desks and feature in the dashboards of motorcars. Better than that, computers would be able to deliver the output of their interaction with us instantaneously and in a form which was easy to use (high-quality 3D graphics or neat spoken summaries).

Some of this has been realized but much of it has been found to be impractical. Voice input does work – in a limited fashion – but does not make a great deal of sense in a busy office; the same applies to voice output. Thumbprint recognition also works but as one major manufacturer recently discovered, cash dispensers equipped with such technology required very frequent cleaning. They found that the thumbprint reader stopped working after being used by people with thumbs covered in the remains of their last fast food meal. Fries and thumbprint readers just do not mix.

In general, at the time of writing we are still sitting at our desks, typing at keyboards and peering at a monitor. After work or college we sit in front of our home multimedia arcade with games controller and remote controls in hand.

There are, of course, numerous exotic, experimental input and output devices which have been developed in research labs and have specialist uses and a number of these will be introduced and reviewed in this chapter.

Box 6-1 Laughter-based input

Laughter-recognition software has been developed at Monah University in Melbourne to make it easier for employees to log on to computers in a network. The software, called SoundHunter, has been designed to recognize a person's voice or laughter and logs that person on to the nearest computer on a network. The voice or laughter is picked up with microphones on each computer and the individual is located by intelligent agents. The agents identify the computer nearest to where the person's voice is loudest. In addition to voice or laughter recognition, the agents listen for footsteps to determine whether a person is moving around the office, and by doing so track their movement to ascertain the direction in which they're going. Using this process, the agents can log users on as far as two computers ahead in the direction in which the user is moving. It is debatable whether this form of voice recognition will take off and how comfortable people would feel laughing (as opposed to screaming with frustration) into a computer.

In order to interact with a computer (or interactive device) we need to be able to communicate with it and it with us. This is done by way of the **user interface**. We communicate with the user interface using one or more **input** devices, while the computer or interactive device communicates with us by way of an **output** device.

This communication can take a very wide variety of forms but in an office context is usually limited to (the default) keyboard, mouse and printer. In the home this is extended to include games controllers and specialist sound equipment (and anything else the high street retailers can sell us).

Other work environments add to this range of devices to include medical instruments (e.g. heart monitors), large-scale plotters and document scanners and a variety of what is usually called multimedia equipment such as digital video-camcorders, graphics tablets and specialist sound processing kit. In a manufacturing context there are a range of tools such as lathes and other cutting tools, CNC (computer numerical control) tools and robots (used in the manufacture of motor vehicles). Finally there are other even more specialist tools such as remote sensing technologies (as used on satellites). Despite this diversity, these technologies are usually divided into input and output devices, though this division is not always as simple as it might appear, for example in the case of force-feedback joysticks, touchscreens or virtual reality.

6.2 User interfaces

The original interfaces to computers would be unrecognizable today and really do not deserve the prefix *user*. The vast majority of personal computers and many small devices have graphical user interfaces, with variants on Microsoft's Windows technologies dominating the market. However, not all computers could be described as 'personal': many computers are used as Web, network or database servers and a number of these are UNIX-based. UNIX is a well-established operating system which exists in a number of different forms, with Linux and BSD (Berkeley Systems Development) being popular forms. While UNIX is usually supplied with a graphical user interface such as X11, at heart it is command based.

Command languages

A command language is simply a set of words with an associated **syntax**. Table 6-1 is a snapshot of the available commands for the BSD implementation of UNIX. In all there are 438 commands in this particular implementation.

TABLE 6-1 Some of the available commands for BSD UNIX

a2p	aclocal	aclocal-1.6	addftinfo
addr	aexml	afmtodit	appleping
appletviewer	apply	apropos	arch
at	at_cho_prn	atlookup	atprint
atq	atrm	atstatus	automake
automake	awk	b2m	banner
basename	bashbug	batch	bc
biff	bunzip2	bzcat	bzcmp
bzdiff	bzegrep	bzfgrep	bzgrep
bzip2	bzip2recover	bzless	bzmore
c2ph	c_rehash	cal	calendar
cancel	cap_mkdb	captoinfo	certtool

One thing which is immediately obvious from this list of commands is their obscurity. What on earth does *addftinfo* do? Or *afmtodit* or *bc* or *biff*? But do remember that to a UNIX expert (usually described as a 'UNIX guru' although other names describe them more accurately) these commands *are* meaningful and convenient. When designing for interaction – know your user – if they are UNIX experts, design for them and not for a first-time user. However, commands and command languages like UNIX have been criticized on the grounds of:

- Having to *recall* the name of a particular command from the range of literally hundreds of possibilities
- Having to *recall* the syntax of the command.

Take, for example, the command to search for a particular file – *grep*. *Grep* stands for **Global Regular Expression Parser** which immediately suggests a file searching utility to a C programmer but not to the average person in the street. Let's look at an extract from the help on *grep* (the following extract was taken from the output from the command *man grep* which means 'give me the manual entry on *grep*'):

'A regular expression is a pattern that describes a set of strings. Regular expressions are constructed analogously to arithmetic expressions, by using various operators to combine smaller expressions.

Grep understands two different versions of regular expression syntax: "basic" and "extended". In GNU grep , there is no difference in available functionality using either syntax. In other implementations, basic regular expressions are less powerful. The following description applies to extended regular expressions; differences for basic regular expressions are summarized afterwards.

The fundamental building blocks are the regular expressions that match a single character. Most characters, including all letters and digits, are regular expressions that match themselves. Any metacharacter with special meaning may be quoted by preceding it with a backslash.'

Grep also takes a number of **arguments** or parameters which affect how it searches, for example *grep –r* to recursively read all files under each directory (folder). In all, *grep* and utilities and tools like it are very powerful but tend to be

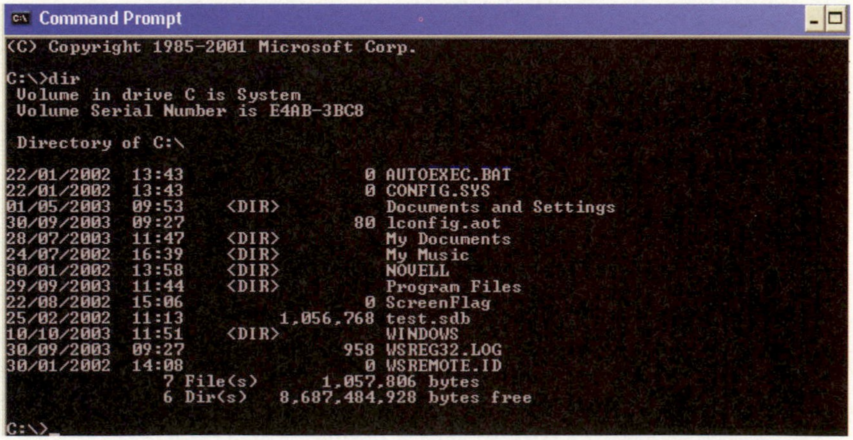

FIGURE 6-1 The enigmatic c:\> prompt in MSDOS

difficult to use. There often seems to be a *perceived* trade-off between ease of use and power but this may indeed be only a perception.

Prior to the creation of Microsoft Windows, the vast majority of the users of personal computers ran the operating system MSDOS. On switching on one's PC, users were faced with the famous (infamous) c:\> prompt. Figure 6-1 is a screenshot of the c:\> prompt – now called the command prompt – which is still part of the Microsoft world. The user was then required to type in a command such as *dir* which listed the contents of the current directory (or folder). A user who had never encountered MSDOS (or even those who had) was continually faced with the problem of having to recall the name of the command to issue next. Let us suppose that we had switched on the PC with the intention of writing a letter. What would we be expected to do to get started? In practice the answer was to type the command *Word*, which started the old MSDOS version of Word – providing, of course, the *path* variable (don't ask) had been set up properly. Moving from the dark ages, we now considers GUIs.

6.3 Graphical user interfaces

Graphical user interfaces (GUIs), which are found on every personal computer, have had an interesting though brief history. Choosing my words carefully so as to avoid being pursued by lawyers, the Microsoft range of Windows GUIs were broadly based (perhaps *influenced* might be a better word) on the Macintosh, which in turn was inspired by work at Xerox PARC, which in turn was developed and built upon early research at the Stanford Research Laboratory and at the Massachusetts Institute of Technology.

WIMPs

WIMP stands for windows, icons, menu and pointer, though it is thought by some to have been a term of abuse used by computer scientists of end-users. A **window** is a means of sharing a computer's graphical display resources among multiple applications at the same time. An **icon** is an image or symbol used to represent a file, folder, application or device, such as a printer. David Canfield Smith is usually credited with coining the term in the context of user interfaces in 1975, while he worked at Xerox. According to Smith he adopted the term from the Russian Orthodox Church where an icon is a religious image. Icons are discussed in greater detail in Chapter 15. A **menu** is a list of commands or options from which one can choose; these are discussed below. The last component is, of course, **pointing devices** of which the mouse is the most widespread. An important aspect of a WIMP environment is the manner in which we use it. This form of interaction is called **direct manipulation** because we directly manipulate the on-screen objects.

Direct manipulation

A direct manipulation interface is one where graphical objects on the screen are directly manipulated with a pointing device. This was first demonstrated by Ivan Sutherland in the Sketchpad system. The *concept* of direct manipulation interfaces for everyone was envisioned by Alan Kay of Xerox PARC in a 1977 article about the *Dynabook*. The first commercial systems to make extensive use of direct manipulation were the Xerox Star (1981), the Apple Lisa (1982) and Macintosh (1984). However, it was Ben Shneiderman at the University of Maryland who actually coined the term 'direct manipulation' in 1982. In essence, direct manipulation depends upon having bitmapped screens so that each picture element or pixel can be used for input and output, and a pointing device.

6.4 The major components of a GUI

Windows

Windows allow a workstation's screen to be divided into rectangular areas which act like separate input and output channels that can be placed under the control of different applications. This allows the user to see the output of several processes at the same time and to choose which one will receive input by selecting its window, usually by clicking on it with a mouse. This is referred to as changing the focus. Early windowing systems were tiled but overlapping windows were eventually suggested by Alan Kay at Xerox PARC (although MS Windows 1, which was released in 1985, supported only tiled windows).

Windowing systems exist in a wide variety of forms but are largely variations on the same basic theme. Microsoft Windows dominate the personal computer

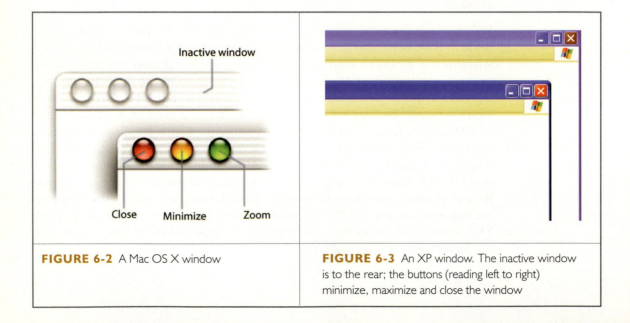

FIGURE 6-2 A Mac OS X window

FIGURE 6-3 An XP window. The inactive window is to the rear; the buttons (reading left to right) minimize, maximize and close the window

market and in turn exist in a variety of forms, although they appear to be converging (at least in terms of appearance) in an XP-like form. There are two other major windowing systems which are widely used. The current Macintosh OS X is proving to be well received (particularly by academics); the X Window System was originally developed at MIT. X is used on many UNIX systems and the latest version is X11R6 (version 11, release 6) which was originally released in May 1994. X is large and powerful and, above all, complex. Figures 6-2 and 6-3 show examples of a Mac OS X window and a Microsoft XP window.

Menus

Most applications running on personal computers are menu-driven. Items are chosen from the menu by highlighting them, followed by pressing <Return> or by simply pointing to the item with a mouse and clicking one of the mouse buttons.

When creating menus, commands should be grouped into menu topics, which are a list of menu items. The user selects a command or option (menu item) from the list, and an action is performed. While menus should be simple, there is little to prevent the over-zealous designer from creating very complex and difficult to navigate menus. Figure 6-4 is a screenshot of the Mac version of a typical **hierarchically** organized menu. In this example, the various options are arranged under a top-level topic (filter) and in turn have series of sub-menus. Figure 6-5 is the equivalent XP version.

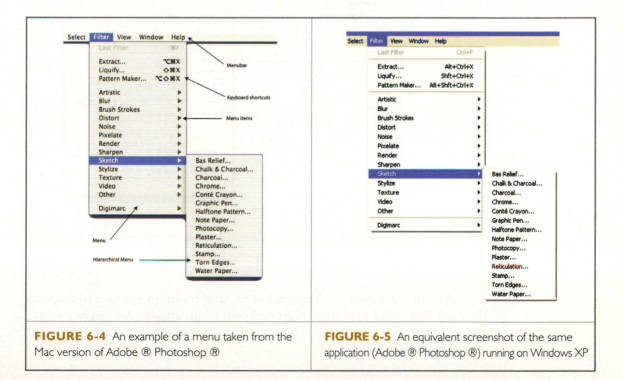

FIGURE 6-4 An example of a menu taken from the Mac version of Adobe ® Photoshop ®

FIGURE 6-5 An equivalent screenshot of the same application (Adobe ® Photoshop ®) running on Windows XP

Hierarchical menus are occasionally also called **cascading menus**. In a cascading menu, the sub-menu appears to cascade out when a choice is made from the higher-level menu.

Comparing Figures 6-4 and 6-5, it is obvious that there is very little to distinguish them. This illustrates the convergence in the appearance of these two 'rival' GUIs.

Another frequently encountered form of menu is the **pop-up**. A pop-up menu is distinguished from a standard menu in that it is not attached to a menu bar in a fixed location (hence the name). Once a selection is made from a pop-up menu, the menu usually disappears. Figure 6-6 is a screenshot of a pop-up menu (or panel). In this case the pop-up menu is also a **contextual menu.** The make-up of contextual menus varies according to the context (hence their name) from which they are invoked. If a file is selected, the contextual menu offers file options. If instead a folder is selected, folder options are displayed.

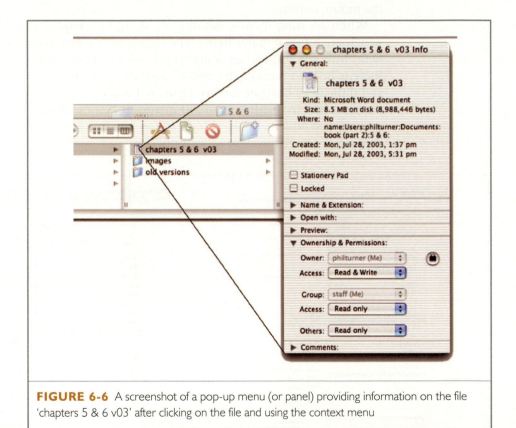

FIGURE 6-6 A screenshot of a pop-up menu (or panel) providing information on the file 'chapters 5 & 6 v03' after clicking on the file and using the context menu

Finally, to aid expert (or frequent) users, it is common practice to associate the most frequently used items with keyboard shortcuts (also known as accelerators in MS Windows systems). Figures 6-7 and 6-8 illustrate shortcuts for both Windows XP and Mac OS X.

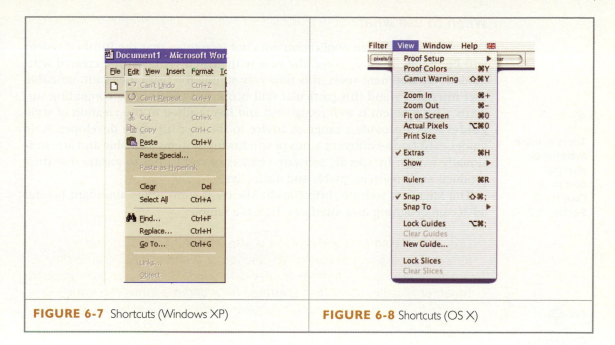

FIGURE 6-7 Shortcuts (Windows XP)

FIGURE 6-8 Shortcuts (OS X)

A miscellany of widgets

Modern graphical user interfaces have as part of their make-up a range of widgets including buttons and radio buttons, sliders, scrollbars and checkboxes. Examples of each can be seen in Figures 6-9 and 6-10. As is clear, the differences between these widgets are mainly aesthetic or cosmetic.

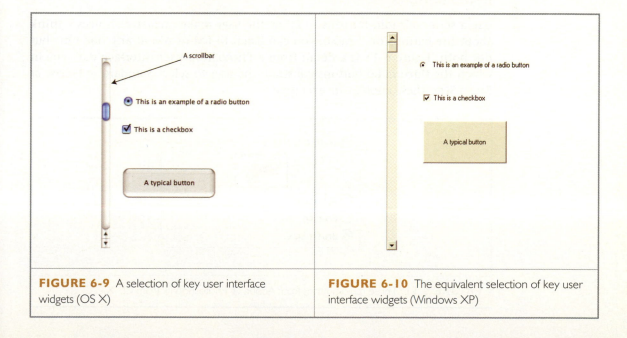

FIGURE 6-9 A selection of key user interface widgets (OS X)

FIGURE 6-10 The equivalent selection of key user interface widgets (Windows XP)

When to use what

Designing a GUI for an application does not guarantee that the finished system will be usable. Indeed, given the ease with which GUIs can be created with modern development tools, it is now very simple to create inelegant, unusable user interfaces – and this particular skill is not just confined to computing students. This problem is well recognized and has resulted in the creation of **style guides** which provide a range of advice to the user interface developer. Style guides exist for the different kinds of windowing systems available and are occasionally written by specific software vendors or companies to ensure that their products are consistent, usable and distinctive.

There is more material on physical design in Chapter 2, Section 2.7

The Microsoft website (http://msdn.Microsoft.com) offers abundant helpful advice on designing user interfaces. Here is a sample:

Chapter 13, Section 13.5 on design languages is also relevant here

> *Grouping of elements and controls is also important. Try to group information logically according to function or relationship. Because their functions are related, buttons for navigating a database should be grouped together visually rather than scattered throughout a form. The same applies to information; fields for name and address are generally grouped together, as they are closely related. In many cases, you can use frame controls to help reinforce the relationships between controls.*

Other advice on user interface design operates at a much smaller level of detail, at the level of individual widgets.

Radio buttons

Use a series of radio buttons to allow the user make *exclusive* choices – think about the buttons on a radio: you can listen to FM or AM at any one time but not both. Figure 6-11 is a detail from a PhotoShop user interface dialogue in which the three radio buttons constrain the user to select Standard *or* Precise *or* Brush Size. These choices are exclusive.

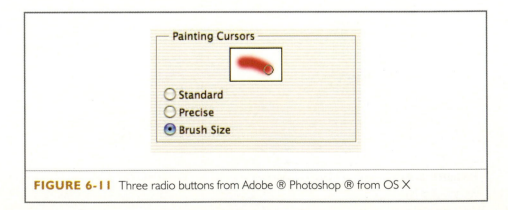

FIGURE 6-11 Three radio buttons from Adobe ® Photoshop ® from OS X

Checkboxes

Checkboxes should be used to display individual settings that can be switched (checked) on and off. Use a group of checkboxes for settings that are not mutually exclusive (that is, you can check more than one box). An example is shown in Figure 6-12.

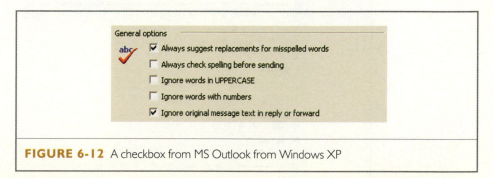

FIGURE 6-12 A checkbox from MS Outlook from Windows XP

Challenge 6-1
You are designing an e-mail client which – among other things – allows users to:

1. Set a series of preferences for incoming mail (download large files on receipt, display first two lines of message body, reject mail from senders not in address book, alert when new mail received ...)

2. Set a colour scheme for the e-mail application (hot colours, water colours or jewel colours).

Would you use radio buttons or checkboxes for these?

Toolbars

A toolbar is a collection of buttons grouped according to function (in this respect they are logically identical to menus). The buttons are represented as icons to give a clue as to their function. Passing the mouse pointer over an icon will usually trigger the associated 'tool tip' which is a short textual label describing the function of the button. Figure 6-13 shows the tool tip 'Rules Wizard' again taken from MS Outlook.

FIGURE 6-13 A toolbar tool tip

Toolbars are also configurable: their contents can be changed and one can choose whether or not they are displayed. Hiding toolbars helps make the best use of the display resources (usually described as the screen real-estate). Figure 6-14 illustrates this.

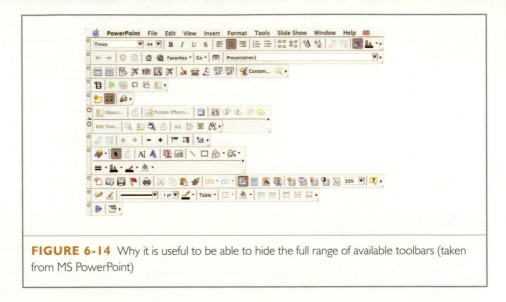

FIGURE 6-14 Why it is useful to be able to hide the full range of available toolbars (taken from MS PowerPoint)

List boxes

A list box is an accurately named widget as it is a box in which files and options are listed. List boxes take a variety of forms and within these forms they offer different ways of viewing the contents – as lists (with more or less detail), as icons or as thumbnails (little pictures of the files' contents). See Figures 6-15 and 6-16.

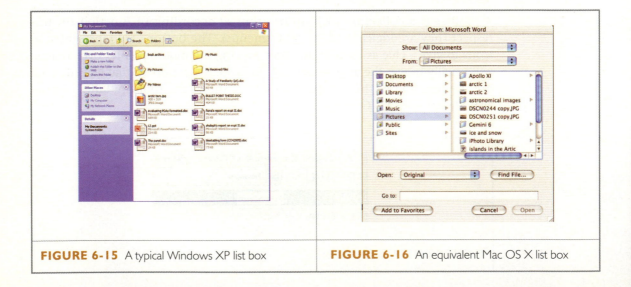

FIGURE 6-15 A typical Windows XP list box

FIGURE 6-16 An equivalent Mac OS X list box

Sliders

A slider is a widget which can return analogue values: rather than setting, say, the volume to 7 on a scale of 10, the user is able to drag a slider to a position three-quarters of the way along a scale. Sliders (Figure 6-17) are ideally suited to controlling or setting such things as volume or brightness or scrolling through a document.

FIGURE 6-17 The RealOne Player ® with two slider controls
(source: courtesy of RealNetworks, Inc)

6.5 Form fill

Form filling is a user interface style which is particularly popular with Web applications. Form fill interfaces are used to gather information such as name and address. Figure 6-18 is a very typical example of a form fill interface. This screenshot is taken from an on-line bookshop. The individual boxes are called **fields** and are frequently marked with an asterisk (*) to indicate that an entry is **mandatory**. This particular user interface is a hybrid as it not only has form fill aspects but has other widgets too, including pull-down menus.

When to use form fill

Form fill interfaces are best used when structured information is required. Examples of structured information include such things as:

- An individual's name and postal address required for mail order services
- Travel details, e.g. the airport from which one is flying, intended destination, time and date of departure
- Number and type of goods, e.g. 10 copies of the DVD 'The Sound of Music'.

Wizards

A wizard is the name given to a style of interaction which leads the user by the metaphorical hand (or pointer) step-by-step through a series of question and answers, pick-lists and other kinds of widgets to achieve a task. In MS Windows wizards are used to install hardware and applications. This style of interaction is widely used by all windowing systems.

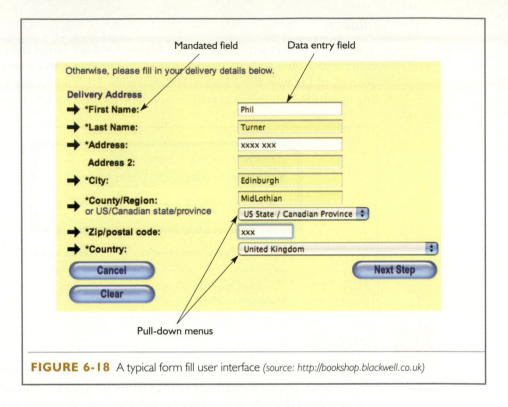

FIGURE 6-18 A typical form fill user interface *(source: http://bookshop.blackwell.co.uk)*

The great strength of wizards is that they present complex tasks in 'bite-sized' pieces. Figure 6-19 is a series of screenshots capturing the steps involved in installing a new item of hardware. This is only one possible route through the process of installing a new item of hardware. Many others are possible.

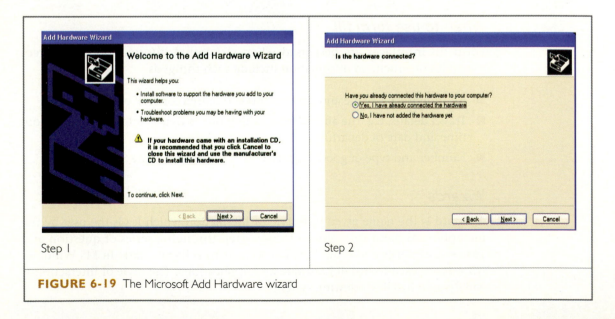

FIGURE 6-19 The Microsoft Add Hardware wizard

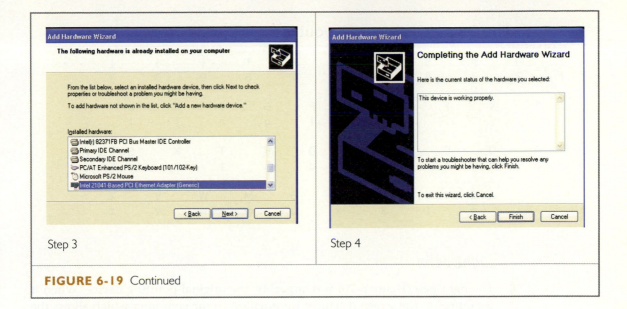

Step 3

Step 4

FIGURE 6-19 Continued

6.6 Input devices

Among the earliest input devices – leaving aside the physical flicking of switches – was the keyboard. Many later input devices support a variety of ways to 'point and click' and were developed in parallel with graphical user interfaces. Others cater for different modes of input such as handwriting or voice.

Keyboards

QWERTY keyboards were invented by C. L. Sholes in 1868. At the time typewriters were relatively crudely manufactured and an alphabetic arrangement of keys tended to result in jams when the keys were struck. By rearranging the keys Sholes solved this problem. DVORAK keyboards (Box 6-2), named after their inventor, offer an alternative presentation of the keys, but have never achieved widespread popularity, probably because of users' familiarity with the conventional arrangement, however inconvenient.

Touchscreens

Touchscreens appear visually identical to a normal monitor but, as the name suggests, are sensitive to the touch of a finger. They function through either infra-red sensitivity or electrical capacitance. Because of their lack of moving or detachable parts, they are suitable for applications intended for public places, and provided the interface is well designed present an appearance of simplicity and ease of use. Remember that in design for touchscreens, screen widgets must be big enough to be selected separately with a finger – so avoid normal-sized drop-down lists and similar objects.

Box 6-2 The Dvorak keyboard layout

!	@	#	$	%	^	&	*	(	)	[	+
1	2	3	4	5	6	7	8	9	0	]	=

"	<	>	P	Y	F	G	C	R	L	?
'	,	.	p	y	f	g	c	r	l	/

A	O	E	U	I	D	H	T	N	S	_
a	o	e	u	i	d	h	t	n	s	-

:	Q	J	K	X	B	M	W	V	Z
;	q	j	k	x	b	m	w	v	z

Light pens

The light pen (Figure 6-20) was, arguably, the original pointing device. When it is pointed at the screen it returns information to the computer which allows the item pointed at to be identified. The first appearance of a light pen was as part of SketchPad. SketchPad supported the manipulation (dragging, resizing and so forth) of objects using a light pen. These ideas were subsequently developed by other researchers at Imperial College London, Stanford and MIT.

Light pens are less expensive than touchscreens, can be armoured (made very robust) and can be sterilized. They have a number of industrial and medical applications.

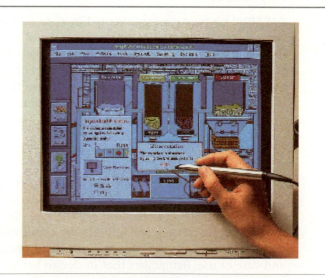

FIGURE 6-20 A light pen *(source: http://www.cw2.co.uk/index.html)*

The mouse

The mouse was developed at Stanford University Research Laboratory in the mid-1960s. Many of the current uses of the mouse were demonstrated by Doug Engelbart as part of his NLS (oNLine System) in 1968. The mouse became the input device of choice for the Xerox Star (1981) and the subsequent Apple Lisa (1982) and Macintosh (1984) (Figure 6-21). The mouse consists of a palm-sized device which is moved over a flat surface such as the top of a desk. At its simplest (and cheapest) it rests on a rubber-coated ball which turns two wheels set at right angles. These two wheels translate the movement of the mouse into signals that the computer to which it is connected can interpret. One or two buttons sit on top of the mouse and are operated with the user's fingers. The mouse has become the default pointing device. More contemporary mouse design includes a thumb-wheel (see Figure 6-22) for scrolling through documents. A mouse may be cordless, using infra-red to communicate with the host computer.

FIGURE 6-21 A Mac one-button mouse. The single button of the traditional Mac is said to have the advantage of 'you always know which button to press'

FIGURE 6-22 A Microsoft two-button mouse with thumbwheel (which is used for scrolling)
(source: Microsoft Intellimouse ® Optical Mouse from http://www.microsoft.com/presspass/images/gallery/hardware/IntelliMouseOptic.jpg © 2004 Microsoft Corporation. All rights reserved. Printed with permission from Microsoft Corporation)

Joysticks

A joystick is a handle which pivots from a central point. Viewing the joystick from above, it may be moved north, south, east and west (and all points between) to control an on-screen pointer, spaceship or any other on-screen object. Joysticks are used mostly for computer games, but they are also found in conjunction with CAD/CAM (computer aided design/manufacture) systems and VR (virtual reality) applications. See Figure 6-23.

FIGURE 6-23 An ergonomically designed games joystick *(source: Microsoft SideWinder ® Precision 2 joystick. Photo by Phil Turner. Printed with permission from Microsoft Corporation)*

Handwriting recognition

In theory, this is an attractive way of inputting data into a computer. Writing with a stylus directly onto a computer's screen or tablet is a natural way of working. The history of handwriting recognition is littered with early promise and a corresponding number of poorly performing systems. Handwriting recognition is found on PDAs (personal digital assistants) and other hand-held devices. Problems with handwriting recognition include the following:

■ It is quite slow.
■ It is quite inaccurate.
■ It requires the user to 'train' the device to recognize your handwriting. Training improves the recognition accuracy of the software.
■ Many people can type faster than writing by hand.

Figures 6-24 and 6-25 illustrate the process as implemented on a HP/Compaq iPAQ handheld.

Other input devices

A **trackball** is another pointing device which is best described as a mouse lying on its back. To move the pointer the user moves the ball. Again, like all other pointing devices, there are one or more buttons which can be used to select on-screen items. Trackballs are often found in public access kiosks because they are difficult to steal and do not require a flat surface to rest upon.

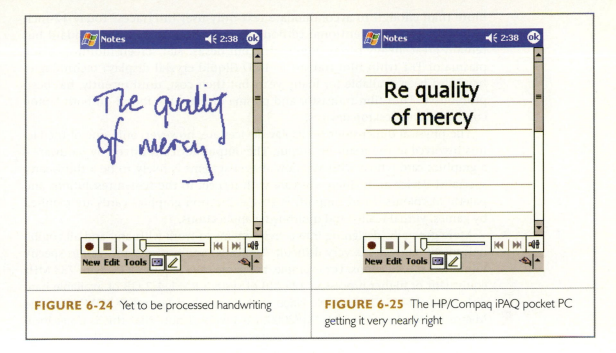

FIGURE 6-24 Yet to be processed handwriting

FIGURE 6-25 The HP/Compaq iPAQ pocket PC getting it very nearly right

Speech/voice recognition

Voice recognition really means dictation rather than the computer understanding instructions. Commercial voice recognition systems are widely available and can be trained to take dictation. Training is required to deal with the nuances of our own voices and accents. This means that voice recognition systems are not only single user systems but single speaker systems too.

Challenge 6-2
Which input devices would you use for a tourist information 'kiosk' application to be sited at an airport in the arrivals area? The system allows users to book hotel rooms, etc., as well as to find information about the area. Explain your choices.

6.7 Output devices

From the perspective of the user interface, technologies for displaying content to people rely primarily on the three perceptual abilities of vision, hearing and touch.

Display devices

The most fundamental output device is the **monitor**. Twenty years ago the default monitor measured a mere 14 inches (diagonal screen size) which was more than enough to accommodate text-only user interfaces. Today 17-inch monitors using conventional cathode ray tube technology are standard but remain great, heavy boxes dominating our desks. Flat screen monitors using plasma or TFT (thin film transistor) LCD (liquid crystal display) technologies have also been available for many years but their cost, until recently, has been prohibitive. Thin film transistor and plasma displays are found on both laptop computers and desktop devices.

The physical dimensions of display devices are, however, only one of the factors involved in the resulting output. The output device is driven by hardware – a graphics card which with Windows-based systems is likely to be a third-party specialist device and which will vary with respect to the screen resolutions and palette of colours it can support. High-specification graphics cards are required by games, virtual reality and multimedia applications.

More generally, designing interactive systems to work with any and all combinations of hardware is very difficult. Typically, applications and games specify minimum specifications. For example, the game *Halo* requires a PC with 733 MHz equivalent or higher processor, 128 MB of system RAM, 1.2 GB of available hard disk space, 32 MB T&L capable video card, 8× speed or faster CD-ROM drive, and Microsoft Windows 98SE/Me/XP/2000. (As I write, I note that this is a specification of a reasonably powerful PC; as you read, it seems entry level, if that.)

Figures 6-26 and 6-27 show two display options.

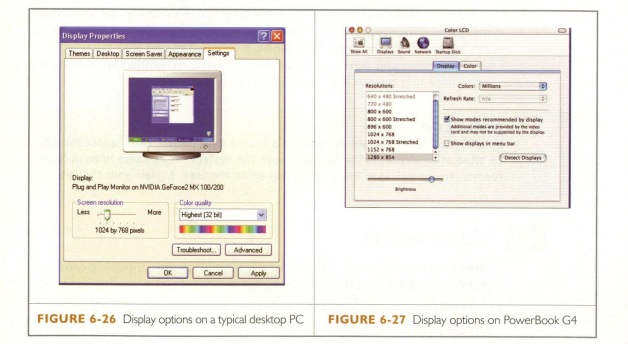

FIGURE 6-26 Display options on a typical desktop PC   **FIGURE 6-27** Display options on PowerBook G4

Data projectors

One way past the problems with restrictive display 'real-estate' is to use a data projector (Figure 6-28). While the resolution is usually less than that of a monitor, the resulting projected image can be huge.

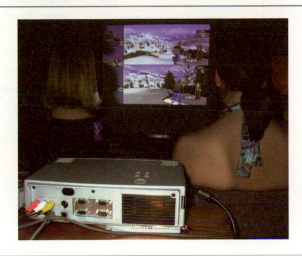

FIGURE 6-28 Game playing in parallel

Sound is discussed at length in Chapter 16

Sound

My computer (a Mac), on start-up, emits a fairly tuneful burst of music which immediately prompts me to hit the mute button. Sound is an output medium which is significantly under-used. Sound is discussed at length in Chapter 16.

Speech

Speech synthesis works well enough (a) to understand what the computer is saying to us and (b) to do a pretty good job at pronouncing all but the most obscure of words. But like sound we generally do not use it. Computers can to a greater or lesser extent produce sounds that resemble human speech. Although they cannot imitate the full spectrum of human cadences and intonations, speech synthesis systems can read text files and output them in a very intelligible, if somewhat dull, voice. Current systems allow the user to choose the type of voice, as can be seen in Figure 6-29.

A **screen reader** produces synthesized voice output for text displayed on the computer screen, as well as for keystrokes entered on the keyboard. Voice-based browsers use the same technology as screen reading software, but are designed specifically for Internet use.

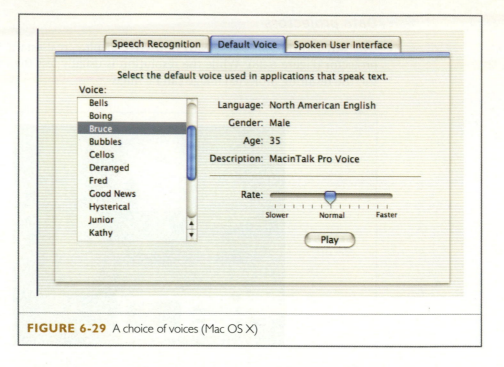

FIGURE 6-29 A choice of voices (Mac OS X)

Printers and plotters

By and large printers and plotters are not of great interest to the HCI professional, largely because modern operating systems take care of them. This was not always the case. Making printers and plotters work was the bane of most system administrators' lives. When Windows 95 first appeared, the fact that it made installing and using printers easy was, for many, a source of great joy.

Both printers and plotters use a variety of technologies to make marks on paper and other media. A printer is a device that prints text or illustrations on paper, while a plotter draws pictures. Plotters differ from printers in that they draw lines using a pen. As a result, they can produce continuous lines, whereas printers can only simulate lines by printing a closely spaced series of dots. Multicolour plotters use different-coloured pens. In general, plotters are considerably more expensive than printers.

Box 6-3 Printers produce copies in 3D

Several companies have developed three-dimensional printers. These machines work by placing layers of a powdery material on top of each other to create a real-life model of a digital image. It is thought that with the use of hundreds and perhaps thousands of layers, everything from 'coffee cups to car parts' could be created. Like putting ink on paper, 3D printers print using powder and binder (glue).

Haptics

Haptic user
interfaces are
considered
further in
Chapter 16

Haptics refer to the sense of touch. However, haptics allow us to be in touch with interactive devices and media in a way which is direct and immediate. Perhaps the most widespread haptic devices are those games controllers which incorporate so-called **force-feedback**. Force-feedback is intended to convey feedback from typically games environments back to the person engaged. So what are the perceived benefits of force-feedback devices?

- Sensations can be associated with interactions, such as feeling driving surfaces or feeling footsteps.
- Sensations can also be used to provide feedback as to the location of other players, objects and so forth.
- Force-feedback can allow the player to feel what it would be like to wield a sword, drive a high-speed car, fly a 'speeder' or engage the Empire with a light-sabre.

A significantly more serious application of force-feedback is NASA's 'Softwalls' initiative in response to the 9/11 terrorist attacks on New York. Softwalls would be used to restrict airspaces by way of the aircraft's on-board systems. The basic idea, attributed to Edward Lee, would prevent aircraft from flying into restricted airspace (such as city centres) and this would be communicated to the pilot by way of the aircraft's joystick. Other examples include the 'silent alert' vibration of a mobile phone and even the feel of a key when pressed.

Challenge 6-3
Which output devices would you use for a tourist information application as described in Challenge 6-2? Explain your choices.

6.8 Virtual reality

The term 'virtual reality' (VR) was coined by Jaron Lanier in 1989, though this was predated by the terms 'artificial reality' (usually attributed to Myron Krueger in the 1970s) and, famously, 'Cyberspace' which appeared in Gibson's novel *Neuromancer* in 1984. Currently the VR literature is littered with terms such as 'virtual worlds', 'virtual environments', 'augmented reality', 'virtuality', 'shared virtual reality' and 'collaborative virtual reality'.

The history of virtual reality is varied and its origin subject to apocryphal stories (VR is said by some to have arisen from the noise made by pilots 'flying' high-fidelity flight simulators – Vrrrhhhmmm! Hence the Vrrrhhhmmm or VR room). However, it does seem likely that various instantiations of VR were developed more or less simultaneously at a number of locations, mainly in the USA.

In consequence, virtual reality is not a unitary phenomenon and there are no agreed definitions. Virtual reality also has a number of synonyms indicating variously its origins and the lack of a clear definition. This new 'reality' can be found instantiated in such things as graphical user interfaces, computer-aided design applications, flight simulators, and arcade games. However, despite this diversity it can be divided into two basic forms, **immersive** and **non-immersive** (or desktop) virtual reality. Immersive virtual reality requires the users to wear a light-excluding helmet (an HMD – **head-mounted display**) which houses the display, and a data glove which facilitates the manipulation of virtual objects within virtual reality. **CAVEs** and **panoramas** offer alternatives to HMDs (see below). Non-immersive virtual reality, in contrast, is displayed on a computer's monitor. While immersive virtual reality has captured the public imagination, desktop virtual reality is more commonly found.

Immersive VR

The main features of immersive VR are:

- Head-referenced viewing provides a natural interface for navigation in three-dimensional space and allows for look-around, walk-around and fly-through capabilities in virtual environments.
- Stereoscopic viewing enhances the perception of depth and the sense of space.
- The virtual world is presented in full scale and relates properly to the human size.
- Realistic interactions with virtual objects via data glove and similar devices allow for manipulation, operation and control of virtual worlds.
- The convincing illusion of being fully immersed in an artificial world can be enhanced by auditory, haptic and other non-visual technologies.

Non-immersive VR

Non-immersive virtual reality (sometimes called desktop virtual reality) can be found in a wide range of desktop applications and games as it does not always require specialist input or output devices. It does, however, often require a specialist graphics card to drive the computationally demanding applications. In terms of market share, games are undoubtedly the most widely used non-immersive virtual reality applications.

6.9 VR input and output devices

In addition to the usual range of input devices, VR researchers and manufacturers have developed a range of novel technologies to match the challenges and opportunities of virtual environments.

Data gloves

We interact with the world in a variety of ways but using our hands must be the most direct. It then follows that a natural way of interacting with virtual environments is also by means of our hands – gloved hands. Gloves equipped with sensors (data gloves) are able to sense the movements of the hand which are translated into corresponding movements in the virtual environment. Data gloves are used to 'grasp' objects in virtual environments or to 'fly' through virtual scenes. Figure 6-30 is an illustration of a force-feedback data glove which uses actuators to 'feed back' an impression of, say, the grasped object.

FIGURE 6-30 A force-feedback data glove *(source: image courtesy: www.5DT.com)*

Head-mounted display

A head-mounted display (HMD) is an essential part of many virtual reality (VR) systems. An HMD is a lightproof and rather heavy helmet isolating the wearer from the world and consists of two colour displays located in line with one's eyes and a pair of stereo earphones. An HMD also has a head tracker which provides information about the user's position and orientation in space. Figure 6-31 offers a view of the interior of an HMD, while Figure 6-32 shows one in use.

The original CAVE was developed at the University of Illinois at Chicago and provides the illusion of immersion by projecting stereo images on the walls and floor of a room-sized (a pretty small room, it should be said) cube. People wearing lightweight stereo glasses can enter and walk freely inside the CAVE.

FIGURE 6-31 An interior view of an HMD

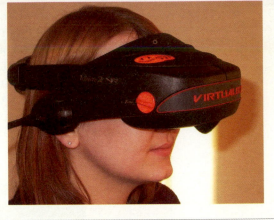

FIGURE 6-32 An HMD

Panorama

A panorama is like a small cinema. The virtual image is projected onto a curved screen before the 'audience' who are required to wear LCD shuttered spectacles (goggles). The shutters on the LCD spectacles open and close over one eye and then the other 50 times a second or so. The positions of the spectacles are tracked using infra-red sensors. The experience of a panorama is extraordinary with the virtual world appearing to stream past the user. Panoramas are expensive and far from portable.

Summary and key points

Many aspects of single user technology, in essence, have not changed very much in the last 30 or so years of computing except to say that everything is much cheaper and mostly works. There has been a steady shift from the old command line user interfaces to graphical, direct manipulation modes of interaction, and this style seems set to be carried through in the current generation of mobile devices. Virtual reality has indeed become reality, though still complex and rather expensive.

Further reading

Technology changes so rapidly that the best places to look for innovations are the academic conferences. The ACM conferences such as DIS (Designing Interactive Systems), CHI (Computer–Human Interaction) and UIST (User Interfaces and Software Technology) are good sources and are available from www.acm.org/dl. Consumer magazines, such as *Stuff*, are also worth a look.

Comments on challenges

Challenge 6-1
Radio buttons for the colour scheme – only one option can be chosen. The incoming mail preferences use checkboxes since multiple preferences can be selected.

Challenge 6-2
For reasons of durability, we would suggest a touchscreen or ordinary monitor with tracker ball and a robust keyboard (for entering data such as name of hotel guest) or an on-screen version (rather tiresome to use). Other options are possible.

Challenge 6-3
The touchscreen used as an output device, plus a small printer embedded in the casing for confirmation of bookings, etc., would probably be more reassuring than just a confirmation number. Sound output (and indeed input) would be possible but is likely to be impractical in the noisy environment of the airport.

Exercises

1. What's so wrong with the old c:\> prompt? As a user new to c:\> what would you do first?

2. A WIMP is always a GUI but a GUI need not be a WIMP. Can you think of an example of a GUI which is not a WIMP?

3. (Advanced) It is frequently said that video cassette recorders (VCRs) are difficult to use. Is this really so, or is it just a complaint from the middle-aged owners of such machines who are alleged to be too lazy (or stupid) to learn to use them? People also often say that they have to wait until their children get home from school before the VCR can be set. Are children and young people better at using technology? If so, why?

4. (Advanced) Design a hand controller for a small (hobbyist) computer-driven telescope. The Clearsky 100GT telescope is a modest 100 mm refracting telescope for the amateur astronomer. The biggest challenge facing the amateur astronomer is in finding faint but interesting star clusters, galaxies and the more remote planets of our solar system (e.g.

▶

Uranus and Neptune). Your task is to design a hand controller which allows the user of the telescope to point it at these objects of interest.

Points to consider: (a) this must be carried out in the dark (which is the best time to see stars); (b) assume that the telescope comes with a database of celestial objects held as a set of three coordinates (x, y and z); (c) as the Earth rotates the sky appears to move too.

Understanding people 2:
Embodied, situated and distributed cognition

Aims

This chapter develops the theme of single user interaction systems by going beyond the bounds of individual cognition. **Embodied interaction**, which is the design of technology that recognizes that we are embodied, that is, we are not merely cognitive systems receiving input from our senses, processing that input and creating motor actions as output. To be embodied is to recognize that we have physical bodies which have evolved and are adapted to a range of activities. Two perspectives on embodied interaction are discussed. The first of these perspectives is traditional and its practitioners would probably be surprised at their discipline being called embodied interaction. The discipline in question is, of course, **ergonomics** which historically is concerned with 'matching the machine to the man'. This should be rewritten as matching the technology and interactive systems to the person. The second example of embodied interaction is the use of avatars to embody individuals in collaborative virtual environments. Another important result of recognizing that interaction is embodied is that interaction always takes place in a context.

After studying this chapter you should be able to understand:

- The ideas of embodied interaction and how they are expressed in ergonomics.
- The importance of **context** in the design of interactive systems and devices. Context is usually defined in terms of the human, physical, organizational, historical and social environment in which a technology is used. Context also plays a major part in determining the range and type of actions we take.
- Three theoretical descriptions of people acting in context. These are **situated action**, **distributed cognition** and **activity theory**.

7.1   Embodied interaction 1: Ergonomics

Embodied interaction and context are very topical themes in HCI. Indeed in the last 10 years or so the whole of the HCI community has discovered that we have bodies and interact with tools, devices and systems in the world. Ergonomics (also called human factors), as distinct from cognitive psychology, deals with the more physiological aspects of our natures. It recognizes, for example, that we have bodies which both facilitate and restrict the range and types of movements we can make. So, for example, ergonomics is interested in reaction times (how quickly we can respond to an alert), visual acuity (the visual detail we can resolve) and reach (literally, concerned with the positioning of controls within our reach). Ergonomics is tremendously important in the design of such things as aircraft cockpits, space suits, vacuum cleaners (Dyson vacuum cleaners have 'ergonomic wands') and the layout of mobile phones (e.g. the Motorola V60 mobile phone is described as having an 'ergonomic, compact design'). Ergonomic design is seen by manufacturers as a major selling point and is also an important aspect of 'inclusive design'. Inclusive design is specifically aimed at including older people in the design process. Older people – particularly in Western Europe – are the greatest growth area for the population. In the UK, for example, the number of people aged 75 years and over is set to double in the next 50 years, so there is a clear need to extend the usefulness of equipment, tools and services designed for the general population to include such people.

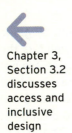

Chapter 3, Section 3.2 discusses access and inclusive design

The science of ergonomics has existed since the Second World War (although work in this area predates WWII, the term 'ergonomics' was not coined until 1948). This is no coincidence, since at that time technically advanced weapons systems were being rapidly developed which required that their design matched human and environmental factors if they were to be used effectively and, paradoxically, safely.

What is ergonomics?

Murrell (1965) defined ergonomics as the scientific study of the relationship between man and his environment: a more contemporary definition would of course include women too. *Environment* includes the ambient environment (temperature, humidity, atmospheric pressure, light levels, noise and so on) and the working environment too (the design of machines, health and safety issues – e.g. hygiene, toxicology, exposure to ionizing radiation, microwaves, etc.).

Ergonomics is multi-disciplinary, drawing on anatomy and physiology, various aspects of psychology (e.g. physiological and experimental), physics, engineering and work studies among others. In everyday life we come across the application of ergonomic design principles in every well-designed interactive system. In the advertisement for a new motor car, we can expect to find reference to its ergonomically designed dashboard (a good, desirable feature) or an adjustable, ergonomic driving seat. In the Mercedes-Benz sales literature for its new coupé we find the following ergonomic description:

> '*Once inside the C-Class Sports Coupé you'll find a wealth of ergonomic detail, designed to live up to the promise of its looks. As if cast from a single mould, the dashboard curves are smooth to the touch ...*'

The term 'ergonomic design' is also extensively used of all manner of office furniture (chairs, desks, lights, footrests and so forth) and office equipment, for example keyboards, monitor stands and wrist rests. Many, if not most of these principles are now embodied in legally binding design guidelines (see Further Reading at the end of this chapter). Figure 7-1 is an illustration of an ergonomically designed keyboard. It is described as ergonomically designed as it reflects the fact that we have two hands – hence the two separate blocks of keys and an integral wrist support. The keyboard has been designed to match the hands and fingers of its intended users.

FIGURE 7-1 An ergonomic keyboard
(source: Microsoft Natural Multimedia Keyboard from http://www.microsoft.com/press/gallery/hardware/Natural MultiMediaKeyboard.jpg © 2004 66Microsoft Corporation. All rights reserved. Printed with permission from Microsoft Corporation)

Anthropometrics

Anthropometrics means literally the measurement of man. While ergonomics has a longer history than HCI, it would be a mistake to perceive it as being old and out of touch – quite the reverse. Ergonomics has much to tell us about the design of interactive devices such as a mobile games console and a PDA (personal digital assistant). Figure 7-2 shows an example of the latter.

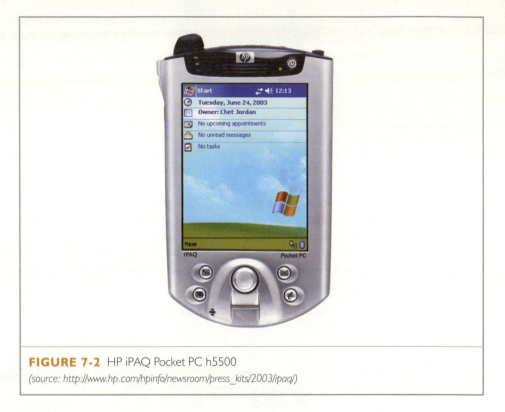

FIGURE 7-2 HP iPAQ Pocket PC h5500
(source: http://www.hp.com/hpinfo/newsroom/press_kits/2003/ipaq/)

Such devices are faced with ergonomic design challenges. For example, we all have relatively *fat* fingers compared with how small buttons can be made. In the world of mobile computing, small is good but too small is bad (too easily lost, too difficult to use, too easily eaten by the dog). Ergonomics can put numbers on what constitutes small and usable and what is *too* small and unusable.

Challenge 7-1
Examine two or three mobile phones. How far have ergonomic considerations been taken into account in the design of their keys?

Without the input from ergonomists, manufacturers are quite capable of designing unusable devices (and frequently do). A common anecdote illustrating this point is the findings of ergonomists evaluating the design of a lathe. A lathe is a tool for turning or shaping wood or metal for which, in this case, the ideal lathe operator would have to be less than 1.5 m tall and 0.75 m wide (at the shoulders) but have a reach of 2.5 m. As very few of us are shaped like this, it is reasonable to assume that the lathe would be very difficult to operate.

Anthropometrics can, for example, tell us the limits (diameter and load-bearing characteristics) of the human wrist for the *average* man and woman.

Box 7-1 The changing role of the thumb

People who have grown up with mobile phones (or Gameboys) tend to use their thumbs when others are more likely to use their fingers. Sadie Plant from Warwick University (*New Scientist*, No. 2315, 3 November 2001) collected data on mobile phone usage in nine cities around the world, including Beijing, Chicago, London and Tokyo. She found that the mainly under-25 age group appear to have experimented with the best way to interact with a mobile phone, one result of which is now to use their thumbs to ring doorbells, push doors and point.

Figures have been compiled from thousands of measurements of different races, different ages and different professions (e.g. office workers vs. manual workers) and drawn up as tables. The same body of data will also tell the designer whether the *average* person can simultaneously press button A while holding down buttons B and C – and whether this is true for both right- and left-handed people.

Occasionally, these measurements and studies can be translated into formulae or laws which can predict the behaviour of human beings. The best-known example of such a law is Fitts' law.

Fitts' law

Fitts' law is a mathematical formula which relates the time required to move to a target as a function of the distance to the target and the size of the target itself, say moving a pointer using a mouse to a particular button. It is expressed mathematically as follows:

$$T_{(time\ to\ move)} = k \log_2(D/S + 0.5)$$

where k ~ 100 ms, D is the distance between the current (cursor) position and the target, and S is the size of the target.

Thus one can calculate the time to move a distance of 15 cm to a button of size 2 cm as

$$T = 100 \log_2(15/2 + 0.5)$$
$$= 0.207\ seconds$$

Fitts' law describes motor control. The smaller the target and the greater the distance, the longer it will take to hit the target. Fitts' law can also be used to calculate how long it would take to type this sentence or more importantly a number of time-critical operations such as hitting the brake pedal of a motor car, or the likelihood of hitting <OK> rather than <Cancel> or more worryingly <Fire> or <Detonate>.

From ergonomics we now turn to another form of embodied interaction.

Box 7-2 Failing to design for children

Professor Peter Buckle, of the Robens Centre for Health Economics at the University of Surrey, has recently raised the alarm that children are risking permanent, painful injuries by using computers set up for adults. Millions of children use equipment designed for adults every day both at school and at home. However, computers, keyboards and the mouse rarely take into account the size of children and this is a major source of problems. Repetitive strain injury (RSI) was a risk, particularly as children's muscles and bones are still developing. 'Most parents wouldn't, for example, have an eight-year-old using a full size cricket bat or an adult bicycle but seem unaware of the possible dangers of children sitting for long periods unsupported, with necks twisted and wrists over extended.' Professor Buckle said that little attention had been paid to students and schoolchildren who use the same equipment, often for hours at a time. 'Worryingly, evidence is starting to show that, for some health problems, we may be leaving it too late before we start helping.' Professor Buckle unveiled research, involving more than 2000 youngsters, showing that 36 percent of 11- to 14-year-olds suffer serious, ongoing back pain.

7.2 Embodied interaction 2: Avatars in CVEs

'A CVE is a computer-based, distributed, virtual space or set of places. In such places, people can meet and interact with others, with agents or with virtual objects. CVEs might vary in their representational richness from 3D graphical spaces, 2.5D and 2D environments, to text-based environments.'

From the introduction to CVE 2000

Collaborative virtual environments (CVEs) mark a shift in interaction with computers in that they provide a space that contains both data and users. They are discussed in more detail in Chapter 30.

The change in interaction hinges on the fact that people are embodied in CVEs by way of an avatar. CVEs are digital landscapes which are inhabited by both data and users in the form of avatars. Avatars are representations of oneself or the adoption of a role or one's persona. In adopting an avatar we become embodied in the CVE. The role of avatars in CVEs is to represent the presence of a user together with their orientation and location.

Examples of avatars

DISCOVER is introduced as a case study in Chapter 9, Section 9.1

Figure 7-3 is an image of an avatar of a member of a ship's crew. This was part of the DISCOVER CVE-based training system which was developed in conjunction with a consortium of major offshore (oil-producing) companies and maritime training organizations. The DISCOVER system was designed to allow trainees to play the part of different members of a ship's crew or key workers on an oil platform (oil rig). When engaged in the training exercises the trainees are effectively embodied in the avatars they have adopted and can be seen to inhabit the bridge or other parts of the ship or platform. So, in practice, the ship's cook can play the role of the captain.

FIGURE 7-3 An avatar on a virtual bridge – a screenshot from the work of the DISCOVER project

Meet Cara ...

Chapter 26 provides more discussion of agents as virtual assistants

Cara (Figure 7-4) is a virtual assistant and while you'll see that clearly she's not a real person, she is designed to be both helpful and attentive. She has been 'trained' on mortgage details and designed to answer most customer questions.

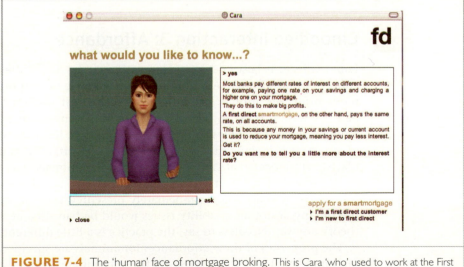

FIGURE 7-4 The 'human' face of mortgage broking. This is Cara 'who' used to work at the First Direct website at www.firstdirect.com/smartmortgage/

Group behaviour

One of the consequences of being embodied in a virtual environment is the like-lihood of social interaction. Salem and Earle (2000) argue that there is a group behaviour that needs to be visually represented. They have developed the con-cept of the 'social circle' which allows for a visual grammar of a social group to be developed. For example, it may prove to be useful to provide a visual clue that indicates whether or not the group is 'full'. If a group is full then perhaps they could be illuminated with a red light source. Other avatars/users would then be able to understand, at a glance, the state of the group. From another perspective groups may be characterized by the type of activities they are engaged in. Casual conversations, for example, may have no control or restric-tion placed upon the participants with respect to interruption and joining or leaving the group. Formal conversations may have more restrictive rules. Participants exchange a token which acts as a moderator of the conversation. Examples of the visual cues as to the status of a group are given in Table 7-1.

TABLE 7-1 Visual cues

Group condition	Visual symbol
Group is closed to newcomers	Emanate a red glow
Group is open to newcomers	Normal
Group is looking for newcomers	Open spaces around the parameter
Group context is social or formal	Dress code of the avatars

Source: Salem, B. and Earle, N. (2000) Designing a non-verbal language for expressive avatars, Proceedings of CVE'00 Conference, pp. 93–101. © 2000 ACM, Inc. Reprinted by permission

7.3 Embodied interaction 3: Affordance

James Gibson is best known in HCI design circles as the man who gave us the concept of **affordance**. An affordance is a resource or support that the environ-ment offers an animal; the animal in turn must possess the capabilities to perceive it and to use it. 'The affordances of the environment are what it offers animals, what it provides or furnishes, for good or ill' (Gibson, 1977). Examples of affordances include surfaces that provide support, objects that can be manip-ulated, substances that can be eaten and other animals that afford interactions of all kinds. This all seems quite remote from HCI but if we were able to design interactive systems which immediately presented their affordances to the user then many, if not all, usability issues would be banished at a stroke. That's the theory anyway. Needless to say, the practice is a little different.

The properties of these affordances for animals are specified in stimulus infor-mation. Even if an animal possesses the appropriate attributes and equipment, it may need to learn to detect the information and to perfect the activities that make the affordance useful – or dangerous if ignored. An affordance, once detected, is meaningful and has value for the animal. It is nevertheless objective, inasmuch as it refers to physical properties of the animal's niche (environmental constraints) and to its bodily dimensions and capacities. An affordance thus exists, whether it is perceived or used or not. It may be detected and used without explicit awareness of doing so. This description was revised in 1986 when Gibson wrote 'An affordance cuts across the dichotomy of subjective–objective and helps us to understand its inadequacy. It is equally a fact of the environment and a fact of behaviour. It is both physical and psychical, yet neither. An affordance points both ways, to the environment and to the observer' (Gibson, 1986, p. 129). So affordances are (confusingly) neither and both in the world and in the mind of the observer.

Figure 7-5 is an illustration of a door. Opening a door is probably the most widely cited example of an affordance in action. The argument is that we 'see' that we can either push or pull open the door from the affordances of the door itself. This might work well for doors, but does it apply to the design of interactive systems?

FIGURE 7-5 An affordance in the world

Challenge 7-2
Find some more affordances in everyday objects. How is the affordance 'presented'? Also try to identify apparent affordances which are misleading.

Donald Norman, who was instrumental in introducing the concept of affordance to HCI, recognized that Gibson's formulation of the concept needs some revision. He has argued that we need to replace the original biological–environmental formulation with a definition which is at one remove, namely perceived affordance (Norman, 1988). He has suggested that the concept of affordances can be extended to a weaker formulation, a user being said to perceive the intended behaviour of the interface widgets such as the knobs and dials of a range of software applications. These intended and perceived behaviours are usually very simple, including sliding, pressing and rotating. He continues, 'real affordances are not nearly as important as perceived affordances; it is perceived affordances that tell the user what actions can be performed on an object and, to some extent, how to do them'. His position is that perceived affordances are 'often more about conventions than about reality' (Norman, 1999, p. 124) and he gives a scrollbar as an example of such a convention.

Figure 7-6 is a screenshot with a number of perceived affordances present. The slider labelled 'Dock Size' affords sliding; the radio buttons ('Position on screen') afford selecting but does the checkbox 'Animate opening applications' really afford checking? What does 'checking' really mean? Are these really affordances or just conventions?

Despite the difficulties in precisely stating what an affordance is, as a concept it is enormously popular amongst researchers. The use of the term *affordance* in anthropology is not unusual (e.g. Cole, 1996; Wenger, 1998; Holland *et al.*, 2001). However, what may be surprising is the extravagant use of the term, going well beyond Gibson's modest conceptualization. Cole (1996), for example, identified a range of affordances offered by a variety of mediating artefacts

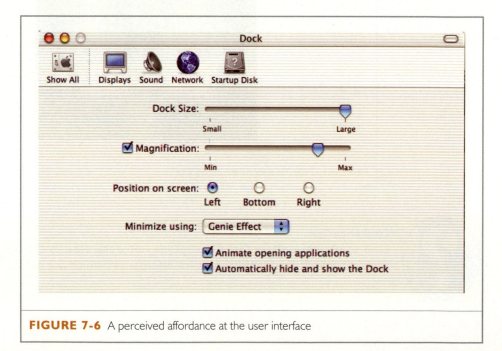

FIGURE 7-6 A perceived affordance at the user interface

including the life stories of recovering alcoholics in an AA meeting (affording rehabilitation), patients' charts in a hospital setting (affording access to a patient's medical history), poker chips (affording gambling) and 'sexy' clothes (affording gender stereotyping). Cole notes that mediating artefacts embody their own 'developmental histories' which is a reflection of their use. That is, these artefacts have been manufactured or produced and continue to be used as part of, and in relation to, intentional human actions. Holland and her colleagues add to this with a discussion of how the men of the Naudada (who are found in Nepal) use the pronoun *ta* (you) to address their wives. This pronoun is the least respectful of all forms of address and is usually reserved for children, dogs and other 'inferiors'. As Holland notes, ' ... pronouns, through their collective use in common practice, have come to embody for, and so impose on, people [...] in Naudada a conception of the tasks to which they are put, and a conception of the person(s) who will use them and be the object(s) of them' (Holland *et al.*, 2001, p. 62). Thus the use of the least respectful form of the pronoun places women as inferior to men, that is, their use affords the maintenance of social structure in their society.

7.4 Theoretical perspective 1: Situated action

The late 1980s and 1990s saw the rise of criticisms of the classic cognitive psychological accounts which we discussed in Chapter 5. For example, Liam Bannon argued for studying people outside the confines of the psychology laboratory, while Lucy Suchman has shown that people respond constructively and perhaps unpredictably to real-world situations.

In 1991 Bannon published a paper entitled 'From human factors to human actors' (Bannon, 1991). The paper was a plea to understand the potential users of collaborative systems as empowered, problem-solving, value-laden, cooperative individuals rather than mere subjects in an 'applied psychology' experiment. In adopting this new perspective we necessarily move out of the laboratory and into complex real-world settings. The argument highlights the differences in perception between treating people as merely a set of cognitive systems and subsystems (which is implied by the term *human factors*) and respecting people as 'autonomous agents' with the capacity to govern their own behaviour. From this point Bannon explores the consequences of this change in perspective. He argues that it involves moving from narrow experimental studies of individual users working on a computer system to the workplace. This too would require changes in techniques from a cognitive and experimental approach to less intrusive techniques with perhaps an emphasis on the observational. Once in the workplace we should study experts and the obstacles they face in improving their practice or competence. There is a need to shift from snapshot studies to extended longitudinal studies. Finally, Bannon argues that we should move from user-centred to user-involved design which places the intended user at the centre of the design process (this is more usually called user-participative or participative design).

There is more about participative design in Chapter 9, Section 9.2

Box 7-3 Ubiquitous computing

Ubiquitous computing is seen by its enthusiasts as being the third generation of computer use. Ubiquitous means 'found everywhere' and ubiquitous computing is really serious about embedding computers everywhere – from coffee cups to washing labels, from children's toys to car keys. Mark Weiser is usually described as the 'father' of ubiquitous computing (often abbreviated to UC or UbiComp). UC is discussed in detail in Chapter 27. Weiser argues that the last 50 years have witnessed two great trends in human–computer relations. The first was the mainframe relationship and this has been followed by the current PC relationship. The next relationship, which has been heralded by the Internet, promises widespread distributed computing, resulting in ubiquitous computing which will be characterized by deeply embedded computation. In the mainframe relationship computers were a scarce resource and had to be shared with others (one computer – many users). Surprisingly this situation still persists today – virtual reality equipment is still relatively scarce and has to be shared, and our weather forecasts rely on simulations run on a 'supercomputer'. The PC relationship began in the 1980s when personal computers began to appear. Weiser has described the personal computing relationship as being 'personal, even intimate. You have your computer, it contains your stuff, and you interact directly. When doing personal computing you are occupied, you are not doing something else.'

It is said that Lucy Suchman's *Plans and Situated Actions* is the most widely quoted book by researchers of collaborative system design. Published in 1987, it is a critique of some of the core assumptions of artificial intelligence (AI) and cognitive science, specifically the role of plans in behaviour, but in doing so it opened the door to ethnomethodology and conversation analysis in HCI. Suchman's starting point – before refuting the planning approach – is to identify the role of planning in AI and the belief of cognitive psychology that this is true of human behaviour too. Simply put, both human and artificially intelligent behaviour can be modelled in terms of the **formulation** and **execution** of **plans**. A plan is a **script**, a sequence of actions.

Box 7-4 'Going for a curry' script

As the national dish of the UK is chicken tikka masala (a kind of creamy curry), let us think about how the British enjoy this dish.

The scene is a Saturday night in any city in the UK. Our potential curry enthusiasts (let's call them *students* for the sake of argument) meet and then drink a great deal of lager which creates an irresistible desire for a curry. The second step is to locate an Indian restaurant. Having gained entry to the restaurant one of the students will ask a waiter for a table. The waiter will guide the party to a table, offering to take their coats as they go. Next the waiter will give the students each a copy of the menu, suggesting that they might like to have a lager while choosing from the menu. The students then decide what they want to eat and order it from the waiter, stopping only to argue over how many poppadums, chapatis or nan breads they want (these are common forms of Indian breads eaten prior to or with a curry). The curry is then served and consumed. Everyone being sated, one of the students asks for the bill. After 20 minutes of heated argument about who had ordered what, the students finally settle the bill and hurry home to ensure that they have a good night's sleep.

Researchers Schank and Abelson (1977) were the first to identify scripts as being a credible means by which we organize our knowledge of the world and more importantly as a means of directing our behaviour (i.e. planning). The advantage of scripts is that they can be adapted to other situations. The above Indian restaurant script is readily adapted for use in a Thai, Chinese or Italian restaurant (i.e. find restaurant, get table, read menu, order food, eat food, pay for meal) and easily adapted to, for example, hamburger restaurants (the order of get table and order food is simply reversed).

Plans are formulated through a set of procedures beginning with a goal, successive decomposition into sub-goals and into primitive actions. The plan is then executed. A goal is the desired state of the system. Figure 7-7 is an illustration of a typical plan (see Chapter 20 for a discussion of task analysis). A plan is associated with a goal (e.g. the desire to go and see a movie). The goal is achieved by way of sub-steps (often called actions) which in themselves may have sub-steps. The sub-steps are **executed** in order 1a, 1b, 2 and 3. Figure 7-8 adds a little to this by recognising that we **monitor** the execution of the plan.

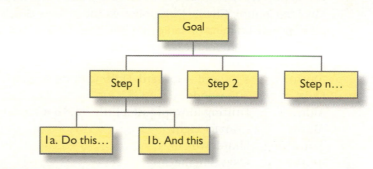

FIGURE 7-7 A simple plan

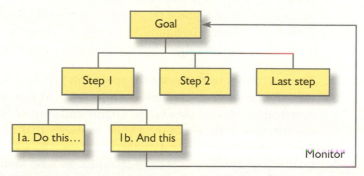

FIGURE 7-8 A more detailed view of a plan and its execution

So what is wrong with planning?

Chapter 25 on navigation also criticises the traditional view of plans

The problems with the planning model as identified by Suchman included the observations that the world is not stable, immutable and objective. Instead it is dynamic and interpreted (by us) and the interpretation is contextual or 'situated'. Thus plans are not executed but rather they are just one resource which can shape an individual's behaviour.

> **Challenge 7-3**
> How do the current generation of graphical user interfaces support behaviour which does not rely on planning?

7.5 Theoretical perspective 2: Distributed cognition

On 20 July 1969, astronauts Neil Armstrong and Buzz Aldrin landed on the Moon. At Mission Control, Charlie Duke followed the process closely (along with 600 000 000 other people listening on radio and watching on TV). What follows is a transcript of the last few seconds of the landing of the Lunar Module (LM).

Aldrin	4 forward. 4 forward. Drifting to the right a little. 20 feet, down a half
Duke	30 seconds
Aldrin	Drifting forward just a little bit; that's good
Aldrin	Contact Light
Armstrong	Shutdown
Aldrin	Okay. Engine Stop
Aldrin	ACA out of detent
Armstrong	Out of detent. Auto
Duke	We copy you down, Eagle
Armstrong	Engine arm is off. Houston, *Tranquillity Base* here. The Eagle has landed.
Duke	Roger, Tranquillity. We copy you on the ground. You got a bunch of guys about to turn blue. We're breathing again. Thanks a lot.

The question is, who landed the spacecraft? History records that Neil Armstrong was the mission commander while Buzz Aldrin was the LM pilot. While Armstrong operated the descent engine and control thrusters, Aldrin read aloud the speed and altitude of the LM ('4 forward', that is, we are moving forward at 4 feet per second), while 250 000 miles away back on Earth, Duke confirms the quantity of fuel remaining (30 seconds). So who landed the LM? In a very real sense they all did; it was a joint activity.

Ed Hutchins has developed the theory of **distributed cognition** to describe situations such as this (Hutchins, 1995). The theory argues that both the cognitive process itself and the knowledge used and generated are often distributed across multiple people, tools and representations. Everyday examples would include:

- A driver and passenger navigating a foreign city using maps and road signs
- The homely task of shopping with the aid of a list and the reminders presented by the supermarket shelves
- Colleagues rationalizing a project budget using an Excel spreadsheet and some unintelligible printouts from Finance.

Internal and external representation

In distributed cognition, resources include the **internal representation** of knowledge (human memory) and **external representations** – potentially anything which supports the cognitive activity, but instances would include gestures, the physical layout of objects, notes, diagrams, computer readings and so forth. These are just as much part of the activity as cognitive processes, not just memory aids (Zhang and Norman, 1994). Hutchins has studied distributed cognition in a range of team-working situations, from Pacific islanders wayfinding between far distant islands to the navigation of US naval ships to aircraft cockpits. In a study of how pilots control approach speeds (aircraft landing speeds), Hutchins (1995) suggests that the cockpit system as a whole in a sense 'remembers' its speed. He argued that the various representations in the cockpit, their physical location and the way in which they are shared between pilots comprise the cockpit system as a whole (Figure 7-9).

The representations employed by the pilots include what they say, charts and manuals and the cockpit instruments themselves. There is also a whole host of

FIGURE 7-9 A typical example of distributed cognition in an aircraft cockpit
(source: Mike Miller/Science Photo Library)

implicit information in aircraft cockpits, such as the relative positions of airspeed indicators and other dials. Hutchins also notes that the various representational states change with time and may even transfer between media in the course of the system's operation. These transformations may be carried out by an individual using a tool (artefact) while at other times representational states are produced or transformed entirely by artefacts.

Different ways in which processes might be distributed

When these principles are applied in the wild, three different kinds of distribution emerge:

Chapter 27
discusses
distributed
information

- Cognitive processes may be distributed across the members of a social group
- Cognitive processes may involve coordination between internal and external structures
- Processes may be distributed through time in such a way that the products of earlier events can transform the nature of later events.

All in all, distributed cognition offers an excellent means of describing how complex systems operate which is well supported by empirical evidence. However, translating these descriptions into the design of interactive systems remains problematic. Hollan *et al.* (2000) showed how insights from a distributed cognition perspective have guided the design of their PAD++ system, but such examples remain few.

7.6   Theoretical perspective 3: Activity theory

In the last decade or so, the focus of much research activity in the broad domain of human–computer systems has moved from the single user at the computer to groups of people interacting with and through a variety of technologies. In parallel with this shift, attention has moved from the usability laboratory to the rich context of everyday work. However, while research and development for individual human–computer interaction has been strongly informed by cognitive accounts of human information processing, as yet no single account of collaborative working has gained widespread acceptance. This is despite the considerable body of literature in the study of work, with researchers drawn from a variety of disciplines including sociologists, anthropologists, psychologists and even computer scientists. As a number of commentators have observed, it may be this very diversity which has prevented the creation of a comprehensive and widely accepted account, theory or model of work – much less collaborative work. This section discusses the adequacy of activity theory in this domain. In recent years a number of prominent researchers have suggested that activity theory might serve as a framework for computer–supported cooperative work (e.g. Kuutti, 1996; Nardi, 1996). However, it remains far from clear how this might be achieved in practice. Activity theory stems from the work of Vygotsky (1978) and his students Luria and Leont'ev, and from its origins in psychology and education has recently gained ground in many other domains, including the study of work (e.g. Engeström, 1995, 1999), information systems and CSCW (e.g. Christiansen, 1996; Heeren and Lewis, 1997; Hasan *et al.*, 1998; Turner and Turner, 2001, 2002) and organizational theory (e.g. Blackler, 1993, 1995).

Not really a theory

Perhaps the first observation to be made of activity theory is that it is not a theory. Instead it is better regarded as a body of thought which has been found relevant not only to psychology and education, but more recently in the understanding of work in organizations and several other fields. It developed from the ideas of the Russian psychologist Vygotsky (1896–1934) and his successors. More recently, Engeström (e.g. Engeström, 1987, 1995) has extended these ideas to include a model of human activity and methods for analysing activity and bringing about change. Most authors would agree that the core features of activity theory, more fully described as CHAT – Cultural Historical Activity Theory – comprise a recognition of the role and importance of culture, history and activity in understanding human behaviour. Other authors do, of course, emphasize different aspects of activity theory variously reflecting their individual research needs and the dynamic, evolving nature of activity theory.

CHAT – a modern formulation of activity theory

The flavour of activity theory employed here draws primarily upon the contemporary work of Engeström which has been adopted and elaborated by many Scandinavian (e.g. Bødker and Christiansen, 1997; Bardram, 1998), American (e.g. Nardi, 1996), Australian (e.g. Hasan *et al.*, 1998) and British researchers (e.g. Blackler, 1993, 1995). Engeström's account of activity theory is probably the dominant formulation in use in the study of information systems, HCI and CSCW research. In such research there is perhaps a greater focus on the role of activity *per se* rather than history and culture. Reflecting this, Engeström has formulated three basic principles, building on the work of earlier activity theorists, which are widely used and cited within the activity theory community. These are, in no particular order: (a) activities as the smallest meaningful unit of analysis (originally identified by Leont'ev); (b) the principle of self-organizing activity systems driven by contradictions; and (c) changes in activities (and by extension the organization hosting them) as instantiations of cycles of expansive learning.

The structure of an activity

Central to activity theory is the concept that all purposive human activity can be characterized by a triadic interaction between a *subject* (one or more people) and the group's *object* (or purpose) mediated by *artefacts* or tools. In activity theory terms, the subject is the individual or individuals carrying out the activity, the artefact is any tool or representation used in that activity, whether external or internal to the subject, and the object encompasses both the purpose of the activity and its product or output. Subsequent developments of activity theory by Engeström and others have added more elements to the original formulation: *community* (all other groups with a stake in the activity), the *division of labour* (the horizontal and vertical divisions of responsibilities and power within the activity) and *praxis* (the formal and informal rules and norms governing the relations between the subjects and the wider community for the activity). These relationships are often represented by an *activity triangle*. Thus activities are social and collective in nature. The use of activity triangles is widespread in the activity theory literature but it must be remembered that this is only a partial representation of an activity. The triangle should be regarded as a nexus, existing as it does in a continuum of development and learning and in turn masking its internal structure. Within the activity are the individual *actions* by which it is carried out. These are each directed at achieving a particular goal mediated by the use of an artefact. Actions, in turn, are executed by means of *operations*: lower-level steps that do not require conscious attention. Thus activities are social and collective in nature (see Figure 7-10).

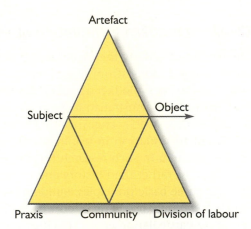

FIGURE 7-10 An activity triangle (sometimes called the activity *schema*)

The internal structure of an activity

Activities are realized by way of an aggregation of *mediated actions*, which, in turn, are achieved by a series of low-level operations. This structure, however, is flexible and may change as a consequence of learning, context or both (Figure 7-11).

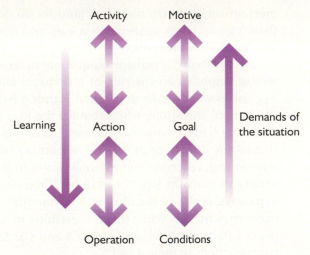

FIGURE 7-11 Structure of an activity

By way of example, consider the process of learning to use a complex interactive device such as a motorcar. The object of the activity is probably quite complex, ranging from and probably including the need to be able to drive because of work commitments, the need to attract the opposite sex, because of peer pressure, because an indulgent parent has given you a car, or the need to participate in a robbery. The activity is realized by means of an aggregation of actions (i.e. obtain driving licence; insure car; take driving lessons; learn the Highway Code; get a job to pay for the petrol and so on). These individual actions in their turn are realized by a set of operations (i.e. get driving licence application form, complete form, write out cheque for the licence, send off licence ...). This, of course, is an incomplete, *static* description of the activity whereas humans are constantly learning with practice, so when first presented with the intricacies of the gear lever (manual gear shift) it is likely that the process of disengaging the engine, shifting gear and re-engaging the engine are under conscious control (thus the action of changing gear is realized by the following operations: depress clutch, shift to the top left, release clutch). Thus the focus of attention is at the operations level but with practice attention will tend to slide down the hierarchy as the action becomes automatic. Over time actions become automatic and the activity itself is effectively demoted to that of an action – unless circumstances change. Such changes might include driving on the right (the British drive on the left), changing the make of motorcar or driving a lorry, or being faced with the possibility of a collision. In such circumstances consciousness becomes refocused at the level demanded by the context.

Thus, this alternative formulation of the nature and structure of an activity is of interest for a number of reasons. Firstly, this theory of activity has, at its heart, a hierarchical task-like structure. Secondly, it introduces the ideas of consciousness and motivation at the heart of the activity. Leont'ev offers a mechanism by which the focus (and locus) of consciousness moves between these various levels of abstraction – up and down the hierarchy depending on the demands of the context.

Activity theory is perhaps unique among accounts of work in placing such a strong emphasis on the role of individual and group or collective learning. Vygotsky's work on developmental learning has been a major influence on the thinking of Engeström, who extended the idea to encompass collective learning which he termed *expansive learning* (Engeström, 1987). Engeström has demonstrated the usefulness of expansive learning with its cycles of internalization, questioning, reflection and externalization in the development of activities in a variety of domains (see, for example, Engeström, 1999). The drivers for these expansive cycles of learning and development are *contradictions* within and between activities. While this is something of a departure from Vygotsky, it has proved particularly valuable to HCI and CSCW researchers. We now consider contradictions in more detail.

Engeström's description of contradictions

Activities are dynamic entities, having their roots in earlier activities and bearing the seeds of their own successors. They are subject to transformation in the light of contradictions. Those contradictions found within a single node of an activity are described as *primary* contradictions. In practice, this kind of contradiction can be understood in terms of breakdowns between actions or sets of actions which realize the activity. These actions are typically poly-motivated, i.e. the same action is executed by different people for different reasons, or by the same person as a part of two separate activities, and it is this poly-motivation which may be at the root of subsequent contradictions. The next category of contradictions are those which occur between nodes and are described as *secondary* contradictions. *Tertiary* contradictions may be found when an activity is remodelled to take account of new motives or ways of working. Thus they occur between an existing activity and what is described as a 'culturally more advanced form' of that activity. A culturally more advanced activity is one which has arisen from the resolution of contradictions within an existing activity and may involve the creation of new working practices (praxis) or artefacts or division of responsibilities. Finally, those occurring between different coexisting or concurrent activities are described as *quaternary* contradictions. From this, it can be seen that a complex and continuing evolving web of contradictions may emerge (Figure 7-12). Primary and secondary contradictions in an activity may give rise to a new activity which in turn spawns a set of tertiary contradictions between it and the original activity, and this may be compounded by quaternary contradictions with coexisting activities.

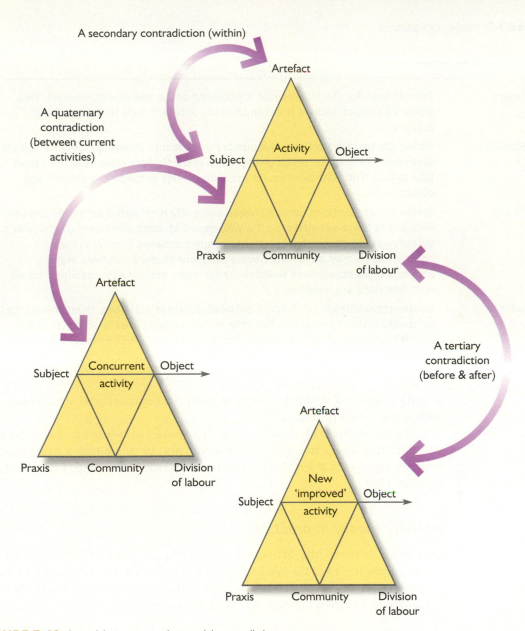

FIGURE 7-12 An activity system and potential contradictions

Concrete examples of contradictions

Table 7-2 holds a set of sample contradictions which might exist within a modern university. A university can be thought of as an activity system, that is, a university can be thought of as the sum of its activities. Put *very* simply, a university comprises teaching, research and (by far the biggest) administration

TABLE 7-2 Sample contradictions

Type of contradiction	
Primary	The set book for the HCI module is outdated and a new one is required. This would be symptomatic of breakdown in the artefact node of the teaching activity.
Secondary	Within the teaching activity, the number of students studying HCI has risen (or dropped) dramatically, which changes the staff–student ratio from the target 20:1 to 50:1. The contradiction (or breakdown) lies between the subject and object nodes.
Tertiary	Tertiary contradictions occur between currently formulated activities and new versions of those activities. So if a Web-based student enrolment (matriculation) system was introduced to replace the academic-based manual system, contradictions may arise from having accurate student numbers. Having accurate student numbers would make for more accurate timetabling. Not all contradictions are negative.
Quaternary	Quaternary contradictions occur between different activities. In all universities (probably without exception) the only reliable growth area is administration, which necessarily causes problems for the other activities of teaching and research.

activities. Table 7-2 details a number of potential contradictions which may exist within and between these activities.

A contradictions analysis such as the one above can be used to direct the evaluation of new interactive systems. (It should also be noted that a contradictions analysis also closely resembles the creation of a rich picture – see Checkland and Scholes, 1999.)

Activity theory in practice

In a study between the School of Computing at Napier University and the Gastrointestinal Unit at the Western General Hospital Trust in Edinburgh a wireless network of personal digital assistants (PDA) has been created. The specific benefits of using such a wireless network of PDAs in the GI unit are expected to be:

- Delivering patients' records, key test results and clinical histories directly into the hands of the clinician and enabling direct data entry at the point of care
- Requesting medical tests
- Access to the GI unit on-line guidelines and drug manuals
- Synchronization with other computers, that is, being able to mutually update files and other materials which the clinician has on his or her desktop
- Portable e-mail, allowing clinicians to read their e-mail on their PDAs off-line at home

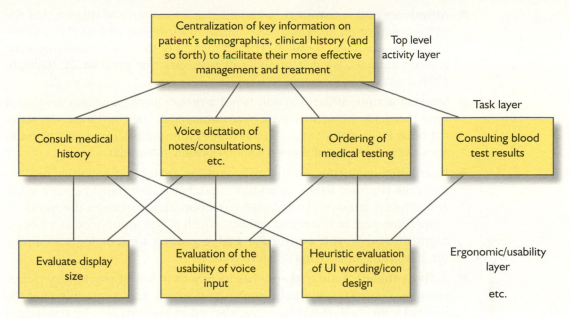

FIGURE 7-13 Evaluating the PDA pilot using activity theory

■ An enhanced means of managing patients both within the hospital context and between general practitioners and hospitals. This work has been partially supported by the ECCI project which itself is looking at improving communications between general practitioners and the hospitals.

In order to determine whether or not these benefits are achieved, it is important to evaluate the usefulness and usability of the network. Activity theory allows us to organize this evaluation effort. Figure 7-13 is a hierarchically organized evaluation framework created for this task.

A fuller account of the evaluation of the PDAs in this clinical setting may be found in Turner *et al.* (2003).

Summary and key points

■ **Ergonomics.** This is primarily concerned with fitting the machine to the person. It draws upon psychology, anatomy, anthropometrics and a host of environmental sciences. It is also mistakenly believed to be a little dated, though it is used by manufacturers as a major selling point for their interactive products.

■ **Embodied interaction.** The design of interactive systems which recognizes the role and importance of the body – which includes the discipline of ergonomics – may be described as embodied interaction. A further example of embodied interaction is the way in which collaborative virtual environments embody their users as avatars.

■ **Affordance and constraints.** An affordance is a resource or support that the environment offers an animal; the animal in turn must possess the capabilities to perceive it and to use it. 'The affordances of the environment are what it offers animals, what it provides or furnishes, for good or ill' (Gibson, 1977).

■ **Situated action.** Situated action is not a theory but a paradigm developed from the highly influential work of anthropologist Lucy Suchman. Her seminal book *Plans and Situated Actions* argues that plans should be treated as resources for action and that we respond flexibly to context.

■ **Distributed cognition.** Distributed cognition argues that cognitive processing is not confined to the individual mind, but is distributed between mind and external artefacts. Distributed cognition exists between the minds of cooperating human actors and artefacts which is best understood as a unified cognitive system with a particular goal, e.g. using a calculator, a shopping list, navigating and driving in a foreign city.

■ **Activity theory.** Activity theory has its origins in Soviet psychology (Marx, Leont'ev, Vygotsky) and places emphasis on society and community, not the isolated individual. It has been popularized in Western HCI by researchers such as Yrjö Engeström, Suzanne Bødker and Bonnie Nardi. It also asserts that human activity itself is the context.

Further reading

Ergonomics

Murrell, K.F.H. (1965) *Ergonomics – Man in his Working Environment.* Chapman & Hall, London.

Embodied interaction

Dourish, P. (2001) *Where the Action Is: The Foundations of Embodied Interaction.* MIT Press, Cambridge, MA.

Winograd, T. and Flores, F. (1986) *Understanding Computers and Cognition: a New Foundation for Design.* Ablex Publishing, Norwood, NJ.

Affordance

Gibson, J.J. (1977) The theory of affordances. In Shaw, R. and Bransford, J. (eds), *Perceiving, Acting and Knowing.* Wiley, New York, pp. 67–82.

Gibson, J.J. (1986) *The Ecological Approach to Visual Perception.* Lawrence Erlbaum Associates, Hillsdale, NJ.

Norman, D. (1988) *The Psychology of Everyday Things*. Basic Books, New York.

Sellen, A. and Harper, R. (2002) *The Myth of the Paperless Office*. MIT Press, Cambridge, MA.

Situated action

Suchman, L. (1987) *Plans and Situated Actions*. Cambridge University Press, New York.

Schank, R. and Abelson, R. (1977) *Scripts, Plans, Goals and Understanding*. Lawrence Erlbaum Associates, Hillsdale, NJ.

Distributed cognition

Hutchins, E. (1995) *Cognition in the Wild*. MIT Press, Cambridge, MA.

Hollan, J., Hutchins, E. and Kirsh, D. (2000) Distributed cognition: toward a new foundation for human–computer interaction research. *ACM Transactions on Computer–Human Interaction*, **7**(2), 174–196.

Activity theory

Nardi, B. (ed.) (1996) *Context and Consciousness: Activity Theory and Human–Computer Interaction*. MIT Press, Cambridge, MA.

Hasan, H., Gould, E. and Hyland, P. (eds) (1998) *Information Systems and Activity Theory: Tools in Context*. University of Wollongong Press, Wollongong, New South Wales.

Engeström, Y. (1987) *Learning by Expanding: an Activity-Theoretical Approach to Developmental Research*. Orienta-Konsultit, Helsinki.

Vygotsky, L.S. (1978) *Mind in Society: the Development of Higher Psychological Processes* (English trans. ed. M. Cole). Harvard University Press, Cambridge, MA.

Monk, A. and Gilbert, N. (eds) (1995) *Perspectives on HCI – Diverse Approaches*. Academic Press, London.

Kaptelinin, V., Nardi, B.A. and Macaulay, C. (1999) The Activity Checklist: a tool for representing the 'space' of context. *Interactions,* **6**(4), 27–39.

Academic journals

Ergonomics is the official journal of the Ergonomics Society and the International Ergonomics Association. It is a multidisciplinary, refereed journal concerned with research into all aspects of the interactions of human beings and their work and leisure, including psychological, physiological, anatomical and engineering design aspects.

Applied Ergonomics contains 'papers [which] reflect the wide range and coverage of ergonomics, embracing analysis and design of tools, products and workplaces, improvements in health and safety, cognitive ergonomics and engineering psychology, and social and work organisation issues.'

Selected ISO standards

Current ISO – International Standards Organization – standards govern the design of aspects of the modern office: less than stimulating for some, perhaps, but of direct relevance to millions of workers. There are standards for the design of VDUs, computer keyboards, office chairs, lighting levels and dozens of other things. Below is a very short selection of current ISO standards relevant to the design and function of visual display terminals.

- **ISO 9241-3.** Ergonomic requirements for office work with visual display terminals (VDTs): Visual display requirements.
- **ISO 9241-4.** Ergonomic requirements for office work with visual display terminals (VDTs): Keyboard requirements.
- **ISO 9241-5.** Ergonomic requirements for office work with visual display terminals (VDTs): Workstation and postural requirements.
- **ISO 9241-6.** Ergonomic requirements for office work with visual display terminals (VDTs): Environmental requirements.
- **ISO 6385.** Ergonomics principles in the design of work systems.
- **ISO 7250.** A basic list of anthropometric measurements.

Comments on challenges

Challenge 7-1
Taking the state of technology at the time of writing, you will probably have observed that the size and layout of many phone keys are too small and cramped for easy and quick operation for anyone with normal-sized fingers. (But with the advent of picture messaging, keys are becoming slightly larger again.) The design is a shifting compromise between ergonomics and style, where designers have decided that style is a more important marketing point. You can find similar trade-offs in many consumer products.

Challenge 7-2
There is a multitude of possible examples. An easy one, leading on from the door handle example, is the near-universal provision of handles on objects designed to be picked up. A counter-affordance is illustrated by door han-

dles such as those pictured on doors designed for *pushing*: not uncommon and very tedious.

Challenge 7-3
For example, some computer systems provide 'wizards' which step users through a sequence of actions without the requirement for planning that sequence. The context-sensitive cornucopia of icons and other widgets presented by most graphical user interfaces also help to suggest what we might do. Most websites – especially e-commerce sites – encourage browsing as well as goal-directed activities.

Exercises

1. Sitting at a workstation/PC (in class, at work or at home), identify the key ergonomic features of the whole setup which (a) have been well designed, and (b) seem to have been designed almost deliberately badly. How would you improve the aspects of those that have been poorly designed?

2. You have been retained as an interaction designer by a mobile phone company. Their concept designers would like to create a combined mobile phone and MP3 player and would like to claim that it has an ergonomic design. How and where would you advise them to begin to create an ergonomic design?

3. (Advanced) Embodied interaction as a way of thinking about designing interactive systems is currently in vogue, but what would disembodied interaction imply? While it is possible to imagine usable systems and unusable systems and aesthetically pleasing and plain ugly designs, what would a disembodied design look like? Is embodied interaction tautological? Or is it emphasizing an aspect of design which is usually ignored?

4. (Advanced) As we have seen, the concept of affordance was originally applied to simple real-world situations. Then Norman suggested that user interface widgets provided perceived affordances (e.g. sliders afford scrolling through a document). But is a perceived affordance just a convention? (We have all learned to use GUIs such as Windows, and a widget such as a slider is just a way one scrolls through a document. These are conventions, not affordances.)

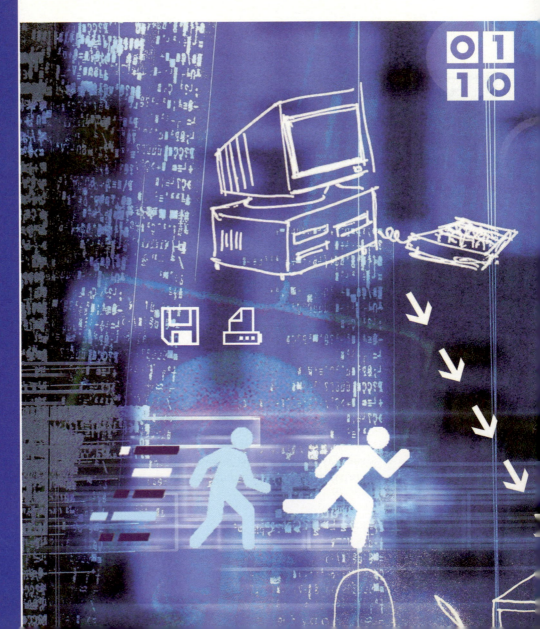

Part III:

Activities and Contexts of Interactive Systems Design

Introduction

In Part III we provide a comprehensive core set of methods and techniques for human-centred interactive systems design. These extend the overview material in Part I of the book and can themselves be further extended by the contents of Part V.

Chapter 8 introduces a scenario-based design method, showing different types of scenarios and illustrating how they are used throughout design. We then go on to detail design techniques for different aspects of the design life cycle in Chapters 9–12. The techniques in these chapters can be used either to support a fully scenario-based design approach, or as the ingredients of a more traditional user-centred process.

Chapter 9 discusses the concept of requirements, and how we go about understanding what users want, dream of, and need. We also introduce a second major case study, the DISCOVER virtual training application. Examples from DISCOVER illustrate Part III alongside the Home Information Centre (HIC) case study, which we introduced in Chapter 4.

Chapters 10 and 11 between them cover the multitude of ways in which emerging designs can be envisioned and communicated. Techniques range from simple sketches to fully functional prototypes, and we also consider the exploration of underlying design concepts and metaphor. Throughout, the focus is on user involvement and there are many examples from our own experience and that of others. Chapter 12, which comprises a thorough introduction to evaluating interactive systems and the essential techniques needed, is followed by a more abstract consideration of the design process in Chapter 13. This distinguishes the activities of physical and conceptual design, including a discussion of the use of a design language.

Finally, the application of the material of the foregoing chapters can be seen in operation in Chapter 14, which is a full description of how the design for the Home Information Centre was achieved using scenario-based design.

We envisage that this part will be used to support a second-level course on the methods of interactive systems design. It can be supplemented by the chapters in Part V, which cover the contextual design method, task analysis and further evaluation techniques. Alternatively, Part III will be a valuable reference for anyone undertaking an interactive systems design project in industry or education.

08   Scenarios

Aims

Scenarios are stories about people undertaking activities in contexts using technologies. They appear in a variety of forms throughout interactive systems design and are a key component of many approaches to design. In this chapter we introduce the ideas of scenarios and develop a method for the design of interactive systems based on scenarios. After studying this chapter you should be able to:

- Understand the different types of scenario
- Appreciate the usefulness of scenarios as a design tool
- Understand the different roles that scenarios have throughout the design process.

8.1   Introduction

Scenarios have been used in software engineering, interactive systems design and human–computer interaction work for many years. More recently scenario-based design has emerged as an important approach to the design of interactive systems in the twenty-first century. Carroll (2000) illustrates how scenarios are used to deal with the inherent difficulty of doing design. Drawing on the task–artefact cycle to show the position in product development, he argues that scenarios are effective at dealing with five key problems of design:

Chapter 2, Section 2.1 introduced our version of the task-artefact cycle

- The external factors that constrain design such as time constraints, lack of resources, having to fit in with existing designs and so on.
- Design moves have many effects and create many possibilities, i.e. a single design decision can have an impact in many areas and these need to be explored and evaluated.

- How scientific knowledge and generic solutions lag behind specific situations. This point concerns *generalities*. In other design disciplines, general design solutions to general design problems have evolved over the years. In interactive systems design this does not happen because the technology changes as soon as, or even before, general solutions have been discovered.
- The importance of reflection and action in design.
- The slippery nature of design problems.

Rosson and Carroll (2002) describe an approach to scenario-based design in which scenarios are used throughout the design process and how they help designers to justify the claims that they make about design issues. Design is

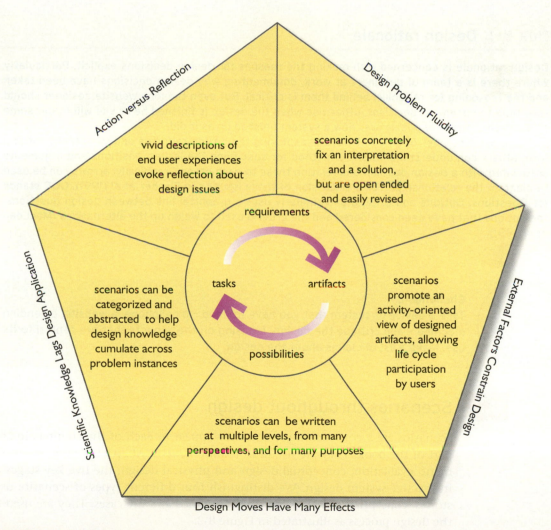

FIGURE 8-1 Challenges and approaches in scenario-based design *(source: after Carroll (2000)* Making Use: Scenario-based Design of Human Computer Interactions, *Figure 3.2, p. 69. Published and reprinted by permission of The MIT Press)*

characterized by trade-offs. There is rarely a simple solution to a problem that solves all the issues. Usually the adoption of one design will mean that something else cannot be achieved. Designers need to document their design decisions so that the trade-offs can be evaluated. Scenarios help by making the rationale for the design explicit (Box 8-1). Designers can record the claims that they make about their designs. *Claims analysis* is an important part of scenario-based design and is used in identifying problems or in thinking through possible future designs (Rosson and Carroll, 2002). The process is simply to identify key features of a scenario and to list good and bad aspects of the design. Rosson and Carroll use a technique of putting a '+' beside good features and a '–' beside bad features. Claims analysis makes the rationale behind a design explicit.

Box 8-1 Design rationale

Design rationale is concerned with making the reasons for design decisions explicit. Particularly where there is a team of designers at work, documenting why design decisions have been taken and the reasoning (or rationale) behind them is critical. But even the lone website designer should take time to document decisions, otherwise when the design is finished he or she will forget some of the details and may puzzle over how a system finished up as it did.

There are a number of different ways of capturing the design rationale and representing it in a form others can understand. IBIS is a method for specifying the issues, positions and arguments associated with a design decision and relating these to each other. Graphically, arrows can be used to diagram the relationships. For a discussion of these issues see Fischer *et al* (1991). QOC stands for Questions, Options and Criteria and similarly uses a graphical link between design questions, the options that have been considered and the criteria used to weigh up the alternatives (MacLean *et al*, 1991).

Challenge 8-1
Take a device or system that you have to hand - a cellphone, a website, a vending machine - and critique the design, focusing on the aspects that are central to its use. Make a list of claims about the design.

8.2 Scenarios throughout design

Scenarios are a core technique and they appear in each of the chapters in this part of the book. They are useful in requirements work, prototyping, envisionment, evaluation, conceptual design and physical design: the five key stages of interactive system design. We distinguish four different types of scenario: user stories, conceptual scenarios, concrete scenarios and use cases. They are used in the design process as illustrated in Figure 8-2.

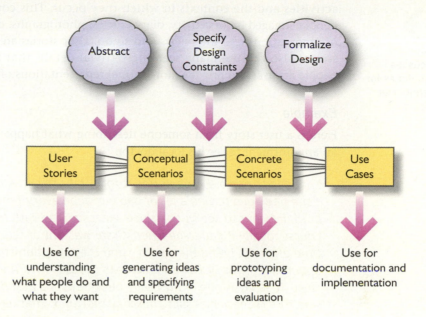

FIGURE 8-2 Scenarios throughout design

At different stages of the design process, scenarios are helpful in understanding current practice and any problems or difficulties that people may be having, in generating and testing ideas, in documenting and communicating ideas to others and in evaluating designs.

User stories are the real-world experiences of people. Conceptual scenarios are more abstract descriptions in which some details have been stripped away. Concrete scenarios are generated from abstract scenarios by adding specific design decisions and once completed these can be represented as use cases. The lines joining the types of scenario indicate the relationships between them. Many user stories will be represented by a few conceptual scenarios. However, each conceptual scenario may generate many concrete scenarios. Several concrete scenarios will be represented by a single use case. The difference between these types is elaborated below.

Figure 8-2 also illustrates three critical processes involved in design and how they interact with the different scenario types. Designers abstract from the details of user stories to arrive at conceptual scenarios. They specify design constraints on conceptual scenarios to arrive at concrete scenarios. Finally they formalize the design ideas as use cases.

User stories

User stories are the real-world experiences, ideas, anecdotes and knowledge of people. These may be captured in any form and comprise small snippets of

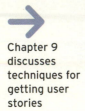

Chapter 9 discusses techniques for getting user stories

activities and the contexts in which they occur. This could include videos of people engaged in an activity, diary entries, photographs, documents, the results of observations and interviews and so on. User stories are rich in context. User stories also capture many seemingly trivial details that are usually left out if people are asked to provide more formal representations of what they do.

Example

Here is a user story from someone describing what happened last time he made an appointment to see his local doctor.

I needed to make an appointment for Kirsty, my little one. It wasn't urgent – she had been having a lot of bad ear-ache every time she had a cold – but I did want to see Dr Fox since she's so good with the children. And of course ideally it had to be when Kirsty was out of school and I could take time off work. I rang the surgery and the receptionist told me that the next appointment for Dr Fox was the next Tuesday afternoon. That was no good since Tuesday is one of my really busy days so I asked when the next one was. The receptionist said Thursday morning. That meant making Kirsty late for school but I agreed because they sounded very busy – the other phone kept ringing in the background – and I was in a hurry myself. It was difficult to suggest a better time without knowing which appointments were still free.

Conceptual scenarios

Conceptual scenarios are more abstract than user stories. Much of the context is stripped away during the process of **abstraction** (see Box 8-2) and similar stories are combined together. Conceptual scenarios are particularly useful for generating design ideas and for *understanding* the requirements of the system.

Example

Once the designer has accumulated a collection of user stories, common elements will start to emerge. In this case a number of stories such as the one above result in the conceptual scenario below describing some requirements for a computerised appointments system.

Booking an appointment
People with any degree of basic computer skills will be able to contact the doctors' surgery at any time via the Internet and see the times which are free for each doctor. They can book a time and receive confirmation of the appointment.

Box 8-2 Abstraction

The process of abstraction is one of classification and aggregation: moving from the details of specific people undertaking specific activities in a specific context using a particular piece of technology to a more general description that still manages to catch the essence of the activity.

Aggregation is the process of treating a whole thing as a single entity rather than looking at the components of something. In most domains, for example, one would aggregate a screen, processor, disc drive, keyboard and mouse and treat this as a single thing – a computer – rather than focusing on the components. However, in another situation one of the components – processor speed, or disc size, say – may prove to be critical and so it would be better to have two aggregations: fast computers and slow computers, say.

Classification is the process of recognizing that things can be collected together, so that dealing with the class of things is simpler (more abstract) than dealing with the individual things. There are no set ways to classify things, so the analyst has to work with the stories that have been gathered and with the users themselves to decide which things belong together and why.

Between them aggregation and classification produce abstractions. Of course there are different degrees of abstraction and it is one of the skills of a designer to settle upon an appropriate level. The most abstract level is to treat everything simply as a 'thing' and every activity as 'doing something', but such an abstract representation is not usually very useful.

As you can see, at this stage, there is little or no specification of precise technologies or how the functions will be provided. The scenario could be made more abstract by not specifying that the Internet should be used or more concrete (that is less abstract) by specifying that the booking should be made from a computer rather than a mobile phone. Finding an appropriate level of abstraction at which to describe things for a given purpose is a key skill of the designer.

Concrete scenarios

Each conceptual scenario may generate lots of concrete scenarios. When designers are working on a particular problem or issue they will often identify some feature that applies only under certain circumstances. At this point they may develop a more specific elaboration of the scenario and link it to the original. Thus one reasonably abstract scenario may spawn several more concrete elaborations which are useful for exploring particular issues. Notes can be added to scenarios that draw attention to possible design features and problems.

Concrete scenarios also begin to dictate a particular interface design and a particular allocation of functions between people and devices. Concrete scenarios are particularly useful for prototyping and envisioning design ideas and for evaluation because they are more prescriptive about some aspects of the technology. However, there is not a clean break between conceptual and concrete scenarios. The more specific the scenario is about some aspects, the more concrete it is.

Example

In the example below, decisions have now been taken concerning drop-down menus, the fact that the next two weeks' details are to be shown, and so on. However, the notes following the scenario show that there are many design decisions still to be taken.

Booking an appointment/01

Andy Dalreach needs a doctor's appointment for his young daughter Kirsty in the next week or so. The appointment needs to be outside school-time and Andy's core working hours, and ideally with Dr Fox, who is the children's specialist. Andy uses a PC and the Internet at work, so has no difficulty in running up the appointments booking system. He logs in [1] and from a series of drop-down boxes, chooses to have free times for Dr Fox [2] displayed for the next two weeks ... [the scenario would continue to describe how Andy books the appointment and receives confirmation]

Notes to booking an appointment/01

1. *Is logging in necessary? Probably, to discourage bogus users, but check with the surgery.*
2. *Free times can be organized by doctor, by time of day, or by next available time. Drop-down boxes will save screen space but may present problems for less experienced users or those with poor eyesight.*

Use cases

A use case describes the interaction between people (or other 'actors') and devices. It is a case of how the system is used and hence needs to describe what people do and what the system does. Each use case covers many slight variations in circumstances – many concrete scenarios. The lines in Figure 8-2 indicate how many concrete scenarios result, after the process of specification and coding, in a few use cases.

Before use cases can be specified, tasks and functions have to be allocated to humans or to the device. The specification of use cases both informs and is informed by the task/function allocation process.

Finally, all the design issues will be resolved and the set of concrete scenarios are then used as the basis of the design. A set of use cases can be produced which specify the complete functionality of the system and the interactions that will occur. There are a number of different ways of representing use cases – from very abstract diagrams to detailed 'pseudo code'. Figure 8-3 shows the 'booking an appointment' use case in a typical format.

See also
Chapter 23 on
task analysis

To make an appointment:
Go to doctors' home page
Enter username and password
Select appointments for specific doctor
Browse available dates
Select suitable date and time
Enter patient's name
Click OK

FIGURE 8-3 Use case for booking an appointment

Box 8-3 Use cases

Despite the fact that use cases have been a core element of software engineering methods since the late 1980s, the concept remains elusive and different authors define a use case in different ways. In a section called 'use cases undefined', Constantine and Lockwood (2001) rage against the lack of clear definition for such a critical term. The definition used in the Unified Modeling Language (UML) – an attempt to provide commonly agreed specification concepts and notation for software engineering – is too lengthy and obscure to repeat here. They also point out that how the use case is specified – in a sort of pseudo programming code as we have done, or simply using the diagrammatic ellipse and named role as some do, or otherwise – also varies considerably between authors and methods.

It is also the case that use cases are used at different levels of abstraction. Constantine and Lockwood's 'essential use cases' are similar to the conceptual scenarios described here and there are others who base a whole design method on use case modelling. We reserve the term 'use case' for describing an implementable system, i.e. enough interface features have been specified, and the allocation of functions between people and the system has been completed, so that the use case describes a coherent sequence of actions between an actor and a system. The term 'actor' is used here because sometimes we need to specify use cases between one part of the system (a 'system actor') and another, but usually the actor is a person.

Challenge 8-2
Find a vending machine or other relatively simple device and observe people using it. Write down these user stories. Produce one or conceptual scenarios from the user stories.

8.3 Documenting scenarios

Chapter 2 describes PACT

Scenarios can become messy, so in order to control the scenarios a structure is needed. We use the PACT framework (people, activities, contexts, technologies) to critique scenarios and to encourage designers to get a good description of the scenario. For each scenario the designer lists the different people who are involved, the activities they are undertaking, the contexts of those activities and the technologies that are being used. We also structure scenario descriptions. Each scenario should be given an introduction. The history and authorship can be recorded, along with a description of how the scenario generalizes (across which domains) and the rationale for the scenario. Each paragraph of each scenario should be numbered for ease of reference and endnotes included where particular design issues are raised. Endnotes are particularly useful in documenting issues raised during the development of the scenario. They are a way of capturing the claims being made about the scenarios (Rosson and Carroll, 2002). Examples of relevant data and media should be collected.

There is a full description of the Edinburgh Festival scenario in Section 14.2

When working in a large design team, it is useful to accompany scenarios by real data. This means that different team members can share concrete examples and use these as a focus of discussion. Another key feature of writing scenarios is to think hard about the assumptions that are being made: to make assumptions explicit or deliberately avoid making things explicit in order to provoke debate. In the Edinburgh Festival scenario in Chapter 4, for example, the couple are deliberately kept gender neutral so discussions about gender issues can be either avoided or confronted. In another scenario an elderly woman with arthritis might be one of the characters, thus foregrounding issues of access and the physically impaired interacting with technology.

Chapter 4 introduces the HIC case study

Finally with these scenarios it is important to provide a very rich context. The guiding principles for scenario writing are people, activities, contexts and technologies. An example of a structured scenario from the Home Information Centre (HIC) case study is given below. Although grounded in a concrete example and in a specific context, this is still quite conceptual in that it is used to generate ideas and designs. It concerns the development of an MP3 music player for the HIC.

Scenario MP3/01 – 'How does that song go again?'

P1. Anne is a freelance arts journalist who works mainly from home. She's writing a piece for a national newspaper about singer-songwriters, and is irritated to find she can't remember the lyrics of a particular well-known song she wants to quote in her article. She knows the name of the singer and the song title, but beyond that, her memory is failing her.

P2. She leaves her desk, hoping a break and a cup of coffee will dispel the block. While in the kitchen, she decides she'll check the HIC for new messages [1]. While she is doing this, she realizes the HIC's MP3 player [2] can help her out.

SCENARIO MP3/01	
Title	'How does that song go again?'
Scenario type	Activity scenario
Overview	People = Single female, computer literate. Works at home.
	Activities = Searching for MP3 tracks by user input.
	Context = Apartment with office/study space where user works from home. HIC is in the kitchen, which is adjacent to the study.
	Technology = The HIC and a PC
Rationale	The opening narrative depicts the contrasts between the 'move around' situation of the HIC and the 'lean forward' usage of a PC workstation. The context is one where the user works at home, and both PC and HIC are in use for different purposes in the same environment. In the scenario, the HIC is used to resolve a query arising directly from use of the workstation. The substantive activity here is the use of the search function to find a specific MP3 track. The use of different search parameters is described. The user interrogates the HIC using keyboard input; future elaborations might deal with other modalities such as voice input.

She remembers she has downloaded the song [3] she needs at some time in the past two months or so, and knows it's still in the HIC's memory [4].

P3. She selects the 'play' function (Level 1 of the HIC's actions bar) [5], which takes her down one level in the HIC interface, to where she can see 'MP3 search' [6]. She selects this and the familiar Rolodex interface comes up, asking her to enter some search details. She can search by entering an artist name, track title, or music genre – these are all elements of an MP3 track's identity which the HIC can recognize. She is about to enter the artist's name, but realizes she has stored several of this singer's tracks in the HIC; to get a unique search result first time, she enters the track name instead, using the keyboard [7].

P4. The HIC quickly finds the track and asks her [8] if she wants to play it now. She does, and selects this option by touching the screen [9]. The MP3 controller appears on the screen, with the selected track already loaded and ready to play.

P5. She touches the 'play' button and listens. She increases the volume [10]. The lyrics she wants come back to her straight away – she can now go back to her desk. She leaves the HIC on [11] (without thinking).

P6. Later on, she has finished her piece and e-mailed it to her editor. But she wants to hear the song again, as it has sentimental memories for her. Fortunately, she has left the HIC on in MP3 mode. All she needs to do is select 'replay' and the song plays again.

P7. She decides she has put in enough time at the computer for the day, and feels like watching some TV. She chooses the TV device on the HIC and settles down to watch the early evening news [12].

Notes to scenario MP3/01

1. Checking messages is peripheral to the MP3 domain, but it is interesting to consider how MP3-related activities fit in with other domains of the HIC. Multiple screen objects will soon start to compete with each other for screen space.

2. 'MP3 player' is meant here in the general sense of the MP3 domain – that is, all the functions relating to MP3.

3. How she has done this is not described here – but see scenario MP3/02 for a more detailed account of this activity.

4. The question of how the HIC stores MP3 and other files is a significant one. One of the popular features of the MP3 format is the ease with which files can be shuffled from one platform to another; this will involve frequent use of saving, copying, deleting and other functions. This may imply the need for some sort of 'File Manager' function in the HIC (cf. scenarios MP3/02, /03, /04).

5. The Actions Bar is now a well-established part of the HIC prototype. Here, Anne goes one level down the HIC's navigation hierarchy to get to the MP3 domain, and her point of entry is the 'play' icon, found on the Actions Bar. But there may be other points of entry too – say, from a 'favourites' menu or similar.

6. The MP3 domain may be made up of different modules – a 'player' with functional controls, a search function, track lists, and so on. Some or all of these may be present on screen at one time; this raises the question of what the 'default' configuration will be: only the basic functional controls? All the different modules? And how will the user call these up or dismiss them as required?

7. Consider other modalities too: handwritten using a stylus and pressure pad? Voice input?

8. How is the search result presented to Anne? It may be in the form of a list, with the results containing the parameters she gave the HIC. The search may return several results, and there should be a way for her to unambiguously select a track from a list. This could be tricky unless the text is at a good size and spacing for touching on a screen – unless some other selection method is used.

9. She is close to the screen – but could she select the option remotely too?

10. Perhaps the HIC could sample the level of background noise in the area, and adjust the playback volume automatically.

11. Is there a screen saver?

12. What happens to the MP3 interface when the TV comes on? Presumably the whole of the HIC's information space will be filled by the TV image. Other functions and controls will need to be cleared from the screen (perhaps returning automatically when the TV is turned off). Or they could be reduced greatly in size, and put onto a display bar on the periphery of the screen. Perhaps there could be a 'bring to front' command (operated remotely, or by voice?) to make other controls available while the TV was still active.

Cross-referencing scenario types

Another aspect of documentation that is useful is to cross-reference the user stories to the conceptual scenarios, through the concrete examples and finally to the use cases. In the HIC case a simple Web-based system was developed as illustrated in Figure 8-4.

Other researchers have suggested similar ideas that capture the multiple views necessary to see how scenarios and claims work together to provide a rich understanding of how a design finished as it did.

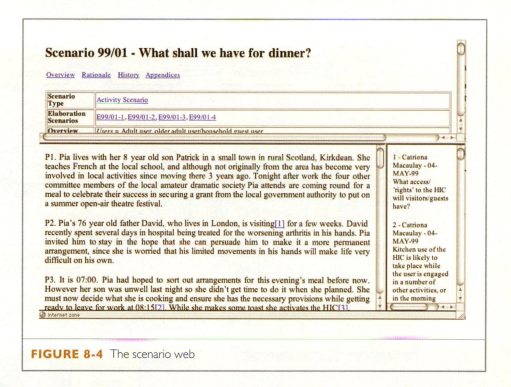

FIGURE 8-4 The scenario web

Chapter 13
discusses the
method in
more detail

8.4 A scenario-based design method

The use of the different types of scenarios throughout design can be formalized into a scenario-based design method. This is illustrated in Figure 8-5 with, once again, products of the design process shown as boxes and processes shown as clouds. Besides the four different types of scenario, four other artefacts are produced during the design process: requirements/problems, scenario corpus, object model and design language. The specification of a system is the combination of all the different products produced during the development process.

Each of the main processes – requirements, envisionment, prototyping, evaluation, conceptual and physical design – is the subject of a chapter in this part of the book. An important thing to notice is the relationship between specifying design

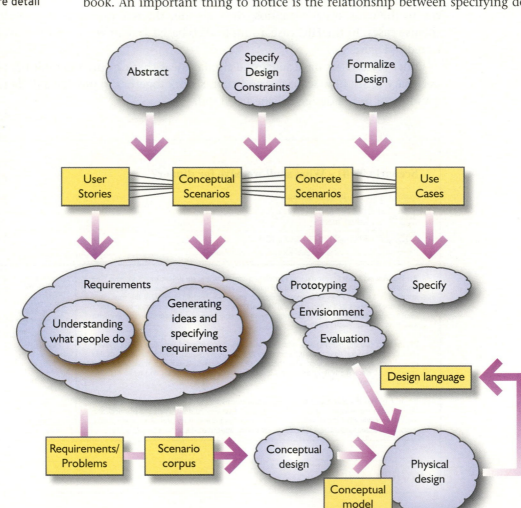

FIGURE 8-5 Overall scenario-based design method

constraints and the use of scenarios. For prototyping, envisionment and most evaluation, the scenarios have to be made more concrete. This means imposing design constraints. However, this does not mean that the designer needs to design a new physical, concrete scenario each time he or she wants to envision a possible design. It may be that designers imagine a scenario with particular design constraints imposed and this helps them evaluate the design. This sort of 'what if … ?' generation and evaluation of concrete scenarios is a common and key aspect of design.

The key products that have not been discussed so far are requirements and problems, scenario corpus, conceptual model and design language. These are briefly introduced below.

Requirements and problems

See
Chapter 12 on
requirements

In the gathering of user stories and during the analysis and abstraction process various issues and difficulties will come to light. These help the analyst/designer to establish a list of requirements – qualities or functions that any new product or system should have. For example, in the HIC example, the device has to be used by the elderly and short-sighted. Another requirement was that it should look good in a living room and should not look or behave like a personal computer running Microsoft Windows. The format of the requirements and problems is a prioritized list of issues, or a more formalized format.

Scenario corpus

In our approach we seek to develop a representative and carefully thought-through set, or corpus, of scenarios. Having undertaken some analysis activities designers will have gathered a wide range of user stories. Some of these will be very general and some will be quite specific. Some will be fairly simple, straightforward tasks; others will be more vague. It is important at some point for the designer to pull these disparate experiences together in order to get a high-level, abstract view of the main activities that the product is to support. These conceptual scenarios will often still be grounded in a real example; the trick is to find an example that shares characteristics with a number of other activities.

The rationale for the development of a corpus of scenarios is to uncover the 'dimensions' of the design situation and to demonstrate different aspects of those dimensions. Dimensions include characteristics of the various domains within which the product will operate (e.g. large and small domains, volatile or static domains, etc.), the various media and data types that need to be accommodated and the characteristics of the people who will be using the system. The corpus of scenarios needs to cover all the main functions of the system and the events that trigger the functions. Different types of interaction need to be present along with any key usability issues. The dimensions include different types of content and how that can be structured, issues of style and aesthetics.

A corpus of scenarios might consist of several scenarios depending on the complexity of the domain. For example, in the HIC study we had 11, and for the MP3 application (which of course is much more specific – just playing, sorting and organizing MP3 files) we had five. The aim is to specify the scenarios at a level of abstraction that captures an appropriate level of generality that will be useful across the range of characteristics that is demonstrated within a domain.

Conceptual model

Chapter 13, Section 13.2 describes object/action analysis

An object or data model results from the process of conceptual modelling, including developing the scenarios and undertaking an object/action analysis of the scenario corpus. The conceptual model shows the main objects in the system, their attributes and the relationships that exist between them. Conceptual modelling is a very important part of interactive systems design that is often overlooked. Having a clear, well-designed conceptual model will make it easier to design so that people can develop a good, accurate mental model of the system. The conceptual model will also form the basis of the information architecture of a system and for any metaphor that is used in the design. Two famous conceptual models are the concept of the spreadsheet and the various objects such as printers, folders, documents, etc. that make up the 'desktop' metaphor of the Windows and Mac OS operating systems.

Design language

We return to this in Chapter 13

The design language produced consists of a set of standard patterns of interaction and all the physical attributes of a design – the colours, shapes, icons and so on. These are brought together with the conceptual actions and objects and the 'look and feel' of the design is completed. A 'design language' defines the key elements of the design (such as the use of colour, style and types of buttons, sliders and other widgets, etc.) and some principles and rules for putting them together. A consistent design language means that users need learn only a limited number of design elements and then they can cope with a large variety of different situations.

Challenge 8-3
Take a look at the operating system that you use on your computer and identify some key elements of the design language that is used.

Summary and key points

This chapter has introduced the main elements of scenario-based design. Scenarios and their different uses in this process have been explored.

■ Scenarios are stories about the interactions between people, activities, contexts and technologies.

■ Scenarios offer an effective way of exploring and representing activities, enabling the designer to generate ideas, consider solutions and communicate with others.

■ Scenarios are used throughout the design process and, as use cases, form part of the formal specification of the system.

Further reading

Carroll, J.M. (ed.) (1995) *Scenario-based Design*. Wiley, New York.

Carroll, J.M. (2000) *Making Use: Scenario-based Design of Human–Computer Interactions*. MIT Press, Cambridge, MA.

Rosson, M.-B. and Carroll, J. (2002) *Usability Engineering*. Morgan Kaufmann, San Francisco.

John (Jack) Carroll has been hugely influential in the area of human–computer interaction over many years and with his wife, Mary-Beth Rosson, has written extensively on scenario-based design. The first of these books is a collection of papers showing how the scenario concept appears in a variety of guises throughout human–computer interaction and software engineering. The second is compiled from many of his writings and presents a thoughtful and coherent approach to developing systems using scenarios. It illustrates how scenarios are appropriate in all the stages of systems development. The third is a practical design book.

Scenarios and use cases appear in a variety of guises in the literature on software engineering, human–computer interaction and interaction design. The ideas of abstract scenarios are very similar to the ideas of essential use cases (Constantine and Lockwood, 2001).

Comments on challenges

Challenge 8-1
Of course this will depend on the device you have chosen and on how you approach the critique. The design principles (Chapter 3) are a good way to think about designs. A critique of a vending machine, for example, might include the claims:

+ Useful for out-of-hours sales
− Limited selection of goods
+ Quick interaction
− Does not always give change
− Mis-operation results in lengthy and time-consuming complaints
− High service costs

Challenge 8-2
A man wearing an overcoat and carrying a backpack came up to the machine and stared at it for two or three minutes. Whilst he was doing this two younger men came up behind him and were trying to look over his shoulder. Finally, he put his hand in his pocket and inserted some money. He pressed two buttons, B and 7, and watched as a packet of crisps was deposited in the tray.

You can imagine a few more stories such as this, resulting in a conceptual scenario along the lines of 'A person comes up to the machine, studies the instructions and what is available, inserts money, presses two buttons and retrieves the goods.'

Challenge 8-3
Key aspects of the design language are standard features of things such as windows and the different types of windows (some that are resizeable, some that are not, etc.). Other features include the design of menus, dialogue boxes, alert boxes and so on. The colours are also consistent and chosen to evoke different feelings in people.

Exercises

1. Find someone using some technology to do something and observe what they do. Now write down the user story associated with that activity. Abstract a conceptual scenario from this one experience, by removing the contextual detail and other details about the specific interface to the technology. Now think of an alternative design for a device

that would allow someone to undertake a similar activity and generate a concrete scenario based on these design constraints. Finally, specify this as a use case.

2. Develop a scenario corpus for people using a vending machine. Consider the dimensions of the usage, the contexts for the interaction and the range of people that you would want to consider.

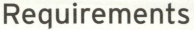

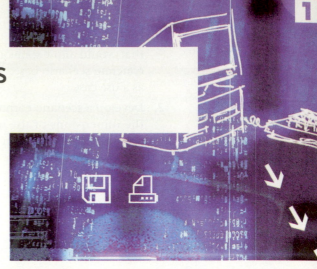

Requirements

Aims

Before creative design can start it is essential that the designer develops a clear and thorough understanding of the *people* who will be involved with the product or system, the *activities* that are the focus of the design, the *contexts* in which those activities take place and the implications for the design of *technologies*: 'PACT'. From this understanding designers generate the requirements for the system that is to be designed. However, it is rarely possible to acquire a thorough understanding of requirements until some design work has been completed. Requirements work, the design process, representations of design and evaluation are tightly interwoven.

Requirements work is about understanding what people do, or might want to do, and about any problems they are having with the current system. It is also about understanding how people do what they do, so that designers can develop technologies that make aspects of everyday life more efficient or more enjoyable.

In this chapter we present the main techniques for understanding people's activities and encapsulating this for design. In software engineering or information systems projects, this is a formal step which is usually termed **user requirements analysis**. After studying this chapter you should be able to:

- Understand what requirements are
- Understand the range of requirements techniques
- Use techniques for understanding people and their activities in context
- Document the results as requirements on interactive technologies.

9.1   # What are requirements?

A requirement is '… something the product must do or a quality that the product must have' (Robertson and Robertson, 1999). Designers will study current activities and gather user stories and soon will have generated a great deal of information about the current situation and about people's aspirations. The task now is to turn this into requirements for a new product or system. Sometimes this is straightforward, but often it will need a creative leap. This is why the analysis/design/evaluation process is so iterative. The accuracy of the guess can only be judged when users or clients review the requirements, something that is best done with the aid of scenarios and early designs or a prototype. Just to further complicate matters, additional requirements will emerge as the design process continues.

Often clients will require a **requirements specification** – a formal document which contains the requirements. Developers also need a clear requirements specification at some point in the development process so that they can cost the project and manage it successfully. Requirements should be expressed in clear, unambiguous language, and worded so that it will be possible to test whether the requirement has been met in the final product.

Conventionally, requirements are divided into two types, **functional** and **non-functional**. Functional requirements are what the system must *do*. For example, in the DISCOVER virtual training environment (Box 9-1):

■ Trainers must be able to modify the virtual environment with events such as fires when the simulation is running.

Or for the HIC home information system:

■ The system must connect to existing content providers.

Or for a multi-function PDA (personal digital assistant):

■ Phone functions must be accessible while connected to the Internet.

Box 9-1 The DISCOVER project

This was a European research and development project concerned with the provision of training to manage safety-critical incidents in the maritime and offshore industries. Incidents such as fires and damage to the structure of ships or offshore platforms, or situations such as ships setting sail with the doors to the hold left open, can be disastrous. Everyone concerned with these areas recognizes the importance of providing appropriate training, but it is almost prohibitively expensive. Current methods require trainees to be co-located at a specialist training site, often equipped with costly physical simulators. DISCOVER aimed to provide a CVE (collaborative virtual environment) in which team training could take place using computer simulations. This would dramatically reduce the need for senior mariners and oil rig workers to have to attend courses at specialist centres. While the system would be made available at such institutions, it was also intended to be used over the Internet from offshore or on board ship. A fuller account of DISCOVER may be found in Turner and Turner (2001).

▶

The project consortium comprised four European marine and offshore training organizations, virtual reality (VR) technology specialists, training standards bodies, a number of employer organizations and the UK university where two of the authors were based. Their role in the project was to establish the requirements for the system.

The approach taken to identifying requirements on the CVE included much fieldwork at training centres. Training sessions were videotaped, transcribed and analysed. Trainees – senior personnel when in their normal roles – were interviewed and debriefed after practice sessions, and other interviews were carried out with assessors, instructors, trainers and the operators of physical simulators of ships' bridges and oil platform control rooms. We found that current training centred on role-playing exercises, allowing trainees to adopt different roles in emergency situations derived closely from real-life incidents. All the training role-plays followed a generic pattern of an incident steadily becoming more serious, the exact plot being adapted dynamically by the trainers depending on the actions and reactions of the 'crew'. Supporting 'technology' ranged from highly realistic, full-size physical simulations to a wooden model of a section through a ship where miniature figures representing crew and passengers could be moved around.

From the earliest stages of our involvement we exploited scenarios coupled with the prototype CVE as the focus of discussions with trainees and tutors. They also proved effective with more senior representatives from the training centres and software developers as an aid to clarifying design issues. Eventually a set of requirements, illustrated by scenarios, were produced and agreed by all concerned. The list was a long one, but core requirements included a strong sense of realism, the ability for tutors to modify elements of the environment in real time, and the ability for tutors to monitor and communicate with trainees. (More about the requirements work can be found in some of the examples used to illustrate this chapter.)

The CVE prototype ran on networked desktop PCs, the only special-purpose equipment being high specification soundcards and audio headsets. The environment represented the interior of a ship (maritime version) or an offshore platform (offshore version). Trainees were represented as avatars in the environment. They were designed to mimic real action as closely as possible, and had access to a small number of interactive objects such as fire extinguishers, alarm panels and indeed bodies. Communication again imitated the real world, being mediated through voice when in the same room, or virtual telephone, walkie-talkie or PA when avatars were not co-present. Tutors were not embodied as avatars, but had the ability to teleport to any part of the environment, to see the location of trainees on a map or through a bird's eye view, to track particular trainees and to modify the environment in limited ways, for example by setting fires or locking doors.

We evaluated the environment from the earliest versions of the prototype, at first concentrating on basic issues of usability such as movement in the environment and later trialling more realistic training scenarios. Evaluation sessions typically required participants to carry out a task or series of tasks, while being observed, and usually videotaped. Immediately after the test sessions short interviews were conducted and in some trials usability and VR-related questionnaires were administered. In brief, the main results indicated that while a lack of realism and flexibility precluded its use for higher-level command-and-control skills, the CVE could support routine low-level training in such activities as learning the layout of a new ship or the procedure for communications in the case of an emergency. (There is more about the DISCOVER evaluation process in Chapters 12 and 22.)

Non-functional requirements are a quality that the system must *have*: they concern the way the functionality operates. These may be the crucial factors in the acceptability, sales or usage of a product. They cover a number of aspects of design, including image, usability, performance, maintainability, security, cultural acceptability and legal restrictions. Here are some non-functional examples.

For DISCOVER:

■ The training environment must be validated by the training standards organizations.

For the HIC:

■ Elderly people with limited dexterity must be able to use the input devices.

For a multi-function PDA:

■ The system must present an up-market, business-like image.

For both types of requirements, note that how the technology will meet the requirement is not specified. This is a later part of the design task. It is best to supplement the list of requirements with some supporting evidence – interview or observation reports, photographs of artefacts, video snippets if practicable. This helps readers of the requirements specification to understand the reason behind items in the list.

Further thoughts: Requirements templates

We strongly advise the use of a standard format, or template, for specifying requirements. The exact presentation of the information is not important, but at a minimum it should include for each requirement:

■ A unique reference number, ideally also coding whether the requirement is functional or non-functional
■ A one-sentence summary
■ The source(s) of the requirement
■ The rationale for it.

As Robertson and Robertson (1999) suggest, there are additional elements which will greatly add to the value of the requirements specification. The most significant of these are:

■ The criteria for measuring whether the requirement has been satisfied
■ A grade for the importance of the requirement, e.g. on a scale of 1–5
■ Dependencies and conflicts with other requirements
■ Change history.

Prioritizing requirements

Requirements should be reviewed with users and clients and modified as necessary. Decisions will almost always be made about the relative priority of the requirements, since few design projects have unlimited resources. One way of doing this is by using the '**MoSCoW rules**'. These classify requirements into:

- **M**ust have – fundamental requirements without which the system will be unworkable and useless, effectively the minimum usable subset
- **S**hould have – would be essential if more time were available, but the system will be useful and usable without them
- **C**ould have – of lesser importance, therefore can more easily be left out of the current development
- **W**ant to have but **W**on't have this time round – can wait till a later development.

The MoSCoW rules are part of the **DSDM** (Dynamic Systems Development) method, a well-used and documented approach which aims to produce usable and useful systems under tight time constraints. The MoSCoW section of the very comprehensive DSDM website can be found at http://www.dsdm.org/en/about/moscow.asp.

Challenge 9-1
Which of these requirements on the HIC are functional and which non-functional? Discuss issues of prioritizing the requirements.

1. Unobtrusive in the home environment
2. Option to print out details
3. Fast download of information
4. Direct 'panic' link to the emergency services
5. Volume control/mute features
6. Customizable to support choice of languages, including those with different character sets
7. Provides e-mail
8. Security for each individual user.

9.2 Participative design and requirements

There has always been much debate about which of the following the requirements activity should be called:

- Requirements gathering, which suggests requirements are lying around waiting to be picked up with little interaction between designer and users
- Requirements generation, which suggests a more creative activity, but tends to de-emphasize links to users' current practice
- Requirements elicitation – our preferred term, since it suggests some user–designer interaction
- Requirements engineering – often used in software engineering projects, usually a very formal approach.

Whichever term you prefer, requirements work involves using a variety of techniques to understand and analyse someone else's needs and aspirations. This is not easy, but talking to people using interviews, observing people and recording their activities on video, organizing focus groups, workshops, etc. will all help the analyst to understand both the requirements for the new design and the problems people are having with the existing system. As we have seen, these activities result in a large number of stories being acquired that form the basis for the analysis work. Recasting several similar stories into more structured scenarios will also help the analyst to understand and generate requirements.

Throughout this book we emphasize the need to take a human-centred approach to design. Firstly, it is important that human characteristics and activities are taken into account. But beyond this, wherever possible, it is right that the people who will use new interactive technologies have an input to the design process itself. We include the qualification 'wherever possible' not because we think that it is ever proper to exclude user interests from the design process, but because in large-scale commercial products it is feasible to involve only a tiny proportion of those who will use the eventual product. The situation is very different from the development of custom-made systems for a small group of people, where it is genuinely feasible for users to act as co-designers and so acquire some 'ownership' of the technology to be introduced.

Further thoughts: The socio-technical tradition

This design philosophy of involving people in the design of their systems is usually attributed to the Scandinavian tradition of worker participation in the management of the workplace. There are also links to the British socio-technical design movement. This started with an emphasis on human considerations in the design of systems to support manual work, such as coal mining, but later evolved methods for user involvement in the design of computer-based systems. The work of Enid Mumford at Manchester, and Ken Eason, Leela Damodoran, Susan Harker and their colleagues at Loughborough University and elsewhere, is central to this development of the socio-technical approach. Methods embodying the socio-technical philosophy included Mumford's ETHICS (Mumford, 1983, 1993), the HUFIT toolkit (Taylor, 1990), which provided a comprehensive, practical set of techniques for working with users, and ORDIT (Eason *et al*. 1996), which aimed to incorporate organizational considerations into systems design.

Challenge 9-2
Incorporating input from users in the requirements process helps to ensure that the eventual technologies have a good fit with the people, activities and contexts they are designed to support. There is also a strong ethical argument for user involvement. Can you think of another reason for doing this?

9.3 Interviews

One of the most effective ways of finding out what people want and what problems they have at the moment is to talk to them! Interviews with all the various stakeholders in the domain is a vital way of gathering user stories. Designers employ a range of different styles of interview. The *structured* interview uses questions which are developed beforehand. The interview follows the wording exactly. Public opinion polls, for example of the sort produced in great numbers before elections, are normally based on structured interviews. Structured interviews are reasonably easy to carry out, simply because of the degree of pre-structuring. However, people are limited to very restricted replies, and it is difficult for the interviewer to follow up the unexpected response. Here is an extract from a structured interview pro-forma about a student information system.

Thinking about the Department's website, about how often would you say that you have used the following features during the last week:

Timetable information	not at all ☐	most days ☐	every day ☐	more than once a day ☐
Staff home pages	not at all ☐	most days ☐	every day ☐	more than once a day ☐
Module information	not at all ☐	most days ☐	every day ☐	more than once a day ☐

Designers very frequently use *semi-structured* interviews. Sometimes, the interviewer is armed with pre-prepared questions, but can reword these as appropriate and explore new topics as they arise. Often, the interviewer simply prepares a checklist, sometimes with suitable prompts such as 'Tell me about the first things you do when you get into the office in the morning …'. Clearly, this free-form approach is more demanding for the interviewer, but the data obtained does generally repay the effort.

An example of such an interview is shown in Figure 9-1, with some annotations about interviewing technique. The interview is designed to start at a high level, then to probe at a greater level of detail. The analyst's checklist of topics to cover for this example included the type of information needed, current sources (paper or online), and specific examples of information needs.

Completely *unstructured* interviews are sometimes used where it is particularly important to minimize designers' preconceptions, or where very little background information is available beforehand. As the term suggests, there are no preset questions or topics beyond the general subject of the project in question.

Challenge 9-3
What sort of information is likely to be missed by interviews? Why?

Interviewer What sort of things do you need information about
in a typical week?

Interviewee Well, I'm afraid I don't always get to lectures – I work
part-time – so I will often need to check what the lecture
covered and important dates for things like coursework hand-ins.
They always seem to be changing tutorial rooms, so I like to check that as well.

Interviewer So you need to find the academic material for lectures you've missed.

Even for the ones I've been to actually. I'm not very good at taking notes.
nd then there's all the information about dates and places and so on ?

do look on the noticeboard but there's such a lot of stuff on there and
ot sure it's always up-to-date or what applies to me. It's a bit easier on
anet but not much.

here do   k for information now? Let's start with the room changes
– you said you checked   oth the noticeboard and the Intranet?

Interviewee Well I do, but ideally I'd ask someone reliable from my group. Then I'd be
sure I was getting the whole story…

Interviewer So what else might you ask about?

> Interviewer reflects back what has been said.

> Interviewer has not foreseen this, but the flexible structure provides the chance to follow up.

FIGURE 9-1 Extract from a semi-structured interview

Stories, scenarios and early prototyping in interviewing

User stories and scenarios have already been introduced in Chapter 8.

They are helpful aids to understanding activities and help avoid having people imagine (or reconstruct) situations in the abstract. For example, people can be asked to recall a typical 'day in the life' or incidents when the current technology does not support what they need to do. This will identify circumstances that the new design must take into account. You will find that people naturally tell stories when describing what they do. One of the training staff being interviewed during requirements work in DISCOVER volunteered an anecdote concerning a trainee who was dismissed from his post after running 'his' ship aground in the physical simulator operated by the training centre. The story emphasized both the realism of current simulators and the serious treatment of performance in the training environment. In turn, this reinforced the importance of requirements for realism in the virtual training environment and the ability to document actions taken within it. The story itself also communicated the requirements to developers very vividly.

Once there is a rough idea of what the new technology might do, discussing a scenario will highlight many issues, from the naming of individual functions to the impact of changes in work practice. Prototypes – anything from paper sketches to semi-functioning products – are very often used to embody scenarios in possible technology. For example, in the later stages of analysis for a shared notebook for engineers, we used simple prototypes created in

PowerPoint coupled with small usage scenarios. These were projected on a screen and discussed in a small group meeting, prompting discussion about the match between our design ideas and the way the engineers currently disseminated information.

Whether or not a prototype is used, the analyst and the user 'walk through' the scenario, while the analyst probes for comments, problems, possible alternatives and suggestions in general. Depending on the outcome of the scenario/prototype walkthrough, modifications and further iterations may be desirable. Where many new issues emerge, it may be the case that the early concepts underlying the scenario or prototype are misconceived, and should be radically rethought.

There is much more detailed material about scenarios and prototypes in design in Chapters 10 and 11

Think aloud commentaries

When it is necessary to know a good deal of low-level detail about current technology, users can be asked to talk through the operations concerned – including their internal cognitive processes – as they use the technology in question. This data, properly termed a 'verbal protocol' (Ericsson and Simon, 1985), can provide helpful *indications* of current problems. It is important to remember, however, that by imposing the requirement to generate a commentary you are interfering with the very process you are attempting to study. Further, not all cognitive processes can be accessed by the conscious mind. The description of the 'contextual interview' in Beyer and Holtzblatt (1998) suggests some ways of alleviating this problem.

There is more about the contextual interview in Chapter 18

9.4 Practical considerations in interviewing

This section contains some practical 'hints and tips' from our experience of interviewing in a variety of analysis situations.

Preparation

Get to know the background. 'Idiot questions' can uncover unspoken assumptions, but use them deliberately, not by accident. Be careful about using people's own jargon until you are sure that you have it right. For work activities, background research might include studying company reports, brochures, websites and organization charts or scanning through software manuals and promotional materials. For home and leisure activities, what is relevant depends very largely on the context.

Keeping track of the interview

Interviewing is hard work and more effective if carried out by a pair of interviewers. One person can take the lead while the other makes notes. Of course, the note-taking burden is relieved if the interview is audio- or video-recorded. In this case, make sure you check the equipment before each session and periodically during the interview. Even when the interview is recorded, notes are still useful, especially if they include regular records of the time, which will help to find key points – it will take you one hour at the least to watch one hour of videotape even without any analysis or transcription. In addition, your notes will be vital if (for example) building work outside has muffled a section of the audio, or the heavy regional accent which was understandable face-to-face proves impenetrable on tape. A full transcription is rarely needed, but if it is, an audio-typist can save hours of your time. The typist will need briefing about any technical terms.

Telling stories

Just because telling stories and listening to them is such a natural thing to do, they can be misleading. As listeners, designers are looking for current problems, scope for improvements or endorsements of early design ideas. As storytellers, users may respond by giving such things disproportionate emphasis. You need to be aware of this in analysing interview data.

Reflection and exploration

Reflecting back during the interview helps confirm that you have understood what has been said. It is often a good idea to have the interviewee review a summary of the interview. This might be because the interviewee's knowledge is central to the new design, or sensitive material is involved, or the context is very unfamiliar. You should also look over the notes of the interview yourself to identify any points which need clarification.

General-purpose exploratory questions

These help the interview along, especially in the early stages or with a taciturn interviewee. Some we have found useful are:

- Tell me about your typical day.
- Tell me three good things about ...
- ... and three bad things.
- What if you had three wishes to make the application better?
- What has gone wrong with the application recently? How did you cope?
- What else should we have asked about?

When to stop

Deciding when to stop interviewing means balancing practical constraints against the comprehensiveness of the data. Certainly, all significant stakeholder groups must be covered. In the case of generic product development, Beyer and Holtzblatt (1998) suggest two or three interviewees per role (or type of stakeholder) across three or four different types of organizations. In many cases, client resources limit the process. With unlimited resources, the general rule is to stop once no new insights are being obtained. In DISCOVER, we interviewed two or three trainers from each of the four training organizations concerned. We also interviewed two representatives of an employer company (others being contacted via an e-mail questionnaire), and two members of different training validation organizations. Trainees themselves were more difficult to interview, because of constraints on their time, but several were interviewed informally in breaks during a training session. This was not an ideal interviewing process, but it is very representative of the level of coverage that is often achieved in practice.

9.5 Obtaining information from people at a distance

Most of the methods we discuss in this chapter involve working with people face-to-face. However, there are ways of obtaining requirements information at a distance. The most common of these is the questionnaire, but there are more ingenious, novel techniques as well.

Questionnaires: a cautionary note

Questionnaires are one way of streamlining the requirements process if a large number of people are to be surveyed and resources are not available to interview them individually. However, constructing a workable questionnaire is surprisingly *difficult* and time-consuming. It is a skilled task to devise the wording of questions when there are no opportunities to detect and clear up misunder-

Challenge 9-4

Consider the following items from a questionnaire about use of the Internet. Are there any problems with the wording? How could the items be improved?

(a) How often do you access the Internet? (tick one)
- Every day
- Most days
- About once a week
- About once a month
- Less than once a month

(b) Please list all types of material which you access frequently using the Internet.

standings as they happen. For this reason they are covered in the advanced material in Chapter 21. For small numbers of people – up to 10 or so – an interview will obtain the same information, and more, in a manageable way. This will consume little or no extra resource if the time required to construct a questionnaire is taken into account.

Cultural probes

'Cultural probes' were developed by Bill Gaver and colleagues (Gaver *et al.*, 1999) in working with elderly people located in three European cities. The overall aim was to design technologies which would foster greater participation in the community by older people. The designers first got to know the groups in person, then introduced them to the cultural probes packages. Each person received a collection of maps, postcards, a disposable camera and booklets – each item being carefully designed to stimulate interest and curiosity, and suggesting ways in which people could use it to send ideas back to the designers. They were '... designed to provoke inspirational responses' (*ibid*, p. 22). Postcards such as that shown in Figure 9-2, for example, asked people to list their favourite devices. The disposable cameras had customized covers which suggested scenes to be captured, such as 'the first person you will see today' or 'something boring'. Over a period of weeks, many of the probe materials were

FIGURE 9-2 Postcard used as a 'cultural probe' (*source: Gaver, W.W., Dunne, T. and Pacenti, E. (1999) Cultural Probes, Interactions, 6(1), pp. 21–29. © 1999 ACM, Inc. Reprinted by permission.*

sent back to the designers, carrying rich data about the lives of the elderly people. Not all items worked out as planned – the authors do not specify which – and the materials were selectively redesigned before being distributed to subsequent participants. All in all, the exercise was highly successful in capturing the general sense of what it meant to be elderly in the communities involved, although it is noted that the results did not have a direct impact on design.

9.6 Working with groups

An alternative to questionnaires for generating a wide range of issues from users in a relatively economical fashion is the focus group. Here a group of people are posed questions by facilitators and encouraged to react to each other's comments. If they are part of a group, users can be asked to describe how they cooperate to manage activities. Members of the group can stimulate each other's memories, and discussion may flow more naturally than in the single user interview. The approach is widely used – the early stages of the Joint Application Development (JAD) method (Wood and Silver, 1995), for example, employ a type of focus group comprising customers and developers in defining the scope and requirements for a new system.

As for single user interviews, the focus group can be enhanced by the use of scenarios and prototypes. However, group discussion may also inhibit comment about sensitive issues, for example deviations from official procedure, and can have the effect of highlighting unusual incidents disproportionately. Many techniques have been developed to support focus groups. One such example is CARD (Collaborative Analysis of Requirements and Design, Tudor *et al.*, 1993; Muller, 2001). Used by Microsoft and Lotus among others, CARD uses physical playing cards with which a group can lay out, modify and discuss the flow of an activity. In the analysis phase, each pre-formatted card contains users' accounts of what is done and why for an individual component of the activity. Requirements on innovations in human practices or technologies can then be discussed around the cards. CARD is also intended to support design and evaluation.

9.7 Observing activities *in situ*

You should complement interview and questionnaire data by observing people's activities as they happen. Interviews and questionnaires provide one side of the story, but it is difficult for people to describe all the details of the relevant aspect of everyday life or work. Sometimes this is because the activity is intrinsically difficult to describe in words – many manual procedures fall into this category – or because it requires complex and subtle cooperation with other people or events. In other cases, an interviewee may describe the 'official' procedure rather than how something is actually done in practice.

Data from observation helps to get round these problems. In its simplest form, the designer can simply ask 'Can you show me how you do that?' during an interview. More complex or larger activities will require someone to spend some time on site observing as unobtrusively as possible. This is best done after some initial interviewing, so you have some idea what it is you are looking at. Everyone at the scene must be informed what is happening and grant their permission in advance, even though they may not be your main focus. Ideally you need to see a range of variations on the normal activity and situations where things go wrong, but this may not be possible in many situations. Here the important point is to identify what you have *not* observed, so you do not over-generalize from your data. If you are lucky enough to be able to choose what you observe, then just as with interviews, the time to stop is when no new information appears. As in interviews, notes should be taken and video recording is very useful, particularly for sharing the observation with other design team members.

In DISCOVER, for example, we observed trainers running exercises using various forms of simulator, some physical and some computer-based. From this we could see how the trainers and trainees interacted, the ways in which the training exercise was adapted in real time in line with trainees' performance, how trainers divided their time between monitoring trainees, talking to them and modifying the simulation, and the way in which even very simple simulations created a very engaging emergency situation. All this helped to shape the design of a virtual reality training environment, and its eventual evaluation.

Chapter 29, Section 29.8 discusses ethnography, the term for long-term, intensive observation and supporting techniques

Of course, observation is not without its difficulties. Being unobtrusive is a skill of its own, and your very presence will naturally tend to make people self-conscious and may alter their behaviour. With time, this effect will decrease. It is much less of a problem where the activity you are observing absorbs all the participants' attention, or if you can find a task to carry out which does not interfere with your data collection. It is also hard to observe effectively where the activity is simply one of people processing data at computers with little or no interaction with other people or artefacts. Here it would be more productive to ask people to demonstrate aspects of interest rather than waiting for them to occur in real time.

Challenge 9-5
Practise your observational skills next time you are working in a small group on a joint task, obtaining the agreement of the rest of the group first. Ideally, the task should involve working with papers, on-line material or some other tangible artefacts. Imagine that you are designing new technology to improve group working. Note how the group interact with each other and the artefacts. Review your notes afterwards from the point of view of identifying requirements on the new design.

9.8   Artefact collection and 'desk work'

Data from interviews, questionnaires and observation will have identified a range of artefacts in the form of things that support an activity. It is often possible to supplement this by collecting artefacts – such as documents, forms or computer printouts, in office settings – or to video or photograph items that cannot be removed.

Figure 9-3 shows the sort of photograph which might be taken and annotated to capture the range of information artefacts used in everyday work in an academic's office. These include:

1. Laptop used for file archiving, calendar, document production, e-mail and Internet
2. Paper notebook – notes of *ad hoc* meetings, also holds currently important papers
3. Print-outs of journal articles
4. CD – current backup
5. (Under mug) miscellaneous documents
6. Sticky notes with 'to do' items, important phone numbers, IP address of laptop
7. Telephone – internal and external calls
8. Desktop PC – older file archive, connection to network backup, used for e-mail/Internet if laptop connection fails.

Sometimes it can be helpful to track a document through a system, noting everyone who interacts with it and how the document is amended at each stage – a technique sometimes known as a 'tracer study'.

FIGURE 9-3 Artefacts on and around an office desk

In a study of a health benefits claim processing system, for example, we collected copies of blank claim forms, standard letters sent to claimants, inter-office memos and the public information leaflet about the benefit. By chance, we also found a copy of an article that provided a valuable insight into health professionals' views in a local newsletter. These artefacts helped to ensure that we had a complete understanding not only of the data processed through the system, but also of their relative importance and significance (what information requests are in bold type, what details have to be verified by a medical practitioner or pharmacist, etc.) and how annotations on the original documents were used as notes of progress through the system. In another medical example, this time in a hospital, Symon *et al.* (1996) show how the very appearance and style of a doctor's handwritten notes on patients' records revealed valuable background details to other staff such as whether the consultation had been carried out in a hurry. All such informal features of the way artefacts are used in practice will make demands on the design of supporting technology.

Understanding activities does not just involve working directly with the people who are doing the activity now or who will be in the future. The designer will need to do plenty of 'desk work' as well. Where the brief is to redesign existing technology such as office systems or home technology products, records of requests for help or user support can be rewarding sources of data about what is confusing or difficult. Similarly, records of bugs reported and change requests often reveal gaps in functionality or presentation. All this can contribute to the new design, but will require interpretation as to which items represent a genuine need for change. Other desk work involves reading procedure manuals and other material about the organization. It involves studying existing software systems to see how they work and what data is kept. Desk work involves collecting and analysing any documents that exist and documenting the movement of documents and the structure of objects such as filing cabinets and ledger books.

Looking at similar products is another way of getting ideas. A **market analysis** looks at similar products that have been produced. This can be useful because the designer can see the product being used *in situ* and can consider the design solutions that others have proposed. This might highlight good and poor solutions for particular design problems. Looking at similar activities complements such an analysis. An activity might be in quite a different setting from the one under scrutiny, but might have a similar structure. For example, looking at a video hire shop might provide inspiration for a car hire application, or looking at an automatic coffee machine might help in understanding an ATM activity.

Challenge 9-6
What artefacts might you collect or photograph relating to people's use of communications technologies in the home? (Hint: think about non-electronic media as well.)

9.9 Requirements and scenarios

Chapter 8
discussed
scenarios in
detail

Requirements are much more easily communicated if they are illustrated by scenarios as well as presented as an organized list. The scenarios are a narrative version of the requirements specification. However, in developing the scenarios you will quite often find that new items need to be added to the requirements list.

Box 9-2 Domain characteristics

The notion of a domain here is that of a 'sphere of activity': some general area that we are interested in. Sometimes the domain will be well specified such as an application to assist with a specific function in an organization: perhaps a website to sell theatre tickets, or a spreadsheet application to help with pricing contracts. Here a software product is to be produced that will not be used elsewhere and so domain characteristics can be utilized in the design. At other times the characteristics of the domain may vary across different situations. For example, if we were developing a software product to help with air traffic control, the domain will have different characteristics depending on whether it is a very busy airport, or a regional airport. At times the domain will be highly volatile (a lot of changes happening quickly), at others it may be quite static. It is likely that different displays and interactions will be needed in these different circumstances. It is important to understand the characteristics of different domains.

In the analysis work for the Home Information Centre (HIC) a number of stories were identified relating to the Edinburgh Festival. An example of a conceptual scenario based on this generic activity is shown below, followed by two others for the HIC and one for DISCOVER.

Scenario HIC/1 – 'What shall we do now?'

A group (not necessarily co-located) of people are trying to decide what to do with some spare time; they want to find out what options for activities are open to them, how much they would cost, whether they can get there in time, etc. A number of versions of this scenario can be developed which stay within this broad framework – e.g. we want to go skiing this weekend, is there anything on at a local pub tonight, what's on at that children's festival and what kind of reviews have the various events had, etc.?

Scenario HIC/2 – 'What shall we have for dinner?'

Someone in the kitchen is trying to decide what to eat for dinner. Variations might include looking for a recipe and then trying to find out where the ingredients can be purchased, or finding a recipe with a given list of ingredients (i.e. what's in the fridge at that moment).

Scenario HIC/3 – 'Entertain me'

A more casual kind of HIC use, someone who has a few minutes to kill so perhaps wants to play a game like cards, or a child who wants to know how many castles there are in the country and when they were built, or someone who wants the answer to a quiz question.

Scenario DISCOVER/1 – 'Refresher course'

Several ship's officers on different ships need to refresh their crisis management skills. Their tutor in a maritime training centre finds a time when everyone is free, then they each run up the DISCOVER training module and practise working as a team, implementing the company's new evacuation procedures.

Chapter 4 introduced the HIC case study

Chapter 8, Section 8.3 has a detailed MP3 scenario

The HIC case study is useful in order to help frame discussions, but it is too big to illustrate the detail of the design process. Hence our main example is just one application of the HIC: an MP3 music application. Questions soon arose relating to the MP3 project. For instance, how much specialized MP3 functionality should the HIC provide? The MP3 domain clearly included playback issues, but went beyond this to encompass displaying and editing MP3 content (tracks), creating playlists and so on. After many discussions with people, gathering their MP3 stories, a conceptual scenario for the MP3 domain was developed.

A person wants to listen to some music on the HIC. The music is in MP3 format and may be stored on the local HIC storage device or may be downloaded from the Web or a content provider. The person can search for tracks, select and organize tracks into playlists and play the tracks in different ways (e.g. randomly, sequentially, from track X and so on).

Similarly, Carroll (2000) describes how he and his colleagues interviewed designers to generate requirements for a video information system and came up with general (conceptual) scenarios such as a 'browsing' scenario or an 'authoring' scenario. In developing an information system for a record shop, conceptual scenarios included the 'make sale', 'take special order' and 'order new stock' scenarios. Finding an appropriate level of abstraction at which to describe activities is a skill designers learn through experience. Different levels of abstraction lead to different insights into the design process.

Challenge 9-7
Write a short conceptual scenario (about 50-150 words) describing how a central remote control device could be used by people with limited mobility to carry out household functions such as drawing curtains, answering the door and so on. The scenario should be aimed towards exploring initial ideas with users.

Summary and key points

In this chapter we have focused on some widely-used techniques for understanding people and activities in context, so we can identify requirements on the design of new technologies. Design starts with understanding the problem in hand, but in the course of achieving that understanding, designers iterate between data and the exploration of new concepts (the next chapter focuses on techniques for exploring and envisioning design). Throughout, the emphasis is on a human-centred process.

- Techniques for understanding people's activities in context include interviews, observation and collecting samples of artefacts, complemented by background research away from the domain of interest.
- Using more than one technique helps to compensate for their individual limitations.
- Requirements work must be documented for communication and use in design; the usual way of doing this is a requirements specification supported by illustrative materials.
- The use of scenarios starts early in the design process, with the construction of conceptual scenarios for exploring requirements and illustrating their application.

Further reading

A number of general-purpose requirements engineering texts have sound advice on the more user-centred techniques as well as a strong grounding in the software engineering process. In particular we recommend:

Sommerville, I. and Sawyer, P. (1997) *Requirements Engineering: a Good Practice Guide*. Wiley, Chichester (Chapter 4).

Robertson, S. and Robertson, J. (1999) *Mastering the Requirements Process*. Addison-Wesley, Harlow (Chapters 5 and 11).

Wixon, D. and Ramey, J. (eds) (1996) *Field Methods Casebook for Software Design*. Wiley, New York.

An excellent, readable introduction to gathering information from fieldwork at user sites, containing many case studies which show how various techniques have been applied and adapted. Unfortunately, at the time of writing it is not easy to obtain a copy to purchase, but your library should be able to track down a copy.

Kuniavsky, M. (2003) *Observing the User Experience – a Practitioner's Guide to User Research*. Morgan Kaufmann, San Francisco.

Contains much sensible, pragmatic material about working with users. Note, however, that most of the examples are oriented towards the design of websites.

Going forward

Rogers, Y. and Bellotti, V. (1997) Grounding blue-sky research: how can ethnography help? *Interactions,* **4**(3), 58–63.

A short introduction to ethnography, a theoretically informed approach to observation, in this case adapted to the design process.

Comments on challenges

Challenge 9-1
Requirements 1, 3, 6 and 8 are all non-functional – they are all *qualities* which the HCI must have, rather than something it actually does. The functional requirements are 2, 4, 5 and 7. Of course, many non-functional requirements do necessitate some underlying functionality – password-controlled entry, for example.

Challenge 9-2
Think about whether it makes a difference to you personally if you are involved in decisions which affect your everyday work or home life. We would expect that you would be more enthusiastic about a holiday, for example, if you have helped to decide whether it should include relaxing on the beach or visiting ancient ruins, staying in a hotel or camping, etc. If people take part in the specification and design of a system, they are more likely to use it effectively once it is implemented. There is strong research evidence to support this.

Challenge 9-3
There are several limitations to interviewing. They include:
- People can only tell the interviewer about aspects of current activities of which they are aware. This excludes parts of the job (or whatever) which are so familiar that they no longer penetrate into consciousness, aspects beyond the interviewees' direct experience, etc.
- Emphasis on correct, official procedures
- Memory
- Difficult to describe complex operations.

▶

Challenge 9-4

(a)

- The focus may not be clear to everyone. E-mail (and older utilities such as FTP – file transfer protocol) run over the Internet, but many people may simply think of the WWW. The question should make it obvious what is intended: perhaps 'How often do you access the WWW (World Wide Web) or use e-mail?'. Better still, use separate questions for each, since usage levels are likely to be different.
- The word 'typically' or 'normally' should be included when asking about usage, unless you are interested in a snapshot of a specific time period.
- There is no provision for 'never'.

(b)

- 'Frequently' is likely to be interpreted in different ways.
- It is much easier for people to check items on a list of possibilities rather than recall them.
- Providing a list also makes it easier to analyse the responses. You can include an 'other – please specify' item to catch any types of material you had not expected.

You may well have identified additional points.

Challenge 9-5

No specific comments – the idea is to gain experience in observation. This variant, where the observer is also part of the group being observed, is termed 'participant observation'.

Challenge 9-6

Possible artefacts to be collected: printouts of typical day's e-mail and e-mail address book, with notes of the contact's relation to the owner of the address book, screen printout showing WWW favourites, etc. And to be photographed: landline phone(s) and fax machines in normal location(s) with any directories, address books, notepads and so on kept near the phone; similarly the home PC if used for communications, etc. Mobile phones are probably only worth photographing if novel features are used which can be captured in the photograph. It would also be useful to draw a sketch plan showing the location of the various communication devices within the home.

Challenge 9-7
A possible conceptual scenario:

A wheelchair-bound person feels rather chilly at home on a late winter's afternoon. He reaches for the home controller and sets the new temperature, then tells the device to close the curtains. Just afterwards, the device alert indicates that someone is at the front door. The person speaks to the caller through the intercom and releases the door lock – again through the home controller.

We would expect the scenario to prompt discussion with potential users about the size and complexity of the device, as well as the relative benefits and drawbacks of using the controller compared with moving around the home.

Exercises

1. You have been commissioned to design an on-line shopping and home delivery system for a new supermarket chain. Your clients want the system to somehow reproduce the best aspects of real shopping without the drawbacks. They want the system to appeal to all adults with access to a home computer. What techniques would be suitable for carrying out a requirements analysis for the shopping application? Explain the reasons for your choices and any potential limitations on the conclusions you could draw from their use.

2. You are defining functionality and interactivity for the next generation of mobile phones. Find a colleague and interview them for up to 15 minutes about the way they use their current mobile phone and what enhanced functionality they might like. You should make notes of points to cover beforehand. Have them demonstrate the way they use the most useful features with and without a running commentary. Take written notes of your interview; also use an audio- or video-recorder if you have one available. (Ask the interviewee's permission first before recording.) Review the data you have collected as soon as possible after the interview.

    • Which questions elicited the most useful data? Why?
    • Did the running commentary provide extra information or did it obstruct the demonstration? Did your interviewee seem comfortable with the process?
    • If you have recorded the interview, how much is missing from your written notes when compared to the recording?

▶

If you have time, carry out a second interview with someone else after reflecting on the results of the first.

3. (More advanced) It is sometimes argued that understanding people's existing activities does not really help to design future technologies, since activities may change radically once the technology is in use.

- Do you agree or disagree with this view? Provide supporting arguments for your position.
- Which requirements elicitation techniques are most likely to be effective in helping users and designers to create the future? Why?

4. (More advanced) Read Lundberg *et al.* (2002) 'The Snatcher Catcher' – an interactive refrigerator, *Proceedings of NordiCHI* '02. (available on-line through the ACM digital library – www.acm.org/dl). Outline a design for a similarly provocative domestic device which is aimed at stimulating people to think about the future directions for home technologies. Explain how your design would facilitate the process.

Envisionment

Aims

Envisionment is concerned with making ideas visible; with externalizing thoughts. Externalization can take all manner of forms: stories and scenarios, presentations, sketches, formal models, software prototypes, cardboard models and so on. Different forms of representation will be more or less useful at different stages in the design process and more or less effective for doing different things. A formal presentation of a design concept for a potential client will look quite different from a sketch of a screen layout intended to explore what something will look like. Envisionment is needed to represent design work to ourselves and to others. It occurs throughout development as the designer generates multiple design solutions and whittles them down to a final product. In this chapter we consider the principal envisionment techniques which (broadly speaking) use text and graphics; in the next chapter, we look at various forms of prototype and the presentation of ideas to clients. But first of all we review ways of thinking about the ideas to be externalized. After studying this chapter you should be able to:

- Exploit the possibilities of different media and metaphors in design concepts
- Use a variety of techniques for envisioning design problems and possible solutions
- Understand the role of concrete scenarios in envisioning design.

10.1 Exploring design concepts

Bill Verplank (Verplank, 2003) is an interaction designer who has been sketching and designing for many years. He argues that interaction design is 'design for human use' and focuses on three main things which he characterizes as

- How do you do?
- How do you feel?
- How do you know?

How do you do?

'How do you do?' is concerned with the ways in which we affect the world. Do you poke it, manipulate it, sit on it? For example, one distinction he highlights is between handles and buttons. Handles are better for continuous control (e.g. trombone), but buttons are better for discrete control (e.g. a piano keyboard). Handles leave you in control (e.g. opening a car door) whereas buttons are more likely to trigger something automatic (e.g. opening an elevator door).

How do you feel?

'How do you feel?' concerns how we make sense of the world and the sensory qualities that shape media. One distinction is Marshall McLuhan's 'hot' versus 'cool'. Marshall McLuhan wrote *Understanding Media* in 1964 and is famed for coining the phrases 'Global Village', 'age of information' and 'the medium is the message'. The book, which was reprinted in 1994, is a whirlwind tour through the media of his time and has much insight into how media would develop in our time. He introduced a distinction between 'hot media' which are more authoritative and exact and 'cool media' which are fuzzy and incomplete. Cool media invite more participation; they require the audience to fill in the gaps, to interpret. Hot media extend a single sense in high definition; they are filled with data. Photography is a hot medium because it is high fidelity, whereas a cartoon is a cool medium, low definition where we fill in the gaps. McLuhan's book is a fascinating if difficult read and he extends the ideas of hot and cool to all manner of concepts such as axes (hot), the 'city slicker' (hot), rural life (cool). Focusing on 'how do you feel' takes us into the areas of satisfaction, affect, enjoyment, involvement and engagement. In his introduction to the 1994 MIT Press edition of *Understanding Media*, Lewis Lapham characterizes McLuhan's ideas as illustrated in Table 10-1. Do not worry too much about understanding these dichotomies; use them as ways of thinking about 'how do you feel'.

Chapter 17 discusses affect and emotion

How do you know?

'How do you know?' concerns the ways that people learn and plan; how designers want users to think. For example, Verplank suggests that one choice is between maps and paths. Paths are good for beginners as they provide step-by-step instructions on what to do. Maps are good for understanding alternatives. They take longer to learn but are more robust and are good for expert skill. Maps offer the chance to take short cuts. Very often, of course, a given system or product will have to accommodate both.

TABLE 10-1 Leitmotifs from McLuhan's *Understanding Media*

Print	Electronic media
Visual	Tactile
Mechanical	Organic
Sequence	Simultaneity
Composition	Improvization
Eye	Ear
Active	Reactive
Expansion	Contraction
Complete	Incomplete
Soliloquy	Chorus
Classification	Pattern recognition
Centre	Margin
Continuous	Discontinuous
Syntax	Mosaic
Self-expression	Group therapy
Typographic man	Graphic man

Source: Lapham (1994) in McLuhan, M. Undertstanding Media: The Extensions of Man, New Edition. Published and reprinted by permission of The MIT Press

Challenge 10-1
What characteristics do you feel belong to the text message as a medium? Be creative!

10.2 Using metaphor to explore design

Chapter 25 on navigation of information space

Paths and maps may be thought of as metaphors for the design of interactions. Different metaphors will lead to different conceptions and designs. Think of the idea of navigating an interactive system, for example. Many people immediately think that navigation is trying to get somewhere specific, but this is only one view (often called 'wayfinding'). We also browse around and explore. If we think of navigation as in a city then we think of roads and signposts, subways that take us invisibly from one part of the space to another, taxis to transport us, or buses that we have to learn about.

Considering one metaphor can stimulate creative leaps into other ways of thinking. For example, during a collaborative design meeting to look at the HIC interface as a 'rolodex' (Figure 10-1), a manual card index device that allowed people to rapidly flip through standard-sized cards, a 'gun barrel' design emerged (illustrated

Box 10-1 Navigation metaphors

Metaphors which might be useful for thinking about navigation have different associations. A wilderness, for example, is frightening, confusing, enchanting. A desert is intimidating and beautiful but has no landmarks. Such metaphors might encourage forging a path, enjoying the scenery and getting out. Wilderness and desert can be included in an overall landscape metaphor where different types of terrain represent different types of information. These metaphors encourage exploration by the user; the system provides a high-level metaphor, but users provide the more detailed structure themselves.

The night sky offers a different sort of space. To the human eye, it contains objects, clusters and patterns and it is very big. It supports the activities of mapping and identifying objects. However, there are relatively few types of object in the night sky (galaxies, stars, planets). It is the configurations and sub-types of these objects which are of interest. Science fiction concepts such as warp drives and worm holes can be used for quick and magic transportation to distant parts of the space. The open sea is another metaphor. It encourages a distinction between surface and depth. Thus it is natural to think of a lot of information as being hidden beneath the surface and only available for viewing if the user dives down. Currents can link continents and islands and take people to unexpected places. People can look for islands of information; archipelagos provide clusters. A museum has been structured to allow free roaming, yet is also structured to facilitate learning. A library is suitable for finding specific information. It is well organized and structured.

These metaphors are not meant to suggest that the interface to a particular product looks like a desert, wilderness or library (though sometimes such explicit interface metaphors can be useful); the idea here is to think about activities in different ways.

in the left-hand part of Figure 10-3). Although the gun barrel idea was rejected, the rolodex concept seemed to capture the idea of searching and retrieving results with an intuitive navigational style of flicking through the 'cards'. In this case the coneptual metaphor of the rolodex translated nicely into a visual representation. So here an interface metaphor seemed wholly appropriate and indeed was implemented as part of the first functional prototype.

Chapter 13,
Figure 13.3
shows the final
implementation

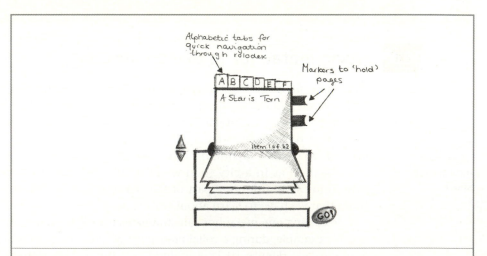

FIGURE 10-1 Sketch of rolodex interface metaphor in HIC project (*Rolodex is a registered trade name, but we use the term in this book to indicate the concept rather than the product*)

10.3 Finding suitable representations

Envisionment is fundamental to effective human-centred design, to enable designers to see things from other people's perspectives and to explore design concepts and ideas with others. Different representations of design ideas are useful at different stages for different people. They help with generation, communication and evaluation of ideas. A sketch 'on the back of an envelope' might be useful for generating an idea and expressing it to a colleague – but it is not so good for giving to a client.

There are many techniques that can be used to help develop an understanding of the design problem and to envision possible solutions. None of these techniques in themselves will lead to the perfect design, but they will all generate some kind of document or representation which can be used in the process of communicating with clients, users and colleagues. It is through communication that design solutions will arise, be evaluated, and (eventually) be transformed into a final product.

Which techniques are used on a particular project will depend on a number of factors: the working style of the development team, the type of project, the resources available and so on. In an ideal world, developers would use a wide variety of representations, but in a two-person company working on a project with a deadline of four weeks this may not be possible.

Choosing suitable representations for the task at hand is one of the skills of a designer; another is making good use of that representation. Representations work by suppressing unnecessary detail, thus ensuring that the significant features of some artefact or activity stand out. A good representation is accurate enough to reflect the features of the system being modelled, but simple enough to avoid confusion. It adopts a style of presentation which is suitable for its purpose. Scenarios are one sort of representation – and their use for this phase of design will be explored later in this chapter – but there are many others.

Consider the following example:

A car designer has been commissioned to produce a new luxury sports car. He or she doodles a few designs on paper and shows them to other designers on the team. They make some comments and criticisms and as a result changes are made. Finally the designer is satisfied with one of the designs and draws up detailed blueprints which are given to the firm's model maker. Scale models are produced and sent to Marketing and Sales for customer reaction. The scale models are also subjected to wind tunnel experiments to investigate the aerodynamics of the design and the results are used in a computer program which will calculate the car's speed and fuel efficiency.

The designer is using four different representations in at least four different ways:

■ The original representations represent a clearing of the mind. In this case they are doodles and sketches which are used to *generate new ideas*, examine possibilities and prompt for questions.

■ The blueprints given to the model maker and the scale model given to the Marketing and Sales Departments are suitable for *accurately expressing ideas* to others.

■ The wind tunnel experiments show representations being used to *test ideas*.

■ The computer model is used to *make predictions*.

Challenge 10-3
Which representations in the example above are being used to explore the problem? Which are being used to communicate ideas?

10.4 Sketches and snapshots

The art of sketching is something that all designers should practise. Ideas and thoughts can be quickly visualized – either to yourself, or to others – and explored. Many an idea has come to fruition 'on the back of an envelope'. The millennium bridge across the River Thames in London was reputedly designed on a paper napkin in a restaurant. Designers do well to carry a sketch book with them so that inspiration can be quickly captured and preserved.

The full scenario is in Chapter 14, Section 14.2

Figure 10-2 shows two visualizations of the Edinburgh Festival scenario. A key design requirement is to display large amounts of data without the need for scrolling (if possible). In the sketches we can see that the designer has been exploring different ideas for displaying and searching through results of a search. The design principle underlying the designs is often referred to as 'focus and context'. Ben Shneiderman has a mantra which he encourages designers to use: 'overview first, zoom and filter, then details on demand' (Shneiderman, 1998, p. 523). On the left is a 'hyperbolic tree' representation of the Festival scenario and on the right is a 'cone tree' representation. Notice how the hyperbolic tree is better for capturing the focus and context principles.

Individual snapshots of a design can be provided to show key moments in an interaction and are particularly useful for exploring the impact of a certain style or design. Snapshots can be single sketches, or frames, from a storyboard (see below) or they can be produced using software. In Figure 10-3 we can see two more examples from the HIC case study. Once again, the aim is to highlight the main result but also to provide a context of related search results. It is clear how the first snapshot has influenced the second, a 'gun barrel' concept.

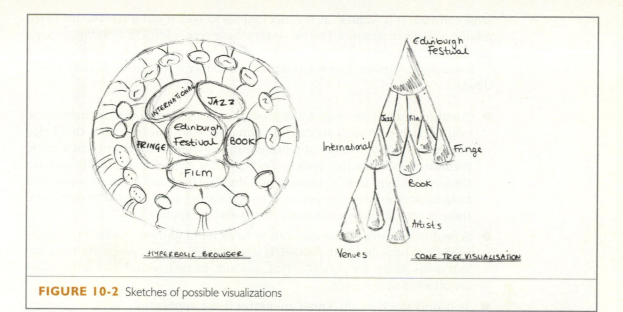

FIGURE 10-2 Sketches of possible visualizations

FIGURE 10-3 Snapshots of alternative designs for searching the HIC

Challenge 10-4
Sketch two different ways in which you might present information about tourist sites on a town's website.

10.5 Storyboards

Storyboarding is a technique taken from film making – using a simple cartoon-like structure, key moments from the interactive experience are represented. The advantage of storyboarding is that it allows you to get a feel for the 'flow' of the experience. It is also a very economical way of representing the design – a single page can hold 6–8 'scenes'. It is often helpful to sketch out a storyboard based around a concrete scenario. The two together are very helpful in working through design ideas with users.

Three main types of storyboarding are commonly found in interactive media design:

■ Traditional storyboarding. A storyboard for a film would usually have some notes attached to each scene expanding on what will happen – this helps overcome the limitations of representing a dynamic experience in a static medium. For interactive systems, notes below each sketch usually contain the relevant steps from a scenario, and the sketches themselves are annotated to indicate interactive behaviour. This is the most usual form of storyboard if there is not a strongly multimedia flavour to the application.

■ Scored storyboards. If the application has a lot of motion graphics the storyboard can be annotated – a sketch is annotated with appropriate notation and notes about, for example, type, colours, images, sound and other issues are attached underneath.

■ Text-only storyboards. These are useful if the application has a lot of very complex sequences. You can specify what images appear, what text accompanies them, any accompanying media, general notes about tone, flow, etc.

Figure 10-4 shows a sketched storyboard for an application of the HIC to playing MP3 music files. The storyboard shows how an interaction might take place. It

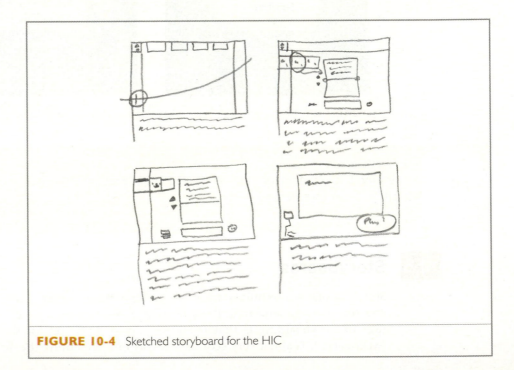

FIGURE 10-4 Sketched storyboard for the HIC

exploits some ideas of marking movement using arrows and lines to indicate change. Figure 10-5 shows part of another storyboard, this time for a website designed to showcase a photographer's portfolio.

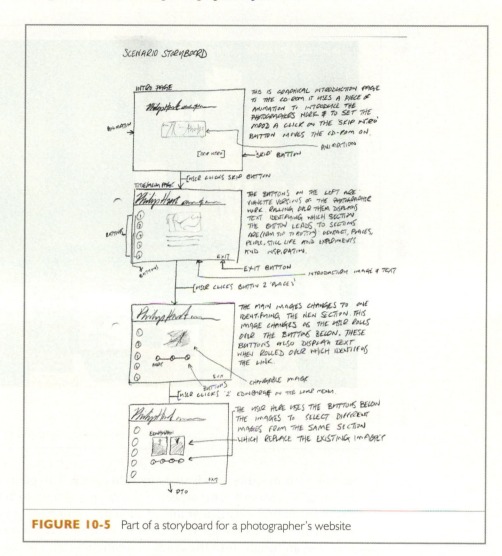

FIGURE 10-5 Part of a storyboard for a photographer's website

10.6 ## Mood boards

Mood boards are widely used in advertising and interior design. Quite simply you gather visual stimuli that capture something of how you feel about the design – photographs and other images, colours, textures, shapes, headlines from newspapers or magazines, quotations from people, pieces of fabric and so on. Attach the stimuli to a pinboard. Even thinking about their arrangement can stimulate ideas. You can put pages from websites you like on mood boards. If you use Blu-tack or something similar then you can add and delete items as your thinking changes. Figure 10-6 shows an example.

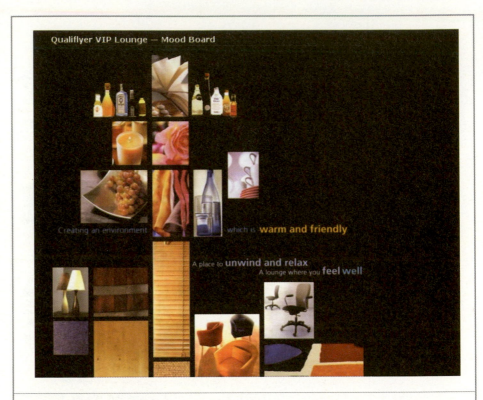

FIGURE 10-6 Mood board
(source: http://perso.wanadoo.fr/Archibald/portfolio/architecture/qualiflyer_concept/mood_board.html)

The rule with mood boards is that 'anything goes'. The point of the board is not to formally represent some aspect of the design, simply to act as inspiration – perhaps promoting a particular line of thought, or providing inspiration for a colour scheme. One technique is to get the client to create a mood board. This can give you an insight into the kinds of aesthetics that are likely to appeal to them. As a variation on the mood board concept, writing down adjectives that describe some aspect of the system can be useful.

10.7 Navigation maps

Navigation is a key feature for many systems. Navigation maps focus on how the user moves through the site or application. The aim is to focus on how users will experience the site. Each page in the site, or location in the application, is repre-

Chapter 25, Section 25.3 discusses navigation for websites

sented with a box or heading and every page that can be accessed from that page should flow from it. A useful tip is to put in all flows possible (i.e. back and forwards from a page) as this will highlight sections where the user can get stranded. Navigation maps can usefully be redrawn many times through the project lifecycle, as poor navigational structure is one of the main reasons people turn off a website. The maps can be used with scenarios to 'walk through' particular activities and are a very good way of spotting poor aspects of design such as 'orphan pages' (pages which are not accessible) or dead ends.

Navigation is important in all manner of applications and products, not just websites. Figure 10-7 shows the navigation map for a mobile phone. More formal and more fully annotated maps can also be developed as illustrated in Figure 10-8. Arrows can be added to lines if the direction of a link is important. An excellent 'visual language' for describing websites is available at Jessie James Garrett's site www.jjg.net/ia/visvocab/.

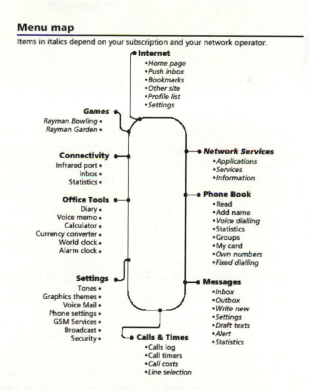

FIGURE 10-7 Mobile phone navigation map *(source: Trium phone manual)*

Challenge 10-5
Construct a navigation map for a website with which you are familiar – perhaps that of your university/college or employer. (If the site is very large, draw a partial map.) Are there any 'dead ends' or complicated routes to important information?

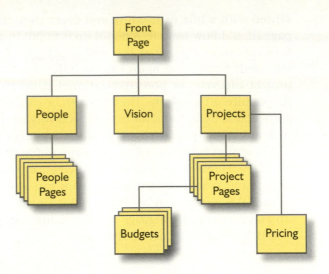

FIGURE 10-8 Navigation map for a website

10.8 Using scenarios in envisionment

At the end of Chapter 9 we saw how conceptual scenarios capturing the essence of new technologies can be used to embody requirements for a new design. In a scenario-based approach, the next stage is to enrich these scenarios with more concrete, contextual details that will prompt discussions and highlight the design decisions to be made. The scenarios should be discussed and evaluated at design team sessions and with the intended users. There are *degrees* of concreteness in scenarios. The most concrete forms are used to envision or evaluate specific interactions. While they are superficially easy to construct, there are a number of ways in which scenarios can be made more effective:

■ Complement the scenarios with some of the more visual envisioning techniques.

■ In a large design team, include real data and materials so people not directly involved can appreciate concrete details.

■ Think hard about underlying assumptions.

■ Include good characterization and develop a number of personas. If this is done well, members of the team start talking about the characters – 'If you design it like that, what will happen when the grandmother tries to use it?'.

■ Provide a rich contextual background – this grounds design decisions in real life, forcing the designer to think about practicality and acceptability.

■ Team members can write their own concrete version of a conceptual scenario that reflects their particular concerns. These can be brought together and overlaps removed.

Personas were introduced in Chapter 2

The aim is to come up with a collection of scenarios that covers all the major uses and functionality of the product. It would be impossible to write scenarios for all possible variations in use and users, but those produced should cover:

- Interactions which are typical of a number of similar use situations
- Design issues which are particularly important for the focus of the project
- Areas where requirements are unclear
- Any aspects which are safety-critical.

Example 1: a simple scenario

Here is a scenario developed for the DISCOVER training application, illustrating some of the software features for tutors. Scenarios such as this were discussed at meetings between user representatives, designers and developers and helped to establish details of technical feasibility and fit with working practice at the training centres. Discussion of a similar scenario revealed substantial differences between expectations of the users that virtual fires (for example) would respond to trainees' behaviour in the environment and technological constraints which meant that only a small number of simple pre-programmed variations would be available.

Terry is a tutor at an oil industry training centre. He is familiar with the DISCOVER VR training system, which he is using for a short practice session with two senior staff on an oil platform. They are shortly to be assessed for a safety-management certificate. The staff have used DISCOVER at the training centre but are now located back at the platform in the North Sea. The three men have already run up DISCOVER in its multi-user mode and have established audio communication, using headsets. Terry uses the drop-down menu to select the trainee Sten to be monitored. By default, his viewpoint is slightly above and behind the head of Sten's avatar, and as Sten moves his avatar through the simulated oil platform Terry's viewpoint changes accordingly. Terry can also move viewpoint independently by selecting the compass icon. Terry speaks to the trainees to give initial instructions for the role-playing scenario – there is a fire in level 2, and the team are to search for crew members who may be trapped or overcome by smoke. The trainees set off, and after 30 seconds or so Terry moves his viewpoint to look behind Sten and observes that Trond (or rather his avatar) is following directly. Terry decides to complicate the situation. He clicks on a spot on the plan of the rig displayed in a window at the bottom of his screen and then on the fire icon from the tutor's palette to set off another fire in the mess hall. A dialogue box appears asking him to specify the scale of the fire and the amount of smoke, presenting the options as radio buttons ...

Structuring scenarios in larger design projects

Chapter 8 discusses scenarios

As already shown in Chapter 8, larger projects and collections of scenarios need a degree of structure to keep them organized. A set of structured scenarios were developed for the MP3 function of the HIC. Following brainstorming sessions, analyses of existing MP3 players and the collection of various stories of the MP3 in use, five scenarios were developed. 'How does that song go again?' is described in full in Section 8.3. The others were:

Title	Activities	Rationale
'Is it on the Web?'	Searching for MP3 audio content on the World Wide Web; downloading and playing back MP3 tracks; file management. Bookmarking favourite websites for future use.	The area of concern is access to Web resources via the HIC. The scenario describes connecting to a Web resource (a website) and downloading MP3 content to the HIC. This involves file management functions including saving and deleting.
'It's my turn now'	Inspecting e-mail; downloading attached files; modifying HIC preferences.	The scenario takes the HIC's MP3 functions as a focus for the kind of conflicts which may arise when several users want to access the HIC at once – to use either the same domain or different domains. Protagonists here access the HIC's functions via personalized user profiles. There is also a description of how access to particular domains of the HIC can be blocked for selected users.
'Play me something while I cook'	Transferring MP3 files to the HIC; saving them to permanent memory; organizing/classifying MP3 files; searching for files by different criteria.	At least two broad areas of functionality are depicted in the scenario: the business of loading new MP3 content into the HIC via different media (including removable discs and the Web); and organizing MP3 files in the HIC using facilities for classifying by different criteria. There is also an account of simple search activities via user input.

Title	Activities	Rationale
'Be our DJ this evening'	Making compilations of MP3 tracks (play lists) within the HIC, and storing them. Editing them. Playing them back in different track orders.	Here the HIC's MP3 functions are used like a jukebox, to provide music for a party. The scenario deals in fairly general terms with the activities involved in making lengthy compilations of MP3 tracks from content already within the HIC.

10.9 Exploring the design space

When writing, thinking about or using scenarios, issues will arise about design features. This is particularly so when reviewing scenarios and other design representations with potential users. It is vital to do this. Very often it is only when people see some sort of concrete representation of the new system and how it will fit (or not) with their lives that they are able to comment meaningfully. Issues may concern the current state of affairs or a future designed position. We have seen how these issues can be highlighted through adding end notes to the scenario descriptions, and notes can also be appended to storyboards and so on. In many cases it will be necessary to revisit the requirements, which in turn may entail further analysis of the current situation.

Carroll's formulation for claims can be found in the advanced evaluation material in Chapter 27

John Carroll (e.g. Carroll, 2000) points out that in design work there are often trade-offs to consider and a design feature may lead to both positive and negative outcomes. He recommends listing positive and negative features of a design alongside a feature, as 'claims'. We have found it useful to identify neutral design features too. One way of highlighting design issues is to undertake a walkthrough using the concrete scenarios to drive the thinking of the designer. Scenarios are very effective at forcing issues into the open, so that claims about designs can be articulated, documented and evaluated.

Refer back to Section 8.3 and consider paragraph P4 of the MP3 scenario and endnotes 8 and 9. How should search results be displayed and selected? Just one of the many decisions associated with this activity is the size of the font used to display artists' names and track titles. Unlike other domains for the HIC such as News, the MP3 domain demands that quite a lot of text is displayed so that the user can make a selection. So font size is a key design issue.

Some of the positive and negative features of using a large font size are:

■ It can be seen from further away (positive).
■ It takes up valuable screen space (negative).
■ It means fewer tracks can be displayed (negative).

There are many variations of techniques that can be used to focus attention on design issues. Listing the actions that people will have to take in order to accomplish a goal using a specific design and identifying the positive and negative aspects of a prototype is one way. Another is to list the options against the design criteria. This technique, known as QOC (Questions, Options, Criteria), is illustrated in Figure 10-9. QOC was developed by Alan MacLean and his colleagues at Rank Xerox (MacLean *et al.*, 1991). The criteria against which the options are ranked need to be developed as part of the design brief and requirements gathering process.

10.10 An outline envisionment process

Here is a suggested series of steps for the envisionment phase, pulling together the wide-ranging material in this chapter.

1. Review requirements and conceptual scenarios
2a. Develop representations of your design ideas. At a minimum these should include concrete scenarios, storyboards developing the main interaction sequences, and snapshot sketches of key screens or other aspects of the product. More complex or creative projects will benefit from the other

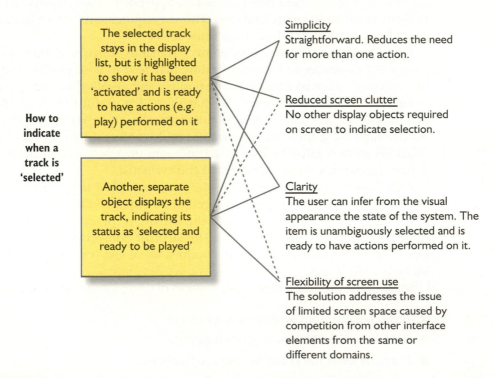

FIGURE 10-9 An example of the QOC (Questions, Options, Criteria) claims method

techniques discussed. Large developments in particular will benefit from the formal structure for concrete scenarios described above.

2b. If your product is a new one, experiment with different metaphors and design concepts through your representations.

2c. Your intended users should be involved in exploring design ideas throughout wherever possible.

3. Resources permitting, explore and document detailed design decisions using a method such as claims analysis or QOC.

4. Reconsider requirements in the light of the developing design, and carry out supplementary analysis where gaps in your background information have been uncovered.

Summary and key points

These are just a few of the many possible envisionment techniques. There are books full of interesting and novel ways of representing aspects of design. For example, 'mind maps' list the main concepts of a design, showing links between them, flow diagrams show the movement of some items or some information through a design, and transition diagrams show how a system changes from one state to another. We discussed an example of a car designer who used sketches, and others in the design process who used scale models, blueprints and so on. We also argued that getting an appropriate representation – appropriate for a particular purpose in a particular context – is important. The different representations will be used alongside other techniques for helping to generate ideas such as brainstorming and other forms of collaborative design. For example, we have found sketching on a whiteboard very effective for a design meeting, as is using a flipchart where pages can be torn off and stuck to the wall. Writing ideas on Post-it notes and sticking them on the walls of a design room is another technique. They can be rearranged to show different collections and 'affinities'. Collaborative writing where a group all work on a single document using a computer and data projector to display the results on a screen can be very effective in producing draft documents.

A key feature of design and of the techniques described here is *not* to sit staring at a blank piece of paper. Getting inspiration from magazines, websites, software systems, other people, similar systems or products and so on, and externalizing ideas through envisionment techniques, is the first step in design. We have also seen in this chapter how thinking about the qualities of different media and underlying metaphors can play a part.

As we noted at the beginning of this chapter, one major envisionment technique remains – prototyping. This is discussed in the next chapter.

- Considering Verplank's design dimensions, the qualities of different media as suggested by McLuhan and underlying metaphors can help to stimulate design thinking.

- Envisionment – the making concrete of design ideas – is a key feature of design. All aspects of the system can and should be envisioned: concepts, functions, structure, interactions.

- Envisionment aids the generation, communication and evaluation of ideas.

- Users should take an active part in envisionment wherever possible – the process allows essential feedback from users themselves and clients.

- Techniques include storyboards, different forms of sketch, mood boards, navigation maps and concrete scenarios.

- Concrete scenarios in particular can be analysed using techniques such as claims analysis and QOC to represent design trade-offs so that decisions can be clearly seen.

Further reading

Browsing the design section of a good bookshop will find numerous books containing ideas to stimulate creativity – which you find helpful is very much an individual preference. Equally, the business section will offer a wide range of published material for enhancing the generation of ideas in group meetings.

McLuhan, M. (1994) *Understanding Media: The Extensions of Man*. MIT Press, Cambridge, MA.
This is not a book for the faint-hearted, nor for those who want some simple answers. It is something of a psychedelic tour through a 1960s view of the coming age of media. It makes you think.

Bill Verplank is at www.billverplank.com

MacLean, A., Young, R., Bellotti, V. and Moran, T. (1991) Questions, options and criteria: elements of design space analysis. *Human–Computer Interaction*, **6**, 201–251.
The original paper describing the elements of QOC. Includes analyses of existing designs and supporting data about the concepts and arguments used by designers during design discussions.

Buckingham Shum, S., MacLean, A., Bellotti, V. and Hammond, N. (1997) Graphical argumentation and design cognition. *Human–Computer Interaction*, **12**, 267–300.
Presents an extensive analysis of the use of QOC. The authors argue that the method provides most support when elaborating poorly understood design spaces, but is a distraction when evaluating well-defined issues.

Comments on challenges

Challenge 10-1
Personal, direct, fun, impromptu, young, quick, pervasive, hot ... occur to me, but there are almost infinite possibilities here. There are no right or wrong answers; it depends on your own perceptions and feelings.

Challenge 10-2
Thinking of physical diaries is one way to come up with possible metaphors: pocket diaries, desk diaries, the diary of personal events that you might keep, the diary of future events in an area such as sports, a diary of events for a local society or club. This might lead to the metaphor of a pocket diary in which the interface had 'pages' that could be 'turned'. The diary of events leads to a wallchart type of display with the days of the month laid out. The personal diary might lead to ideas such as secrecy and security, being able to write free-flowing text rather than having a regimented date- and event-driven design that a business diary suggests.

Challenge 10-3
The sketches and doodles are being used to explore the problem space. The computer simulation is also being used in this way and so the scale model put into the wind tunnel is an essential part of that representation. Both the blueprints and the scale model sent to Marketing are being used to communicate ideas. The blueprints and the scale model are both used for communication, but the blueprints are inappropriate for communicating with Marketing. Marketing people are interested in the physical shape of the design, but the model maker requires a more precise description of the designer's ideas in the form of blueprints. Also notice that the representations must be accurate enough for their purpose, highlighting the important features but ignoring the irrelevant aspects. In the wind tunnel, the interior design of the car is unimportant, so the scale model takes no account of this.

Challenge 10-4
Many different ideas are possible here. Examples could include a simplified interactive map, a text listing by category, a montage of clickable images, etc. Remember that what you are doing here is trying out ideas, so don't spend time adding too much detail or creating a work of art.

Challenge 10-5
No specific comments here, but make sure that you have shown the direction of links on the map where they are important. If there are multiple links to the same target, the map can be simplified by adding a note such as 'all pages link back to home page' and omitting the links themselves.

Exercises

1. Write a scenario for the home control device introduced in Challenge 10-9. You should use the formal structure introduced in this chapter. Choose three of the design features from the scenario and list the positive and negative aspects as described in Section 10.9.

2. Mood boards are usually constructed out of physical materials, but they can also be made in software. Using any software application that allows the inclusion of visual, audio and text components, make a mood board to explore the following concepts:

   - A website for seaside holidays targeted at one-parent families
   - A website for adventure holidays targeted at active, affluent over-sixties.

   This can be done as a single-person exercise, but works best as a small group project.

3. (More advanced) We argue strongly in this book for users to be involved as closely as possible in the envisionment process. Develop some bullet points setting out a counter argument – that designers 'know best'.

11 Prototyping

Aims

The last chapter introduced the general concept of envisioning designs, and introduced a range of different envisionment techniques. In this chapter we explore the main remaining technique – prototyping and its variations. We also discuss how to present designs effectively to clients. Finally, we provide examples of how different types of representations and prototypes have supported different types of design project. After studying this chapter you should be able to:

- Select and use appropriate prototyping techniques
- Understand the main factors in communicating designs effectively
- Appreciate the use of different envisionment techniques in human-centred design projects.

11.1 Different types of prototype

A prototype is a concrete but partial representation or implementation of a system design. Prototypes are used extensively in most design and construction domains. This may be to demonstrate a concept (e.g. a prototype car) in early design, to test details of that concept at a later stage and sometimes as a specification for the final product. A prototype may be made of something as simple as paper, cardboard or other suitable material, or it may be developed using a sophisticated software package.

Box 11-1 Prototyping the lunar lander

The engineers in the Apollo missions built a full-size cardboard prototype of the lunar landing module to test the position and size of the windows in relation to the field of view of the astronauts. This experimentation led to the design decision that the astronauts would stand (not sit) inside the lander – thus allowing windows to be smaller and saving crucial weight.

In our domain of interactive systems design, representations such as the screen sketches discussed in the previous chapter and simple early prototypes blend into each other. But the main distinguishing characteristic of a prototype is that it is *interactive*. Something happens when the user 'presses' a 'button' – even if the button is drawn on paper and the action consists of a menu on a Post-it note being added by the designer. The appropriateness of a prototype will depend on a number of factors such as whom the prototype is aimed at, the stage of the design process and what features the designer is looking to explore.

→

The evaluation process itself is the subject of Chapter 12

For the design team representations like navigation maps and PACT statements might be meaningful, but for clients and end-users some form of prototype is crucial for capturing the outcomes of the envisioning techniques we have discussed so far. The prototype might seek to highlight just the interface, or some crucial aspect of the functionality. Prototypes are first and foremost a way of involving people and clients in evaluating your design ideas. There are two main kinds of prototyping – low fidelity (lo-fi) and high fidelity (hi-fi).

Hi-fi prototypes

Hi-fi prototypes are similar in look and feel, if not necessarily in functionality, to the anticipated final product. They are produced in software, whether in the development environment which will be used for implementation or in packages which will allow interactive effects to be mocked-up easily. Hi-fi prototyping has the following features:

■ It is useful for detailed evaluation of the main design elements (content, visuals, interactivity, functionality and media) – for example, hi-fi prototypes can be used in usability studies to establish whether people can learn to use the system within a specified amount of time.

■ It often constitutes a crucial stage in client acceptance – as a kind of final design document which the client must agree to before the final implementation.

■ It is generally developed fairly well into the project when ideas are beginning to firm up, unless there is some crucial issue that needs to be resolved before any other work can proceed.

A problem with developing hi-fi prototypes is that people believe them! This is dangerous if the designer has not checked details and thought through ideas clearly beforehand. A simple error – perhaps in the name of a customer, or of a product – can completely ruin a prototype because clients or potential users will get confused. If everything else seems real why aren't the customers our real customers? It is no good saying 'we were going to fix that' or 'that is just a place holder'. For hi-fi prototyping accurate detail is vital. Another problem with hi-fi prototyping is that it suggests such a system can be implemented. We have found it impossible to implement some effects that were prototyped using Macromedia Director. Facilities can be mocked-up and a video made which again can prove impossible to implement. Finally, inevitably a certain degree of effort and time is consumed in producing the prototype. If this is in the eventual development environment, developers can be understandably reluctant to discard work on features rejected in exploring the prototype.

Figure 11-1 shows the final prototype for the searching part of the HIC interface. This was produced using Macromedia Director and an integrated database that allowed for a certain amount of interaction. The aim of the prototype was to get the reaction of people to the main concepts – the rolodex itself and how to navigate through the system. One additional feature that had been introduced was that the results of previous searches appeared as smaller rolodexes. These are shown towards the left-hand side. The other main concepts were the category bar at the top of the screen, the activity bar on the left and the object and content providers bar on the right-hand side.

More detail on the HIC in Chapter 14

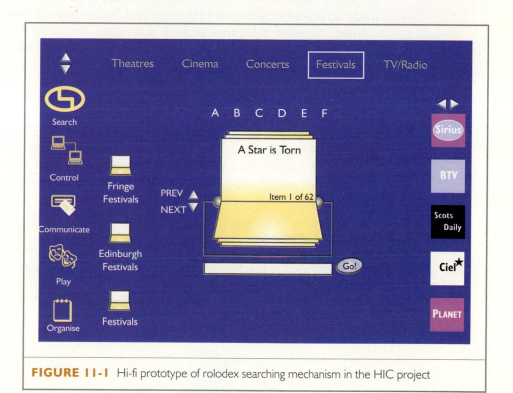

FIGURE 11-1 Hi-fi prototype of rolodex searching mechanism in the HIC project

Lo-fi prototypes

Lo-fi prototypes – often termed paper prototypes, since that is what they are usually made from – on the other hand, have the following features.

- They are more focused on the broad underlying design ideas – such as content, form and structure, the 'tone' of the design, key functionality requirements and navigational structure.
- They are designed to be produced quickly, and thrown away as quickly.
- They capture very early design thinking and should aid, not hinder, the process of generating and evaluating many possible design solutions.

The products of some of the envisioning techniques discussed previously are kinds of lo-fi prototypes in some respects. However, the most usual form of this sort of prototype is a series of 'screenshots' which the user can 'walk through' (for example, a button on screen shot 1 can be 'clicked' and the user is instructed to pull up screen shot 6, etc.). How the prototype is implemented is in theory limited only by your imagination, in practice by time and the materials readily to hand. Very flexible prototypes can be produced simply and quickly using screen-sized pieces of stiff paper and index cards or Post-its in different colours. Permanent features of each screen are drawn on the card; dynamic items such as dialogue boxes or menus use the cards or Post-its, cut to size as necessary. More ambitiously, overlays of acetates can simulate dynamic features, or allow users to write comments using wipe-off pens. But it is really important not to spend too much time doing this – the whole point is the low investment in the prototype build. If you are spending a good deal of time trying to replicate design details on paper, you should probably be using a hi-fi software prototype instead.

Figure 11-2 illustrates a lo-fi prototype developed to explore ideas for a tool to allow households to communicate directly with local government. One feature

Box 11-2 Paper prototypes

Paper prototypes are widely used in practice. A survey of 172 usability professionals conducted in 2002 asked how important they considered the technique to be in their work (Snyder, 2003). The responses are shown in the chart below – a 'useless' option was included but no-one chose it. (The percentages do not sum to 100 percent because of rounding.)

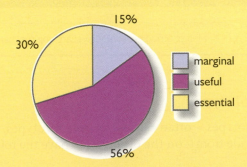

FIGURE 11-2 Paper prototype of a messaging screen for a home communications centre

to note here is the small acetate just visible at top left, which allows users to record suggested changes.

The main practical issues with designing paper prototypes are as follows.

- Robustness – if a paper prototype is to be handled by lots of people it needs to be tough enough to survive.

- Scope – focus on broad issues and key elements; if you are trying to tell too detailed a story it can be hard for users to understand.

- Instructions – there is a trade-off between adding enough detail for someone to able to use the prototype without the designer helping (in which case the boundary between the design ideas and the supplementary information can be hard to see) and adding so much detail that it needs someone to talk the user through it (which may affect the user's responses).

- Flexibility – have parts of the paper prototype adjustable so that people viewing it can 'redesign it' on the fly, e.g. by using sticky notes to represent parts of the screen where the user can move elements around or add new items.

Challenge 11-1
You are a designer working on a new interface to a supermarket's on-line shopping system. The client wants a complete revamp of the site. Your team leader in your own organization, a software developer, is unconvinced of the value of using lo-fi prototypes to explore ideas. Write the text of a short e-mail to convince her that this is a good idea. (Only the main part of the text arguing the case is required.)

Working through the prototype with users

In using the prototype, designers sit alongside the users to make the prototype 'work' if it is a lo-fi version. It helps to have two designers, one to 'play computer' and one to make notes. Whatever the type of prototype, record comments and design issues as they arise. Videotape can sometimes be useful if there is likely to be a substantial quantity of detailed feedback for other members of the team.

People find it difficult to react to a prototype if it is just placed in front of them devoid of any context. Some sort of structuring narrative is required. The most common strategy is to have users step through a scenario using the new application or to try carrying out one of their current tasks if the application is to replace an earlier system. For interface design details, set the scene by suggesting what someone would be trying to do with the software at that particular point, for example 'You are interested in buying the shirt shown on this screen but want to know more about the material – show me what you would do now.' It is always best if users interact with the prototype themselves, even if only by pointing to a paper button. This promotes engagement with the questions to be explored, and avoids any danger of the person running the prototyping session misinterpreting responses. But there will be cases where this is not feasible. Perhaps the prototype software is fragile, or the prototype is at a very early stage with very little genuine interactivity. Here designers can act under the user's directions – or maybe even run a 'movie' produced in software such as Director or Flash to simulate a usage session. The movie can be paused as appropriate for discussion. What is happening here is of course early evaluation, so many of the techniques discussed in Chapters 12, 21 and 22 are appropriate.

11.2 Prototypes and participatory design

Lo-fi prototypes are an essential part of participatory design because people cannot always understand formal models, but they can explore and evaluate ideas through engaging with prototyped systems. Users can also be directly involved in prototype design. During the development of the HIC we ran a workshop with schoolchildren from a school in Dumfries and Galloway in Scotland. It was decided to use the existing scenarios as stimuli in a participatory design workshop with a group of 20 high school students. Using the 'what will we do tonight' scenario as a basis, we spent a morning working with the students. The scenario was adapted to make it more relevant to the participants – the students were asked to imagine that they and a group of friends had won a trip to the city for the day and had to plan their activities.

We asked participants to use a range of supplied craft materials and information examples to create a mock-up of how they thought the HIC would look and operate. A number of lo-fi prototypes were quickly produced (Figures 11-3 to 11-5).

11.3 Different approaches to functionality in prototypes

There are several other types of prototype that it is useful to distinguish. A full prototype provides full functionality, but at a lower performance than the target system. A horizontal prototype aims to go across the whole system, but deals only with top-level functions, so much of the detail is omitted. In contrast a vertical prototype implements the full range of features, from top to bottom, but is

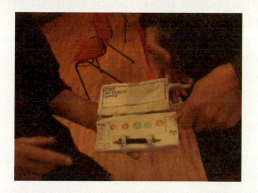

FIGURE 11-3 HIC mock-up in clay (and pencil!)

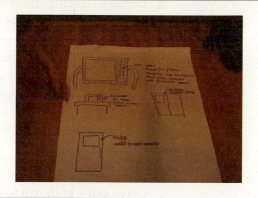

FIGURE 11-4 Storyboard

FIGURE 11-5 Remote control mock-up

applied to only a small number of functions of the overall system. Combinations of these are common. Evolutionary and incremental (a more step-wise version of evolutionary) prototypes eventually develop into the full system.

As with so many aspects of design the designer has to consider the trade-offs in terms of time, resources, the aim of the evaluation, the stage of the project and so on. Indeed, when reflecting on how and what to prototype, the designer should think in terms of the PACT elements – people, activities, contexts and technologies. Who is the prototype aimed at? What is the designer trying to achieve with the prototype? What stage of the project are things at and what is the context for the use of the prototype? What technologies (hi-fi or lo-fi) are appropriate?

Rosson and Carroll (2002) highlight some of these trade-offs:

PACT is introduced in Chapter 2

■ High-quality graphics and animation can be used to create convincing and exciting prototypes *but* may also lead to premature commitment to some design decision.

- Detailed special-purpose prototypes help to answer specific questions about a design, *but* building a meaningful prototype for each issue is expensive.
- Realistic prototypes increase the validity of user test data, *but* may postpone testing, or require construction of throw-away prototypes.
- Iterative refinement of an implementation enables continual testing and feedback, *but* may discourage consideration of radical transformations.

Prototyping is used throughout the design process.

- 'Requirements animation' is a term used to describe the use of prototyping to illustrate requirements. Used at an early stage, a quick prototype can be developed and shown to the client/users for comment on the general design.
- Rapid prototyping (also known as 'throw-it-away' prototyping) is common in user interface design where software such as PowerPoint or Macromedia Director is used to illustrate concepts. The prototype will be 'thrown away' because implementation will be in a different language. However, as one famous quotation in software development has it, 'You will throw away your first few designs, so you might as well plan to throw them away in the first place'.

Prototyping and design documentation

One of the purposes of prototyping is to clarify or verify requirements, which will usually need adjustment once clients and users have a realistic design to review and explore. It is important to remember to update the requirements list, noting why and when the requirements were modified, and having any clients agree and sign off the changes. Clients should be advised beforehand if the modifications resulting from prototyping will change delivery dates or costs – almost certainly the case. If scenarios, sketches or other representations are part of the definitive design documentation, they should be updated as well.

Challenge 11-2
Imagine you are presenting your ideas for a diary tool on a PDA to a small team of developers from the PDA manufacturer. What type of prototype would you use?

11.4 Prototyping tools

Given the wide range of uses for prototyping and the large number of occasions when it is used, it is not surprising that there are a wealth of software 'tools' that can be used. A good prototyping tool should:

- Allow easy, rapid modification of interface details or functionality
- For designers who are not programmers, allow direct manipulation of prototype components
- For incremental and evolutionary prototypes, facilitate reuse of code
- Not constrain the designer to default styles for interface objects.

Useful tools for requirements animation include paper, PowerPoint (e.g. for illustrating main screens) and drawing packages. Data manipulation languages such as SQL can be effective in animating the functionality of a system, and vertical or horizontal prototypes can be built using simple application builders such as Visual Basic, the Borland development environment, the Java development environment and so on.

Throw-it-away (rapid) prototyping emphasizes rapid evaluation and changing requirements. Useful software here includes Macromedia Director and similar tools, Visual Basic, PowerPoint, hypermedia tools and Web tools such as Dreamweaver or Flash. For evolutionary and incremental prototyping there is a compromise between production and prototyping and a long-term view of system development, so a development environment that can be used for implementation is needed. Reuse of code is likely and hence object-oriented languages are suitable.

Prototyping functionality in software has its own pitfalls. For example, if the user interface prototype diverges from the functional prototype it may not be possible for them to be brought together. Indeed this is what happened in the HIC case study and we finished up with an interface prototype which was low in functionality and a functional prototype which had a pretty poor interface! Other dangers include users being unable to evaluate functionality because the user interface is distractingly difficult – something that happened in DISCOVER, where early prototype users found it so difficult to move around the virtual environment that reviewing the training functionality was practically impossible. People found it impossible to find their way around fixtures and fittings (as in the virtual bridge in Figure 11-6), became irretrievably stuck midway up a virtual staircase or entangled themselves with railings. We recovered the situation by refocusing the early evaluation sessions on interaction mechanisms and considering functionality much later, when the worst problems had been resolved. Incidentally, this illustrates the value of prototyping with users as early as possible in the process. The software designers themselves had naturally experienced no problems with virtual movement.

Challenge 11-3
What are the advantages and disadvantages of prototyping software at the very early stages of development?

FIGURE 11-6 The virtual bridge in the DISCOVER CVE

11.5 Presenting designs

Presenting design ideas clearly and appropriately is a key skill of the designer. The design process is a long one with many different stages, there are many different people involved and there are many different reasons for giving a presentation. The combination of these will affect what sort of presentation and what sort of representation is suitable.

If the ideas are aimed at senior management, for example, then it is likely that the focus is on vision, concepts and key features of design. People in this position are generally concerned with strategic issues rather than detail, so a presentation to management should focus on impact, image and concept. If the presentation is aimed at the client then one would expect a bit more detail and some idea of how it works. If the presentation is aimed at end-users then it is most likely to concentrate on the detail of the design and the workings of the system. If presenting to end-users it is important to beware of misconceptions about current activities. It is very easy for people to lose credibility with such an audience if an unrealistic scenario or example is used.

The purpose of the presentation is equally important. If the aim is getting the contract then the presentation should focus on the big selling point and what it is that distinguishes your design from the others. If the contract is organized and the aim is agreeing the concept, then the focus will be on restating the client's brief, clarifying requirements and scoping the area. Where the presentation is concerned with evaluating a general design idea, or with testing major design features with users, then it must be focused on eliciting an appropriate response.

If the prototype or design is still at the concept stage, broad images of the system are appropriate with little functionality except in key areas. An early design will emphasize the design principles and the basis of the *design language*. It will show how the parts fit together, basic navigational features and so on. If it is a detailed design then the correct size is important along with the proposed shapes, colours and text.

Finally it is important to be clear about what is being highlighted by the presentation. Is it the functionality and events, or is it the interactions and usability with the focus on look and feel, or ease of use? If the focus is on content and structure, then attend to what information is there, and how is it organized, whereas if it is style and aesthetics then the focus is on features such as enjoyability, visual and tangible design and use of media.

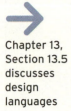

Chapter 13, Section 13.5 discusses design languages

11.6 Envisionment in practice

In this section we revisit some of the material in this chapter and the previous one to show how different envisionment techniques have been combined in some of our own projects.

Redesigning a CAD (Computer Aided Design) package

This example dates from the mid-1980s, when a command language-based engineering drawing system was being updated with a graphical user interface (GUI). This might seem to be of historical interest only, but to our certain knowledge legacy systems are still being converted to GUIs. In this case, users were largely quite happy with the command language interaction. It had the advantage of being extremely efficient for expert users – and most users were well practised – and freeing a very large proportion of the screen for the engineering drawing itself. The software vendor producing the package, however, decided to update the software with a fashionable GUI and to support non-English speaking users by allowing interaction through icons rather than text (see Figure 11-7). (The design challenges in doing this for some very abstract functions were near-impossible, but that is another story.) Our first visualization technique was a full-size paper prototype, simply comprising a sheet of paper delineating the screen and the areas proposed for permanent icons and drop-down menus, together with cut-outs of icons and menus which could be moved around the screen. This helped to get a quick impression of how much space would be required – a good deal – and alternative layouts.

Once an initial design had been decided, an evolutionary prototype was discussed with customers who visited the development site for training or to discuss custom modifications, sales consultants and support engineers. All were concerned about compromising drawing space. The result was a final design which minimized the range of controls permanently displayed, and allowed users to choose between command language and GUI interfaces.

FIGURE 11-7 Icon 'buttons' used in the paper prototype for a redesigned CAD package

Exploring distributed working in automobile design

Here we were in the early stages of designing a system to allow automobile design engineers to work together with their colleagues in production engineering who were located many miles away. The ideas and the technology were quite new for the people concerned. We conducted an intensive initial requirements analysis which produced a number of scenarios incorporating use of the technology in familiar work practices, being careful to use the industry-specific technology wherever possible. These were discussed at a two-day workshop with representatives from the design groups, their managers, IT specialists from the industry and software developers. The results were much clearer requirements for the functionality to be provided and great enthusiasm for the ideas.

Later in the project a realistic hi-fi prototype was produced using Macromedia Director and discussed in detail with individual users. Here the main focus was the details of user interface design.

Summary and key points

Prototyping brings designs to life for both designers and the people who will use the new designs. The prototype can be anywhere along the spectrum of technical sophistication, be put together in half an hour or take several days of programming. Aim to fit the prototype to the design situation you find yourself in, but beware of bring carried away with your own ingenuity. The point is to explore ideas, not to build an entire parallel system or product. Prototyping is never a substitute for a good requirements analysis, nor should versions of software prototypes slide uncontrolled into the final product. But used properly it is at the heart of a human-centred design process.

- Prototyping may focus on a vertical or horizontal slice through the system, or cover the whole system, and may evolve into a final product or be thrown away and re-engineered.
- The presentation of ideas is a key aspect of design. The form of the presentation and the content need to be considered given the audience and the stage of the product's development.
- Different techniques for envisionment will suit different types and scales of project.
- Lo-fi prototyping explores initial concepts and broad ideas; hi-fi prototyping is more suitable for detailed evaluation of 'look and feel' and functionality.
- One of the main purposes of prototyping is to evaluate designs with users.

Further reading

Rudd, J., Stern, K. and Isensee, S. (1996) Low vs. high fidelity prototyping debate. *Interactions*, **3**(1), 76–85.
A readable exploration of the issues.

Rosson, M.-B. and Carroll, J. (2002) *Usability Engineering*. Morgan Kaufmann, San Francisco.
Chapter 6 covers prototyping.

Snyder, C. (2003) *Paper Prototyping: The Fast and Easy Way to Design and Refine User Interfaces*. Morgan Kaufmann, San Francisco.
Everything you always wanted to know about paper prototyping. A great source of ideas and practical tips.

Comments on challenges

Challenge 11-1

It would be a good idea to emphasize how the paper prototype would allow radically different concepts to be explored – and eliminated – cheaply and quickly, rather than rejecting weak ideas only when they had been realized in software.

Challenge 11-2

Presumably the idea here is to impress the management with the quality of the design work and to 'get the contract'. The prototype is probably going to be hi-fi with respect to size. Management will want to see how the ideas work on the small screen of a PDA. The prototype will also have to get over the principles of the design effectively. This might be a novel way of interacting – turning the 'pages' using a pen, for example. Or there might be some special functionality that the designer wants to get over: a facility to zoom to the next appointment, perhaps. The designer should identify these key elements that need to be communicated and prototype them using a hi-fi tool such as Director or Flash. The designer might also take along some paper prototypes of other concepts and designs in order to get more involvement and feedback on ideas. It is all a matter of judgement and resources, trying to 'sell' some of the ideas and concepts (so that the contract can be secured) and exploring others.

Challenge 11-3

Advantages:

- Can gather good feedback from users when there is still plenty of time to modify the design
- Fosters a sense of user involvement
- Can provide a realistic impression of the end-product
- May be possible to develop the prototype into the final product.

Disadvantages:

- May have distracting usability problems
- Developers may be reluctant to discard software to accommodate redesigns
- Can inhibit some more technophobic users
- Can appear too 'finished' to generate comment.

You will probably have thought of others.

Exercises

1. You have been asked to develop a website for a local radio station and have gone to meet the radio station manager and one of their leading DJs. What envisionment techniques would you use during and after this meeting? Outline some initial ideas for alternative design concepts.

2. Using plain paper, coloured pens and different coloured Post-its, create a paper prototype for the screen of the home control device for the concrete scenario you developed in Exercise 1 of Chapter 10.

12 Evaluation

Aims

We have seen how designs are developed by means of envisionment and proto-typing of the system's structure and behaviour. We have stressed how this process is an iterative and exploratory one, where designers move between design concepts and their physical expression. Throughout, we have stressed how evaluation is central to this process, but we have not yet discussed how to do this in any detail. This chapter introduces evaluation as a key element of interactive systems development, discusses different purposes and styles of evaluation and provides simple but effective evaluation techniques. The major focus in this chapter is usability: other aspects of evaluation are explored later in the book in Chapters 21 and 22.

After studying this chapter you should be able to:

- Understand the role of evaluation
- Define what needs to be evaluated for particular contexts
- Conduct and report a basic usability evaluation.

12.1 Evaluating interactive systems design

By evaluation we mean reviewing, trying out or testing a design, a piece of soft-ware or a product to discover whether it is learnable, effective and accommodating – our design principles from Chapter 2 – for its intended user population.

The designer is concerned not just with surface features such as the meaning-fulness of icons, but also with whether the application is fit for its purpose – anything from entertainment to routine order processing.

Box 12-1 Definitions of usability

There are many of these, many of which have similar underlying philosophies. Indeed in Chapter 3 we offered three slightly different ways of conceptualizing usability. International standard ISO 9241 part 11 defines usability as 'The extent to which a product can be used by specified users to achieve specified goals with effectiveness, efficiency and satisfaction in a specified context of use.'

We discuss some of these issues in Chapter 22, Section 22.4

The techniques in this chapter will allow you to evaluate many types of applications. Some applications do not sit easily with this approach – particularly those intended to entertain, to provoke (as in the case of some art installations), to make a lifestyle statement or to be adopted and personalized as part of people's everyday domestic life.

Challenge 12-1

Collect several advertisements for small, personal technologies such as that shown in Figure 12-1. What claims are the advertisers making about design features and benefits? What issues does this raise for their evaluation?

Design

The image of sophistication. The T100's crisp, clean simplicity is its strength: very small and light, it's as eye-catching as a jewel, but without the high price tag.

FIGURE 12-1 Sony Ericsson T100 mobile phone *(source: http://www.sonyericsson.co.uk/)*

In our human-centred approach to design, we evaluate designs right from the earliest idea. For example, as we have seen, very early ideas for the HIC were mocked-up and reviewed by a group of potential users, to be followed later by more realistic prototyping and user testing of a partially finished system and finally by evaluation of the near-complete device in its intended home setting.

Basic evaluation step-by-step

The table below summarizes the main steps in undertaking a simple but effective evaluation project. Each is then explained in the material which follows in this chapter.

Step	Material in this chapter and elsewhere in this book
1. Establish the aims of the evaluation, the intended users and context of use for the software; obtain or construct scenarios illustrating how the application will be used	Chapters 8–11, this section
2. Select evaluation methods – should be a combination of expert review and end-user testing	12.2, 12.3, 12.4, 12.5; see also further methods in Chapters 21 and 22
3. Carry out expert review	12.2
4. Plan user testing; use the results of the expert review to help focus this	12.3
5. Recruit users and organize testing venue and equipment	12.3
6. Carry out user testing	12.4 and 12.5
7. Analyse results, write up and report back to designers	12.6

Evaluation is concerned with different issues at different times during the development of a product or system. The steps above are applicable to all of these. The key is to consider what information you are trying to obtain.

Obtaining feedback to inform early design concepts

You may need to evaluate initial concepts, especially if the application is novel for your users. Here quick 'paper' prototypes can help, or even software if this can be produced rapidly. Evaluations of competitor products or previous versions of technology can also feed into the design process at this stage.

Deciding between different design options

During development, designers have to decide between options, for example between voice input or touchscreen interaction for a shared electronic household wall-planner or between different sequences for order processing functions. In DISCOVER, we had to decide between cursor keys, mouse or joystick for moving around the virtual environment.

Checking for usability problems

Testing will identify potential problems once a stable version of the technology is available. This needs to respond when the user activates a function, but not all the data processing components (for example) may be fully operational. Alternatively, the system may be completely functional, but only in some parts. What is important is that there is still time to fix problems. What happens all too frequently is that you are asked to check that interaction is 'user friendly' just before development is completed. Very often all that can be changed are minor issues such as the position, colour or labelling of on-screen buttons. It is best to be helpful in these circumstances. If you make a note of problems which could have been solved easily if identified sooner, you can exploit these examples (tactfully) to justify evaluation work at an earlier stage in the next project.

Evaluation of the types described above is sometimes termed **formative evaluation**, because the results help to form – or shape – the design.

Assessing the usability of a finished product

This may be to test against in-house guidelines, or formal usability standards such as ISO 9241, or to provide evidence of usability required by a customer, for example the time to complete a particular set of operations. Government departments and other public bodies often require suppliers to conform with accessibility standards and health and safety legislation. In DISCOVER, employers of the personnel to be trained in the virtual environment required evidence that such training was just as effective as its classroom equivalent.

This type of evaluation is sometimes termed **summative**.

As a means of involving people in the design process

In participatory design approach, users help designers set the goals for the evaluation work. Involving users has great benefits in terms of eventual uptake and use of the technology. (Of course, this applies only to technology which is tailor-made for defined user communities, rather than off-the-shelf products.) For example, in a redevelopment of a Web-based gallery showcasing the work of disadvantaged artists, as many of the artists themselves as possible were involved in evaluating the new designs, thus preserving the sense of community which the site aimed to embody (Macleod, 2002).

Assessing use in practice

Researchers undertake long-term evaluations as a means of understanding the success of particular technologies. Such an approach is relatively rare in commercial practice, though indirect data are often collected and used to inform the next release of a product. These might include problems reported by customers or end-users, customer reactions to salespersons' pitches or requests for modifications.

12.2 Expert evaluation basics

The most widely used form of expert review, heuristic evaluation, involves experts checking the application systematically against a list of principles, guidelines or 'heuristics' for good design. Usability heuristics draw on psychological theory and practical experience.

There are many sets of heuristics to choose from, both general purpose (e.g. the long-established lists in Hix and Hartson, 1993, and Shneiderman, 1998, and the participatory heuristics included in Chapter 27) and those relating to particular application domains, for example heuristics for Web design.

Here is a brief list of the design principles – or heuristics – which we introduced in Chapter 3. You should refer back to that chapter for the details.

1. Visibility	7. Feedback
2. Consistency	8. Recovery
3. Familiarity	9. Constraints
4. Affordance	10. Flexibility
5. Navigation	11. Style
6. Control	12. Conviviality

The list can be summarized by the three over-arching usability principles of learnability, effectiveness and accommodation – if time is very short, a quick review of the design against this triad can produce reasonably useful results as we saw in Chapter 4.

Challenge 12-2
Carry out a quick review of the controls for a domestic device, e.g. a stove, microwave or washing machine, for learnability, effectiveness and accommodation. Refer back to Section 3.6 for a detailed explanation of these principles.

How many evaluators?

Ideally, several people with expertise in interactive systems design should review the interface. Valuable insights can also be gained from technical authors and support and help desk staff. It has been well documented (Nielsen, 1993) that lone evaluators will find only around 35 percent of usability problems. Nielsen goes on to suggest that the optimal number of evaluators (in cost–benefit terms) is around five, but this is infeasible in many situations and worthwhile results can be obtained even if only one expert is used. Each expert notes the problems and the relevant heuristic, and suggests a solution where possible. It is also helpful if a severity rating, say on a scale of 1–3, is added, according to the likely impact of the problem. Evaluators work independently and then combine results. They may need to work through any training materials users will be given, or at least be briefed by the design team about the functionality. The scenarios used in the design process are valuable here.

Unless there is no alternative, you should not evaluate your own designs. It is extremely difficult to ignore your knowledge of how the system works, the meaning of icons or menu names and so on, and you are likely to give the design the 'benefit of the doubt' or to find obscure flaws which few users will ever happen upon.

A basic heuristic evaluation step-by-step

Step	Notes
0. Establish the aims of the evaluation and the intended users and context of use for the software.	The IMPACT model – described in Section 12.3 – will help you do this.
1. Select heuristics.	Add specific heuristics as necessary.
2. Brief evaluators about the technology and how it is intended to be used.	Design scenarios very useful here; training may be necessary for complex applications. A member of the design team may need to be available during the session to help evaluators.
3. Evaluators independently make a first pass through the design.	Aim is to gain an impression of how the system fits together and its overall design.
4. Evaluators independently examine the design in more detail, working through typical or critical scenarios.	Review against each heuristic, and focus on areas which are particularly important or are typical of a set of similar interactions. A standard problem report form is useful.
5. Evaluators produce a consolidated list of prioritized problems linked to heuristics and suggested solutions.	Adding solutions and severity ratings increases the chance of having the problem fixed. Evaluators should review the list to remove any problems which, although difficulties in theory, are unlikely to inder a sensible user.

The results of the expert review also guide the focus of testing with users.

12.3 The IMPACT model for user evaluation

While expert analysis is a reasonable first step, it will not find all problems, particularly those which result from a chain of 'wrong' actions or are linked to fundamental misconceptions. Woolrych and Cockton (2001) discuss this in detail. Experts even find problems which do not really exist – users overcome many minor difficulties using a mixture of common sense and experience. So it is really important to complete the picture with some real people trying out the interaction design. The findings will always be interesting, quite often surprising and occasionally disconcerting. From a political point of view, it is easier to convince designers of the need for changes if the evidence is not simply one 'expert' view, particularly if the expert is relatively junior. The aim is to trial the design with people who represent the intended target group in as near realistic conditions as possible.

The decisions to be made in planning can be encapsulated in the acronym 'IMPACT' – we are after all concerned with assessing the 'impact' of technology on users. As well as the now familiar components of PACT – People, Activities, Context and Technologies – we now have Intention and Metrics.

Intention

Deciding the aim(s) for evaluation helps to determine the type of data required. It is useful to write down the main questions you need to answer. Early concept evaluation, in DISCOVER for instance, entailed questions such as:

- Do the trainers understand and welcome the basic idea of the virtual training environment?
- Would they use it to extend or replace existing training courses?
- How close to reality should the virtual environment be?
- What features are required to support record keeping and administration?

The data we are interested in at this stage is largely qualitative (non-numerical). We might, however, want to determine the relative strength of opinions. Rating scales (see Section 12.5) are a simple way of doing this. By contrast, the comparison of two different evaluation designs usually entails much more focused questions, for example in the DISCOVER case:

- Is it quicker to reach a particular room in the virtual environment using mouse, cursor keys or joystick?
- Is it easier to open a virtual door by clicking on the handle or selecting the 'open' icon from a tools palette?

Figure 12-2 shows the evaluation in progress. Underlying issues were the focus on speed and ease of operation. This illustrates the link between analysis and evalua-

FIGURE 12-2 A trainer evaluating the DISCOVER CVE training system. He is consulting the scenario used to structure the evaluation

tion – in this case, it had been identified that these qualities were crucial for the acceptability of the virtual learning environment. With questions such as these, we are likely to need quantitative (numerical) data to support design choices.

The above material has illustrated the sort of questions which are important for two of the many possible evaluation intentions. But these are only examples: you will need to consider each situation individually. Ideally, the focus should be discussed with designers and clients or end-users as appropriate.

Metrics (and measures)

What is to be measured and how? Table 12-1 shows some common usability metrics and ways in which they can be measured, adapted from the list provided in the usability standard ISO 9241 part 11 and using the usability definition of 'effectiveness, efficiency and satisfaction' adopted in the standard. There are many other possibilities.

Such metrics are helpful in evaluating many types of applications from small mobile communication devices to office systems. In most of these there is a task – something the user wants to get done – and it is reasonably straightforward to decide whether the task has been achieved successfully or not. There is one major difficulty: deciding the acceptable figure for, say, the percentage of tasks successfully completed. Is this 95 percent, 80 percent or 50 percent? In some (rare) cases clients may set this figure. Otherwise a baseline may be available from comparative testing against an alternative design, a previous version, a rival product, or the current manual version of a process to be computerized. But the evaluation team still has to determine whether a metric is *relevant*. For example, in a complex computer-aided design system, one would not expect most functions to be used perfectly at the first attempt. And would it really be meaningful if design engineers using one design were on average two seconds quicker in completing a complex diagram than those using a competing design? By contrast,

TABLE 12-1 Common usability metrics

Usability objective	Effectiveness measures	Efficiency measures	Satisfaction measures
Overall usability	Percentage of tasks successfully completed Percentage of users successfully completing tasks	Time to complete a task Time spent on non-productive actions	Rating scale for satisfaction Frequency of use if this is voluntary (after system is implemented)
Meets needs of trained or experienced users	Percentage of advanced tasks completed Percentage of relevant functions used	Time taken to complete tasks relative to minimum realistic time	Rating scale for satisfaction with advanced features
Meets needs for walk-up and use	Percentage of tasks completed successfully at first attempt	Time taken on first attempt to complete task Time spent on help functions	Rate of voluntary use (after system is implemented)
Meets needs for infrequent or intermittent use	Percentage of tasks completed successfully after a specified period of non-use	Time spent re-learning functions Number of persistent errors	Frequency of reuse (after system is implemented)
Learnability	Number of functions learned Percentage of users who manage to learn to a pre-specified criterion	Time spent on help functions Time to learn to criterion	Rating scale for ease of learning

Source: ISO 9241-11:1998 Ergonomic requirements for office work with visual display terminals (VDTs), extract of Table B.2

speed of keying characters may be crucial to the success of a mobile phone. There are three things to keep in mind when deciding metrics:

- Just because something can be measured, it doesn't mean it should be.
- Always refer back to the overall purpose and context of use of the technology.
- Consider the usefulness of the data you are likely to obtain against the resources it will take to test against the metrics.

The last point is particularly important in practice.

Challenge 12-3
Why is learnability more important for some applications than for others? Think of some examples where it might *not* be a very significant factor in usability.

Further thoughts: Engagement

Games and other applications designed for entertainment pose different questions for evaluation. While we may still want to evaluate whether the basic functions to move around a game environment, for example, are easy to learn, efficiency and effectiveness in a wider sense are much less relevant. The 'purpose' here is to enjoy the game, and time to complete, for example, a particular level may sometimes be less important than experiencing the events that happen along the way. Similarly, multimedia applications are often directed at intriguing users or evoking emotional responses rather than having the achievement of particular tasks in a limited period of time. In contexts of this type, evaluation centres on probing user experience through interviews or questionnaires. Read and MacFarlane (2000), for example, used a rating scale presented as a 'smiley face vertical fun meter' when working with children to evaluate novel interfaces. Other measures which can be considered are observational: the user's posture or facial expression, for instance, may be an indicator of engagement in the experience.

People

The most important people in evaluation are users. Analysis work should have identified the characteristics of intended users, but sometimes you will have to work with the designers to obtain this information. Relevant data can include knowledge of the activities the technology is intended to support, skills relating to input and output devices, experience, education, training and physical and cognitive capabilities.

The issue is discussed further in Chapter 27

You need to recruit at least three and preferably five people to participate in tests. They should be typical of the intended users. Nielsen's recommended sample of 3–5 users has been accepted wisdom in usability practice for over a decade. However, some practitioners and researchers advise that this is too few. We consider that in many real-world situations obtaining even 3–5 people is difficult, so we continue to recommend small test numbers as part of a pragmatic evaluation strategy.

However, testing such a small number only makes sense if you have just one main type of target user – for example, experienced users of a customer database system, or computer games players aged between 16 and 25. If you have several different user groups, then you will need to run 3–5 people *from each group* through your tests. For example, in DISCOVER we tested the virtual training environment with both tutors and trainees. If your product is to be demonstrated by sales and marketing personnel, it is useful to involve them as a special type of user group. Finding users should be straightforward if you are developing an in-house application. Otherwise they can be found through product user groups, focus groups established for marketing purposes or, if necessary, through advertising. Students are often readily available, but remember that they are only representative of a particular segment of the population. If you have the resources, payment can help recruitment. Inevitably, your sample will be biased towards cooperative people with some sort of interest in technology, so bear this in mind when interpreting your results.

If you cannot recruit any genuine users, and you are the designer of the software, at least have someone else try to use it. This could be one of your colleagues, a friend, your mother or anyone you trust to give you a brutally honest reaction. Almost certainly, they will find some design flaws. The data you obtain will be limited, but better than nothing. You will, however, have to be *extremely* careful as to how far you generalize from your findings.

Finally, consider your own role and that of others in the evaluation team if you have one. You will need to set up the tests and collect data, but how far will you become involved? Our recommended method for basic testing requires an evaluator to sit with each user and engage with them as they carry out the test tasks. We also suggest that for ethical reasons and in order to keep the tests running, you should provide help if the user is becoming uncomfortable, or completely stuck. The amount of help which is appropriate will depend on the type of application (e.g. for an information kiosk for public use you might only provide very minimal help), the degree of completeness of the test application and in particular whether any help facilities have been implemented.

Activities

It is equally important to consider typical activity with the technology. Concrete scenarios are reused here. They should cover typical uses of the technology, and rare but critical events. For example, in the evaluation of a bank auto teller (ATM), scenarios might be created for withdrawing money, obtaining a mini-statement and forgetting to remove one's bank card. Use scenarios to set the scene for users, and to draw up the list of actions which they will undertake.

Contexts

All the elements of IMPACT contribute to the context of the evaluation. But what we are specifically concerned with here is the wider social and physical context which may affect the way the technology is used. This may include:

- Patterns of activity – is this just part of another activity? Is the user's work monitored? Do users have control of pace or order in which tasks are undertaken? Is use likely to be interrupted? Is use voluntary?
- Assistance – are other people around to help out if there are problems?
- Is the technology single user or to be used with others (as in many games) or in co-working?
- The physical set-up of the technology – at a desk, on a small portable device, as a free-standing information kiosk, as a display in a car or other vehicle …?

■ The wider physical environment – inside or outside, noisy or quiet, hot, humid or cold, are there unusual lighting conditions ...?

■ Social norms – are users likely to feel time-pressured by others waiting to use the application, as in the case of an auto teller or a ticket machine? Are users expected to be particularly accurate ...?

Consideration of these points will help to make the evaluation as ecologically valid (i.e. close to the context of use) as possible and guide the metrics to be applied.

You will need a place where the context of use can be recreated as far as possible, the technology can be installed, there is space for you and anyone else helping you with the evaluation, and you will not be disturbed. If you are undertaking a good deal of evaluation work, a dedicated usability laboratory could be justified, but most of us do not have that luxury.

Technologies

Near the end of the development process, you should be evaluating on a machine or device which is as near as possible to that on which the product will be delivered. For networked applications, you should also take into account issues such as network speed and reliability. A good example where this is an issue is in the evaluation of Internet-based multimedia applications. Loading time for a video segment may be evaluated as acceptable if the video file is in local storage, but discouragingly long when the application is running over a domestic Internet connection.

Also decide the technology to support the user tests. At a minimum, you will need pen and paper for recording observations (see next section) and printed copies of any instructions or other materials for users and expert evaluators. You may also want to make video or audio recordings.

The test plan and task specification

Having considered each of the IMPACT elements, a plan should be drawn up to embody the decisions. The plan specifies:

■ Aims of the test session

■ Practical details including where and when it will be conducted, how long each session will last, the specification of equipment and materials for testing and data collection and any technical support that may be necessary

■ Numbers and types of user

■ Tasks to be performed with a definition of successful completion. This section also specifies what data should be collected and how it will be analysed.

You should now conduct a pilot session and fix any unforeseen difficulties. For example, task completion time is often much longer than expected, and instructions may need clarification.

12.4 A minimal Cooperative Usability Evaluation

This section shows how to apply one illustrative usability testing technique. Cooperative Usability Evaluation was developed by Andrew Monk and colleagues (Monk *et al.*, 1993) at the University of York (UK) as a means of maximizing the data from a simple testing session. The technique is 'cooperative' because users are not passive subjects but work as co-evaluators. It has proved a reliable but economical technique in diverse applications. The table below and the sample questions are edited from Appendix 1 in Monk *et al.* (1993).

Step	Notes
1. Using the scenarios prepared earlier, write a draft list of tasks.	Tasks must be realistic, do-able with the software, and explore the system thoroughly.
2. Try out the tasks and estimate how long they will take a user to complete.	Allow 50 percent longer than the total task time for each user test session.
3. Prepare a task sheet for the users.	Be specific and explain the tasks so a novice user can understand.
4. Get ready for the test session.	Have the prototype ready in a suitable environment with a list of prompt questions, notebook and pens ready. An audio recorder would be very useful here.
5. Tell the users that it is the system that is under test, not them; explain the procedure and introduce the tasks.	Users should work individually – you will not be able to monitor more than one user at once. Start recording if equipment is available.
6. Users start the tasks. Have them give you a running commentary on what they are doing, why they are doing it and difficulties or uncertainties they encounter.	Take notes of where users find problems or do something unexpected, and their comments. Do this even if you are recording the session. You may need to help if users are stuck or have them move to the next task.
7. Encourage users to keep talking.	Some useful prompt questions are provided below.
8. When the users have finished, interview them briefly about the usability of the prototype and the session itself. Thank them.	Some useful questions are provided below. If you have a large number of users, a simple questionnaire may be helpful.
9. Write up your notes as soon as possible and incorporate into a usability report.	

Sample questions during the test session:

1. What do you want to do?
2. What were you expecting to happen?
3. What is the system telling you?
4. Why has the system done that?
5. What are you doing now?

Sample questions after the session:
1. What was the best/worst thing about the prototype?
2. What most needs changing?
3. How easy were the tasks?
4. How realistic were the tasks?
5. Did giving a commentary distract you?

12.5 Data capture techniques for usability evaluation

Section 9.3 describes the basics of these techniques and should be read before applying them in evaluation

As we can see from the instructions for Cooperative Evaluation, the same basic techniques used for obtaining information from people in the analysis stage are used in evaluation. The questions and any observation checklists are now, of course, geared to people's use of the new system, but the same general considerations apply in their design. A typical deployment of these techniques in usability testing would be to have test users work through one or more scenarios, then be interviewed by a member of the evaluation team or complete a short questionnaire about the experience. An evaluator may also observe users and will often ask questions during the process.

Interviewing in usability evaluation

Interviews are reviewed in Chapter 9, Section 9.4

Short individual interviews after testing are very valuable in clarifying user reactions, or amplifying the answers to questionnaire items. You could also interview users in a group – this can save time and users will prompt each other – but beware of people dominating the discussion. Some typical generic questions are included above in the Cooperative Evaluation section. Other topics might be:

- Clarity of function presentation
- Adequacy of functionality
- Clarity of feedback and any system messages
- Any particular difficulties encountered

- Whether the user would choose to use the application
- Realism of test tasks
- Clarity of test instructions.

An alternative to Cooperative Evaluation is to videotape the test session and then talk through with users what was happening. This helps to avoids distraction during the test session but does run the risk of *post hoc* rationalizations.

Challenge 12-4

Why are interviews and questionnaires (see below) insufficient to collect a full spectrum of data from an evaluation session?

Designing questionnaires for usability evaluation

Questionnaires are fully discussed in Chapter 21, Section 21.1

Questionnaires can gather basic background data about user characteristics and reactions after the test session. The usual cautions apply to their construction and analysis. Relevant user characteristics should have been identified when planning the testing and a set of check-boxes or short free-text answers can be used to collect this data. User perceptions of interaction design are usually collected through rating scales, for example using this five-point scale:

1. Strongly agree
2. Agree
3. Neutral
4. Disagree
5. Strongly disagree.

The scale is attached to each of a number of statements such as:

I always knew what I should do next (*tick one box*)

1. Strongly agree	2. Agree	3. Neutral	4. Disagree	5. Strongly disagree

Icons were easily understandable

1. Strongly agree	2. Agree	3. Neutral	4. Disagree	5. Strongly disagree

The destination of links was clear

1. Strongly agree	2. Agree	3. Neutral	4. Disagree	5. Strongly disagree

Chapter 14, Section 14.8 illustrates some of these ideas in the HIC case study

Make the questionnaire items as specific as possible. A probe statement such as 'The system was easy to use' does provide a general impression but gives very little information for redesign if you do not supplement it. Another approach is to devise 'bipolar' rating scales with individual labels for particular aspects of the software. These take longer to construct, but are helpful in probing specific reactions. For example:

The screen layout was (*circle one number*)
Neat and clear   1   2   3   4   5   Cluttered

Operation of functions was
Consistent   1   2   3   4   5   Inconsistent

Several ready-made and validated usability questionnaires are available, for example QUIS (Questionnaire for User Interface Satisfaction) from the University of Maryland (www.lap.umd.edu/QUISFolder/quisHome.html) and SUMI (Software Usability Measurement Inventory) from the University of Cork (http://www.ucc.ie/hfrg/questionnaires/sumi/index.html). These are 'industrial strength' instruments and there is normally a fee for their use. Others may be found in textbooks and the Web, but in the latter case be sure that their source is a reliable one.

Observation in usability evaluation

It is difficult for people to verbalize all their perceptions. People may not know why they find certain aspects difficult, or be reluctant to admit confusion, or simply be unable to recall their thought processes. For this reason it is best to sit with users as they carry out the test tasks, noting their actions and reactions. It may be less obtrusive to videotape the sessions, with the added benefits that the recordings can be replayed for analysis and are very effective in communicating results to designers.

12.6 Reporting usability evaluation results to the design team

However competent and complete the evaluation, it is only worthwhile if the results are acted upon. Even if you are both designer and evaluator, you need an organized list of findings so that you can prioritize redesign work. If you are reporting back to a design/development team, it is crucial that they can see

Box 12-2 An example small-scale evaluation

This is the process implemented by a postgraduate student to evaluate three different styles of user interface for the editing functions on photo-CDs. It is not a perfect example, but rather illustrates making the best use of limited resources.

Four experts reviewed the three interfaces in stage 1. Stage 2 consisted of a small number of short interviews of potential users designed to elicit typical uses for the software. These were used to develop scenarios and test tasks. Finally, stage 3 was a detailed end-user testing of the interfaces. This focused on exploration of the issues identified by the experts and was structured around the scenarios and tasks derived from stage 2. Stages 1 and 3 are described here.

Each person carrying out the heuristic evaluation had experience of interface evaluation and a working knowledge of interface design. They familiarized themselves with a scenario describing the level of knowledge of real users and their aims in using the products, together with a list of seven generic usability heuristics, then examined the software. They spent approximately one hour per interface and explored all functions, listing all usability issues discovered.

User testing involved a group of three males and three females aged between 25 and 35. Half were students and half were professionals; they had a varying degree of PC experience. With such a small sample, it was impossible to reflect the entire spectrum of the target population, but it was considered that these would provide a reasonable insight into any problems. After drawing up a test plan, scenarios and tasks were derived from background interview data and task analysis (see Chapter 20), supplemented by the results of the expert evaluation. Five main tasks were identified. Since the software was for home use, the tests were carried out in a home environment using equipment equivalent to that identified for the target population. Users undertook the testing individually and were reassured that the focus was on not on their skills but on any problems with the software. Written instructions emphasizing this and listing the five tasks were supplied, together with a scenario to set the scene. Each session lasted no more than 45 minutes to avoid fatigue.

Each user started with simple tasks to gain familiarity with the interface. The main tasks consisted of selecting an image and performing a number of typical editing tasks. For example, users were asked to select a specific image and edit it by rotating it the correct way round, switching to black and white, cropping the picture and adjusting the brightness and contrast before saving the new image. The intention was to give an overview of the functionality and a chance to learn the more complicated tools. Parts 3 and 4 of the tests asked the users to perform almost identical tasks to those already achieved. The aim here was to monitor the 'learnability' of the interface. The test was completed by accessing the slideshow option of each interface. Where possible, the user was also asked to attempt to import images from the hard disk. No help except that available from the software was provided.

Each sub-task required the user to rate the functions on a scale from 1 (easy) to 5 (difficult) before proceeding to the next. During the session, the evaluator noted user behaviour and verbalizations. Users were prompted to verbalize where necessary.

Finally, the user undertook a short task based on the operation of a mobile phone – intended as an indicator of competence in operating a commonplace artefact – before completing a brief questionnaire. This collected details of experience of PCs and software packages.

immediately what the problem is, how significant its consequences are, and ideally what needs to be done to fix it.

The report should be ordered either by areas of the system concerned, or by severity of problem. For the latter, you could adopt a three- or five-point scale, perhaps ranging from 'would prevent user from proceeding further' to 'minor irritation'. Adding a note of the general usability principle concerned may help designers understand why there is a difficulty, but often more specific explanation will be needed. Alternatively, sometimes the problem is so obvious that explanation is superfluous. A face-to-face meeting may have more impact than a written document alone (although this should always be produced as supporting material) and this would be the ideal venue for showing *short* video clips of user problems.

Suggested solutions make it more probable that something will be done. Requiring a response from the development team to each problem will further increase this probability, but may be counter-productive in some contexts. If your organization has a formal quality system, an effective strategy is to have usability evaluation alongside other test procedures, so usability problems are dealt with in the same way as any other fault. Even without a full quality system, usability problems can be fed into a 'bug' reporting system if one exists. Whatever the system for dealing with design problems, however, tact is a key skill in effective usability evaluation.

Challenge 12-5
Design a simple one-page pro-forma for a usability evaluation summary.

Summary and key points

This chapter has provided an overview of what needs to be considered in evaluating interactive systems using the IMPACT framework, with practical guidance in using simple but effective expert and end-user techniques. We have illustrated some of these with the real-life example of evaluating a user interface. We have seen that:

- Differing aims for evaluation require different questions to be answered
- Expert review and end-user testing are both effective, but should be used together as complementary methods
- Almost any degree of user testing can reveal useful insights, but care must be taken in generalizing from a small number of users
- Factors to take into account in user testing can be summarized as Intention, Metrics, People, Activities, Context and Technologies (IMPACT)

- The Cooperative Usability Evaluation method affords a practical way of testing usability in an economical manner
- Data collection techniques for evaluation mirror those for analysis.

Further reading

Monk, A., Wright, P., Haber, J. and Davenport, L. (1993) *Improving Your Human–Computer Interface: a Practical Technique*. BCS Practitioner Series, Prentice-Hall, New York and Hemel Hempstead.
This book includes a full description of cooperative usability evaluation. It may now be hard to purchase but should be available through libraries.

Doubleday, A., Ryan, M., Springett, M. and Sutcliffe, A. (1997) A comparison of usability techniques for evaluating design. *Proceedings of DIS '97 Conference*, Amsterdam, Netherlands. ACM Press, New York, pp. 101–110.
This compares the results of heuristic evaluation with user testing in the evaluation of an information retrieval interface. A good example of the continuing stream of research into the relative efficacy of different approaches to evaluation.

Nielsen, J. (1993) *Usability Engineering*. Academic Press. New York.
Nielsen's classic exposition of his 'discount' approach. Highly practical, but as discussed in this chapter and in Chapter 21, later work has suggested that the results obtained can have some limitations.

Comments on challenges

Challenge 12-1
The 'answer' to this of course depends on the material collected. But you will probably have found adverts appealing to aspirational needs and desires – status, style and so on – which standard usability techniques do not deal with particularly well. We discuss some of these issues in Chapter 17 and their evaluation in Chapter 22.

Challenge 12-2
The control panel for our dishwasher is very simply designed. It has four programmes, each of which is listed and numbered on the panel with a brief explanatory label (e.g. 'rinse') and a rather less self-explanatory icon. The dial to set the programme has starting points labelled with the programme numbers. The design is learnable – even without the handbook it is clear what each programme does and how to select it. It is also effective – I can

easily select the programme and the movement of the dial shows how far the cycle has progressed. It is accommodating to some extent in that I can interrupt the process to add more dishes, but fails (among other deficiencies here) to cope with the needs of partially sighted or blind users – something that could apparently be done fairly simply by adding tactile labels.

Challenge 12-3

Learnability – in terms of time taken to become familiar with functionality – can be less crucial, for example, when the application is intended for intensive, sustained long-term use. Here people expect to invest some effort in becoming acquainted with powerful functionality; also the overall learning time is relatively small compared with that spent using the software productively. Applications for professionals, such as computer-aided design, desktop publishing, scientific analysis software and the myriad of products intended for use by computer programmers, fall into this category. This doesn't mean that overall usability and good design cease to matter, but there will be more emphasis on issues such as fit to activity rather than superficial ease of learning.

Challenge 12-4

Among the reasons are:

- Users have to recall their experience, which may be difficult and introduce distortions.
- It is difficult to describe all aspects of interaction verbally.
- Users may tell the interviewer what they feel is expected.

Challenge 12-5

Points to consider here:

- A very short summary
- Structure (by topic, severity or some other ordering principle)
- A rating scale for severity
- Brief suggested solutions
- Links to supporting data
- Space for explanations where necessary.

Exercises

1. Using the list of heuristics from Section 12.2, carry out a heuristic evaluation of the features dealing with tables in your usual word processor and the phone book in your cellphone.

2. Think about the following evaluation. A call centre operator answers enquiries about insurance claims. This involves talking to customers on the phone while accessing their personal data and claim details from a database. You are responsible for the user testing of new database software to be used by the operators. What aspects of usability do you think it is important to evaluate, and how would you measure them?

   Now think about the same questions for an interactive multimedia website which is an on-line art gallery. The designers want to allow users to experience concrete and conceptual artworks presented in different media.

3. (More advanced) Identify any potential difficulties with the evaluation described in Box 12-3. What would you do differently?

4. (More advanced) You are responsible for planning the evaluation of an interactive toy for children. The toy is a small, furry, talking animal character whose behaviour changes over time as it 'learns' new skills and in response to how its owner treats it, for example how often it is picked up during a 24-hour period. The designers think it should take around a month for all the behaviours to develop. Children interact with the toy by speaking commands (it has voice recognition for 20 words), stroking its ears, picking it up, and pressing 'spots' on the animal's back which are, in effect, buttons triggering different actions. No instructions will be provided; children are intended to find out what the toy does by trial and error.

   Design an evaluation process for the toy, explaining the reasons behind your choices.

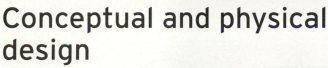

13 Conceptual and physical design

Aims

Conceptual design is a key aspect of interactive systems design. The methods for requirements, envisionment, prototyping and evaluation that we have described may be sufficient for designers and users to arrive at a final design. Applying general design principles (Chapter 3) and undertaking a PACT analysis will certainly improve the probability of that design being successful. Sometimes the designer is also the implementer of a system, or the development is on a small scale and so no further documentation is needed before development proper can start. But often this is not enough. And frequently the design has to be represented in a more structured form that can be given to a programmer to write software. In this chapter we discuss the importance of conceptual design and show how scenarios can be used to guide a structured conceptual design and how a physical design including interaction patterns is developed. We also introduce the idea of a design language.

After studing this chapter you should be able to:

- Understand the nature of conceptual and physical design
- Undertake an object/action analysis
- Produce a conceptual model of a new system or product using scenarios
- Describe how the system will look and behave through specifying the design language
- Specify a design in a form that can be implemented by programmers using use cases.

13.1 Conceptual and physical design

Figure 13-1 is the lower part of Figure 8-5 which we used earlier to illustrate the whole of the design process. It illustrates the processes of conceptual and physical design and the products of design that are produced at this stage. The

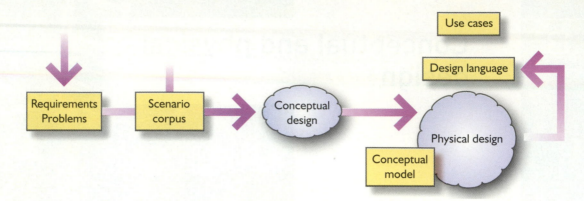

FIGURE 13-1 Conceptual and physical design

minimum system specification is a conceptual model, a set of use cases and a design language. Conceptual design is concerned with arriving at an abstract description of the system – its logic, functions, structure and content – but not with how the structure and functions are to be physically realized. Physical design is concerned with who does what (with the allocation of functions between people and artefacts), how the artefacts will look and how they behave.

The distinction between conceptual and physical design does not dictate that conceptual design should be finished before physical design starts. Analysts and designers will iterate between these two levels of design description and will fix on some physical design decisions in order to understand the conceptual level better. A good deal of early physical design happens during the envisionment process. This iteration will involve various kinds of evaluation with people so that we can check that the design really does meet their needs. The advantage of designing at the conceptual level before details of the physical design are fixed, however, is that it avoids the problem of 'design fixation' and maintains a wide design space in which alternatives can be considered for as long as possible.

Box 13-1 Design space

Design can be thought about through the concept of a design space. A design space constrains a design in some dimensions whilst allowing exploration of alternatives in others (Beaudouin-Lafon and Mackay, 2003). Designers always work within constraints, whether these are financial or functional, but they need to take care not to impose too many constraints too early in the process. This is when they can ignore ideas for designs because of design fixation – settling on a design idea or a design constraint that prevents them from exploring possible alternatives. Brainstorming is a good way of expanding the design space.

Clear conceptual design is central to developing systems that are understandable. Designers need to ensure that their conception of the system is easily learnt by people and fits with their expectations and preferences. This is so that the users can develop a clear 'mental model' of the system.

Mental models,
Chapter 5,
Section 5.11

For example, in any windows application most of us would expect to find a menu that allows us to open files, close files and create new files. Moreover we might expect it to be called 'File'. Logically we would expect to find these functions grouped together somewhere and if the designer has understood and applied sensible design guidelines (Chapter 3) then this should be the case. But often we have to spend a long time looking for some function, or we do not know about the existence of some function, because the designer has put it somewhere unexpected. The lack of standards for the menus of mobile phones, for example, results in the need to search the whole structure for an expected command.

Challenge 13-1
Critique the menu structure for the mobile phone in Figure 10-7. Is everything where you would expect to find it? Does the design provide a clear mental model for you?
Where would you expect to find the 'Sort' command in MS Word?

Figure 13-2 illustrates the problem. As Norman set out in his classic exposition of the issues (Norman, 1986), designers have some conception of the system they have produced. This may or may not be the same as what the system actually does. Moreover in a system of any large size, no single designer will know everything that the system does. Designers design a system's image that they hope will reveal the designer's conception to the users. The problem is that it is only through the system image – the user interface, the behaviours of the system and any documentation – that the designer's conception can be revealed. Users interact with the system image and from this have to derive their conception (their 'mental model') of what the system is and what it does. A clear, logical and consistent conceptual design will be easier to communicate to people who use the system and hence they will develop a clearer conception of the system themselves.

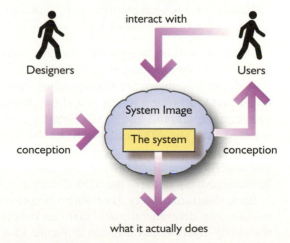

FIGURE 13-2 The system image

The HIC case study is in Chapters 4 and 14

A good mental model will more likely be formed by users of a system if the designer has used consistent language, and has thought carefully about the logical functions of the system and how they are grouped together. In the HIC case study the conceptual model separated actions, objects/content providers, and categories. The physical design instantiated this structure by arranging the actions on the left-hand bar, the objects and content providers on the right-hand bar and categories along the top. Another key aspect of the conceptual design was the searching mechanism. This was realized physically as a rolodex (Figure 13-3).

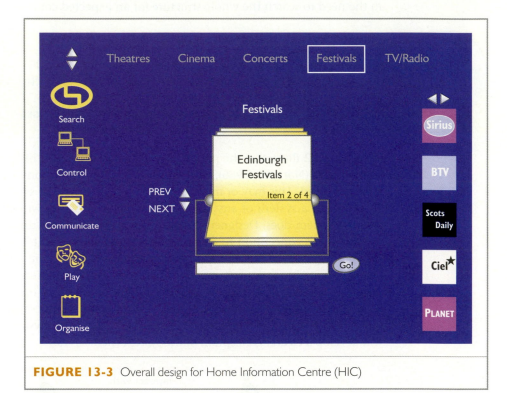

FIGURE 13-3 Overall design for Home Information Centre (HIC)

Entity-relationship models are also discussed in Chapter 20, Section 20.5 and Chapter 27, Section 27.3

Designers will often represent the conceptual model of a system using a diagrammatic technique such as an entity–relationship model or object model. Figure 13-4 shows two alternative conceptual models of the same thing, an ATM. In the upper part is an object model that shows the relationships between the concepts person, card, account and ATM. A person may ask about an account, the card is inserted into the ATM and so on. In the lower part is an entity–relationship model. This is more complex, but captures more of the semantics of the situation. The model distinguishes between the concept of a user and the owner of the card. It distinguishes a usage of the ATM and the accounts which may be accessed.

Such diagrams rarely exist without some further explanation and entity–relationship diagrams in particular can become quite formalized. For example, the entity–relationship diagram in Figure 13-4 includes a notation showing the participation conditions (optional or mandatory) of entities in relationships and

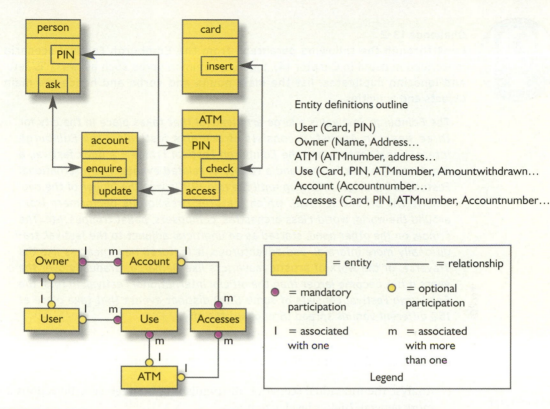

Entity definitions outline

User (Card, PIN)
Owner (Name, Address...
ATM (ATMnumber, address...
Use (Card, PIN, ATMnumber, Amountwithdrawn...
Account (Accountnumber...
Accesses (Card, PIN, ATMnumber, Accountnumber...

FIGURE 13-4 Two conceptual models of an ATM: object model above and entity–relationship below

some outline definitions of the entities in terms of the attributes that they contain. Attributes can be shown on the diagram as ovals if required. It is not the intention to explore all the details of conceptual modelling techniques here. Books are available on object modelling (e.g. van Harmelen, 2001) and on entity–relationship modelling for interface design (Benyon, Green and Bental, 1999). The point to note is that such techniques can be very useful in externalizing the conceptual structure that underlies a design.

In website design it is usual to produce a 'site map' – a conceptual model of the site's structure. Conceptual modelling using a formalism such as an object model can be a very powerful tool in helping the designer to think about the details of a design. By externalizing the objects and relationships in a system the designer can see more clearly whether the logic of a design works.

13.2 Conceptual design using scenarios

A good way of doing conceptual design is to undertake an object/action analysis of the scenario corpus. For each of the scenarios in the corpus the analyst works through the scenario descriptions, identifying the various objects that are mentioned and the various actions that are performed. Objects are often indicated by nouns or noun phrases and activities and actions by verbs.

Challenge 13-2
Look through the following paragraph from the Edinburgh Festival scenario (described in detail in Chapter 14). Ignoring common verbs such as 'was', 'is', etc. and ignoring duplicates, list the main nouns and verbs and hence the main objects and activities.

The Edinburgh Festival is a large arts festival that takes place in the city for three weeks in August. It consists of two arts festivals – the Edinburgh International Festival and the Edinburgh Festival Fringe – a book festival, a film festival, a jazz festival and a variety of related events. The International Festival is the original, and up until the mid-1980s was the bigger of the two. This is the official festival, which features prestigious performers from around the world, world-class orchestras, composers, ballet troupes, etc. The Fringe, on the other hand, started as an unofficial adjunct to the festival, traditionally more informal, and adventurous. It featured new theatres like the Traverse, or the work of artistic mavericks like Demarco. Gradually over the years it has become larger than the official International Festival. In total the Edinburgh Festival consists of some 1200 distinct events that take place at 150 different venues spread throughout the city.

Working with a corpus of scenarios in this way requires four stages:

1. Analyse the individual scenarios, distinguishing between specific actions and more general, higher-level activities.

2. Summarize objects and actions from each scenario, merging similar or identical actions where necessary.

3. Bring together the analyses from the individual scenarios, collating them into summarized objects, actions and more generic activities.

4. Merge actions and objects where they are identical and give them a single name.

← The concept of a scenario corpus is described in Chapter 8

Objects and actions in MP3 example

← Scenario MP3/01 is in Chapter 8, Section 8.2

Table 13-1 shows how part of Scenario MP3/01 – 'How does that song go again?' – is analysed. Activities are shown in the far left column referencing the paragraph number. Where these appeared to be made up of a sequence of individual sub-activities, these are identified in column 2. Actions and objects derived from these appear in columns 3 and 4. Comments are included in column 5. Of course this is only a fraction of the analysis of the MP3/01 scenario analysis used here to illustrate the idea.

Table 13-2 shows a portion of the collated results across all the scenarios. A tally of the number of occurrences of each action (column 1) and object (column 2) is kept. Various notations are used to indicate questions, slightly different views or uses of the terms and so on. The aim of this analysis is to *understand* the objects and actions in a domain. It is vital to note that there is no definitive or 'right' answer here. The object/action analysis is just another way of exploring the design space.

TABLE 13-1 Object/action analysis of part of scenario MP3/01

Activity	Consists of sub-activities	Action	Object	Comments
Search for MP3 track by name P3	Go to Search function P3	Go to	Search object	'Search object' – may need revision?
	Enter query (track name) P3	Enter (*user input*) Confirm	Search object Query	
Play track P4	Select search result (MP3 track) P4	Select	Search result (*track*)	= MP3 track No 'browse search result' formula here, as it is specified that search result contains only one object (track)
	Play track P4	Play (*start play*)	Track	'Play' does not imply playing complete track – track may be paused, stopped, fast-forwarded, etc. 'Start Play' may be the better term

Actions that could be thought of as generically similar can now be grouped together, prior to the final distillation stage. This requires careful attention, to avoid mistakenly merging together slightly different actions. The guiding principle is to look for conceptual or functional parallels among the actions, indicating likely candidates for grouping. The table is annotated with comments, documenting the criteria applied in making the groupings. Here, each grouping of actions is merged and given a single name. In each case this is the generic term which will be used from this point on. Table 13-3 illustrates this process with the actions of 'select' and 'choose'.

So, the object/action analysis has resulted in a generic action of select and an understanding of the various objects that can be selected: Track, Playlist, Playlist Catalogue, Query result. This could be represented as an object, or entity–relationship model as illustrated in Figure 13-5. This may be read as a Playlist Catalogue consisting of many Playlists, though each Playlist is on just one Playlist catalogue. A Playlist consists of many Tracks. Each Track is on just one Playlist and one Tracklist. A Track may be the result of a Query. Notice how, by developing a con-

TABLE 13-2 Portion of consolidation of objects and actions in MP3 domain with number of occurrences in parentheses

Scenarios MP3/01 to MP3/05: activities and objects decomposition - stage 3 (A) (all actions and objects collated)

All actions	All objects
...	...
Go to (21)	Playlist (30)
[Go to] (1)	Playlist catalogue (2)
Load (1)	Playlist catalogue (7)
Modify (4)	Query (4)
Move (1)	Search object (9)
(*Move*) (1)	Search result (Track) (1)
Name (2)	Search result (3)
Name (*user input*) (4)	Set up (1) [scenario MP3/03]
Open (3)	Track (32)
Pause (2)	Track (*MP3 file*) (1)
Play (*start play*) (7)	Track list (1)
Repeat (*replay*) (1)	Tracks (9)
Re-save (*save*) (1)	Tracks (*MP3 files*) (1)
Save (8)	Tracks list (9)
[Select] (1)	[Tracks list] (2)
Select (*specify*) (1)	...
[Select (*specify*)] (3)	
...	

TABLE 13-3 Considering the various uses of actions select and choose

[Select] (1)	7	'Select', '(*specify*)', 'Choose' all describe a user's action of
Select (*specify*) (1)		• selecting an item or group of items from a list or other display object
[Select (*specify*)] (3)		• selecting an option from a menu of other actions.
		Here, the HIC has determined the list of possible options/interactions available to the user, and is presenting it to the user (in a number of possible forms and modalities).
Choose (1)	1	
Choose (*specify*) (1)	1	

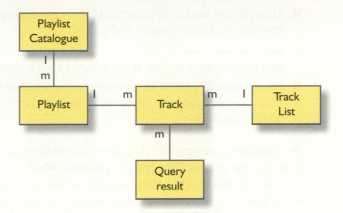

FIGURE 13-5 Possible conceptual model for MP3 example

ceptual model, we are able to raise and discuss issues. You may disagree with some of the assertions above. This is fine. This is exactly why making the conceptual model explicit is useful.

Box 13-2 Object modelling

Object models, or entity–relationship models, represent the main objects of interest in a domain and the relationships between them. There are many books devoted to such conceptual models and the techniques can be used to explore the conceptual structure, not simply to document it. There is an important distinction in conceptual models between the specific instances of an object and the class or type of object. In the MP3 example, an instance of the object type Track might be 'Moondance' and another instance might be 'Gloria' (both songs by Van Morrison as it happens). What makes us group these things together as an object type called Track is that they have certain characteristics in common such as a track name, a duration and so on (classification is discussed briefly in Chapter 8, also see discussion in Chapter 23). Relationships between objects are expressed in terms of how many instances of an object can be related to how many instances of another object. Typically we are not interested in exactly how many instances, but rather whether a relationship exists between one or many instances. The conceptual model is annotated with a 1 if an instance can be related to only one other instance or an m if it can be related to many.

13.3 Physical design

As we discussed in Chapter 2, physical design is concerned with how things are going to work and with detailing the look and feel of the product. Physical design is about structuring interactions into logical sequences and about clarifying and presenting the allocation of functions and knowledge between people and devices. Physical design is concerned with taking this abstract representation and translating it into concrete designs.

There are three components to physical design:

- Operational design is concerned with specifying how everything works and how content is structured and stored.

- Representational design is concerned with fixing on colours, shapes, sizes and information layout. It is concerned with style and aesthetics.

- Interaction design in this context is concerned with the allocation of functions to humans or to technology and with the structuring and sequencing of the interactions.

In operational design, the designer concentrates on how to input data and commands, the events that trigger actions, what feedback is provided and how people will know what they are able to do. The system must be able to reveal what state it is in – that is, what actions are legitimate at any point. Either the designer must make the system state visible (or otherwise perceptible) or it must be made observable if the person takes some action.

Ergonomics and psychology, Chapter 5; dialogue design, Chapter 6

Representational design is more concerned with the layout of screens, the overall mood and metaphor of the design, the 'story' the design is telling. This is where mood boards are useful, but it also includes selecting colours, graphics and text fonts that are clear and consistent.

Interaction design needs to take on board the limitations of people in terms of their memory capacity, physical characteristics and so on. Commands have to be decided upon, organized and structured into logical sequences; the 'information architecture' of the system needs to be clarified. Commands and responses have to be organized into human–computer 'dialogues'.

Information architecture, Chapter 23

There is, of course, a close relationship between the design of interactions and operational design, as the allocation of functions to persons or to devices effectively determines the operation of the device. The next two sections discuss these aspects of physical design in terms of designing interactions and of developing a 'language' for the design.

13.4 Designing interactions

The design of interactions is critical to interactive systems design. The conceptual design should be as independent of an implementation as possible. The move from conceptual to physical design requires designers to allocate functions and knowledge to persons or to devices and hence to create interactions. For example, in the case of the MP3 player there have to be actions that select tracks and that play tracks, that modify playlists or that load playlists. But this does not say who does what. For example, the selection of a track can be left to a random function of the MP3 player. Playlists may be bought from a content provider, or created by the system based on statistics such as how often they are played.

In designing interactions – i.e. allocating functions to people or to devices – designers need to consider the capabilities of people and the constraints on what they can do. People will forget things over time. They will forget things in working memory in a very short time. They are not good at following long lists of instructions, at carrying out boring tasks repeatedly and so on. On the other hand, people are good at improvising and at dealing with ambiguity and incomplete information. On the whole, the capabilities of technology are just the reverse.

But it is not just a question of efficiency. The interaction should be engaging, enjoyable and fulfilling. Moreover, if the system supports working life, it should help to create satisfying and meaningful jobs, while a product for home use has to fit lifestyle and desired image.

Of course, in a very real sense this whole book is about designing interactions, so prototyping, evaluation and envisioning design ideas are critical. In this chapter we aim to provide more formal methods to help in this process. The first of these is interaction patterns and the second reviews a number of models for structuring interactions.

Interaction patterns

The idea of 'patterns' – perceived regularities in an environment – has been adopted by designers of interactive systems and appears as interaction patterns. As with architectural patterns (see Box 13-3), interaction patterns can be identified at many different levels of abstraction. For example, on most PCs if you double-click on something it opens it; if you right-click, it displays a menu of operations you can perform. Macintosh computers have only a single mouse button so the 'right-click' pattern is unknown to Mac users. Most playing devices such as VCRs, DVDs, cassette players and MP3 players on a computer have a play, stop, fast forward and rewind interaction pattern. Patterns build up into the complex interactions that we are familiar with of menus and mice: patterns of layout of menus, of the highlighting when the mouse rolls over an item, flashing when an item is selected and so on. General usability patterns have been identified which to a large extent are similar to design guidelines, but the advantage that patterns have over guidelines is the rich description and examples that go with them. In the HIC the main interaction pattern was to select an object on the right-hand bar and then select an activity from the activity bar (or vice versa). Another pattern was to touch the scroll buttons and the bars would rotate.

Box 13-3 Alexandrian patterns

In architecture Christopher Alexander (Alexander, 1979) has been very influential in introducing the idea of architectural patterns. These are regular good design ideas. For example, it is a good idea to have small parking lots in a neighbourhood because very large parking lots are ugly and disrupt the neighbourhood. It is a good idea to have pavement cafés in a city where people can sit outside because it creates a nice atmosphere. It is a good idea to have a low wall next to an open area so people can sit on it.

Alexander's patterns for architectural features are at different levels of abstraction – from patterns for walls to patterns for whole cities. Each pattern expresses a relation between a certain context, a certain system of 'forces' which occurs repeatedly in that context (i.e. a particular problem) and a solution which allows these forces to resolve themselves. Patterns, therefore, refer to other patterns and are part of larger patterns. For example:

▶

- GALLERY SURROUND proposes that people should be able to walk through a connecting zone such as a balcony to feel connected to the outside world.
- OPENING TO THE STREET says that people on a sidewalk should feel connected to functions inside a building, made possible by direct openings.

Patterns are embodied as concrete prototypes rather than abstract principles and tend to focus on the interactions between the physical form of the built environment and the way in which that inhibits or facilitates various sorts of behaviour within it. Pattern languages are not value neutral but instead manifest particular values in their names and more explicitly in their rationales.

Alexander specified over 200 patterns in his book. Pattern 88 (adapted from Erickson, 2003) is shown below. Notice how it refers to other patterns (numbered) and how there is a wealth of rich, socially based description.

88 Street Café

[picture omitted]

... neighborhoods are defined by Identifiable Neighborhood (14); their natural points of focus are given by Activity Nodes (30) and Small Public Squares (61). This pattern, and the ones which follow it, give the neighborhood and its points of focus, their identity.

The street café provides a unique setting, special to cities: a place where people can sit lazily, legitimately, be on view, and watch the world go by.

The most humane cities are always full of street cafés. Let us try to understand the experience which makes these places so attractive. We know that people enjoy mixing in public, in parks, squares, along promenades and avenues, in street cafés. The preconditions seem to be: the setting gives you the right to be there, by custom; there are a few things to do that are part of the scene, almost ritual: reading the newspaper, strolling, nursing a beer, playing catch; and people feel safe enough to relax, nod at each other, perhaps even meet. A good café terrace meets these conditions. But it has in addition, special qualities of its own: a person may sit there for ...

[nine paragraphs of rationale omitted]

Therefore:
Encourage local cafés to spring up in each neighborhood. Make them intimate places, with several rooms, open to a busy path, where people can sit with coffee or a drink and watch the world go by. Build the front of the café so that a set of tables stretch out of the café, right into the street.

[diagram omitted]

Build a wide, substantial opening between the terrace and indoors – OPENING TO THE STREET (165); make the terrace double as A PLACE TO WAIT (150) for nearby bus stops and offices; both indoors and on the terrace use a great variety of different kinds of chairs and tables – DIFFERENT CHAIRS (251); and give the terrace some low definition at the street edge if it is in danger of being interrupted by street action – STAIR SEATS (125), SITTING WALL (243), perhaps a CANVAS ROOF (244).

[text omitted] ...

Patterns are described in some general format. The format used in the HIC case study is illustrated in Table 13-4 which shows the interaction pattern for the Edit function in the MP3 application. Each pattern is described in this standard way, given a name and description, an indication of the problems it addresses, the design rationale or forces that act on the design decision, and the solution that has been adopted. Patterns will typically refer to other patterns and be referenced by other patterns.

TABLE 13-4 An interaction pattern for the edit action

Interaction pattern: Edit	
Description	Edit the contents of a HIC entity (Conceptually associated with 'Sort' – *q.v.*)
Examples	Adding MP3 tracks to a playlist Adding a URL (Web address) to an MP3 Favourites List Moving tracks to different positions within a playlist Moving MP3 tracks from one genre list to another Removing a track from a playlist
Situation	Some entities – lists and categories, for instance – have constituent objects associated with them. The user will want to change what these are, and the way they are organized within the 'umbrella' entity.
Problem	How does the user know which entities are editable, and if so, how to perform the 'Edit' action on them? How will the user select the components of the entity which are to be the subject of the edit? If objects are removed from an entity, will this mean they are permanently deleted from the HIC? Is it the 'umbrella object' which is actually edited, or its constituent objects? (For instance, a list, or its entries?)
Forces (i.e. issues affecting the problem and possible solutions)	The object(s) to be edited will be displayed on the screen. If the user requires to move the position of items within an object, or move an item from one object to another, all the relevant objects will have to be on the screen. The size of the objects, and of the screen, presents a limitation. Some items may be difficult to isolate (select) on the screen due to their small size or close proximity to each other, and this may make them difficult to edit – for example, text strings in a list. Alternative modalities could be offered other than screen touch. Editing may involve more than one step: select > edit > go/confirm. There should be clear feedback telling the user the changes they are about to make. There should probably be a means of cancelling or escaping from the action.

▶

Solution

The graphical interface signals to the user (perhaps by means of a familiar or self-explanatory symbol) whether an entity can be edited. It may also be clear from the context which items are likely to be editable (for instance, the user would expect playlists to be editable).

There are several possible means of editing. The user could select items one by one or in groups, and use a 'Go' action to complete the process (suitable for touchscreen, remote control or perhaps voice activation). Or she could 'drag and drop' objects to edit them (suitable for touchscreen). Items being edited could change their appearance – perhaps change colour.

If the object being edited (such as a list) is larger than the available screen space, it could be divided into contiguous sections. A suitable device for displaying this might be the scrolling 'rolodex' device already established in the present HIC prototype.

Resulting situation

It is clear to the user which objects of the HIC can be edited; the interaction pathways for editing them are apparent (if more than one step is involved, the sequence should be apparent). Clear feedback is given during the Edit action, and the screen is updated afterwards to reflect the new situation.

Notes

This pattern is conceptually associated with 'Sort', the important distinguishing factor being that 'Edit' can change the number and identity of the constituent objects in an entity, while 'Sort' simply rearranges (categorizes) them.

It also has links with 'Delete'. It is unclear at this stage whether removing an MP3 track from, say, a playlist or a track list, actually deletes it from the HIC entirely, or merely from that list (*qua* display object). Is the original file kept in another part of the HIC's file management space?

Challenge 13-3
Look at the interaction patterns on a cellphone that you have available. What combination of buttons and displays does what? Identify the 'select' key or select pattern. Identify the 'move down' pattern. Does it always work in the same way or are there different patterns for 'move down a menu' and 'move down through some text'? Compare the existence of patterns in phone design to those in the design of car controls.

Structuring interactions

In many design situations there will be a need to provide a structured 'dialogue' between the system and the user. The system may need to elicit particular pieces of data in a particular sequence, or to guide the user through a series of actions, or to present a number of related options together. Dataflow diagrams are a good way of showing the logical steps required to complete some interaction. The example in Figure 13-6 shows the steps needed to complete a simple transaction

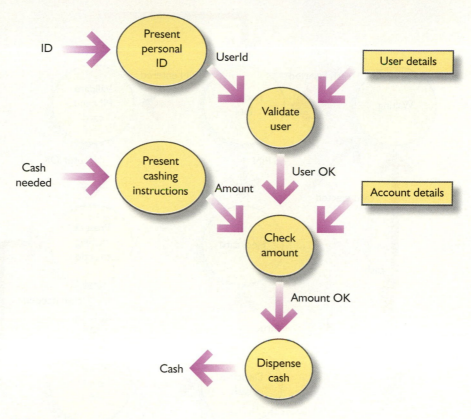

FIGURE 13-6 Dataflow diagram

with a cash machine. It shows the data needed to go in, the processes (shown as circles) that need to be undertaken and the data that flows out. It also shows the stores of data (boxes) that will be needed. With a logical flow diagram such as this, designers can debate where the human–computer interface should be and where certain functions should take place. Notice that this representation is as independent of technology as possible. Some data, called 'ID', is needed but this representation does not say that this should be a card and PIN. It could be, but it could equally be some new technology such as iris recognition, or fingerprint recognition.

Several other methods are available for representing interactions. Sequence models (Chapter 18) are one; task structure diagrams (Chapter 20) are another. Use cases (Chapter 8) can be used to describe the interactions, as can simple tabular layouts that show user actions on one side and system responses on the other. Another common diagrammatic technique is the state transition network (STN). This shows how a system moves from one state to another depending on the actions by the user. Figure 13-7 shows an STN for the ATM example. Notice both the similarities and the differences between the two representations. STNs come in a variety of forms and can be powerful techniques for thinking about and creating interactions.

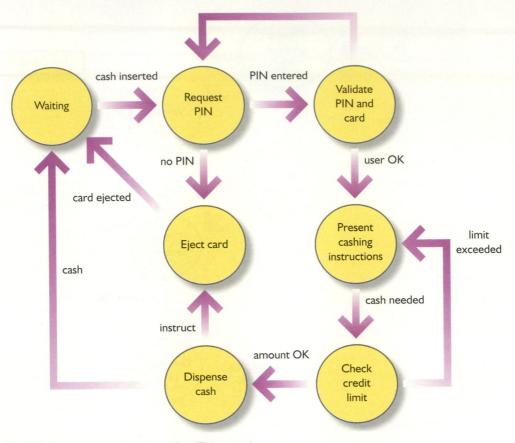

FIGURE 13-7 State transition network for ATM example

13.5 Design languages

A design language consists of the following:

- A set of *design elements* such as the use of colour, styles and types of buttons, sliders and other widgets
- Some *principles of composition* (i.e. the rules for putting them together)
- Collections of *qualifying situations* – contexts and how they affect the rules.

A consistent design language means that people need only learn a limited number of design elements and then they can cope with a large variety of different situations. A design language is how designers build meaning into objects enabling people to understand what things do and to make distinctions between different types of object.

Any language provides a way of expressing things and design languages are ways of expressing design concepts. Languages are useful for particular purposes if they have appropriate elements and appropriate organizing principles and use an appropriate medium for both expression and transmission.

Box 13-4   Design languages

Rheinfrank and Evenson (1996) stress that design languages have most impact when they have become deeply embedded and when people use them and exploit them unconsciously. Their method for design includes developing a design language through:

- Characterization - the process of describing existing assumptions and any pre-existing design languages
- Reregistration - the creation of a new assumption set through exploring trends and needs through field research
- Development and demonstration - using storyboards, prototypes and other envisioning techniques
- Evaluation of the reactions to the design
- Evolution of the language over time. No matter how good a design, it will only last so long - until circumstances force it to be revisited.

Design languages help to ensure transparency, helping people to understand what is going on inside a device. They also afford transferability of knowledge from one device to another. The user of one Nokia phone can generally expect to find similar design on another phone. This also means that people will more readily see opportunities to use a device or function and will expect certain behaviours, structures or functions. Finally, people will identify with a style, which helps to define their identity; they act through the design language.

Of course the interaction patterns are a key part of the design language. Together with the representational aspects of the design they define the whole 'look and feel' of the product or system.

Design language for the MP3

The MP3 application would have to fit in with the overall design language of the HIC, but could also have its own features. The key aspect of the HIC's design language was the rolodex for displaying and accessing search results and the object, action and category bars. In previous work on the HIC, the problem of how to select text items from a rolodex list had not been considered in depth. This was a significant issue, particularly in a touchscreen environment where serious functional constraints were imposed by the size and proximity of text in the display. Selecting by simple touch was probably the most intuitive solution. However, all but the smallest fingers would find it hard to pick a track unambiguously unless the text was large and widely spaced. One possible solution that was proposed is shown in Figure 13-8.

The user can drag the track into the white slot in the module (A) to select it. In this instance, the interaction can take two possible courses: users either drag the track into the slot and take their finger away, resulting in the track being loaded; or they can abort the selection, in which case the track returns automatically to its position in the rolodex. This 'recoverability factor' is one of the basic design principles.

Whether the interaction is completed or aborted, the text item changes colour from black (B) to orange (C) while it is in transit, to indicate it is 'active'.

Chapter 3, Section 3.6 discusses design principles

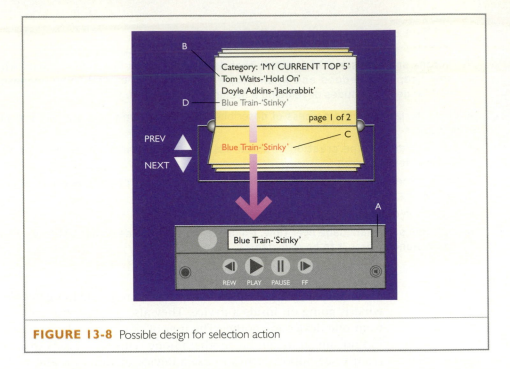

FIGURE 13-8 Possible design for selection action

A dimmed version of the track name (D) remains in the rolodex while the track is being dragged. Thus the proposed language elements are dimming of selected items, dragging to select, changing the colour to indicate selection, and so on.

Summary and key points

Conceptual and physical design will happen in any system development, and conceptual modelling, in particular, is a key activity for designers. In this chapter we looked at the importance of conceptual modelling and presented a scenario-based method that can help. Of course not all design projects will need to analyse the scenarios in this detail, but all projects will need to consider the conceptual model because it is this that leads to people developing their own conceptual model – their mental model – of the system. In addition to developing the conceptual model we have highlighted the need for designing interactions and packaging design ideas into a design language.

- Designers need to complete both conceptual design and physical design.
- Designers can understand objects and actions in the existing, proposed system by analysing the scenario corpus.
- Designing interactions is concerned with allocating functions to people or devices and hence arriving at a set of interaction patterns.
- Designers should ensure that there is a consistent design language in terms of both the patterns of interaction and representational aspects of design.

Further reading

Rheinfrank, J. and Evenson, S. (1996) Design languages. In Winograd, T. (ed.), *Bringing Design to Software*. ACM Press, New York.
A good chapter on design languages and how they have been used in everything from houses in Nantucket to knitting patterns.

van Harmelen, M. (ed.) (2001) *Object Modeling and User Interface Design: Designing Interactive Systems*. Addison-Wesley, Boston, MA.
This book is a collection of papers providing different methods for conceptual and physical design. Constantine and Lockwood's chapter 'Structure and style in use cases for user interface design' covers much the same ground as presented here but is wholly based around use cases. Constantine and Lockwood define 'essential' use cases that are basically the same as our conceptual scenarios. William Hudson's chapter 'Toward unified models in user-centred and object-oriented design' gives a very comprehensive overview of different methods and how they might all be brought together.

Graham, I. (2003) *A Pattern Language for Web Usability*. Addison-Wesley, Harlow.
An excellent example of the development of a pattern language, this time to help designers to design good websites.

Comments on challenges

Challenge 13-1
Some of the design seems quite strange. For example, why is 'voice dialling' under 'phone book', or 'alarm clock' under 'office tools'? Even if you feel these are sensible places to put these commands, there is no inherent logic, nor is there any standard. I would expect to see 'inbox' under 'calls and times' and why is there a small, three-item menu called 'connectivity'?

The 'Sort' command in MS Word is under the 'Tables' menu even though Word allows you to sort all manner of things. Most people would think it is under Tools or Format.

Challenge 13-2
Nouns: arts festival, city, three weeks, August, Edinburgh International Festival, Edinburgh Fringe Festival, book festival, film festival, jazz festival, related events, performers, orchestras, composers, ballet troupes, theatres, the Traverse, mavericks, Demarco, events, venues. Verbs: takes place, consists of, features, started.

The main objects are the same as the nouns; there are the different types of festival and events, different types of performers, theatres, and venues. We also know a bit more about some of these: 1200 events, 150 venues, etc. The main activities express relationships between the objects. In this way the underlying conceptual model of the domain begins to emerge.

Events *take place* at a venue/theatre. A festival *consists of* events and *features* performers, and so on.

Challenge 13-3
Most phones will have these standard patterns, though exactly how they are implemented varies widely between different makes and varies over time. Preferences shift from four-way rocker keys to arrow keys and back again. Presumably designs will settle down at some stage as they have done, for example, in the design of car controls, which were highly non-standard but which now have similar patterns of interaction – for signalling, for windscreen washing, turning the lights on, and so on.

Exercises

1. Discuss the underlying conceptual model for the following activities: using an ATM; buying a plane ticket on the Web; using a public information kiosk; setting a VCR to record a programme.

2. In the design of electronic calendars, there are lots of functions such as making regular appointments (say an appointment every Wednesday at 3 pm). In shared calendar systems appointments can be made by other people. There are even some systems that let software 'agents' make appointments. Discuss issues of the allocation of functions between people and software in the context of electronic calendars.

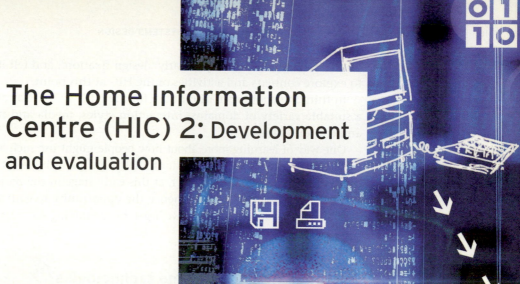

14 The Home Information Centre (HIC) 2: Development and evaluation

Aims

In this chapter we revisit the Home Information Centre (HIC) case study introduced in Chapter 4 and provide a detailed description of the development and evaluation of the first full interface prototype. The aim is to show what developing a real system is like, so there is quite a lot of detail. We do not claim that all the design decisions were good ones, but we do show how they happened and often why they happened. The chapter has been compiled from the various reports that were produced by different members of the design team. To a large extent these have been left as they were originally written so we do not inadvertently clean everything up and make it seem easy! The chapter should be read *critically* and used as a basis for discussion.

After studying this chapter you should be able to:

- Describe the conceptual and physical design of a large interface prototype
- Appreciate how scenarios are used in such a design project
- Discuss approaches to evaluation.

14.1 Scenarios: the first prototype

Recall that the Home Information Centre (HIC) was a concept for a new device. It was not to be a TV for the 'lean back' environment of the living room, nor a PC for the 'lean forward' environment of the home office. It was to address both of these and more, new functions in the 'move around' environment of infotainment. That was the basic brief for this project.

In Chapter 4 we looked at the evaluation of three interface prototypes. Before we got to that stage we had developed the first prototype, P0. This would be a conceptual tool, a set of scenarios of use. We were reluctant to fix too soon on a physical design, being wary of early 'design fixation', and felt it was much better to explore contexts and activities of the HIC at this point.

In thinking about scenarios of use for the HIC, we were aware that we needed a suitable variety of domains, interaction styles, media and modalities, people and contexts of use.

One way of learning more about how people might use such a device as the HIC would be to undertake naturalistic studies of people using existing media in their 'infotainment' activities. However, at this early stage in the project we were under considerable time pressure and hence the opportunity to gather real 'user stories' would have to wait. Accordingly, we began by identifying some conceptual scenarios.

Further thoughts: Home technologies

Subsequently we did undertake such studies of people and technologies in their home and this led to a number of interesting findings regarding technologies in the home and how people use them within the social and physical spaces. A special issue of the journal *Cognition, Technology and Work* (volume 5, number 1, May 2003) is devoted to home technologies and includes a description of these findings. A method for investigating technology in household use was also produced.

The scenario corpus

As we have seen (Chapter 2), a useful structure for thinking about interactive systems design is the PACT approach: people, activities, contexts and technologies. Conceptual scenarios are abstract descriptions of the PACT elements in some domain. For the HIC design, we brainstormed ideas at a number of internal workshops about how the HIC might be used and finished up with three general, highly abstract uses for the HIC – information, communication and entertainment. From these abstract ideas, 11 scenarios were developed that looked at more specific activities, contexts and people, and explored the range of information content, input, output, media and communication abilities of the HIC technology. For both of these, distinguishing between the 'what' (i.e. the content) and the 'how' (the functions) was important.

Early ideas about communication centred on how the HIC might be used as a sort of 'Post-it' system: one member of the family might leave a message for another. The HIC would also be used as a videophone, e-mail system, etc. The informational scenarios concerned activities such as going sailing, going skiing (hence finding out about the weather) or going out to a restaurant or show. The entertainment scenario led to ideas that users might like to watch TV on demand alongside a chat room, say. Other scenarios included integration with other devices, such as heating control and home security. The children doing homework was another; investigating, finding out, doing crosswords and quizzes, ordering videos, photographs and so on.

In developing the various, more concrete versions of the abstract activities, we were aware from a high-level PACT analysis of the need to cover the different people – children, people with disabilities (e.g. arthritis, short-sightedness), as well as the young and wealthy who would be the early adopters of such technology. We also needed to cover a variety of domains and information spaces – e.g. those with rapidly changing information against those with static information, different media such as maps, voice, sound output, and so on. Eleven scenarios constituted the final scenario corpus that was used in the project:

- What shall we have for dinner?
- What shall we do now?
- News and e-books
- Entertain me
- Messageboard
- Traffic
- New users
- Housekeeping
- Payment
- I cannot programme my video because ...
- Planning ahead.

Challenge 14-1
Take one of the scenario ideas above, undertake a PACT analysis and brainstorm how the scenario might unfold.

A future workshop

One important thing about developing prototypes is using them. The scenario corpus was used internally within the project team to generate ideas and discuss the details of functionality. The scenarios were also taken outside the team and used as the basis of 'future workshops'. Future workshops are one of the design methods advocated in the participatory design approach to the design of interactive systems. This approach has a long tradition, particularly in Scandinavia, going back to the late 1970s.

A future workshop comprises three stages:

1. Critique – a group brainstorming session that tries different approaches to the activities/problems being addressed by the proposed system. A set of themes arising out of this stage is used in stage 2, Fantasy.

2. Fantasy – the emphasis here is on creative solutions/ideas, no matter how unrealistic. From these a number of fantasy themes are generated and these are then used to drive stage 3.

3. Implementation – the groups work out what would be necessary in order to produce a real solution to some of the fantasy themes generated (e.g. by producing a mock-up or a storyboard).

The prototypes from this were described in Chapter 10

Using the 'What shall we do now?' scenario as a basis, we spent a morning working with four groups of students through these three stages. The scenario was supplemented with introductory presentations and written materials and adapted to make it more relevant to the participants; the students were asked to imagine they and a group of friends had won a trip to the city for the day and had to plan their activities.

The results of this session were quite telling. The group focused on the need for the HIC to be personalized. They wanted mobility in the system and they emphasized the communication function over the informational function of the HIC.

A more concrete scenario

At this stage in the project it was important to pick one of these scenarios to orient the various project teams around (ultimately, more fully detailed versions of the scenarios would drive specification of the HIC interface). We suggested the informational scenario 'What shall we do now?' was the best one to start with because it covered lots of different data types which would help all the project partners. A key feature of the scenario-based design approach that we were following is that all partners in the project would be required to use the scenario and they would need appropriate data to work with. There had to be data for the people doing the data mining, data for the people developing the interface, data for the speech recognition people, and so on. Additionally, the 'What shall we do now?' scenario covered various user types (young/old, etc.) rather well. Another of the informational scenarios, 'What shall we have for dinner?', was far less applicable to children, for example, and we saw children as potentially significant users of the HIC. The range of activity types (finding out something, communicating with others, booking tickets on-line, etc.) in the scenario also provided the opportunity for a variety of interaction possibilities to be investigated. The remaining scenarios would allow us to investigate other data types (e.g. pictures/video), use contexts (e.g. hands and eyes occupied elsewhere), activity types (e.g. games, controlling another device such as a TV) and input/output devices not covered in the first scenario.

Developing the scenario

At one of the workshops, one group took the 'What shall we do now?' scenario and discussed it in more detail. The extract below is taken from the notes of this meeting and gives an idea of how the scenario discussion generated ideas and questions. The overall context for the scenario was the large arts festival that takes place in Edinburgh every August. It was envisaged that the HIC would be an ideal device for finding out what was going on so the people could decide 'What shall we do now?'.

Early on there was a need to make it more concrete, to focus on a specific context of use. The discussion at the workshop switched rapidly between high-level concerns and the details of a concrete interaction. It is summarized below.

1. The couple should be aged 20–30. They lived in Edinburgh. It was August and the Edinburgh Festival was in full swing. The couple knew about the Edinburgh Festival and wanted to check out what was on that evening. They did not have much time.

2. What sort of a query would they enter? Broad categories of shows such as 'comedy', time constraints such as 'starting after 6 pm', specific artists or shows or a specific venue (because a venue might have a particular specialism)?

3. What would be on the HIC? For example, would there be text only, or pictures/icons? Would there be advertising? Would the users enter a free-form query or browse through an on-line catalogue? This was an issue that the content or service provider would need to deal with. If this is the case then setup issues are raised. Perhaps users would select a favourite provider, then they would need to be able to add and remove them.

4. The modality of the input was considered. Would the HIC have hand-writing recognition? Voice input for free-form queries, a keyboard, remote keyboard or on-screen keyboard?

5. Once the name of the actor/venue, etc. had been input, the user would get some display on the HIC which was dependent on the amount of results of the query and the list of categories. Would the categories be generated automatically, or be preset?

6. Queries would need a response time of 5–10 seconds. The user would make a selection 'check out show times' – perhaps by touching an icon, perhaps by saying 'show times'. They might be using a remote control – how far could the person be from the screen?

7. Once the HIC had displayed the show time, venue, names of actors, any reviews of the show, etc., the person might want to make a booking. The display would be dependent on the history of the interaction and the visualization of the query history (or at least this should be accessible). Then all the issues of how to go back, up, etc. through the interaction history would need to be addressed.

8. The booking of tickets would probably require a different service or content provider. Would the HIC then 'lose control' of the interface or could the HIC provide its own to someone else's (e.g. the Festival Theatre's) website and on-line booking facility? How would the user input their name, credit card, address, etc.? Preferably this would be automatic.

9. Would the HIC be able to show the number of seats remaining for a show? Would the tickets be printed on a local printer? There was a need for a function of the HIC that automatically kept the user informed of a changing situation: an interface agent perhaps, or just part of the interface?

10. The brainstorming continued – what if there was a need to contact friends about the show, send them details of the location, etc.? They might want to meet for a drink nearby – in which case could the HIC access a webcam in the pub to see how busy it was?

11. Issues of traffic then arose. How long would it take to get there? What about providing bus or taxi information? The need to have the HIC provide a map or print instructions was recognized – and this should be able to happen from different locations.

12. The group changed the context to explore other areas such as going skiing or sailing, but apart from the issue of scale – the information space of skiing is much larger than the information space of the Edinburgh Festival – few new issues arose. How to update the service or content providers was important and there was some discussion about security, personalizing the HIC, etc.

The results of these discussions were taken away from the workshop and put alongside some real data from the previous year's festival. Fliers for shows, brochures advertising events and the details from the whole festival programme were used to provide real examples of the sort of data that the HIC in this scenario would have to deal with (Figure 14-1). The final version of the scenario is shown in the next section.

FIGURE 14-1 Example fliers from the Edinburgh Festival

14.2 The Edinburgh Festival scenario

The ideas that had been developed finally finished up as the scenario shown below. Although it is quite concrete, with some interface features described and a wealth of context, there are many design features which have not been agreed. These are recorded as footnotes (or end-notes) to the scenario. One of the features of the design method is that these footnotes force the designers to consider further design issues.

Scenario name

What shall we do now?

Scenario history

Version	Date	Author	Description
1	20 April 2004	D. Benyon	Discussed at Struer meeting
1.1	4 May 2004	D. Benyon	Modified following discussions at Struer

Scenario type

Activity scenario

PACT

People – young, wealthy, no children

Activities – searching for information, making bookings, meeting friends

Context – flat in Edinburgh, assume fast Internet connection

Technology – HIC as currently specified

Rationale

This scenario has been developed as part of the prototype P0 deliverable. It is intended to provide a rich description of a general context of use of the HIC. The scenario is deliberately vague with respect to a number of features such as input and output media and modalities, how the content is provided, etc., in order to stimulate discussion about such things. More concrete forms of the scenario are expected to be produced to illustrate a range of media/modalities. The scenario is also intended to provide a rich source of data so that issues concerning the semantics of the information space may be considered.

Scenario

1. Jan and Pat are a couple in their mid-thirties. Pat is a university lecturer in Cultural Studies and Jan is an accounts manager at Standard Life insurance. They live in the Stockbridge area of Edinburgh in a two-bedroom flat overlooking the river. It is 12.00 noon on 15 August. Jan and Pat are sitting in their large, airy kitchen/dining room. The remains of pizza and mixed salad mingle with a pile of newspapers on the kitchen table. Jan and Pat have recently returned from a holiday on the island of Zante and, apart from checking their e-mail, have not gone back to work. They decide that they would like to go to see one of the events that is happening as part of the Edinburgh Festival.

2. The Edinburgh Festival is a large arts festival that takes place in the city for three weeks in August. It consists of two arts festivals – the Edinburgh International Festival and the Edinburgh Festival Fringe – a book festival, a film festival, a jazz festival and a variety of related events. The International Festival is the original, and up until the mid-1980s was the bigger of the two. This is the official festival, which features prestigious performers from around the world, world-class orchestras, composers, ballet troupes, etc. The Fringe, on the other hand, started as an unofficial adjunct to the festival, traditionally more informal and adventurous. It featured new theatres like the Traverse, or the work of artistic mavericks like Demarco. Gradually over the years it has become larger than the official International Festival. In total the Edinburgh Festival consists of some 1200 distinct events that take place at 150 different venues spread throughout the city.

3. Jan activates the HIC[1] and chooses 'Edinburgh Festival'[2]. The HIC connects to the different content providers who are registered as providing content about the festival. The display shows five categories of information – Times of Events, Specific Artists, Specific Events, Specific Venues, Types of Events – a catalogue and a query facility[3].

4. 'What sort of thing do you fancy doing?', asked Jan. 'Hmmm, something funny, perhaps', Pat replied, 'Richard Herring, maybe, or Phil Kay? Stewart Lee? I guess we ought to check out the International Festival as well'. Jan entered the query 'What do we have for Richard Herring, or Stewart Lee'.

---

[1] How the HIC is activated is not considered here. Different methods may lead to different versions of the scenario.

[2] So, 'Edinburgh Festival' is a 'thing' in, or accessed by, the HIC. It could be some sort of plug-in provided by a third-party content provider. For example, the *Guardian* newspaper might provide a free CD-ROM for its readership, Jan and Pat may have downloaded the data from a website, or the data may be physically resident on some remote machine, or on Pat and Jan's computer.

[3] Again the modality of these are not specified. The query facility could be spoken, typed on a remote keyboard or an on-screen keyboard, written by hand or in some other form such as a query agent. The catalogue facility could be represented in a number of different ways.

5. The HIC displays *Excavating Rita, King Dong vs. Moby Dick* and *This Morning with Richard not Judy II*[4] along with a display[5] of categories of further information: TV Reviews, Newspaper Reviews, and Times of Events[6]. Jan makes the selection[7] of Times of Events. The HIC responds with details of the events it has retrieved, displaying the data Title, ShortDescription, Venue, FromDate, ToDate, ExceptDates, Days, StartTime, Duration, Cost, ConcessionCost[8]. 'What do you think?', said Jan. 'Check out *Excavating Rita* and *This Morning with Richard not Judy II*', replied Pat. 'Well, there may not be any tickets left for *This Morning with Richard not Judy II*, I'll check'. Jan specifies that the HIC should monitor the number of tickets left for *This Morning with Richard not Judy II*[9]. The display shows 24 tickets left. 'You had better check *Excavating Rita* as well'. 'OK'. Jan instructs the HIC to monitor TicketsLeft for *Excavating Rita* as well. The display shows 45. The display highlights that the value of TicketsLeft for *This Morning with Richard not Judy II* has changed to 20, then to 18. 'Hmmm, *This Morning with Richard not Judy II* is selling fast, I don't think we are going to make that. Is there anything else?', says Pat.

6. 'Well, hundreds of things, actually', Jan responded; 'Let's see. At 1 pm we have 'Verdi's Macbeth', a lunchtime talk at the Queen's Hall, or an archive recording of Sir John Barbirolli at 2.15. The Nimo Twins in 'Posh Spice Nude' at the Gilded Balloon, that's at 1.30 …'. Jan continues to browse the listings, jumping to read reviews, watch snippets of TV Reviews, check times and so on[10]. The display highlights changes in the TicketsLeft for *Excavating Rita*, now down to 35. At 12.30 the display indicates that *This Morning with Richard not Judy II* has started. 'Well, we had better do something', said Pat; 'Let's go for *Excavating Rita* and book our tickets now'. Jan selects *Excavating Rita* and 'booking' and the Booking Office at the Pleasance Theatre is displayed[11].

---

[4] How this data is presented is a major issue. We do not know how far our users are from the display.

[5] There are a number of issues concerned with things such as response time here. Will the HIC display some sort of 'busy' icon, provide information on how long the result of the query will take, present data gradually, etc.?

[6] There are many possible categories and ways of presenting and interrelating the data. Ideally the categories will be automatically generated.

[7] Once again, modality is not specified – Jan could touch an icon on the screen, say 'Show Times', use a remote control and click the 'Go' button, etc.

[8] See data dictionary for more details about these data items. (Not included here.)

[9] This raises the whole issue of agent-based interaction. Will the HIC have an agent (anthropomorphic or not) or will it be possible to specify these sorts of things through the general 'intelligence' of the HIC technology? Jan could instruct an agent to monitor some attribute of the data – TicketsLeft in this case – or the system could facilitate this type of facility in other ways.

[10] An issue here is how the display builds up and how a trace of the various queries and browsing is presented. It would or might be desirable to have some way of showing links between artists, shows, venues, type of event and so on.

[11] Note that at this point we have 'gone outside' the HIC and are at the mercy of the Pleasance Theatre's interface design for their booking system.

7. The booking form has fields for Name, Address, PhoneNumber, PostCode and CreditCard type, ExpiryDate and Number. Jan selects 'personal profile' on the HIC[12], confirms that the details should be Jan's, and the data is entered onto the booking form[13]. 'Just a minute', says Pat, 'Kat and Toni might like to come. Why don't you check?'. Jan activates the phone[14] and selects Kat and Toni[15]. The number is dialled and Toni answers. 'We are going to see *Excavating Rita* with Richard Herring at the Pleasance. Do you fancy coming? It starts at 3.30 and there are only 35, sorry 32 tickets left'. 'Sure', says Toni, 'We'd love to. I'll come on-line'[16]. Jan returns to the booking form and specifies four tickets. The total credit card amount is calculated and displayed. Jan confirms the transaction and receives a confirmation number.

8. Jan sees that Toni is on-line and changes to the conferencing system that they both use. Jan enters the message[17] that they have the tickets and suggests meeting for a drink beforehand. There is some discussion about the location, pubs versus restaurants versus cafés, food or not, etc.[18] Toni indicates that the area is not familiar. 'I'll see if there is a map', says Jan.

9. Jan selects the Specific Venues category, selects the Pleasance Theatre[19], and selects map. A map showing the area is displayed. All the restaurants, cafés, pubs, etc.[20] are shown. Jan selects Pubs and the display changes to remove the other eating and drinking places. The pubs are highlighted and referenced[21]. Jan selects three or four pubs in turn and gets information about the pub type, distance from the Pleasance, etc. Jan returns to the conference and sends the message to Toni that there is the Pleasance Courtyard, but it will be packed[22], or the Southsider. It's a 10-minute walk, but it serves Maclays which is a nice beer.

10. Toni says that some help getting there would be useful. Jan attaches the map to a message and sends it to Toni. When Toni gets it, the HIC at Toni's end is able to provide instructions about how to get to the Southsider. 'See you in the pub in an hour, then', says Pat, 'but you had better get started. I just checked the traffic on the Dalkeith road and it's terrible'.

[12] Again this could be a personal agent or other way of providing profile data.
[13] This happens automatically, presumably.
[14] This is probably part of the HIC, but could be the regular phone, of course. How it is activated is up for debate.
[15] By Name from an address book, through their personal profile, or whatever.
[16] Or perhaps Toni is automatically 'on-line' in answering the phone.
[17] This may be spoken interaction, it does not have to be typed.
[18] Ideally the HIC will be able to pick up on keywords used in such conversations and use these in subsequent searches.
[19] Again this would probably be the default given the history of this interaction.
[20] As per their conversation, earlier.
[21] There's another issue about categories here. Maxine's is categorized as a wine bar, but could just as easily be classified as a pub.
[22] Or perhaps looks at the Courtyard in real time through the Pleasance Cam!

Challenge 14-2
Using the footnotes recorded against the Edinburgh Festival scenario, discuss possible design decisions, or design trade-offs that will have to be made.

14.3   Functional requirements

Having evaluated the existing prototypes, it was evident that before finalizing any design ideas it was necessary to understand the HIC and the generic actions of the system. That is, it was important to establish some high-level functional requirements: what the system had to do. As we discussed in Chapter 13, a good method of establishing requirements is to undertake an object/action analysis of the scenarios.

The idea in doing this analysis was to acquire a more in-depth understanding of the HIC. By identifying the activities, actions and objects within the scenarios it was hoped to give an outline of the potential utilization of the HIC. By listing these activities, it also gives an indication of how often particular activities and actions could be carried out and how many objects require being present on the screen at the same time. The HIC needed to be as accessible and simple as possible for the user. This information would give an indication as to whether access to particular actions, objects and activities needed to be always present on the screen and therefore immediately available to the user. It would also highlight actions, activities and objects that were less utilized and therefore need not be accessed in one mouse click, but could be available through hidden dock methods or slide-on submenus.

The analysis of the scenarios also reveals other aspects of the HIC. As we move throughout the scenarios, the user does not quit or close down the information pages or searches, but continues on to the next activity. In many instances in the scenarios, the user wants to return to a previous page or search or to toggle between levels of information. For example, in the scenario 'Traffic', the user looks up travel options for getting to the museum. She then moves on to printing transport times and prices, e-mails her teacher, switches back to the location map which she prints out, and then switches back to the TV.

There are two main issues here. Firstly, how will all of the information be shown on the screen if the manipulation of windows is to be ruled out (which was an early design requirement)? The current page in view must be large enough to enable viewing at a distance; the elements must all be large enough to be touchable. This points to the display of one page at a time.

Secondly, if the HIC shows one page at a time, the use of a back button to reach previous pages of information will not be a sufficient solution to navigating these pages. In some scenarios the user may have accessed more than 17 levels of information or pages, in order to complete a fairly simple task. Utilizing only Back and Next would not allow enough flexibility, and the user could easily get lost in the information space.

To enable the user to toggle between two or three pages or levels of information, there must be some form of visual feedback and labelling to enable the user to easily identify the route they have taken through the information space. The user must also be able to easily return to or go forward through the history of their actions. As the use of windows is not an option, devising a history bar for the interface would accommodate the user's needs and would clearly visualize and label the user's path of navigation.

Object/action analysis

As we discussed in Chapter 13, a useful technique for understanding the concepts involved in a system is to undertake an object/action analysis of the scenario corpus. This was the next activity undertaken in this project. The initial object/action analysis resulted in four categories of object:

- **Information display objects**: display-only data which has been searched for or queried. The data is non-editable and provided by content providers, etc.
- **Category objects**: includes lists and catalogues, changeable dependent on the providers that are subscribed to on the HIC. Restrictions or enhancements may also be applied to individual users' preferences.
- **Functions/user control objects**: controls and tools which are basic to the HIC and enable functionality of the system, i.e. preferences, payment, setup, etc.
- **Physical objects**: devices which are displayed on screen or controlled by the HIC.

Details of the objects and actions in the different categories are listed in Tables 14-1 to 14-4. These were extracted from all the scenarios, not just the Edinburgh Festival Scenario.

TABLE 14-1 Information display objects and actions

Objects	Actions
Information display	Select
	Select links
Catalogue	None
Details of events display	Specify
Reviews display	Jump, browse
Programme guide	Asks, narrows search
Traffic information	Asks, checks, directs, picks
Presentation display	None

TABLE 14-2 Category objects and actions

Objects	Actions
TV channel display	Select
On-line shopping	Check, adjust, confirm
Map facility	Asks, selects
Services display	Uses
Category display	Select
TV Reviews display	None
Booking form	Confirm, enter, specify
Content providers display	Select connect
Subscribers list	Select
News setup display	Selects, instructs
Books category	None
Payment form	Selects
	Enters, verifies, sends
Search	Asks
	Looks around
	Narrows down
	Streams
TV control display	Setup

TABLE 14-3 Functions/user objects and actions

Objects	Actions
Messages	Directs
	Instructs, attaches
	Enters (verbal)
	Instructs
	Sends
	Creates
Calendar	Checks
E-mail facility	Writes (written)

▶

Objects	Actions
Print facility	Has the HIC write out
	Has the HIC print out
Setup display	Select
	Select, answer
	Select, enter
Help function	Asks
Query facility	Input
	Asks
Personal profile	Select
	Create filter
	Confirm
Phone	Select
Subscribers list	Select
Payment section	Selects, sets up, inputs, confirms

TABLE 14-4 Physical objects and actions

Objects	Actions
Radio	Streams
Video display	Follow links
Audio display	Follow links
Animation display	Follow links
Clock	Check
CD player	Set
	Play
Internal camera	Record
Conferencing system	Enter into
TV display	None
Phone	Select

Collating objects and actions

From the data collected through an analysis of the scenarios, a list of the actions was made with a count of the number of times these actions occurred in the scenarios. This helped to identify repetition in actions, actions that represent a series of actions rather than singular actions, and any actions which are performed by the system rather than by the user.

Table 14-5 shows these actions. Table 14-6 shows the actions which remain after the repetitive actions have been condensed under one action title. For example, 'Answers', 'Enters', 'Writes', 'Inputs' and 'Specifies' in the context of the scenarios all describe the action of 'inputting' information into the HIC in a variety of modal forms. The action 'Inputs' therefore remains in this second table as the word that best describes the generic action performed.

Table 14-7 includes the generic actions 'Down', 'Back', 'Forward' and 'Navigate', which were not listed in the scenarios. In looking at the actions which describe a number of actions rather than the singular, it was noted that these actions similarly describe 'on screen' and 'off screen' navigational actions which would be replaced by and accommodated in these additional actions.

TABLE 14-5 Simplification of the data – stage 1

Action	No.	Action	No.
Answers	1	Plays	1
Enters	6	Sets up (series of actions)	2
Writes	1	Connects	1
Inputs	2	Up	1
Specifies	2	Narrows down (series of actions)	2
Verifies	1	Jumps (series of actions)	1
Confirms	5	Creates (series of actions)	3
Selects	17	Streams	1
Picks	1	Adjusts (series of actions)	1
Links	3	Sets	2
Looks up (series of actions)	1	Sends	2
Looks around (series of actions)	1	Attaches	2
Browses (series of actions)	1	Records	1
Uses	1	Checks	4
Asks	7	Directs	2
Wants	1		
Instructs	3		

TABLE 14-6 Simplification of the data – stage 2

Action	No.	Action	No.
Inputs	12	Adjusts (series of actions)	1
Confirms	10	Plays	1
Selects	21	Connects	1
Instructs	13	Up	1
Browses (series of actions)	3	Streams	1
Sets up (series of actions)	2	Sets	2
Narrow down (series of actions)	2	Sends	2
Jumps (series of actions)	1	Attaches	2
Creates (series of actions)	3	Records	1

TABLE 14-7 Simplification of the data – stage 3

Action	No.	Action	No.
Inputs	12	Down	
Confirms	10	Up	
Selects	21	Back	
Instructs	13	Forward	
Plays	1	Navigate	
Connects	1		
Sends	2		
Attaches	1		
Records	1		

Generic actions

The actions listed above form the basis of the functions required for the HIC at this stage. Many actions in the initial list taken from the scenarios have been discarded as the words used describe the same actions in a variety of ways. For example, the actions 'Verify' and 'Confirm' in the context of the scenarios describe the actions of reading feedback data from the HIC and confirming the information is correct. Therefore these have been narrowed down under the action of 'Confirm'.

Challenge 14-3
Develop a simple e-mail scenario for the HIC and then look at the commands above. Are there sufficient commands to deal with e-mail?

14.4 Conceptual design

The results of the analysis of the scenarios and evaluations of some early interface prototypes (Chapter 4) resulted in a number of conceptual and physical design decisions. Three important decisions are described here. Notice that although the design is primarily conceptual at this point (i.e. we are concerned with what is required rather than how it will look and behave), it is natural to undertake some physical design as part of this process.

Chapter 4 discusses the three prototypes

The category bar

The wealth of information that was going to be included in the HIC, probably from third-party content providers, had to be categorized to give it some form of order. In interface prototype C (*Recipes*) the designer had utilized categorization to develop four headings in the history. These categories now needed to be looked at further. The designer had listed 'work', 'household', 'email & web' and 'entertainment'.

However, it was not clear why these were chosen, nor how they related to the general domains in which the HIC would be used. The use of the standard terminal colours – red, blue, yellow and green – was liked by the industrial partner, and these seemed to be the most effective colours to use in categorizing the information. This meant that all domains would have to be grouped into four categories. The domains listed in the scenarios were as follows:

- Recipes
- Travel Planner
- Traffic
- Culture
- Find a Place
- News
- TV/Radio Programmes
- On-line Shopping

The following categories were defined from this list:

- Culture – includes the Culture and TV/ Radio Programmes domains.
- News – includes the News domain.
- Household – includes the Recipes and On-line Shopping domains.
- Travel – includes the Travel Planner, Traffic and Find a Place domains.

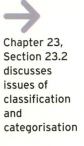

Chapter 23, Section 23.2 discusses issues of classification and categorisation

Each of the categories listed above was now colour coded and represented as buttons on a bar, as shown in Figure 14-2. To aid association for the user, the information contained within these categories would also incorporate the colour chosen to identify that category.

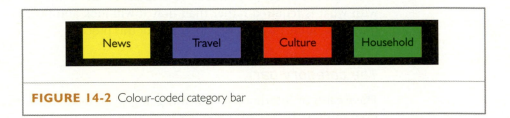

FIGURE 14-2 Colour-coded category bar

Amalgamating a user history and category bar

From problem solving and reworking the ideas of Prototype B – *Festivals* (which uses previous page history as a top bar), and Prototype C – *Recipes* (which uses category history as a top bar), we now have two separate solutions: a history bar and a category bar, which will occupy the top half of the interface. These will integrate so that when the HIC opens, the category bar is displayed in the top part of the screen. If the user clicks on a category, they are presented with that category's history bar which is now shown on top of the category bar. As the user progresses through pages in that category's information space, appropriately labelled and coloured arrows increment to show the user's history. In Figure 14-3, we see the user has initially chosen the blue travel category and has progressed through three pages in the Travel information space.

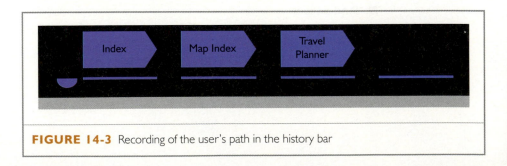

FIGURE 14-3 Recording of the user's path in the history bar

User controls and physical objects

Many of the objects within the HIC do not require any generic actions of the system to be performed upon them. It therefore seemed appropriate that they be grouped together on the interface. The majority of these facilities still needed to be easily accessible. For example, in one of the scenarios, the user wants to send a message to another user and attaches a picture taken with the internal camera to the message before sending it. This implies that both the messaging function and the internal camera have to be present on the screen at all times or be accessible to the user through a hidden dock.

The user controls and physical objects within the HIC that this applies to are as follows:

- Auxiliary objects – include objects external to the HIC but controlled by it: TV, Radio, CD and Video
- Functions – include those objects within the HIC which are utilized alongside other functions: Telephone Functionality, Conferencing System, Internal Camera
- Subscribers – information providers
- Time – Alarm and Clock
- Print
- Users – Home Banking, User Preferences, messages (Message Board, Email and My Notes)
- Help
- Search

As the auxiliary objects and functions had been identified and grouped together under these headings, it seemed sensible to separate them to different areas of the screen. Two slide-on hidden docks were designed to accommodate each of the groupings (Figure 14-4), with a marker which moves along to indicate the selected object.

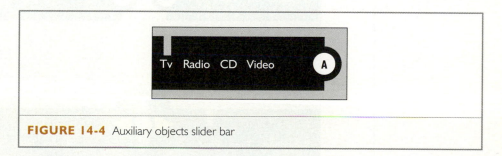

FIGURE 14-4 Auxiliary objects slider bar

Challenge 14-4
Before reading further, spend some time sketching your design of the overall interface, given information that is available. What would be the key conceptual model behind the design? What mental model are you trying to engender in the users?

14.5 An interface design

The various design ideas were then brought together into the first comprehensive interface prototype. This is described here. The category bar and history bar were devised to occupy the top part of the interface, and the navigation controls both needed to be central for the user to get easy feedback whilst utilizing the system – an important design principle.

Combining the slide-on hidden dock and the navigation controls at the bottom of the interface keeps the main part of the screen free for the display of information (see Figure 14-5). The idea of all the control being allocated to the border of the screen meant that the two sliding hidden docks containing the functions and auxiliary objects were placed to the left and right of the screen to slide out when needed (see Figure 14-6).

← Design principles are listed in Chapter 3

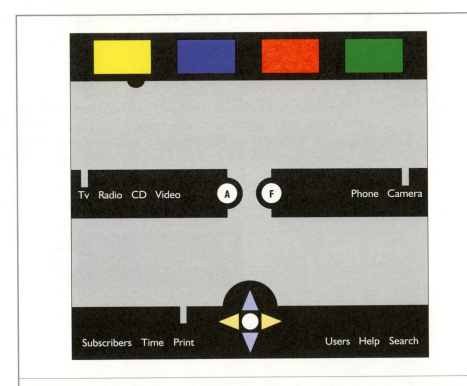

FIGURE 14-5 First layout with hidden docks extended

FIGURE 14-6 First layout with hidden docks

The idea of the sliding docks was a good one, but the two slide bars intruded somewhat into the main space. There was also the possibility of applying all of these objects to one location rather than splitting them up into groupings. This was another idea worth mocking-up: see Figure 14-7. The immediately obvious problem with this design was its use of pop-up menus which were not intended to be used within the HIC interface, as they are too reminiscent of a PC interface.

Evaluation of first solutions

These designs were brought back to the main interface design team who met together and discussed the ideas. This section provides a summary of this discussion.

Feedback on user history

The general consensus was that this was an effective solution for visualizing the activity history. The prominence of the history bar, however, was thought to be over-accentuated, given that it may not always be needed. As it stood, the history bar was tied in with the navigation of the categories. It was decided at the meeting that the history should be a separate entity, perhaps shown as a hidden dock that could be utilized upon request.

One design possibility was to have four history arrows mapping onto the four categories. This would allow the use of forward and fast forward, back and fast

FIGURE 14-7 Layout with objects applied to bottom area only

back functions to be included on the history bar, enabling the user to go through the previous and next history pages either one at a time or four at a time.

Feedback on auxiliary objects/functions slide-on bars

It was immediately pointed out that the bars impose too much upon the central information space as they moved out horizontally. The suggestion of having them slide vertically was made. The group was also not sure about the categorization of these objects. One of the designers suggested that the activities Search and Print, which were allocated to the bottom bar, should be grouped at the left side of the interface. This seemed a much more coherent separation of the objects. He also suggested that the right-hand bar could include the lists of the content providers subscribed to on the HIC. This would enable the user to click on an activity, for example Search, and then to click on a content provider, such as the Scotsman, and search the Scotsman information space. A sketch produced at this meeting is shown in Figure 14-8.

This design decision turned out to be fundamental to the HIC concept. The separation of objects and actions and the provision of a central information

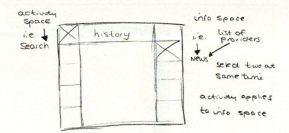

FIGURE 14-8 Activity and providers bar sketch

space was felt to provide potential users with a clear and simple conceptual model: objects on one side and actions on the other. Such a simple and clear model should go a long way to ensuring the interface was 'intuitive'.

The question then arose of what to do if there are lots of content providers subscribed to by the user. How could they be shown on a bar without the use of scrolling of lists? The use of a rotating bar was suggested to deal with this.

On the left-hand side of the display there would be an activities bar which initially was thought to include:

- Search
- Print
- Go To
- My Space (for saving information to)
- Bin

The buttons would be labelled in white text, utilizing rollovers to highlight the text to indicate that these areas include some interaction.

Feedback on bottom bar with navigation

The layout and design of the bottom bar was liked by the team, but the user functions and physical objects now needed to be allocated to it. The grouping of these objects needed to be looked at further as they now all had to be contained around the navigation controls which would remain in the centre of the bar.

Developing the bars

In problem-solving the three-dimensional aspect of the design, the initial idea was to develop a two-sided bar which would rotate when required to reveal further options. The category bar (at the top) would rotate to reveal the history as required, the provider bar (on the right-hand side) would rotate to provide further options, and the activity bar (on the left-hand side) would rotate to provide further activities (Figure 14-9).

FIGURE 14-9 Screen shot from rotating bar animation

Development of the two-sided bar

As it stood, the navigation bar at the bottom, the activity bar and the provider bar would slide on as needed. But how would the user realize that these bars had more than one side to them? An animation was needed in which the hidden docks would slide in, rotate, then rotate back and slide out to demonstrate the functionality of these bars to the user.

The next realization was that only five content providers could feasibly fit onto a provider bar and still be legible because of the necessity to include a logo and title for each provider. This meant that with a two-sided bar only 10 providers could be shown. It was likely that the user would subscribe to more than 10 providers; 15 was more of a realistic number. A three-sided bar therefore needed to be developed. The design team referred to this as a 'Toblerone' after a famous chocolate bar.

Development of the 'Toblerone' bar

The development of a prototype to show the opening screen and the functionality of the two spinning Toblerones that were also hidden docks (the activity and provider bars on the left and right) was the next stage of development (Figure 14-10). The bottom bar at this stage did not require further dimensions, so remained as a one-sided bar.

After development of this prototype it was realized that the idea of a three-sided Toblerone would allow the category bar to have a menu on one side which lists the domains within that category for the user to choose from. This would mean that when the user clicks on a category, the bar could spin to reveal a menu. With three sides, the category bar could still have the history on one of the sides. Instead of the history bar being only relevant to the category the user was looking at, the bar would show the history of all the pages the user had vis-

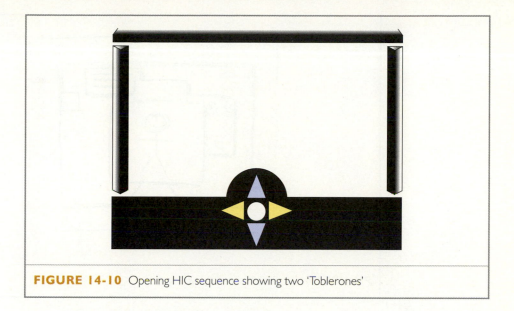

FIGURE 14-10 Opening HIC sequence showing two 'Toblerones'

ited within all of the categories. For example, it could show two blue arrows from the Travel category, one from the yellow News category, a red search arrow from the Culture section and a green arrow from the Household category.

The necessity of this bar to be available on screen at all time meant that this bar would not take the form of a hidden dock.

14.6 Finalizing ideas

At the following design meeting, one of the designers suggested a solution for the presentation of pages within the information space where the three-dimensional illusion of the interface could be developed further, the idea being that the information space in the centre of the interactive controls could contain several layers of information or several page levels. This would accentuate the idea of the path the user had followed through the information space with the past (previous pages) being displayed behind the present (present page) in descending order, the furthest away being the smallest graphically (see Figure 14-11). By continuing to use black as the background colour for all pages, there would be no representation of an outline on each page (avoiding any similarity to windows), therefore accentuating the three-dimensionality of the central information space.

If we look at the sketch in Figure 14-11, level 1 is shown as the largest page on the screen. Level 2 is slightly smaller, level 3 slightly smaller still and so on. The user is also able to click on the previous levels, bringing them to the front. If level 2 is clicked upon, it will come to the front, thus occupying the space previously held by level 1. Level 1 will then occupy the space of level 2.

This manipulation and interaction of the levels can be further developed so that the user can drag the levels to an activity in the activity bar, and the activ-

FIGURE 14-11 Sketch showing two levels

ity would automatically be carried out. For example, if the user had clicked on a content provider such as the *Scotsman* newspaper, it would come into focus as level 1. If the user were then to drag the page (level 1) to the search button in the activity bar, a search would be provided on the contents of the *Scotsman*. The search would then be in focus as level 1 and the *Scotsman* page would occupy level 2. This action can be applied to any of the activities on the bar. For example, drag a level to Print and the page will be printed; drag the level to the bin and the page will be sent to the bin.

In mocking-up different layouts, with the information being displayed on different levels of varying sizes with no outside border, it was impossible to give a sense of distance or the illusion of three dimensions. Because the pages or levels could be displaying graphics and text of any size, when reduced to indicate a sense of distance, some graphics appeared larger than those that were conceptually less far away. If the levels had different coloured backgrounds, the objective could have been achieved. The best solution to the problem was to have all of the previous levels the same size, but let their position around the level in focus indicate their distance (Figure 14-12). The level numbers depreciate in a clockwise manner, i.e. the bottom left graphic is level 2, and the top right level is level 6.

Finalising the bottom bar

The entire interface had now been decided except for the functionality of the bottom bar of the HIC. At this stage of development, for the purpose of testing, many functions did not have to be included and so therefore were no longer an issue for this prototype. The Users button was not to be represented, as prototype P1 was not addressing the issue of multi-users.

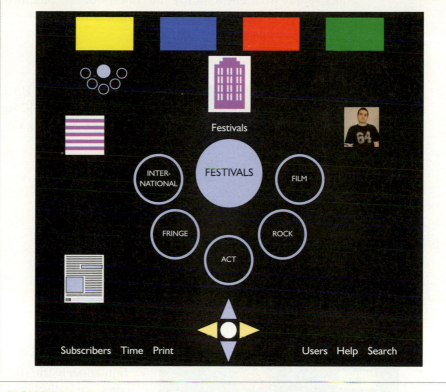

FIGURE 14-12 Mock-up levels layout showing six levels

The external devices (or physical objects as they have been called previously) were to be contained within the bottom bar. The need for them to take up as little space as possible and the need for easy access meant that the utilization of a Toblerone style button was going to be the best solution. By grouping the objects (TV, Radio, CD, Camera, Video and Phone) together under the button labelled Devices, when the user clicked on this button only this area of the bar would spin to reveal the other sides of its Toblerone with the devices labelled individually on the other two sides.

The messaging function would also occupy space on this bar. Again, because it contained a sub-menu, it would employ the use of a spinning Toblerone to contain its other elements on its other sides.

Building the final prototype

The final part of this exercise was to develop a relevant scenario to demonstrate the functionality of the prototype, which could be used in evaluations with users. This was adapted from the Edinburgh Festival scenario. In order to give the user an easy to follow account of the interface, it seemed that the most effective way would be to utilize the concept of the 'Picture Story' rather than to give a merely textual illustration of its functionality. The picture story is shown in the next few pages.

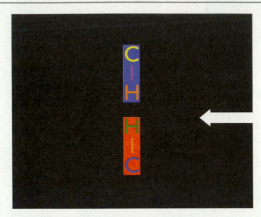

(1) *Click on screen (black area only)*

Jan activates the HIC, which is displaying the HIC logo on standby mode, by clicking on the screen. (1)

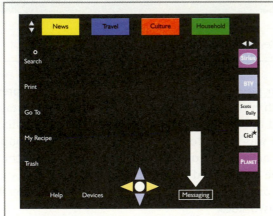

(2) *Click on message bar (edge only)*

Immediately the HIC's navigation interface is displayed on the screen. Jan decides to quickly check her messages, so clicks on the message bar (2), which reveals the choice of composing or collecting messages. Jan can see that there are no new messages, so closes the message bar by clicking the bar edge. (2)

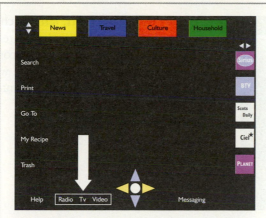

(3) *Click on TV to reveal TV remote*

Pat suggests to Jan that there may be some interesting coverage of Festival events reviews on the local STV lunchtime news, so Jan clicks on the devices bar to reveal the TV facility. (3)

(4) *Change channel (left and right arrows)*

When clicked upon, the TV is instantly activated and a remote control is displayed on the HIC screen. Jan changes the channel (4), which is currently set to Channel 1, to Channel 3, the Scottish Television station …

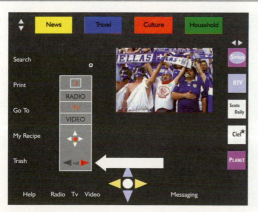

(5) *Adjust volume*

… and adjusts the volume. (5)

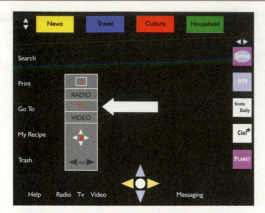

(6) Switch off (centre red button)

After the news report, Jan switches off the TV facility on the 'virtual' remote (6) and decides to look at her content providers to see if any of them will contain relevant festival information.

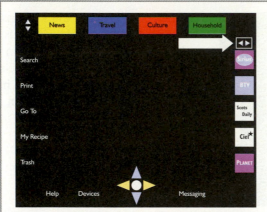

(7) Providers bar (left and right)

Jan clicks on the provider's bar and looks at the various providers (7). The bar spins round to reveal the various providers they have subscribed to.

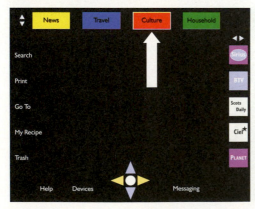

(8) Category bar, click on 'Culture'

Pat suggests that it might be better to view the information from a group of providers rather than just one, so Jan then goes to the category bar and clicks on the category 'Culture' (8) which encompasses the subcategory of 'Festivals'.

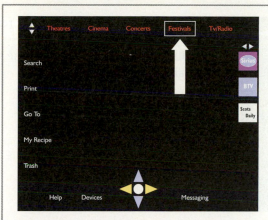

(9) *Click on 'Festivals'*

The category bar spins to reveal the domains within the culture bar, and Jan can see that only three content providers supply information in this category. Jan clicks on 'Festivals' (9) on the top bar, and a page is displayed which shows the festivals that Jan can look up.

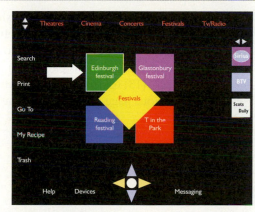

(10) *Edinburgh Festival*

Jan clicks on 'Edinburgh festival' (10) and a new page is displayed which shows the various Edinburgh Festivals. The previous display shrinks and moves to the bottom left of the display.

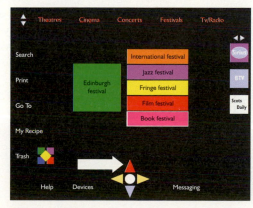

(11) *'Up' button*

Jan moves across the room to make a cup of coffee and uses the remote control to control the HIC. Jan presses the 'Up' (11) button on the remote (click on Up on the lower bar) until the Fringe festival title is highlighted.

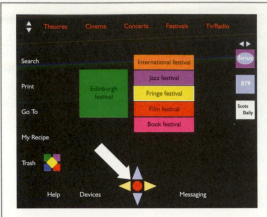

(12) *'Select' button*

Jan presses 'Select' (12) on the remote (click on Select) and a page is displayed which categorizes the ways Jan can look up fringe shows.

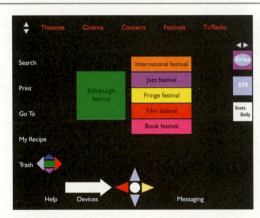

(13) *'Back' button*

Jan can see the previous pages she has looked at in the background behind the current page, and decides to go back to the previous page. Jan presses 'Back' (13) on the remote and the previous page now comes to the front.

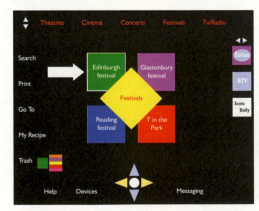

(14) *Previous display*

The Festivals page is displayed and the Edinburgh Festivals display replaces it in the bottom left corner.

Challenge 14-5
Evaluate this first interface. How logical is the structure? How intuitive do you think the interface is? What is the navigation object doing at the bottom of the screen? Why are some objects along the bottom and others down the side? Is this a sensible distinction?

14.7 The second interface design

A number of changes were made between the first and second interface designs. These included changing the categories of actions on the left-hand bar and dropping the bottom bar altogether.

One important concept to arise from the first prototype was the idea of a history. Previous queries could be displayed on the screen, gradually disappearing into the distance as they got older. Another member of the design team began to look at this and at the overall concept of searching. The initial ideas for having a novel searching interface had been developed and critiqued over a long period. A number of the relevant sketches have been discussed elsewhere in this part.

The final design was based on the concept of a 'rolodex' (Figure 14-13). This design avoided the PC-centric design feature of having scrolling windows with all the concomitant window management activities and we felt that it was a more engaging design, suitable for a relaxed home environment. The concept

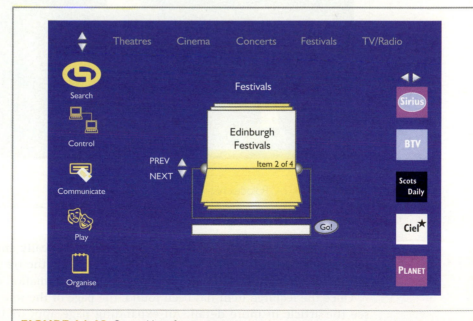

FIGURE 14-13 Second interface prototype

behind the finalized rolodex is such that the user may 'flip' page by page through results until the required item is found. This is done by simply touching the 'Prev' or 'Next' icons to the left of the rolodex. At any stage the user may select an item by touching the page of the rolodex or by selecting 'Go!'.

Bringing together the concept of history and the concept of the rolodex resulted in the idea of having a history of previous searches represented with smaller rolodexes. When the person selects 'Go!' an animation of the rolodex shrinking in size and moving to the bottom left-hand corner of the screen is provided. A new rolodex is presented with the items relevant to the previously selected item, and searching through the information may be performed in exactly the same manner with the new data.

One further concept was added. If any category of the search returns more than 20 results the system then presents the user with a 'rolodex tree' (see Figure 14-14). This is based on the idea of a cone tree. See Chapter 24, Section 24.4.

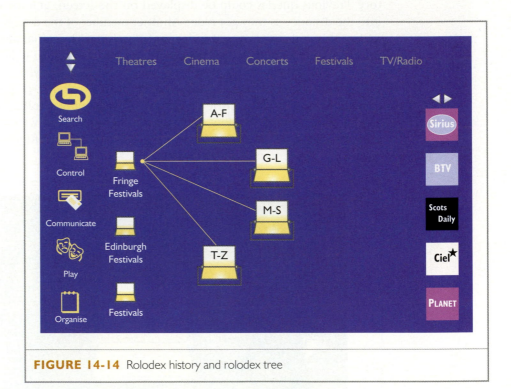

FIGURE 14-14 Rolodex history and rolodex tree

In this case the rolodex tree is categorized alphabetically and any miniature rolodex may be touched for selection. This then fades the tree and a new full-size rolodex is again presented to the user with the information contained in it.

Once the required item has been found, the page of the rolodex is pressed to see the article in more detail. An expanding page appears from within the rolodex, looking like a card from a card index in order to maintain the visual metaphor, that offers a complete description of the item selected (Figure 14-15). To return to the items in the rolodex, the user would press the small rolodex titled 'Items' at the top-left corner of the screen.

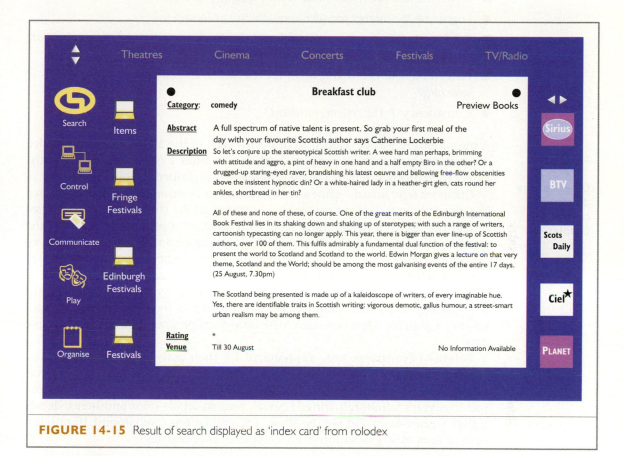

FIGURE 14-15 Result of search displayed as 'index card' from rolodex

14.8 Evaluation of the second prototype

The second prototype embodied a number of key concepts that would now have to be evaluated with some real people. Designers can only come up with their best ideas. As soon as these are in a coherent form, they need to be evaluated with potential users of the system. A full working visual prototype from which the screen shots in Figures 14-14 and 14-15 are adapted was developed in Macromedia Director. This included a real database of articles from the *Scotsman* newspaper on the Edinburgh Festival so that people could undertake real searches.

As with the rest of the case study, the evaluation process is not presented as a perfect model to follow, but rather to stimulate discussion of the approaches used. The evaluation was aimed towards the key areas of the interface. In this case the designers were particularly interested in:

- **System learnability:** *Does the design of the interface help or hinder the user?*
- **Toolbars:** *Was animation of toolbars effective? Overall concept good?*
- **Icons:** *Are they understandable? Is their meaning obvious?*
- **Logos:** *Are the content provider logos effective as identifiers?*
- **Rolodex:** *Is the general concept of the rolodex liked? Is it effective? Does it facilitate searching?*
- **Categorization:** *Is breaking down the search into categories an effective means of searching?*
- **Consistency:** *Is the system consistent?*

Questionnaire design is covered in Chapter 21

A questionnaire was developed to deal with each of the above areas. It included 20 statements for which people could choose from 1 (meaning strongly disagree) to 5 (strongly agree). The questionnaire is explained in Table 14.8.

Questions were mixed – some were expressed in a positive fashion and others in a negative fashion to prevent people simply ticking all the strongly agree or disagree boxes; they had to read and think about each question. A section at the start of the questionnaire established the background of the participant. A further list of three open-ended questions was included at the end of the questionnaire. A comment box was also included for additional suggestions that evaluators could make.

The evaluation took place in a vestibule area of the university where many people were passing. A physical prototype of the HIC with a 15-inch touchscreen monitor set into a portable television-sized MDF casing was programmed with the sample data.

Potential evaluators were approached for their assistance and then taken through the main functions of the HIC. They were then given a concrete scenario to work through in which they were to find a performance from the previous year's Edinburgh Fringe Festival, read an article on it and hence decide if they wished to go and see the show. The evaluations took around 10 minutes each. A total of 50 evaluations were completed over two days.

Evaluation results

Just a few of the results are explored here. The bar chart (Figure 14-16) outlines the responses to each question: whether the user agreed with the question, disagreed with it, or was indifferent (neither agreed nor disagreed). 'N' indicates a negative question, hence if a high proportion disagree it is a good design feature. 'P' indicates a positive question, hence if people agree this is a good feature. The assumption was made that if a person chose agree or strongly agree, then the response was classed as agreeing with the question. If a person chose disagree or strongly disagree, then the response was classed as a disagree. This method filtered out all the halfway votes which may have influenced the answer unfairly.

It can be seen through this chart that in general all responses were of a positive nature. Some aspects of the system were more positive than others. The data was used for a number of related evaluations. The aspects that this evaluation focuses on are in particular the use of rolodexes for searching, the rolodex tree, the categorization of data and the general ease of use of the system.

TABLE 14-8 A brief explanation of the questionnaire

Feature	Question numbers	Question: concept	Question: design	Comments
System	1, 2	Design	To evaluate system as a whole	Do users like the system? Do they find it easy to use?
System integration	3, 4	Consistency	Is system consistent?	Is design too cluttered or ambiguous?
System learnability	5, 6	System should be easy to learn	Does design of interface help or hinder user?	System is designed with ease of use uppermost. These questions will give important feedback on this issue
Searching	7, 8	More than one way to search	Rolodex or content provider logo: any preference?	HIC allows user to search for information in more than one way. Will user even realize this?
Toolbars	9, 10	Animation, i.e. movement idea, sides	Arrows too big or small, colour	Aim: to try to cut out scrolling
Icons	11	To do away with text	Icons understandable and meaning obvious?	Icon meaning may be ambiguous. Do people readily understand them?
Logos	12	Use of pictures to symbolize company	Colour, font, legibility	Aim: to cut out writing and associated problems; to make content providers more recognizable
Touchscreen	13, 14	Touch as in feel, feedback	Design facilitates use of touchscreen	Aim: to reduce amount of peripherals (mouse, keyboard, etc.)
Colours used by the system	15	Colours should be pleasing to the eye, and for categories map onto colours on remote	Aesthetics: shape, colour	Will people like very basic colour used? Makes the design boring?
Rolodex	16	Helps user visualize size of search	Shape, size, legibility of rolodex itself	To make searches more interesting and help user visualize amount of information returned by their search criteria
Categories	17	Quick way to search, without having to be too specific	Category names, e.g. culture, household	To let user search without having to put in specific search criteria. Aim is also to show some kind of history
Consistency	18-20	Design should be conceptually and physically consistent	Selection/searching mechanism, colours	Also external consistency

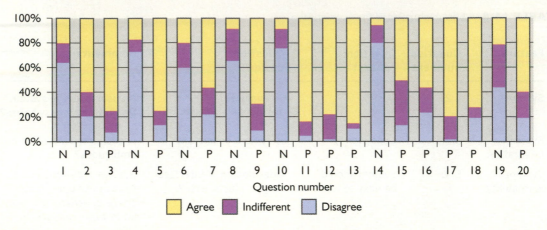

FIGURE 14-16 Overall results from the questionnaire: averages over 50 evaluations (see Table 14-8 and text)

Results indicated that a general liking was found for the rolodex concept, although a significant minority felt quite strongly against it. A few negative comments were as follows:

■ 'Rolodex too slow, no way to jump through lots of data ...' (Questionnaire 34)
■ '... should be as life-like as possible (putting in markers, taking out cards, leafing through them)' (Questionnaire 36)

Some positive feedback was as follows:

■ 'Very intuitive' (Questionnaire 38)
■ 'The rolodexes and menus were very good for browsing ...' (Questionnaire 41)
■ 'The rolodex idea is very good. Selection of alphabet would improve it.' (Questionnaire 10)

The question that asked whether the rolodexes helped gain an overview of the information available was posed and the outcome is shown in Figure 14-17.

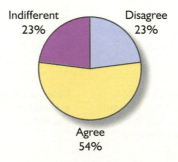

FIGURE 14-17 Overall response to question whether rolodexes helped gain an overview

Through a study of the many comments made regarding the interface by those who took part in the evaluations, it was clear that the first prototype was quite successful and that many of the main concepts of the interface were worth pursuing. Areas of improvement and amendment are necessary, in particular:

- Larger arrows. At present the arrows on the toolbars are too small for convenience.
- Markers. A point made by many was that a marker system should be introduced to the rolodex, i.e. some way of holding a page of the rolodex. Perhaps have a colour-coded tag at the side of the page of the rolodex.
- Alphabetical search. It was suggested by a few that displaying an alphabetic search at the top of the rolodex would be a good idea. This would save searching through each individual item one by one.
- Order of colours for category buttons. To conform to a standard they should be red, green, yellow, then blue.

Challenge 14-6
Critique this evaluation. What do you think is good about it? What could have been improved?

Summary and key points

In this case study we have focused on the interface design for a novel device – the Home Information Centre. We have deliberately left the discussions much as they were during the design process so that you can see how discussions move, fluctuating between very detailed concerns and very high-level or conceptual concerns. We have not 'tidied up' the process. Much of what is in this chapter has been taken from reports that were produced at the time. What we have tried to do is to tell a story of a design, the key points being:

- How scenarios were developed to explore the design space of the HIC device
- How the scenarios were analysed in order to understand the main functionality the device required
- How the key design concepts were developed through prototyping ideas, evaluating them and redesigning them
- How key design concepts were realized physically and how the physical design affected the conceptual design and vice versa
- How a physical design was evaluated, focusing on some key aspects of the design.

Further reading

There are not many books that provide good case studies of doing interactive systems design and it is difficult to get at papers reporting designs. The proceedings of the ACM Designing Interactive Systems, DIS, conferences (1995, 1997, 2000, 2002 and 2004) do contain some design cases and it is also worth looking at the CHI series of conferences for design cases. Both are available from the ACM digital library.

Comments on challenges

Challenge 14-1

Of course you will have chosen different examples, but you should have thought about the variety inherent in any of these scenarios. For example, the 'What shall we have for dinner?' scenario might include

● People – a young girl with her grandmother who is visiting for a while

● Activities – investigating recipes, finding out what could be cooked with the food that is in the house, dealing with allergies to particular foods and finding alternatives, finding simple or complex recipes, finding particular types of food

● Contexts – making something quickly, cooking for lots of people, cooking for just one or two

● Technologies – the basic HIC design is a constraint, but there is a need to consider the content (i.e. information about recipes). Is there a video showing how to make things, are there links to on-line chat rooms, recommendations for others or from famous chefs, etc.?

Challenge 14-2

There are of course many design issues that are raised and hence many design options that can be considered to deal with them. One issue, for example, concerns how much the system can know about the different people – e.g. where they live, what the roads are like, how you can travel from one place to another. Such data is available (e.g. for in-car travel systems), but how the different content from different providers can be linked together by the HIC is a challenge. There would presumably have to be some standard 'mark-up' language used such as XML. This would allow interoperability between the different applications.

Challenge 14-3

There is not obviously a 'read' command at the moment. 'Write' did appear in Table 14-5 but became merged with another command. It is difficult to see from the lists of commands exactly what each would do, and certainly before the design goes much further it would be a good idea to specify what is meant by each of these in more detail, perhaps in the form of an interaction pattern (Chapter 13).

Challenge 14-4
The key conceptual model to emerge from the analysis was the concept of the object and action as described later in this chapter. Other key concepts included the interaction history and categories.

Challenge 14-5
Once again it is interesting to notice how physical design is needed to evaluate conceptual issues. Looking at the physical design it is difficult to see, conceptually, the difference between the objects on the bottom and the objects on the side bars. The reasons for separating them are no longer clear. The structure, then, is still a bit confusing and illogical. More work is needed to refine the design.

Challenge 14-6
The evaluation was quite effective, though probably could have been better. All too frequently these things are rushed near the end, but for its purpose – to get general feedback on the interface concepts – it was probably sufficient. Importantly, it was undertaken with real potential users and there was a good spread of people who used the system. The task was relatively quick to do, which is important from the pragmatic perspective, and the results provided both qualitative and quantitative data.

Exercises

1. Another thorny problem that a device such as the HIC creates is the issue of filing, storing and retrieving data, whether these are e-mail messages, MP3 files, photos or other objects. Consider how to design an effective filing system that does *not* require users to understand and use a hierarchical system such as on the Mac or PC that uses files and folders.

2. During this project we also investigated how to provide good access to all the content that people would be accessing. We concluded that there would always be a need for content providers to mark up content aimed at a specific audience. Just as news is reported in many different ways, so all the HIC's content would come from subscribing to a content provider. Discuss what a content provider might offer and what the business model might be for providing this service.

Part IV:

Psychological Foundations for Interactive Systems Design

Introduction

This part of the book considers advanced issues in the cognitive and affective aspects of the design of interactive systems. We start with Chapter 15 which revisits and greatly extends the introductory material on memory and attention in Part II, linking theoretical issues to practical design issues. We also discuss human error and how it can be minimized with careful design. Key guidelines are included for both these important areas.

Chapter 16 moves on to consider two of the less well-used modalities in interactive systems: hearing and haptics. The chapter begins with an explanation of the workings of hearing and auditory perception, then considers how the auditory modality can be exploited in designing interaction. Design guidelines are again included. The next part of the chapter deals with the role of the sense of touch and related capabilities such as proprioception – the ability to sense the position and movement of the body, relating the material to the design of tangible and wearable computing. Current examples from this rapidly developing field complement the more theoretical material.

Finally in this part, Chapter 17 turns to affective computing – applications which monitor and respond to human emotions, and may synthesize emotion themselves. Devices which facilitate human affective communication are also considered here. As for the other chapters in this part, material on the theory of human affect and emotion is balanced by discussion of current applications. The chapter ends by describing practical methods for designing for one particular human emotion – pleasure.

The material in this part is generally aimed at final-year undergraduate teaching and learning or an introductory postgraduate course. That being said, some of the more applied elements could supplement material at earlier stages. Among the possibilities for making use of these chapters are:

- As 'the psychology of interaction' element of a second or third module in interactive systems design or related areas. Each chapter is substantial, so would support at least two lectures. Visual perception is not revisited in these chapters, so Chapter 5 (which deals with this topic) would need to be reviewed if not previously covered.
- Selected elements as a supplement to the introductory interactive systems design material, in Parts I and II, either delivered through lectures or as self-study material.
- As a resource for dissertation or project work.

15

Memory, attention and making mistakes

Aims

This chapter provides considerably more detail on the importance of memory and attention in the design of interactive systems. After studying this chapter you should be able to describe:

- The importance of memory and attention and their major components and processes
- How interactive systems are being designed to take advantage of how human memory works
- The key design guidelines for designing for memory and attention
- Attention and awareness; situation awareness, attracting and holding attention
- The characteristics of human error, mental workload and how it is measured
- Memory, attention and error-avoidance design guidelines.

This material extends the introduction to memory and attention in Chapter 5, but is intended to be read as a stand-alone chapter.

15.1 What is memory?

It is said that a goldfish has a memory that lasts only three seconds. Imagine this were true of you: everything would be new and fresh every three seconds. Of course, it would be impossible to live or function as a human being. This has been succinctly expressed by Blakemore (1988):

'... without the capacity to remember and to learn, it is difficult to imagine what life would be like, whether it could be called living at all. Without

memory, we would be servants of the moment, with nothing but our innate reflexes to help us deal with the world. There could be no language, no art, no science, no culture.'

In introducing memory we begin with a brief discussion of what memory is *not* and in doing so we hope to challenge a number of misconceptions.

Firstly, memory is not just a single, simple information store – it has a complex, and still argued over, structure. Most people are aware of the short-term–long-term memory divide: short-term memory is very limited but is useful for holding such things as telephone numbers while we are dialling them. In contrast, long-term memory stores, fairly reliably, our names and other biographical information, the word describing someone who has lost their memory, and how to operate a cash dispenser. This common-sense division reflects the most widely accepted structure of memory, the so-called **multi-store model** (Atkinson and Shiffrin, 1968) which is illustrated below. However, it should be noted that this model is a simplification and does not necessarily reflect the current state of thinking and understanding in memory research.

Secondly, memory is not a passive repository; indeed it is quite the reverse: memory comprises a number of active processes. When we remember something we do not simply file it away to be retrieved whenever we wish. For example, we will see that memory is enhanced by deeper or richer processing of the material to be remembered.

Thirdly, memory is also affected by the very nature of the material to be remembered. Words, names, commands or images for that matter which are not particularly distinctive will tend to interfere with their subsequent recognition and recall. Game shows (and multiple-choice examination questions) rely on this lack of distinctiveness. A contestant may be asked:

'For €10000 can you tell me ... Bridgetown is the capital of which of the following?

(a) Antigua
(b) Barbados
(c) Cuba
(d) Dominica'

As the islands are all located in the Caribbean they are not (for most contestants) particularly distinctive. However, this kind of problem can be overcome by means of **elaboration** (e.g. Anderson and Reder, 1979). Elaboration allows us to emphasize similarities and differences among the items (see Section 15.3 for more detail).

Fourthly, memory can also be seen as a **constructive process**. Bransford, Barclay and Franks (1971) were able to show that we construct and integrate information from, for example, individual sentences. In an experiment they presented a group of people with a series of thematically related sentences and then presented them with a second set of sentences, asking 'Have you seen this sentence before?'. They found that most people estimated that they had seen approximately 80 percent of these sentences before. In fact *all* of the sentences were new. Bransford, Barclay and Franks concluded that people are happy to say that they recognized sentences they have not seen providing they are *consistent* with the theme of the other sentences.

Finally, many researchers would now argue that memory cannot be meaningfully studied in isolation, as it necessarily underpins all other aspects of cognition (thinking). For example, object recognition relies on memory; the production and understanding of language relies on some form of internal lexicon (or dictionary); finding our way about town relies on an internal representation of the environment, sometimes described as a cognitive map; the acquisition of skills often begins with internalizing and remembering instructions. Of course, having said that memory cannot be studied in isolation did not stop the pioneers of psychology from trying to do so. The early psychologist Ebbinghaus, at the end of the nineteenth century, famously used lists of nonsense syllables (such as *waj, duk, sep*) to assess his own memory for material devoid of context or meaning. Such approaches are no longer used, as the role of prior knowledge and understanding are now seen to be centrally important. Now we turn to the conventional account of memory.

15.2 How memory works

Memory is usually divided into a set of **memory processes** and a number of different types of **memory stores**. Table 15-1 is a summary of the main memory stores and their sub-components and associated processes. Figure 15-1 is an illustration of this multi-store model of the memory (note the role of attention).

Memory stores: working memory

As we have already noted, working memory, first identified and named by Baddeley and Hitch (1974), is made up from three linked components, namely a **central executive**, a **visuo-spatial sketchpad** and an **articulatory loop** (also called the phonological loop). The central executive is involved in decision making, planning and related activities. It is also closely linked to managing our ability to perform more than one thing at a time (*cf.* Section 15.9 which discusses the role of attention). The articulatory or phonological loop can be thought of as behaving like a loop of audio tape. When we are trying to dial an unfamiliar telephone number or repeating a phrase in a foreign language, we tend to repeat the string of numbers (or words) either out loud or silently to ourselves. This process is called **rehearsal**. When we are doing this we are making use of the articulatory loop, which can also account for our experience of the **inner voice**. The analogy of the audio tape is useful as it allows us to see that the articulatory loop is limited in both capacity and duration.

TABLE 15-1 A summary of the structure of memory

Main components	Key processes associated with this particular store
Sensory stores	
The **iconic** store (visual) and the **echoic** store (auditory) are temporary stores where information is held before it enters working memory.	The contents of these stores are transferred to working memory within a fraction of a second.
Working memory (WM)	
Working memory is made up from three key elements: the **central executive**, the **articulatory loop** and the **visuo-spatial sketchpad**. The central executive is involved in decision making, the articulatory loop holds auditory information and the visuo-spatial sketchpad, as the name suggests, holds visual information.	**Rehearsal** is the process of refreshing the contents of WM, such as repeating aloud a phone number. The contents of WM are said to **decay** (are lost/forgotten) if they are not rehearsed. Another way of forgetting from WM is **displacement** which is the process by which the current contents of WM are pushed out by new material.
Long-term memory (LTM)	
Long-term memory comprises the following: **Semantic** memory. This holds information related to meaning. **Procedural** memory. This stores our knowledge of how to do things such as typing or driving. **Episodic** and/or **autobiographical** memory. This may be one or two different forms of memory that are related to memories personal to an individual such as memories of birthdays, graduation or getting married. **Permastore**. This has been suggested by Bahrick (1984) as the name for the part of LTM which lasts for our lifetime. It stores the things you never forget.	**Encoding** is the process by which information is stored in memory. **Retrieval** is the means by which memories are recovered from long-term storage. **Forgetting** is the name of a number of different possible processes by which we fail to recover information.

The visuo-spatial sketchpad (also called the scratchpad) is the visual and spatial information equivalent of the articulatory loop and has been linked to our **mind's eye**. We use our mind's eye to visualize a route through a town or building or for the mental rotation of figures (visualize a coin and then rotate it to see what is on the other side). The visuo-spatial sketchpad is also limited in capacity

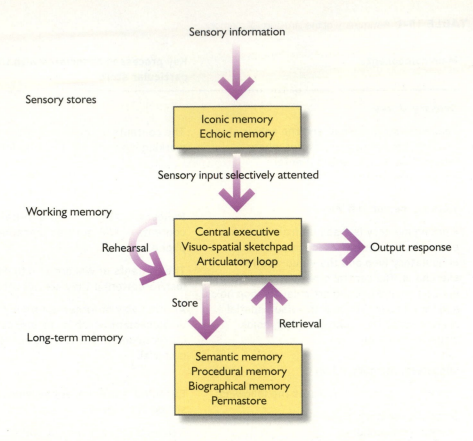

FIGURE 15-1 A schematic model of multi-store memory (*Source: after Atkinson and Shiffrin, 1968*)

**More about
7 ± 2 in
Section 15.5**

and duration unless refreshed by means of rehearsal. Finally, the capacity of working memory itself is approximately three or four items (e.g. MacGregor, 1987; LeCompte, 1999) where an item may be a word or a phrase or an image. It should be noted that older textbooks and papers suggest that the limit of short-term memory is 7 ± 2 items, sometimes called the *magical number* 7: this is now known to be incorrect.

Box 15-1 Distinguishing between short-term and working memory

In their multi-store model of memory, Atkinson and Shiffrin (1968) distinguish between short- and long-term memory (reflecting William James's primary and secondary memory division 70 years earlier). While the term **short-term memory** (STM) is still widely used, we have chosen to employ the term **working memory** (WM) instead. STM is usually characterized by a limited, temporary store for information before it is transferred to long-term memory, while WM is much more flexible and detailed in structure and function. Our use of WM instead of STM also better reflects our everyday experience.

Memory stores: long-term memory

Long-term memory has an effectively unlimited capacity and memories stored there may last as long as an individual's lifetime. The coding (the internal representation) of the information held by it is primarily semantic in nature, that is, it is stored in terms of its meaning, e.g. knowledge of facts and the meaning of words (contrast this with the binary encoding of information in a computer). However, research has indicated that other forms of encoding are present too; for example, memories of music or the bark of a dog are encoded as auditory information, and similarly haptic (touch) encoding allows us to remember the feeling of silk and the sting of a cut. Finally, olfactory (smell) and gustatory (taste) encoding allows us to recognize and distinguish between the smell and taste of fresh and rotten food.

In addition to semantic memory, long-term memory includes other kinds of memories such as **episodic** or **autobiographical** memory (memory of our personal history, for example our first kiss, graduation day, the death of a parent) and **procedural memory** (e.g. the knowledge of how to ride a bike, type, play the euphonium). This neat three-way division of long-term memory into component parts – semantic, episodic and procedural – has been questioned by Cohen and Squire (1980) who argued that the real distinction is between 'knowing how' (declarative memory) and 'knowing that' (procedural memory), but in practice there is little between these two accounts.

Challenge 15-1
Contrast listing the components of a bicycle (e.g. frame, wheels, etc.) with knowing how to ride a bicycle (e.g. sitting on the saddle and pedalling) and with your memory of the first time you rode a bicycle (e.g. How old were you? What sort of day was it? Who else was there?). Which is hardest to describe?

15.3   How do we remember?

In everyday English, to remember means both to retrieve information ('I think her birthday is the 18th June') and to store information in memory ('I'll remember that'). To remove this ambiguity we will use the terms **store** and **encode** to mean place in memory, and **retrieve** and **recall** to mean bring back from memory.

If what we want to store is not too complex (that is, it does not exceed the capacity of working memory) we will typically **rehearse** it, that is, repeat the string of words either aloud or using our inner voice. This is useful for remembering unfamiliar names or strings of numbers or words such as a foreign phrase, for example 'Dos cervezas, por favor'. This technique exploits the **articulatory loop** of working memory. Similar strategies are also used to remember, for a short time, the shape of an object or a set of directions. The capacity of working memory can effectively be enhanced by **chunking** the material to be remembered first. Chunking is the process by which we can organize material into meaningful groups (chunks). For example, an apparently random string of numbers such as 00441314551234 may defeat most people unless it is *chunked*. This particular number may be seen to be a telephone number made up from the code for international calls (0044), the area code for Edinburgh (131) and the prefix for Napier University (455), leaving only 1234 to remember. Thus the string of numbers has been reduced to four chunks.

So how do we remember things for longer periods? One answer is **elaboration** which has been developed as an alternative view of memory in itself. The **levels of processing** (LoP) model proposed by Craik and Lockhart (1972) argues that rather than focusing on the structural, multi-store model of memory we should emphasize the memory processes involved. The LoP model recognizes that any given stimulus (piece of information) can be processed in a number of different ways (or levels) ranging from the trivial or shallow all the way through to a deep, semantic analysis. Superficial processing may involve the analysis of the stimulus's surface features such as its colour or shape; a deeper level of analysis may follow which may test for such things as whether the stimulus (e.g. cow) rhymes with the word 'hat'. The final and deepest level of analysis is the semantic, which considers the stimulus's meaning – does the word refer to a mammal?

Finally, we are able to retrieve stored information by way of **recall** and/or **recognition**. Recall is the process whereby individuals actively search their memories to retrieve a particular piece of information. Recognition involves searching our memory and then deciding whether the piece of information matches what we have in our memory stores.

15.4 How and why do we forget?

There are numerous theories of forgetting. However, before we discuss their strengths and weaknesses we begin with another key distinction, namely the difference between **accessibility** and **availability**. Accessibility refers to whether or not we are able to retrieve information which has been stored in memory, while the availability of a memory depends on whether or not it was stored in memory. The metaphor of a library is often used to illustrate this difference. Imagine you are trying to find a specific book in a library. There are three possible outcomes: (a) you find the book (the memory is retrieved); (b) the book is not in the library (the memory is not available); or (c) the book is in the library but has been misfiled (not accessible). There is, of course, a fourth possibility, namely that someone else has borrowed the book, which is where the metaphor breaks down!

As we described earlier, information is transferred from working memory to long-term memory to be stored permanently, which means that availability is the main issue for working memory while accessibility is the main (potential) problem for long-term memory.

Challenge 15-2
Demonstrating recency and the serial order effect. The serial position curve is an elegant demonstration of the presence of (a) a short/long-term divide in memory and (b) the primacy and recency effects in forgetting. This is easily demonstrated. First create a list of, say, 20 to 30 words. Present them in turn (read them or present them on a screen – try using PowerPoint) to a friend, noting the order in which the words were presented. At the end of the list, ask them to recall as many of the words as they can. Again note the order of the words. Repeat this process with another 6–10 people. Plot how many words presented first (in position 1) were recalled, then how many in positions 2, 3, 4, etc., up to the end of the list.

Moving on from these distinctions we now consider forgetting from working memory.

Forgetting from working memory

The first and perhaps oldest theory is **decay theory** which argues that memory simply fades with time, a point which is particularly relevant to working memory which maintains memories for only 30 seconds or so without rehearsal. Another account is **displacement theory** which has also been developed to account for forgetting from working memory. As we have already seen, working memory is limited in capacity, so it follows that if we were to try to add another item or two to this memory, a corresponding number of items must be squeezed out.

Forgetting from long-term memory (LTM)

We turn now to more widely respected theories of forgetting from long-term memory. Again psychology cannot supply us with one, simple, widely agreed view of how we forget from LTM. Instead there are a number of competing theories with varying amounts of supporting evidence. Early theories (Hebb, 1949) suggested that we forget from *disuse*. For example, we become less proficient in a foreign language learned at school if we never use it. In the 1950s it was suggested that forgetting from LTM may simply be a matter of decay. Perhaps memory engrams (= memory traces) simply fade with time, but except in cases of explicit neurological damage such as Alzheimer's disease no evidence has been found to support this.

A more widely regarded account of forgetting is **interference theory** which suggests that forgetting is more strongly influenced by what we have done before or after learning than the passage of time itself. Interference takes two forms: **retroactive interference** (RI) and **proactive interference** (PI).

Retroactive interference, as the name suggests, works backwards. That is, newer learning interferes with earlier learning. Having been used to driving a manual-shift car, spending time on holiday driving an automatic may interfere with the way one drives after returning home.

In contrast to RI, proactive interference may be seen in action in, for example, moving from word processor v1 to v2. Version 2 may have added new features and reorganized the presentation of menus. Having learned version 1 interferes with learning version 2. Thus earlier learning interferes with new learning. However, despite these and numerous other examples of PI and RI, there is surprisingly little outside the laboratory to support this theory.

Retrieval failure theory proposes that memories cannot be retrieved because we have not employed the correct retrieval cue. Recalling the earlier library metaphor, it is as if we have 'filed' the memory in the wrong place. The model is similar to the tip of the tongue phenomenon (Box 15-2). All in all, many of these theories probably account for some forgetting from LTM.

Box 15-2 The tip-of-the-tongue phenomenon

Researchers Brown and McNeill (1966) created a list of dictionary definitions of unfamiliar words and asked a group of people to provide words which matched them. Not surprisingly, not everyone was able to provide the missing word. However, of those people who could not, many were able to supply the word's first letter, or the number of syllables or even words which sounded like the missing word itself. Examples of the definitions are:

- Favouritism, especially governmental patronage extended to relatives (nepotism)
- The common cavity into which the various ducts of the body open in certain fish, birds and mammals (cloaca).

15.5 Designing for working memory

Having considered how memory works, we can now turn to the challenges and opportunities presented by working memory.

Chunking

As we have already noted, there is an outdated but widely quoted design guideline based on *Miller and his magic number*. Miller (1956) found that short-term memory is limited to only 7 ± 2 bits of information. The first point to remember is that *this is no longer accepted*. Miller was working at a time when memory was less well understood and more recent work indicates that the real capacity of working memory is closer to three or four items; indeed Cowan has recently argued for 4 ± 1 (Cowan, 2002). However, Miller's observations about chunking are still entirely relevant (recall our discussion of the Edinburgh telephone number in Section 15.3). Chunking, it will be remembered, is the process of grouping information into larger, more meaningful units, thus minimizing the demands on working memory. Chunking is a very effective way of reducing **memory load**.

An example of chunking at the user interface is the grouping of meaningful elements of a task into one place (or dialogue). Think about setting up a standard template for a document. Among the things we have to remember to do are printing the document on the printer we wish to use, setting document parameters such as its size and orientation, setting the print quality or colour setting, and so on. Figure 15-2 is a familiar example of a chunked dialogue. (It should be noted that this example of chunking is enhanced by the use of a visual representation which also aids recognition.) In this figure we see the task of setting up a Word page organized into four tabbed dialogues (here a *tab* is equivalent to a *chunk*) with each tab collecting together relevant and related elements into meaningful chunks, namely margin settings, paper size, paper source and layout.

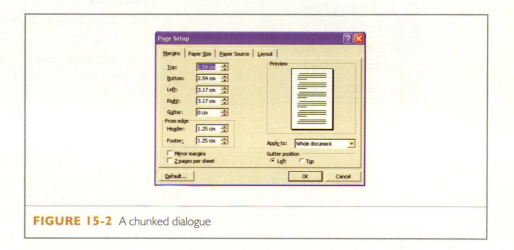

FIGURE 15-2 A chunked dialogue

Another implementation of chunking can be seen in Figure 15-3. Here a large number of formatting options (font, alignment, border and document setting) have been chunked into a single, expandable dialogue. The ▶ symbol indicates that the selection will expand if selected. Having clicked on the *Alignment and Spacing* button, the chunked dialogue expands to unpack a number of related options.

Another use of chunking can be found in the various attempts at grouping Web pages into natural chunks such as *books*. WebBook was developed by Card and his colleagues to help users of the Web manage the material they had found (Card *et al.*, 1996). They chunked separate Web pages into *books*.

Time limitations

As we have seen, working memory is also time limited. These memories are surprisingly short-lived, and even in ideal conditions they will persist for only 30 seconds. So, it is essential to make important information presented to the user

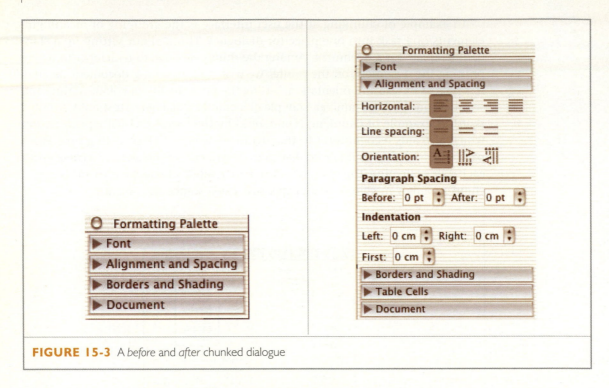

FIGURE 15-3 A *before* and *after* chunked dialogue

persist (Figure 15-4); that is, do not flash an alert such as 'Cannot save file' onto a screen for a second or two and then remove it. Get the user to click 'OK' – even if she does not think that it is. 'OK' is this instance really means 'I acknowledge the message'.

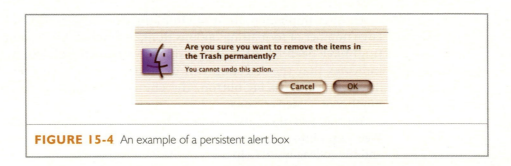

FIGURE 15-4 An example of a persistent alert box

The same should apply to the display of status information. Figure 15-5 is a screenshot from Microsoft Word indicating that the author is on page 10 of 32, is working in page layout mode, is at word 3951 of 11834 and so forth.

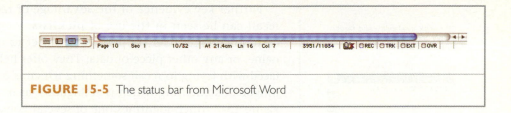

FIGURE 15-5 The status bar from Microsoft Word

Designing for recognition versus recall

As we have seen, it is much easier to recognize something than to recall it. Mandler (1980) found that recall-based systems were a major source of frustration for novices using old-style command-line interfaces (see Box 15-3) . Novices prefer menus because they can scroll through the list of options until a particular command is recognized. Expert users, however, have been reported as being frustrated in scrolling through a series of menus (particularly nested menus) and often prefer keyboard shortcuts instead (e.g. <alt>-F-P-<return> instead of select File menu / Print / OK). Interactive systems should be designed to accommodate both styles of working.

Box 15-3 Command line interfaces

Prior to the widespread use of graphical user interfaces, most user interfaces resembled Figure 15-6.

```
●●●            Terminal — tcsh (ttyp1)
Last login: Wed Feb 26 09:50:41 on console
Welcome to Darwin!
[pc162050:~] philturner% ls -la
total 80
drwxr-xr-x  18 philturn  staff     612 Feb 26 10:20 .
drwxrwxr-t   6 root      wheel     204 Dec 31 13:46 ..
-rw-r--r--   1 philturn  staff       3 Dec 17 23:37 .CFUserTextEncoding
-rw-r--r--   1 philturn  staff   12292 Feb 26 10:20 .DS_Store
-rw-r--r--   1 philturn  staff   20480 Feb 22 15:40 .FBCIndex
drwxr-xr-x   3 philturn  staff     102 Feb 22 15:40 .FBCLockFolder
-rw-r--r--   1 philturn  staff       0 Feb 14 15:11 .MCXLC
drwx------  31 philturn  staff    1054 Feb 26 11:44 .Trash
-rw-r--r--   1 philturn  staff      21 Feb 26 10:20 .lpoptions
drw-rw----   2 philturn  staff      68 Jan 18 23:26 .qt
drwx------  11 philturn  staff     374 Feb 26 11:44 Desktop
drwx------  20 philturn  staff     680 Feb 25 17:15 Documents
drwx------  31 philturn  staff    1054 Jan 30 23:50 Library
drwx------   7 philturn  staff     238 Feb 22 15:40 Movies
drwx------   7 philturn  staff     238 Feb 22 15:40 Music
drwx------   9 philturn  staff     306 Feb 22 15:40 Pictures
drwxr-xr-x   4 philturn  staff     136 Dec 17 23:37 Public
drwxr-xr-x   6 philturn  staff     204 Dec 23 20:05 Sites
[pc162050:~] philturner%
```

FIGURE 15-6 A UNIX user interface

Commands are typed at a terminal. The command used here was **ls –la** which is a request to list (ls) the contents of the current directory (folder). The command takes several parameters, the letters **l** and **a**, which modify the output to produce a long listing of the directory detailing dates, file ownership, permissions and so forth, and the **a** which lists all files which begin with a dot. The operating system is UNIX-based and has by some been described as 'obscure'. This interface relies heavily on the user to *recall* the available commands.

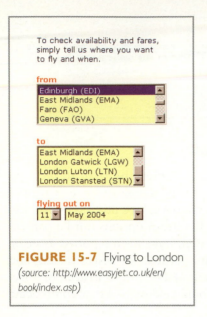

FIGURE 15-7 Flying to London
(*source: http://www.easyjet.co.uk/en/ book/index.asp*)

Further key evidence of the advantage of recognition over recall can be seen in the use of **picklists**. Picklists have two clear advantages over simply asking a user to recall a specific name, or any other piece of data. They offer help when we are faced with trying to recall something which is on the tip of our tongue or something which is ambiguous (as in the example of Figure 15-7 which identifies one of several London airports) or which may be difficult to spell. Consider the next two examples: imagine you are trying book a flight from Edinburgh to London. You know that the target airport is not London Heathrow but one of the others and are confident that you will be able to recognize the specific airport without difficulty from the list more easily than from unaided memory. Figure 15-7 is an image of a standard Web pull-down picklist.

London Stansted is easier to recognize than trying to remember (a) how to spell it – *Stanstead, Standsted* or *Stansted*? – and (b) the official airline abbreviation (STN). The use of a picklist can also significantly improve the spelling of the documents we produce. Current versions of Microsoft Word identify misspelled words by underlining them with a red wavy line. Left-clicking on the word drops down a picklist of alternative spellings. This approach has also been adopted by modern visual (software) development environments where not only misspelled commands are identified but the syntax of commands is checked. Figure 15-8 is an illustration of this.

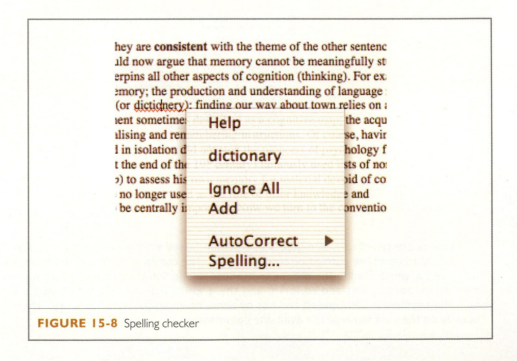

FIGURE 15-8 Spelling checker

The recent use of **thumbnails** is another example of how recognition is more effective than recall. Figure 15-9 is a screenshot of the *My Pictures* of a computer running the Windows XP operating system. The folder contains a number of thumbnails, that is, very small (thumbnail-sized) images of the contents of the files in the folder. The files were placed there some weeks before this text was written but each is immediately recognizable as images used in the chapter.

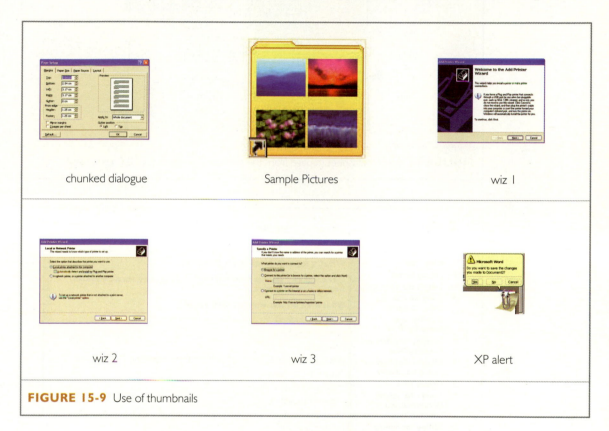

chunked dialogue

Sample Pictures

wiz 1

wiz 2

wiz 3

XP alert

FIGURE 15-9 Use of thumbnails

Manuals, help and extending memory

Figure 15-10 is an image of a datasheet from Gemini 10 dating from the mid-1960s (one of the last two-man American spacecraft). The datasheet is a classic *aide-memoire*, a way of extending or distributing memory beyond the mere individual. Writing down a reminder of instructions is one of the most effect ways of extending our memories. Help systems, manuals, quick reference guides and other such devices serve a similar purpose and as such are excellent examples of distributed cognition.

Designing and writing help systems, manuals and tutorials is a thankless task. There is good evidence that end-users do not consult them (men in particular) and there is the strong sense that they never tell you what you want to know. More modern help systems (e.g. Figure 15-11) are, of course, hyperlinked and fully searchable.

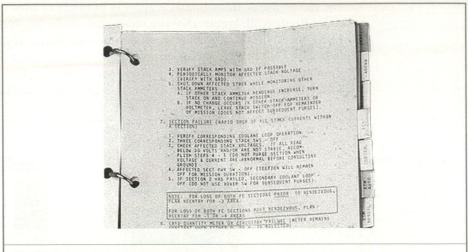

FIGURE 15-10 A datasheet (a page from the manual) from Gemini 10 (*source: NASA*)

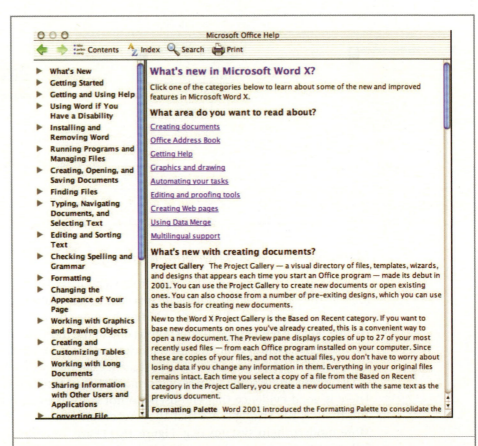

FIGURE 15-11 Microsoft Office help

15.6 Icons

A picture is said to be worth a thousand words. Icons are little pictures – so is there any evidence that they are worth anything approaching a thousand words? Icons are used to represent features and functions on everything from software applications, DVD players and public information kiosks to clothing (as those incomprehensible washing symbols on the back of the label). Icons are generally regarded as being useful in helping people to recognize which feature they need to access. Icons first appeared on the Xerox Star (Box 15-4) and became an important research issue in the 1980s and early 1990s, though since then there has been considerably less interest.

The use of icons is now ubiquitous, but their design, apart from a small number of standard items (see further reading at the end of this chapter), is a hotch-potch of the use of metaphor, direct mapping and convention. The use of **metaphor** can be seen in the cut, copy and paste operations. These three operations relate to a time when in preparing a text it was not unusual to cut out elements of a document using scissors and then physically paste them into

---

Box 15-4 The Xerox Star

It is widely recognized that every graphical user interface owes a debt to the Xerox Star work-station. Launched as the 8010 Star information system in April 1981, it was designed to be used by office workers and other professionals to create and manage business documents such as memos, reports and presentations. The Star's designers took the perspective that their intended users were primarily interested in their jobs and not in computers *per se*. Thus from its inception a central design goal was to make the computer effectively invisible to the end-users.

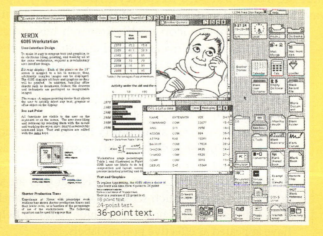

FIGURE 15-12 The Xerox Star user interface (*source: courtesy of Xerox Ltd.*)

another document (*copy*, of course, works in a similar but non-destructive manner). The use of **direct mapping** is probably the simplest technique in the design of icons and involves creating a more or less direct image of what the icon is intended to represent. Thus a printer icon looks like a printer. Finally **convention** refers to a more or less arbitrary design of an icon in the first instance, which has become accepted as standing for what is intended over time. This can lead to anachronisms. For example, the icon representing the function *save* on the Mac that I am using to write this is a representation of a floppy disc (Figure 15-13) despite the fact that the machine is not fitted with a floppy disc drive. Figure 15-14 shows further examples of icons.

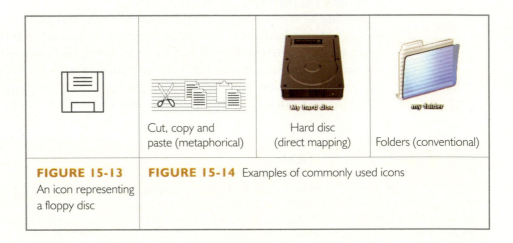

| | Cut, copy and paste (metaphorical) | Hard disc (direct mapping) | Folders (conventional) |

FIGURE 15-13
An icon representing a floppy disc

FIGURE 15-14 Examples of commonly used icons

However, the two most important design issues for icons are legibility (whether or not one can discriminate between icons) and interpretation (what it is that the icon is intended to convey). The legibility aspect refers to icons not always being viewed under ideal conditions (e.g. poor lighting, screen resolution or the size of the icon itself). Research has indicated that under such conditions it is the overall global appearance of the icon which aids discrimination, so icons should not be designed so that they differ only with respect to one small detail. Figure 15-15 illustrates two icons which differ only by the placement and direction of the arrow head.

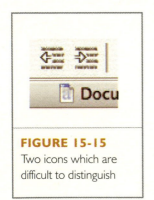

FIGURE 15-15
Two icons which are difficult to distinguish

The interpretation of the icon is a non-trivial issue. The icon may indeed be recognized as an object but remain opaque as to its meaning. Brems and Whitten (1987) for this reason caution against the use of icons which are not accompanied by a textual label. Do remember, however, that one reason why icons are used is that they are succinct and small (i.e. do not take up too much screen space); adding labels removes this advantage. Solutions to this problem include **balloon help** and **tool tips** which have appeared as effective pop-up labels.

Further thoughts: Types of consistency

Consistency, which has sometimes been called the 'principle of least astonishment', is not just about putting dialogue elements, such as buttons, in the same place on every screen. Consistency aids learning. If a user can associate the relationships between commands (whether they are accessed by way of icons, menus, buttons or a command line) and how the system responds then learning is facilitated, that is, we are more likely to remember. It is useful to divide consistency into two parts, namely **syntactic** and **semantic** consistency. **Structural** or **syntactic** consistency concerns such things as the order within a sequence of actions, so for example, within the MS Windows environment, a single left mouse click on an object (icon or file) selects that object, a double left mouse click opens that object, while a single right mouse click opens the object's context menu. These sequences apply to *all* objects within the environment and hence may be described as syntactically similar. The Mac environment is similarly consistent but with a different syntax. However, in both environments there are notable inconsistencies; perhaps the most famous is found in the Mac where dragging an icon representing a disc to the trash can ejects it.

15.7   Horton's icon checklist

William Horton (of William Horton Consulting, Inc.) has produced a detailed checklist designed to help the icon designer avoid a whole raft of common mistakes. We reproduce his top level headings here together with a sample question for each issue (see Horton's tutorial on designing icons and visual symbols in CHI '97).

Understandable
Does the image spontaneously suggest the intended concept to the viewer?

Familiar
Are the objects in the icon ones familiar to the user?

Unambiguous
Are additional cues (label, other icons, documentation) available to resolve any ambiguity?

Memorable
Where possible, does the icon feature concrete objects in action? Are actions shown as operations on concrete objects?

Informative
Why is the concept important?

Few
Is the number of arbitrary symbols less than 20?

Distinct
Is every icon distinct from all others?

Attractive
Does the image use smooth edges and lines?

Legible
Have you tested all combinations of colour and size in which the icon will be displayed?

Compact
Is every object, every line, every pixel in the icon necessary?

Coherent
Is it clear where one icon ends and another begins?

Extensible
Can I draw the image smaller? Will users still recognize it?

For further information on this approach to icon design see http://www.horton.com/.

15.8 What is attention?

This section will introduce theories of attention and how attention has been studied in much more detail than in Chapter 5. Attention is a pivotally important human ability and is central to operating a machine, using a computer, driving to work or catching a train. Failures in attention are a frequently cited reason for accidents: car accidents have been attributed to the driver using their mobile phone while driving; aircraft have experienced 'controlled flight into terrain' (to use the official jargon) when the pilots have paid too much attention to the 'wrong' cockpit warning, and control room operators can be overwhelmed by the range and complexity of instruments to which they must attend. Clearly we need to be able to understand the mechanism of attention, its capabilities and limitations, and how to design to make the most of these abilities while minimizing its limitations.

This section has a strong *engineering* and *ergonomics* flavour. Attention is an aspect of cognition which is particularly important in the design and operation of safety-critical interactive systems (ranging from the all too frequently quoted control room operator through to inspection tasks on mundane production lines). While there is no single agreed definition of attention, Solso (1995) defines it as 'the concentration of mental effort on sensory or mental events', which is typical of many definitions. The problem with definitions in many ways reflects how attention has been studied and what mental faculties researchers have included under the umbrella term of attention. However, the study of attention has been split between two basic forms, namely **selective attention** and **divided attention**. Selective (or focused) attention generally refers to whether or not we become aware of sensory information. Indeed, Cherry (1953) coined the term **the cocktail party effect** to illustrate this (Box 15-5).

Box 15-5 The cocktail party effect

Cherry (1953), presumably while at a cocktail party, had noticed that we are able to focus our attention on the person we are talking to while filtering out everyone else's conversation. This principle is at the heart of the search for extra-terrestrial intelligence (SETI), which is selectively listening for the alien radio signals against the background of natural radio signals.

Studies of selective attention have employed a *dichotic* listening approach. Typically participants in such experiments are requested to shadow (repeat aloud) one of the two voices they will hear through a set of headphones. One voice will be played through the right headphone while another is played through the left – hence *dichotic*. In contrast to selective attention, divided attention recognizes that attention can be thought of in terms of mental resources (e.g. Kahneman, 1973; Pashler, 1998) which can in some sense be divided between tasks being performed simultaneously (commonly referred to as *multi-tasking*). For example, when watching television while holding a conversation, attention is being split between two tasks. Unless an individual is very well practised, the performance of two simultaneously executed tasks would be expected to be poorer than attending to just one at a time. Studies of *divided* attention might employ the same physical arrangements as above but ask the participant to attend (listen to) both voices and, say, press a button when a key-word is heard spoken in either channel.

Box 15-6 The Stroop effect

Stroop (1935) showed that if a colour word such as 'green' is written in a conflicting colour such as red, people find it remarkably difficult to name the colour the word is written in. The reason is that reading is an automatic process which conflicts with the task of naming the colour of the 'ink' a word is written in. The Stroop effect has also been shown to apply to suitably organized numbers and words.

Try saying aloud the colour of the *text* – not the word itself:

Column 1	Column 2
RED	RED
GREEN	GREEN
BLUE	BLUE
RED	RED
GREEN	GREEN
RED	RED

You should find that saying the *colour* of each word in column 1 is slower and more prone to error owing to the meaning of the word itself. The word 'red' interferes with the colour (green) it is printed in and vice versa.

15.9 How attention works

To date there have been a number of different accounts or models of attention. The earliest date from the 1950s and are characterized by likening attention to a bottleneck. Later theories have concentrated on an allocation model which treats attention as a resource that can be spread (or allocated) across a number of different tasks. Other views of attention have concentrated on the automatic/controlled processing divide and on sequential/parallel processing. As in most aspects of psychology, there is no single account of attention; instead there is a mosaic of complementary views.

'Bottleneck' theories of attention

We begin with Broadbent's single-channel theory of attention (Broadbent, 1958). He proposed that information arriving at the senses is stored in short-term memory before being **filtered** or selected as being of interest (or being discarded), which in practice means that we attend one particular channel and ignore others. This information (this channel) is then processed by a limited capacity processor. On being processed, instructions may be sent to motor effectors (the muscles) to generate a response. The presence of short-term memory, acting as a temporary buffer, means that information which is not selected is not immediately discarded either. Figure 15-16 is an illustration of Broadbent's model. Broadbent realized that we might be able to attend this information stored in the short-term memory, but switching between two different channels of information would be inefficient. (It has been observed by a number of researchers that Broadbent's thinking reflects the technology of his day, as in many ways this single-channel model of attention is similar to the conventional model of a computer's central processing unit (CPU) which too has a single channel and is a serial processing device – the *von Neumann* architecture.) This original single-channel model (sometimes referred to as a **bottleneck** account of attention) was refined and developed by Broadbent's co-workers and others (Triesman, 1960; Deutsch and Deutsch, 1963; Norman, 1968) but remained *broadly* similar.

Triesman argued for the **attenuation** of the unattended channel, which is like turning down the volume of a signal, rather than an on–off switch. In Triesman's model competing information is analysed for its physical properties, and for sound, syllable pattern, grammatical structure and meaning, before being attended. The later Deutsch and Deutsch (1963) and Deutsch–Norman (Norman, 1968) models completely rejected Broadbent's early selection model, instead arguing for a **later-selection** filter/**pertinence** account. Selection (or filtering) only occurs after all of the sensory inputs have been analysed. The major criticism of this family of single-channel models is their lack of flexibility, particularly in the face of a competing allocation model discussed below. It has also been questioned as to whether any single, general purpose, limited capacity processor can ever account for the complexity of selective attention. The reality of everyday divided attention presents even greater problems for such accounts. As we have just discussed, models of selective attention assume the existence of a limited capacity filter capable of dealing with only one information channel at a time. However, this is at odds with both everyday experience and experimental evidence.

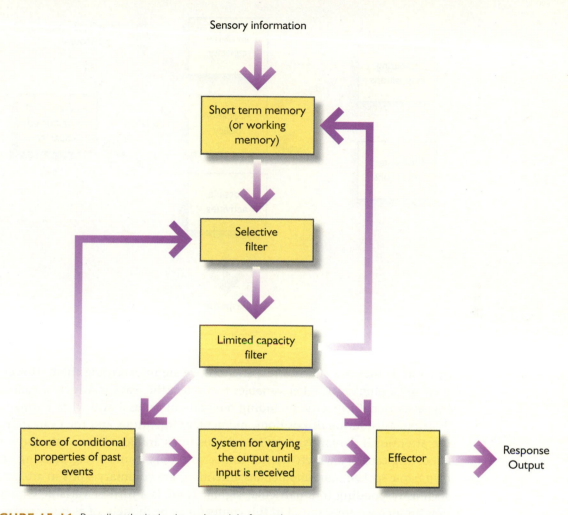

FIGURE 15-16 Broadbent's single-channel model of attention

Attention as capacity allocation

Next we briefly discuss an example of a group of models of attention which treat attention as a limited resource that is allocated to different processes. The best known is Kahneman's **capacity allocation** model (Kahneman, 1973). Kahneman argued that we have a limited amount of processing power at our disposal and whether or not we are able to carry out a task depends on how much of this capacity is applied to the task. Of course, some tasks require relatively little processing power and others may require more – perhaps more than we have available. This intuitively appealing account does allow us to explain how we can divide our attention across a number of tasks depending upon how

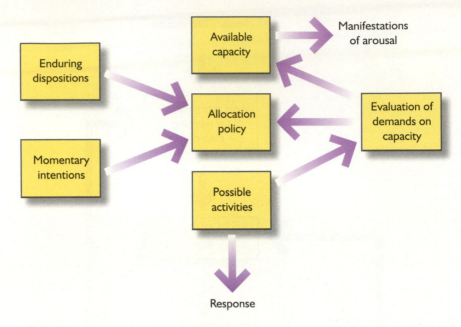

FIGURE 15-17 Kahneman's capacity allocation model

demanding they are and how experienced we are in executing them. However, there are a number of other variables that affect the ways in which we allocate this attentional capacity, including our state of arousal and what Kahneman describes as enduring dispositions, momentary intentions and the evaluation of the attentional demands. Enduring dispositions are described as the rules for allocating capacity which are not under voluntary control (e.g. hearing your own name spoken), and momentary intentions are voluntary shifts in attention, such as responding to a particular signal. There is a further variable which is how aroused we are. Arousal in this context may be thought of as how awake we are. Figure 15-17 is a diagram of the capacity allocation model in which we can see the limit capacity; the central processor has been replaced by an allocation policy component that governs which of the competing demands should receive attention. While Kahneman portrays attention as being more flexible and dynamic than the single-channel models, he is unable to describe how attention is channelled or focused. Similarly he is unable to define the limits of what is meant by 'capacity'.

Automatic and controlled processing

In contrast to the foregoing models of attention, Schneider and Shiffrin (1977) have observed that we are capable of both automatic and controlled information processing. We generally use **automatic processing** with tasks we find easy (and this, of course, is dependent upon our expertise in this task) but use **controlled processing** on unfamiliar and difficult tasks.

Schneider and Shiffrin distinguish between controlled and automatic processing in terms of attention as follows. Controlled processing makes heavy demands on attention and is slow, limited in capacity and involving consciously directing attention towards a task. In contrast, automatic processing makes little or no demand on attention, is fast, unaffected by capacity limitations, unavoidable and difficult to modify, and is not subject to conscious awareness.

Schneider and Shiffrin found that if people are given practice at a task, they can perform it quickly and accurately, but their performance is resistant to change. An example of apparent automaticity in real life occurs when we learn to drive a car. At first, focused attention is required for each component of driving, and any distraction can disrupt performance. Once we have learned to drive, and as we become more experienced, our ability to attend simultaneously other things increases.

Moving from this very brief treatment of models of attention, we now consider how a wide range of internal and external factors can affect our ability to attend.

Factors affecting attention

Of the factors which affect our ability to pay attention to a task, stress is the most important. Stress is the effect of external and psychological stimuli on us and directly affects our level of arousal. Arousal is different from attention in that it refers to a general increase or decrease in perceptual and motor activity. For example, sexual arousal is typified by heightened levels of hormonal secretions, dilation of the pupils, increased blood flow and a whole range of mating behaviours.

Stressors (stimuli which cause stress) include such things as noise, light, vibration (e.g. flying through turbulence) and more psychological factors such as anxiety, fatigue, anger, threat, lack of sleep and fear (e.g. think about the days before an examination). As long ago as 1908, Yerkes and Dodson found a relationship between performance of tasks and level of arousal. Figure 15-18 is an illustration of this relationship – the so-called Yerkes–Dodson Law. There are two things to note about this relationship. Firstly, for both simple and complex tasks there is an optimal level of arousal. As our level of arousal increases, our ability to execute a task increases until we reach a point when we are too aroused and our performance falls off sharply. Secondly, simple tasks are more resistant to increased levels of arousal than are complex tasks. The other aspect of this is the skill of the individual involved. A simple task to a highly skilled individual is likely to be seen as complex to a less skilled or able individual.

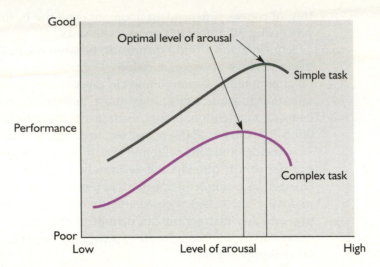

FIGURE 15-18 The Yerkes–Dodson law

15.10 Designing for attention

There are two key issues in designing for attention. Firstly, we need to balance providing the user with important, relevant and timely information while not swamping or overloading him or her. This reflects the limited capacity of attention. Secondly, we must be able to *attract* and *engage* the user's attention at times in a manner which, again, does not distract the user without unnecessary detail.

Attracting and holding attention

Attracting attention is a simple enough matter – flash a light, use some other form of animation, ring a bell, and our attention is directed at that stimulus. It is, of course, possible to alert someone as to where to direct their attention. An air traffic controller's attention, for example, might be directed to a potential collision.

However, the challenge of attracting and holding attention is to do so in a manner which:

- Does not distract us from the main task, particularly if we are doing something important, such as flying an aircraft or operating a complex or hazardous tool
- In certain circumstances *can* be ignored while in other circumstances *cannot* and *should not* be ignored (Figure 15-19)
- Does not overwhelm the user of a system with more information than they can reasonably understand or respond to.

But do think about the wording (Figure 15-20) …

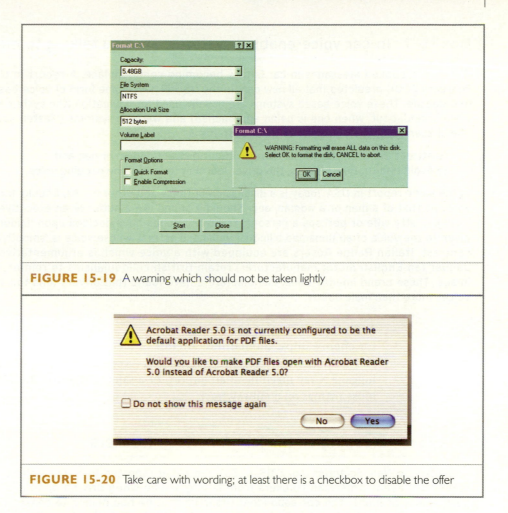

FIGURE 15-19 A warning which should not be taken lightly

FIGURE 15-20 Take care with wording; at least there is a checkbox to disable the offer

Wikman *et al.* (1998) have reported differences in the performance of inexperienced (novice) and experienced drivers when given a secondary task to perform while driving. The drivers were asked to do such things as changing a cassette tape, operating the car radio or using a mobile (cell) phone. Unsurprisingly the novice drivers were distracted more (allocated their attention less effectively) than the experienced drivers. Experienced drivers took their eyes off the road for less than three seconds while novice drivers were found to weave across the road.

Vigilance

Vigilance is a term applied to the execution of a task wherein an individual is required to monitor an instrument or situation for a signal. Perhaps the classic example of a vigilance task is being on watch on board a ship. During the Second World War mariners were required to be vigilant in scanning the horizon

Box 15-7 In-car voice-enabled systems: are you talking to me?

The use of spoken messages in-car is now becoming commonplace. A report in *USA Today* (15 February 2001) predicted that all new cars in the US will have some form of voice-based system by mid-decade. These voice-based systems are usually used for navigation (the system will speak the word 'roundabout' when one is being approached) and warning systems ('Fasten your seat belt'). The challenge for the designers of these systems is

(a) to attract the attention of the driver without distracting him or her, and
(b to avoid habituation – that is, the driver learning to ignore the nagging voice.

In the same report in *USA Today* is a discussion of these and other issues. Should, for example, the voice be that of a man or a woman, and 'Should it sound like a butler or an executive assistant? A loving, chatty wife or perhaps a personal trainer?'. Honda have decided upon 'Midori' – the name given to the voice of an unnamed bilingual Japanese actress whose voice is 'smooth as liqueur'. In contrast, Italian Range Rovers are equipped with a voice which is argumentative in tone, and Jaguar (an English motor manufacturer) retain British colloquialisms to reinforce their brand image. These brand images aside, manufacturers have found that drivers tend to listen to female voices more than male voices.

for enemy ships, submarines, aircraft or ice-flows. Wartime aside, vigilance is still an important element of many jobs – consider the role of the operator of a luggage X-ray machine at an airport, or a safety inspector checking for cracks or loose fittings on a railway track.

Box 15-8 Sleeping on the job: American truckers

In a letter to *New Scientist* (no. 2319, p. 53) Jon Laver reported that research had been undertaken to prevent American truckers from falling asleep when driving on long straight roads, particularly at night. The correspondent reported that he had helped to construct a prototype system which would deliver a mild but effective electric shock to the driver if he showed signs of dropping off. The system used measures of the driver's brainwaves – theta waves, specifically, which are produced during sleep. Theta waves were also produced when the driver became annoyed or angry such as when he had just received an electric shock.

Mental workload

Mental workload addresses issues such as how busy is the user or operator? How difficult are the tasks assigned to him or her – can he or she be able to deal with an additional workload? A classic example of this occurred in the 1970s when it was decided to remove the third crew member from a flight team on board a medium to large passenger jet. The Federal Aviation Administration now requires measures of the mental workload on the crew prior to the certification of a new aircraft or new control system.

Turning now to design issues in respect of mental workload, the first observation is that a discussion of mental workload does not necessarily equate workload with overload. Indeed the reverse is often true: just consider the potential consequences of operator/user boredom and fatigue (Wickens and Hollands, 2000, p. 470). There are a number of different ways in which workload can be estimated, one of which is the NASA TLX scale. This scale (Table 15-2) is a subjective rating procedure that provides an overall workload score based on a weighted average of ratings on six sub-scales.

TABLE 15-2 Measuring workload

Title	Endpoints	Description
Mental demand	Low/end	How much mental and perceptual activity was required (e.g. thinking, deciding, etc.)? Was the task easy or demanding, simple or complex?
Physical demand	Low/high	How much physical effort was required (e.g. pushing, pulling, etc.)? Was the task easy or demanding, slack or strenuous, restful or laborious?
Temporal demand	Low/high	How much time pressure did you feel due to the rate or pace at which the tasks or task elements occurred? Was the pace slow and leisurely or rapid and frantic?
Performance	Perfect/failure	How successful do you think you were in accomplishing the goals of the task set by the experimenter (or yourself)? How satisfied were you with your performance in accomplishing these goals?
Effort	Low/high	How hard did you have to work (mentally and physically) to accomplish your level of performance?
Frustration level	Low/high	How insecure, discouraged, irritated, stressed and annoyed as opposed to secure, gratified, content, relaxed and complacent did you feel during your task?

Source: Wickens and Hollands, (2000), Table 11.1, p. 468

Visual search

Visual search has been researched extensively by psychologists and ergonomists and refers to our ability to locate particular items in a visual scene. Participants in a visual search study, for example, may be required to locate a single letter in a block of miscellaneous characters. Try to find the letter 'F' in the matrix in Figure 15-21.

E	E	E	E	E	E	E	E
E	E	E	E	E	E	E	E
E	E	E	E	E	E	E	E
E	E	E	E	E	E	E	E
E	E	E	E	E	E	E	E
E	E	E	E	E	E	F	E
E	E	E	E	E	E	E	E

FIGURE 15-21 A matrix of letters

This is a good example of how perception and attention overlap and an understanding of the issues involved in visual search can help in avoiding interactive systems such as that shown in Figure 15-22.

Research has revealed that there is no consistent visual search pattern which can be predicted in advance. Visual search cannot be presumed to be left to right, or clockwise rather than anticlockwise, except to say that searching tends to be directed towards where the target is expected to be. However, visual attention will be drawn towards features which are large and bright and changing (e.g. flashing, which may be used for warnings). These visual features can be used to direct attention, particularly if they have a sudden onset (i.e. a light

FIGURE 15-22 A practical example of the challenge of visual search. As the designer of this page, where do you expect your customers (in this case) to begin?
(*source: www.lastminute.com, 22 January 2004*)

being switched on, or a car horn sounding). Megaw and Richardson (1979) found that physical organization can also have an effect on search patterns. Displays or dials organized in rows tended to be scanned from left to right (just as in reading western languages, but raising the question of cultural bias – would the same be true for those cultures who read from right to left or from top to bottom?). Parasuraman (1986) has reported evidence of an **edge effect** wherein during supervisory tasks (that is, the routine scanning of dials and displays) operators tended to concentrate on the centre of the display panel and tended to ignore the periphery. As Wickens and Hollands (2000) note, research into visual scanning behaviour has yielded two broad conclusions. Firstly, visual scanning reveals much about the internal expectancies that drive selective attention (*cf.* Section 15.9). Secondly, these insights are probably most useful in the area of diagnostics. Clearly those instruments which are most frequently watched are likely to be the most important to an operator's task. This should guide design decisions to place the instruments in prominent locations or to locate them adjacent to one another.

Box 15-9 Just how long is it reasonable to wait?

It is generally accepted that delays of less than 0.1 second are taken to be effectively *instantaneous*, but delays of a second or two may be perceived by the user of an interactive system as being an interruption in the free flow of his or her interaction. Delays of more than 10 seconds present problems for users. Minimizing delay is important in the design of websites for which numerous, often contradictory, guidelines have been published. Here are two perfectly reasonable suggestions:

- The top of your page should be meaningful and fast.
- Simplify complex tables as they display more slowly.

Signal detection theory

It is late at night. You are asleep alone in your apartment. You are awoken by a noise. What do you do? For many people the first thing to do is to wait and see (as it were) whether they hear the noise again. Here we are in the domain of **signal detection theory** – was there really a signal (e.g. the sound of breaking glass by the local axe-murderer) and if so, are we to act on it – or was it just the wind or a cat in the dustbin? Signal detection theory (SDT) is applicable in any situation in which there are two different, non-overlapping states (i.e. signal and noise) that cannot be easily discriminated – that is, for example, did a signal appear on the radar screen, did it move, has it changed size or shape? In such situations we are concerned with signals which must be detected, and in the process one of two responses may be produced – e.g. 'I detected the presence of a signal, so I shall press the stop button', or 'I failed to see anything, so I shall continue to watch'. This may vary in importance from the trivial, e.g. recognizing that a job has been printed (the printer icon has disappeared from the application's status bar), through to the safety-critical, e.g. a train driver spotting (or not) a stop light.

The following compelling examples of the importance of SDT have been identified by Wickens and Hollands (2000): the detection of a concealed weapon by an airport security guard; the identification of a malignant tumour on an X-ray plate by a radiologist; and a system malfunction detected by a nuclear plant supervisor. Their list goes on to include identifying critical incidents in the context of air traffic control, proof-reading, detecting lies from a polygraph (lie detector) and spotting hairline cracks in aircraft wings, amongst other things. SDT recognizes that an individual faced with such a situation can respond in one of four ways: in the presence of a signal, the operator may detect it (hit) or fail to detect it (miss); in the absence of a signal, the operator may correctly reject it (correct rejection) or incorrectly identify it (false alarm). This is illustracted in Table 15-3.

TABLE 15-3 SDT decision table

		State	
		Signal	Noise
Response	Yes	Hit	False alarm
	No	Miss	Correct rejection

The probability of each response is typically calculated for a given situation and these figures are often quoted for both people and machines. So, a navigational aid on board an aircraft (e.g. ground collision radar) might be quoted as producing false alarms (also called false-positives) at a rate of less than 0.001 – one in a thousand. Similar figures are quoted as targets for medical screening operators (e.g. no more than 1 in 10000 real instances of, say, breast cancer should be missed while 1 in 1000 false alarms are acceptable).

Box 15-10 Transcript from Apollo XIII: barber-poles and the Moon

The Apollo flights to the Moon in the late 1960s and early 1970s are excellent examples of both user-centred design and brilliant and innovative ergonomic design. One of the innovations can be found in the design of the Apollo spacecraft which used *barber-poles* to provide status information to the astronauts. A barber-pole is a striped bar signalling that a particular circuit or function is active (for example, the communication system – the *talkback system*), or as can be seen in the transcript below, measures of liquid helium and the state of the electrical systems. In the transcript we see that Jim Lovell reports to Mission Control that main bus '*B is barber poled and D is barber poled, helium 2, D is barber pole*':

55:55:35 – Lovell: 'Houston, we've had a problem. We've had a main B bus undervolt.'

55:55:20 – Swigert: 'Okay, Houston, we've had a problem here.'

...

55:57:40 DC main bus B drops below 26.25 volts and continues to fall rapidly.

55:57:44 – Lovell: *'Okay. And we're looking at our service module RCS helium 1. We have – B is barber poled and D is barber poled, helium 2, D is barber pole, and secondary propellants, I have A and C barber pole.'* AC bus fails within 2 seconds.

Interestingly, the use of a barber-pole can be found in modern operating systems. For example, the Mac OS X system uses barber-poles (Figure 15-23).

FIGURE 15-23 Barber-pole, Mac OS X

15.11 Cognitive work analysis: cognition in action

Cognitive work analysis (CWA) has evolved from the work of Jens Rasmussen and his colleagues (Rasmussen, 1986, 1987; Vicente and Rasmussen, 1992) originally working at the Risø National Laboratory in Denmark. Originally formulated to help in the design of systems concerned with the domain of process control, where the emphasis is on controlling the physical system behind the human–computer interface, it provides a different and powerful view on the design of interactive systems. CWA has been used in the analysis of complex real-time, mission-critical work environments, e.g. power plant control rooms, aircraft cockpits and so on.

The approach is also known as 'the Risø genotype' (Vicente, 1999) and relates closely to ecological interface design (Vicente and Rasmussen, 1992). Flach (1995) provides a number of perspectives on the issues and includes chapters by others originating from the Risø National Laboratory, including Vicente, Rasmussen and Pejtersen. One principle underlying CWA is that when designing computer systems or any other 'cognitive artefact' we are developing a complete work system, which means that the system includes people and artificial artefacts. Seeing the whole as a work system enables designers to recognize that this system is more than the sum of its parts; it has emergent properties.

Another key principle of CWA is that it takes an ecological approach to design. Taking an ecological approach recognizes that people 'pick up' information directly from the objects in the world and their interaction with them, rather than having to consciously process some symbolic representation. In CWA, there is much discussion over the similarities between the ecological psychology of Gibson (1986) and designing systems that afford certain activities. The emphasis is on taking a user-dependent view of the analysis and design, recognizing the skills and knowledge that the user will have.

Chapter 3, Section 3.3 discusses the people-technology system, which is the same idea

In the domain in which CWA was formulated, process control, it is vital that the operator has a correct view of the operation and status of the plant and that he or she can correctly identify any component that is malfunctioning. A key feature of the approach is to understand the domain-oriented constraints that affect people's behaviours and to design the environment so that the system easily reveals the state it is in and how that state relates to its purpose. CWA provides a structural representation of a domain.

CWA is complex

CWA is very complex and comprises a set of techniques and models. CWA techniques include such things as

- Task analysis (including sequencing and frequency)
- Workload analysis (flow of work, identification of bottlenecks).

In short, there is a strong emphasis on work analysis and job design.

The range of modelling in CWA is also complex and comprehensive. Modelling in CWA is made up from six different kinds of modelling, each of which breaks down into further levels. For example, a work domain analysis has five further levels of abstraction, describing

- The functional purpose of the system
- The priorities or values of the system
- The functions to be carried out by the system
- The physical functionality of the system
- The physical objects and devices.

The abstraction hierarchy

CWA describes a system, subsystem or component at five levels of abstraction. At the top level is the system's purpose; the analysis takes an intentional stance. Taking the design stance, CWA distinguishes between the abstract function and the generalized function of the system. The abstract function concerns the capabilities that it must have in order to achieve its purpose, and the generalized function describes the links between the physical characteristics and that abstract function. At the physical level of description CWA distinguishes the physical function from the physical form of the system.

For example, a car's purpose is to transport people along a road. Therefore it must have the abstract functions of some form of power, some form of accommodating people and some form of wheels. These abstract functions may be provided by the generalized functions of a petrol engine, some seats and some wheels with pneumatic tyres. Physically the engine might be realized as an eight-cylinder fuel-injected engine, the seats are of a size to accommodate people and the tyres have an ability to take the weight of the car and its passengers. The physical forms of these functions are the features that distinguish one type of car from another and concern the different arrangements of the engine components, the colour and material of the seats and the characteristics of the tyres.

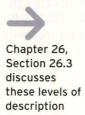

Chapter 26, Section 26.3 discusses these levels of description

A work domain analysis describes the whole system in these terms and describes each of the subsystems, components and units in these terms. For example in describing the car, we could describe each of the engine's subsystems (fuel system, ignition system, etc.), its components (the petrol tank, feed tubes, injector mechanism, etc.) and the basic units which make up the components. At each level of the hierarchy the connection going up the hierarchy indicates why some system or component exists, whereas the relationship looking down the hierarchy indicates how something is achieved. The chain of 'hows' describes the means by which something happens and the chain of 'whys' describes the reasons for the design – the ends or teleological analysis. Hence the whole physical functioning of the domain is connected with its purpose.

So, the car can transport people because it has an engine which is there to provide the power. The engine needs a fuel system and an ignition system because the fuel system and the ignition system provide power. This discussion of means and ends can continue all the way down to an observer looking under the car bonnet, saying 'that pipe takes the fuel from the fuel tank to the fuel injection system but because it is broken this car has no power so it cannot transport us until it is fixed'.

CWA in action

Benda and Sanderson (1999) have used the first two levels of modelling to investigate the impact of a new technology and working practice. Their case study concerned an automated anaesthesia record-keeping system. They undertook a work domain analysis and an activity analysis in work domain terms. For the work domain analysis:

- The output was the relationships between purpose, functions and objects.
- Changes representable at this level were changes to the functional structure of this domain.

For the activity analysis in work domain terms:

- The output was the coordination of workflow.
- Changes representable at this level were changes to procedure and coordination.

Based on these analyses Benda and Sanderson successfully predicted that the introduction of the automated anaesthesia record-keeping system would take longer to use and place additional constraints on the medical team.

15.12 Human error

Human error is studied in a wide variety of ways. Some researchers conduct laboratory investigations while others investigate the causes of major accidents after the event. A typical example of a laboratory study is that by Hull *et al.* (1988) who asked 24 ordinary men and women to wire an electric plug. They found that only five succeeded in doing so safely, despite the fact that 23 of the 24 had wired a plug in the previous 12 months. In analysing the results of this study it was found that a number of different factors contributed to these failures, including:

Chapter 5, Section 5.11, discusses mental models

- Failure to read the instructions
- Inability to formulate an appropriate mental model
- Failure of the plug designers to provide clear physical constraints on erroneous actions. This last point was regarded as the most significant.

Unhappily error is an inescapable fact of life. Analysis of the causes of major accidents has found that human error is primarily responsible in 60–90 percent of all major accidents (Rouse and Rouse, 1983; Reason, 1997). This figure is consistent with the findings of commercial organizations: for example, Boeing, the aircraft manufacturer, estimate that 70 percent of all 'commercial airplane hull-loss accidents' are attributable to human error (www.boeing.com/commercial/aeromagazine/aero_08/index.html).

Understanding action slips

Research conducted by Reason (1992) has given insight into everyday errors. In one study he asked 36 people to keep a diary of action slips (i.e. actions which

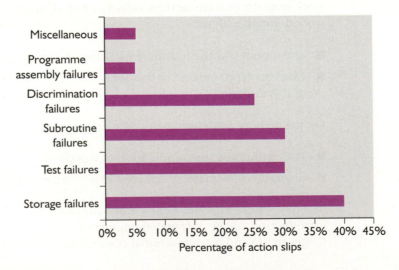

FIGURE 15-24 Five categories of action slips (*source: after Reason, 1992*)

have deviated from what they intended) for a period of four weeks. Analysis of the reported 433 slips revealed that storage failures (e.g repeating an action which has already been completed) were the most frequently reported. Figure 15-24 summarizes the key findings of this study and Table 15-4 describes each type of action slip (the miscellaneous errors are too diverse to discuss).

TABLE 15-4 Action slips

Type of action slip	Description
Storage failures	These were the most common and involved errors such as repeating an action which has already been completed, e.g. sending the same e-mail twice.
Test failures	These refer to forgetting what the goal of the action was, owing to failing to monitor the execution of a series of actions, e.g. starting to compose an e-mail and then forgetting to whom you are sending it.
Subroutine failures	These errors were due to omitting a step in the sequence of executing an action, e.g. sending an e-mail and forgetting to attach the attachment.
Discrimination failures	Failure to discriminate between two similar objects used in the execution of an action resulted in this category of error, e.g. intending to send an e-mail and starting Word instead by mistake.
Programme assembly failures	This was the smallest category, accounting for only 5 percent of the total. They involved incorrectly combining actions, e.g. saving the e-mail and deleting the attachment instead of saving the attachment and deleting the e-mail.

Each of these slips (and there are other classifications of errors) presents challenges for the interactive systems designer. Some can be reduced or managed, others cannot.

Reducing action slips

A good example of the use of prompts is **wizards** (we have seen these already in Chapter 5). Wizards prompt the user and help her recall the steps which she must take to complete a task, such as installing a printer. In the image of the sequence in Figure 15-25 we see a user being prompted systematically to provide information to allow the operating system to install a printer. The advantage of this approach is that the user need only supply relatively small amounts of information at any one time and has the advantage of an error correction system (i.e. use of the *Back* and *Next* steps).

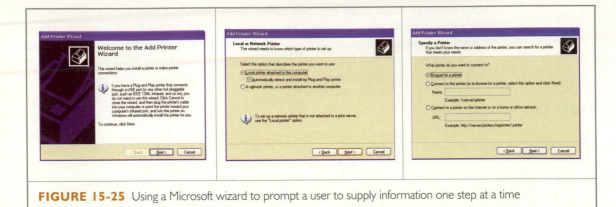

FIGURE 15-25 Using a Microsoft wizard to prompt a user to supply information one step at a time

One of the most demanding tasks in the work of an academic is marking coursework and examination scripts and tabulating the results without making mistakes. Figure 15-26 is a snapshot of a spreadsheet designed by Professor Jon Kerridge of the School of Computing, Napier University, to help reduce errors in this process. It is an example of good practice in this kind of manual tabulation of data as it employs a number of semi-automated checks (with corresponding error messages): in the column labelled *Checked* is a *note* indicating that an error message will appear if 'either the mark inserted for a question is more than the maximum mark obtainable for that question or ...' . The author of the system has annotated the spreadsheet using *comments* and has used a series of *if statements* to check the inputted data. So, for example, marks should be entered for three questions only and an error is signalled if this number is exceeded.

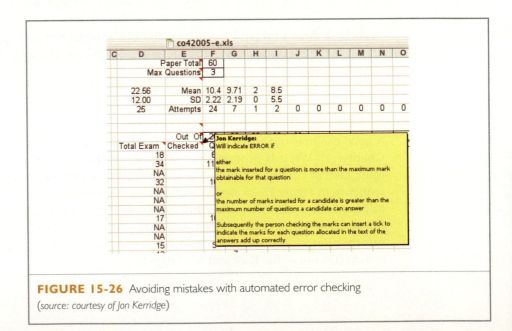

FIGURE 15-26 Avoiding mistakes with automated error checking
(*source: courtesy of Jon Kerridge*)

15.13 Design guidelines

The following design guidelines have been drawn (and edited) from Reason and Norman's design principles for minimizing error (*cf.* Reason, 1990, p. 236).

Error avoidance design guidelines

E1.   Use knowledge both in the world and in the head in order to promote a good conceptual model of the system on the part of its users; this requires consistency of mapping between the designer's model, the system model and the user's model.

E2.   Simplify the structure of tasks so as to minimize the load upon vulnerable cognitive processes such as working memory (see Section 15.2), planning or problem solving.

E3.   Make both the execution and the evaluation sides of an action visible. Visibility in regard to the former allows users to know what is possible and how things should be done; visibility on the evaluation side enables people to gauge the effects of their actions.

E4.   Exploit natural mappings between intentions and possible actions, between actions and their effects on the system, between the actual system state and what is perceivable, and between the system state and the needs, intentions and expectations of the user.

E5.   Exploit the power of constraints, both natural and artificial. Constraints guide the user to the next appropriate action or decision.

E6.   Design for errors. Assume that they will happen, then plan for *error recovery*. Try to make it easy to reverse operations and hard to carry out non-reversible ones. Exploit forcing functions such as wizards which constrain the user to a limited range of operations.

E7.   When all else fails, standardize actions, outcomes, layouts, displays, etc. The disadvantages of less than perfect standardization are often compensated for by the increased ease of use. But standardization for its own sake is only a last resort. The earlier principles should always be applied first.

Error message design guidelines

Em1.   Take care with the wording and presentation of alerts and error messages.

Em2.   Avoid using threatening or alarming language in messages (e.g. fatal error, run aborted, kill job, catastrophic error).

Em3.   Do not use double negatives as they can be ambiguous.

Em4.   Use specific, constructive words in error messages (e.g. avoid general messages such as 'invalid entry' and use specifics such as 'please enter your name').

Em5.   Make the system 'take the blame' for errors (e.g. 'illegal command' versus 'unrecognized command').

Em6. DO NOT USE ALL UPPERCASE LETTERS as it looks like you are shouting – instead, use a mixture of uppercase and lowercase.

Em7. Use attention grabbing techniques cautiously (e.g. avoid over-using 'blinks' on Web pages, flashing messages, 'you have mail', bold colours, etc.).

Em8. Do not use more than four different font sizes per screen.

Em9. Do not over-use audio or video.

Em10. Use colours appropriately and make use of expectations (e.g. red = danger, green = OK).

Memory design guidelines

M1. Organize information into a small number of 'chunks'.

M2. Try to create short linear sequences of tasks.

M3. Use persistence, so do not flash important information onto the screen for brief time periods.

M4. Do not 'overwrite' the contents of working memory by giving additional tasks to the users.

M5. Organize data fields to match user expectations or to organize user input (e.g. the automatic formatting of phone numbers).

M6. Provide reminders or warnings of the stage the user has reached in an operation.

M7. Provide ongoing feedback on what is happening and/or what has just happened.

M8. The user interface should behave in consistent ways at all times for all screens.

M9. Terminology, icons and use of colour should be consistent between screens.

Challenge 15-3
What is wrong with the error message in Figure 15-27? How would you reword it?

Unexpected critical error: can't start program

OK

FIGURE 15-27 An unexpected error message

Summary and key points

We have seen that memory is divided into a number of different stores, each of different size, make-up and purpose. Information arriving at the senses is held very briefly in the *sensory stores* before moving on to *working memory*. Working memory (the modern equivalent of short-term memory) holds three or four items for up to 30 seconds unless *rehearsed*. Information may subsequently be stored in the *long-term memory* store with additional processing. The contents of long-term memory last a long time (minutes, hours, days, even years) and are held in several different types of memory, including memory for skills (*procedural memory*), *semantic memory* which holds the meaning of words, facts and knowledge generally, *autobiographical memory* which holds our personal experiences, and finally *perma-store* which holds information which literally may last a lifetime.

Turning to how these limitations and capabilities have been translated into design features at the user interface, firstly we have seen the need to *chunk* material to reduce the load on working memory; secondly, the importance of designing for *recognition* rather than *recall* has been highlighted; and finally, we have discussed the importance of *icons* as aids to memory.

We have learned that attention can be thought of in terms of being *divided* or *selective*. Divided attention refers to our ability to carry out more than one task at a time, though our ability to carry out multiple tasks also depends upon our skill (expertise) and the difficulty of the task. In contrast, selective attention is more concerned with focusing on particular tasks or things in the environment. We have also seen that the design of interactive systems which recognizes the limitations of attention is largely in the domain of safety-critical systems (e.g. aircraft cockpit design, X-ray machines) where abilities to *detect signals* and undertake *vigilance* tasks are of particular importance. Cognitive work analysis has been discussed as a technique which aims to integrate aspects of human cognition with design of the wider system.

It should come as no surprise that we make errors while using interactive devices. These errors have been classified and described by a range of researchers, *storage failures* being the most common. While all errors cannot be prevented, measures can be taken to minimize them using devices such as *wizards* and automated error checking.

Further reading

Reason, J. (1990) *Human Error*. Cambridge University Press, Cambridge.
Perhaps a little dated now but a highly readable introduction to the study of error.

Wickens, C.D. and Hollands, J.G. (2000) *Engineering Psychology and Human Performance* (3rd edn). Prentice-Hall, Upper Saddle River, NJ.
One of the definitive texts on engineering psychology.

Going forward

Ericsson, K.A. and Smith, J. (eds) (1991) *Towards a General Theory of Expertise.* Cambridge University Press, Cambridge.
This is an interesting collection of chapters written by experts in expertise.

Baddeley, A. (1997) *Human Memory: Theory and Practice.* Psychology Press, Hove, Sussex.
An excellent introduction to human memory.

Vicente, K.J. (1999) *Cognitive Work Analysis: Toward Safe, Productive, and Healthy Computer-based Work.* Lawrence Erlbaum Associates, Mahwah, NJ.
An excellent introduction to cognitive work analysis.

International standards for the design of icons

■ **ISO/IEC DIS 11581-1:** Icon symbols and functions – Part 1: Icons – general.

This contains a framework for the development and design of icons, including general requirements and recommendations applicable to all icons.

■ **ISO/IEC DIS 11581-2:** Icon symbols and functions – Part 2: Object icons.

This contains requirements and recommendations for icons that represent functions by association with an object, and that can be moved and opened. It also contains specifications for the function and appearance of 20 icons.

Comments on challenges

Challenge 15-1
The most difficult of these to describe is usually the procedural knowledge of how to ride a bicycle. Most people find the other two aspects reasonably easy. Procedural knowledge is notoriously difficult to articulate – hence the advisability of having users *show* you how they perform particular tasks rather than try to *tell* you.

Challenge 15-2
The plot should resemble Figure 15-28. Words presented first, second, third, ... are recalled well, as are the last four or five words. The twin peaks represent recall from long-term (*primacy*) and working memory (*recency*) respectively. This is a well-known effect and explains why, when asking directions or instructions, we tend to remember the beginning and end but are very vague about what was said in the middle.

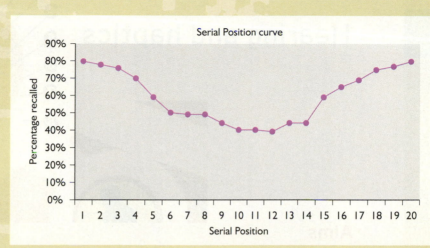

FIGURE 15-28

Challenge 15-3
This error message violates a number of good practice guidelines. 'Critical' sounds scary. 'Can't start program' is not helpful – what is the user supposed to do next? How does the user avoid the error in the future? See the guidelines above. Perhaps a better form of wording might be 'System problem encountered. Please restart application'.

Exercises

1. As wizards can be used to prevent action slips being made, does it make good sense to use them for all dialogues with the system or application? When would you *not* use an error-preventing dialogue style such as wizards?

2. Compare and contrast how you would design a Web browser for recall as compared to one for recognition. What are the key differences?

3. (Advanced) You are responsible for designing the control panel for a nuclear reactor. Operators have to monitor numerous alerts, alarms and readings which (thankfully) indicate normal operating conditions almost all the time. If and when an abnormal state is indicated, the operator must take remedial action immediately. Discuss how you would design the control panel to take into account the qualities of human attention.

4. (Advanced) How far (if at all) does psychological research into the mechanisms of human memory support the effective design of interactive systems? Give concrete examples.

16   Hearing and haptics

Aims

This chapter discusses two of the less exploited interaction modalities. It begins with an introduction to auditory perception and why it is important to the design of interactive systems. We then turn to the role of touch, haptics and kinaesthesia. After studying this chapter you should be able to describe:

- How hearing and auditory perception work
- How interactive systems are being designed to take advantage of how human auditory perception works
- The key design guidelines for designing for audition
- The role of touch, haptics and kinaesthetics
- Designing for tangible computing.

16.1   Sound and hearing

The first distinction to be made is between *hearing* and *audition* (*auditory perception*). Just as vision is concerned with the physiological and neurological processing of light (with visual perception being the extraction of meaning from the patterns of light), hearing is the processing of variations in air pressure (sound) and auditory perception is the extraction of meaning from the patterns of sound, for example recognizing a fire alarm or holding a conversation.

What is sound?

Sound comes from the *motion* (or vibration) of an object. This motion is transmitted through a *medium* (such as air or water) as a series of *changes in pressure*. Figure 16-1 is an illustration of a single (pure) sound wave. The height of the

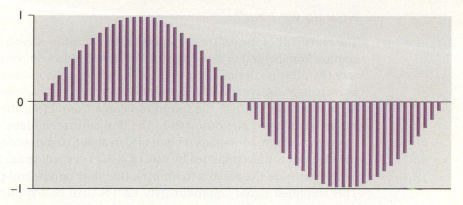

FIGURE 16-1 A pure sound wave

wave is a measure of the sound's loudness; the time from peak to peak is its frequency (or pitch).

Loudness

The heights of the peaks (and the depths of the troughs) indicate how loud the sound is. Loudness is measured in decibels (dB). On the decibel scale, the smallest audible sound (near total silence) is 0 dB. The decibel scale is logarithmic, which means that a sound of 40 dB is 10 times louder than the same sound at 30 dB.

It should be noted that prolonged exposure to any sound above 85 dB will cause hearing loss.

Near total silence	0 dB
A whisper	15 dB
Normal conversation	60 dB
A car horn	110 dB
A rock concert	120+ dB

Frequency

The frequency of the sound wave is the pitch of the sound – low frequency sounds like the rumble of an earthquake have a very low pitch, while high frequency sounds like those of screaming children have a high pitch. Human hearing is quite limited in terms of the range of frequencies we can detect and as we get older we tend to lose the ability to hear higher-pitched sounds. So while children may be able to hear a dog whistle or the sound of a bat's echo location, adults usually cannot. (The Pipistrelle bat emits its echo-location signals at about 45 kHz, whereas the Noctule bat uses a lower frequency of about 25 kHz or so.) The range of hearing for a typical young person is 20 to 20,000 hertz.

How do we hear?

The outer part of the ear (or *pinna*) is shaped to capture sound waves. If a sound is coming from behind or above the listener, it will reflect off the pinna in a different way than if it is coming from in front of or below the listener. The sound reflection changes the pattern of the sound wave which is recognized by the brain and helps determines where the sound has come from. From the pinna, the sound waves travel along the ear canal to the tympanic membrane (the *eardrum*). The eardrum is a thin, cone-shaped piece of skin about 10 mm wide. The movement of the eardrum is then amplified by way of *ossicles* (a small group of tiny bones). The ossicles include the *malleus* (hammer), the *incus* (anvil) and the *stapes* (stirrup). This amplified signal (approximately ×22) is then passed on to the *cochlea*. The cochlea transforms the physical vibrations into electrical signals.

The cochlea is a snail shell-shaped structure and is made up from a number of structures including the scala vestibuli, the scala media, the basilar membrane, and the organ of corti. Each of these structures contributes to the transduction of the sound waves into complex electrical signals which are transmitted by way of the cochlear nerve to the cerebral cortex, where the brain interprets them. The structure is shown in simplified form in Figure 16-2.

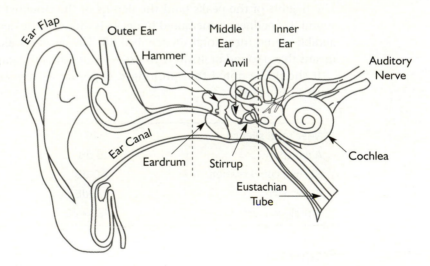

FIGURE 16-2 The structure of the human ear

16.2   Auditory perception

Auditory perception can be divided into (a) transduction, (b) auditory grouping processes, (c) scene analysis, and (d) interpretation. *Transduction* is the translation of sound vibrations into neural impulses by the ear and has been described above. *Auditory grouping processes* are the processes by which sound elements are:

- segregated into separate streams
- integrated into sound in coherent streams.

The next phase of auditory processing involves the extraction of perceptual properties as a part of *scene analysis*. These auditory streams are then *interpreted* by our brains to create the experience of the auditory environment. All of these steps are highly complex and beyond the scope of this chapter. The interested reader should refer to a specialist text such as McAdams and Bigand (1993) – see the Further reading at the end of the chapter.

Box 16-1   Some key terms

hertz	The basic unit of frequency. 1 Hz = 1 cycle per second.
Pitch	The property of the experience of sound by which sounds can be ordered on a musical scale, i.e. by which sounds can be judged relatively high or low.
Timbre	Relates to the quality of a sound. Timbre depends on the frequency and amplitude of partials, and on how they change over time.
Tone	A sound wave that evokes a sensation of pitch.

16.3   Using sound at the user interface

The following section is based closely on Stephen Brewster's chapter on 'Non-speech auditory output' in *The Human–Computer Interaction Handbook* (Brewster, 2003). The main headings are Brewster's.

Vision and hearing are interdependent

While comic book superheroes may acquire super-sensitive hearing on the loss of their sight, for the rest of us ordinary mortals our visual and auditory systems have evolved to work together. It is interesting to contrast the kinds and range of information our eyes and ears provide. Sight is a narrow, forward-facing, richly detailed picture of the world, while hearing provides information from all around us. An unexpected flash of light or a sudden movement orients our heads – and hence our hearing – to source; the sound of a car approaching from behind makes us turn to look. Both sound and vision allow us to orient ourselves in the world.

Reduce the load on the user's visual system

This design guideline and the next two are very closely related. It is now recognized that modern, large or even multiple-screen graphical interfaces use the human visual system very intensively – perhaps over intensively (see Figure 16-3). To reduce this sensory overload, key information could be displayed using sound, again to redistribute the processing burden to other senses.

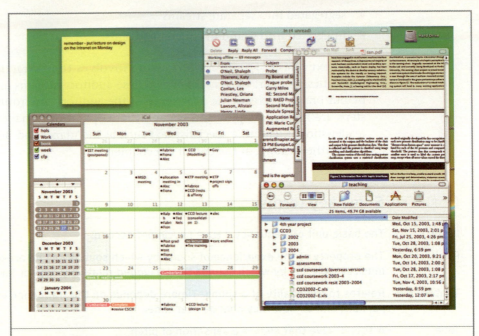

FIGURE 16-3 A typical visually cluttered desktop

Challenge 16-1
Suggest three different ways in which information belonging to a typical desktop could be displayed using sound.

Reduce the amount of information needed on screen

One of the great design tensions in the creation of mobile and ubiquitous devices is to display a usable amount of information on a small screen – small as in palm-sized, or pocket-sized, or carried or worn without a course in body building. The problem is that we live in an information-rich society. When moving information from one place to another was expensive, the telegram ruled. Send money. Urgent. Now we are likely to send a three-part multimedia presentation complete with streamed video, with the theme of send money, urgent. Mobile and ubiquitous devices have very small screens which are unsuited to viewing large bodies of data. To minimize this problem, information could be presented in sound in order to free screen space.

Reduce demands on visual attention

Again in the context of mobile and ubiquitous devices, there is an uneasy and at present unsatisfactory need to switch from attending the world – crossing the road, driving a car, following a stimulating presentation – to paying attention to

Attention is discussed in Chapters 5 and 15

the display of such devices. As we have seen earlier, the UK government made it an offence from December 2003 to both drive a car and use a mobile phone (hands-free phones excepted). The need for visual attention in particular could be reduced if sound were used instead.

The auditory sense is under-utilized

We listen to highly complex musical structures such as symphonies and operas. These pieces of music comprise large complex structures and sub-structures. This suggests that there is, at least, the potential of using music to successfully transmit complex information.

Sound is attention grabbing

While we can look away from an unpleasant sight, the same is not true of an unpleasant sound. The best we can do is to cover our ears. This makes sound very useful for attracting attention or communicating important information.

To make computers more usable by visually disabled users

While screen readers can be used to 'read' on-screen textual information they cannot easily read graphical information. Providing some of this information in an auditory form can help alleviate this problem. See Box 16-2.

Box 16-2   A mobile phone for the blind

In late 2003, the first mobile phone designed specifically for blind and partially sighted people went on sale in Spain. The phone has been created by a Spanish company, Owasys. It has no visual display at all but uses a speech synthesizer to read everything that would normally appear on the screen. As well as giving audio feedback from button presses, the phone can send and receive text messages and will speak the name or number of incoming callers.

Challenge 16-2
Can you think of possible disadvantages to augmenting the user interface with sound? Or circumstances where it would be inappropriate?

16.4   Examples of auditory user interfaces (AUIs)

To date most research on AUIs has concentrated on the use of either earcons or auditory icons. **Earcons** are musical sounds designed to reflect events in the interface. For example, a simple series of notes may be used to indicate a folder. Opening that folder (opening the folder = an event) might be represented as that series of notes rising in pitch, while closing it (another event) might be played in reverse. In contrast, **auditory icons** reflect the argument that we make use of many sounds in the everyday world without thinking about their musical content. The sounds used in these interfaces are caricatures of everyday sounds, where aspects of the sound's source correspond to events in the interface. Opening a folder in this case might be marked by the sound of a file drawer opening.

Earcons

Earcons are abstract, musical tones that can be used in structured combinations to create auditory messages. They were first proposed by Blattner *et al.* (1989) who defined earcons as 'non-verbal audio messages that are used in the computer/user interface to provide information to the user about some computer object, operation or interaction'. Earcons are based on musical sounds.

Numerous studies of the usefulness of earcons in providing cues in navigating menu structures have been conducted. The following study, from Brewster (1998), involved the creation of a menu hierarchy of 27 nodes and four levels with an earcon for each node. Participants in the study were asked to determine their location in the hierarchy by listening to an earcon. Results of this and similar experiments showed that participants could identify their location with greater than 80 percent accuracy. This suggests that earcons were a useful way of providing navigational information.

Given their usefulness, one proposed use for earcons is in telephone-based interfaces where navigation has been found to be a problem.

Earcon design guidelines

These design guidelines have been adapted from the work of Brewster, Wright and Edwards (1993). They are quoted more or less verbatim.

- **Timbre**. Use synthesized musical instrument timbres. Where possible use timbres with multiple harmonics. This helps perception and avoids masking.
- **Pitch**. Do not use pitch on its own unless there are very big differences between those used. Some suggested ranges for pitch are maximum 5 kHz (four octaves above middle C) and minimum 125–150 Hz (an octave below middle C).
- **Register**. If this alone is to be used to differentiate earcons which are otherwise the same, then large differences should be used. Three or more octaves difference give good rates of recognition.
- **Rhythm**. Make rhythms as different as possible. Putting different numbers of notes in each rhythm was very effective. Very short notes might not be noticed, so do not use less than eighth notes or quavers.
- **Intensity**. Although intensity was not examined in this test, some suggested ranges are maximum 20 dB above threshold and minimum 10 dB above

threshold. Care must be taken in the use of intensity. The overall sound level will be under the control of the user of the system. Earcons should all be kept within a close range so that if the user changes the volume of the system no sound will be lost.

■ **Combinations**. When playing earcons one after another, leave a gap between them so that users can tell where one finishes and the other starts. A delay of 0.1 second is adequate.

Auditory icons

One of the most famous examples of auditory icons is the SonicFinder developed for Apple. The SonicFinder was a developed as an alternative to the Macintosh Finder (equivalent to Explorer in MS Windows). The SonicFinder used sound in a way that reflects how it is used in the everyday world. Users were able to 'tap' objects in order to determine whether they are applications, disks or folders, and it was possible to gauge their size depending upon how high-pitched they sounded (small objects sounded high-pitched while large objects sounded low-pitched). Movement was also represented as a scraping sound.

Soundtrack

Soundtrack (a novel form of graphical user interface) has an unusual screen layout comprising eight 'auditory windows'. Each window had a sound associated with it which was heard as the cursor was moved into that window. The sounds were arranged according to their musical pitch. The windows had names too, and the name could be elicited (in synthetic speech) by pressing the mouse button within the window. Each window had a particular role; four of them corresponded to menus, for instance. A second level of interaction was reached by double-clicking the mouse. That would cause the current window to become subdivided into a number of components (auditory items). Each of those had a sound and a name, just as the windows had, as well as an action, which was performed if the user double-clicked the item.

Soundscapes

The term 'soundscape' is derived from 'landscape' and can be defined as the auditory environment within which a listener is immersed. This differs from the more technical concept of 'soundfield', which can be defined as the auditory environment surrounding the sound source, which is normally considered in terms of sound pressure level, duration, location and frequency range. Soundscapes are potentially important features of virtual environments and have already been used to create a greater sense of presence (being there) when experiencing virtual environments (see for example Turner *et al.*, 2003).

Challenge 16-3

We use background sound to a surprising degree in monitoring our interaction with the world around us. For example, I know that my laptop is still writing to a CD because it makes a sort of whirring sound. If my seminar group are working on problems in small groups, a rustling of papers and quiet-ish murmuring indicates all is well, complete silence means that I have baffled people, and louder conversation often means that most have finished. At home, I can tell that the central heating is working as it should by the background noise of the boiler (furnace) and the approximate time during the night by the volume of traffic noise from the road.

Make a similar – but longer – list for yourself. It might be easier to do this over a couple of days as you notice sounds. Read over your list and note down any ideas for using sound in a similar way in interaction design.

16.5 Problems with sound

Sound is not widely used at the user interface except for specialist purposes. The reason for this are remarkably easy to understand. First of all is the issue of *annoyance*. Visualize a large open-plan working environment filled with PCs and the office workers complete with headphones (or ear defenders). There are clearly a number of practical issues with computers making a noise while we interact with them. On a day-to-day basis most people have the feedback 'beeps' on their mobile phones disabled and most have the ring-tone volume turned down (the reverse appears to apply to phone users travelling by public transport).

A further issue is the question of *discrimination*. While it is easy to talk about discriminating between low and high pitched tones, it is quite another to discriminate between quite low and fairly low tones. There are a number of open questions about how well we can distinguish between different tones in context (in a busy office or a noisy reception area) and this is made worse by the obvious fact that sounds are not persistent. One of the strengths of the graphical user interface is the persistence of error messages, status information, menus and buttons. Auditory user interfaces are, in contrast, transient.

16.6 What is haptic perception?

Haptic perception has become in recent years an area of significant research. Again we distinguish between the *sense* of touch, and haptic *perception* which is the interpretation of this sense (see Figure 16-4). Haptic perception starts with touch which is sensed by receptors lying both beneath the skin surface (cutaneous receptors) and in the muscles and joints (kinaesthetic receptors). This sense provides the data about objects and surfaces in contact with the individual. It should also be remembered that heat and vibration can also be sensed from a source with which we are not in direct contact. Haptic perception provides a rich 'picture' of an individual's immediate surroundings and is essential to manipulating objects.

Box 16-3 Key terms for haptics

Haptic	Relating to the sense of touch.
Proprioceptive	Relating to sensory information about the state of the body (including cutaneous, kinaesthetic and vestibular sensations).
Vestibular	Pertaining to the perception of head position, acceleration and deceleration.
Kinaesthetic	The feeling of motion. Relating to sensations originating in muscles, tendons and joints.
Cutaneous	Pertaining to the skin itself or the skin as a sense organ. Includes sensation of pressure, temperature and pain.
Tactile	Pertaining to the cutaneous sense but more specifically the sensation of pressure rather than temperature or pain.
Force feedback	Relating to the mechanical production of information sensed by the human kinaesthetic system.

Source: after Oakley et al. (2000)

In HCI, the term haptics refers to both sensing and manipulating through the sense of touch (Tan, 2000). The keyboard and mouse are haptic input devices. Tan divides haptics into two components – *tactile sensing*, that is, sensing via the outsides of our bodies (skin, nails and hair) and *kinaesthetic sensing* which concerns the knowledge we have of our body's position. As I type I am aware of my forearms resting on the table, the crick in my neck and the looseness of my shoes on my feet – this information is provided by the **proprioceptic** nerves. Unlike visual perception and audition which can be thought of as input systems, the haptic system is *bidirectional*. Activities such as the reading of Braille text by the blind require the use of both the sensing and manipulation aspects of the haptic system. Tan notes that historically, work on haptic systems display has been driven by the need to develop 'sensory-substitution systems for the visually or hearing impaired'.

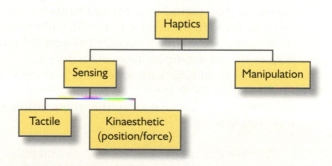

FIGURE 16-4 Defining haptics
(source: after Tan, H.Z. (2000) Perceptual user interfaces: haptic interfaces, Communications of the ACM, 43(3), pp. 40–41. © 2000 ACM, Inc. Reprinted by permission)

Designing for touch

It was the author Aldous Huxley who invented the notion of going to the *feelies* in his novel *Brave New World*. The feelies were the haptically enhanced cinema – not only could we watch the action and screen but feel it too. This notion did see a realization in the movie *Earthquake!* released in the 1970s where, in specially equipped cinemas, the deep rumble of an earthquake could be felt, and also in some theme park rides.

16.7 Tangible interaction

GUIs are discussed in Chapter 6

Tangible means being able to be touched or grasped and being perceived through the sense of touch. Tangible interaction is a practical application of haptics. Tangible interaction has given rise to TUIs – tangible user interfaces, which have a structure and logic both similar to and different from GUIs.

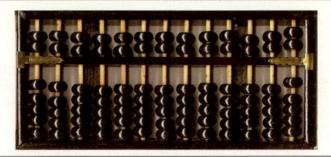

FIGURE 16-5 An abacus, which combines tangible input, output and the data being manipulated *(source: http://www.sphere.bc.ca/test/sruniverse.html. Courtesy of Sphere Research Corporation)*

Most of the work to date has been confined to the major research laboratories, for example the Media Lab at MIT (the Massachusetts Institute of Technology – http://mit.edu), which have constructed advanced prototype systems. Many of these systems have been used in fairly specific domains, for example urban planning (Urp) and landscape architecture (Illuminating Clay) among others. (Illuminating Clay is described in Section 16.9.) While many of these systems may never become commercial products, they do illustrate the state-of-the-art in tangible interaction design.

So what is tangible interaction and how does one go about designing a TUI rather than a GUI? Where better to begin than with the people at the MIT Tangible Media Lab who describe their vision for the future of HCI in the following way:

'Tangible Bits is our vision of Human Computer Interaction (HCI) which guides our research in the Tangible Media Group. People have developed sophisticated skills for sensing and manipulating our physical environments. However, most of these skills are not employed by traditional GUI (Graphical User Interface). Tangible Bits seeks to build upon these skills

by giving physical form to digital information, seamlessly coupling the dual worlds of bits and atoms. Guided by the Tangible Bits vision, we are designing "tangible user interfaces" which employ physical objects, surfaces, and spaces as tangible embodiments of digital information. These include foreground interactions with graspable objects and augmented surfaces, exploiting the human senses of touch and kinaesthesia. We are also exploring background information displays which use "ambient media"- ambient light, sound, airflow, and water movement. Here, we seek to communicate digitally-mediated senses of activity and presence at the periphery of human awareness.'

(http://tangible.media.mit.edu/projects/Tangible_Bits)

So their 'goal is to change the "painted bits" of GUIs (graphical user interfaces) to "tangible bits", taking advantage of the richness of multimodal human senses and skills developed through our lifetime of interaction with the physical world.'

Further thoughts: Why tangible interaction?

There are a number of good reasons why we should think about adopting (or at least exploring the possibilities of) tangible interaction. First of all, if we could remove the divide between the electronic and physical worlds we potentially have the benefits of both. We could have all the advantages of computation brought to us beyond the confines of the graphical display unit and have them, as it were, present-to-hand. Present-to-hand could also be taken literally by putting information and computation literally 'in our hands' (we are after all discussing tangible interaction). Finally, and this is proving to be a recurrent theme in this chapter, there may be advantages in off-loading some of the burden of our computation (thinking and problem solving) by (a) accessing our *spatial cognition* and (b) adopting a more concrete style of interaction (like sketching, which provides a more fluid and natural style of interaction). As we saw in Chapter 7, graspable, physical objects provide stronger (real) affordances as compared to their virtual equivalents.

16.8 Tangible user interfaces (TUIs)

More of Ishii's work is discussed in Chapter 28

This introduction to TUIs has drawn heavily on a recently published chapter entitled 'Emerging frameworks for tangible user interfaces' by Ullmer and Ishii (2002) to which the reader is directed. Hiroshi Ishii is a leading light in the world of tangible computing. Ullmer and Ishii begin by noting that 'TUIs couple physical representations (e.g. spatial manipulable physical objects) with digital representations (e.g. graphics and audio), yielding interactive systems that are computationally mediated but generally not identifiable as "computers" *per se*'. In plain English, if we want to use an on-screen, virtual tool – say a pen – we would use a real, physical pen which in some sense has been mapped on to the virtual equivalent. Picking up the real pen would then be mirrored in the computer by the virtual pen being raised or becoming active. Drawing with the real pen would result in an equivalent virtual drawing which might be displayed on a screen and represented as a data object. Now let's think about this beyond pens – think about the entire contents of your real desktop being mirrored and represented in a computer.

TUIs are different from GUIs in many different ways but here are three important ones:

- TUIs use *physical representations* – such as modelling clay (see Illuminating Clay in Section 16.9) – and physical drawing boards rather than *pictures* of them displayed on monitors. So, for example, instead of having to manipulate an image using a mouse and keyboard on a screen, people can draw directly onto surfaces using highlighter pens.

- As these tangible, graspable elements cannot, of course, perform computation on their own, they must be linked to a digital representation. As Ullmer and Ishii put it, playing with mud pies without computation is just playing with mud pies.

- TUIs *integrate representation and control* which GUIs keep strictly apart. GUIs have a MVC structure – Model–View–Control. In traditional GUIs we use peripheral devices such as a mouse or keyboard to *control* a digital representation of what we are working with (the *model*), the results of which are displayed on a screen or printer or some other form of output (the *view*). This is illustrated in Figure 16-6.

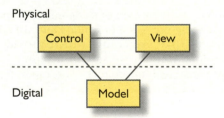

FIGURE 16-6 Model–View–Control

TUIs in contrast have a more complex model which can be seen in Figure 16-7. This is the MCRpd model. The control and model elements are unchanged but the view component is split between Rep-p (physical representation) and Rep-d (digital representation). This model highlights the tight linkage between the control and physical representation. This MCRpd model is realized in the prototypes described in the section below.

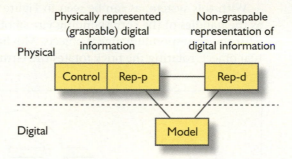

FIGURE 16-7 MCRpd

16.9 | Getting a feel for tangible computing

Bricks

The Bricks system is a good example of a graspable user interface (for graspable read tangible). Bricks was developed by Fitzmaurice, Ishii and Buxton and reported as long ago as 1995 (Fitzmaurice *et al.*, 1995). It was designed to allow the manipulation of digital objects by way of physical 'bricks'. The bricks, which are approximately the size of Lego bricks, are placed and operated on a large, horizontal computer display surface called the *Active Desk*. For Fitzmaurice, Ishii and Buxton, a *graspable, tangible* object is an object composed of both a physical and a virtual object. The physical object or objects were designed to act as the *handle* of a virtual object. Figure 16-8 is an image of a rectangle drawn in a graphics package showing its handles. Handles are the points by which one can 'get hold of' the rectangle in order to move it, resize it and so on.

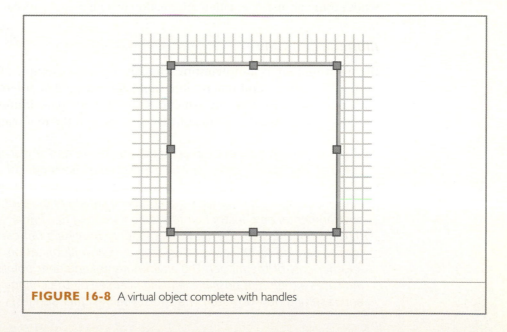

FIGURE 16-8 A virtual object complete with handles

With this system, as can be seen in Figure 16-9, a brick or group of bricks act as the handles of the corresponding virtual object. The bricks are tightly coupled with the corresponding digital objects. Moving the physical brick moves the virtual object; rotating the brick rotates the virtual object.

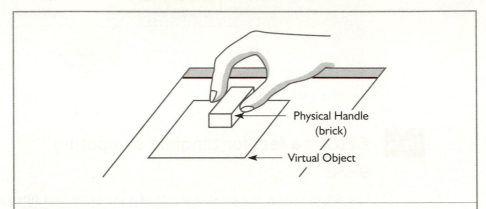

Physical Handle (brick)

Virtual Object

FIGURE 16-9 An image from Bricks: laying the foundations for graspable user interfaces (*after Fitzmaurice, G.W., Ishii, H. and Buxton, W.A.S. (1995) Bricks: laying the foundations for graspable user interfaces, Proceedings of CHI '95 Conference, Denver, CO, 7–11 May, pp. 442–49. © 1995 ACM, Inc. Reprinted by permission*)

A key technical challenge for TUIs lies with tracking the positions of the physical representations themselves and reflecting those changes in the virtual (digital) representation. In the Bricks system Ascension Flock of Birds, 6D input devices were to simulate the graspable objects. Each receiver is a small 1-inch cube that constantly sends positional and orientation information to a high-end workstation.

Illuminating Clay

Illuminating Clay is an interesting, though specialist example of tangible computing. It is a later and much more sophisticated implementation than Bricks but essentially builds on the same underlying principles. Illuminating Clay is introduced and placed in context by its creators with the following scenario:

'A group of road builders, environment engineers and landscape designers stand at an ordinary table on which is placed a clay model of a particular site in the landscape. Their task is to design the course of a new roadway, housing complex and parking area that will satisfy engineering, environmental and aesthetic requirements. Using her finger the engineer flattens out the side of a hill in the model to provide a flat plane for an area for car parking As she does so an area of yellow illumination appears in another part of the model. The environmental engineer points out that this indicates a region of possible landslide caused by the change in the terrain and resulting flow of water. The landscape designer suggests that this

landslide could be avoided by adding a raised earth mound around the car park. The group tests the hypothesis by adding material to the model and all three observe the resulting effect on the stability of the slope.

Piper, Ratti and Ishii (2002)

In the Illuminating Clay system, the physical, tangible objects are made of clay. Piper *et al.* (2002) experimented with several different types of modelling material including Lego blocks, modelling clay, Plasticine, Silly Putty and so on. Eventually they found that a thin layer of Plasticine supported by a metal mesh core worked best. This clay was then shaped into the desired form by the landscape specialists (see Figure 16-10). The matte white finish also proved to be highly suitable as a projection surface onto which the digital elements of the system were projected. Ordinarily, people working with landscapes would create complex models using computer aided design (CAD) software and then run simulations to examine, for instance, the effects of wind flow, drainage and the position of powerlines and roads. With Illuminating Clay, the potential consequences of the landscape are projected directly (for example, as in the scenario above a patch of coloured light) onto the clay itself.

FIGURE 16-10 An image from Illuminating Clay
(source: Piper, B., Ratti, C. and Ishii, H. (2002) Illuminating Clay: a 3D tangible interface for landscape analysis, Proceedings of CHI '02 Conference, Minneapolis, MN, 20–25 April, pp. 355–62. © ACM, Inc. Reprinted by permission)

The coupling between clay and its digital representation is managed by means of a ceiling-mounted laser scanner and digital projector. Using an angled mirror the scanner and projector are aligned at the same optical origin and the two devices are calibrated to scan and project over an equal area. This configuration ensures that all the surfaces that are visible to the scanner can also be projected upon.

Thus Illuminating Clay demonstrates the advantages of combining physical and digital representations for landscape analysis. The physical clay model conveys spatial relationships that can be directly manipulated by the user's hands. This approach allows users to quickly create and understand highly complex topographies that would be time-consuming using conventional CAD tools.

Challenge 16-4
Suggest other application areas where Illuminating Clay may be useful.

16.10 Interactive workbenches

Interactive workbenches are a group of related technologies which track the position and movements of objects on a flat 'tabletop'. The workbenches are interactive in that they respond to user input with a graphical response (or output). A number of these prototype systems have been developed and include Bricks (Fitzmaurice *et al.*, 1995), described above, DigitalDesk (Wellner, 1993), SenseTable (Patten *et al.*, 2001) and Urp (Underkoffler and Ishii, 1999). The Actuated Workbench developed by Pangaro *et al.* (2002) is described in a little detail below.

The Actuated Workbench

Pangaro, Maynes-Aminzade and Ishii (2002) from the MIT Media Lab have built and described a system they have called the Actuated Workbench (AW). The AW is a device that uses an array of magnets to move objects on a table in two dimensions. It is intended for use with existing tabletop tangible interfaces, providing an additional feedback loop for computer output, and helping to resolve inconsistencies that otherwise arise from the computer's inability to move objects on the table. Other interactive workbenches are primarily input devices. Users are able to manipulate objects on the 'tabletop' which are reflected in changes in a corresponding digital object. This is fine for input, but output in such cases tends to be limited to a sound or change in the accompanying visual display. The Actuated Workbench is different in that it physically moves the objects on the tabletop by manipulating an array of magnets hidden below. See Figures 16-11 and 16-12. A schematic view of how this works is reproduced in Figure 16-13. The technical complexity of these workbenches is not to be underestimated.

16.11 Wearable computing

Most of us encounter computers on desktops in offices or at college. We also find computers (as games consoles) in the bedrooms of teenagers, in the pockets of the white coat of a clinician (as a PDA – personal data assistant) and in all manner of household devices (as microprocessors in washing machines, microwaves, DVD players and so forth). We do not, however, often find computers

FIGURE 16-11 The Actuated Workbench uses an array of electromagnets to move a magnetic puck across a table surface *(source: Pangaro et al., 2002 © 2002 ACM, Inc. Reprinted by permission)*

FIGURE 16-12 An overhead view of the electromagnets
(source: Pangaro et al., 2002 © 2002 ACM, Inc. Reprinted by permission)

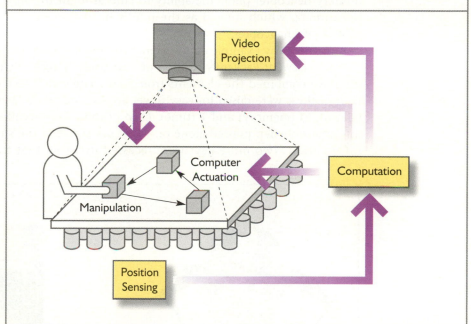

FIGURE 16-13 A schematic representation of the operation of the Actuated Workbench *(source: after Pangaro, G., Mayes-Aminzande, D. and Ishii, H. (2002) The Actuated Workbench: Computer-controlled actuation in tabletop tangible interfaces, Proceedings of UIST '02, Paris, 27–30 October, pp. 181–90. © 2002 ACM, Inc. Reprinted by permission)*

in our clothing or as part of our clothing. But this is set to change. Wearable computers (or wearable computing) has actually been around in a variety of experimental and prototype forms since the 1960s – see Figure 16-14.

So what is wearable computing? Steve Mann, one of the pioneers of wearable computing, defines it as follows:

'A wearable computer is a computer that is subsumed into the personal space of the user, controlled by the user, and has both operational and interactional constancy, i.e. is always on and always accessible. Most notably, it is a device that is always with the user, and into which the user can always enter commands and execute a set of such entered commands, and in which the user can do so while walking around or doing other activities.'

Mann (1998)

The topic of wearable computing is also discussed in Chapter 17 which discusses affective computing

We begin our review of wearable computing by considering its origins.

Early wearable computers

In one early project (dating from the mid-1960s) at Bell Helicopter Company, the head-mounted display was coupled with an infra-red camera that would give military helicopter pilots the ability to land at night in rough terrain. An infra-red camera, which moved as the pilot's head moved, was mounted on the bottom of a helicopter.

A further early example of a wearable computer was the HP-01 (Figure 16-15). This was Hewlett-Packard's creation of a wristwatch/algebraic calculator; its user interface combined the elements from both. The watch face had 28 tiny keys. Four of these were raised for easy finger access. The raised keys were D (date), A (alarm), M (memory) and T (time). Each of these keys recalled the appropriate information when pressed alone or, when pressed after the shift key, stored the information. Two more keys were recessed in a way that they would not be

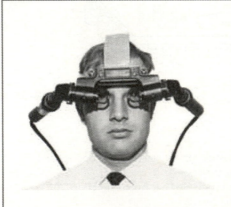

FIGURE 16-14 (Probably) the first head mounted display (HMD), dating from 1967 *(source: http://www.sun.com/960710/feature3/alice.html © Sun Microsystems. Courtesy of Sun Microsystems, Inc.)*

FIGURE 16-15 The HP-01 algebraic watch *(source: The Museum of HP Calculators. http://www.hpmuseum.org)*

pressed accidentally but could still be operated by finger. These were the R (read/recall/reset depending on mode) and S (stopwatch) keys. The other keys were meant to be pressed with one of two styluses that came with the watch. One of these was a small unit that snapped into the clasp of the bracelet.

Spacesuits

Perhaps the ultimate wearable is the spacesuit. Whether this is the genuine article as used by astronauts or something more fanciful from science fiction, the spacesuit encompasses and protects the individual while providing (at least) communication with the mother ship or with command and control. While the Borg in *Star Trek* may have enhanced senses, today's spacesuits are actually limited to a single-line text display and a human voice relay channel. These limitations reflect the practical issues of power consumption and the demands of working in a vacuum. NASA and its industrial collaborators are trying to create extra-vehicular activity – EVA (space walk) – support systems using head-up displays (mounted in the helmet), wrist-mounted displays and modifications of the current chest-mounted display and control system. The work continues to balance the requirements of utility, reliability, size and mass. Figure 16-16 is an illustration of some of the key components of this particular type of wearable computer system or spacesuit.

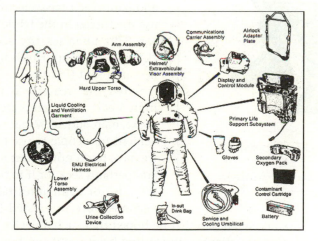

FIGURE 16-16 The major components of a spacesuit
(source: http://starchild.gsfc.nasa.gov/docs/ Star Child/space_level2/spacesuit.html.)

FFW – Future Force Warrior

We now move from the peaceful exploration of space to something much more terrifying: the Future Force Warrior. The FFW has been described as the US army's flagship project, designed to create 'A Formidable Warrior in an Invincible Team, able to See First, Understand First, Act First, & Finish Decisively.'

FIGURE 16-17 The soldier of the future – FFW
(*source: Army Soldier Systems Center*)

The FFW initiative aims at creating 'a lightweight, overwhelmingly lethal, fully integrated individual combat system, including weapon, head-to-toe individual protection, netted communications, soldier worn power sources, and enhanced human performance' – the last word in wearables (Figure 16-17).

The FFW system will be equipped with *power vision*, a networked (i.e. intra-squad local area network) distributed sensor and communication array including GPS (Global Positioning System). A flip-down display on the helmet allows the soldier (sorry, warrior) to scan the surroundings in the darkness, using *thermal* and *night-vision sensors* connected to his weapon. This display also provide a real-time situation map that can locate both friend and foe.

Biomedical applications

Philips Research has developed underwear (bras and pants) that can monitor heart rate or blood pressure and, at the first sign of a problem, telephone for help. The bra and pants each have electrodes built into their fabric and use the thread in the fabric to send data to a microprocessor. This analyses the signals and detects dangerous changes in heart rhythm. A spokesman from Philips Research said that the device would be able to work out whether the wearer was taking exercise and disregard high heart rates generated by physical exertion. The spokesman added: 'What we have ended up with is convenient for people to use in an unobtrusive way. ... What we have to do now is test it on a larger number of people, and perhaps seek for it to be approved in Europe. ... There are a lot of companies taking this direction as people become more interested in preventive medicine.' The spokesman said that he hoped that such a device would not simply be useful to give to patients with existing heart problems, but would eventually be used by a wider public. He said he expected other measurements, such as blood pressure, could also be taken by the clothing. And he promised that the hi-tech underwear would be as convenient as normal clothing. 'It can be put through the washing machine – and ironed if necessary.' However, it could be some years before the technology becomes widely available.

Body Wearable Computer

Figure 16-18 shows a technician equipped with a head mounted display and a Body Wearable Computer (BWC) being used to survey the severity and location of damaged heat tiles on the STS – Space Transportation System (usually known as the Space Shuttle). The BWC is a battery-powered computer system worn on the user's body (on a belt, backpack or vest). It is designed for mobile and hands-free operations.

E-textiles

Another interesting line of research into wearables is to integrate the computing or communications elements themselves into the very substance of fabrics rather than as external modules. Research into the general area of 'intelligent materials' has facilitated solutions using fabrics with conductive properties. Such fabric systems can be used to enable sensing and control applications in sectors as diverse as wearables (Figure 16-19), furniture, flexible keyboards (Figure 16-20) and mobile gaming. The fabric is flexible, durable, washable and capable of being fully integrated into fabric assemblies.

FIGURE 16-18 Body Wearable Computer or BWC
(source: http://science.ksc.nasa.gov/ payload/projects/ borg/shuttle.html.NASA)

FIGURE 16-19 A jacket with integrated controls *(source: www.eleksen.com. Courtesy of Eleksen Ltd)*

FIGURE 16-20 A flexible keyboard *(source: www.eleksen.com. Courtesy of Eleksen Ltd)*

16.12   The six attributes of wearable computing

Steve Mann has identified what he calls the six informational flow paths associated with wearable computing (Mann, 1998). These informational flows are essentially the key attributes of wearable computing (the headings are Mann's):

1. **Unmonopolizing** of the user's attention. That is, they do not detach the wearer from the outside world. The wearer is able to pay attention to other tasks while wearing the kit. Moreover, the wearable may provide enhanced sensory capabilities.

2. **Unrestrictive** to the user. The wearer can still engage with the computation and communication powers of the wearable computer while walking or running.

3. **Observable** by the user. As the system is being worn, there is no reason why the wearer cannot be aware of it continuously.

4. **Controllable** by the user. The wearer can take control of it at any time.

5. **Attentive** to the environment. Wearable systems can enhance environmental and situational awareness.

6. **Communicative** to others. Wearable systems can be used as a communications medium.

Challenge 16-5
Carry out an Internet search and find at least two more examples of wearable computing. From the information available, how far do the applications embody Mann's six key attributes?

16.13   Final thought: haptics meets hearing

A new mobile phone has just been announced which requires the user to put their finger into their ear. The Japanese telecoms company NTT DoCoMo has developed a wearable mobile phone that uses the human body to make calls. Called Finger Whisper, the device is built into a narrow strap worn on the wrist like a watch. To answer a call on the Finger Whisper phone, to make a call or hang up, the user simply touches forefinger to thumb and then puts their forefinger in their ear. Electronics in the wristband convert sound waves into vibrations, which are carried through the bones of the hand to the ear so that the Finger Whisper user can hear the other caller. A microphone in the wristband replaces the cellphone's usual mouthpiece, and instead of dialling a number, the user says it out loud. Voice recognition technology turns the command into a dialled number. The company said it was too early to say when the Finger Whisper phone might go on sale. However, it should be noted that the prototype is currently the size of a kitchen cupboard.

Summary and key points

There is no doubt that sound could play an important role in the design of user interfaces. The work which has been carried out to make sound useful and usable at the interface is convincing but still has not been adopted by the major user interface designers.

TUIs offer a new way of thinking about and interacting with computers. While the keyboard and mouse of the typical PC offer a tangible interface, true TUIs embodying the MCRpd model are still only available as advanced prototypes.

Finally, wearables, while very much in their infancy, offer an interesting hands-free way of interacting with both computers and the environment.

Further reading

Ullmer, B. and Ishii, H. (2002) Emerging frameworks for tangible user interfaces. In Carroll, J.M. (ed.), *Human–Computer Interaction in the New Millennium*. ACM Press, New York.
A useful introduction to the tangibles domain.

More advanced

Blauert, J. (1997) *Spatial Hearing*. MIT Press, Cambridge, MA.

McAdams, S. and Bigand, E. (1993) *Thinking in Sound*. Oxford University Press, Oxford.
The titles of these two volumes are entirely descriptive of their contents. Recommended for those who need to investigate this area in depth.

Comments on challenges

Challenge 16-1
Here are three possibilities. There are of course many more. All would need careful design.

1. Voice read-out of calendar reminders.
2. Different audio tones to distinguish levels in the file system hierarchy.
3. Readout of senders and first lines of incoming e-mail, so one could do other physical jobs around the room while listening to a new batch of messages. Even better with voice command input.

Challenge 16-2
See Section 16.5, 'Problems with sound'.

Challenge 16-3
The list you produce will be individual to you and your circumstances. An idea which comes to mind is attaching an unobtrusive humming to a file search or other lengthy operations, perhaps changing in pitch as it nears completion.

Challenge 16-4
Any area where the design of physical objects has to be checked for particular properties or against guidelines is a possibility. One might be the design of car bodies, which – at least until relatively recently – are 'mocked-up' full-size in order to check for wind resistance, etc. Designers make modifications to the mock-up by hand and then check in a wind tunnel.

Challenge 16-5
The results here will depend on the applications found.

Exercises

1. Design a sonically enhanced interface for a *simple* game in the form of a general knowledge quiz for children. The quiz is presented as a set of multiple-choice questions. If time is short, confine yourself to one screen of the game. This is much more fun done in presentation software such as PowerPoint or any of the multimedia software packages if you are familiar with them.

2. Discuss the advantages and disadvantages of augmenting the user interface with (a) sound and (b) haptics. In your view, which has the most potential and why? Support your argument with specific examples.

Affective computing and pleasure

Aims

In a recent special issue of an academic journal devoted to affective computing, Rosalind Picard quotes a MORI survey which found that three-quarters of computer users admit to swearing at computers (Picard, 2003). This chapter focuses on the role of emotions (often termed **affect** in this context) in interactive systems design. We first introduce theories of human emotion and demonstrate their application in technologies which respond to emotion, or can generate 'emotions' themselves. The chapter ends with considering one particular emotion – pleasure – and how we can design pleasing devices. After studying this chapter you should be able to describe:

- The physical and cognitive accounts (models) of emotion
- The potential for **affective computing** in interactive systems design
- Applications of affective computing
- Approaches to designing pleasurable products.

You should also be aware of the current research issues in affective computing which include:

- Sensing and recognizing human affective/emotional signals and understanding affective behaviour
- Synthesizing emotional responses in interactive devices
- Designing interactive systems which communicate or evoke emotions.

There are, of course, other aspects of affective computing but these not particularly relevant to the design of interactive devices and systems.

Emotion has both a cognitive and a physical aspect; accordingly this chapter should be read in conjunction with Chapter 16 which considers haptics.

Much of the material in the first part of this chapter draws heavily on Rosalind Picard's excellent book *Affective Computing* (Picard, 1997) to which the interested reader is directed.

17.1 Introduction

There are three basic aspects to affective computing which, put simply, are as follows.

1. Getting computers to recognize human emotions and react accordingly. A good example of this might be the use of a sensor in a motor car to detect whether or not the driver is angry or stressed. Sensors could be used to pick up on the fact that the driver is perspiring, is holding the steering wheel in a vice-like grip or has elevated blood pressure or heart rate. As statistics show that stress and anger are major contributory factors in road accidents, the car may then offer counselling, refuse to start (or something equally infuriating) or phone ahead to the emergency services. Another couple of examples, suggested by Picard and Healey (1997), are (a) the creation of an intelligent Web browser which responds to the wearer's degree of interest on a topic that the wearer found interesting, until it detected the interest fading, and (b) an affective assistant agent that could intelligently filter your e-mail or schedule, taking into account your emotional state or degree of activity.

2. Synthesizing emotion, that is, giving the impression of computers behaving or reacting with emotion. Here an example might be a machine showing signs of distress when a system crash has just destroyed several hours' work. The notion permeates much science fiction. A classic instance here is HAL, the onboard computer on the spaceship in Arthur C. Clarke's novel *2001: A Space Odyssey* (Clarke, 1968). In Kubrick's film version HAL's voice eloquently expresses fear as Dave, the astronaut, considers switching 'him' off. HAL's 'death' is agonizingly slow and piteous:

   'Dave, stop. Stop, will you? Stop, Dave. Will you stop, Dave? Stop, Dave. I'm afraid. I'm afraid, Dave. Dave, my mind is going. I can feel it. I can feel it. My mind is going. There is no question about it. I can feel it. I can feel it. I can feel it. I'm afraid.'

   In the film the dialogue is particularly poignant when contrasted with the unchanging expression of Hal's 'eye'.

3. Designing interactive systems which communicate or evoke human emotions. Designing for pleasure is one aspect of this – and commercially crucial for small consumer devices such as phones – but others include devices

which allow people to communicate affect at a distance, and the creation of virtual environments which support the treatment of phobias or attempt to evoke the feelings associated with particular places.

Whether or not computers could ever actually feel emotion is beyond this discussion, but science fiction novels such as *Do Androids Dream of Electric Sheep?* by Philip K. Dick (1968) offer interesting discussions of such themes. So why should we be interested in emotion? At first sight, the idea of 'giving' computers emotion seems to be counter-intuitive. Computers are the epitome of logic and the idea of acting emotionally has strong negative connotations – just think of Star Trek's Mr Spock. There is no denying that emotion (affect) has traditionally had a bad press.

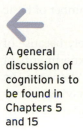

A general discussion of cognition is to be found in Chapters 5 and 15

The other side of the argument is the recognition that emotions are part of day-to-day human functioning. Emotion plays a significant part in decision making, social interaction and most aspects of what we would describe as cognition such as problem solving, thinking and perception.

Increasingly, these human activities and functions are supported by interactive systems, so an understanding of how emotion works can help us design systems which recognize, synthesize or evoke emotions. Or computers with affective capabilities might be more effective than conventional technology in making decisions with incomplete data – circumstances where affect helps human beings to respond quickly. Needless to say we must now turn to what psychologists have concluded over the years. Be warned that the research findings are less well agreed than many other aspects of human behaviour.

Challenge 17-1
Is it ethical to attempt to manipulate people's emotions through technology? Do new technologies differ from older media such as films in this respect?

17.2 Psychological theories of emotion

What are the basic human emotions? Ekman, Friesen and Ellsworth (1972) are widely quoted researchers who identified six basic emotions, namely, fear, surprise, disgust, anger, happiness and sadness. These are generally regarded as being universal – that is, recognized and expressed (facially at least) in the same way in all cultures. Ekman and Friesen (1978) went on to develop the 'facial action coding system' (FACS) which uses facial muscle movements to quantify emotions; an automated version of FACS has also been produced (Bartlett *et al.*, 1999). FACS is still the most widely used method of detecting emotion from facial expression.

Similar work has been undertaken by Plutchik (1980) who has argued for eight pairs of basic or primary emotions which can be combined to produce secondary emotions. In Figure 17-1 we can see that disgust and sadness combine to give the experience of remorse.

But what do we mean by basic or primary emotions? For Ekman this means that they have adaptive value (that is, they have evolved for some purpose), they are, as we have already said, common to everyone irrespective of culture and individual differences, and finally, they all have a quick onset – that is, they appear or start quickly. There is indeed some evidence of different patterns of activity in the ANS (the autonomic nervous system, which links organs such as the heart and stomach to the central nervous system embodied in the brain and spinal cord) for some of the basic emotions. Clearly it would be useful for the designers of affective systems if there is indeed a relatively small number of basic emotions to recognize or simulate.

However, the idea of basic emotions has been challenged, largely because of methodological issues. The main flaw, it is argued, is that the experiments of Ekman and others required participants to make a 'forced choice' between the eight emotions when identifying facial expressions rather than having a completely free choice of emotion terms. (This issue recurs in Section 17.3 in the discussion of one of Picard's experiments.) Instead of the eight emotions model, Russell and his colleagues propose that variations in just two dimensions – greater or lesser degrees of pleasure (or 'valence') and arousal – can describe the range of affective facial expressions (Russell and Fernandez-Dols, 1997). For

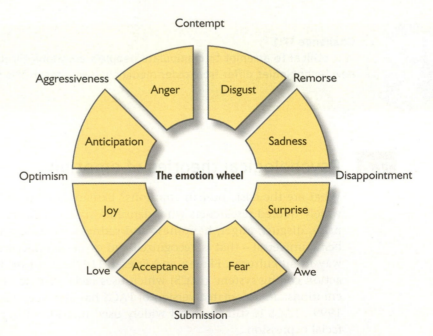

FIGURE 17-1 The 'emotion wheel' (*source: after Plutchik, 1980*)

example, 'happy' and 'content' lie at the pleasure end of the pleasure/displeasure dimension and entail slightly positive and slightly negative degrees of arousal respectively.

Both the Ekman and Russell approaches continue to be used in affective computing research and development.

It is generally agreed that emotions have three components:

- The *subjective experience* or feelings of fear and so on.

- The associated *physiological changes* in the ANS and the endocrine system (glands and the hormones released by them). We are aware of some but not all of these (e.g trembling with fear) and have little or no conscious control of them.

- The *behaviour* evoked, such as running away.

Box 17-1 Virtual environments

Consideration of these three aspects of emotions can be seen in the evaluation of virtual environments, as discussed in Chapter 22. Researchers evaluating the impact of a 'precipice' in the virtual environment might capture data on people's reported experience through questionnaires and interviews, their physiological changes through various sensors, and behaviour through observation. In convincing virtual environments reports of fear, increases in heart rate and retreat from the 'precipice' have all been found. In this context the self-report measures are often termed 'subjective', and behavioural and physiological measures 'objective'. However, as we shall see from this chapter, the so-called objective measures require a degree of interpretation by researchers, thereby introducing a substantial degree of subjectivity.

Beyond the simple cataloguing of emotion and its components are the various attempts to account for them. This, until relatively recently, was the province of philosophers until the early psychologists decided to try their hands at it. Probably the first of these were James and Lange.

The James–Lange theory

This theory, which dates from the 1890s, argues that action precedes emotions and the brain interprets the observed action or actions as emotions. So, for example, we see an axe-wielding maniac walking towards us: in response our pulse rate rises, we begin to sweat and we quicken our step – we run for our lives. These changes in the state of our body (increased pulse, sweating and running) are then interpreted as fear. Thus from interpreting the state of our bodies we conclude that we must be afraid.

This is summarized in Figure 17-2 but is obviously a rather crude model. What bodily state, for example, corresponds to the emotional state 'mildly disappointed but amused'?

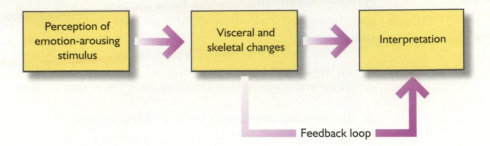

FIGURE 17-2 The James–Lange theory of emotion

The Cannon-Bard theory

Two psychologists working in the 1920s, Cannon and Bard, disagreed with the James–Lange theory and argued that when an emotion-arousing stimulus is first perceived, then actions follow from cognitive appraisal. They also noted that the same visceral changes occur in a range of different emotions. In their view, the thalamus (a complex structure in the brain) plays a central role by interpreting an emotional situation while simultaneously sending signals to the autonomic nervous system (ANS) and to the cortex which interprets the situation. The ANS is responsible for the regulation of unconscious functions like heart rate and the secretion of hormones such as adrenaline. This is shown in Figure 17-3.

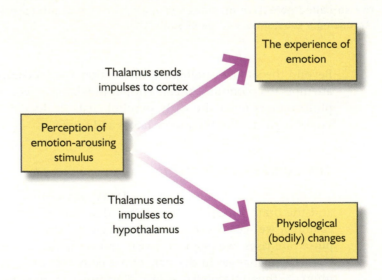

FIGURE 17-3 The Cannon–Bard theory

Cognitive labelling and appraisal theories: Schachter–Singer and Lazarus

On a more contemporary note, Schachter and Singer conducted a series of experiments in the 1960s, basically working along the same lines as James and Lange. However, Schachter and Singer favoured the idea that the experience of emotions arises from the **cognitive labelling** of physiological sensation. However, they also believed that this was not enough to explain the more subtle differences in emotion self-perception, i.e. the difference between anger and fear. Thus, they proposed that, once the physiological symptoms or arousal have been experienced, an individual will gather information from the immediate context and use it to modify the label they attach to the sensation. Figure 17-4 is an illustration of the Schachter and Singer model of emotion.

In a series of classic experimental studies they tested these ideas. The most famous of their studies was the adrenaline experiment (Schachter and Singer, 1962). In this experiment they told the participants that they would receive an injection of a vitamin (adrenaline is not a vitamin) and then test to see whether it had affected their vision. They also divided the participants into four groups:

- *Group A*: these people were given accurate information as to the effect of the 'vitamin', that is, sweating, tremor, feeling jittery.

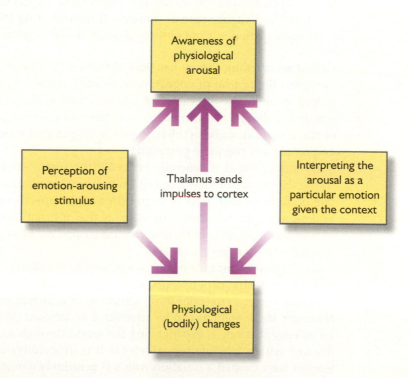

FIGURE 17-4 The Schachter–Singer theory

- *Group B*: they were given false information as to the effect of the 'vitamin', namely, itching and headaches.
- *Group C*: these people were told nothing.
- *Group D*: this group served as a control and were actually injected with saline (which has no side effects) and were also told nothing.

Before the (fake) vision test, the experimenters exposed everyone to an emotion-arousing stimulus which in practice was invoked by a stooge – a laughing, happy individual who fooled around or an angry, bad-tempered person who was seen to rip up a questionnaire. The participants were then asked to rate to what degree they had joined in with the stooge's behaviour and to report on how they felt. As expected, groups A and D said that they felt less likely to join in, while groups B and C said that they shared the stooge's apparent emotional state.

There have been several criticisms and qualifications of the theory arising from later research:

- The situation in the experiment is atypical, in that there is usually much less ambiguity about what is happening.
- We base our labelling of the emotion not just on the behaviour of others, but on our own past experiences and many other sources of information.
- Unexplained emotional arousal tends to be experienced as negative – for example, a vague sense of unease – thus indicating that the nature of emotional experience is not entirely determined by cognitive labelling.

Cognitive labelling theory has been developed further by Lazarus (1982), who proposed the notion of **cognitive appraisal**. According to cognitive appraisal theory some degree of evaluation of the situation always precedes the affective reaction, although this can be unconscious and does not prevent the immediacy of the sensation. Zajonc (1984), however, argues that some emotional responses do precede any cognitive processing.

In conclusion, it is generally believed that some cognitive evaluation occurs in the experience of emotion, but there is no overall agreement about the relative dominance and order of cognition and the affective reaction. For our work as designers, the 'take-home message' is that *it is not enough to induce emotional arousal, but the context of the arousal must support the identification of the particular emotion which it is intended to evoke*.

As a concrete instance of this, we return to the design issues for virtual environments. Many experiments have shown that events or features in the environment can engender some sensation of anticipation, or fear, or whatever. However, those feelings can be attenuated or labelled differently because of the knowledge that one is experiencing the world through an HMD (head-mounted display) within a laboratory. Moreover it is (hopefully) unlikely that one's colleagues have created a situation which is genuinely dangerous. Computer games minimize this problem by creating a strong narrative (or story) and a good deal

Box 17-2 The EMMA project

The EU-funded EMMA project is investigating the relationship between presence (the sense of 'being there') and emotions. EMMA uses tools such as virtual reality, intelligent agents, augmented reality and wireless devices to provide ways of coping with distressing emotions for users, including people with psychological problems. Emotions are stimulated through engagement with a virtual park, which changes in accordance with the emotion involved. Figure 17-5 shows the winter view of the park, designed to evoke sadness.

FIGURE 17-5 The 'sad' park developed in the EMMA project
(source: http://www.psychology.org/The%20EMMA%20Project.htm.
Courtesy of Mariano Alcañiz)

of interaction, both of which help to reduce the influence of the real world beyond the virtual one. It is necessary to use similar stratagems in the design of virtual worlds intended to evoke an emotional response, whether this is for entertainment, therapy, training or some other purpose.

17.3 Detecting and recognizing emotions

If technologies are to act upon human emotions, the first step is to recognize different affective states. As we have already seen from the psychology of emotion, human emotional states have physiological, cognitive and behavioural components. Behavioural and (some) physiological changes are of course most apparent to the outside world, unless we deliberately choose to disguise our feelings. Some signs of our affective state are more easily detected than others, however, as shown in Table 17-1. But while some of the physiological changes are obscure to other people, unless they are extremely physically close or have special monitoring equipment, they are virtually all accessible to a computer armed with the appropriate sensors.

TABLE 17-1 Forms of sentic modulation

Apparent to other people	Less apparent to other people
Facial expression	Respiration
Voice intonation	Heart rate, pulse
Gesture, movement	Temperature
Posture	Electrodermal response, perspiration
Pupilary dilation	Muscle action potentials
	Blood pressure

Source: adapted from Picard (1998) Affective Computing, *Table 1.1, p. 27. Published and reprinted by permission of The MIT Press*

However, detecting changes and attributing them to the correct emotion are two radically different problems. The second is much more intractable than the first, and one which causes much misunderstanding between people as well as potentially between people and machines.

Box 17-3   What if boredom couldn't be disguised?

We are of course capable of disguising the more overt symptoms of socially unacceptable emotions. Writing in the *Observer* newspaper of 7 September 2003, the columnist Victoria Coren speculates thus: 'What if (just as you blush when you're embarrassed or shiver when you're cold) you automatically removed your trousers when you were bored? The world of polite feigned interest would be dead and gone. You could smile all you liked as the boss made small talk – but no use, the trousers would be off... Everyone would have to try harder and waffle less... As things stand, boredom is too easily disguised, but we have tamed our wilder instincts.'

Basic capabilities for recognizing emotion

Technologies which successfully recognize emotion need to draw upon techniques such as pattern recognition and are likely to need to be trained to individual users – as for voice input technologies. The list below is reproduced from Picard (1997, page 55) and sets out what capabilities a computer requires to be able to discriminate emotions.

- **Input**. Receiving a variety of input signals, for example face, hand gestures, posture and gait, respiration, electrothermal response, temperature, electrocardiogram, blood pressure, blood volume, and electromyogram (a test that measures the activity of the muscles).

- **Pattern recognition**. Performs feature extraction and classification on these signals. For example, analyses video motion features to discriminate a frown from a smile.

- **Reasoning**. Predicts underlying emotion based on knowledge about how emotions are generated and expressed. This reasoning would require the system to reason about the context of the emotion and a wide knowledge of social psychology.

- **Learning**. As the computer 'gets to know' someone, it learns which of the above factors are most important for that individual, and gets quicker and better at recognizing his or her emotions.

- **Bias**. The emotional state of the computer, if it has emotions, influences its recognition of ambiguous emotions.

- **Output**. The computer names (or describes) the recognized expressions and the likely underlying emotion.

Progress has been made on many of these dimensions. Sensors and software which detect physiological changes such as heart rate, skin conductivity and so forth have long been available. However, there are practical issues with relying on this sort of data alone. The sensors themselves are too intrusive or awkward for most everyday uses, and the data requires expert analysis – or intelligent systems – to interpret the significance of changes. Also, individual physiological signs tend to indicate a general increase in arousal rather than specific emotions, and the same combinations of physiological signs can belong to different emotions – the signs of disgust and amusement are very similar, for example. Hence the need for the detection of other physical signs and/or pattern recognition to support computers in recognizing emotions.

Box 17-4 StartleCam

StartleCam is a wearable video camera, computer and sensing system, which enables the camera to be controlled via both conscious and preconscious events involving the wearer. Traditionally, a wearer consciously hits record on the video camera, or runs a computer script to trigger the camera according to some prespecified frequency. The system described here offers an additional option: images are saved by the system when it detects certain events of supposed interest to the wearer. The implementation described here aims to capture events that are likely to get the user's attention and to be remembered. Attention and memory are highly correlated with what psychologists call arousal level, and the latter is often signalled by skin conductivity changes; consequently, StartleCam monitors the wearer's skin conductivity. StartleCam looks for patterns indicative of a 'startle response' in the skin conductivity signal. When this response is detected, a buffer of digital images, recently captured by the wearer's digital camera, is downloaded and optionally transmitted wirelessly to a Web server. This selective storage of digital images creates a 'flashbulb' memory archive for the wearable which aims to mimic the wearer's own selective memory response. Using a startle detection filter, the StartleCam system has been demonstrated to work on several wearers in both indoor and outdoor ambulatory environments.

Recognizing emotions in practice

Pattern recognition was exploited in work by Picard and her team which was designed to explore whether a wearable computer could recognize a person's emotions over an extended period of time (Picard *et al.*, 2001). Over a period of 'many weeks', four sensors captured

- an electromyogram (indicating muscle activity)
- skin conductance
- blood volume pulse (a measure of arousal)
- respiration rate.

By using pattern recognition algorithms, eight emotions were distinguishable at levels significantly higher than chance. This does not mean, however, that computers can recognize people's emotions with reliable accuracy – the main reason being that the recognition software was constrained to a forced choice among the eight defined emotions. But as Picard notes, even partial recognition can be helpful – provided that the wrong emotion is not positively identified. Elsewhere at MIT work has been targeted at identifying rather more diffuse emotions such as 'the state you are in when all is going well with the computer' as contrasted with 'the state you are in when encountering annoying usability problems' (Picard, 2003). There is clear value here for developing applications which mitigate user frustration.

Tracking changes in facial expression offers another means of extending the data from physiology. In one recently reported experiment, for example, Ward, Bell and Marsden (Ward *et al.*, 2003) used a commercially available facial tracking package. The software works by tracking facial movements detected from a video of the face. The findings suggested the following.

- Facial expressions change in response to even relatively minor interaction events (in this case low-key surprising and amusing events, where the latter produced a weaker reaction).
- These changes were detected by the tracking software.

The authors concluded that the approach has potential as a tool for detecting emotions evoked by interacting with computers, but best performance in recognizing emotions (rather than simply tracking physical changes) is likely to be more successful with a combination of data sources.

Most applications of computer recognition of emotion lie in the development of systems which moderate their responses to respond to user frustration, stress or anxiety. However, there are worthwhile applications in domains beyond computing *per se*. One of the most significant of these is healthcare, where taking account of affective state is a vital element of patient care. In tele-healthcare, however, the clinician's scope for doing this is rather limited. Tele-healthcare is used for such applications as collecting 'vital signs' such as blood pressure, checking that medication has been taken or compliance with other medical directions. Lisetti *et al.* (2003) report early work on an application designed to improve affective information in this context. The system models the patient's affective state using multiple inputs from wearable sensors and other devices such as a camera. The identified emotions are then mapped on to intelligent agents which are embodied as avatars. The personal avatar is then able to 'chat' to the patient to confirm the emotions identified, and also to reflect this state in supplementing textual communication between patient and clinician (Figure 17-6).

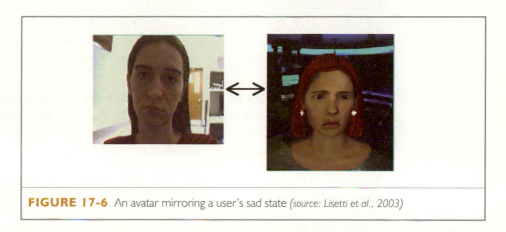

FIGURE 17-6 An avatar mirroring a user's sad state *(source: Lisetti et al., 2003)*

Preliminary results showed 90 percent success in recognizing sadness, 80 percent success for anger, 80 percent for fear and 70 percent for frustration.

Affective wearables

Wearables are discussed in general in Chapter 16, Section 16.11

'An affective wearable is a wearable system equipped with sensors and tools that enables recognition of its wearer's affective patterns' (Picard, 1997, page 227). Wearable computers are not merely portable like a laptop or a Walkman but can be used whether we are walking, standing or travelling. Wearables are also always on (in every sense). At present a wide range of prototypes of affective wearables already exist, though they are far from complete or polished and require regular attention/maintenance. To date most studies of affect involve the use of artificially induced emotion in the laboratory. One of the clear advantages to the design and use of affective wearables is that they can supply information on affect naturalistically. Affective wearables provide an opportunity to study and test theories of emotion. Currently, the most common examples of affective wearables are affective jewellery.

Figure 17-7 is an illustration of a piece of affective jewellery, in this instance an earring which also serves to display the wearer's blood volume pressure using photo-plethysmography. This involves using an LED to sense the amount of

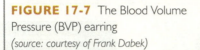

FIGURE 17-7 The Blood Volume
Pressure (BVP) earring
(source: courtesy of Frank Dabek)

FIGURE 17-8 Sampling biometric data
with a wearable device
(source: courtesy of Frank Dabek)

blood flow in the earlobe. From this reading both the heart beat and constriction of the blood vessel can be determined. In practice, the earring proved to be very sensitive to movement but future applications might include being able to gauge the wearer's reaction to consumer products.

Figure 17-8 is a further example of a system which can sample and transmit biometric data to larger computers for analysis. The data is sent by way of an infra-red (IR) link.

Challenge 17-2
We have established that affect stems partly from physiological sensations such as increases in pulse rate, perspiration and so on. Given that sensors exist to detect these changes, how could these phenomena be exploited in the design of interactive games? You should consider acceptability to users alongside technical feasibility.

Whether computers could ever be said to *experience* emotions has long been a matter for debate and is largely beyond the scope of this chapter, but in some ways this fascinating question does not fundamentally affect thinking on how to design for affect. We now move on to investigate what it means for a computer – or any other interactive system – to express emotion.

17.4 Expressing emotion

This is the other side of the affective computing equation. As we have seen, humans express emotions through facial expressions, body movements and posture, smaller-scale physiological changes and changes in tone of voice – which can be extended to the tone and style of written communications. With interactive systems, there are several aspects to consider:

- How computers which apparently express emotion can improve the quality and effectiveness of communication between people and technologies.

- How people can communicate with computers in ways which express their emotions.

- How technology can stimulate and support new modes of affective communication between people.

Can computers express emotion?

There is little argument that computers can *appear* to express emotion. Consider the expressions of the Microsoft Office Assistant – in Figure 17-9 he is 'sulking' when ignored by one of the authors. Whether such unsophisticated anthropomorphism enhances the interactive experience is debatable at best. As well as the irritation provoked in many users, there is a risk that people may expect much more than the system can provide.

Many of the more visible outward expressions of emotion introduced in Section 17.2 can be mimicked by computing applications. Even very simple facial models have been found capable of expressing recognizable emotions. A representative instance of this strand of research is reported by Schiano and her colleagues (Schiano *et al.*, 2000). The experiment tested an early prototype of a simple robot with 'a box-like face containing eyes with moveable lids, tilting eyebrows, and an upper and lower lip which could be independently raised or lowered from the center.' The face was made of metal and had a generally cartoon-like appearance – most of the subtle changes in facial folds and lines which characterize human emotions were missing. Despite these limitations human observers were able to identify the emotions communicated successfully.

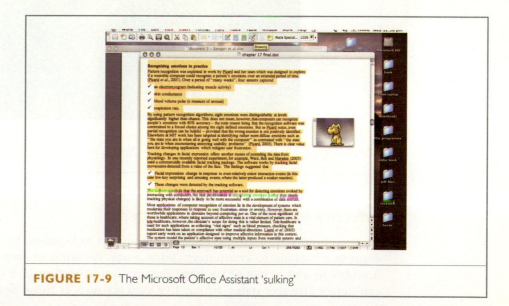

FIGURE 17-9 The Microsoft Office Assistant 'sulking'

The impact of even limited emotional expression is illustrated again by an experimental application at MIT, the 'relational agent' (Bickmore, 2003). This was designed to sustain a long-term relationship with users who were undertaking a programme to enhance exercise levels. The agent asked about, and responded to, users' emotions and expressed concern by modifying text and bodily expression where appropriate. The computer did not disguise its limited empathetic skills, nor were users really convinced of the reality of the 'feelings' displayed, but nevertheless the agent was rated significantly higher for likeability, trust, respect and feelings that it cared for them than a standard interactive agent.

By contrast, 'Kismet' (Figure 17-10), an expressive robot developed at MIT, provides a much more complex physical implementation. It is equipped with visual, auditory, and proprioceptive (touch) sensory inputs. Kismet can express apparent emotion through vocalization, facial expression, and adjustment of gaze direction and head orientation.

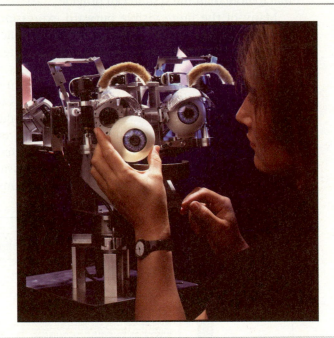

FIGURE 17-10 The Kismet robot *(source: Sam Ogden/Science Photo Library)*

Affective input to interactive systems

So, if computers can express apparent emotions to humans, how can humans express emotions to computers, aside from swearing or switching off the machine in a fit of pique? We have already seen in Section 17.3 that computers can detect affective states. Interactive systems such as those described in that section generally aim to monitor human affective signs unobtrusively so as to identify current emotions. But what if the human wants to communicate an emotion more actively, perhaps to influence the actions of her character in a game?

The affective, tangible user interface developed in the SenToy project (Paiva *et al.*, 2003) affords an imaginative treatment of this type of input problem. Manipulating the SenToy doll (Figure 17-11) so that it performs prespecified gestures and movements allows users to modify the 'emotions' and behaviour of a character in a game. Users can express anger, fear, surprise, sadness, gloating and happiness through gestures which are picked up by the doll's internal sensors and transmitted to the game software. Sadness, for example, is expressed through bending the doll forwards, while shaking it with its arms raised denotes anger. Actions carried out by the game character reflect the emotion detected.

In preliminary user trials with adults and children, sadness, anger and happiness were easily expressed without instruction, while gloating – requiring the doll to point and perform a little dance – was particularly difficult. In playing the game itself, this time with instructions for the gestures, all the emotions except surprise were expressed effectively. People became very involved with the game and the doll, and generally enjoyed the experience.

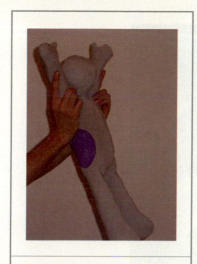

FIGURE 17-11 The SenToy affective interface
(source: Paiva et al., 2003)

Enhancing human affective communication

Researchers have also turned their attention to enhancing emotionally toned communication between people. Developments fuse highly creative conceptual design with (sometimes very simple) technology. Sometimes the idea is to convey a particular emotion – generally a positive one – but more often the aim is to foster emotional bonds through feelings of connection. Like much else in the affective computing field, these innovations are very much in their infancy at the time of writing with few realized in their final form.

A representative set of examples, designed for 'telematic emotional communication', is described by Tollmar and Persson (2002). Rather unusually in this domain, the inspiration behind the ideas comes not only from the designers or technologists, but also from ethnographic studies of households and their use of artefacts to support emotional closeness.

There is more about ethnography as a design technique in Chapter 29

They include '6th sense' (Figure 17-12), a light sculpture which senses body movement in the vicinity. If there is continuous movement for a time, the lamp sends this information to its sister lamp in another household. This lights up, indicating someone's presence in the first houehold – an unobtrusive way of staying in touch with the movements of a friend or family member.

FIGURE 17-12 6th sense

(source: Tollmar, K. and Persson, J. (2002) Understanding remote presence, Proceedings of 2nd Nordic Conference in HCI, NordiCHI' 02, Aarhus, October, pp. 41–49. © 2002 ACM, Inc. Reprinted by permission)

Further thoughts: Is affective computing possible or desirable?

Writing in the 2003 Special Issue on Affective Computing of the *International Journal of Human–Computer Studies*, Eric Hollnagel argues thus:

'Emotions can provide some kind of redundancy that may improve the effectiveness of communication. The affective modality of communication can furthermore be expressed by different means such as the grammatical structure (a polite request versus an order), the choice of words, or the tone of voice (or choice of colours, depending on the medium or channel). Yet neither of these represents affective computing as such. Instead the style of computing – or rather, the style of communication or interaction – is effectual. It does not try to transmit emotions as such but rather settles for adjusting the style of communication to achieve maximum effectiveness.

In work, people are generally encouraged to be rational and logical rather than affective and emotional. Indeed, every effort in task design, ergonomics, procedures and training goes towards that. From the practical perspective the need is therefore not to emulate emotions but to be able to recognize and control emotions. (This goes for human–human communication as well as human–machine interaction.) In cases where emotions are considered an advantage, they should be amplified. But in cases where they are a disadvantage (which include most practical work situations), they should be dampened. All work, with or without information technology, aims to produce something in a systematic and replicable manner – from ploughing a field to assembling a machine. Affects and emotions usually do not contribute to the efficiency of that but are more likely to have a negative influence. In contrast, art does not aim to produce identical copies of the same thing and emotions or nonlogical (not replicable) procedures and thinking are therefore valuable.

In conclusion, affective computing is neither a meaningful concept nor a reasonable goal. Rather than trying to make computers (or computing) affective, we should try to make communication effectual. Rather than trying to reproduce emotions we should try to imitate those aspects of emotions that are known to enhance the effectiveness of communication.'

Source: Hollnagel (2003), p. 69

17.5 Potential applications and key issues for further research

Table 17-2 is a list of potential 'areas of impact' for affective computing. 'Foreground' applications are those in which the computer takes an active, usually visible, role; in 'background' applications the computer is a more backstage presence.

Despite lists such as that in Table 17-2 which identify a compelling range of *potential* applications, affective computing is still a developing area. There are fundamental issues which remain to be clarified. Perhaps the most salient for interactive systems designers are:

- In which domains does affective capability make a positive difference to human–computer interaction, and where is it irrelevant or even obstructive?

- How precise do we need to be in identifying human emotions – perhaps it is enough to identify a generally positive or negative feeling? What techniques best detect emotional states for this purpose?

- How do we evaluate the contribution of affect to the overall success of a design?

TABLE 17-2 Potential 'areas of impact' for affective computing

	Human–human mediation	Human–computer interaction
Foreground	**Conversation** • Recognizing user emotional states **Wireless-mobile devices** • Representing–displaying user emotional states **Telephones** • Speech-synthetic affect and voice **Video teleconferences** • Affective iconics	**Graphical user interface** • Adaptive response based on physiological detection **Wearable computers** • Remote sensing of physiological states **Virtual environments** • Emotional capture and display **Decision support** • Affective elements of decision-making
Background	**Portholes (video/audio links between offices or other spaces)** • Affective interchanges – adaptive monitoring **Electronic badges** • Affective alert and display systems **Avatars** • Creation of personality via synthetic emotional content	**Smart house technology** • Sensors and affective architectures **Ubiquitous computing** • Affective learning **Speech recognition** • Monitoring voice stress **Gaze systems** • Movements and emotion detection **Intelligent agents** • Social and emotional intelligence

Source: adapted from McNeese (2003)

17.6 Designing for pleasure

While pleasure may not be a primary emotion, the giving and receiving of pleasure is, well, ... pleasurable. This section considers some of the practical techniques which can be used to create interactive systems which evoke pleasure.

While interactive systems were largely confined to the workplace, designing positively for pleasure was not a high priority for HCI designers – although phrases such as 'easy and pleasant to use' might appear in requirements specifications, in practice this often really meant 'not actively unpleasant to use'. Expectations are rather higher for systems we pay for ourselves and choose to enhance our personal lives. That being said, there is often no good reason why work systems should not be pleasing and even fun to use. Chao (2001), for instance, had the ingenious idea of adapting the computer game Doom as a process management application. Load on the system is managed by shooting the rampaging monsters which represent processes. This may seem an unduly violent approach, but as Chao points out, it mirrors the original UNIX command such as 'kill' (see Figure 17-13).

FIGURE 17-13 Killing a process in Chao's PSDoom application
(source: Chao, D. (2001) Doom as an interface for process management, Proceedings of CHI'01 Conference, Seattle, WA, 31 March–5 April, pp. 152–58. © 2001 ACM, Inc. Reprinted by permission)

Product designers in other domains have long been concerned with building in pleasure as a key marketing point, and as we have argued, pleasure is a focus for many design situations which were once much more dominated by the more functional aspects of usability. The Apple PowerBook G4 used by one of the authors of this chapter has clearly been designed with pleasure in mind. The G4 is advertised as being lightweight and elegant (it is only 3 cm thick) and – as originally launched – had a distinctive and attractive titanium shell. While all of these features contribute to the laptop's usability, they also contribute to the pleasure of owning, using and (perhaps) being seen with it. In Box 17-5 is some text from a magazine advertisement for a mobile phone – see how the functionality takes second place – and also the playful reference to tactile pleasures.

Patrick Jordan's book *Designing Pleasurable Products* illustrates the growing synergies between product design techniques and more traditional HCI and human factors. He argues effectively that designing for pleasure can be as important as ensuring that an interactive device is usable. Jordan describes pleasure as being 'the condition of consciousness or sensation induced by the enjoyment or anticipation of what is felt or viewed as good or desirable; enjoyment, delight, gratification'. In the context of interactive devices or products, designing for pleasure contributes to 'emotional, hedonistic and practical benefits' (Jordan, 2000, p. 12).

Box 17-5 Designed for desire

From the moment you slide back the cover of the SL55 you're smitten. You'll discover it's more than just a pretty face, with polyphonic ring tones, a full colour screen and MMS picture messaging.

The new SL55. Nothing without your touch.

Be inspired.

Source: ad for Siemens SL55 mobile phone, *Observer Magazine*, 23 November 2003

Jordan's approach draws heavily on the work of Lionel Tiger, who is an anthropologist and has developed a framework for understanding and organizing thinking about pleasure. This framework is discussed at length in Tiger's book *The Pursuit of Pleasure* (Tiger, 1992). Tiger has argued that there are four dimensions or aspects of pleasure. These are *physio*-pleasure, *socio*-pleasure, *psycho*-pleasure and *ideo*-pleasure. As you will see, the way these are conceptualized does not always fit neatly with psychological theories of emotion, and different aspects of pleasure cannot always be partitioned cleanly. That being said, the four dimensions do form a useful checklist for designers. We now discuss each in turn briefly.

Physio-pleasure

More about ergonomics and anthropometrics – body measurement data – in Chapter 7

This is concerned with the body and the senses. Physio-pleasure arises from touching or handling devices or from their smell – think about the smell of a new car, or the pleasingly solid but responsive feel of a well-designed keyboard. This sort of pleasure is also derived from using devices which fit seamlessly with the human body – although this is more usually noticed when the fit is less than ideal. The physical fit of technology to people has long been a central concern for ergonomists working on the design of new products.

Socio-pleasure

Socio-pleasure arises from relationships with others. Products and devices which have a socio-pleasurable aspect either facilitate social activity or improve relationships with others. A very obvious example is the key role which text messaging has rapidly acquired in enhancing social communication for many people. Others are the devices for person-to-person affective communication described in Section 17.4. Pleasure derived from enhanced status or image is also considered a socio-pleasure, and of course is much exploited by the vendors of successive generations of small personal technologies.

Psycho-pleasure

Psycho-pleasure (short for psychological pleasure) refers to cognitive or emotional pleasure in Tiger's framework. Given that pleasure is an emotion in itself and any emotion – as we have just seen – has a cognitive component, this is a rather circular definition. If not too closely inspected, this dimension of pleasure is useful for pulling together sources of pleasure such as the perceived ease of use and effectiveness of a device and the satisfaction of acquiring new skills. For some people, learning a complex programming language generates a degree of satisfaction which would never be obtained from moving icons around the screen in a GUI.

Ideo-pleasure

Ideo-pleasure (ideological pleasure) concerns our values – things one holds dear or meaningful – and aspirations. We are more likely to enjoy using items which fit our value system. Aspects which come readily to mind here might include a respect for careful craftsmanship and design, the desirability or otherwise of having an obviously expensive device, and our perceptions of the trading ethics of the supplier (for example, commercial software as against freely available shareware). A recent series of IBM advertisements on British television seems to be aiming to invoke ideo-pleasure by emphasizing the professionalism and reliability of a well-established company.

The four dimensions in practice

It should be remembered that these four dimensions are simply a method of structuring design thought rather than a description of the nature of pleasure itself.

Let's see how they work by returning to the example of the G4 laptop and analysing it against Tiger's four pleasures.

- Physio-pleasure. The machine is light, the texture of the titanium shell is pleasing and the keyboard is responsive. (Incidentally, the pleasure rather diminishes when the G4 has been dropped a small distance and the light titanium shell acquires a crumpled corner, making it wobble in use.)
- Socio-pleasure. Certainly when first released, owning a G4 might be thought to enhance image as it distinguishes the owner as someone with the discernment to adopt a stylish remodelling of the laptop. There is also a certain socio-pleasure in being part of a small (rather administratively inconvenient) group of Apple devotees among a much larger community of PC users in our particular workplace.
- Psycho-pleasure. The G4 provides relatively seamless integration between different media and so generates satisfaction from streamlining many work tasks.
- Ideo-pleasure. For some consumers, Apple products remain an embodiment of independence, creativity and free-thinking – attributes inherited from the early image of the corporation. Whether this is still an accurate perception is not the point: it is enough that people feel that it is so.

Box 17-6 Pleasure and culture

The make-up of the different aspects of pleasure, particularly ideo-pleasure, varies between different cultures. Much work on identifying the characteristics of different ethnic and national cultures has been carried out by the anthropologist Geert Hofstede. Hofstede (1994) described five key dimensions along which cultures vary. Very much summarized, these are:

- Power-distance – how far people accept that power and influence are distributed unequally in society
- Individualism – how far people see themselves as distinguishable from wider society
- Masculinity – reflecting values of toughness and achievement
- Uncertainty avoidance – how far ill-defined and ambiguous situations are tolerated
- Long-term orientation – the extent to which people see the present in the context of the future.

Hofstede's extensive research was able to classify nations along these dimensions. To take just a couple of illustrations, some continental European countries are uneasy with uncertainty, respect authority and are not very individualistic, whereas the US and the UK display the reverse characteristics. Clearly what gives pleasure would be rather different for these two cultural groups.

Challenge 17-3
Using Tiger's classification, what do you consider is the main pleasure evoked by the design of one of the interactive devices/systems you enjoy owning or using? If possible, compare your response to those of one or more colleagues for a similar device.

Pleasure, PACT and personas

Requirements analysis is discussed in Chapter 9

Analysing existing products is all very well as a way of thinking about the different aspects of pleasure, but how can we use these ideas to help generate new design concepts? A little thought suggests that a pleasure-focused design is likely to be more appropriate in some circumstances than in others. A PACT analysis of the design space is helpful as a starting point, coupled with the design brief if you have one, and the results of requirements work. (The PACT concept was introduced in Part I and revisited in Part III. As you will remember, the acronym stands for People, Activities, Contexts and Technologies.)

We have already encountered personas in Chapter 2.

Having scoped the possibilities for pleasure, how should we decide on what in particular might delight our users? The features that contribute to pleasure of course vary from individual to individual and from person to person: one way of dealing with this is to construct **personas** or profiles of typical users and use them to refine design thinking. Here they are used to embody the four pleasures and stimulate design thinking. Personas embody the relevant characteristics of people who are typical of intended users for the product – essentially, they are archetypes. They are constructed from data gathered through interviews, focus groups, observations and often market-research related activities. Following Jordan's worked examples, let us consider a persona-based four-pleasure analysis for 'Mary'. Mary is a single, 28-year-old Irish woman working as a research assistant in a university department in a British university. In this example, her persona has been constructed to embody the educated, lively women who are expected to purchase and use a new multi-functional PDA (personal digital assistant).

Table 17-3 holds a partial profile for Mary which could be used to analyse how far different aspects of the PDA's design match these pleasures.

TABLE 17-3 Mary's four pleasures

Physio	Socio	Psycho	Ideo
Swimming under water	Going out for a drink with friends	Reading travel literature	Supportive of animal rights
Making ceramics (e.g. pots)	Enjoys working as part of a team	Wearing 'classically' cut clothes	Being with friends and family
		Listening to folk music	
		Getting things done efficiently	

Other methods to support designing for pleasure

Many of the conventional design methods described in Part II of this book can be adapted to incorporate a focus on pleasure. Jordan (2000) suggests a number of variations – here are just two examples.

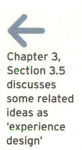

Chapter 3, Section 3.5 discusses some related ideas as 'experience design'

The pleasure checklist and the pleasure with products index

This involves developing sets of three or four statements for each of Tiger's four pleasures as applied to the design, for example 'this would make my life easier' (psycho-pleasure), 'the use of recycled materials pleases me' (ideo-pleasure) and 'my friends would be envious when they saw me using this' (socio-pleasure). For a deeper understanding, the checklist can be complemented by a list of specific product features to be checked according to whether they are liked or disliked. Jordan also helpfully provides a full, validated, pre-prepared questionnaire – the 'Pleasure with Products (General Index)'.

Laddering

This market-research derived technique can be effective for getting at people's underlying motivations and values, and is thus particularly suitable for exploring ideo-pleasure. The idea is that starting from a specific like or dislike about the product, a series of 'why' questions are put to a participant until they can explain no further. There is a strong resemblance to a conversation with a three-year-old, as can be seen from the example below, so some participants may find the experience exhausting and there is a risk that people provide artificial explanations simply to pacify the interviewer! However, it does have the advantage of directly linking specific features to aspects of pleasure. Here is an example laddering interview based on some of our work in introducing PDAs to a medical context (Turner et al, 2003). The interview content is fictitious, but the point about size was a real concern.

> *Investigator*: Please tell me something you don't like about this product.
> *Participant*: I don't like the size.
> *Investigator*: What don't you like about the size?
> *Participant*: It's too small.
> *Investigator*: Why is being small a bad thing?
> *Participant*: Because it could easily drop out of my pocket and get lost.
> *Investigator*: What is particularly bad about losing the PDA?
> *Participant*: Losing control of patients' personal medical data.
> *Investigator*: Why do you want to control medical data?
> *Participant*: Because security of medical data is vital.
> *Investigator*: Why is security vital?
> *Participant*: Because otherwise there would be no trust between doctor and patient.
> *Investigator*: Why is trust between doctor and patient important?
> *Participant*: It just is.

A 'ladder' can then be constructed linking features to perceived cost–benefits and, ultimately, values. In this case:

Trust between doctor and patient is important

↑

Confidentiality is central to trust

↑

Potential undesirable consequences for confidentiality

↑

Easy to misplace

↑

Small size

Other approaches

Researchers have also developed more visual ways for participants to relate design features to aspects of pleasure. Antikainen, Kälviäinen and Miller (2003) describe the 'Visual Research Package'. This comprises graphically based computer software which – among other things – allows participants to organize pictures of design variants along a 'pleasing–unpleasing' scale, or to match designs to types of users. The results can then be analysed by the software, and interpreted alongside interview data which is collected after participants have completed the computer. There is no reason, of course, why a similar process could not be conducted by hand. Another computer-based measure is exploited by Desmet and Dijkhuis

(2003) in their design of a more desirable wheelchair for children. This is the PrEmo self-report instrument, which represents seven pleasant and seven unpleasant feelings through different animated cartoon characters (Figure 17-14). Participants select those which best correspond to their own emotions.

FIGURE 17-14 Four of the characters from the PrEmo instrument – fascination, satisfaction, disgust and contempt
(source: Desmet, P. and Dijkhuis, E. (2003) A wheelchair can be fun: a case of emotion-driven design, Proceedings of DPPI '03 Conference, Pittsburgh, PA, 23–26 June, pp. 22–27. © ACM, Inc. Reprinted by permission)

However, given the elusive, subtle and personal qualities of pleasure, you are likely to gather richer results from approaches which prompt unconstrained exploration and free-form comment than from strongly task-based and structured techniques. Several possibilities are described in more detail in Chapter 22 – which is about evaluation – but briefly they are:

- Co-discovery – having participants explore and discuss an application in pairs.
- Conversation to camera – participants tell their thoughts about a product to a video-camera. This can be less inhibiting for some people than describing personal feelings face-to-face.
- Participant diaries, which can be in written or digital media, and help to capture the evolving relationship with the system.

Summary and key points

In this chapter we have explored the theory of emotions and seen how this has been applied to the developing field of affective computing. We have discussed what is required for technologies to display apparent emotion, to detect and respond to human emotions and to support human affective communication – potentially a very diverse and technically advanced set of capabilities – but we have suggested that an approximate identification and representation of emotion may suffice for many purposes. Applications have been identified which range from affective communication to support telemedicine to interacting with games. In the last section we concluded by outlining practical techniques for designing for one particular emotion – pleasure – which expand the traditional repertoire of human-centred designers.

Further reading

Jordan, P.W. (2000) *Designing Pleasurable Products*. Taylor & Francis, London.
A practical and interesting guide to designing for pleasure, closely informed by the author's own experience and with many real-life examples. Includes a ready-made 'pleasure' questionnaire.

Picard, R.W. (1998) *Affective Computing*. MIT Press, Cambridge, MA.
A stimulating discussion of the theoretical and technological issues grounded in (then) state-of-the-art research at MIT.

International Journal of Human–Computer Studies, no. 59 (2003) – special issue on Affective Computing.
Includes review papers, opinion pieces, theoretical treatments and applications and so provides an excellent snapshot of the state of affective computing in the early twenty-first century.

Norman, D.A. (2004) *Emotional Design: Why We Love (or Hate) Everday Things*. Basic Books, New York.
A very readable account of the relationship between emotions and design.

More advanced/specialized

Tiger, L. (1992) *The Pursuit of Pleasure*. Little, Brown & Co., Boston, MA.
A comprehensive exposition of the framework on which much of Jordan's research is based.

Proceedings of Designing Pleasurable Products and Interfaces, 23–26 June 2003, Pittsburgh, PA (available through the ACM digital library)
Another snapshot of current developments, this time on products which evoke pleasure and methods to support their design. Note that much of the material is not concerned with interactive systems *per se*, but many of the ideas can be applied to this domain.

Comments on challenges

Challenge 17-1
There are many possible arguments here. Our view on this is that it is probably acceptable as long as people can choose whether to use the technology, they are aware that the technology has affective aspects and they can stop using it at any point. Among the differences from older media are the interactive nature of new technologies and the possibility that giving technology reactions and expressions which mimic human emotions may mislead people into inappropriately trustful behaviour.

Challenge 17-2
It would be possible, for example, to detect that a games player's state of arousal had remained unchanged since starting the game and step up the pace accordingly, or conversely to slow things down to provide a calmer interlude after a sustained period of high arousal readings. I would guess that people might prefer not to wear (and fix, and calibrate) physical sensors, so perhaps non-contact monitoring, e.g. of facial expression, might be an acceptable solution.

Challenge 17-3
As you will probably find, in our context, Tiger's classification is a useful guide to thinking about pleasure rather than a hard-and-fast set of categories. You are likely to find that people's responses vary – even for an identical product – so think about how such information could be used to guide design choices.

Exercises

1. How far is it necessary to understand the theory of human emotions in order to design affective technologies? Illustrate your answer with examples.

2. Develop a storyboard showing the proposed use of an affective operating system designed to respond when it detects frustration and tiredness in its user.

3. Consider a standard desktop PC and a small interactive device such as a palmtop, mobile phone or digital camera. Choose recent examples.

   (a) Analyse each device against Tiger's four principles, attempting to determine which (if any) the designers were intending to evoke, and note the results of your analysis.

   (b) Conduct a PACT analysis for each of the two products you have chosen. (PACT – People, Activities, Contexts and Technologies – was introduced in Part I.) Taking account of the results of this, discuss whether pleasure should be an important design feature for the technologies in question. Explain your reasons.

   (c) Which requirements, design and evaluation techniques best support capturing the concept of pleasure? What modifications are required to conventional techniques? (You may need to refresh your memory by a quick review of Part III of this book.)

Part V:

Techniques for Interactive Systems Design and Evaluation

Introduction

Part V revisits interactive systems design methods and extends the material which we presented in Part III.

We start with a condensed version of Beyer and Holtzblatt's Contextual Design method. The method is well used by practitioners. Our lighter-weight version takes the main steps in the process for interactive systems design and presents them in a form usable by students and for smaller projects or small (or single-person) design teams. This material forms Chapters 18 and 19, which are intended to be read as a pair. Contextual design as presented here is a complement to the design process described in Part III, although it draws on the same human-centred philosophy and shares many of the same basic techniques.

Chapter 20 is a review of the many forms of task analysis, when and where the technique is best applied, and step-by-step instructions for conducting a hierarchical task analysis.

Chapters 21 and 22 return to evaluation, perhaps the main element of interactive systems 'design' work in practice. Chapter 21 offers a wider selection of 'general purpose' techniques to complement those in Chapter 12, and introduces the reader to some currently contentious issues. Special-purpose evaluation techniques, including those for CSCW, VR and small devices, comprise Chapter 22.

We envisage that Chapters 18 and 19 would form the basis of a module or part-module on the contextual design method. Chapter 20 can be added into any module where task analysis is covered, although the background material is best suited to more advanced modules. The evaluation techniques in the final pair of chapters are intended mainly for reference in practical work, but could also play a part in more advanced teaching. The issues discussed at the end of Chapter 21, however, should be included in any teaching beyond that of basic techniques.

Contextual Design 1:
The Contextual Interview and work modelling

Aims

This chapter and the next introduce **Contextual Design – CD** (Beyer and Holtzblatt, 1998). The two chapters should be read in sequence. In this chapter we introduce the first two elements of Contextual Design, namely, the **Contextual Inquiry** and **work modelling.** Beyer and Holtzblatt described CD as '... an approach to defining software and hardware systems that collects multiple customer-centred techniques into an integrated design process. CD makes data gathering from customers the base criteria for deciding what the system should do and how it should be structured.' The method is a well-documented and practical set of tools and techniques which have been quite widely used by practitioners. It is a self-contained method, and can be regarded as an alternative **user-centred design** approach to that described in Chapters 8 to 14. One of the great strengths of contextual design is that its range of tools and techniques can be used in an *ad hoc* manner – in a variety of different contexts as the analyst or designer requires.

Although its creators have focused on building generic systems (e.g. hotel booking systems which work for most medium-sized hotels, or medical records systems which will work for most small doctors' surgeries) it has the advantage of being very flexible and can be applied in many different contexts.

This is a strongly *practical* chapter and will be illustrated throughout by an extended worked example. Occasionally parallel examples will be provided too. After studying this chapter you should be able to:

- Conduct a Contextual Inquiry
- Create the five different work models, namely
  - Flow models
  - Sequence models
  - Artefact models
  - Cultural models
  - Physical models.

Contextual Design is a comprehensively documented method, which takes the authors more than 470 pages to explain in their *Contextual Design* handbook (Beyer and Holtzblatt, 1998). Necessarily, these two chapters provide only 'edited highlights' and draw heavily on Beyer and Holtzblatt's own material. Among the omissions here are the more team-focused techniques, since we are very aware that many user-centred design students and practitioners work as singletons. That being said, the material in these two chapters is enough to get you started with a small-scale CD project.

In this and the next chapter there are no separate exercises at the end of the chapters. Instead and in the spirit of Contextual Design we have embedded (contextualized, if you like) a series of challenges in each of the chapters.

18.1 Introduction

The Contextual Design method was developed by consultants Karen Holtzblatt and Hugh Beyer drawing on their extensive user-centred design experience at DEC (Digital Equipment Corporation) and elsewhere. The method is a mixture of:

- Familiar techniques with a new twist, such as the contextual interview
- Established techniques integrated into the method, such as paper prototypes and scenarios
- Novel modelling techniques for representing work practice and the new design, such as the flow model and the user environment diagram
- Team building and data sharing techniques – which are not treated in this book.

On being an analyst/designer

As a starting point to learning and applying the methods of Contextual Design perhaps the single most important aspect to be grasped is one of attitude. Your role is one of a proactive analyst, a 'detective', an 'archaeologist', in short someone who is attempting to make sense of a real-life working situation. Specific

Further thoughts: The roots of user-centred techniques

A little history. Many of the techniques in contextual design originated in the Scandinavian participatory design movement of the early 1980s. This was very much a politically informed initiative, with the emphasis on workplace democracy and empowering workers as co-designers of work practice and the tools supporting it. Techniques such as paper prototyping were invented so that workers – the future end-users – were not disadvantaged in working with technologists. The most influential of such initiatives was the work of Pelle Ehn and colleagues in the UTOPIA project (Bødker *et al.*, 1987). Since that date, the techniques have been adopted and adapted by practitioners elsewhere in Europe and the USA. However, much of the emphasis on worker ownership and empowerment has been lost along the way. As adapted in Contextual Design, paper prototypes and other user-focused techniques aim simply to create a more effectively designed system which may or may not enhance its users' working lives. Moreover, users are no longer co-designers but sources of data for the design team. The focus is on producing efficient, well-grounded systems for customers or clients.

working situations are made up of people who know their jobs much better than you, the analyst, ever will; it is your job to understand theirs, to understand their responsibilities, the tools they use, where they work and why they do what they do. Having understood this, your job is then to design for an interactive system or application which matches the needs of its intended users. Its intended users are people engaged in purposive work.

Ideally, applying Contextual Design is a team activity as it requires a wide range of skills ranging from the technical to what are often described as 'people skills' – the ability to talk to people and make sense of what they do (and do not) say.

Why Contextual Design?

There are other discussions of context in Part I and Chapter 8

Why *Contextual* Design rather than some other form of design? To understand this we need to define and consider the importance of context. Context is often defined as the 'human, physical, organizational, historical and social environment in which a technology is used'. There are, of course, numerous other definitions and contextual design makes no claims to offer a sole solution to the problem of context.

Contextual Design is a practical design method which focuses on fitting software and hardware solutions to the human, physical (and so forth) environment. Many of the horror stories concerned with yet another government IT (information technology) disaster can be traced to a poor match between the system and the context of its use.

So far we have given a very high-level (vague) description of context because context varies with, errh, context and what is essential in one context may be a mere detail in another (and vice versa).

Challenge 18-1

What contextual factors might you take into account in designing a customer database for the following?

- A small multimedia start-up company
- An insurance company call centre
- A hospital surgical unit.

Hint: think about the conditions under which the database is likely to be used.

Contextual Design supports the designer in finding out about context and translating these factors into the design of products which meet customers' needs. Note the term *customer*: in CD, a customer is anyone who uses the system in question either directly or indirectly – it's a similar concept to the term 'stakeholder' often found in user-centred design. In CD *user* is generally only used for those who use the technological system themselves.

When should Contextual Design be used?

Contextual Design is written as a method for the design of generic products across a particular customer sector. For example, the aim might be to develop an administration system for small to medium-sized hotels such as the one we focus on in these two chapters. As well as keeping data customer-centred, CD supports designers in collecting data from different organizations and sites and distilling common elements. CD is also intended to be used by a design team, which means that its models (for example) are helpful for sharing data and interpretations as well as recording them. This does not mean that CD cannot be used for smaller projects, but you are likely to find that using all the techniques recommended on a one-person project for a small company is not worthwhile. Indeed, the method is designed to be modular. Among the smaller projects we have been involved in where a slimmed-down version of CD has proved beneficial have been an administration system for a voluntary organization, a redesigned customer information system for an airport, and a revamped customer enquiry system for a satellite television company. The process is really intended for redesigning work practice, although some aspects could be useful in other contexts – a physical model of home layout, for example, could be helpful when considering home technologies.

The first stage in CD is CI – **Contextual Inquiry**.

18.2 Contextual Inquiry

Contextual Inquiry (CI) is the name given to the first stage of Contextual Design. It is essentially a combination of a focused interview and observation. As Holtzblatt and Beyer observe,

'The core premise of CI is very simple: go where the customer works, observe the customer as he or she works, and talk to the customer about the work. Do that, and you can't help but gain a better understanding of your customer.'

CI is made up from a number of techniques which are designed to help the analyst understand what it is your client needs. (In these chapters we use the term 'analyst' to refer to someone finding out about existing work, and 'designer' when we reach the later stages. Of course, analyst and designer may be the same person in practice.) CI brings together a number of techniques including interviewing (called, unsurprisingly, the **Contextual Interview**), artefact collection and observation under one unifying theme or philosophy.

There are four guiding principles of contextual inquiry which are:

- Context
- Partnership
- Interpretation
- Focus.

Context

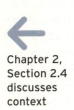

Chapter 2, Section 2.4 discusses context

Here the advice is to go to the customer's workplace and observe how work is actually carried out. This allows the analyst to experience the rich everyday detail of work. It is best to focus on concrete data and tasks rather than generalized abstraction, for example to steer customers away from statements like 'usually ...' or 'in our group, we ...'. Occasionally these observations may need to be supplemented by retrospective explanations ('When I saw you checking the bill against the bar receipts, why was that exactly?') from the customer.

Partnership

One of the core premises of CD – and of its Scandinavian ancestors – is that analyst and customer are expert in their different fields. The analyst should be looking for patterns and structure in the work while the customer contributes her knowledge of how the work really gets done. As redesign ideas occur, they can also be discussed. Thus customers can genuinely influence the analyst's interpretations of the work and design ideas based upon it. The relationship is characterized by Beyer and Holtzblatt as the **master–apprentice model**. The customer 'teaches' the analyst by doing the work and talking about it while working. This helps avoid some problems of tacit (implicit, unspoken) knowledge. The periods of observation should be interspersed with discussion. This is well illustrated with a couple of quotations from Beyer and Holtzblatt themselves:

'One customer said he would not use a manual's index to find the solution to a problem: "It's never in the index." He could not say what led him to this conclusion ... All his bad experiences were rolled up into one simple abstraction: it's not there. But when we watched him looking things up, we could see that he was using terms from his work domain, but the index listed parts of the system. We learned what the problem was and what we could do to fix it.'

'A customer was unable to describe how she made her monthly report. When asked to create it, she pulled out her last report and started filling in the parts. The old report was her reminder of how to create the next one.'

Beyer and Holtzblatt (1998, p. 44)

Interpretation

The hotel case study is introduced in Section 8.3

It is not enough simply to observe and document: the analyst must interpret workplace data so that it is properly understood. For example, in our hotel case study, the receptionist can be seen crossing off guests' names on a paper list as they arrive as well as updating data on-screen. Why should this be happening, and what does this mean for a redesigned system? Possible reasons might be:

- The on-line guest data system is unreliable
- Not all reservations are on the system
- The receptionist isn't confident she is using the system properly
- It is easier for other staff to consult a paper copy.

The analyst should reflect her interpretations back to the customer and listen to the response. Be prepared to be wrong.

Focus

Each site visit and interview needs a focus, though concentrating on one part of the work helps to see detail but at the expense of other aspects. If there is a team of analysts, sharing data in the group can help to avoid the problem. While the interview is happening, one sign of an over-narrow focus might be unexpected actions by the customer. In our experience, the opposite difficulty commonly occurs when customers divert conversation into areas of their job which are not pertinent to the problem in hand. In this case, a few tactful prompts usually help to refocus. If not, treat the information as useful general background to organizational life and culture.

Practicalities of the Contextual Interview

As for any work at customer sites, it is essential to have a notebook and ideally a tape-recorder or video-camera. The first 15 minutes or so should take care of the usual introductions, the obtaining of permissions, explanations of the process and the focus for the interview.

Then the Contextual Interview itself follows. Its length will depend on the nature of the job and the time available, but around 2–3 hours' mixed conversation and observation is not unusual. In many jobs, your interviewee may move around the workplace – be prepared to follow them. You should try to observe as many different types of everyday tasks as possible, but some will be more difficult to see 'live' than others. Here are some suggestions for capturing this sort of data.

- Intermittent, unscheduled and brief tasks, e.g. recovering from a system crash:
  - Have customers note the event, save any related artefacts, then discuss in a follow-up interview.
- Uninterruptible work, e.g. a training session or client meeting:
  - Videotape or take detailed notes and review later with the customer.
- Very lengthy collaborative projects, e.g. major engineering design projects:
  - Interview different customers at different stages in the process
  - Collect project documents and other artefacts and walk through the process with customers.
- Focused, fine-grained tasks, such as interacting with a complex piece of software:
  - Videotape and review later with customer. A word of warning: while video recording may seem an attractive solution to capturing data, it should be treated with caution. The appeal of simply pointing a camera at your customer (or whoever) and reviewing the data later must be balanced against the fact that an hour's videotape will take significantly longer to analyse off-line than an hour – perhaps twice or three times as long.

Chapter 2, Section 2.3 presents more on activities in general

Finally, use the last 15 minutes of the interview to review what you have learned, remembering to ask your interviewee what you might have missed.

More about interviewing in general in Chapter 9

Who to interview?

Beyer and Holtzblatt's rule of thumb is that for a product designed to support work in different organizations, two or three people should be interviewed for each work role in each of four to six organizations. The organizations should ideally represent the diversity to be found in the market sector, in terms of technological sophistication, size, physical organization and so forth. In practice, we find that we often have to be flexible about who we see. Customer organizations do not always supply the 'right' people, and contextual inquiry sessions often suggest other people who should be involved.

Challenge 18-2

Think about a medium-sized, neighbourhood restaurant. Imagine you are planning a contextual inquiry for a system which will allow waiting staff to take orders on a hand-held device which can then be downloaded to a PC and displayed in the kitchen. The system also generates bills and keeps track of which dishes have been sold. The restaurant personnel comprise:

- The owner, who runs the business and devises menus in consultation with the chef
- The chef, who runs the kitchen, devises menus and new dishes, orders supplies
- Two under-chefs, who cook the food and deliver the dishes to waiting staff
- A part-time baker, who comes in the early morning, leaving before lunch preparation starts
- Three waiting staff, who take orders from customers to the kitchen and serve food
- A wine waiter
- Two washers-up
- A part-time cleaner
- A part-time book-keeper, who prepares the accounts.

List which people you would interview and what aspects of their jobs you would focus upon.

18.3   Contextual Design: work modelling

The next stage of the CD process is to document the raw data obtained from interviews and observation as a set of models. The models each represent a different facet of work. We illustrate the models through a case study which we introduce here.

The Swan Hotel case study

You are a member of a small team of analysts, designers and developers and your employer has won a contract to specify, design and implement an integrated booking, billing and inventory system for small hotels. We now assume that you have conducted your contextual inquiry, having interviewed key members of staff, collected artefacts and observed the running of the hotel.

Your client requires a generic hotel booking system which needs to be simple, easy to use and geared to small, privately owned hotels rather than large hotel chains. The system needs to be linked to the Web as small hotels generate much of their business that way. Currently, small hotels typically have a mixture of simple paper-based booking systems (in the form of a large diary), a paper-based inventory system and a PC-based billing system. You are able to visit a number of different small hotels, observe how they work, interview their staff and will have access to examples of their paperwork, accounts, bills and other documentation.

What follows is a description of the Swan Hotel which one of the team has already visited. We focus on the role of the receptionist for the examples which follow.

The Swan Hotel

The Swan Hotel is a small family-owned establishment located in northern England. The Swan has 12 double rooms, one small suite complete with a f our-poster bed, a restaurant/breakfast room and a public bar. The hotel is very busy and always fully booked during the summer months and offers short breaks during other times of the year. Older customers who particularly like the friendly atmosphere and helpful staff make up a substantial proportion of the guests.

The hotel team is made up from a core of permanent staff including the *general manager* (also the owner), the *catering manager*, the *bar manager*, the *receptionists* and the *rooms manager*. *Waiters* and *waitresses*, *cleaning* and *bar staff* are usually employed on a seasonal basis. More staff are employed during the summer and fewer in the winter.

Reception is located opposite the main entrance and is manned from 0700 until 2230 by two shifts of receptionists. A member of the bar staff looks after the reception between 2230 and midnight.

The receptionists are responsible for the following tasks.

- *Checking-in guests*. This involves checking their names against the details in the booking system, allocating them a room and issuing the key from the key board.

- *Checking-out guests*. This involves preparing their bills, including totalling the cost of their room or rooms and any bar and restaurant bills, settling the bill by taking payment usually by way of credit or debit card, and returning the room key to the key board.

- *Bookings*. This involves accepting bookings, responding to requests as to the availability of rooms and cancelling bookings. Most communication is by telephone but occasionally faxes are received, particularly to confirm bookings. Surface mail is also received containing written confirmations. Increasingly, however, e-mail is beginning to replace some of the phone calls and letters.

- *Maintaining the website*. The general manager is keen on using the WWW for attracting fresh business, advertising the restaurant and promoting special offers such as short breaks (these are weekend breaks for couples and are typically inclusive of an evening meal).

- *Taking bookings for dinner* from the guests and any member of the general public wishing to eat in the hotel.

- Giving a warm, friendly *welcome* to the guests, helping with tourist enquiries and generally being the *main point of contact*.

- The receptionists are responsible to the general manager or her deputy, the rooms manager.

Challenge 18-3
What are the main aspects of work at the Swan Hotel which it is important to understand?

18.4 Flow models

A flow model in CD represents how work is broken up across people and how it is coordinated to get the whole job done. A flow model is drawn from a particular point of view (e.g. the receptionist or the general manager). This means that there may be several flow models – one for each point of view – which will agree in broad terms but will not be identical. You will have to resolve these differences before you can begin the design. This process of consolidation is described in the next chapter.

Note that flow models are not the same as the *dataflow* models often used in structured systems design. These are briefly discussed in Chapter 13.

Components of a flow model

The following list is adapted from Beyer and Holtzblatt (1998, p. 91).

- *Individuals* – who is involved. At this stage we are thinking about individuals themselves rather than generalized roles. They are labelled with an identifier such as 'user 1', 'user 2' and so on, and with job title rather than personal names.
- *Responsibilities* belonging to each individual, e.g. booking rooms.
- *Groups* – a group is more than one person with the same responsibilities. They can be considered as a group if the outside world interacts with all its members in a similar way. The receptionists are a group.
- *Flow* – how people communicate to get the work done, whether by informal chat or more formal artefacts such as invoices.
- *Artefacts* – the 'things' that are processed or support the work. They can be tangible objects, such as memos, or more rarely intangibles such as important conversations where key points are agreed.
- The *communication topic* or *action*, such as a request for a room.
- *Places*, such as meeting rooms, are shown if they are central to coordinating the work.
- *Breakdowns* – problems in communication and coordination.

Constructing a flow model

Step 1

The first step in constructing a flow diagram is to show the individuals who do the work or are directly involved with the work. So, in this example, the guests of the hotel are included as they are important in understanding the operation of the hotel.

A flow model is constructed from the particular *point of view* of an interviewee. Figure 18-1 illustrates this; in this case we have chosen to centre the flow model on one of the receptionists (User 1 or U1), shown as an ellipse or bubble. We would also draw a diagram based on the information from the other receptionists, but this is not shown here. Other relevant roles are drawn as a set of annotated ellipses. The annotation comprises a brief description of the person's responsibilities (e.g. makes the tea, is the union representative). Do the same for groups.

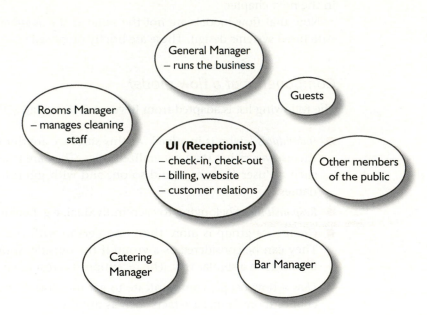

FIGURE 18-1 Constructing a flow model, step 1

Step 2

The flow – communication between people – is shown by arrows on the diagram with arrowheads indicating the direction of the communication. Remember to include informal communications where these contribute to the work. Label the arrows with either the topic of the communication for an informal process, or the artefact used in a more formal communication. Artefacts are shown in boxes on the arrows. In Figure 18-2 we can see some communications which are mediated through artefacts and some which are not.

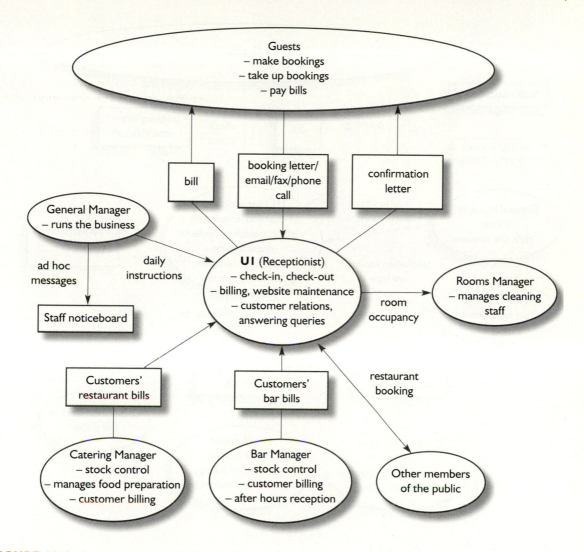

FIGURE 18-2 Constructing a flow model, step 2

Add locations and shared information spaces where they are significant. Here we have the noticeboard in the staffroom which is used for *ad hoc* communications to all staff.

Step 3

Finally, show any breakdowns – problems in communication or coordination – by a lightning flash, in red. The flash has a label briefly detailing the problem. The completed diagram is shown in Figure 18-3.

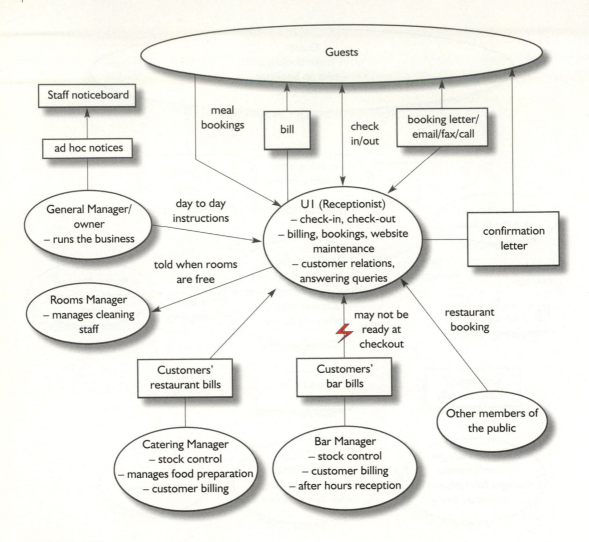

FIGURE 18-3 The completed flow model

Box 18-1 Hints and tips for creating flow models

- Represent every contact people make.
- Note what responsibilities people take on – even those that are not part of their job.
- Look at the action people take without thinking.
- Represent locations, things and systems when they make a place to coordinate.
- The real interactions between people reveal glitches in the work.

Source: Beyer and Holtzblatt (1998)

Challenge 18-4
The model above was drawn from the perspective of the 'morning' receptionist (User 1), who works from 0700 until 1500. The 'evening' receptionist (User 2) works from 1430 until 2230. She does not normally deal with checking-out, since latest checkout time is 1030. However, she is responsible for informing the catering manager of all restaurant bookings. This is done by means of a handwritten list handed over at about 1800, with later bookings being passed on by internal phone or by the receptionist herself. (Occasionally, bookings 'get lost' if reception is very busy with new guests.) Otherwise her job is similar to that of the other receptionist. Draw a flow model from the point of view of the 'evening' receptionist.

18.5 Sequence models

See Chapter 20 on task analysis. Section 20.3 describes HTA – a similar idea to a sequence model

A sequence model represents work tasks. These are ordered and unfold over time. They can be shown as a sequence of steps of actions. Again, they are drawn from a particular point of view and you are likely to construct several different versions for some tasks at least.

Components of a sequence model

The following list is adapted from Beyer and Holtzblatt (1998, p. 99).

■ The *intent* (or purpose) that the sequence is intended to achieve. There will always be one main intent and usually several subsidiary intents.

■ The *trigger* which causes the sequence of actions. The main intent and the trigger are a pair. The intent is the reason why a sequence action is taken, the trigger is the event which sets it off. One cannot exist without the other. There is only one trigger for each sequence.

■ A series of *steps* which achieve the intent. There should be enough detail to allow a colleague to implement software to support the activity without having to ask you for help.

■ Any *breakdowns* or problems.

In practice, the level of detail will vary according to the focus of the project. If you are concentrating on the main features of work for a new system, then a diagram such as that shown in Figure 18-4 is suitable. But much lower-level detail would be required if the focus was on the redesign of a user interface, and you would show steps at the level of 'select week from on-screen calendar', for example.

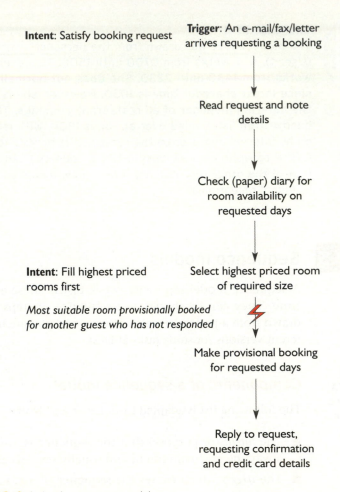

FIGURE 18-4 A simple sequence model

Box 18-2 Hints and tips for creating sequence models

- Capture actions at the level that matters for your project.
- Customers' actions are never purposeless.
- Watch how automation removes effective prompts to action.
- Find intents implied by actions.

Source: Beyer and Holtzblatt (1998)

Sequence models are not always simply linear (i.e. step1 → step 2 → step 3). Sometimes people need to loop back and carry out a task more than once, or there may also be decision points where different steps are taken depending upon circumstances. In such cases the sequence model may require the addition of *loops* or *branches*.

Constructing a sequence model

Step 1

From the contextual inquiry data, identify each main task which is carried out and express it as an intent. There will be a set of intents for each individual. Reviewing the data against people's responsibilities (shown on the flow diagram) can be a good way of finding intents. Put each intent on the top left of a new sequence model.

The concept of an 'event' is the same as a 'trigger'. See Chapter 13, Section 13.4

Step 2

Identify the trigger which sets off the sequence. In Figure 18-4 the trigger is an incoming booking request. Triggers can also be time-based – at the Swan Hotel, the guests' bar bills are passed to reception when the bar closes at 1 am – or rather more vague, such as the receptionist taking advantage of a quiet moment to send promotional offers to previous guests. Add the trigger to the model as the first step in the sequence.

Step 3

Add the steps taken to achieve the intent, linking the steps with arrows and showing any loops or branches.

Step 4

Review the steps, looking for any subsidiary intents which influence the way the sequence is carried out. In the example below, the receptionist has a subsidiary intent to maximize bookings for the most expensive rooms, so she looks for these first and offers them to the customer. Put the subsidiary intents down the left-hand side opposite the relevant steps.

Step 5

Identify any breakdowns and add them. There is one in Figure 18-5 where the most suitable room is already provisionally booked.

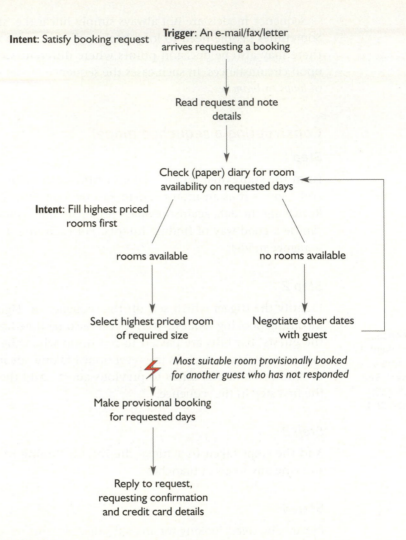

Intent: Satisfy booking request   **Trigger**: An e-mail/fax/letter arrives requesting a booking

Read request and note details

Check (paper) diary for room availability on requested days

Intent: Fill highest priced rooms first

rooms available   no rooms available

Select highest priced room of required size   Negotiate other dates with guest

Most suitable room provisionally booked for another guest who has not responded

Make provisional booking for requested days

Reply to request, requesting confirmation and credit card details

FIGURE 18-5 A branched sequence model with a loop

Challenge 18-5
Draw a sequence model for checking-out a departing guest (from the point of view of the guest). Remember to consider possible breakdowns in the process.

18.6   Artefact models

Artefacts are the things people use or create in their work. As part of the Contextual Inquiry, collect the artefacts themselves, or photographs or photocopies of the objects, or simply sketch them. Interpreting artefacts is rather like detective work – you are looking for evidence as to how everyday work practice is actually carried out, and you will need to confirm your deductions with customers.

Relevant artefacts are of many different types. In the Swan Hotel case study, they include:

- The bookings diary
- The bar till roll
- Bar and restaurant bills
- The room key board
- The website.

In a hospital, artefacts involved in daily patient care might be:

- Current patient notes
- Patient records
- Forms requesting tests and reporting results
- Bedside equipment monitoring vital signs
- The whiteboard where bed occupancy and patient status is displayed for all staff to see
- The loose pieces of paper on which nurses make their own notes when taking over a patient at shift changes.

Often, the interface to a computer system is a key artefact. The artefact model consists of the artefact itself – if already in a suitable paper format – or a sketch, photo, photocopy or scanned version of it, labelled to indicate aspects of interest. The model has at least two uses. It can be used to tease out details of how work is done currently, preferably with customers. Later in the design process it provides basic information as to what data or other material is currently held/processed/communicated, its current organization, and problems occurring. Sometimes (but not always) the current artefacts can be used as a basis for the data structures for the new system. There is one model per stakeholder for each artefact.

Components of the artefact model

The following list is adapted from Beyer and Holtzblatt (1998, p. 105).

- The *information* content itself, e.g. the rooms booked and guest details in the bookings diary

■ The *structure* of the object into different *parts*, showing different usages, who gets involved, and the information intended for different users. Many government forms have a blank part labelled 'for official use only'. Expenses claim forms commonly have sections for the claimant, the person authorizing the claim, and the finance department.

■ Informal *annotation* of the artefact, e.g. the use of Post-it notes and handwritten notes (often a clue that the artefact is not supporting the work adequately)

■ The *presentation* of the artefact – the general style, the use of colour and fonts. Contains clues both to organizational image and values and to the relative importance of different parts of the artefact

■ Note any aspects which change over *time*

■ Note *when* it was created, *what* it is used for, and *by whom*.

■ Finally, any *breakdowns* in its use.

Constructing an artefact model

Step 1

Collect artefacts or images of them as you carry out Contextual Interviews. Identify, in consultation with customers, the most significant and/or typical examples.

Step 2

Check with customers that you understand the role of the artefact in the work and its affordances and constraints by walking through the process of using it.

Step 3

Annotate the model to highlight the relevant aspects of the list above.

Box 18-3 Hints and tips for creating artefact models

- Artefacts capture traces of people's work practice
- Structure reveals how the work is organized
- Content is the trail left by real events
- Presentation directs the eye and reveals importance

Source: Beyer and Holtzblatt (1998)

Figures 18-6 to 18-8 show three examples of models of very different types of artefact. Figure 18-6 shows the bookings diary for the Swan Hotel (drawn from the point of view of the receptionist). Figure 18-7 shows a standard baggage label as attached at airport check-in desks (from the point of view of the check-in staff). Lastly, Figure 18-8 shows a room booking form for a small charitable organization (from the point of view of the manager).

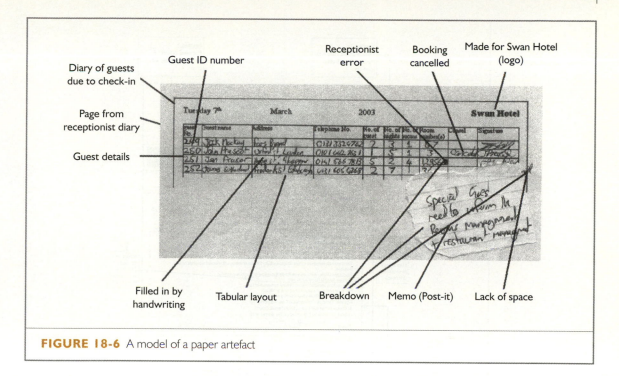

Diary of guests due to check-in

Guest ID number

Receptionist error

Booking cancelled

Made for Swan Hotel (logo)

Page from receptionist diary

Guest details

Filled in by handwriting

Tabular layout

Breakdown

Memo (Post-it)

Lack of space

FIGURE 18-6 A model of a paper artefact

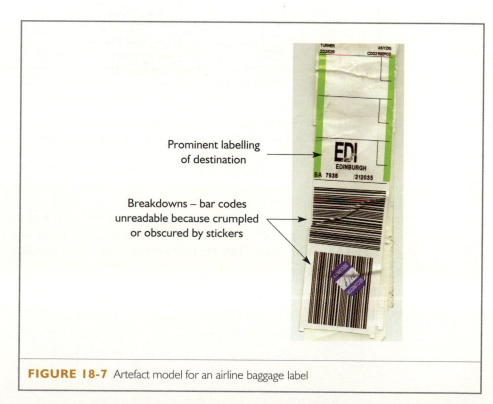

Prominent labelling of destination

Breakdowns – bar codes unreadable because crumpled or obscured by stickers

FIGURE 18-7 Artefact model for an airline baggage label

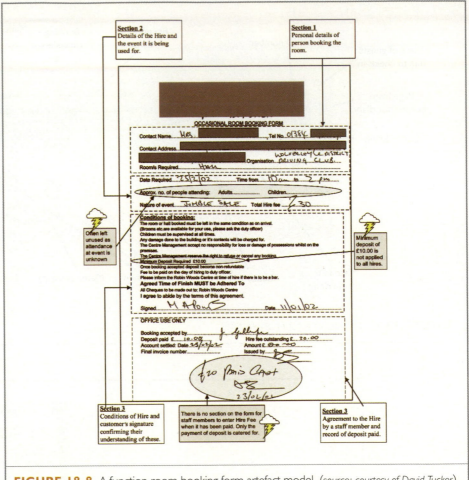

FIGURE 18-8 A function room booking form artefact model *(source: courtesy of David Tucker)*

Challenge 18-6
Construct an artefact model based on your own diary or scheduler. Photocopy a typical page (or grab a screenshot if your diary is on-line) and annotate it. Better still, get a copy of a page from another person's diary or scheduler.

18.7 The cultural model

Work takes place in a culture which defines people's expectations, wishes, organizational policies and values and indeed the whole approach to the work. It is 'the way we do things around here'. Achieving a good fit between customer culture and systems which support the work is essential for a design to be successful. Some organizations initially restricted internal e-mail communications because of the way organizational hierarchies seemed to be undermined, for example. Often cultural assumptions are unspoken and invisible, even though there may be cultural divides between different parts of a customer's organization. A typical instance of this occurred in a CD project with the visitor services unit of an international airport. Information staff employed by the airport itself saw their function as assisting visitors with hotel (and other) information most suited to their needs, whereas those operating as part of the city's tourist information bureau promoted only those suppliers who had paid for the service. The cultural model makes these issues explicit. In some ways it is quite similar to a *rich picture*.

Rich pictures were discussed in Chapter 2

Components of the cultural model

The following list is adapted from Beyer and Holtzblatt (1998, p. 109).

■ *Influencers* – people or bodies which affect the way work is done, typically managers, customers or competitors of the organization being studied, or regulatory bodies. The Swan Hotel is influenced by its competitors – other small hotels in this popular tourist area, and more generally those competing for the lucrative short-break market – and the owner/manager's insistence on individual guest care as the Swan's key selling point. They are shown as bubbles in Figure 18-9. A pervasive, shared organizational culture can be shown as a large arc around the rest.

■ The *extent* to which the work is affected by the influencers, indicated by the degree of overlap between bubbles. At the Swan, the way receptionists interact with customers is heavily influenced by the values of the owner/manager, but much less directly by competing hotels.

■ The *direction* of the influence, shown as arrows.

■ *Breakdowns* arising from cultural issues. One problem at the Swan is that the aim to provide individual service tends to be undermined by the need to keep prices competitive.

Typical cultural influences include national or international standards and policy, organizational policy on technology platforms and the ethos encapsulated in mission statements. Other elements to be included are the attitudes and concerns of the individual involved.

Constructing a cultural model

The cultural model is drawn for each individual.

Step 1

Start with the bubble for the individual concerned and add bubbles for other groups or individuals who affect the way work is done. Label each bubble with job title or name of the group, institution and so forth.

Step 2

Arrange the bubbles to reflect the extent of the influence (although this can be difficult to show if there are many influencers). Add arrows labelled with what the influence is.

Step 3

Add the outer arc showing overall company culture, if such a shared culture exists.

Step 4

Identify any significant breakdowns with red lightning symbols.

Box 18-4   Hints and tips for creating cultural models

- The cultural model speaks the words that people think but don't say.
- An organization's culture is not reflected in its organization chart.

Source: Beyer and Holtzblatt (1998)

Figure 18-9 shows the cultural model for the Swan Hotel from the point of view of the receptionist.

Challenge 18-7
Construct a cultural model for an organization you are part of or have worked for in the past, from your own perspective. What are the major influences on the organization? Perhaps they are legal or governmental or maybe they have a strong business basis. What kind of image does the organization aim to project to the rest of the world and what kind of image does it actually have?

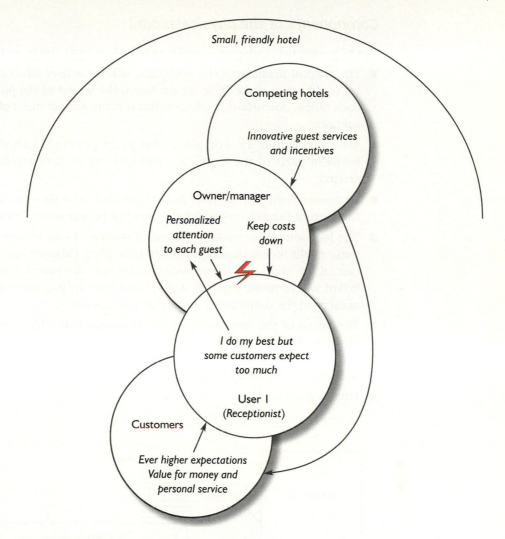

FIGURE 18-9 A cultural model for the Swan Hotel

18.8 The physical model

The physical model is a representation of where the work takes place. It is not an exact floor plan, but rather shows the key features of the workplace – large or small, open plan or a network of offices, new or old. Is equipment supporting the work conveniently located? Is there a focal point such as a coffee machine where people congregate? The physical model helps to show why work is carried out in a particular way – perhaps people don't print out documents very often because the printer is a long way down the corridor. It also indicates physical features which may need an equivalent in a computer system – the receptionist at the Swan can see room occupancy at a glance simply by looking at the key board which is on the wall at the side of her desk.

Components of the physical model

The following list is adapted from Beyer and Holtzblatt (1998, p. 117).

- The *physical structures* of the workplace, insofar as they affect the way work is (or could be) carried out. So for the Swan, the layout of the public rooms and back offices downstairs is relevant, but not the arrangement of the bedrooms upstairs.

- *Movement* within the workplace – the paths of people's regular movements between parts of the workspace and how significant artefacts are moved around.

- *Communications* and *computer technologies* and *networks* – the latter being just the parts of the network which connect the people we are concerned with.

- The location of *key artefacts* created or processed – in a conventional office, these might include desktop, whiteboards, filing cabinets and so forth. In the case of the Swan, notable items would include the rooms booking diary, the board where room keys are stored when not in use, the stack of bills for guests and the noticeboard in the manager's office.

- The *layout* of the workplace. In the Swan example, this would include the position of the receptionist's desk opposite the stairs and front door – so that she can see guests arriving and leaving – but not the low table with the vase of flowers at one side of the lobby.

- Finally, *breakdowns*.

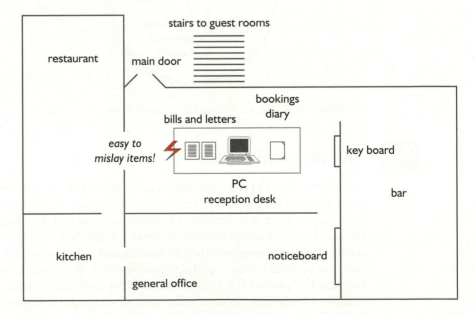

FIGURE 18-10 The physical model for the Swan Hotel

The physical model is shown in Figure 18-10. Note that this model is very simple, but indicates the receptionists' position at the hub of the hotel. It can be seen that everyone – staff and guests – moving around the hotel will pass the reception desk.

Challenge 18-8
Draw the physical model of the office based on the images provided (Figures 18-14 to 18-16) at the end of the chapter.

Summary and key points

Each of the five models presents a different perspective on work. These perspective are interlocked, so a person has a role, undertakes tasks and exchanges information with others. These tasks are discharged in sequence by the use of artefacts. This is all carried out in a cultural context and is constrained by the physical environment.

We have now reviewed the **Contextual Inquiry** approach to gathering information about current work practice, and represented the findings in five different **models**, each representing a different facet of work.

- The **flow** model shows individuals, their working relationships, and the information and artefacts which support the work process.
- The **sequence** model details how tasks are carried out.
- The **cultural** model shows how work is constrained by organizational values and concerns.
- The **physical** model illustrates work in relation to the physical environment.
- The **artefact** model identifies key features of the concrete objects which are produced or processed.

The models support designers in several ways:

- By documenting complex contextual data coherently and systematically.
- The process of drawing the models identifies gaps in customer data.
- By supporting the sharing of data between designers.

So far, we have considered models drawn from an individual perspective. In the next chapter, we see Contextual Design's approach to the consolidation of different perspectives and the design of new systems.

Further reading

Beyer, H. and Holtzblatt, K. (1998) *Contextual Design*. Morgan Kaufmann, San Francisco.

The primary reference for this chapter. The philosophy behind CD and all the component techniques are explained in a very accessible and practical way.

Going forward

Spinuzzi, C. (2002) A Scandinavian challenge, a US response: methodological assumptions in Scandinavian and US prototyping approaches. *Proceedings of SIGDOC '02 Conference*, Toronto, 20–23 Oct. ACM Press, New York, pp. 208–215. A thought-provoking review of the way user-centred techniques have diverged from their roots in workplace democracy.

Comments on challenges

Challenge 18-1
Some suggestions are below. You have probably thought of additional factors – but take care that you keep to relevant issues.

- A small multimedia start-up company
  - Small customer base
  - Likely that staff mix and match roles, so all may use the customer database, but only intermittently
  - Located in a compact office suite, but may be a need to access the database while visiting customer sites.
- An insurance company call centre
  - Used while staff are interacting with customers over the phone
  - Very large volume of customer data – often the same claim or enquiry dealt with by several different staff
  - Staff use database continuously
  - High pressure on staff to meet targets for sales and closing cases
  - Large numbers of staff, many part-time and with high turnover.
- A hospital surgical unit
  - Accuracy and reliability are safety-critical
  - No time for training sessions
  - Highly pressured environment
  - Need for access at different locations in the unit
  - Environmental hazards such as bodily fluids.

Challenge 18-2
We would interview everyone except the baker, the washers-up and the cleaner, who don't really have any involvement in the work we are considering. The book-keeper is not directly part of the process but will very likely use the sales data, as will the owner.

Challenge 18-3
Essentially, the processes of managing bookings, keeping track of guest charges during the stay and checking in and out – not just the mechanics of these operations, but how they are carried out and what is used to support the process. The functions will be the core of the new system, but the 'how' information will ensure that the new system supports the way the work actually happens without being constrained by artificial obstacles presented by the current system.

Challenge 18-4
Figure 18-11 shows the relevant *part* of our version of the model. Yours may differ in detail, but should show dinner bookings being communicated to the catering manager and the breakdown if these are forgotten. The guest

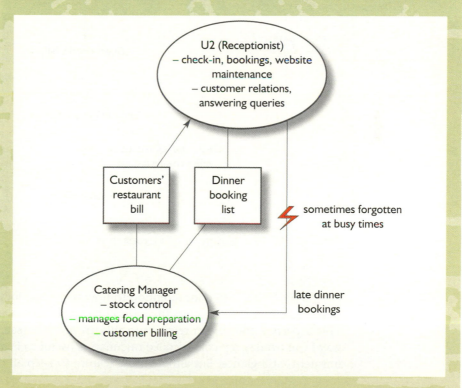

FIGURE 18-11 Part of a flow model for the 'evening' receptionist

billing process can be omitted, since this is not usually part of the 'evening' receptionist's job. Note that the exact shape of the symbols, arrowheads, choice of fonts and so on are not important.

Challenge 18-5
Figure 18-12 shows a typical sequence model for a guest checking out.

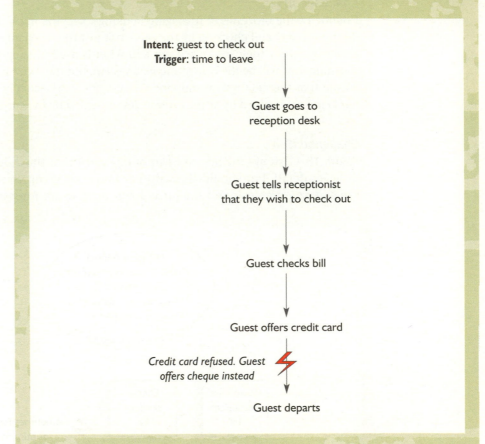

Intent: guest to check out
Trigger: time to leave

Guest goes to
reception desk

Guest tells receptionist
that they wish to check out

Guest checks bill

Guest offers credit card

*Credit card refused. Guest
offers cheque instead*

Guest departs

FIGURE 18-12 Sequence model for guest checking out

Challenge 18-6
Key points here are to draw attention to how the diary does (or doesn't) help in the task of organizing one's time. Don't be diverted into annotating all possible aspects if they aren't relevant to this. In my case (see Figure 18-13) the way I can overlay my colour-coded calendars is useful so I can see all my commitments at a glance. But although the feature to keep all day appointments

confined to the top of the page keeps the page uncluttered, I have also been caught out booking new meetings on days which are apparently free but are really already taken up. Part of my job is concerned with organizing external speakers for research seminars, and I usually need to look at the overall schedule for these in isolation – hence their representation as a separate calendar.

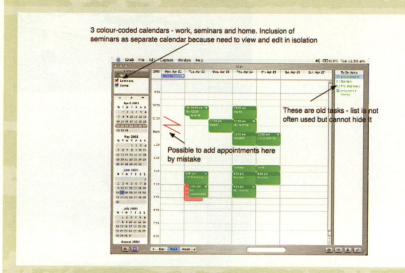

FIGURE 18-13 An artefact model of a personal calendar application

Challenge 18-7
You should be representing all the individual roles (but not named people), groups and institutions which affect your functioning within the organization. Remember that you may be a source of influence yourself!

Challenge 18-8
Figures 18-14 to 18-16 are from an office at Napier University. The faces of the people in the office have been obscured. The office is the administrative centre for the School of Computing. One of its main functions is to receive coursework submissions from the School's students. The office is staffed with six administrators, three of whom can be seen in Figure 18-14. One of the students can be seen in Figure 18-16.

The key point to check for here is that you have included the main physical aspects of the environment which support or constrain the work. Don't waste time drawing an exact floor plan. You might need to make some areas proportionately larger than their real space in order to show more detail.

FIGURE 18-14 Looking into the administrative (private) area from the counter

FIGURE 18-15 Looking left from behind the counter

FIGURE 18-16 Looking along the counter

19 Contextual Design 2:
From models to design

Aims

This chapter continues the Contextual Design process and must be read after Chapter 18 (otherwise it will not make a great deal of sense). At the end of the last chapter we had shown how the analysts can create a set of five models of existing work practice, using data gathered from different customers or customer sites. Now we set out how these are consolidated into a common set of issues and models. This information is then used to drive the design of a new system grounded in the contextual data. The chapter concludes with some brief case studies where CD has been applied.

After studying this chapter you should be able to:

- Identify the commonalities in contextual data using the affinity diagram and an informal consolidation process
- Produce designs for a new system using storyboards and to drive the user environment design (UED)
- Evaluate designs with customers using paper prototyping.

19.1 Introduction

This chapter concentrates on the practical skills of creating an affinity diagram, how to consolidate our understanding of work, and how to create storyboards and the user environment design (UED). It then moves from the UED to discuss the practical use of prototyping and user interface design – all with the distinctive flavour of contextual design. Generally speaking we adhere to the methods and sequence of stages recommended by Beyer and Holtzblatt (1998) with the following main exceptions:

- Beyer and Holtzblatt correctly emphasize the team-based nature of Contextual Design (and the need for a team room). This is true of the larger-scale, commercial application of their method, but does not necessarily suit small projects or students of the method.

- While Beyer and Holtzblatt suggest that affinity diagrams are best created by the design team, we have found that getting the users to do it themselves works very well.

- In line with our scaled-down approach, we treat consolidation and the creation of a design vision much more informally than in the canonical Beyer and Holtzblatt method.

- We do not discuss the latter stages of Contextual Design which concern the implementation and rollout of the system.

You are, of course, free to follow full-scale, orthodox Contextual Design if you so choose and then consulting the *Contextual Design* book is essential. We would certainly recommend this for large, multi-customer projects and large design teams.

In this as in the previous chapter there are no separate exercises at the end of the chapters. Instead and in the spirit of Contextual Design we have embedded a series of challenges in each of the chapters.

19.2 The affinity diagram

Affinity diagrams are brilliantly simple and effective. Figure 19-1 is an illustration of three maritime trainers (an Englishman, a German and a Dane) creating an affinity diagram from their requirements, needs, wishes and hopes on a technical system to support safety-critical training (this was part of the DISCOVER project which was introduced in Chapter 9).

FIGURE 19-1 Creating an affinity diagram

Constructing an affinity diagram

1. Write each separate requirement, wish, need (whatever) ideally on a Post-it note. Make sure this is fairly succinct – a word or two, a sentence at most, but not your CV.

2. Repeat until you have perhaps several hundred (in the above example, there were well in excess of 300 Post-its).

3. The affinity diagram is built bottom-up by identifying common themes and structure. So, rather than providing the affinity diagrammers with predefined headings, they should define their own.

4. The Post-its should then be affixed to a wall in groups, as the groupings emerge. In Figure 19-1 we used a mixture of whiteboards and flipcharts to maximize the use of space. During this process it is not unusual to discard duplicate or near-duplicate requirements.

5. Remember to record the groups and headings.

Affinity diagrams are an effective way of designing information architectures, which are described in Chapter 23

Figure 19-2 is part of the output from the affinity diagramming process for the DISCOVER project. The three maritime trainers grouped the requirements on the system under the headings of (design of the) accommodation (on a ship) and (design of the) avatars. The orange Post-it is at the top level of the grouped themes, with the grey Post-its being at an intermediate level. The yellow Post-its detail individual requirements.

The creation of an affinity diagram is the first step in the design process as we can begin to see already the features, properties and expected behaviours of parts of the new system. As you can see from Figure 19-2, parts of it naturally map to potential menu structures for the user interface to the interactive application which is specified here.

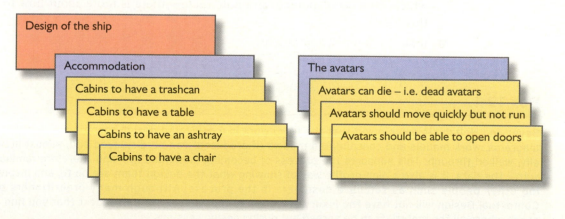

FIGURE 19-2 A partial affinity diagram for the DISCOVER training system

19.3 Consolidation

From a practical point of view, consolidation is the most difficult part of the Contextual Design method. In a full-scale Contextual Design project, we will have generated a series of models reflecting the points of view of the stakeholders across the particular work contexts we are studying. In the Swan Hotel case study (Chapter 18) we would have created, for example, sequence models from the points of view of the guests, receptionists, managers and so forth. More than this, we may have multiple versions of these models from other hotels we have studied too.

Contextual Design requires that we bring together (consolidate) all the different kinds of models – flow, sequence, artefact, physical and cultural, all the different points of view. During the consolidation process, we are looking for ways in which the system can be redefined. This is a non-trivial task as in addition to defining the behaviour of the interactive system we intend designing, we are also changing the way people do their jobs.

While it is practical to consolidate, that is, identify and pull out common features between two or three different models, in our experience this is a very demanding exercise if you have dozens of different models. The process requires a considerable degree of iteration. The output from the full consolidation process is a consolidated flow model, a series of consolidated sequence models, a series of consolidated artefact models and similarly consolidated physical and cultural models. In our lighter-weight approach to modelling and design, we do not suggest constructing formal consolidated models, but instead that you

■ Review the work models that have been created – if different people have created different models, they should each step through their models with the rest of the team. The best place to start is with flow models, then sequence models, using artefact, physical and cultural models to fill out the more process-oriented data.

■ Look for common problems, bottlenecks and any effective workarounds which have been adopted, and note them – there is more about how to do this below.

■ Brainstorm possible solutions.

Box 19-1

Beyer and Holtzblatt recommend that the team work in a dedicated design room in which affinity diagrams, work models and consolidated models (if produced) can be displayed and, almost literally, walked through. This supports the process of becoming immersed in – and therefore familiar with – the data. It is also a high-profile way of showing what the design team are up to, and involving other people such as software designers in the process. Although many practitioners of Contextual Design will not have the luxury of a room to themselves, we do suggest that you find a space where all the material can be spread out during design sessions.

In the next sections we suggest particular aspects from the various models which will help to generate new design ideas. The material is edited from Beyer and Holtzblatt's treatment of consolidation.

Further thoughts: The tension between context and generalization

The early stages of the contextual design method are deeply grounded in real work. People are interviewed and observed in their working environment, and models are drawn which reflect real practice. But once consolidated models are produced, some of this rich detail and variation is, inevitably, lost in the process. This is not an issue which is unique to contextual design but applies to any analysis and design method which produces generalized models. The fact that abstraction and generalization necessarily loses context was one of the stimuli for other attempts to preserve contextual data such as the patterns of cooperative interaction proposed by researchers at Lancaster University (further discussed in Chapter 29). However, the tension between designing to fit one particular situation perfectly and the need to produce systems which can be used across similar instances of a given context remains fundamentally irresolvable.

Using flow models to review roles

The flow model is the best starting point for an overview of work practice and people's roles within it. In considering how a redesigned interactive system could better support the work, you will be looking to the following:

- Recognize that people switch roles and that different people may share the same role – most people have more than one role at work. An example from the Swan Hotel would be the bar staff, who also act as receptionist late in the evening, so a consistent interface between bar and reception system functions would be a good idea. University academics are typically required to be researchers, teachers and administrators – sometimes, it seems, all at once.

- Minimize overloaded roles, where people have so many conflicting tasks that it is impossible to carry out any of their roles effectively. Parts of these roles are good places to consider full or partial automation, or reallocating tasks between roles. Note that here you are moving from interactive systems design to job design, quite another area of expertise. It is essential that if you suggest changing the make-up of people's jobs, you do this in close consultation with the customer organization concerned. It may also be a good idea to involve management consultants as part of the design team.

- Avoid 'role isolation' where roles are so segregated that information sharing and communication become problematic. This can be alleviated by making sure that artefacts that communicate between roles have sufficient information. The receptionist booking dinner for a special anniversary may need a checkbox on the form to say that the couple have priority for a special table. If the receptionist was responsible for both reception and table allocation (reasonably enough, the job of the restaurant manager) there might be no such need.

■ As a sanity check, review the ideas for change against the fundamental purposes of the customer organization. The hotel aims to keep its rooms at maximum occupancy through providing an attractive 'product' and keeping guests content. Giving guests the impression that they exist mainly as a number on a computer is unlikely to improve their satisfaction.

Sequence models as sources of ideas for redesign

Your first question should be whether the activity depicted in the sequence diagram can be automated altogether. In the Swan Hotel case study, it is unlikely that activities dealing with guests can be completely computerized, but 'backstage' activities such as checking stock levels present more possibilities. Where an activity apparently can be automated, you should carefully check through all the implications before finally deciding. It may be, for example, that the catering manager uses the stock check as a way of keeping an eye on how the kitchen is running.

Given that an activity is to be kept, then consider:

■ Can the intent be achieved in a more effective way, perhaps by part-automation? There is no need, for example, for the receptionist at the Swan to check for available rooms manually when taking a booking request. (The original sequence model from Chapter 18 is shown again in Figure 19-3.)

■ Are all current steps necessary?

■ The different ways in which different role holders undertake the activity in the sequence. Some versions may be more effective than others, and thus a source of ideas for redesign. Other variations may be unavoidable, and scope for them built into the design.

■ All subsidiary intents. Make sure redesign ideas still satisfy them. For example, the subsidiary intent of booking higher-priced rooms first would have to be embodied in an automatic allocation process.

■ Eliminate all unnecessary steps and breakdowns. Dealing with the breakdown in the sequence model in Figure 19-3 where a guest has not yet confirmed a reservation is difficult to avoid, however. One partial solution might be for a provisional reservation to lapse after a certain (short) period of time; the room is then made available again.

■ The new design ideas should not create *more* work – walk through the new process to ensure that you have not done this.

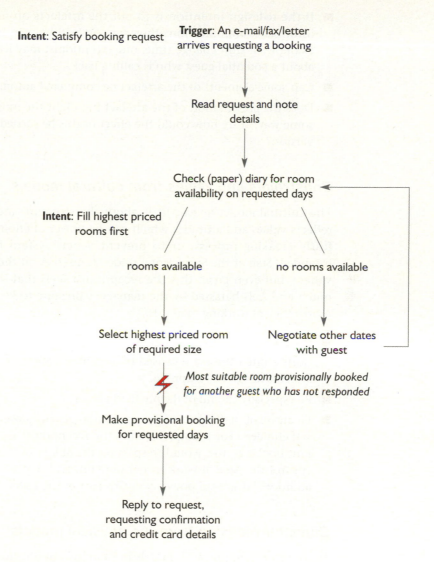

Intent: Satisfy booking request   **Trigger**: An e-mail/fax/letter
arrives requesting a booking

Read request and note
details

Check (paper) diary for room
availability on requested days

Intent: Fill highest priced
rooms first

rooms available   no rooms available

Select highest priced room   Negotiate other dates
of required size   with guest

*Most suitable room provisionally booked
for another guest who has not responded*

Make provisional booking
for requested days

Reply to request,
requesting confirmation
and credit card details

FIGURE 19-3 The original sequence model for the receptionist booking a room

Reconsidering artefacts

Artefact models embody the structure of the work the artefact supports and the
underlying intents. They will also give you clues as to where the process – or the
current artefacts – do not work well. Perhaps some sections of a form are never
used, or conversely, explanatory notes are written on it. In the model of the
bookings diary for the Swan Hotel (Figure 18-6), we can see, for example, that
there is no space for additional notes about bookings. Aspects to consider in
reviewing the role of artefacts in the new design include:

■ If the redesign intention is to put the artefacts on-line, consider how any informal communications they support will happen in the new system. For example, at shift change time, one receptionist may leave a note for the next about a potential guest who is calling back.

■ Can some elements of the artefact be completed automatically?

■ Does the presentation of the artefact highlight the most important aspects in some way? If so, how could the effect of this be carried through to an on-line version?

Constraints and values from cultural models

The cultural model reveals little about the structure and process of work, but reflects values and attitudes which can be powerful enough to prop up a manifestly creaking process, or to prevent a new system from ever working as intended. Staff at the Swan Hotel pride themselves on the hotel's friendly atmosphere, but even given this the receptionist feels that some guests expect too much and feels harassed by the manager's pressure to keep costs down through more efficient working methods.

■ Look for areas where sensitive use of interactive systems can alleviate irritations – often these are caused by communication problems which a careful systems design can improve.

■ Be especially careful of deeply held values.

■ Be aware of the impact of proposed changes on power relationships between stakeholders. For example, if only the receptionist were able to make restaurant bookings, this would trespass on the ability of the restaurant manager to control the pace of work in her domain, and hence give the receptionist an additional degree of power over this part of the hotel.

Clues for redesign from the physical models

As we have seen, physical models hold more clues to how people actually carry out their work in the environment in which they find themselves. Frequently used artefacts are ready to hand; other items may be relegated to the back of the cupboard. The hotel bookings diary is prominent on the receptionist's desk, for example, while the board where room keys hang provides an easy overview of which rooms are currently occupied. As we have seen in the last chapter (see Figure 18.10), everyone passes in front of the reception desk, so the receptionist is always aware of what's happening, and acts as a hub for passing on messages. But written messages get lost on the cluttered desk. When thinking about redesign from this perspective, you need to be aware of how the environment both helps and hinders the work. In particular:

- Do not waste time attempting to design an on-line equivalent of parts of the physical environment which already support work well.

- Consider the impact of proposed changes on the way tasks are currently supported by physical features.

- Look for breakdowns which can be fixed by the new system.

- Consider how the physical environment might be modified – although this is ultimately much more a decision for the customer organization, you should make recommendations where they seem justified.

Challenge 19-1
Your ideas for redesigning the hotel system include a change to reprogrammable plastic key cards – which the guest is intended to carry with him or her – from the traditional keys which hang on the board in reception when the guest leaves the hotel. Also, the move to a computerized system will involve printing out accounts for each guest on check-out. The only printer is currently in the office behind reception. Are there any negative consequences of these proposals? If so, what are they?

19.4   Developing a vision

In the full version of the Contextual Design method, Beyer and Holtzblatt place great emphasis on the creation of the 'vision' as an intensive, cooperative activity for the design team. The vision is a mixture of sketch and text which encapsulates the main points of the new system, from its main functions to its impact on customer organizations and the way people do their jobs. It is the main creative act in the CD process.

In our lighter-weight version of the approach for interactive systems designers, the vision remains a crucial step. You may very well, however, be working in a single-person team. You will also probably be focusing on the interactive system itself rather than matters of job or organization design – although of course you should always take account of such issues.

Your task is to decide what the new system should do – but not yet how it should be presented to its users, which happens at a later stage. Since this is a creative process, there is no one 'textbook' way of arriving at good ideas for the new system, although the ideas about design envisionment described in Chapters 10 and 24 of this book may help. At this stage you should aim to:

- Review the ideas that have been captured in the informal consolidation process against the models of work and any other contextual data you have collected.

- Establish how the client – the hotel – wants to project an image of itself through its information system. The cultural model may be helpful here. Where does the hotel see itself in relation to the market? Is it up-market or a cheap and cheerful, backpacker hostel?

■ Outline the vision – the *main* functionality of the new interactive system.

■ Involve all members of the design team – if you have one – in the creation of the agreed vision.

This being achieved, we move on to define how the new design works in detail. Contextual Design does this through the following means:

■ Capturing strands of interaction in storyboards

■ Developing a structure for the system in the user environment design (UED)

■ Paper prototyping with users.

The next sections describe each of these steps.

Challenge 19-2
Using everything you have learned about the Swan Hotel and your own experiences of hotels, develop your vision for the hotel's new information system. Is it going to be 'flash and hi-tech' or 'warm and friendly' (middle-aged) and what will its main functions be?

19.5 Constructing a storyboard in Contextual Design

We introduced the idea of storyboards with the material on envisionment in Chapter 10

In Contextual Design, storyboards are used to ground the vision of the new system in work practice to make sure it fits with the larger system. They show how real tasks would actually work in a graphical way.

While many storyboards in user interface design tend to focus on what happens on the screen of the device, CD storyboards have a wider perspective, and incorporate significant interactions both between users and also between users and other artefacts – rather more like a strip cartoon. The example in Figure 19-4 demonstrates this. This particular example is a high-level encapsulation of the vision for the new design, showing the ease of the new check-in procedure. As your design develops, you would need to sketch a more detailed version working through the individual steps.

You will need the agreed vision for the new interactive system, the ideas from your informal consolidation process, the affinity diagram and the work models.

Step 1

■ Identify the key user tasks which will be supported in the new system. Choose one.

■ Review the models and affinity diagram for any issues relevant to the task.

1) On arrival at the hotel, the guest goes straight to the Reception desk.

2) At the Reception desk, the receptionist types details of the guest into the computer and checks the guest in.

3) The receptionist asks for a credit card from the guest as a deposit.

4) The receptionist then gives the guest the key to their room.

FIGURE 19-4 A hotel storyboard showing a high-level impression of the registration process *(source: © Fiona Carroll, reproduced with kind permission)*

Step 2

■ Produce a detailed redesign for the task using text and/or diagrams – do not attempt the storyboard itself just yet. You might find it helpful to draw this as a new sequence model.

■ Consider alterative options and select that which deals with the intent for the task and any associated issues most effectively.

– For example, in redesigning the restaurant booking procedure for the hotel, either (a) only the receptionist, (b) only the restaurant manager, or (c) any staff may take bookings, entering the booking into terminals linked to the central bookings list.

– Options (a) and (b) may cause some inconvenience for the customer but may need fewer terminals and avoid clashing bookings; option (c) may be more expensive and requires all staff – including casual workers – to be trained but is flexible and foolproof. You can see that both technological and human design solutions are being considered here.

Step 3

■ Step through the redesign against the original sequence models. Check that the intents are met.

Step 4

■ Sketch the storyboard, one frame for each step in the task sequence.

■ Include interaction between people, automatic and manual steps as well as interactions with the system.

■ This is not the place to consider the details of user interface design – where screens are included, just include a rough sketch of how they might be presented.

Step 5

■ Repeat for all the key tasks.

■ Review the storyboards with the rest of the design team, if you have one.

Challenge 19-3
In the style of Figure 19-4 develop a detailed storyboard for a guest checking out and paying their bill.

19.6 The user environment design (UED)

Having worked through the Contextual Design process, we now have

■ An affinity diagram

■ Directions for the new design from the consolidation process

■ A vision of what the eventual system might look and behave like

■ Storyboards.

Other approaches to this design stage are covered in Chapter 13

The question is how to turn this into a finished design which meets user/customer needs and is usable by the team who will implement it. Contextual Design's answer is to create a **user environment design (UED)**.

The UED is a user-centred, high-level design for the interactive application which we are intent on implementing. It is user-centred in that it does not use obscure (computing) notation but plain English with a few boxes and connecting arrows. It should be easily understood by a non-expert such as the person who will use the finished system. The UED is used to guide the detailed design of the system, the design of the user interface and the management of the development process (if required, though this is not described in this chapter).

A UED is required because storyboards are not sufficient in themselves for this. Each storyboard captures only a single thread of the new process, and so cannot ensure that the overall work structure and system organization are coherent. Designing an interactive system piecemeal may result in its functions being partitioned in a sub-optimal manner.

In the hotel example, separate storyboards may have been developed for a guest making an advance room booking and for making an advance dinner booking. But what if some guests want to do both at the same time? Developing these different elements separately may result in a poorly designed system with the receptionist having to switch between different parts of the booking system to achieve these simple tasks. Creating and using a user environment design helps to avoid this undesirable state of affairs.

UED basics

The UED is a diagram which represents the structure of the new design. It is:

- based on the underlying structure and sequence of the work itself
- a shared resource for designers, developers and project managers
- constructed before user interface design takes place
- similar in some ways to a website navigation map (but much more comprehensive), or – as Beyer and Holtzblatt suggest – to the floor plan of a building.

Chapter 24 discusses navigation maps

At its simplest a UED comprises a number of **focus areas** (if the UED is a floor plan, then the focus areas are places or rooms). The focus areas are the places in the system which support particular parts of the work. A focus area collects functions and work objects into one place to support a particular part of the work. However, it does not include functions which affect just the UI (e.g. re-arrangement of tool bars). Focus areas should be named with a simple active phrase (e.g. compose message) which is the *purpose statement* and is numbered so that it can be referenced unambiguously. Note that a focus area is not equivalent to a software module as this is a developer's view of the process.

Figure 19-5 is an illustration of a focus area. Each focus area comprises primarily:

- A *purpose statement*. This is what it sounds like. A purpose statement is a brief plain English statement describing the purpose of the focus areas.
- *Functions*. These enable the user to do the work. The functions are identified and described with a short phrase. These functions are invoked either by the user (e.g. enter new customer) or automatically by the system (e.g. create new customer order number). The latter are shown as unfilled bullet points in the UED, thus o.
- *Objects*. Work objects are the things the user sees and manipulates in the focus area. These might include people and artefacts.
- *Links*. These are pointers to other related focus areas.

2. Check-in guest
Register new guest

Functions
- Retrieve room booking
- Confirm room booking details
- Allocate room
- Print guest card
- Take credit card details
- Open guest account

Links
> Reserve restaurant table
> Bill guest

Objects
Guest
Room allocations
Guest card

Constraints
Allow simultaneous check-ins

Issues
Password protection?
Project corporate image

Roles
Receptionist

FIGURE 19-5 A sample focus area to support a guest check-in

Other elements of focus areas which may (or may not) be needed are as follows:

- *Constraints* in implementation on the focus area, e.g. speed and reliability
- *Issues* which might include ideas for UI, unresolved problems and so on
- *Hidden focus areas*, which are parts of the system that the user knows about but doesn't have to interact with (e.g. keeping of statistics in a helpdesk system); these are represented with dotted lines
- *Roles*, a list of the users whom you expect to use this focus area.

Building the UED from storyboards

The UED is constructed from the storyboards. The UED is, effectively, a representation of all the storyboards into one single, unified structure. It is constructed by walking through each storyboard frame by frame, identifying new focus areas and adding functions, links (and so forth) to existing focus areas. It is also worth checking for the following:

- Overlapping focus areas
- Unnecessary functions
- Function areas that contain only links – remove them
- Focus areas that contain more than one task – simplify them.

Let's look at a practical example, using the four-frame storyboard we saw earlier in Figure 19-4. Walking through this storyboard, we can observe:

Frame 1.   The guest arrives at the reception desk and announces 'I have a reservation and I wish to check in'. The receptionist stops what she is doing and asks for the guest's name.

Frame 2.   The receptionist then consults the hotel's information system *and* accesses the database to match the guest's name against reservations. The name is found and the receptionist updates the database to indicate that the guest has arrived and allocates a room to her.

Frame 3.   The receptionist then asks the guest for her credit card in order to secure payment. The card is swiped and its details are entered into the hotel's information system.

Frame 4.   Finally, the receptionist gets the room key from the key board and hands it to the guest.

This then can be translated into the following partial UED which can be seen in Figure 19-6.

Checking the UED with a walkthrough

Having created a UED it needs to be checked. This, ideally, is a group activity (or failing that, get a friend to listen to you walking through it). Things to check for are as follows.

1. Are focus areas coherent?
2. Support *one* task in overall activity.
3. Check for focus areas without an obvious purpose.
4. Avoid single-function focus areas.

Challenge 19-4
Complete the focus area for 'Check-out guest' in Figure 19-6. Ensure that all the components of the focus area are accounted for.

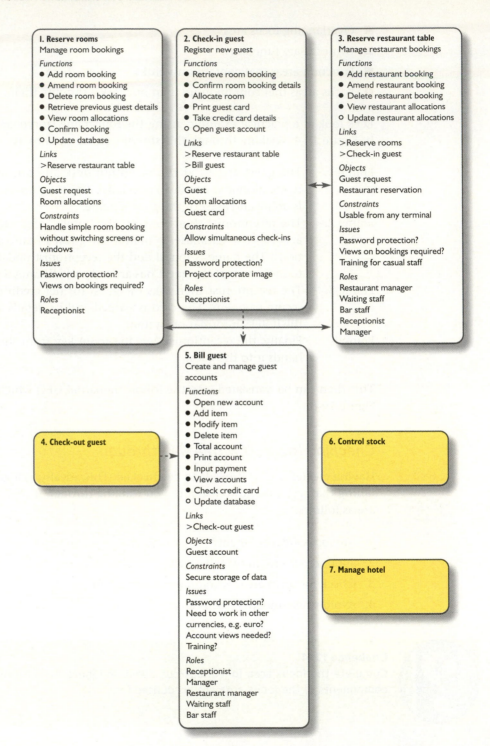

1. Reserve rooms
Manage room bookings

Functions
- Add room booking
- Amend room booking
- Delete room booking
- Retrieve previous guest details
- View room allocations
- Confirm booking
○ Update database

Links
>Reserve restaurant table

Objects
Guest request
Room allocations

Constraints
Handle simple room booking without switching screens or windows

Issues
Password protection?
Views on bookings required?

Roles
Receptionist

2. Check-in guest
Register new guest

Functions
- Retrieve room booking
- Confirm room booking details
- Allocate room
- Print guest card
- Take credit card details
○ Open guest account

Links
>Reserve restaurant table
>Bill guest

Objects
Guest
Room allocations
Guest card

Constraints
Allow simultaneous check-ins

Issues
Password protection?
Project corporate image

Roles
Receptionist

3. Reserve restaurant table
Manage restaurant bookings

Functions
- Add restaurant booking
- Amend restaurant booking
- Delete restaurant booking
- View restaurant allocations
○ Update restaurant allocations

Links
>Reserve rooms
>Check-in guest

Objects
Guest request
Restaurant reservation

Constraints
Usable from any terminal

Issues
Password protection?
Views on bookings required?
Training for casual staff

Roles
Restaurant manager
Waiting staff
Bar staff
Receptionist
Manager

4. Check-out guest

5. Bill guest
Create and manage guest accounts

Functions
- Open new account
- Add item
- Modify item
- Delete item
- Total account
- Print account
- Input payment
- View accounts
- Check credit card
○ Update database

Links
>Check-out guest

Objects
Guest account

Constraints
Secure storage of data

Issues
Password protection?
Need to work in other currencies, e.g. euro?
Account views needed?
Training?

Roles
Receptionist
Manager
Restaurant manager
Waiting staff
Bar staff

6. Control stock

7. Manage hotel

FIGURE 19-6 Work in progress on a UED for a hotel system (shaded boxes and their links to be completed)

The UED and user interface design

The UED has collected all the functions from storyboards and organized them into coherent areas of focus. User interface design, from the perspective of contextual design, is primarily concerned with accessing the functions identified in the focus areas of the UED. Since much of the rest of this book is about methods and principles for user interface design, we do not discuss how this is done any further, except to note the following points:

- The contents of a focus area in the UED *may* translate into one screen or one window, but this is not necessarily so – sometimes it will make for better interaction design to split the presentation of the functions.

- When designing the details of interaction, remember that different roles may use the same focus area, so design for the skills and tasks of each role.

- You should review your design against the issues captured in the affinity diagram and work models.

19.7 Paper prototyping

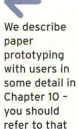

We describe paper prototyping with users in some detail in Chapter 10 – you should refer to that chapter for further information

As the user interface design develops, Contextual Design uses paper prototypes as the means of communicating with users and bringing them back into the design process. A paper prototype essentially animates the user interface design. It is constructed using a sheet of paper or, better, card of the right size to represent the screen and the main items which are permanently displayed. Post-its, acetate transparencies and similar removable media are used to mimic transient and movable windows, drop-down menus and so forth, or to try out alternative layouts for more permanent screen elements.

The Beyer and Holtzblatt book also has detailed instructions for paper prototype construction. In contextual design paper prototypes are employed in the following ways:

- Having users walk through their existing tasks (and new/revised ones which are supported by the new interactive system) as the designer makes the prototype 'work'.

- Probing users for the reasons why they take particular actions with the prototype, and what they expect to happen.

- Taking notes of user reactions, suggestions and confusions – having a second designer involved in the session helps here.

- At an early stage of design, involving users in the review of the general scope and organization of functionality.

- As the design develops, checking the effectiveness of a more complete and detailed user interface design.

- Using a 'replay' of the user prototyping session to communicate user responses to the rest of the design team.

The prototyping session itself should be structured in a similar way to the Contextual Interview (see Chapter 18) with an introduction to the process, the prototype walkthrough, and a concluding session confirming interpretations of the data which has been captured. The resulting feedback is then used to revise both the UED and the user interface design as appropriate.

Challenge 19-5
Create a paper prototype which represents the process of checking out from the hotel. Ensure that you design the screens for both billing and payment.

So, now we have completed a lightweight version of Contextual Design from the initial analysis of the Contextual Inquiry to a structure for a new interactive system documented with the UED and an initial design which has been prototyped with users. Now we turn to a number of case studies documenting the use of contextual design in the real world.

19.8 Applications of Contextual Design

Karen Holtzblatt and Hugh Beyer, and their company InContext Enterprises, have run many Contextual Design seminars for practitioners. The method – or parts of it – has been enthusiastically taken up by practitioners, especially in the US. This section gives a taste of the way the method has been used. Table 19-1 summarizes four large-scale case studies which are reported in published material. It can be seen that in these examples, practitioners select elements of the CD process according to the needs of the situation. (It should be noted that most reported studies – not just those summarized here – tend to concentrate on the upstream 'inquiry' part of the process rather more than the downstream 'design' techniques.) Sometimes other techniques – usually more familiar to the design team – are used to augment the process. Enhancement of communication is a key benefit. This applies both within the team, where cross-disciplinary membership is thought invaluable, and to those outside the team, who are kept involved at regular intervals in an often lengthy process. Finally, the need for a clear focus is stressed throughout.

As designed, CD is a strongly team-based process with particular strengths in consolidating data between organizations. This is reflected in the case studies just discussed. However, we have experience of its successful use in several small, single-person projects, including designing new interactive systems for a sales support system in a DIY store, the administration of a local charity, and the provision of information for passengers at an airport. In these small projects, the main advantage of the method has been the provision of a detailed and systematic structure for gathering and modelling contextual data.

TABLE 19-1 Four large-scale case studies of contextual design

Authors	Project summary	Elements of CD used	Benefits/limitations/lessons learned	Team
Cleary (1999)	Main purpose to evaluate CD, in two projects relating to management of network devices. Located at Cabletron Systems, Inc. – vendor of high-performance hardware and software systems.	Dedicated resource room. Contextual Interviews with customers, interpretation sessions, sequence models, flow models, minimal use of physical models, artefacts 'looked at' in interpretation sessions, affinity diagrams. 'Open House' sessions for others to discuss data. Consolidated sequence and flow models. Envisionment and storyboarding.	Good synergy in the multi-disciplinary team. Immersion in the data. Much better understanding of customer views within and beyond team. Main lessons: • Establish clear focus for inquiry • Have developers participate in interviews and interpretation • Report interim results to stakeholder • Digest data into manageable form for colleagues outside the team.	Usability manager (leader), three developers, QA engineer, three usability specialists, one usability trainee. Personnel changed over project lifetime but able to get up to speed quickly.
Rockwell (1999)	Project to develop tools for use by systems administrators supporting a new operating system. Hewlett-Packard, Enterprise systems group.	'Contextual Inquiries' at customer sites. Interpretation sessions, individual and consolidated physical, sequence and flow models. Collection of artefacts. Envisionment and lo-fi software prototypes. Also standard usability testing techniques.	Synergy and focus in the team. Little design reworking required. Clear rollout strategy. Adoption of CD by other teams. Good customer reaction to the product. Easy to integrate with standard usability and development methods. Main lessons: • Decide clear focus • Foster take-up by demonstrating success on small projects • Integrate with established approaches • Gain management buy-in.	Unspecified engineers and managers.

TABLE 19-1 Four large-scale case studies of contextual design

Authors	Project summary	Elements of CD used	Benefits/limitations/ lessons learned	Team
Page (1996)	New version of WordPerfect word-processing software.	Visits to user sites, Contextual Interviews, interpretation sessions, flow, sequence and physical models. Affinity diagram, consolidated models, redesigned work models, user environment design, paper and software prototypes.	Logical, systematic way of understanding users. Expanded to other business areas once potential demonstrated. Cross-disciplinary team improved effectiveness. UED effective long-term blueprint. Main lessons: ● Output does not have to be perfect, nor does the process ● Check progress daily ● Revisit users often ● Report to others as the work develops, choosing the most effective techniques (in this case, the software prototype) ● Emphasize that ideas come from real customer data.	Specialists in software development, human factors, documentation, usability and marketing.
Coble et al. (1996)	Requirements generation for physician's clinical workstation.	Contextual Interviews at physicians' workplaces, observers from outside the team in some sessions. Interpretation session, producing sequence, flow and cultural models, also user profiles and lists of detailed observations and issues. Consolidated flow and cultural models, affinity diagram. Also document containing prioritized requirements, augmented by scenarios. Presentation to technical team using illustrated scenarios.	Management support for process; reuse of findings in other project activities. Accurate, comprehensive data including some findings which could not have been obtained without CI. Strong relationship with physicians. Main lessons: ● Involve a larger, cross-disciplinary team ● Schedule more analysis time.	Three-person user interface team, including physician who did not participate in data gathering.

Summary and key points

This chapter provided a number of additional practical techniques for transforming the work models, which were the primary output of the last chapter, into a design suitable for further development and implementation.

We began with the affinity diagram which helped to create logical groupings of functions for our new interactive system. This was followed by what we have described as 'informal consolidation', which is a cut-down version of the full process, after which we invited the analyst–designers to create a vision of the new system. This vision of the new system should reflect both the required functionality and how the customer would like to present themselves to the world (their image).

The design itself is high level, user-centred and referred to as the user environment design (UED). The UED is created by systematically analysing the storyboards detailing the use of the new system.

The UED is then used to guide the creation of a series of paper (or software, but paper is better) prototypes which are used to present the design to the customer.

Further reading

Beyer, H. and Holtzblatt, K. (1998) *Contextual Design*. Morgan Kaufmann, San Francisco.
Again, the primary reference for this chapter. The elements of contextual design which have been omitted from this chapter are, not surprisingly, to be found in the full text.

More advanced

The references in Table 19-1 are highly recommended for insight into the use of contextual design in practice.

Comments on challenges

Challenge 19-1
Possible undesirable consequences include (a) the receptionist will be unable to check room occupancy at a glance (traditional keys are usually hung from a board); (b) plastic keys are easily lost and as guests think that they are cheap and easily replaced will take less care with them; and (c) as the only printer is behind reception, the receptionist will be required to leave the front desk whenever she is required to print off a bill or receipt.

Challenge 19-2
'Flash and hi-tech' does not seem to fit well with the cosy image of the hotel which the cultural model reflects. A more suitable, if middle-aged, image might be 'small, friendly and (but?) efficient'. We suggest the main functionality might be:

- A room allocation system which lists available rooms for specified dates but allows the receptionist the final choice
  - integrated with a guest database holding details of previous stays and preferences.
- A guest accounts system which links accommodation, restaurant, bar and any other charges to a specified room, which will produce
  - an itemized bill on check-out and a printed receipt
  - stock control systems (probably).

Challenge 19-3

The storyboard should include (a) the guest checking-out and returning their key; (b) the receptionist producing the bill; (c) the guest checking the bill – maybe querying an item; (d) the guest offering their credit card; (e) the receptionist processing the card; (f) a receipt being produced and the guest taking their leave.

Challenge 19-4

The check-out focus area might include the items listed in Table 19-2.

TABLE 19-2 Contents of check-out focus area

Purpose statement	Check out guest and prepare bill
Functions	Prepare bill Review bill Get payment Produce receipt De-allocate room (hidden) Cancel standing arrangements of guest (hidden)
Links	Manage hotel Stock control Bill guest
Objects	Guest Bill Payment Rooms allocation
Constraints	Must be simple, quick and accurate
Issues	Handling queries from guests
Roles	Receptionist

Challenge 19-5

The most important thing about a paper prototype is its use. A good paper prototype should be (a) easily modified and (b) sufficiently flexible to allow the movement of dynamic items. Do not worry too much about the fine detail as the software will look different. The prototype should be tried out with a potential user and comments collected.

20 Task analysis

Aims

The notion of a 'task' has been central to work in human–computer interaction since the subject started. Undertaking a task analysis is a very useful technique – or rather set of techniques – for understanding people and how they carry out their work. Looking at the tasks that people do, or the tasks that they will have to do because of some redesigned system, is a necessary part of human-centred design. This chapter provides some philosophical background on what task analysis is and where it fits in to interactive systems design. It then provides practical advice on doing different types of task analysis. After studying this chapter you should be able to:

- Understand the difference between goals, tasks and actions
- Undertake a hierarchical task analysis
- Undertake a procedural cognitive task analysis
- Understand the importance of considering a structural view of a domain.

20.1 Goals, tasks and actions

Some authors consider 'task analysis' to encompass all manner of techniques (such as interviewing, observation, development of scenarios, etc.). We do not. We consider task analysis to be a specific view of interactive systems design that leads to specific techniques. Chapters 18 and 19 presented a method for doing design and Part III of this book presented many generic techniques for understanding requirements, envisioning solutions and evaluating designs. Most of these consider tasks in the sense that they consider what people have to do. This chapter looks more formally at the concept of task, how to undertake task analyses and what benefit designers might get from such analyses. In the final section we look at the importance of understanding a structural perspective of a domain.

The distinction between the key concepts in task analysis – goals, tasks and actions – may be identified as follows:

A task is a goal together with some ordered set of actions.

We called this the people-technology system in Chapter 3, Section 3.3

The concept of task derives from a view of people, or other agents, interacting with technologies trying to achieve some change in an application domain. Taken together the people and technology constitute what is sometimes called a 'work system' which is separate from the 'application domain'. Dowell and Long (1998) emphasize that the application domain (or simply 'domain') is an abstraction of the real world, i.e. some abstract representation (such as a database). Importantly task analysis is concerned with some aspects of the performance of a work system with respect to a domain. This performance may be the amount of effort to learn a system, to reach a certain level of competence with a system, the time taken to perform certain tasks, and so on. This conceptualization is shown in Figure 20-1.

Diaper's full definition of task analysis (Diaper, 2004) is:

'Work is achieved by the work system making changes to the application domain. The application domain is that part of the assumed real world that is relevant to the functioning of the work system. A work system in HCI consists of one or more human and computer components and usually many other sorts of thing as well. Tasks are the means by which the work system changes the application domain. Goals are desired future states of the application domain that the work system should achieve by the tasks it carries out. The work system's performance is deemed satisfactory as long as it continues to achieve its goals in the application domain. Task analysis is the study of how work is achieved by tasks.'

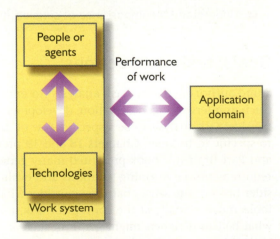

FIGURE 20-1 Task analysis is concerned with the performance of work by a work system

This view of the separation of work system and domain is not shared by everyone (and we revisit it in Chapter 27) but this definition does result in some useful task analysis techniques for systems analysis and design. These are discussed in Sections 20.3–20.5.

Goals

A goal is a state of the application domain that a work system wishes to achieve. Goals are specified at particular levels of abstraction.

This definition allows for artificial entities such as technologies or agents or some combination to have goals. For example, we might be studying the organizational goals of a company, or the behaviour of a software system in terms of its goals. It is not just people who have goals; the work system as a whole may have goals. For this reason the term 'agent' is often used to encompass both people and software systems that are actively and autonomously trying to achieve some state of the application domain. The term 'technology' is used to encompass physical devices, information artefacts, software systems and other methods and procedures.

For example, an agent might have a goal such as to write a letter, to record a programme on TV, or to find the strongest mobile phone signal. The assumption is that the domain is in one state now – no letter written, the TV programme not recorded, the signal not confirmed as the strongest – and the agent has to undertake some activities, i.e. some tasks, in order to get it into the required state.

Usually a goal can be achieved in a variety of different ways. So the first thing the agent has to decide is which technology to use to achieve the goal. For recording a TV programme, for example, an agent could use the following technologies:

Chapter 27 on devices and information artefacts

States and state transitions were introduced in Chapter 13

- Ask a friend to record it
- Press 'Rec' on the VCR
- Set the timer using a manual setting
- Set the timer using the 'videoplus' codes that are provided in the TV guide.

Of course the agent needs to know quite a lot about each of these technologies and the pros and cons of each and will select different ones at different times depending on the circumstances. The agent may misunderstand some of the technologies and so may not take the optimum course of action. The selection of a technology will depend on the agent's knowledge of the functions, structure and purpose of particular technologies; and this knowledge may be quite erroneous. Once a technology has been decided upon, the tasks can now be defined.

Chapter 15, Section 15.11 discusses cognitive work analysis, which is concerned with understanding what means are needed to achieve certain ends

Tasks and actions

A task is a structured set of activities required, used, or believed to be necessary by an agent to achieve a goal using a particular technology. A task will often consist of subtasks where a subtask is a task at a more detailed level of abstraction. The structure of

an activity may include selecting between alternative actions, performing some actions a number of times and sequencing of actions.

The task is broken down into more and more detailed levels of description until it is defined in terms of actions. Actions are 'simple tasks'. Whereas a task might include some structure such as doing things in a particular sequence, making decisions as to alternative things to do (selection) and doing things several times (iteration), an action does not. This structure is often called a plan or method.

An action is a task which has no problem solving associated with it and which does not include any control structure. Actions and tasks will be different for different people.

Chapter 6. Activity theory has similar constructs called activities, actions and operations

For example, in the case of recording a TV programme, if the programme is just about to come on it might be best to press 'Rec' on the VCR which would start recording immediately. This brings its own problems as the VCR might be tuned to the wrong channel or might not have enough tape in it. Alternatively the agent could set the timer manually. Using a 'videoplus' numbering system is more laborious as the agent has to turn the TV on to use the on-screen menu system. If the agent is not very well informed about the operation of the system, the agent may fiddle around selecting the VCR channel and finally getting to the on-screen programming and so on. The agent may do things that are strictly unnecessary because the agent had a poor conceptualization (a 'mental model') of the device.

> **Challenge 20-1**
> Write down the task structure for manually recording a programme using a VCR. Think about the decisions that an agent would need in order to undertake this task and about the differences between tasks and actions for different agents with different knowledge. Discuss with a friend or colleague.

Task analysis methods can be divided into two broad categories: those concerned with the logic of the task – the sequence of steps that need to be undertaken by a work system to achieve a goal – and those concerned with cognitive aspects. Cognitive task analysis is concerned with understanding what cognitive processes the work system will have to undertake in order to achieve a goal. Cognition is concerned with thinking, solving problems, learning, memory, and the representations of things that people are assumed to have in their heads: 'mental models'.

Chapter 5 on cognition and mental models

People also have knowledge of how to do things in general and how to do things with specific technologies. People make use of things in the environment (such as displays on a computer screen or notes on a piece of paper) as part of the cognitive processes. Cognitive task analysis has a long-established tradition in human–computer interaction with a large number of methods coming from a variety of slightly different backgrounds. Most of the theoretical treatments presented in Chapters 5 and 7 have resulted in some technique applied to the design or evaluation of interactive systems.

In terms of the goals, tasks and actions, we need to consider both the goal–task mapping (knowing what to do to achieve some goal) and the task–action mapping (knowing how to do it). There is also a need to consider the goal formation stage – knowing that you can do something in the first place. In addition to this procedural knowledge, people have structural knowledge. Structural knowledge concerns knowing about concepts in a domain and knowing how those concepts are related. This sort of knowledge is particularly useful when things go wrong, when understanding the relationships between the components in a system will help with trouble-shooting.

20.2 Task analysis and systems design

There are many views on, and methods for, task analysis and task design. As noted previously, some authors equate task analysis with the whole of systems development. Others equate methods of task analysis with methods of requirements generation and evaluation. Yet others distinguish task analysis (understanding existing tasks) from task design (envisioning future tasks). Diaper and Stanton (2004a) provide a comprehensive overview of 30 different views. One thing that people agree upon is that a task analysis will result in a task model, though as we will see these models can take very different forms.

Balbo, Ozkan and Paris (2004) emphasize the expressive power of different methods in their taxonomy of task analysis techniques. For example, they focus on whether a technique captures optionality (is a task mandatory or optional in pursuing a goal?), parallelism (can tasks be performed in parallel?) or non-standard actions such as error handling or automatic feedback. They also classify methods along the following axes:

- The goal of using the notation – by which they mean the stage in the development life cycle; is it best for analysis, design, evaluation and so on?

- Its usability for communication – some task analysis techniques can be very hard to read and understand, particularly those that are based on a grammar rather than graphical notation.

- Its usability for modelling tasks – task analysis methods have to fit into the software development process and be used and understood by software engineers. It has long been a problem that software engineers do not have ready access to a good task analysis technique. Some methods are intended to assist in the automatic generation of systems (see Further thoughts box overleaf).

- The adaptability of a task analysis technique to new types of system, new aims or new requirements (e.g. a task analysis technique aimed specifically at website design may not be very adaptable). To what extent is the technique extensible to other purposes?

Further thoughts: Model-based user interface design

One particular branch of task analysis concerns the formal representation of systems so that the whole system, or part of it, can be automatically generated by a computer system from the specification or model. Work on model-based design has continued, without much success, in several areas. In user interface design several systems have been tried (see Abel *et al.*, 2004, for a review) that represent systems at the domain level, an abstract level of description and the physical level of different styles of widget such as scroll bars, windows, etc. One aim of the model-based approaches is to enable different versions of a system to be automatically generated from the same underlying model. For example, by applying different physical models an interface for a WAP phone, a computer and a PDA could be generated from the same abstract and domain models. Stephanidis (2001) uses this approach to generate different interfaces for people with varying levels of ability.

Model-based approaches have also been tried in software engineering for many years (e.g. Benyon and Skidmore, 1988) again with limited success. The screen-design systems that automate the generation at the physical layer (such as Delphi, Borland and VB) have been highly successful, but automatically linking this to an abstract level of description proves difficult.

Diaper and Stanton (2004b) make an important observation regarding many task analysis techniques, namely that they are usually mono-teleological. That is to say, they assume that the agent or work system has a single purpose which gives rise to its goal. Teleology is the study of purposes, causes and reasons, a level of description of activities that is missing from most task analysis approaches. In reality, of course, people and work systems may be pursuing multiple goals simultaneously.

Task analysis is an important part of systems development, but it is a term that encompasses a number of different views. It is undertaken at different times during systems development for different purposes.

■ During analysis, for example, the task analysis should aim to be as independent as possible from the device (or technology), for the aim is to understand the essential nature of the work in order to inform new designs.

■ During the design and evaluation of future tasks, task analysis focuses on the achievement of work using a particular technology (i.e. a particular design) and hence is device dependent.

During analysis, task analysis is concerned with the practice of work, with the current allocation of function between people and technologies, with existing problems and with opportunities for improvement. During design and evaluation task analysis is concerned with the cognition demanded by a particular design, the logic of a possible design and the future distribution of tasks and actions across people and technologies.

Scenario-
based design
is described in
Chapter 8

Task analysis is in many ways similar to scenario-based design, for tasks are just scenarios in which the context and other details have been stripped away. Task analysis is best applied to one or two key activities in a domain. Task analysis is not quick or cheap to do, so it should be used where there is likely to be the best pay-off. In an e-commerce application, for example, it would be best to do a task analysis on the buying-and-paying-for-an-item task. In designing the interface for a mobile phone, key tasks would be making a call, answering a call, calling a person who is in the address book and finding your own phone number.

In the rest of this chapter we look at three task analysis techniques. The first is based on **hierarchical task analysis (HTA)** and is concerned with the logic of a task. The second, based on the **goals, operators, methods, selection rules (GOMS)** method, is concerned with a cognitive analysis of tasks, focusing on the procedural knowledge needed to achieve a goal. This is sometimes called 'how to do it' knowledge. The third, **ERMIA**, focuses on understanding structural knowledge, sometimes called 'what it is' knowledge.

20.3 Hierarchical task analysis

Hierarchical task analysis (HTA) is a graphical representation of a task structure based on a structure chart notation. Structure charts represent a sequence of tasks, subtasks and actions as a hierarchy and include notational conventions to show whether an action can be repeated a number of times (iteration) and the execution of alternative actions (selection). Sequence is usually shown by ordering the tasks, subtasks and actions from left to right. Annotations can be included to indicate *plans*. These are structured paths through the hierarchy to achieve particular goals. For example, making a call using a mobile phone has two main routes through the hierarchy of tasks and subtasks. If the person's number is in the phone's address book then the caller has to find the number and press 'call'. If it is not, the caller has to type the number in and press 'call'.

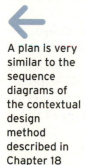

A plan is very
similar to the
sequence
diagrams of
the contextual
design
method
described in
Chapter 18

HTA was developed in Hull during the 1960s and has appeared in a variety of guises since then. Stanton (2003) gives an up-to-date account. Figure 20-2 illustrates a typical HTA diagram for the goal of recording a TV programme. It uses the tasks and subtasks from the solution to Challenge 20-1.

There are a number of notational conventions that can be used to capture key features of the tasks. We recommend using an asterisk in the box to show that an action may be repeated a number of times (iteration) and a small 'o' to show optionality. The plans are used to highlight sequencing. Others (e.g. Stanton, 2003) like to show decision points as parts of the plans.

HTA is not easy. The analyst must spend time getting the description of the tasks and subtasks right so that they can be represented hierarchically. For example, tasks 1.1, 1.2 and 1.3 of Figure 20-2 are not hierarchical, although at first sight they appear so. Ensuring there is enough tape may require rewinding the tape, which will require inserting the tape into the VCR. Moreover, task 1.1 will

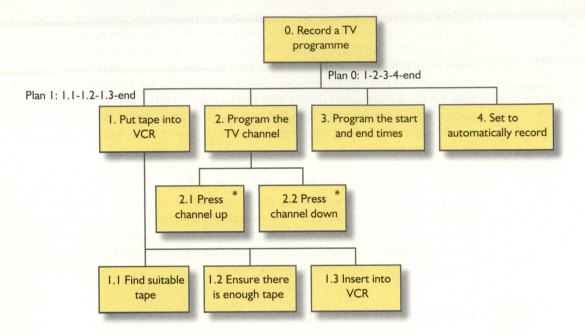

FIGURE 20-2 HTA for programming a VCR

presumably involve making some judgement about how much tape is left. Like most things in interactive systems design, undertaking a hierarchical task analysis is highly iterative and you will not get it right first time. The analyst should return to the task list and try to redefine the tasks so that they can be represented hierarchically.

HTA appears in many different methods for interactive systems design. For example, Stanton (2003) uses it as part of his method for error identification. He develops an HTA model of a system and then works through the model looking for possible error situations. At the action level (bottom level of an HTA), people might make a slip such as pressing the wrong button. What happens if they do this? At the task and subtask levels the analyst can consider what type of task it is and hence what types of error might occur.

Annett (2004) provides a step-by-step guide to how to do an HTA:

Chapter 15, Section 15.12 discusses human error

1. Decide on the purpose of the analysis. This is typically to help with systems design or to design training materials.
2. Define the task goals.
3. Data acquisition. How are you going to collect data? Observation, getting people to use a prototype, etc.
4. Acquire data and draft a hierarchical diagram.
5. Recheck validity of decomposition with stakeholders.

6. Identify significant operations and stop when the effects of failure are no longer significant.

7. Generate and test hypotheses concerning factors affecting learning and performance.

Lim and Long (1994) use HTA slightly differently in their HCI development method called MUSE (Method for Usability Engineering). They illustrate their approach using a 'Simple ATM' example as shown in Figure 20-3. This shows that the 'Simple ATM' consists of two subtasks which are completed in sequence: Present Personal ID and Select Service. Present Personal ID consists of two further subtasks: Enter Card and Enter PIN. In its turn, Enter PIN consists of a number of iterations of the Press Digit action. Select Service consists of *either* Withdraw Cash *or* Check Balance. Each of these is further re-described (indicated by the dotted line, but not shown in this example). Notice that this HTA does not have a goal as its top level, but instead has the name of a system.

HTA can be highly effective in helping people to really understand the structure of tasks – either existing tasks or new, proposed task structures. This type of analysis can be represented in ways other than the structure chart. For example, the user action notation (UAN) (Hix and Hartson, 1993) represents each task as a separate box with the overall goal at the top of the box and the actions listed underneath with the distribution of user and system tasks shown in two columns. Figure 20-4 shows an example for part of the ATM. Other columns can be included in the table such as showing the interface state and when the system connects to background computation.

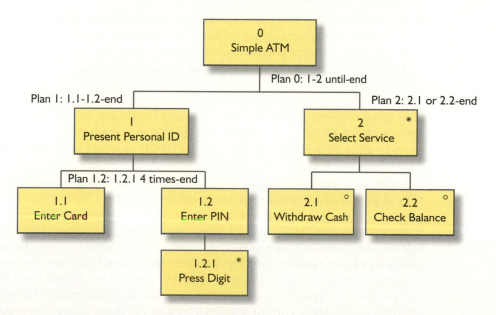

FIGURE 20-3 Hierarchical task model for a portion of an ATM

Task: Present personal ID	
User Actions	*Interface Feedback*
	Welcome message
Insert card	'Please enter PIN' message
Press digit	Beep + display *

FIGURE 20-4 Illustrating user action notation (UAN)

20.4 GOMS – a cognitive model of procedural knowledge

GOMS is the most famous and long-lasting of a large number of cognitive task analysis methods. It focuses on the cognitive processes required to achieve a goal using a particular device. The aim is to describe tasks in terms of the following:

- **Goals** – what people are trying to do using some system, say make a call using a cellphone.
- **Operators** – the actions that the system allows people to make, such as clicking on menus, scrolling through lists, pressing buttons and so on.
- **Methods** – sequences of subtasks and operators. Subtasks are described at a more abstract level than operators – things such as 'select name from address book' or 'enter phone number'.
- **Selection rules** – the rules that people use to choose between methods of achieving the same subtask (if there are options). For example, to select a name from an address book a person could scroll through the names or type in the first letter and jump to a part of the address book.

There are many different 'flavours' of GOMS, focusing on different aspects of a task, using different notations, using different constructs. In this book we do not claim to teach GOMS as a method, but just to alert readers to its existence and provide some illustrative examples. Kieras (2004) provides his version and John (2003) provides hers.

Looking at the constructs in GOMS, it is clear that the method is applicable only if people know what they are going to do. John (2003) emphasizes that selection rules are 'well-learned' sequences of subgoals and operators. GOMS is not a suitable analytical method where people are problem-solving. Also it is mainly applicable to single user–system interactions where it can give accurate estimates of performance and help designers think about different designs.

John (2003) gives the example of a GOMS analysis in project Ernestine. She and co-worker Wayne Gray constructed 36 detailed GOMS models for telephone operators using their current workstation and for them using a new proposed workstation. The tasks such as answer call, initiate call and so on are broken

Chapter 5, Section 5.1 provides more detail on the KLM model which is closely related to GOMS

down into the detailed operations that are required, such as enter command, read screen and so on. Times for these operations are then allocated and hence the overall time for the task can be calculated.

The new workstation had a different keyboard and screen layout, different keying procedures and system response time. The company believed the new workstation would be more effective than the old. However, the results of the modelling exercise predicted that the new workstation would be on average 0.63 second slower than the old. In financial terms this cost an additional $2m a year. Later field trials were undertaken which confirmed the predicted results.

John (2003) provides much more detail on this story, but perhaps the most important thing is that the modelling effort took two person-months and the field trial took 18 months and involved scores of people. A good model can be effective in saving money. A portion of the model is shown in Figure 20-5.

Undertaking a GOMS analysis shares with HTA the need to describe, organize and structure tasks, subtasks and actions hierarchically. As we have seen, this is not always easy to do. However, once a task list has been formulated, working through the model is quite straightforward. It is also important to note that

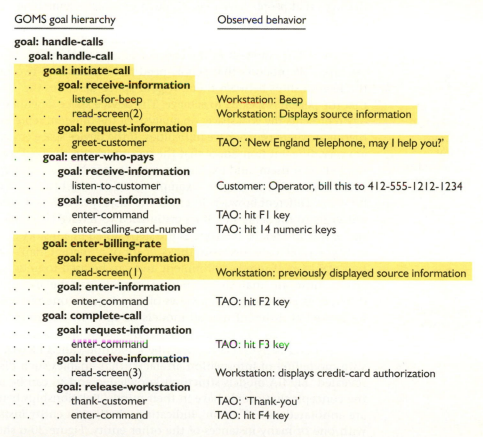

GOMS goal hierarchy	Observed behavior
goal: handle-calls	
. **goal: handle-call**	
. . **goal: initiate-call**	
. . . **goal: receive-information**	
. . . . listen-for-beep	Workstation: Beep
. . . . read-screen(2)	Workstation: Displays source information
. . . **goal: request-information**	
. . . . greet-customer	TAO: 'New England Telephone, may I help you?'
. . **goal: enter-who-pays**	
. . . **goal: receive-information**	
. . . . listen-to-customer	Customer: Operator, bill this to 412-555-1212-1234
. . . **goal: enter-information**	
. . . . enter-command	TAO: hit F1 key
. . . . enter-calling-card-number	TAO: hit 14 numeric keys
. . **goal: enter-billing-rate**	
. . . **goal: receive-information**	
. . . . read-screen(1)	Workstation: previously displayed source information
. . . **goal: enter-information**	
. . . . enter-command	TAO: hit F2 key
. . **goal: complete-call**	
. . . **goal: request-information**	
. . . . enter-command	TAO: hit F3 key
. . . **goal: receive-information**	
. . . . read-screen(3)	Workstation: displays credit-card authorization
. . . **goal: release-workstation**	
. . . . thank-customer	TAO: 'Thank-you'
. . . . enter-command	TAO: hit F4 key

FIGURE 20-5 GOMS analysis *(source: after John, 2003, p. 89, part of Figure 4.9)*

GOMS can be used as the keystroke model described in Chapter 5. Times can be associated with the various cognitive and physical actions and hence one can derive the sort of predictions discussed by John (2003).

Challenge 20-2
Write a GOMS-type description for the simple ATM (Figure 20-3).

20.5 Structural knowledge

Task analysis is about procedures. But before a person sets about some procedure they need to know what types of things can be accomplished in a domain. For example, if I am using a drawing package I need to know that there is a facility for changing the thickness of a line, say, before I set about working out how to do it. I need some conception of what is possible, or what is likely. So in this section, instead of focusing on the steps that people have to go through to achieve something (hence looking at a procedural representation), we can look at the structural knowledge that people have and how an analysis of this can help in designing better systems.

Chapter 5, Section 5.10 discusses mental models. Also see Chapter 15, Sections 15.1 – 15.5

Payne (2003) shows how the concept of a 'mental model' can be used to analyse tasks. He proposes that people need to keep in mind two mental spaces and the relationships between them. A **goal space** describes the state of the domain that the person is seeking to achieve. The **device space** describes how the technology represents the goal space. An analysis of the different representations used can highlight where people have difficulties. If the device space employs concepts that are very different from those that the person uses in the goal space, then translating between them, and explaining why things happen or why they do not, is made more difficult. A good example of this is the history mechanism on Web browsers. Different browsers interpret the history in different ways and some wipe out visits to the same site. If a person tried to retrace their steps through a Web space, this will not be the same as the steps stored in a history.

Chapter 25 discusses mental maps

Payne (2003) also discusses the concept of a 'mental map' which is analogous to a real map of some environment and can be used to undertake tasks. He discusses how an analysis of mental models can be useful in highlighting differences between people's views of a system. In one piece of empirical work he looked at different mental models of an ATM and found several different accounts of where information such as the credit limit resided.

Green and Benyon (1996) describe a method called ERMIA (entity–relationship modelling of information artefacts) that enables such discrepancies to be revealed. ERMIA models structural knowledge and so can be used to represent the concepts that people have in their minds. Relationships between the entities are annotated with '1' or 'm', indicating whether an entity instance is associated with one or many instances of the other entity. Figure 20-6 shows the different beliefs that two subjects had about ATMs in a study of mental models undertaken by Payne (1991).

S14: network of interconnected intelligent machines, everything stored on the card

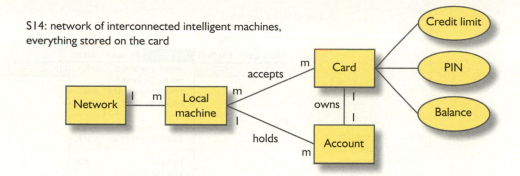

S15: central machine with local 'dumb' clients, nothing on the card except the PIN

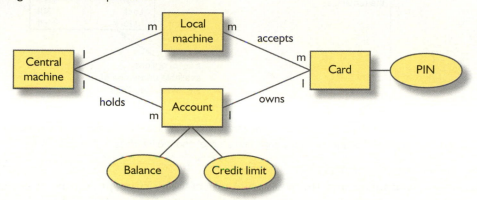

FIGURE 20-6 Comparison of two mental models of ATMs described by Payne (1991) *(source: after Green and Benyon, 1996)*

The designer's model and system image is presented in Chapter 13

ERMIA uses an adaptation of entity–relationship modelling to describe structures. Entities are represented as boxes, relationships by lines, and attributes (the characteristics of entities) by circles. In Figure 20-7 we can see a typical menu interface. What are the main concepts at the interface?

Menu systems have two main concepts (entities). There are the various menu headings, such as File, Edit, and Arrange, and there are the various items that are found under the headings, such as Save. More interestingly, there is a relationship between the two kinds of entity. Can we imagine an interface that contains a menu item without a menu heading? No, because there would be no way to get at it. You have to access menu items through a menu header; every item must be associated with a heading. On the other hand, we can imagine a menu which contained no items, particularly while the software is being developed.

This, then, is the basis of ERMIA modelling – looking for entities and relationships and representing them as diagrams (see Figure 20-8). Benyon, Green and Bental (1999) provide a practical guide to developing ERMIA models, and Green and Benyon (1996) provide the background and some illustrations. A key feature of ERMIA is that we use the same notation to represent the conceptual aspects of

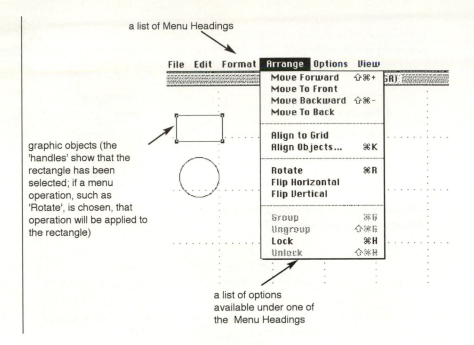

FIGURE 20-7 A simple drawing program, showing the document being created (a drawing, currently consisting of a rectangle and a circle) and the interface to the application

a domain and the perceptual aspects. The conceptual aspects concern what people think the structure is and what the designer thinks the concepts are. The perceptual aspects concern how the structure is represented perceptually. In the case of menus we have the concepts of menu header and menu item and we represent these perceptually by the bold typeface and position on a menu bar and by the drop-down list of items. A different perceptual representation is to represent the menu using a toolbar.

Returning to the relationships between menu headers and menu items, each menu heading can list many items, while each item is normally found under only one heading – in other words, the relationship of heading to item is one to many (written 1:m).

Is it strictly true that the relationship between menu items and menu headers is 1:m? Not quite; by being forced to consider the question precisely, we have been alerted to the fact that different pieces of software are based on differing interpretations of the interface guidelines. There is actually nothing to prevent the same menu item being listed under more than one heading. So an item like 'Format' might be found under a Text heading and also under the Tools heading; the true relationship between heading and item is therefore many to many, or m:m as it is written.

Many-to-many relationships are inherently complex and can always be simplified by replacing the relationship with a new entity that has a many-to-one

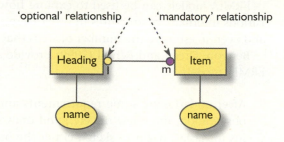

FIGURE 20-8 ERMIA structure of a menu system containing headers and items. The relationship between heading and item is 1:m (that is, each heading can refer to many items, but an item can be associated with only one heading). For items, the relationship is mandatory (that is, every item must have a heading), but a heading can exist with no associated items

relationship with each of the original entities. This is a surprisingly powerful analytical tool as it forces the designer to consider concepts that would otherwise remain hidden.

Look again at the top diagram in Figure 20-6 and consider the m:m relationship between local machine and card. What is this relationship and does it help us understand anything? The answer is that the relationship represents a transaction: a usage of a local machine by a card. There is nothing particularly interesting in this except perhaps that it means that the local machine will not store long-term details of the card but just deals with transaction details.

ERMIA represents both physical and conceptual aspects of interfaces, which enables comparisons to be made and evaluations to be carried out. Like GOMS and HTA this enables the analyst to undertake model-based evaluation (see the Further thoughts box in Section 20-2). Because ERMIA presents a clear view of the different models, it can be used as part of the process of reasoning about the models. If we have a designer's model that the designer wishes to reveal, he or she can look at the model of the interface and see to what extent the 'intended' model shows up. Similarly one can gather different user views, in the manner of Payne's work, and compare them to the designer's view, making the models and their possible differences explicit through ERMIA. A related approach is the 'cognitive dimensions' framework (Blackwell and Green, 2003).

Box 20-1 Model-based evaluation

Model-based evaluation looks at a model of some human–computer interaction. It can be used either with an existing interface or with an envisaged design. It is particularly useful early in the design process when designs are not advanced enough to be used by real users or when testing with real users is uneconomic or otherwise infeasible. The process involves the designer working through a model of a design, looking for potential problems or areas which might prove difficult. ERMIA can be used like this and GOMS was used in this way in Section 20.4.

Chapter 27 looks at using ERMIA with distributed information

ERMIA models can be used to explore how people have to navigate through various information structures in order to retrieve specific pieces of information and even to estimate the number of steps that people will need to take.

Benyon, Green and Bental (1999) provide a step-by-step guide to developing ERMIA models.

1. After undertaking some requirements and analysis work as usual (through observation, interviewing, etc.) and drawing up some representative scenarios (or tasks), begin to sketch either the perceptual aspects or the conceptual aspects of the interface.

2. Identify the major entities and their relationships with one another.

3. Begin to sketch out the entities and relationships.

4. Replace any m:m relationship with a new entity. Do not worry if you cannot think of a name for it at first. Think about what it is.

5. Iterate and work with the sketch, analysing and identifying more relationships and looking for the characteristics (or attributes) of the entities.

Challenge 20-3
Draw an ERMIA model for the World Wide Web. List the major entities that the Web has and begin to sketch the relationships. Spend at least 10 minutes on this before looking at our solution.

Summary and key points

Task analysis is a key technique in interactive system design. The focus may be on the logical structure of tasks, or the cognitive demands made by tasks procedurally or structurally. Task analysis encompasses task design and it is here that it is probably most useful, as an analysis of a future design is undertaken to reveal difficulties. Task models can also be used for model-based evaluations.

■ Task analysis fits very closely with requirements generation and evaluation methods.

■ Task analysis focuses on goals, tasks and actions.

■ Task analysis is concerned with the logic, cognition or purpose of tasks.

Further reading

John, B. (2003) Information processing and skilled behaviour. In Carroll, J.M. (ed.), *HCI Models, Theories and Frameworks*. Morgan Kaufmann, San Francisco. This provides an excellent discussion of GOMS.

Annett, J. (2004) Hierarchical task analysis. In Diaper, D. and Stanton, N. (eds), *The Handbook of Task Analysis for Human–Computer Interaction*. Lawrence Erlbaum Associates, Mahwah, NJ.

Green, T.R.G. and Benyon, D.R. (1996) The skull beneath the skin: entity–relationship modelling of information artefacts. *International Journal of Human–Computer Studies*, **44**(6), 801–828.

Going forward

Carroll, J.M. (ed.) (2003) *HCI Models, Theories and Frameworks*. Morgan Kaufmann, San Francisco.
This is an excellent introduction to many of the key task analysis methods and includes a chapter by Steve Payne, 'Users' mental models: the very ideas', a good chapter on cognitive work analysis by Penelope Sanderson, and the chapter by Bonnie John on GOMS.

Diaper, D. and Stanton, N. (eds) (2004) *The Handbook of Task Analysis for Human–Computer Interaction*. Lawrence Erlbaum Associates, Mahwah, NJ.
A very comprehensive coverage of task analysis with chapters from all the major writers on the subject. There is a good introductory chapter by Diaper and two good concluding chapters by the editors.

Benyon, D.R., Green, T.R.G. and Bental, D. (1999) *Conceptual Modelling for Human–Computer Interaction, Using ERMIA*. Springer-Verlag, London.
The 'how-to-do-it' book on ERMIA.

www.cl.cam.ac.uk/~afb21/CognitiveDimensions
The website for cognitive dimensions work.

Comments on challenges

Challenge 20-1

The overall goal of this activity is to have the VCR record a TV programme. This will involve the following tasks: (1) putting a tape into the VCR, (2) programming the right TV channel, (3) programming the right time to start and stop the recording, and (4) setting the VCR to automatically record. Task 1 will involve the following subtasks: (1.1) finding a suitable tape, (1.2) ensuring there is enough tape to record onto, and (1.3) inserting the tape into the VCR. Task 1.1 will involve all manner of considerations such as whether it is OK to record over some other programme. Similarly task 1.2 may involve just a visual scan of the amount of tape – maybe it should be rewound to the beginning of the tape, or perhaps you need to watch some of what is already on the tape to find out where that programme ends. Different VCRs will have different facilities to help (or hinder) you in making this decision. Task 1.3 should be straightforward, but someone who is unfamiliar with a particular VCR might get the tape round the wrong way, it may be necessary to eject a tape that is already in the VCR and so on. A simple action for the expert – insert the tape – may be quite a lengthy task for the novice.

Challenge 20-2

GOMS goal hierarchy	Observed behaviour
Goal: present personal ID	
Goal: insert card	
Goal: locate slot	Card inserted
	Screen displays 'enter PIN'
Goal: enter PIN	
Recall number	
Locate number on keypad	Press key
	Beep + *
Repeat 4 times	

Challenge 20-3

The major entities you should have thought of are Web pages and links. Then there are websites. There are many other things on the Web; files are one type of thing, or you may have thought of different types of file such as PDF files, Word files, GIFs, JPEGs and so on. Overall, though, the Web has quite a simple structure, at least to start with. A website has many pages, but a page belongs to just one site. A page has many links, but a link relates to just one page. This is summarized in Figure 20-9.

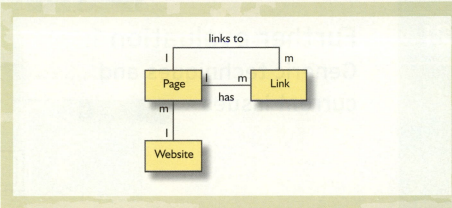

FIGURE 20-9

As soon as we have this basic structure we start questioning it. What about 'mirror' sites? A link can point to a whole website, so we should include that in our model. How are we defining a page? Or a site? This will affect how we model things. What about within-page links? And so on.

Exercises

1. Undertake an HTA style analysis for phoning a friend of yours whose number you have in the phone's address book. Of course the actual actions will be different for different phones. If you can, compare your solution to someone else's. Or try it with two different phones.

2. Now translate the HTA into a GOMS analysis. What different insights into the task does this give you?

21

Further evaluation 1:
Generic techniques and current issues

Aims

This chapter and Chapter 22 are a complementary pair. Together, they supplement the basic evaluation techniques described in Chapter 12. They are intended to be used as a resource for study or practical evaluation in a variety of circumstances and as such it is not necessary to read the whole chapter in order to apply an individual technique (but see the introduction below). The material provides you with enough information to appreciate the underlying issues, to understand what the techniques involve – and in most cases to apply them – and where to find further details.

Towards the end of this chapter (Section 21.4) you will find a discussion of current debates and practice in evaluation. This is recommended for anyone needing a deeper understanding of what evaluation techniques can and cannot deliver.

After studying this chapter you should be able to:

- Appreciate the uses of a range of generally applicable evaluation techniques designed for use with and without users
- Apply the techniques in appropriate contexts
- Be aware of current issues in evaluation and the limitations of what can be achieved.

Chapter 22 extends our coverage of evaluation with information about special-purpose approaches designed for particular domains.

21.1 Introduction: establishing the context for evaluation

As we stressed in Chapter 12, before undertaking an evaluation project it is vital to clarify objectives, and to plan the work to provide usable feedback.

Recapping briefly from Chapter 12, establishing evaluation objectives means considering each of the elements of the 'IMPACT' framework.

- *Intention*: Clarify the aim(s) for the evaluation project.
- *Metrics and measures*: What is to be measured, how and why? Be careful that each planned measure actually helps to answer evaluation questions.
- *People*: What is the target population for the technology being evaluated? How will they be represented in evaluation work?
- *Activities*: What activities will be supported by the technology? Use scenarios to set the scene for users (and expert evaluators), and to draw up the list of actions which they will undertake.
- *Contexts*: What aspects of the wider social and physical context may affect the way the technology is used? How will they be taken into account in evaluation?
- *Technologies*: What hardware and software will be used to deliver the product? How far can or should these be used in the evaluation? What tools are needed to support the evaluation process itself?

It would be useful to read Sections 12.1, 12.3 and 12.5 before embarking on techniques from this chapter

21.2 Further techniques for evaluation with users

This section introduces a wider range of approaches to working with users in evaluation.

Questionnaires and checklists

Whenever we ask students to suggest data collection techniques, the questionnaire is the first to be mentioned. Some form of questionnaire is included in many student projects. In the majority of these questionnaires it is hard to see how any usable information could have been obtained. This is because questionnaires are *not* an easy option for capturing evaluation data (or any other user-related material). All this being said, you may decide that a questionnaire is indeed the best option. Perhaps you need to collect a large amount of quantifiable data, or to capture responses from users who cannot be involved more directly. If so, read on …

A good questionnaire is time-consuming to construct so that all the items:

- are understandable
- are unambiguous

- collect data which actually answers evaluation questions
- can be analysed easily.

Challenge 21-1
What is wrong with the question 'How many people share your PC?' Compose a question which would be more effective in gathering data about (a) how many people share a PC with others and (b) how many other people this is.

Response rates to questionnaires can be very low indeed – return rates of under 10 percent are common if the intended respondents have no particular stake in the design of the technology or incentive to participate. Where questionnaires are administered as part of a face-to-face evaluation session most people will complete them, but people who take them away to finish in their own time very often don't.

Finally, analysing the data requires thought and time. If most users have awarded feature 'A' 5 out of 7 for usefulness but feature 'B' 6 out of 7, does this really mean that feature B is better? Or is it enough that both features score above the mid-point? Maybe feature A was misunderstood – without a follow-up question the data is difficult to interpret. This is easy to do in an interview, but would add significantly to the length of a questionnaire. Where users have been given the opportunity to express opinions as unstructured answers, you will need to devise a scheme for classifying this material so that it is usable.

You should first consult Section 12.5 which introduces some basic issues in the design of evaluation questionnaires. The 'hints and tips' in Box 21-1 (an edited version of Robson, 1993, pp. 247–252) should help you to produce more worthwhile questionnaires. If the questionnaire is very lengthy, however, or targeted at a very large group, then we strongly recommend you consult a reference such as Oppenheim (2000) or an expert in questionnaire design.

Perhaps the most important piece of advice is to pilot the questionnaire in draft form with a few people who are similar to the target group. It is always surprising how an apparently simple question can be misunderstood.

← Chapter 14, Section 14.8 evaluates on interface using a questionnaire. Criticise this.

Box 21-1   Hints and tips for design of evaluation questionnaires

Specific questions are better than general ones

General questions (a) tend to produce a wider variety of interpretation by respondents; (b) are more likely to be influenced by other questions; and (c) are poorer predictors of actual behaviour.

General: List the software packages you have used.

Specific: Which of these software packages have you used?

Visual Basic ☐   Word ☐   Excel ☐   PowerPoint ☐

Closed questions are usually preferable to open questions

Closed questions help to avoid differences in interpretation. Open questions are more difficult to analyse, but can be useful, for instance, when seeking comments in the respondent's own words, when not enough is known to construct closed questions, and for potentially sensitive items.

Open: People look for different things in a job; what sort of things are important to you in your job?

Closed: People look for different things in a job; which <u>one</u> of the following five things is most important to you?

good pay ☐
a feeling of achievement ☐
ability to make your own decisions ☐
good people to work with ☐
job security ☐

Consider a 'no-opinion' option

If there is no such option people may manufacture an opinion for the questionnaire.

Mobile communications technology has made life easier. Do you agree, disagree or not have an opinion?

Agree ☐   Disagree ☐   No opinion ☐

However, a middle choice may encourage a non-committal response. One strategy is to omit the middle choice and follow up with an 'intensity item' which separates out strong from mild feelings.

Do you think mobile communications technology has made life easier or more difficult? Please tick the number which reflects your opinion.

Easier   1   2   3   4   More difficult

How strongly do you feel about this?

Extremely strongly   1   2   3   4   5   Not at all strongly

Vary the orientation of rating scales or intersperse with other questions

If a questionnaire contains a lot of similar scales, all of which have, say, the 'good' end at the left and the 'bad' end at the right, people may go down the page ticking each scale in the same place. Either reverse some scales or put some other types of question in between.

Appearance, order and instructions are vital

The questionnaire should look easy to fill in, with plenty of space for questions and answers. Initial questions should be easy and interesting. Middle questions cover the more difficult areas. Make the last questions interesting to encourage completion and return of the questionnaire. Keep the design simple and give clear instructions, repeating them if confusion seems possible. Ticking boxes is less confusing than circling answers.

Add introductory and concluding notes

The introduction should explain the purpose of the survey, assure confidentiality and encourage reply. The concluding note can ask respondents to check they have answered all questions,

▶

encourage an early return of the questionnaire with the deadline date (and return details, if not using a pre-addressed envelope), offer to send a summary of the findings, if appropriate, and thank them for their help.

Make return easy

Using internal mail is often easiest (include a pre-addressed envelope). Or arrange for a box to be placed in a convenient place to be collected by you. For people who habitually use e-mail, an e-mail questionnaire can be one of the easiest ways to get a good response rate. The Web is also worth considering. Postal returns should of course include a pre-paid return envelope.

Source: edited from Robson (1993), pp. 247-252

We have already introduced heuristic evaluation in Chapter 12

A simpler alternative to questionnaires, particularly where a quick impression is needed, is to have users select yes/no answers against a checklist of attributes of the technology, such as 'I feel confident in using this' or 'Features always work in a consistent way'. This is relatively rapid to produce and administer, but obviously loses detail.

Participatory heuristic evaluation

In Chapter 22 we will see some versions of heuristic evaluation intended for special contexts

This is helpful for introducing the user perspective into early evaluation, but does add to the time needed.

The developers of participatory heuristic evaluation (Muller *et al.*, 1998) claim that it extends the power of the technique without adding greatly to the effort required. An expanded list of heuristics is provided, based on those of Nielsen and Mack (1994). The extra items provide real-world context by introducing considera-tion of users' jobs and tasks (heuristics 12–15 in the list in Box 21-2). The procedure for the use of participatory heuristic evaluation is just as for the expert version (explained in Chapter 12), but users are involved as 'work-domain experts' alongside usability experts and must be briefed about what is required.

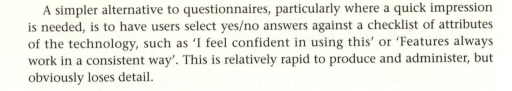

Box 21-2 Heuristics for participatory heuristic evaluation

System status

1. **System status.** The system keeps users informed about what is going on through appropriate feedback in a reasonable time.

User control and freedom

2. **Task sequencing.** Users can select and sequence tasks (when appropriate), rather than the system taking control. 'Wizards' are optional and under user control.

3. **Emergency exits.** Users can:
    - easily find quick 'emergency exits' from mistakes, and are informed clearly of the consequences
    - access undo and redo operations.
4. **Flexibility and efficiency of use.** Shortcuts/accelerators are available, but are unseen by the novice. Users can tailor frequent actions. Alternative means of operation are available to support individual differences, e.g. in physical or cognitive ability, culture or language.

Consistency and relevancy

5. **Match between system and the real world.** The system uses familiar terminology and concepts, rather than system-oriented terms. Messages are presented in a natural and logical order.
6. **Consistency and standards.** Each term or image is used consistently. The conventions of the 'house style', operating system or platform are followed.
7. **Recognition rather than recall.** Objects, actions and options are visible. The user does not have to remember information from one part of an operation to another. Instructions are clearly visible or easily retrievable whenever appropriate.
8. **Aesthetic and minimalist design.** The overall design is pleasing to the eye; no more information is presented than is needed.
9. **Help and documentation.** The system is intuitive and can be used for most common tasks without documentation. Where needed, documentation is easy to search, is task-oriented and lists concrete steps to be carried out. Large manuals have multiple means of locating material (tables of contents, indexes, searches, etc.).

Error recognition and recovery

10. **Help users recognize, diagnose and recover from errors.** Error messages indicate the problem precisely and suggest a solution. They are expressed in plain language. Users are not blamed for the error.
11. **Error prevention.** The design prevents errors happening wherever possible.

Task and work support

12. **Skills.** The system supplements users' skills and knowledge rather than replacing them.
13. **Pleasurable and respectful interaction.** The user's interactions enhance the quality of work, leisure or home experience. The design reflects personal and/or professional roles and identities.
14. **Quality work.** The system supports the user in delivering high quality work (if appropriate). Attributes of quality work include timeliness, accuracy, aesthetics and completeness.
15. **Privacy.** The system helps the user to protect personal or private information.

Source: edited from Muller et al. (1998)

Co-discovery

Co-discovery is a naturalistic, informal technique which is particularly good for capturing first impressions. It is best used in the later stages of design.

The standard approach of watching single users interacting with the technology, and possibly 'thinking aloud' as they do so, can be varied by having users explore new technology in pairs. For example, a series of pairs of people could be given a late prototype of a new digital camera and asked to experiment with its features by taking pictures of each other and objects in the room. This tends to elicit a more naturalistic flow of comment, and people will often encourage each other to try interactions which they may not have thought of in isolation. It is a good idea to use people who know each other quite well. As with most other techniques, it also helps to set users some realistic tasks to try out.

Depending on the data to be collected, the evaluator can take an active part in the session by asking questions or suggesting activities, or simply monitor the interaction either live or using a video-recording. Inevitably, asking specific questions skews the output towards the evaluator's interests, but does help to ensure that all important angles are covered. The term 'co-discovery' originates from Kemp and van Gelderen (1996) who provide a detailed description of its use.

Evaluation without being there

This section suggests some ideas for when participants cannot come to the evaluation site. Relatively finished software is required.

With the arrival of Internet connectivity, users can participate without being physically present. If the application itself is Web-based, or can be installed remotely, instructions can be supplied so that users can run test tasks and fill in and return questionnaires in soft or hard copy. In many cases the software can be programmed to collect usage data such as options selected or links followed – something that is very commonly done for Web applications – and the user's screen can be exported to the display of the person running the evaluation. Users can also take part in more interactive evaluation sessions supported by text conferencing, chat applications or full video conferencing.

The approach developed by Hartson and colleagues (e.g. Hartson and Castillo, 1998) at Virginia Polytechnic Institute and State University centres around user reporting of 'critical incidents' as they happen, or very shortly afterwards. A critical incident is anything related to the application that disturbs the task in hand. Immediate reporting overcomes some of the difficulties in data from post-use questionnaires, where problems may be forgotten or mis-remembered. The critical incident report is amplified by sequences of the user's screen at the time from a screen capture application. More about this approach can be found at http://research.cs.vt.edu/usability/projects/remote%20evaln/remote%20evaln.htm.

Physical and physiological measures

We have just seen how users can be involved at a distance in evaluation. This section is about direct physical and physiological measures as indications of a user's reactions. Again, it is best used on near-completed applications.

For example, eye-movement tracking can show users' changing focus on different areas of the screen. This can indicate which micro features of a user interface have attracted attention, and in which order, or capture larger-scale

FIGURE 21-1 A participant being eye-tracked
(*source: Mullin et al., 2001, p. 42. Courtesy of Jim Mullin*)

gaze patterns indicating, for example, the relative degree of use of video and shared workspaces in conferencing applications. Eye-tracking equipment is head-mounted or attached to computer monitors, as shown in Figure 21-1.

Physiological techniques in evaluation rely on the fact that all our emotions – anxiety, pleasure, apprehension, delight, surprise and so on – generate physiological changes. Some psychophysiologists argue that the physiological reaction (e.g. increased heart rate) comes first, and we then label the sensation (e.g. fear). But the debate is a complex one, and all we need to know here is that emotion does have a physical manifestation.

The most common measures are of changes in heart rate, the rate of respiration, skin temperature, blood volume pulse and galvanic skin response (an indicator of the amount of perspiration). All are indicators of changes in the overall level of arousal, which in turn may be evidence of an emotional reaction. Sensors are attached to the participants' body (commonly the fingertips) and linked to software which converts the results to numerical and graphical formats for analysis.

Which particular emotion is being evoked cannot be deduced from the level of arousal alone, but must be inferred from other data such as facial expression, posture or direct questioning. Thus physiological reaction is rather a blunt instrument for measuring emotional response and we strongly recommend that the help of a psychophysiologist is obtained when using such techniques.

Applications are usually in circumstances where direct questioning would interfere with the interaction being evaluated, and post-trial interviews or questionnaires are thought to be inaccurate because users may be unaware of their emotional response during the trial session. A practical example is in assessing the degree of stress imposed by degradation of video and/or audio quality in networked multimedia applications, as described by Wilson and Sasse (2001). However, as these authors point out, not all physiological measures are useful for all types of interactive tasks. Mullin *et al.* (2001) includes a detailed discussion of these issues.

Another current application is in the assessment of the degree of presence – the sense of 'being there' – evoked by virtual environments (see Figure 21-2).

There is more about the role of emotion in interactive systems design in Chapter 17

FIGURE 21-2 A 20-foot 'precipice' used in evaluating presence in virtual environments (*source: Insko, 2003*)

There is more on the evaluation of presence in Chapter 22

Typically, startling events or threatening features are produced in the environment and arousal levels measured as people encounter them. Researchers at University College London and the University of North Carolina at Chapel Hill (Usoh *et al.*, 1999; Insko, 2001; Meehan, 2001) have conducted a series of experiments when measuring arousal as participants approach a 'virtual precipice'. In these circumstances changes in heart rate correlated most closely with self-reports of stress.

Controlled experiments – a note

Small-scale user evaluations of the type we have discussed so far in this chapter and in Chapter 12 do no more than *indicate* where problems lie or which design is preferable. (See the further discussion of this point in Section 21.4.) It is sometimes necessary to gather precise, statistically validated, quantitative data from an evaluation project. Typically, this will be to demonstrate reliably that one version of a design is 'better' than another according to chosen metrics, or that no more than a certain proportion of errors are made or some similar claim. To do this it is necessary to run properly designed and controlled experiments and analyse them with statistical tests. You will need some basic understanding of probability theory, of experimental theory, and of course of statistics. Daunting as this might sound, it is not so very difficult given a good textbook. *Experimental Design and Statistics* (Miller, 1984) is a widely-used text, and we also recommend Robson (1994). The Robson book is now out of print but may still be held by libraries or available second-hand.

21.3 Predictive evaluation without users

This section extends the 'expert' based techniques introduced in Chapter 12 with two more structured methods. These are not necessarily more difficult to apply than the heuristic-based techniques, but they do require a close attention to detail and – especially for the cognitive walkthrough – a reasonable amount of time.

Claims analysis

Claims analysis is a well-respected method which should be initiated in the early stages of design but can then be used throughout the process.

One of the ways in which scenarios can be extended is to document them with 'claims' about design features. Claims document the envisaged positive effects of the feature but also potential undesirable consequences. Here is the canonical form for a claim, from Carroll (1992) – note that in practice the consequences need not be limited to the psychological:

Scenarios were introduced in Section 8.2.

> *IN < situation > , <a feature >*
> *CAUSES < 'desirable' psychological consequences>*
> *BUT MAY ALSO CAUSE < 'undesirable' psychological consequences >*

And here is an example – in this case concerning supplementary audio feedback in navigating a mobile phone interface:

Claims are also discussed in Chapter 10

> *IN < use by new users> , <audio feedback >*
> *CAUSES < increased ease of navigation>*
> *BUT MAY ALSO CAUSE < embarrassment in public spaces >*

In other words, for users learning to use the device, or where the visibility of the display is restricted, audio feedback may support navigation, but may also cause embarrassment if used in public.

The simple act of composing claims forces the designer to consider the likely advantages of the feature, and is thus an early evaluation technique in itself. It is also possible to use claims to guide the focus of an expert review or user testing.

The cognitive walkthrough technique

This is a rigorous paper-based technique for checking through the detailed design and logic of steps in user interaction. It is used once a full description of user interaction has been completed, but normally before software has been built.

Formal usability inspections are the user interaction version of the formal code inspections carried out by software development companies. Just as code 'inspectors' walk through program code line-by-line with programmers to identify errors in program design and coding, each interactive step in concrete scenarios can be checked for usability flaws. Giving the usability inspection some structure helps to avoid conflict between inspectors and designers: the cognitive walkthrough is the best-established technique here, although practitioners tend to develop tailored versions of structured inspection to suit their own circumstances.

In essence, the cognitive walkthrough entails a usability analyst stepping through the cognitive tasks a user must carry out in interacting with technology. Originally developed by Lewis *et al.* (1990) for applications where users browse and explore information, it has been extended to interactive systems in general (Wharton *et al.*,1994). Aside from its systematic approach, the great strength of the cognitive walkthrough is that it is based on well-established theory rather than the trial and error or a heuristically based approach.

Inputs to the process are:

For concrete scenarios, see Chapter 8

Hierarchical task analysis was described in detail in Chapter 20

■ An understanding of users, their tasks, skills and abilities – the people element of a PACT analysis (for PACT, see Chapter 1)

■ A set of concrete scenarios representing both (a) very common and (b) uncommon but critical sequences of tasks

■ A complete description of the user interface – this should comprise both a representation of how the interface is presented to the user, e.g. screen designs, and the correct sequence of actions for achieving the scenario tasks, usually as a hierarchical task analysis (HTA).

Box 21-3 An extremely short summary of the theory underlying the cognitive walkthrough

The technique is based on a theoretical model of how users learn new technologies. However, deep familiarity with the theory is not required to carry out the walkthrough, since its steps are specified in detail. In brief, the theory is that users start with a goal – for example, to find out the times of flights between Manchester and Edinburgh – and some sort of plan as how to achieve the goal – for example, to find an option that appears to relate to timetables and, through this, to interrogate the system. Users then look for apparently relevant actions, activate the most probable option, consider the system response and decide whether the right effect has been achieved. The cycle then repeats for the next action.

Having gathered these materials together, the analyst asks the following four questions for each individual step in the interaction (this is the version from Wharton *et al.*, 1994, p. 106):

■ Will the user try to achieve the right effect?

■ Will the user notice that the correct action is available?

■ Will the user associate the correct action with the effect that the user is trying to achieve?

■ If the correct action is performed, will the user see that progress is being made towards solution of the task?

If any of the questions is answered in the negative, then a usability problem has been identified and is recorded, but redesign suggestions are not made at this point. If the walkthrough is being used as originally devised, this process is carried out as a group exercise by analysts and designers together. The analysts step through usage scenarios and the design team are required to explain how the user would identify, carry out and monitor the correct sequence of actions. Software designers in organizations with structured quality procedures in place will find some similarities to program code walkthroughs.

Challenge 21-2
A joint walkthrough session between evaluators and designers can work well, but there can be drawbacks. Suggest what these might be and how you might overcome them.

Several cut-down versions of the technique have been devised. Among the best documented are:

■ The 'cognitive jogthrough' (Rowley and Rhoades, 1992) – video records (rather than conventional minutes) are made of walkthrough meetings, annotated to indicate significant items of interest, design suggestions are permitted, and low-level actions are aggregated wherever possible.

■ The 'streamlined cognitive walkthrough' (Spencer, 2000) – designer defensiveness is defused by engendering a problem-solving ethos, and the process is streamlined by not documenting problem-free steps and by combining the four original questions into two (*ibid.*, p. 355):

– Will the user know what to do at each step?

– If the user does the right thing, will they know that they did the right thing, and are making progress towards their goal?

Both these two approaches acknowledge that detail may be lost, but this is more than compensated by enhanced coverage of the system as a whole and by designer buy-in to the process. Finally, the cognitive walkthrough is very often practised (and taught) as a technique executed by the analyst alone, to be followed in some cases by a meeting with the design team. If a written report is required, the problematic interaction step and the difficulties predicted should be explained.

A basic cognitive walkthrough step-by-step

Since its invention, the term 'cognitive walkthrough' has been attached to many techniques which involve a structured consideration of a user's cognitive activity in using technology. In Table 21-1 we set out a generic, simplified cognitive walkthrough. We use a variant of Spencer's (2000) two questions for each step:

■ Will the user know what to do?

■ If the user does the right thing, will they know that they have achieved progress towards their goal?

TABLE 21-1 Generic simplified cognitive walkthrough

Step	Notes
0. Establish context-of-use for the technology and generate detailed concrete scenarios.	Scenarios should cover most common envisaged usage and particularly critical operations.
1. Obtain a detailed description of the user interface.	Should show how the interface is presented to the user, e.g. screen designs and the correct sequence of actions for achieving the scenario tasks, usually represented as a hierarchical task analysis (HTA). Although much of this should be available as design documentation, in practice the analyst may have to prepare this herself. (See Chapter 20 for how to do HTA.)
2. Walk through each scenario. For each interaction step, check: ● Will the user know what to do? ● If the user does the right thing, will they know that they have achieved progress towards their goal?	It is important to apply experience and common sense at this stage, taking into account user skills and background knowledge.
3. If the answer to either of these questions is no, document the problem.	Many problem actions may be essentially similar; in this case simply reference the first instance of the problem. A simple proforma for problem recording is useful here.
4. Review the findings with designers and/or prepare a written report.	Redesign suggestions are not strictly part of the cognitive walkthrough technique, but are likely to improve the chances of action being taken.

An example

This example shows a partial cognitive walkthrough applied to an audio menu – the telephone enquiries and booking line for FreeFly. FreeFly customers collect points from spending with affiliated companies and exchange them for flights or tickets for leisure facilities.

Scenario

Alex has accumulated some FreeFly points, but is not sure how many. He wants to know whether he has enough for a return flight from Manchester to Edinburgh and to find out details of the timetable. He has not yet decided whether to spend just the day in Edinburgh or to stay overnight. This is a family visit and could be arranged for more or less any dates. The choice is thus likely to depend on the possibilities afforded by the timetable. Alex has a FreeFly ID number, but has not used the FreeFly phone enquiry line before. He tends to be rather wary of such services, preferring to speak to a human operator or consult printed material. He phones FreeFly to find out the possibilities.

Partial interface description relating to the scenario

This describes the options presented in the part of the system which is covered in the scenario and how they relate to the intended sequence of customer (user) actions. It corresponds to an annotated screen layout for a screen-based system. Customer actions are shown in *italics*, system actions are preceded thus >>. The letters (**b**) cross-refer to the HTA diagram in Figure 21-3 and the walkthrough results.

Phone FreeFly number
>> Enter your FreeFly ID number using the keys on your phone followed by the hash key. (**b**)
Key ID number (**c**)
Key hash (**d**)
>> To check your points press 1, to amend your details press 2, to check availability and book domestic flights press 3, to check availability and book international flights press 4, to book for other FreeFly promotions press 5, to hear special offers press 6, to speak to an advisor press 7, to hear the choices again press 8.
Key 1 (**e**)
>> Your points total is [points total]. To end the call press 9 ... [5 seconds pause] ... To speak to an advisor hold the line.
Key 9 (**f**)
>> To check your points press 1, to amend your details press 2, to check availability and book domestic flights press 3, to check availability and book international flights press 4, to book for other FlyFree promotions press 5, to hear special offers press 6, to speak to an advisor press 7, to hear the choices again press 8.
Key 3 (**g**)
>> All our advisors are busy. Your call is important to us and is held in a queue. Please wait and we will be with you as soon as possible.
>> Music plays for 15 seconds.
>> All our advisors are busy. Your call is important to us and is held in a queue. Please wait and we will be with you as soon as possible.

>> Music plays for 15 seconds.

>> Your call is important to us and is moving up in the queue. Please continue to hold.

>> Music plays for 15 seconds; cycle of 'hold' messages repeats.

>>[Human] advisor answers. Customer requests and receives timetable details, chooses a flight and completes the booking.

Figure 21-3 shows the hierarchical task analysis (HTA) corresponding to the above options and actions. This shows the task sequence if the goal is achieved as intended. (Note – there are many styles of presenting an HTA. This is one possibility.)

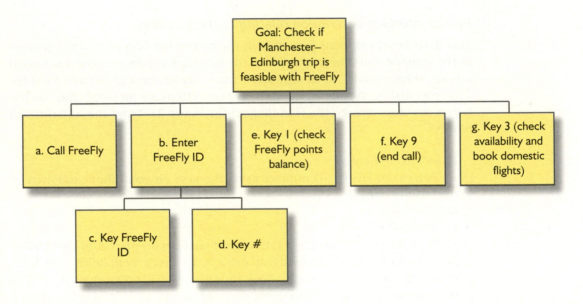

FIGURE 21-3 HTA for checking points and making a timetable enquiry

Walkthrough results

The results of the walkthrough are shown in Table 21-2. For completeness, both 'pass' and 'fail' comments are shown in this example, although 'pass' comments can be omitted if time is short. A table such as this can be used as an appendix to a walkthrough report, but the content should be summarized to make a succinct report of issues and recommendations to the design team.

Limitations of the cognitive walkthrough

A full cognitive walkthrough can be extremely time-consuming if applied exhaustively to substantial systems. Other difficulties may include the production of realistic scenarios and action sequences for novel products and the limitations of the emphasis on novice users. The whole procedure is also heavily

TABLE 21-2 Results of the cognitive walkthrough

Step	Walkthrough questions	Comments
(a) Call FreeFly	Will the user know what to do?	Yes. User is doing this because it is suggested in FreeFly membership documents.
	If the user does the right thing, will they know that they have achieved progress towards their goal?	Yes. Usual ringing tone followed by voice prompts.
(b) Enter FreeFly ID	Will the user know what to do?	Yes, assuming they have their number to hand.
	If the user does the right thing, will they know that they have achieved progress towards their goal?	Yes. Menu is presented.
(c) Key FreeFly ID	Will the user know what to do?	Yes.
	If the user does the right thing, will they know that they have achieved progress towards their goal?	Possibly, but no response is obtained until 'hash' is entered. (Design suggestion – prompt for 'hash' if correct number of digits entered and pause of more than 3? seconds.)
(d) Key #	Will the user know what to do?	Probably – some people may not know which key is 'hash'. (Suggestion – replace 'hash' by star key.)
	If the user does the right thing, will they know that they have achieved progress towards their goal?	Yes. Menu is presented.
(e) Key 1	Will the user know what to do?	Yes. First option on the menu and bears a clear correspondence to user's goal.
	If the user does the right thing, will they know that they have achieved progress towards their goal?	Yes. Points balance is presented.
(f) Key 9	Will the user know what to do?	No. Not obvious. 'End call' suggests terminating the call altogether, not returning to other options. Customer is probably not expecting to speak to an advisor but to listen to timetable details. (Design suggestion – reword as 'choose another option'.)

▶

Step	Walkthrough questions	Comments
	If the user does the right thing, will they know that they have achieved progress towards their goal?	Yes. Menu is presented.
(g) Key 3	Will the user know what to do?	Probably not. No option seems suitable for the goal of hearing the points cost of flights and the timetable, which are in fact accessible under option 3. Also, this is a long list and even if customer decides on option 3 after hearing all options, they may not remember the option number. (Design suggestions – reword option 3 'label' to 'flight costs, availability and bookings' or provide a new option; split the list into two separate menus.)
	If the user does the right thing, will they know that they have achieved progress towards their goal?	Yes, customer is informed call has reached a queue and someone answers eventually. However, there is no information as to expected waiting time or place in queue. (Suggestion – add this information to 'queue' message.)

reliant on a theoretical model of human action based on goal-directed planning. Many HCI theorists, notably and influentially Lucy Suchman (1987), reject such a model, arguing that behaviour is fundamentally situated in context and therefore triggered by environmental cues rather than planned in advance. From such a viewpoint, the formal cognitive walkthrough is fundamentally flawed. Finally, the limited model of the user's world employed in the cognitive walkthrough cannot take into account conditions of real use, for example interruptions which may hinder the interactive process or experience of other applications which may help. Nonetheless, the technique remains reasonably widely used in industry and continues to be researched and developed further by academics and practitioners.

21.4 Current issues in evaluation

Designers can choose from an impressive array of techniques for different evaluation problems, many of which we have described in this book. But while applying the individual techniques is often straightforward, deciding what conclusions can be drawn is not. This section discusses why. There are no easy solutions to these issues: rather the point is to be aware of their existence and thoughtful in the application of evaluation results.

'Discount usability' and the role of controlled user testing

We presented a discount evaluation in Chapter 4

In Chapter 12, we suggested that around five users are enough for basic usability testing. This follows the 'discount usability engineering' approach pioneered by Jakob Nielsen (1993) and enthusiastically followed by many time-pressured evaluation practitioners. We also recommended that this number should be extended where user groups subdivided along relevant characteristics such as pre-existing skills. Increasingly, however, both academics and practitioners have argued that testing a small number of people is at best of limited use and at worst misleading. Ken Dye of Microsoft, for example, observed in a keynote address to the British HCI conference in 2001 (Dye, 2001) that the company has found it necessary to have large numbers of users to avoid problems of being swamped by individual differences between users. Taking a different slant, Woolrych and Cockton (2001) contend that the formula underlying the 'five users' advice is flawed because it depends on assumptions of low variation between the 'discoverability' of problems, the type of user tasks and the characteristics of the users themselves.

The issue here is that users of a discount approach need to be absolutely clear about what can and cannot be claimed about the results. Testing small numbers of users will help to *identify* and *diagnose* problems in interaction design. But it will not *prove* (or *disprove*) that the product is usable, enjoyable or meets any other criterion of interest to the designer or client, nor *predict* how the user population at large will react. Statistical constraints do not allow us to assume that because four out of five test users found no usability problems this will also be true for 80 percent of the real user population.

Heuristic evaluation has similar limitations. Part of the difficulty lies in its apparent ease of use. This means that it is a relative simple (although tedious) task even for novice evaluators to produce a list of design flaws with their related heuristics, and it is for this reason we include it as a basic technique in Chapter 12. However, as we observed briefly in that chapter, not all the issues identified will translate into genuine problems for users, and some problems may be missed.

Woolrych and Cockton (2000) conducted a large-scale trial of heuristic evaluation. Evaluators were trained to use the technique, then evaluated the user interface to a drawing editor. The editor was then trialled by users. Comparison of findings showed that many of the issues identified by the evaluators were not experienced by users (false positives), while some severe difficulties were missed by the inspection against heuristics. There were a number of reasons for this. Many false positives stemmed from a tendency to assume no intelligence or even commonsense on the part of users (what the authors memorably characterize as the 'misrepresentation of users as helpless imbeciles'). As for 'missing' problems, these tended to result from a series of user mistakes and misconceptions, often relating to a set of linked items, rather than isolated misunderstandings. Sometimes heuristics were misapplied, or apparently added as an afterthought. Woolrych and Cockton conclude that the heuristics add little advantage to an expert evaluation and the results of applying them may be counter-productive. They (and other authors) suggest that more theoretically informed techniques such as the cognitive walkthrough offer more robust support for problem identification. It is very evident that heuristic evaluation is not a complete solution. At the very least, the technique must be used together with careful consideration of users and their real-life skills and tasks, and ideally, as suggested in Chapter 12, in combination with user testing.

Limited user testing and heuristic evaluation therefore are valuable as *formative* evaluation, to help the designer improve user interaction. They should not be used as a *summative* assessment, to make claims about the usability and other characteristics of a finished product. If that is what we need to do, then we must carry out properly designed and controlled experiments with a much greater number of users. However, the more controlled the testing situation becomes, the less it is likely to resemble the real world, which leads us to the question of 'ecological validity'.

Challenge 21-3

You have just completed a small evaluation project for a tourist information 'walk-up-and-use' kiosk designed for an airport arrivals area. A heuristic evaluation by you (you were not involved with the design itself) and a technical author found 17 potential problems for users, of which seven were graded severe enough to require some redesign and the rest were fairly trivial.

You then carried out some user testing. You had very little time for this, testing with only three users. The test focused on the more severe problems found in the heuristic evaluation and the most important functionality (as identified in the requirements analysis). Your test users – again because of lack of time and budget – were recruited from another section of your own organization who are not directly involved in interactive systems design or build, but who do use desktop PCs as part of their normal work. The testing took place in a quiet corner of the development office.

Participants in the user evaluation all found difficulty with three of the problematic design features flagged up by the heuristic evaluation. These problems were essentially concerned with knowing what information might be found in different sections of the application. Of the remaining four severe problems from heuristic evaluation, one person had difficulty with all of them, but the other two people did not. Two out of the three test users failed to complete a long transaction where they tried to find and book hotel rooms for a party of travellers staying for different periods of time.

What, if anything, can you conclude from the evaluation? What are the limitations of the data?

Further thoughts: Ecological validity

In real life, people multitask, use several applications in parallel or in quick succession, are interrupted, improvise, ask other people for help, use applications intermittently and adapt technologies for purposes the designers never imagined. We have unpredictable, complex but generally effective coping strategies for everyday life and the technologies supporting it. The small tasks which are the focus of most evaluations are usually part of lengthy sequences directed towards aims which change according to circumstances. All of this is extremely difficult to reproduce in testing, and often deliberately excluded. So the results of most user testing can only ever be indicative of issues in real-life usage. Practitioners and researchers are not unaware of this problem and a number of solutions have been proposed. They include:

- Ethnographically informed observations of technologies in long-term use (although this is more often undertaken earlier in the design–evaluation cycle) – see Chapter 29
- Having users keep diaries, which can be audio-visual as well as written – there is more about this in Chapter 17
- Collecting 'bug' reports – often these are usability problems – and help centre queries.

Evaluation in practice

A survey of 103 experienced user-centred design practitioners conducted in 2000 (Vredenburg *et al.*, 2002) indicates that around 40 percent of those surveyed conducted 'usability evaluation' (i.e. testing with users), around 30 percent used 'informal expert review' and around 15 percent used 'formal heuristic evaluation' (Table 21-3). These figures do not indicate where people used more than one technique. The popularity of informal expert review is interesting, since data (not included in Table 21-3) indicated that it was not felt to have a strong impact on end products. As the authors note, some kind of cost–benefit trade-off seems to be in operation. Table 21-3 shows the benefits and weaknesses perceived for each method. For busy practitioners, the relative economy of review methods often compensates for the better information obtained from user testing. Clearly the community remains in need of methods which are both light on resources and productive of useful results.

Indeed the Vredenburg survey supports our own experience that user-centred specialists working in organizations where usability is a new area of concern, and/or where resources are very limited, will find their main role is as an expert evaluator. Often this entails being asked by a designer to 'approve' an interface in a near-complete state. While this is far from ideal, such a review process can feed in useful suggestions for future designs and kick-start the process of infiltrating user-centred practice into the earlier stages of development.

TABLE 21-3 Perceived costs and benefits of evaluation methods. A '+' sign denotes a benefit, and a '−' a weakness. The numbers indicate how many respondents mentioned the benefit or weakness.

Benefit/weakness	Formal heuristic evaluation	Informal expert review	Usability evaluation
Cost	+ (9)	+ (12)	− (6)
Availability of expertise	− (3)	− (4)	
Availability of information			+ (3)
Speed	+ (10)	+ (22)	− (3)
User involvement	− (7)	− (10)	
Compatibility with practice			− (3)
Versatility			− (4)
Ease of documentation			− (3)
Validity/quality of results	+ (6)	+ (7)	+ (8)
Understanding context	− (10)	− (17)	− (3)
Credibility of results			+ (7)

Source: adapted from Vredenburg, K., Mao, J.-Y., Smith, P.W. and Carey, T. (2002) A survey of user-centred design practice, Proceedings of CHI' 02 Conference, Minneapolis, MN, 20–25 April, pp. 471–78, Table 3. © 2002 ACM, Inc. Reprinted by permission

Summary and key points

This chapter has provided a further range of formal and informal evaluation techniques which can be applied in a variety of circumstances. Carefully constructed questionnaires, for example, will play a part in many user-based evaluations, but are most cost-effective when collecting data from a large number of users. Those working with limited resources may find participatory heuristic evaluation can strike a balance between user-based and expert-based methods. By contrast, where reliable, predictive data is required, full-scale usability experiments may be considered worthwhile. Physiological measurements – usually obtained under experimental conditions – have become increasingly used recently, and may overcome some of the drawbacks of users reporting on their reactions.

We concluded with a discussion of current debates in evaluation practice, drawing attention to the limitations of small-scale usability testing, the problem of ecological validity and actual real-world practice.

Further reading

The British HCI Group's website www.usabilitynews.com often carries current debates about usability evaluation.

Woolrych and Cockton (2001) carry forward their work on the limitations of discount usability engineering approaches, while Jakob Nielsen's website www.useit.com carries his latest thinking on their value.

Going forward

The tutorial provided at the HCI 2001 conference is an excellent introduction to the use of physiological methods, although focusing on issues of audio and visual quality. It can be accessed at www-mice.cs.ucl.ac.uk/multimedia/projects/etna.

Wharton *et al.* (1992) provide a detailed account of the full cognitive walk-through procedure which is recommended for those wishing to understand the underlying principles in more depth.

Comments on challenges

Challenge 21-1
This question was actually included in a probe about PC availability. It was expected that if the respondent shared the PC with one other person, they should answer '1'; if two other people then '2' and so on. It was apparent, however, from the responses that some people counted themselves in their figures, so replying with '2' if only one other person used the machine. It was impossible to decide in many cases which counting strategy had been adopted.

Challenge 21-2
Potential difficulties include over-defensiveness on the part of the designers and consequently lengthy explanations of design rationale and a confrontational atmosphere. It would be a good idea to hold a preliminary meeting to diffuse these feelings from the start. Also, asking the *designers* the walk-through questions may help people to identify issues themselves rather than feeling under attack.

▶

Challenge 21-3
It is likely that the three problems found in both evaluations are genuine, not merely induced by the testing procedures. You cannot really conclude very much about the remaining four, but should review the relevant parts of the design. The difficulties with long transactions are also probably genuine, and unlikely to have been highlighted by heuristics. In all these cases you should ideally test the redesigns with real representative users.

Exercises

1. You are evaluating the usability of a new e-mail utility designed for use on a PDA, firstly during early design before a working software prototype exists and later when the prototype is fully functional. The interface uses input from a stylus and includes an on-screen keyboard. Voice input and output are also provided. Describe what techniques you would use, why, and the major problems foreseen. *Hint*: It would help to consult Chapter 12 as well as the present chapter for this exercise.

2. Prepare a report for the development manager of a small software producer setting out the advantages and disadvantages of discount usability evaluation and your recommendations as to whether this approach should be adopted by the organization.

3. Consider your current e-mail tool. Carry out a cognitive walkthrough for the task of sending a message with file attachment to multiple recipients. Assume users are generally PC/Mac literate but not familiar with this particular e-mail utility. You should write a scenario and carry out an HTA before performing the walkthrough itself.

22

Further evaluation 2:
Special contexts

Aims

This chapter complements Chapter 21 with special-purpose evaluation techniques devised for particular domains and types of product. As before, this is not intended to be read straight through, but consulted as a resource. We provide material which will support the evaluation of the following:

- Virtual environments
- Small mobile devices
- CSCW (computer-supported cooperative work) systems
- Home and leisure products.

For some of these applications, techniques are relatively mature and exist as checklists, frameworks, walkthroughs and so forth which are ready to be applied. But for mobile and home devices in particular, approaches to evaluation are still very immature. For these domains we introduce research into novel evaluation techniques.

22.1 Evaluating virtual environments

Virtual environments introduce an extra layer for evaluation: not only are there (sometimes) a selection of generic interface widgets such as menus, but the user must also interact with objects and people within the environment. Special-purpose variants of the cognitive walkthrough have been developed to deal with this.

The work of the European-funded COVEN project (Tromp *et al.*, 1998), for example, concerns collaborative virtual environments (CVEs). A series of sets of cognitive walkthrough questions are provided dealing with different aspects of action and collaboration in the CVE. The full walkthrough is a significant undertaking, and you should consult the COVEN documentation if you wish to use the technique. As an example, the questions relating to communicating with other users are set out below.

- Can the user locate the other user(s)?
- Can the user recognize the identity of the other user(s), tell the other users apart?
- Are the communication channels between the users effective?
- Are the actions of the other user(s) visible and recognizable?
- Can the user act on a shared object while keeping the other user(s) in view? Can the user easily switch views between the shared object, other locations/objects of interest and the other user(s) (sweep from one to the other)?
- Can the user get an overview of the total shared space and all other users in it?
- Can the user tell when there are interruptions in the attention of the other user(s) to the CVE?

Evaluating presence

Designers of virtual reality – and some multimedia – applications are often concerned with the sense of presence, of being 'there' in the virtual environment rather then 'here' in the room where the technology is being used. A strong sense of presence is thought to be crucial for such applications as games, those designed to treat phobias, or to allow people to 'visit' real places they may never see otherwise, or indeed for some workplace applications such as training to operate effectively under stress. This is a very current research topic, and there are no techniques which deal with all the issues satisfactorily. The difficulties include:

- The sense of presence is strongly entangled with individual dispositions, experiences and expectations. Of course this is also the case with reactions to any interactive systems, but presence is an extreme example of this problem.
- The concept of presence itself is ill-defined and the subject of much debate among researchers. Variants include the sense that the virtual environment is realistic, the extent to which the user is impervious to the outside world, the retrospective sense of having visited rather than viewed a location and a number of others.
- Asking people about presence while they are experiencing the virtual environment tends to interfere with the experience itself. On the other hand, asking questions retrospectively inevitably fails to capture the experience as it is lived.

The measures used in evaluating presence adapt various strategies to avoid these problems, but none are wholly satisfactory. The various questionnaire measures, for example the questionnaire developed by NASA scientists Witmer and Singer

(1998) or the range of instruments developed at University College and Goldsmiths' College, London (Slater, 1999; Lessiter *et al.*, 2001) can be cross-referenced to measures which attempt to quantify how far a person is generally susceptible to being 'wrapped up' in experiences mediated by books, films, games and so on as well as through virtual reality. The Witmer and Singer Immersive Tendencies Questionnaire (Witmer and Singer, 1998) is the best known of such instruments. However, presence as measured by presence questionnaires is a slippery and ill-defined concept. In one experiment, questionnaire results showed that while many people did not feel wholly present in the virtual environment (a re-creation of an office), some of them did not feel wholly present in the real-world office either (Usoh *et al.*, 2000). Less structured attempts to capture verbal accounts of presence include having people write accounts of their experience, or inviting them to provide free-form comments in an interview. The results are then analysed for indications of a sense of presence. The difficulty here lies in defining what should be treated as such an indicator, and in the layers of indirection introduced by the relative verbal dexterity of the participant and the interpretation imposed by the analyst.

Other approaches to measuring presence attempt to avoid such layers of indirection by observing behaviour in the virtual environment or by direct physiological measures such as those described in Chapter 21.

Challenge 22-1
What indicators of presence might one measure using physiological techniques? Are there any issues in interpreting the resulting data?

22.2 Evaluating small mobile devices

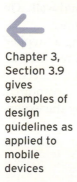

Chapter 3, Section 3.9 gives examples of design guidelines as applied to mobile devices

Small mobile devices, whether mobile (cell) phones, portable music players, PDAs or hybrids of these, test the creativity of the evaluator. The whole essence of the device is that it can be used almost anywhere. Often, this means on the move, and/or while engaging in almost any of the multitude of activities of which human beings are capable. One way of dealing with all this complexity is to look at the underlying issues which affect use, which might range from the ergonomics of small keypad design to the matter of mental workload – the amount of mental effort required to operate the device. Mental workload is an important factor for the designers of mobile devices because of their use in conjunction with other activities, even if the activity in question is simply walking along the street.

An example: evaluating gesture input and audio feedback for a Pocket PC application

The GIST (Glasgow Interactive Systems) group at the University of Glasgow and their collaborators elsewhere have carried out a great deal of recent work on mobiles. We have included an example of their work here since it shows neatly how new evaluation techniques can be devised to extend established usability approaches. The full account can be found in Pirhonen *et al*. (2002).

The design concepts to be tested were a new gestural (touch) and audio-based interface for the Windows Media Player running on a Hewlett-Packard iPAQ Pocket PC. In brief, two approaches were taken, a classic usability experiment gathering quantitative data and a video-based study capturing qualitative information about users' behaviour.

The usability experiment required participants to wear the iPAQ running either Media Player or the experimental 'TouchPlayer' while walking up and down a corridor. A series of prespecified tasks were carried out by the participants as they walked, for example 'Find the song Wonderwall'. The measures taken are a good example of combining standard usability metrics with special-purpose techniques designed to address particular aspects of the context of use. They were:

■ Overall time to complete the experiment

■ Time to complete each individual task

■ Erroneous input gestures

■ Mental workload

■ Percentage of normal walking speed achieved.

Mental workload was measured using the TLX (Task Load indeX), a questionnaire developed at NASA and widely used elsewhere. In this case an 'annoyance' scale was added, since earlier research had suggested that audio feedback could be irritating for users. Walking speed was measured since it was considered that the more intrusive the use of the device was, the slower people would walk. On all measures, the TouchPlayer proved more successful in usability terms.

The companion study tested the TouchPlayer again, this time using a 'stepper' machine to simulate walking on level ground or upstairs. This represented an attempted compromise between real-world walking conditions and the need to capture high-quality video data so that small scale behaviours could be captured. This time the participants were given individual task instructions by the experimenter, which were tailored to be as naturalistic as possible. During part of the experiment different audio feedback sounds were introduced. This time the data collection undertaken was:

■ Interviews about relevant personal background and experience of media players

■ Asking participants to indicate when they noticed a change in the nature of the audio feedback

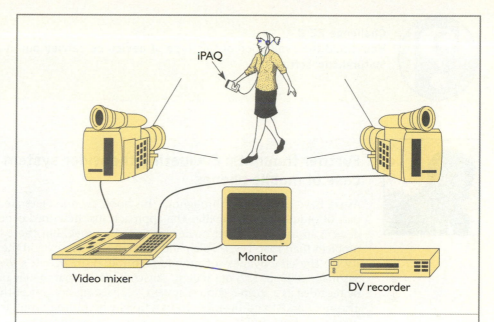

FIGURE 22-1 Capturing video of the TouchPlayer in use
(*source: after Pirhonen, A., Brewster, S. and Holguin, C. (2002) Gestural and audio metaphors as a means of control for mobile devices*, Proceedings of CHI'02 Conference, *Minneapolis, MN, 20–25 April, pp. 291–298, Fig. 7. © 2002 ACM, Inc. Reprinted by permission*)

- Having participants sketch their understanding of the user interface
- Capture of video (overall view and close-up of the interface in use) and audio from the experimental sessions – Figure 22-1 shows the video setup.

Space prevents us from reporting the results themselves here, but they are discussed in detail in the original paper. As for the techniques themselves, all proved practical, and provided rich, detailed information about the performance in use of the interface design. However, the two different experimental sessions uncovered different but complementary types of information. To summarize:

Usability test data	Qualitative 'naturalistic' data
• More precise	• Lower precision but wider scope
• Could use statistical analysis	• Detail about individual interface elements
• Showed overall effect on the user, in particular on user on the move	• Data about gesture and use of sounds
• Allowed comparison of current and new designs	• Data about tentative, therefore unsuccessful, gestures not picked up by the device

Challenge 22-2
How could the evaluation of this type of device be carried out in an even more 'naturalistic' setting?

Further thoughts: Evaluating the wider system – the case of mobile phones

As we have emphasized throughout this book, technologies are fast becoming part of ordinary domestic life. The approach just described copes with mobile devices in use while their owners are on the move, but there is more to the problem than that. Leysia Palen and Marilyn Salzman extend the idea of usability to 'the effectiveness of mobile technology in people's *lives*' (Palen and Salzman, 2002, p. 127, our italics). The core idea is that mobile phone use must be regarded as a socio-technical system – consisting not just of the handset, but also network(s) and business transactions, the billing arrangements, special offers and deals, and so on. Phone users' understanding of these aspects of their phone makes a radical difference to the usability of the devices themselves.

Palen and Salzman worked with 19 people in the first six weeks of their use of their new phones. None had previous experience of mobiles. Call records were collected and the techniques used to gather data from users were as follows:

■ *Interviews*: Three interviews were held over the period, each being video-taped. Interview 1 had users explore their phones for the first time, interview 2 focused on changes in behaviour and use, while interview 3 picked up further changes and participants' understanding of their bills.

■ *Voicemail diaries*: Users were invited to call a dedicated voicemail line with their experiences. The list of issues to comment on included when they first used their phones in a new environment or in an unexpected way, periods when they did not use their phones at all, when they used a new feature or when they had a problem.

The data showed a wide range of problems encountered by new users. There were some genuine usability problems with the handsets, but many difficulties were thought by users to stem from the handset when in fact they were the results of misunderstandings about network services available, signal coverage or charging regimes. A strong theme here was difficulty with the terms used in the phone documentation, some inherited from computing, e.g 'scroll' and 'icon', others used in special ways in the phone context, e.g. 'roaming'.

The results provide ample support for the case for evaluating technologies which deliver services in their wider context. Palen and Salzman sum up the position neatly: 'The user's experience of a technology is ultimately dependent on the actions and reactions that occur within the larger socio-technical system.' (*ibid.*, p. 148)

← Chapter 3, Section 3.4 discusses some of these issues in terms of acceptability

The authors conclude that both approaches were both necessary and useful to capture the range of usability data required.

22.3 Evaluating CSCW and groupware

The main discussion of CSCW (Computer Supported Cooperative Work) forms Part VII of this book, but we discuss evaluation here. CSCW and groupware (the now rather dated term for technologies which support working groups) present a formidable challenge for evaluation. There are a number of interwoven reasons.

- The technology must be effective at (at least) three different levels: for the individual user, the working group and the overall organization. Of course, most work-based technologies have some impact beyond the individual user, but for CSCW, co-working is the very essence of the system.

- Group working practice takes time to adjust to change, but most evaluation techniques take a snapshot at the time a system is introduced.

- Stakeholders in the system may have different perceptions of the benefits of the technology, depending on whether it brings improvements for the person concerned or simply causes more work. On-line shared diaries (calendars) are a classic example, often obliging staff to keep the diary up-to-date with their movements, so that administrators can arrange meetings quickly and easily.

- There are few tried-and-tested techniques. As we will see, there are ways of attacking aspects of the problem in isolation, but even approaches which aim to provide an overall framework will not provide simple answers.

All this means that CSCW evaluation is a complicated activity, requiring careful planning and a good deal of time. We start our review with a variant of the familiar heuristic approach. Then we move on to the problem in more detail, concluding with a brief account of the METATAQ framework, which claims to provide a complete, integrated solution.

Heuristics for groupware

Given that technology for groupworking and academic research into computer supported cooperative work has been around since the late 1980s, it is surprising that only recently have heuristics appeared for groupware evaluation. The heuristics in Box 22-1 stem from the long-standing groupware research in Saul Greenberg's group at the University of Calgary (Baker et al., 2002). The procedure is essentially similar to using any other set of heuristics, but the authors note that it is a good idea for inspectors to use applications in pairs, so that the collaborative features can be explored more easily. The explanations in Box 22-1 have been condensed from the original, which provides more examples and other additional material. Note that the heuristics only relate to groupware which supports real-time collaboration.

Box 22-1 Heuristics for groupware evaluation

1. Provide the means for intentional and appropriate verbal communication

The prevalent form of communication is verbal conversation. This has been termed *intentional communication* and usually happens in one of three ways.

(a) People talk explicitly about what they are doing and where they are working within a shared workspace.
(b) People overhear others' conversations.
(c) People listen to the running commentary that others tend to produce alongside their actions.

2. Provide the means for intentional and appropriate gestural communication

Explicit gestures are used to directly support conversation and convey task information. Intentional gestural communication can take many forms.

3. Provide consequential communication of an individual's embodiment

A person's body interacting with a physical workspace *unintentionally* provides awareness information about what's going on, who is in the workspace, where they are, and what they are doing. This is fundamental for creating and sustaining teamwork, and includes:

(a) *Actions coupled with the workspace*. These include gaze awareness (where someone is looking), seeing someone move towards an object, and hearing sounds as people go about their activities.
(b) *Actions coupled to conversation*. These are the subtle visual or audio cues picked up from our conversational partners that help us continually adjust our verbal behaviour.

4. Provide consequential communication of shared artefacts

Consequential communication also involves information *unintentionally* given off by physical artefacts as they are manipulated. Seeing and hearing an artefact as it is being handled helps to determine what others are doing to it. Identifying the person manipulating the artefact helps to make sense of the action and to mediate interactions.

5. Provide protection

Concurrent activity is common in shared workspaces but it introduces the potential for conflict. People should be protected from inadvertently interfering with the work of others. Collaborators must be able to keep an eye on their own work, noticing what effects others' actions could have and taking actions to prevent certain activities.

6. Manage the transitions between tightly and loosely coupled collaboration

Coupling is the degree to which people are working together. People continually shift back and forth between *loosely* and *tightly coupled collaboration* where they move fluidly between individual and group work. To manage these transitions, people need to maintain awareness of what others are doing. This allows people to recognize when tighter coupling could be appropriate, e.g. when they have reached a stage in their task that requires another's involvement.

7. Support people with the coordination of their actions

An integral part of face-to-face collaboration is how group members mediate their interactions by taking turns and negotiating the sharing of the common workspace. Coordinating actions involves making some tasks happen in the right order and at the right time while meeting the task's constraints. Within a shared workspace, coordination can be accomplished via explicit communication and the way objects are shared.

8. Facilitate finding collaborators and establishing contact

Most meetings are *informal*: unscheduled, spontaneous or initiated by one person. In everyday life, these meetings are facilitated by physical proximity since co-located individuals can maintain awareness of who is around. People frequently come in contact with one another through casual interactions (e.g. bumping into people in hallways) and are able to initiate and conduct conversations effortlessly. In electronic communities, the lack of physical proximity means that other mechanisms are necessary to support awareness and informal encounters.

Adapted from Baker et al (2002)

Beyond heuristics: an affordance-based approach

Affordance is one of the design guidelines described in Chapter 3, Section 3.6. It is also discussed in Chapter 7, Section 7.3

One way of structuring the complex CSCW evaluation problem is to partition the issues by levels of affordance. Affordance, very briefly, it is the way an artefact or technology supports particular behaviours or activities. Affordances do not have to be learned, but rather are implicit in the properties of the artefact. Thus a table affords placing objects upon it, a user interface button affords clicking, a door handle affords pulling and so forth. The concept was originally developed as a theory of perception by the ecological psychologist Gibson (1977), then extended to the usability of computing devices in Don Norman's classic work *The Psychology of Everyday Things* (Norman, 1988). We can extend the idea to include affordances for meaningful user tasks – in this case cooperative activity – and to the fitness of an artefact for its intended purpose, including organizational goals. Affordances of this last type, which we term cultural affordances, are particular to people belonging to the culture or group concerned and so necessitate their involvement in design, and more pertinently here, evaluation.

In the next three subsections we consider techniques for evaluating each type of affordance, illustrating their application with examples from our evaluation of the DISCOVER collaborative virtual environment case study which was introduced in Chapter 9.

Evaluating affordances for individual usability

CSCW systems must be usable in the ordinary way – icons and terms must be comprehensible, feedback perceptible and so on. Not only will usability problems hinder co-working, but much group activity is interwoven with strands of individual work, for example preparation of material to share with other people. In our CVE-based training system, DISCOVER, tutors had to modify features in the environment as the simulation was running, as well as keeping a log of trainees' actions in the CVE. We were also concerned with the affordances of such features as the use of the mouse click as a means of opening doors, setting off fire extinguishers and generally activating objects in the virtual environment.

The straightforward user testing techniques we introduced in Chapter 12 have their place here, and will need little adaptation. If necessary, some testing can take place before the cooperative features are fully functional.

In the DISCOVER project, the emphasis was to obtain basic usability data with minimal resources. Early trials largely employed 'proxy' participants who resembled the eventual user population in relevant skills and experience. This allowed us to conserve the scarce resource of 'real' users for more polished versions of the software and fitness-for-purpose issues later. Users undertook simple but realistic tasks, monitored by observers. Post-trial questionnaires were compiled and administered, adapting usability items from standard usability instruments and the VRUSE questionnaire for virtual environments (Kalawsky, 1999). The trials were supplemented by usability inspections structured by standard heuristics. In the event, most usability problems were identified by a quick expert check of the interface, but the other techniques were able to provide substantive data to back up these observations.

Evaluating affordances for cooperative tasks

Here we are concerned about how easy it is for people to work together through the CSCW system. The focus will vary with context, but typical questions include:

■ Are people sufficiently aware of each other's actions and communications?
■ Are the communication resources sufficient for meaning to be conveyed effectively?
■ Can people collaborate on shared objects without extra work to compensate for the deficiencies of the technology?

Many existing tools for evaluating group performance focus on communication and derive from observational techniques in social psychology. Thus it is possible to examine the structure of conversations – turn-taking, the length and number of 'turns' for each individual, the length of pauses, the use of non-verbal signals and direction of gaze being typical aspects to be measured. Similarly the content of conversations can be scrutinized – how often are others in the group explicitly addressed or referenced, or how do people talk about artefacts in a shared workspace?

Conversational structure can indicate how easily group activity 'flows' and whether the system supports participation by all. Content analysis can pinpoint, for example, whether lengthy explanations are necessary to allow people to act on a shared workspace object. Below we can see an example of this sort of conversation, from a study reported by Hindmarsh *et al.* (1998). This evaluated a desktop collaborative virtual environment designed to explore issues of mutual awareness. Users Sarah and Kate are acting through their avatars to arrange furniture in a virtual room.

> S: You know this desk-thing?
> K: Yeah?
> S: Can you see – what I'm pointing at now?
> (K turns to find S)
> K: Er, I can't see you, but I think –
> S: It's like a desk-thing.
> K: Er – where've you gone? heh heh heh
> S: Erm, where are you?
> K: I've – th- I can see
> S: Tur- oh, oh yeah. You're near the lamp, yeah?
> K: Yeah.
> S: And then, yeah turn around right. And then it's like I'm pointing at it now, but I don't know if you can see what I'm pointing at?
> K: Right yeah I can see.

Slightly edited from Hindmarsh *et al.* (1998), p. 220

Users can also be asked about co-working through questionnaires or interviews, and about more elusive aspects such as their sense of 'social presence' – the feeling that the group were together as in a shared physical environment. The COVEN material discussed earlier in this chapter is a good source of questions in this area.

Returning to our case study, trainees in the DISCOVER environment needed to be able to find each other, to communicate with fellow trainees and tutors, to monitor what others were doing and to interact with various items in the environment, for example to pick up a 'body' overcome by smoke. Tutors had to monitor activity in the CVE to provide guidance and post-training feedback, to communicate with trainees and to modify interactive objects in the CVE such as the location of fires.

Aspects of communication and coordination were initially evaluated in parallel with individual usability. Once the software was stable and more co-working features had been added, more complex trials were carried out. As before, 'proxy' users were used to test basic affordances for coordination and communication. They undertook collaborative tasks similar to those undertaken in a normal training situation. Short post-use questionnaires were administered using items derived from a task analysis. For users adopting the role of tutor, tasks and questionnaire items explored affordances for such pedagogic actions as setting task goals, monitoring trainees and giving feedback. Again, observers monitored the progress, or occasionally lack of progress, of the scenario, supported by checklists mirroring the questionnaire content.

The final version of the software was evaluated with experienced tutors from one of the training organizations involved. (Evaluation techniques had been planned for trials with 'real' trainees, but in the event personnel could not be made available. This work continued outside the project at one of the training organizations.) Tutors undertook a realistic training scenario, authored by one of the training organizations. They took turns to play tutor and trainee roles. They were observed and completed a post-trial questionnaire incorporating the collaborative and pedagogic aspects as before. These trials were videotaped for further analysis of evaluation data.

Evaluating cultural affordances – the organizational level

Beyond the issues of small group working, we are concerned with how far organizational benefits are achieved, for example improved time to process orders, or reduction in travel to meetings. It is here that the relative benefits for different stakeholder groups are most naturally considered. A user cost–benefit analysis (Eason, 1988) provides one way of doing this. In brief, changes in role and tasks are identified for each stakeholder group and an estimate made of whether each change brings a cost or benefit (or a mixed outcome). Organizational 'winners' and 'losers' can then be identified and steps taken to remedy problems. More material on this technique can be found at http://www.lboro.ac.uk/departments/hu/groups/hfsd/ucdm.html.

Where the organization is receptive, treating CSCW evaluation as an occasion for learning can be highly productive. The SESL (Systemic Evaluation for Stakeholder Learning) method developed by Magnus Ramage (Ramage, 1999) is designed to support such a project. The aim is to facilitate learning outcomes for all stakeholders during the evaluation process itself.

At the organizational level, many of the standard approaches used by information systems specialists are applicable, and provide a perspective lacking in many CSCW case studies. Common techniques include:

■ Monitoring the actual use of the system after implementation

■ Assessing how far planned benefits have been achieved

■ Questionnaire surveys of users covering intentions to use (pre-implementation), usage levels and perceptions of benefits (both post-implementation).

Overall evaluation conclusions are rarely simple. Organizational goals may be met by the new CSCW system while failing to enhance individual jobs, or perhaps advantaging some staff at the expense of others. It is our responsibility as evaluators to carry out properly designed studies, and to report on the results clearly and accurately, but in the end the conclusions reached are a matter for the owners of the CSCW system. The case study in Box 22-2 is a striking example of this.

The purpose of the DISCOVER CVE was the learning of emergency management skills for offshore and maritime contexts. It was also essential that stakeholders could trust that the skills learnt would transfer to real emergencies. The evaluation of affordances for fitness for purpose can only be undertaken

Box 22-2 Evaluating a collaborative system for fraud detection

This is a typical tale of mixed results in CSCW evaluation. The system in question was designed to support administrative staff checking claims for a state benefit in order to detect possible cases of fraud. The work involved cooperating with other benefit agencies and communicating with claimants as well as the individual task of checking the claims themselves. Before the new technology was introduced, each member of the team was responsible for a case from start to finish, and also took their turn in staffing a telephone enquiry line for the public. The work was thought to be satisfying, with enough variety to avoid monotony. With the advent of the new system, jobs changed so that each person specialized in just one part of the process, and new, rather tiresome tasks were introduced such as feeding claim forms into a scanner (and then unjamming it). There were also design flaws in the user interface – such as the need to turn one's head to read text displayed at a 45° angle – and enigmatic buttons and commands. Finally, each worker's throughput rate was automatically monitored and made available to the group manager.

We were asked by the group manager to assess 'how well the system is working' and by one of the designers of the system to evaluate its usability. From interviews and observation of the system in use, the usability flaws were easily picked up, as were the changes for the worse in job design. However, despite these issues the group manager himself considered the new technology a great success, since throughput had improved and therefore the organizational goal of detecting fraud more economically and effectively had been met.

with individuals from the community concerned: we had to be opportunistic about this given their limited availability. In one early trial, we had access to several maritime officers (including the captain of a well-known passenger ship) who completed questionnaires probing their confidence in the future use of the system as well as taking part in debriefing sessions. More substantive evaluation for perceived fitness for purpose focused firstly on data from the tutor sessions already discussed. Here data was collected through custom-designed questionnaire items, post-trial discussions and analysis of verbalizations and behaviour from the video record. As for pedagogic effectiveness, trials had been planned with trainees in an employer organization that would incorporate realistic training scenarios with checkpoints for the display of specific management behaviours at appropriate times. These were to be complemented by observational measures of team effectiveness. Sadly, however, lack of project resources prevented this final stage of evaluation.

A comprehensive framework: the MEGATAQ approach

The MEGATAQ guidelines and techniques – produced by an EU funded project – provide a tightly specified approach to CSCW evaluation (Andriessen, 2002). The guidelines cover the broad spectrum of issues involved, but are designed to be modular so that only the most relevant need be used in any given application. The approach is most suitable for large organizational CSCW projects, where the degree of structure provided would reduce the evaluation to manageable proportions. The MEGATAQ components are:

- The Evaluation Process Model, which specifies the steps of a user-oriented evaluation process
- The Behavioural Reference Model, which specifies relevant issues
- Evaluation methods and tools – a catalogue of techniques to support the design and evaluation process.

The overall contents of the evaluation process and issues in the Behavioural Reference Model are similar to those we have already discussed in this section. The supporting documentation contains a great deal of detailed advice. To give a flavour of the material, the Evaluation Process Model in diagrammatic form is shown in Figure 22-2. The catalogue of techniques includes checklists specifically developed as part of MEGATAQ which support the following:

- Construction of scenarios
- Identification of stakeholders and their success criteria
- Description of the technical system and infrastructure
- Description of existing contexts of use
- Identification of evaluation criteria
- A first evaluation of implemented systems.

There is also a useful inventory of other validated tools developed outside MEGATAQ, such as measures of the quality of working life and evaluation checklists for multimedia design.

22.4   Evaluation beyond the workplace

Many interactive systems and products are designed for use outside the workplace. Some ideas for their evaluation – using voicemail diaries, for example – have been illustrated in the material about mobile phones. But there are a range of other issues and approaches to think about, and we consider them here.

Evaluation at home

The cultural probes described in Chapter 9 are relevant here

People at home are much less of a 'captive audience' for the evaluator than those at work. They are also likely to be more concerned about protecting their privacy and generally unwilling to spend their valuable leisure time in helping you with your usability evaluation. So it is important that data gathering techniques are interesting and stimulating for users, and make as little demand on time and effort as possible. This is very much a developing field and researchers continue to adapt existing approaches and develop new ones. Petersen, Madsen and Kjaer (2002), for example, were interested in the evolution over time of relationships with technology in the home. They used conventional interviews at the time the technology (a new television) was first installed, but followed this

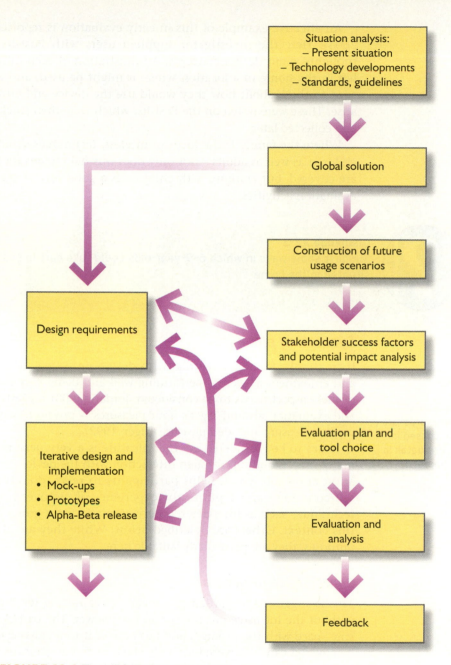

FIGURE 22-2 The MEGATAQ process model
(source: http://www.ejeisa.com/nectar/megataq/4.3/2.htm, after Figure 2.1)

by having families act out scenarios using it. Diaries were also distributed as a data collection tool, but in this instance the non-completion rate was high, possibly because of the complexity of the diary pro-forma and the incompatibility between a private diary and the social activity of television viewing.

An effective example of this in early evaluation is reported in Baillie (2002, 2003). Here the investigator supplied users with Post-its to capture their thoughts about design concepts. An illustration of each different concept was left in the home in a location where it might be used, and users were encouraged to think about how they would use the device and any issues that might arise. These were noted on the Post-its, which were then stuck to the illustration and collected later.

Where the family is the focus of interest, techniques should be engaging for children as well as adults – not only does this help to ensure that all viewpoints are covered, but working with children is a good way of drawing parents into evaluation activities.

Challenge 22-3
Suggest some ways in which 6–9-year-olds could take part in evaluation activities situated in the home.

Evaluating pleasure

The 'four pleasures' are discussed in more detail in Chapter 17

Increasingly, we are concerned with designing systems which afford pleasure and enjoyment as well as performing well and being easy to use, so evaluation of these aspect needs to be considered. Jordan (2000) suggests structuring design and evaluation around Tiger's 'four pleasures' – physio-pleasure, socio-pleasure, psycho-pleasure and ideo-pleasure (Tiger, 1992).

Issues to be considered are that pleasure is a very personal emotion, and in many cases is built up through interaction with the device. So we need an evaluation approach which helps participants to relax, does not make them feel self-conscious, and captures the experience of use over time. Some standard techniques such as interviews, observation and focus groups can be adapted to this context. Others are described below. While they are also useful for other purposes, they are particularly suitable here.

Conversation to camera

This is suggested by Jordan as a means of capturing feelings about a product without the intrusive presence of an interviewer. The participant is inside a private space with the product, and talks about it to a video camera. The topics to be covered can be covered on a checklist or the conversation left undirected – which has the merit of not forcing comments on aspects which participants do not feel are very important. Depending on the focus of the evaluation, the 'conversation' can take place after the product has been used for a while or as participants discover it for the first time. The technique has the advantage of being relatively natural, but for this reason may elicit some irrelevant material. Two people can be asked to comment on the product together, which may produce more conversation but can be skewed by a dominant participant.

Diaries

Whether text-based, video or audio, diaries can be a good way of getting at longer-term experiences. It helps if participants have a prompt list of points to cover, and it is often a good idea for the evaluator to remind people at reasonable interviews. It can be difficult to motivate people to persist with a long-term diary. Periodic incentives as well as a final payment or gift can help here.

Questionnaires

Finally, questionnaires are often used in this context. Jordan (2000) provides a validated special-purpose questionnaire which includes such items as 'I would miss this product if I no longer had it', 'I feel excited when using this product' and 'I am proud of this product'.

Summary and key points

This chapter has presented a diverse selection of evaluation techniques to suit different circumstances, some of which are relatively well established, others the subject of continuing research. What all have in common, however, is that they ground evaluation in real contexts of use. It is likely that none will fit your own evaluation circumstances exactly, so do as other practitioners do – consider what you really need to evaluate, review what is already available, and extend or adapt where necessary. Of course, this is most effective when you have a good working knowledge of both theoretical and practical aspects of your application context – so read the relevant chapters in the rest of this book!

Further reading

This is all specialized material in keeping with the nature of this chapter's contents.

Willcocks, L. and Lester, S. (1998) *Beyond the IT Productivity Paradox: Assessment Issues*. Wiley, Chichester.
This provides a good overview on the evaluation of workplace information technologies and use from the information systems perspective.

Robson, C. (1994) *Experiment, Design and Statistics in Psychology*. Penguin, London.
An excellent guide to techniques for the design of usability evaluation experiments. You will need to extrapolate their application to the context of interactive systems evaluation.

The ACM series of GROUP and CSCW conferences provide a multitude of examples of CSCW evaluations in research and industrial settings.

Comments on challenges

Challenge 22-1

You need to refer back to Chapter 21 for a discussion of physiological measures. Changes in heart-rate, breathing rate and skin conductance (among other things) will all indicate changes in arousal levels. The issues include teasing out the effects of the virtual environment from extraneous variables such as apprehension about the experiment itself, or something completely unrelated which the participant is thinking of.

Challenge 22-2

One possibility would be to have people use the device over a period of several weeks and log their experiences in a diary – which could be Web-based, video-based or mediated by a dedicated voice mailbox as well as the conventional paper format. An example of the last for mobile phone usage is described immediately below the challenge. A shorter-term option might include an observer accompanying the participant as they used the device while walking down the street – the observer could purposely distract the participant at intervals in some trials. Of course, you may well have thought of other plausible variations.

Challenge 22-3

One technique which has been tried is to have the children draw themselves using the technology in question – perhaps as a strip cartoon for more complicated operations. Older children could add 'thinks' bubbles. Possibilities are limited only by your imagination.

Exercises

1. How do we know that the criteria we use for evaluation reflect what is important to users? Suggest some ways in which we can ground evaluation criteria in user wants and needs.

2. An organization with staff in geographically dispersed offices has introduced desktop video-conferencing with the aim of reducing resources spent on 'unnecessary' travel between offices. Working teams often involve people at different sites. Before the introduction of video-conferencing, travel was regarded as rather a nuisance, although it did afford the

opportunity to 'show one's face' at other sites and take care of other business involving people outside the immediate team. One month after the introduction of the technology, senior managers have asked for a 'comprehensive' evaluation of the system. Describe what techniques you would adopt, what data you would hope to gain from their use, and any problems you foresee with the evaluation.

3. Critically discuss the strengths and weaknesses of the 'standard' user evaluation techniques of task-based interviews and observation in settings beyond the workplace. What additional methods could be used in these domains?

Part VI:

Information Spaces

Introduction

There are many different types of information spaces, from huge spaces such as the World Wide Web or an interactive museum to tiny spaces such as a wristwatch or a train timetable. Sometimes seemingly small spaces are remarkably large. A mobile phone, for example, may easily have dozens of functions.

In this part we go inside the idea of an information space and explore how information is organized, structured and displayed. We look at how people find their way through the forests of information that surround them and how they search for things. If we think of information as being like a forest, or perhaps a wilderness, then we think of people enjoying a walk and admiring the view, of trying to find particular spots or trying to find areas where they might stop and rest a while. How can such notions inform our design?

One important motivational reason for thinking about information *spaces* is that we are increasingly surrounded by information and increasingly carrying or wearing computing and communication devices. Human–computer interaction started in the early days of computers with screens. The predominant view was of a computer user sitting outside a world of information, staring into this world, trying to figure things out, trying to retrieve information. Since the early 1990s things have changed radically and people have moved from outside to inside the worlds of information. We *go to* websites, using Internet *Explorer*. We *navigate* around a website; clicking on a link *takes us* to another site. We are inside this space and moving through it. So, the first thing we do in this part, in Chapter 23, is to look at *architecture*: information architecture. In Chapter 25 we look at navigation of information *spaces*: how we can support people moving through, exploring and understanding information spaces. In between, in Chapter 24, we look at information *design*, at website design and at the design of visualizations. Chapter 26 introduces us to another new and emerging feature of information spaces: *agents*. Information spaces are not just full of information; they include autonomous things called agents that have certain things they want to do. Once we understand agents we can look, in Chapter 27, at a new view of computing: at ubiquitous, or pervasive, computing and the formation of distributed information spaces.

Many traditional analysis and design techniques for human–computer interaction rely on the person-outside-the-computer view. Bringing people inside the space changes our views on how to design. This new view of designing interactive systems is more akin to interior design, or landscape architecture, or urban planning, than it is to science or engineering. We, as designers, are creating aesthetic, enjoyable and engaging spaces for people to travel through information.

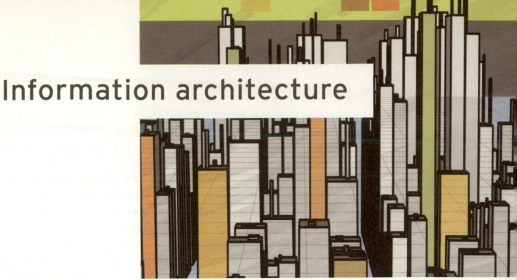

23 Information architecture

Aims

Information architecture is concerned with the structural design of information spaces. Although the term is usually applied to website design, it is just as applicable to the design of any information space. In this chapter we explore the concept of an information space and how the architecture of that space can be developed. We apply the ideas more specifically to website design.

After studying this chapter you should be able to:

- Describe the characteristics of information spaces
- Discuss the importance of information design
- Understand the key issues of information architecture
- Design the organizational structure for a website.

23.1 Information spaces

An information space is some combination of things – objects, displays, people, signs, icons, sounds and so on – that is used by someone to provide information. Information spaces allow people to plan, manage and control their activities. For example, consider the signage system that might be employed in an airport. This is an information space that could consist of TV monitors showing the times of departures and arrivals, announcements made over a system of loudspeakers, signs showing gate numbers, directional signs, information signs and people staffing an information desk. Another example of an information space is a website. Here there are various artefacts and devices such as the Web browser, the type of computer and operating system, connection method and other programs that are available on a particular computer. There is the design of the site itself with the labels, menu structure, organizational structure, and so on. There is the content of the site – the words, pictures, video and sound files and so on – that people access and there are other people who can be contacted through the site. Sometimes information spaces are designed specifically to support a well-defined activity. For example, a train timetable is an information space designed to support travelling by train (e.g. Figure 23-1). An address book on a cellphone is an information space designed to support the activity of storing and retrieving contact details. Such small, specialized information spaces are sometimes referred to as 'information artefacts'.

TRAIN	Rapid 37	Express 7	Express 929 Sprinter	Special Express 5	Rapid 59
Departure BKK	15:00	18:00	19:25	19:40	22:00
Arrival Chiangmai	05:00	07:10	06:10	07:55	11:30
2nd class upper berth FAN	411.-	461.-	n/a	481.-	411.-
2nd class lower berth FAN	461.-	531.-	n/a	551.-	461.-
2nd class upper berth AIR	n/a	581.-	n/a	601.-	n/a
2nd class lower berth AIR	n/a	651.-	n/a	671.-	n/a
2nd class seat, FAN	311.-	331.-	n/a	n/a	311.-
2nd class seat, AIR	381.-	n/a	471.-	n/a	381.-

FIGURE 23-1 Train timetable information artefact (*source: www.thailine.com/contact/trainair/page6.html*)

However, more often than not activities make use of general-purpose information spaces that include many information artefacts. On the other hand information spaces have to serve multiple purposes. In the airport, the information space has to support all the activities that go on at an airport such as catching planes, finding the right gate, meeting people who have landed, finding lost luggage, and so on. The website has to support people browsing through the site, or going to specific parts of the site. A typical website is shown in Figure 23-2. Pause for a moment to think about the multiple purposes and activities that this site would support – even through it is all about a single area, namely travel.

Conceptual and physical features

An information space or information artefact consists of two parts: a conceptual information structure and an interface onto that structure. It is only through an interface that the conceptual information can be accessed. For example, in order to enable the activity of catching a train, a timetable information artefact is created. The designer decides what conceptual information is useful for this activity – train times and stations, say – and then considers how to provide access to this

FIGURE 23-2 A typical travel website has to support many different activities (*source: www.expedia.co.uk*)

information. One option is a paper timetable, another is a speaking timetable, another is an electronic display. Different interfaces have different structures and provide operations to manipulate those structures. They also physically store the content, the instances of the conceptual objects, in some order. The features of the interface affect how information is retrieved and what people have to do to access information.

A paper timetable, for example, lays out the times and stations in a tabular format. This structure allows a person to undertake a number of operations, such as scanning across the columns or up and down the rows, and allows searching by arrival time. A talking timetable provides a different interface onto the same conceptual structure (times and stations of the train journeys), but this only allows a serial search; the person has to wait for the required times to be spoken and cannot actively scan the interface.

The situation is illustrated in Figure 23-3, this time using a clock information artefact. An analogue clock face and a digital clock face provide different displays of the conceptual information concerning hours and minutes. Analogue clocks can be quickly scanned and approximate times can be easily judged. A speaking clock is a third interface (Figure 23-3).

Information architecture is concerned with the design of information spaces. Designing interfaces is one critical aspect as one display may not succeed in conveying all the conceptual information that is needed by a person to support an activity. Even if all the information is presented, it may be structured in such a way as to make the information hard to use. For example, using an earlier version of the site in Figure 23-2, if a person selected 'ferries' and then 'select outward route', well over 100 options were presented in a drop-down menu.

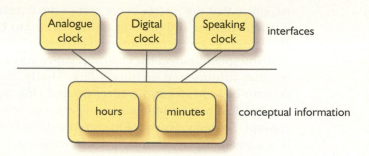

FIGURE 23-3 Different interfaces to the same underlying conceptual information

These were in alphabetical order. This is acceptable if you know the name of the port (e.g. you need to look at 'Piraeus' to find ferries from Athens), but still searching through over 100 items takes time.

Designing the conceptual structure of an information space is also critical. Note that this conceptual structure is designed. Some designer, an information architect, has *chosen* a conceptual structure to represent some activity. Just as the design of the interface may make life difficult, so the design of the conceptual information structure may not be what is required. For example, using the site www.ferrybooker.com, 'the UK's one-stop shop for ferries …' you would be forgiven for thinking that you could not get a ferry from Scotland to the Western Isles, because it does not appear under 'select route'. This is an example of the conceptual information either not being available or being in a place that is difficult to access.

Information architecture is concerned with conceptual information structures and physical displays. It is concerned with the relationships between these and to what extent the information space allows people to plan, monitor and control their activities.

Challenge 23-1
Think about the information structure of an address book on a cellphone. Find a real example and look at the interface. What activities are easy to do with the phone and what activities are hard to do?

Levels of description

The process of designing an information space may be seen as follows. Some designers recognize something about a domain, a 'sphere of activity'. They choose to conceptualize its structure in a particular way and develop a conceptual representation of the domain. In order to access this conceptualization, various interfaces are created. Each interface reveals something about the underlying structure. However, the interfaces that have been created are now part of the domain and can then be considered in a similar fashion. The designers recognize that the interfaces are part of the domain, conceptualize the interface in some manner and provide an interface onto this new conceptual structure. This produces another information artefact.

If you spent time on the challenge above you will understand some of the difficulties information architects face. Firstly, how do you conceptualize the domain of addresses and contact details? One big issue is whether you have a separate first name and family name concept or whether you just have a 'name' concept. Secondly, you need to consider the interface. In the case of a cellphone it is a small display, with facilities to scroll up and down. Almost certainly the content (names and contact details) will be organized in alphabetical order of name – how annoying when you just have a number and cannot remember whose number it is. Once you have the address book (however it is designed) you need to create a new information artefact to let people know it is there. So an item on a menu, or an icon on a screen, called 'address book' (or something similar) is created. Once there are a few functions like this, the information architect will need to group them together and create another information artefact. This might be a menu called 'Tools', say, which includes Address Book, Calculator, and other functions.

In theory this can continue indefinitely with information artefacts being created on top of one another, revealing different aspects of the underlying domain. In practice, people tend to specialize in a particular level of discourse about information artefacts and lower levels effectively disappear from their experienced world. For example, one view of the world of computers deals with the physical arrangement of files on discs, with the workings of disc access times and transfer rates, memory allocation and so on. For most of us such a view is not experienced; instead it is presented to us through information artefacts such as computer operating systems. The graphical user interfaces which are so ubiquitous provide another view into the operating system and so our activities consist of dragging icons, double-clicking and using menus to issue commands. The car mechanic experiences a different world from the driver. The surgeon experiences a different world from the patient. Recognizing these different levels of information artefact is important in order to establish a shared level of abstraction within which we can discuss our needs and concerns. The idea is illustrated in Figure 23-4.

Deciding the level of description, the interface and how the activity is conceptualized is fundamental to information architecture. Physically any information artefact will allow various manipulations of the physical structures. For example, a table structure facilitates scanning down rows and columns, whereas the serial structure of speech output does not allow this. With cellphones it is pressing the right buttons that is difficult and the need for extensive scrolling because of the small screen.

Moreover, different information artefacts provide different facilities for moving around *within* an object and moving *between* objects. On a word processor scrolling allows people to move within a document object. Selecting the name of a document from the 'window' menu allows people to move between documents.

The Further thoughts box in Chapter 8, Section 8.2 discussed levels of abstraction

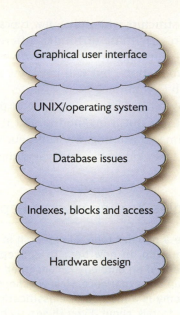

FIGURE 23-4 Different levels of information artefact

23.2 The structure of information space

Information architects have to abstract some aspect of a domain and choose how this should be presented to people. The first thing they must do, then, is to decide how to conceptualize the activity. This is known as defining an ontology. The ontology – the chosen conceptualization – is critical and will affect all the other characteristics of the information space.

Deciding on an ontology for some domain of activity is deciding on the conceptual entities, or objects, and relationships that will be used to represent the activity. Choosing an appropriate level of abstraction for this is vital as this influences the number of entity types that there are, the number of instances of each type and the complexity of each object.

■ A *coarse-grained* ontology will have only a few types of object, each of which will be 'weakly typed' – i.e. will have a fairly vague description – and hence the objects will be quite complex and there will be a lot of instances of these types.

■ Choosing a *fine-grained* ontology results in a structure which has many strongly typed simple objects with a relatively few instances of each. In a fine-grained ontology the object types differ from each other only in some small way; in a coarse-grained ontology they differ in large ways.

For example, consider the ontology that you (acting as an information architect) choose to help with the activity of organizing the files in your office. Some people have a fine-grained structure with many types (such as 'Faculty Research Papers', 'Faculty Accommodation', 'Faculty Strategy', etc.) whilst others have a coarser structure with only a few types (such as 'Faculty Papers'). These different structures facilitate or hinder different activities. The person with the fine-grained ontology will not know where to put a paper on 'Faculty Research Accommodation', but will have less searching to do to find 'Minutes of April Research Committee'.

In my office I have a large pile of papers. This makes filing a new paper very easy – I just put it on the top. But it makes retrieval of specific papers much more time-consuming. My colleague carefully files each paper she receives, so storage takes longer but retrieval is quicker.

Box 23-1 Ontologies, taxonomies and epistemologies

Ontologies have become a popular topic of research in recent years because of issues over the vast amounts of information on how best to conceptualize activities associated with this. Philosophically the concept of an ontology is concerned with what things exist, with the nature of those things that make up our experience. How we choose to group these together is the concern of taxonomies. A taxonomy is a method of classification. Both ontology and taxonomy provide philosophers with plenty to talk about. Even things such as plants are not organized into a single agreed taxonomy, but rather several taxonomies coexist. Epistemology concerns how we come to know things, with the nature of knowledge and of knowing.

Challenge 23-2
Look at the travel website (Figure 23-2) again and write down the top-level ontology that the designer has chosen. Is this a good design? Think of some activities you might want to undertake and critique the design. Is it easy to find the information you want? If not, why not?

Characteristics of information spaces

The key feature about designing information spaces is to achieve a good relationship between the conceptual structure (the ontology), the physical characteristics of the interfaces and display objects and the activities that people are doing. Inevitably there will be trade-offs arising from the constraints of technologies and how the many different activities that people are undertaking can be supported by the information space design. Understanding key aspects of the information space (as it is *designed*, note – not as it *is*) will help designers avoid major problems. These characteristics are discussed below.

Volatility

Volatility is concerned with how often the types and instances of the objects change. In general it is best to choose an ontology that keeps the types of object stable. Given a small, stable space, it is easy to invent maps, or guided tours to present the contents in a clear way. But if the space is very large and keeps changing then very little can be known about how different parts of the space are and will be related to one another. In such cases interfaces will have to look quite different. Volatility is also important with respect to the medium of the interface and how quickly changes in the conceptual information can be revealed.

For example, consider the information space that supports train journeys. The ontology most of us use consists of stations, journeys and times. An instance of this might be 'The 9.10 from Edinburgh to Dundee'. This ontology is quite stable and the space fairly small so the train timetable information artefact can be produced on paper (as in Figure 23-1). The actual instances of the journeys such as the 9.10 from Edinburgh to Dundee on 3 March 2004 are subject to change and so an electro-mechanical display is designed that can supply more immediate information. The volatility of the objects (which in itself is determined by the ontology) demands different characteristics from the display medium.

Size

The size of an information space is governed by the number of objects which in turn is related to the ontology. Recall that a fine-grained ontology results in many object types with fewer instances of each type, and a coarse-grained ontology results in fewer types but more instances. A larger space will result from a finer-grained ontology, but the individual objects will be simpler. Hence the architecture should support locating specific objects through the use of indexes, clustering, categorization, tables of content and so on. With the smaller space of a coarse-gained ontology the emphasis is on finding where in the object a particular piece of information resides. A fine-grained ontology will require moving *between* objects; a coarser grain requires moving *within* the object. The physical

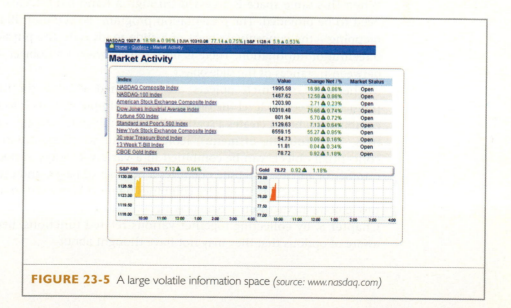

FIGURE 23-5 A large volatile information space *(source: www.nasdaq.com)*

organization of the information artefact and the functions provided to manipulate types and instances will determine how effective the design is.

For example, a common design issue in developing a document to go onto a website is whether to chop it up into small pieces and link these together with hyperlinks or whether to keep a long document through which people have to scroll. Navigating within a Web document uses scrolling; navigating between documents (or parts of documents) uses linking.

Conceptual and physical objects

Any information space will be populated by a variety of objects and devices. For example, we can consider the Web to be populated by objects such as websites, Web pages, links, GIF files, PDF files, Word files and so on. This is our ontology. In addition to these conceptual objects, there are physical/perceptual devices that are used to interact with this space – Web browsers, mice, scrollbars, radio buttons, drop-down menus and the like. The relationship between physical/perceptual devices and conceptual objects is critical to the design of the space. A hand-held computer provides a very different display than a 21-inch computer screen and so the interaction with the content will be different. The perceptual devices, or 'widgets', provided in information spaces also have a big impact on the ease of use of an information space.

A good mapping between conceptual and physical objects generally results in better interaction. This relationship between the conceptual and physical objects and the conceptual and physical operations that are available in the interface objects fundamentally affects the usability of systems. For example, the arrangement of windows showing different applications needs to be controlled in the limited screen space provided by a typical computer display. When this same space is accessed through a hand-held device, different aids need to be provided. The presentation program 'PowerPoint' illustrates a good mapping – the conceptual object of a slide maps onto the physical object of a screenful of information. There is no scrolling within an object – movement is between instances of the slide object.

The way in which objects are combined is also significant. At the physical/perceptual level the organization of simple widgets into more complex combination boxes creates a spatial phenomenon that will offer certain possibilities. The grouping of menus, icon bars and so on is important. Similarly conceptual objects can be combined in a variety of ways. A book combines a number of articles, a website organizes a number of pages, and even a seemingly simple object such as an invoice combines name, address and so on. The formatting palette in Microsoft products is a good example of this and was discussed in Chapter 5. By collecting together various related functions, people are made aware of options that they may not have thought about.

Topology

The topology of an information space concerns both conceptual and physical objects.

■ The conceptual structure will dictate where conceptual objects are, that is how things are categorized.

■ The physical topology relates to the movement between and through physical objects and how the interfaces have been designed.

A website again provides a good illustration of these issues. How many times have you been to a website and tried to find some information only to give up or eventually stumble across it in what seems to you to be a strange place? This is all down to the conceptual information design of the site – the conceptual topology. In many websites it is very difficult to get a clear view or understanding of the topology, especially as websites often try to serve too many different user groups, each of which will have a different conception of what should be near to what.

Looking at the site map (Figure 23-6) provided by the travel site, we can see that 'cruises' appear on the tabs at the top but are not in the site map. A number of the categories in the site map are different from those in the tabbed selection bar. This indicated a confused topology.

Once the conceptual topology has been determined, the designer needs to consider how to present the interface to that and, as we saw earlier, the ways in which instances are organized has a large impact on the number of steps needed to reach a specific instance.

FIGURE 23-6 Site map for travel site (*source: www.expedia.co.uk*)

Distance

Conceptual and physical distance results from the conceptual and physical topologies chosen by the designer. The notion of distance relates to both the ontology and the topology of the space, with the ontology coming from the conceptual objects and the topology coming from how these are mapped onto a physical structure.

In my word processor, it is a 'long way' from working on a drawing to changing the margins. There are many clicks involved and these two activities are clearly in different parts of the overall information space. One of my favourite examples is my travel alarm clock. This provides a small information space for supporting the activity of getting me up in the morning when I am travelling. The clock has a usual LCD display and just two buttons. In order to change the time on this clock I have to press one button seven times and then hold the next button while it loops through the minutes.

Direction

Direction can be important in information spaces – particularly when moving between instances of an entity as there is always some sense of next and previous. For example, the alarm clock does not have a facility for going back. If you miss the time you were aiming for, you have to cycle through all the numbers again. In e-mail messages or diary appointments there is the sense of next and previous, but it is sometimes difficult to work out which is which – particularly when this has to be mapped onto a physical interaction that is based on moving up or down through a list. Is 'up' equal to next, or is it down? Immersive and desktop virtual reality (VR) spaces exploit the concept of geographical movement, and notions of distance and direction have a much clearer mapping onto our experiences from the geographical world.

VR is discussed and illustrated in Chapter 28

Media

Some spaces have a richer representation that may draw upon visual, auditory and tactile properties, while others are poorer. Issues of colour, the use of sound and the variety of other media and modalities for the interaction are important components of the information space.

Design

If the space has a coherent design it is easier to convey that structure to users. Other spaces have grown without any control or moderation. In the former case, often called moderated spaces, it is possible for the careful designer to create cues helping the user to orient herself in the space, and being aware of the relationship between the present view and other locations. In non-moderated spaces, where no one is in control of the design of the individual nodes or places, nor of their interrelations, this is not possible. For example, the Web as a whole is unmoderated so it does seem rather like a wilderness. The only way to find anything is through the keyword search or through following links. Individual websites are typically designed with maps and signs.

Of course, we are all designers of information spaces as we all file documents or other things, whether electronically or not. But designs go out of date and organizational structures change. Returning to a place where you have filed things after a period of time can be quite unnerving as you try to figure out why you filed things in a particular place. The next time you put something in a drawer while saying to yourself 'I'll remember that', consider a more careful design of the information structure.

Agents

Agents are discussed in more detail in Chapter 26

In some spaces, we are on our own and there are no other people about. In other spaces we can easily communicate with other people (or 'agents') and in still other spaces there may not be any people now, but there are traces of what they have done. The availability of agents in an information space is another key feature. If there is a person behind the ticket counter at the railway station you do not have to consult the timetable. In other spaces previous visitors might have left information that we make use of. For example, the organization of a library is something deliberately given to us from people who have tried to make our search task easier. When we look at the books on a shelf, the well-thumbed volume might attract us. Here we can see traces of previous activity left unintentionally by people over the years.

Making use of other people to help in navigation is discussed in Chapter 25, Section 25.4

Summary

The concept of an information space is a useful one because it does not distinguish between interactive and non-interactive devices, instead focusing on the structure of the space and how that structure can be accessed through an interface. One of the things an information architect needs to consider is this relationship between people, their activities and the information spaces that will support their activities. But each of these is itself very complex – people have different skills and carry different devices with them, their activities are wide ranging and the information space has to support this diversity. The information architect has to consider how best to conceptualize a space and how best to reveal that, bearing in mind the characteristics and level of description of the space.

23.3 The information architecture of websites

Websites are good examples of the sort of information spaces that many information architects are involved with creating today. As we saw in Chapter 3, there are many different types, or genres, of websites such as news sites, shopping sites, entertainment sites and information sites. These different types of site have to serve many different purposes for many different people. Getting an information architecture that is robust enough to serve such multiple interests is difficult and website 'information architects' are in great demand. The features of websites will clearly vary widely. However, there are some commonalities in terms of the main characteristics of information spaces, as illustrated in Table 23-1.

TABLE 23-1 Information space characteristics of websites

Characteristic	Website issues
Volatility	Some sites such as the stock exchange site (Figure 23-5) are of course highly volatile. News sites are more volatile than information sites. The key issue is to get the structure – the information architecture – as stable as possible.
Size	Large sites are exactly why information architecture for websites has become so important. There are many very large websites.
Conceptual and physical objects	Here there is little variation. The conceptual objects are pages, files, documents and so on (and different sorts of these – e.g. PDF files, GIF files, etc.). Physically sites are distinguished by their use of implementation method. Simple HTML sites have different physical objects for use at the interface than dynamic HTML sites, or Flash sites (see Box 23-2).
Topology	The topology is another key element of information architecture as it determines how easy or otherwise it is to move through a site.
Distance	The information architecture will determine how many clicks it takes to get from one part of the site to another.
Direction	Direction plays an important part of the navigational schemes employed in a site. We return to this in Chapter 25.
Media	Websites can make use of the full range of media, though simple HTML sites are static.
Design	Websites should be carefully designed. Information architects contribute to this.
Agents	Whether or not other agents are available on a website is another key aspect of design which we refer to as 'social navigation'. See Section 25.4.

Box 23-2 Implementing websites

Websites are implemented on the Internet by specifying the layout of the pages in a language known as the Hypertext Mark-Up Language (HTML) which is itself a variant of the Standard Graphical Mark-up Language (SGML). As a mark-up language HTML suffers from not having much functionality. Essentially it is a publishing language which describes how things are laid out, but not how they should behave. For this reason the Web itself suffers from some awkward interactions when real interactivity is required (such as submitting forms to a database). More recently dynamic HTML has been developed that allows functions more commonly associated with a graphical user interface such as a 'drag and drop' style of interaction. It is also possible to embed interactive displays into an HTML page by writing a 'movie' in the programming language Flash. Once again this facilitates new methods of interaction such as drop-down menus. One might expect this to develop rapidly over the next few years.

Information architecture for websites is to do with how the content of the site is organized and described. Of course it has to be organized and described for some purpose, so many authors include the design of navigation systems as part of the information architecture. We prefer to deal with this separately in the context of navigation as a whole. Others still might include the design of the information layout as part of the information architecture. We cover this in Chapter 24, Information Design. This allows us to concentrate here on the key structural aspects of websites: how to organize the content (i.e. create a taxonomy), how to label the items and categories, how to describe the content in the site and how to present the architecture to users and to other designers. To borrow the title of Christina Wodtke's book, we are engaged in 'Information Architecture: Blueprints for the Web' (Wodtke, 2003).

Classification schemes

Further thoughts: Classification is difficult

These ambiguities, redundancies and deficiencies recall those attributed by Dr Franz Kuhn to a certain Chinese encyclopedia entitled *Celestial Emporium of Benevolent Knowledge*. On those remote pages it is written that animals are divided into (a) those that belong to the Emperor, (b) embalmed ones, (c) those that are trained, (d) suckling pigs, (e) mermaids, (f) fabulous ones, (g) stray dogs, (h) those that are included in this classification, (i) those that tremble as if they were mad, (j) innumerable ones, (k) those drawn with a very fine camel's hair brush, (l) others, (m) those that have just broken a flower vase, and (n) those that resemble flies from a distance.

Source: Jorge Louis Borges, essay: 'The Analytical Language of John Wilkins'

As we have seen, the choice of an ontology or classification scheme is crucial to how easy it is to retrieve an instance of an object. The ontology is fundamental as it affects how things can be organized. Rosenfeld and Morville (2002) distinguish between exact organization schemes (of which there are three – alphabetical, chronological and geographical) and ambiguous schemes that use subjective categorization. Norman Shedroff (2001) suggests that there are seven organizational schemes: alphabets, locations, time, continuums (i.e. using some rating scale to rank instances), numbers, categories, and randomness.

Alphabetical is a very common organizational scheme, of course, and is exploited in all manner of information artefacts such as phone books, book stores, and directories of all kinds. Although at first sight an alphabetical organization is straightforward, it is not always easy, especially where forenames and surnames are muddled up, or where rogue characters can get into the name. Where is a '.' in the alphabet, or a '-'? Another occasion when alphabetical organization breaks down is when the formal title of a company or organization is not the same as the informal name. Looking in the paper-based phone directory for the phone number for Edinburgh City Council recently I finally found it under 'C' for 'City of Edinburgh'! There was not even an entry under 'E' pointing to the entry under 'City'.

Chronological organization is suitable for historical archives, diaries and calendars and event or TV guides (see Figure 23-7).

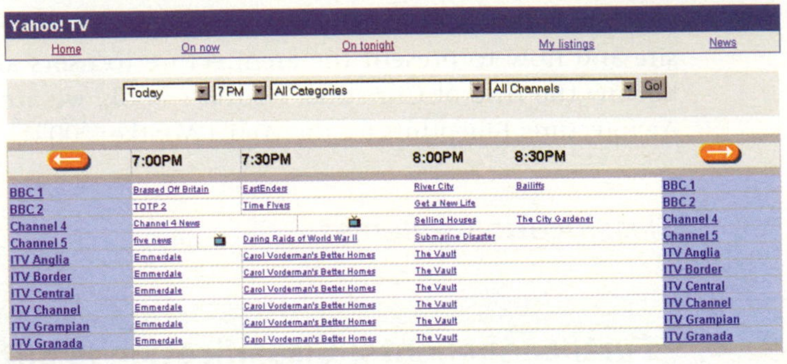

FIGURE 23-7 Yahoo! TV guide *(source: reproduced with permission of Yahoo! Inc. © 2004 by Yahoo! Inc. YAHOO! and the YAHOO! logo are trademarks of Yahoo! Inc.)*

Geographical organization suits travel subjects, social and political issues and regional organizations such as wine sites, local foods, etc. Problems can arise, of course, when one's geography is not good enough. The time zones on my calendar program are organized geographically (I think) which makes finding certain time zones very difficult (see Figure 23-8).

Organization by *topic* or subject is another popular way to structure information, but here it is important to prototype the names of topics with the potential users of a site. Often a topic structure used by people internal to an organization is different from those from outside.

Task organization structures the website by particular activities that people may want to do ('Buy ticket'; 'Contact us').

Audience is another popular structuring method. This can be very effective when there are a few well-defined different types of user. 'Information for staff', 'Information for students', and so on, helps different users find their part of a site.

Hybrid schemes can be (and often are) used to mix these types of organization together. Other authors suggest that there are other organizational schemes. For example, Brinck *et al.* (2002) include 'department' as a scheme. They give the following example to illustrate the differences:

- Task-based: 'Buy a Car'
- Audience: 'Car Buyers'
- Topic-based: 'Cars'
- Department: 'Sales Department'

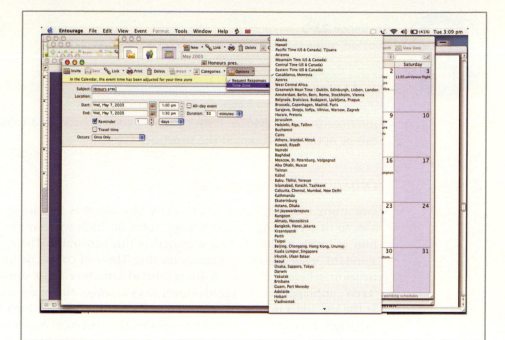

FIGURE 23-8 Time zones feature in MS Entourage, presumably in some geographical sequence

Faceted classification

Any information space can be described in terms of three key features: its dimensions, the facets (or attributes) of those dimensions and the values that these facets can take. The dimensions come from the ontology – the major concepts in the site. So, the travel site illustrated in Figures 23-2 and 23-5 has dimensions of cars, flights, hotels and on. Each of these has certain common facets (such as price) but also may have its own unique facets: flights go from one city to another, hotels are located in a single city (but may be part of a chain), cars generally are rented and returned to the same location but may exceptionally be returned elsewhere. Ferries have a different pricing structure from planes which have a different structure from trains. Each of these attributes, or facets, can take certain values. The name of a city, for example, could be just about anything, but the name of an airport could be restricted to a known list of official airports. Classification in terms of the facets of dimensions works particularly well in small, clearly defined spaces. Music sites classify music in terms of its main facets such as genre, artist and title. Recipe sites will have facets such as country/region, main ingredient, course/dish and so on. Wodtke (2003) points out, though, that once such a site includes things such as cooking utensils, the sharing of facets across such different entities as utensils and recipes is no longer possible. Faceted classification has an important impact on the user

Challenge 23-3
Consider some classification schemes for a music website.

interface that is provided. With clear and known facets and values the interface can be optimized to exploit the structure.

Organizational structures

One thing that a designer can be quite sure about is that he or she will not be able to fit everything onto one page. Some decision will have to be taken about how to break up the site to accommodate this constraint. There are a number of standard organizational structures for this. These of course tie in with the classification schemes chosen. A **hierarchical** structure (also sometimes called a '**tree**', although it is an upside-down tree) arranges the pages with a single root at the top and a number of branches underneath, each of which has several sub-branches. For example, in a music website, the root page might be called 'home', then branches under that might be 'Classical', 'Rock', 'Jazz' and so on, each of which would be split into sub-genres. Hierarchies are a very common organization and lead naturally to the technique of providing a 'you are here' sign. Figure 23-9 shows a page from a music website. In the pale yellow area on the left is 'Home > Music >' telling the visitor where he or she is in the hierarchy.

Rosenfeld and Morville (2002) point out the need to consider the granularity of the ontology as this leads to the breadth vs. depth debate in website design. Often the same material can be organized as a deep structure – only a few main branches but many sub-branches – or as a shallow and broad structure with many branches and only a few sub-branches. As a general rule, six to eight links per category is about right, but the nature of the content and how it would naturally be divided up by the people who will be visiting the site must also be considered.

FIGURE 23-9 Hierarchical organization of Music site

(source: www.pricegrabber.com. Courtesy of PriceGrabber.com, LLC)

The problem with a hierarchical structure is that no matter what classification scheme is chosen, some item will not fit nicely into it, and the designer will want to put it under two or more headings. As soon as this happens, the nice clean structure of a hierarchy breaks down. Soon the hierarchy becomes a **network**.

Networks are structures in which the same item may be linked into several different hierarchies. It is a more natural structure but also a more confusing one for people to understand. Often the visitor to a website navigates down through a hierarchy and so develops a reasonably clear view of the site structure. However, in a network they may then go back up another branch or may jump from one part of the site to another. In such cases understanding the overall logic of the site is much more difficult. Organizing pages into a **sequence** is ideal for dealing with a straightforward task structure such as buying a product or filling in a series of questions. The different structures are illustrated in Figure 23-10.

← That is, they develop a clear 'mental model'. See Chapter 5, Section 5.10

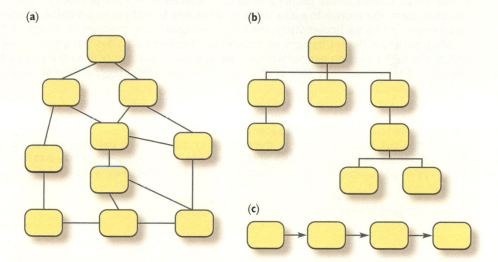

(a)   (b)   (c)

FIGURE 23-10 Common organizational structures: (a) = network, (b) = hierarchy, (c) = sequence

Box 23-3 The importance of classification

This is a portion of an article on Jared Spool's UIE website in which UIE investigated different ways of classifying clothes. UIE is a commercial company that investigates usability issues in websites. Their site contains several interesting articles. Here they describe a study investigating shopping sites with 44 users.

'Among the thirteen sites we studied, we found five different department-page designs. Most listed the departments in a left navigation panel, with the galleries for that department listed in the center. (Look at Macy's department pages – http://www.macys.com – by clicking on Women, then Tops.)

However, some got clever. For example, the Gap and Victoria's Secret (http://www.gap.com, http://www.victoriassecret.com) both used a menu-based department that wasn't a separate page, but instead used menus at the top of the screen.

Old Navy (http://www.oldnavy.com) used a combination department and gallery page where sometimes the left nav contains galleries and sometimes it contains products. (Try clicking on Girls, then Accessories. Compare that to clicking on Girls, then Skirts & Dresses.)

Lands' End (http://www.landsend.com) used a design that had both product descriptions and departments. (Click on Women's, then Swimwear to see their department page design.)

Finally, Eddie Bauer (http://www.eddiebauer.com) combined text lists of all the products in the department with a toggle to see the pictures for a gallery. (Click on Women, then Sweaters. Click on View Photos to see a specific gallery.)

After realizing that there were five basic types, we got very excited about seeing if the different types made a difference. While we'd expect differences between individual sites, it wasn't clear that we'd see if an entire type of design outperformed others.

After watching people shopping on the sites, we compared their behaviors. (As with many of our e-commerce studies, these users came to our facilities with a list of products they wanted to buy. We gave them the money to make the purchases and told them to purchase as much on their list as possible. In this particular study, there were 44 users who shopped for a total of 687 products.)

Studying the different designs on apparel and home goods sites turned out to be a good thing. Out of the 687 shopping expeditions that we observed, users only used the search engine 22% of the time. That means that 78% of the time they used the categorization scheme to locate their desired products.

We found the sites with the standard left-nav design, such as Macy's, actually performed the worst, selling the least amount of product. Lands' End's design performed the best, with Old Navy's combination design being second.

It turned out, in our study, that the number of pages that a user visited before they put something into their cart was inversely proportional to purchasing. The more pages they visited, the less they bought. (Remember, our users knew exactly what they wanted and were ready to make a purchase.)'

Source: http://www.uie.com/Articles/strategies_categories.htm

Metadata

Metadata means data about data and in the case of websites this means data about the content of the site. Wodtke (2003) suggests that there are three types of metadata for describing websites.

- Intrinsic metadata describes the factual, technical nature of the data files. It covers things like file size, resolution of graphics, type of file, etc.
- Administrative metadata is concerned with how the content should be treated. It might include details of the author, date of origin, dates of any revisions, security issues and so on.
- Descriptive metadata highlights the facets of the thing, the ways it is classified and so on, so that it can be found and related to other items of content.

Metadata is easily seen and indeed is used by search engines on the Web to locate and rank pages for relevance to a search term entered. Figure 23-11 shows how some metadata is specified in HTML.

```
<!DOCTYPE HTML PUBLIC "-//W3C//DTD HTML 4.0
Transitional//EN">
<html>
<head>
    <meta http-equiv="content-type"
content="text/html;charset=iso-8859-1" />
    <meta name="keywords" content="stock photography, stock
images, digital images, photos, pictures, advertising, gallery,
digital photography, images, sports photography, graphic design,
web design, content" />
    <meta name="copyright" content="All contents © copyright.
All rights reserved." />
```

FIGURE 23-11 Example HTML tags

For example, an image on a photo library website will have a description below it showing how the picture is categorized. The website will allow users to refine their search based on these keywords. I could, for example, request more images of the person shown in the photograph. Other developments include developing standards for Web metadata such as Dublin Core (see box below).

Further thoughts: Semantic Web

Semantic Web is an initiative of the World Wide Web Consortium (W3C) 'to create a universal medium for the exchange of data. It is envisaged to smoothly interconnect personal information management, enterprise application integration, and the global sharing of commercial, scientific and cultural data'. The underlying assumption is that objects on the Web need to be processable automatically by computer. This would enable such things as artificial agents (Chapter 26) to search out objects and exchange information with them.

XML stands for 'extensible mark-up language'. It provides a more flexible description of objects than HTML. Dublin Core describes intrinsic properties of Internet resources. It is an approach to providing standard metadata. RDF stands for the 'Resource Description Framework' which aims to provide an application-independent form for processing metadata. Web Ontology is a standard Web classification scheme.

Together these are the enabling technologies that would bring about the Semantic Web. More details can be found at http://www.w3.org/2001/sw/Activity.

Vocabularies

A taxonomy is a classification scheme. There are many different types that serve many different purposes. One of the most famous is the Dewey Decimal Classification that is used to classify books in libraries. It is a hierarchical structure that divides books into 10 top-level categories such as:

000   computers, information and general reference
100   philosophy and psychology
200   religion

and so on. Within each classification more levels can be added with decimal points: 005 is computers, 005.7 is information architecture and so on. Of course all schemes get out of date and it is perhaps strange that religion gets as much space in the scheme as computers. In our library there are several rows of shelves devoted to the 005 classification, but only part of a row devoted to 200.

One of the problems with devising a taxonomy is that different people use different concepts to organize things. Another is that people use different words and terms to refer to the same thing. There are synonyms and homonyms. There are slight variations of meaning and often it is difficult to find a home for an instance of something. A thesaurus is a book of synonyms and semantic relationships between words. Similarly in information architecture there is often a need to define a thesaurus to help people find what they are looking for. Rosenfeld and Morville (2002) suggest the structure illustrated in Figure 23.12.

The preferred term is at the centre of the structure. It needs to be chosen carefully so that it will be recognized and remembered by the people using the site. Far too often these terms are chosen by administrative staff and reflect an administrative view of things. Our university has a heading 'Facilities Services' on its website rather than 'Catering', and the library is now a 'Learning Information Service'. Different nationalities will use different words. The preferred term should be linked to any number of variant terms. These are synonyms that people might be expected to use, or follow or type into a search engine. Narrower terms describe sub-categories of the term (sometimes called siblings) and these are related to other terms (sometimes called cousins). Moving up the hierarchy takes us to a broader term.

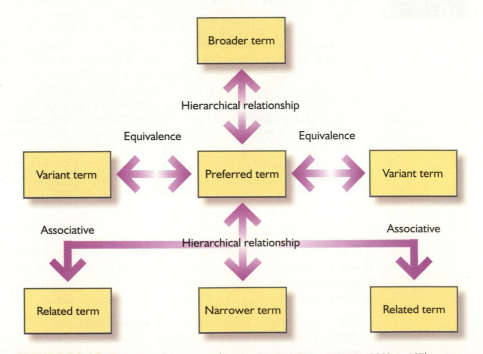

FIGURE 23-12 Structure of thesaurus (*source: after Rosenfeld and Morville, 2002, p. 187*)

Specifying all these relationships is a lengthy but important activity for the information architect. This structure will be used to explain the conceptual structure to people using the site and to people administering the site. It will be used in displaying the content on the page, as part of the navigation system and to help people searching. This scheme also helps to provide functionality such as 'may we also suggest' on a shopping site. The scheme will be used to provide category information for people, navigation bars and the 'breadcrumbs' that show where you are on a site. We return to these when discussing navigation. You can see the scheme at work on sites such as Yahoo! (Figure 23-13). Look at the different categories returned when searching for 'cheese' on Yahoo!.

2. I Love Cheese! 📇
all about the yellow stuff, from the American Dairy Association.
Category: Dairy > Cheese
www.ilovecheese.com/ - 18k - Cached - More pages from this site

3. CheeseNet 📇
cheese information resource, includes a world cheese index, literature, ar
Category: Dairy > Cheese
www.cheesenet.info/ - 16k - Cached - More pages from this site

4. String Cheese Incident 📇
a sacrilegious mix of bluegrass, calypso, salsa, afro pop, funk, rock, and
Category: Rock and Pop > String Cheese Incident
www.stringcheeseincident.com/ - 2k - Cached - More pages from this site

5. Amazon.com: Books: Who Moved My Cheese? An Amazing Way
Who Moved My Cheese? ... Editorial Reviews Amazon.com Change can
curse, depending on your perspective. The message of Who Moved My C
www.amazon.com/exec/obidos/tg/detail/-/0399144463?v=glance - 85k - C

6. Steak and Cheese 📇
galleries of pictures, movies, and programs.
Category: Tasteless Humor
www.steakandcheese.com/ - 2k - Cached

7. Chuck E. Cheese's 📇 (NYSE: CEC)
where a kid can be a kid.
Category: Shopping > Children > Parties
www.chuckecheese.com/ - 4k - Cached - More pages from this site

FIGURE 23-13 Searching for 'cheese' on Yahoo! (*source: reproduced with permission of Yahoo! Inc. © 2004 by Yahoo! Inc. YAHOO! and the YAHOO! logo are trademarks of Yahoo! Inc.*)

23.4 Conclusion

Information architecture is a key feature of websites. Information architecture is concerned with getting the right structure for the site, presenting that structure, to people and helping people find their way through the structure. In order to design a structure, an information architect will use all the user-centred design techniques that are useful elsewhere in the design of interactive systems. This will include profiling the users of the site by developing personas, developing scenarios of use, generating requirements through interviews, questionnaires and observations. It will involve developing prototype schemes and evaluating them. Since information architecture is concerned with how concepts are structured, methods such as card sorting and concept or topic sketching can be particularly useful (see Box 23-4). Developing an affinity diagram (Chapter 18) is another excellent technique for designing an information architecture.

Box 23-4 Concept organization

Concept organization methods include both top-down approaches and bottom-up approaches. With a top-down approach the information architect identifies the main dimensions of the area through discussions with people and looking at similar sites to see which schemes have been used. Bottom-up approaches include card sorting, where items of content are grouped together. This is best done in a group. People write their items on a 'Post-it' note and then put them together into groupings (classifications) by sticking them onto a whiteboard. (See Chapter 18 on developing an affinity diagram for more detail.) Alternatively, issues can be written on cards and arranged on the floor. Examples of real content (e.g. recipes if it is a recipe site, music artist and titles if it is a music site, etc.) can similarly be grouped and hence the main dimensions for the organization grows. Another approach is to develop 'mind maps' – growing the concepts on a large whiteboard and drawing the links between concepts.

Summary and key points

In this chapter we have explored the concept of an information space, both in general and as applied to websites. Information spaces have some structure – whether by accident or by design. The structure of the space will have a huge impact on what that space is useful for and how enjoyable it is for people to spend time in the space.

- Information spaces are developed by designers who need to consider how to abstract and represent some sphere of activity.

- Information spaces have characteristics such as their size, volatility and so on that depend crucially on the ontology that the designer has chosen to represent the activity.

- The information architecture of websites is concerned with how the content of the site is organized, classified and presented.

Further reading

Wodtke, C. (2003) *Information Architecture: Blueprints for the Web*. New Riders, Indianapolis, IN.
A highly readable and practical account of information architecture for the Web.

Garrett, J.J. (2003) *The Elements of User Experience*. New Riders, Indianapolis, IN.
A very approachable little book that packs a lot of good advice into a small package. It does not go into information architecture in any great detail, but covers the basics of Web design very well.

Going forward

http://www.boxesandarrows.com
For information architecture chat and articles.

Rosenfeld, L. and Morville, P. (2002) *Information Architecture for the World Wide Web*. O'Reilly, Sebastopol, CA.
A more comprehensive book than Wodtke's but it is less accessible for a general reader. It covers much more ground in terms of thesauri, but sometimes the detail obscures the message.

Brinck, T., Gergle, D. and Wood, S.D. (2002) *Designing Web Sites that Work: Usability for the Web*. Morgan Kaufmann, San Francisco.
An excellent book on Web design in general.

Comments on challenges

Challenge 23-1
Clearly this will depend on the particular cellphone that you are looking at. If possible, look at more than one. Often there is room for several numbers such as work, home and mobile, but of course you have many entries which do not have all of these. The instances are stored in alphabetical order by first letter of name, but some provide a first name and a last name. Many provide a facility to jump to a part of the address book when typing in the first letter of a name, but few allow people to do this on either first name or last name. Issues of what is easy or more difficult to do can vary tremendously according to the number of entries (or instances) that there are. Searching 10 or 20 is very different from searching 100 or 200.

Challenge 23-2
The tabs across the top of the site represent most of the main ontology with a few other concepts presented in the right-hand bar and on the left-hand bar. We do not know how much research went into this design, so perhaps 'deals' is exactly what people want at the top level; they are certainly the main thing that is advertised in the window of a travel agent. Having maps separate from guides is perhaps unusual. The top-level bar of the UK site is shown again in Figure 23-14.

FIGURE 23-14 Expedia main bar – UK site *(source: www.expedia.co.uk)*

As a comparison of preferred terms, vocabularies and structure, the US site is shown below (Figure 23-15).

FIGURE 23-15 Expedia main bar – US site (*source: www.expedia.com*)

Challenge 23-3
The obvious answer to this is to organize by music genre – pop, classical, jazz and so on. The problem is that many bands slip between categories. There are soon hybrid categories to deal with, such as jazz-funk or techno-garage or classic-rap. Then there are all the compilations, special deals, Christmas albums and so on. One of the best ways to think about classification is to go into a record store and see what they do. Or of course visit on-line stores.

Exercises

1. Take a familiar place, such as your university or college, or a department store, and think about the information space. What conceptual and physical objects are there in the space? What is its topology? Think about the other characteristics of information spaces (distance, direction, etc.) in this place. Concentrate on the *information space* (signs, notice boards, help desks, etc.), not the physical space.

2. Look at some different clothes shopping sites (see examples in Box 23-3) and think about how to describe clothes. Draw up a thesaurus for men's knitwear.

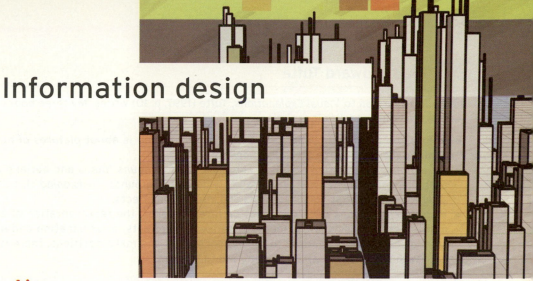

24 Information design

Aims

Information design is concerned with many different things: icon design, instruction design (manuals, information messages, etc.), selecting fonts and graphical layouts, and the meanings that people attach to such displays. Information design is concerned with things as diverse as the design of maps, signage systems in museums, labelling systems, instruction guides and so on. Often information design is concerned with non-interactive devices and displays, but sometimes it is concerned with interactivity. At other times it is concerned with dramatic visualizations of complex data.

After studying this chapter you should be able to:

- Understand the broad area of information design
- Understand the role of metaphor in information design and design appropriate metaphors
- Undertake the design of websites
- Understand interactive visualizations.

24.1 Introduction

Jacobson (2000) argues that the key feature of information design is that it is design dealing with meanings rather than materials. Information design is essentially to do with sense-making, with how to present data (often in large amounts) in a form that people can easily understand and use. Information designers have to understand the characteristics of the different media being used to present data and how the medium affects how people move through structures. This concept of *moving through* an information space is very important and we return to it in the next chapter.

Box 24-1 Edward Tufte

In the introduction to *Visual Explanations*, Tufte (1997, p. 10) writes 'My three books on information design stand in the following relation:

- *The Visual Display of Quantitative Information* (1983) is about *pictures of numbers*, how to depict data and enforce statistical honesty.
- *Envisioning Information* (1990) is about *pictures of nouns* (maps and aerial photographs, for example, consist of a great many nouns lying on the ground). *Envisioning* also deals with visual strategies for design: colour, layering and interaction effects.
- *Visual Explanations* (1997) is about *pictures of verbs*, the representation of mechanism and motion, or process and dynamics, or causes and effects, of explanation and narrative. Since such displays are often used to reach conclusions and make decisions, there is a special concern with the integrity of the content and the design.'

Information design is traditionally traced back to the work of Sir Edward Playfair in the eighteenth century and to the work of the French semiologist Jacques Bertin (1981). Bertin's theories of how to present information and on the different types of visualizations have been critical to all work since. The work of Edward Tufte (1983, 1990, 1997) shows just how effective good information design can be (see Box 24-1). He gives numerous examples of how, in finding the best representation for a problem, the problem is solved. Clarity in expression leads to clarity of understanding. He describes various ways of depicting quantitative information such as labelling, encoding with colours or using known objects to help get an idea of size. He discusses how to represent multivariant data in the two-dimensional space of a page or a computer screen and how best to present information so that comparisons can be made. His three books are beautifully illustrated with figures and pictures through the centuries and provide a thoughtful, artistic and pragmatic introduction to many of the issues of information design.

Figure 24-1 is one of Tufte's designs that shows a patient's medical history involving two medical and two psychiatric problems.

Beck's map of the London Underground is often cited as an excellent piece of information design. It is praised for its clear use of colour and its schematic structure – not worrying about the actual location of the stations, but instead concerned with their linear relationships. The original map was produced in 1933 and the style and concepts have remained until now. However, it is interesting to note how nowadays – with the proliferation of new lines – the original structure and scheme is breaking down. With only a few underground lines, the strong visual message could be conveyed with strong colours. With a larger number of lines the colours are no longer easily discernible from one another. Figure 24-2 shows the map from 1933 and the current version.

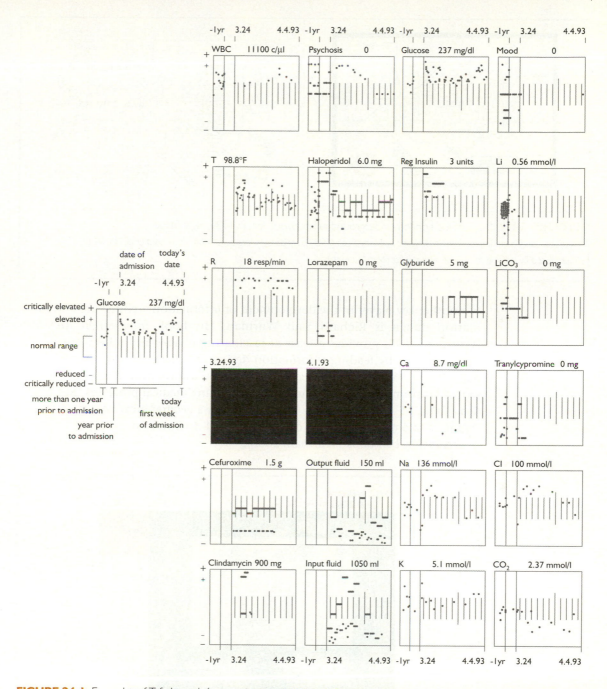

FIGURE 24-1 Examples of Tufte's work (*source: after Tufte (1997), p. 110 and p. 111. Courtesy of Edward R. Tufte and Seth M. Powsner*)

FIGURE 24-2 Maps of the London Underground rail network: left, in 1933; right, now

(sources: London Underground map designed by Harry Beck (1933); London Underground Map. Registered User No. 04/E/1424. Reproduced by kind permission of London's Transport Museum)

Another key player in the development of information architecture and information design is Richard Saul Wurman. His book *Information Architects* (Wurman, 1997) provides a feast of fascinating images and reflections on the design process by leading information designers. Wurman's own contribution dates from 1962 and includes a wide variety of information design cases from maps comparing populations, to books explaining medical processes, to his *New Road Atlas: US Atlas* (Wurman, 1991), based on a geographical layout with each segment taking one hour to drive. Figure 24-3 shows an example from his *Understanding USA* book (Wurman, 2000).

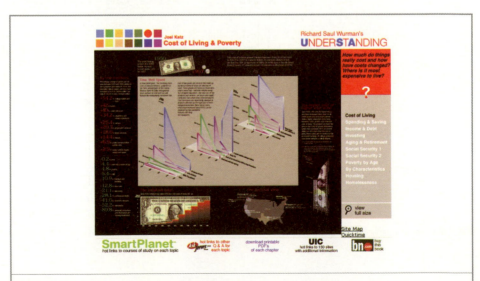

FIGURE 24-3 Illustration from Richard Saul Wurman's book *Understanding USA*

(source: Wurman, 2000, designed by Joel Katz)

Further thoughts: Museum design

The design of museums and other exhibition spaces that the public can wander through at their leisure provides an excellent example of information design at work. The exhibit labels must be informative and clear. There need to be motivational features to draw people in to the exhibits. A rich and integrated signage system is needed to help people find their way through the exhibits, understand the organizational structure and know where to go and where they have been. People need to be able to find answers to their questions but also need to be stimulated to find out more. Once at an exhibit the museum curators will often want people to stay there, spend time and get the maximum benefit and enjoyment from the exhibit. Museum design is about mixing education with entertainment.

Chapter 5, Section 5.6 discussed the *Gestalt* principles

A number of authors are keen to ground information design in theory – particularly theories of perception and cognition. Indeed, some of these theoretical positions such as *Gestalt* principles (closure, proximity, etc.) are useful. General design principles of avoiding clutter, avoiding excessive animations and avoiding clashing colours also help make displays understandable. Bertin's theories and modern versions such as that of Card (2003) are useful grounding for anyone working in the area. Card (2003) provides a detailed taxonomy of the various types of visualization and provides details on different types of data that designers can deal with. He also discusses the different visual forms that can be used to represent data.

Chapter 13 presented some ideas on design languages and design patterns

Essentially, though, information design remains a design discipline rather than an engineering one. There are many methods to help designers understand the problems of information design in a particular context (and taking a human-centred view is the most important), but there can be no substitute for spending time critiquing great designs and looking at the reflection of designers on their creative and thinking processes. Readers are encouraged to follow up the references at the end of this chapter.

When developing a scheme of information design in a given context, designers should realize that they are developing visual 'languages'. The visual language of information design is an important part of these. Designers will imbue colours, shapes and layouts with meanings that people have to come to understand.

24.2 Metaphors in design

Section 10.2 discusses metaphor

Another key aspect of information design is finding an appropriate metaphor. Metaphor is generally seen as taking concepts from one domain (called the source domain, or the vehicle) and applying them to another (the target, or tenor). Recall your schooldays and how you studied 'The ship ploughed through the waves', or 'The President marshalled his arguments to defend his position'. The first of these likens a ship moving through the sea to a plough moving through a field. It suggests the waves are like the furrows. It has connotations of strength and how the ship is pushing aside the sea. For some people it connotes speed of movement. In the second we see arguments likened to a battle, arguments being marshalled as if they were soldiers, the President's position being analogous to a castle or other physical place that needs defending.

In the development of interactive systems we are constantly trying to describe a new domain (a new application, a different design, new interactive facilities) to people. So we have to use metaphor to describe this new domain in terms of something that is more familiar. After a while the metaphorical use of a term becomes entrenched in the language to such an extent that people forget it ever was a metaphor.

Challenge 24-1
Consider some of the familiar computing concepts: 'windows', 'cut and paste', 'bootstrap', 'open' a 'folder', 'close' a 'file'. Make a list of these metaphors. Try to write down where they came from.

Metaphor is not just a literary thing, it is fundamental to the way we think. Lakoff and Johnson (1981, 1999) and their colleagues have worked on their theories of metaphor for over 20 years. They describe a philosophy of 'experientialism' or cognitive semantics. They argue that all our thinking starts from the metaphorical use of a few basic concepts, or 'image schemas', such as containers, links and paths. A container has an inside and an outside and you can put things in and take things out. This is such a fundamental concept that it is the basis of the way that we conceptualize the world. A path goes from a source to a destination. The key to experientialism is that these basic concepts are grounded in spatial experiences. There are other basic 'image schemas' such as front–back, up–down and centre–periphery from which ideas flow.

An important contribution from this view is that metaphors are much more than a simple mapping from one domain to another. It is a much more complex affair. Take the idea of a window as it appears in a computer operating system. We know a computer window is different from a window in a house. It shares the idea of looking *into* a document, as you might look *into* a house, but when you open it, it does not let the fresh air in. It is only ever a window into, or onto, something. Moreover it has a scroll bar which a window in a house does not. In a similar fashion we know that the trash can, or the recycling bin, on a computer screen is not a real trash can. The connotations of recycling files are really quite complex.

The contribution that Fauconnier and others have made (e.g. Fauconnier and Turner, 2002) is to point out that what we call 'metaphors' in design are really **blends**. A blend takes input from at least two spaces, the characteristics of the domain described by the source and the characteristics of the target that we are applying it to. So a computer window takes elements from the domain of house windows and elements of the functioning of a computer trying to get a lot of data onto a limited screen display. The metaphor of a folder is a blend from the domain of real folders which you keep papers in and the domain of computer files which have a physical location on a disc. Figure 24-4 illustrates this idea.

The blend that results from bringing two domains together in this way will have some features that were not in the original domains. Blends have an *emergent structure* that results from bringing two sets of concepts (from the source and target domains) together. So, the computer window has different features from both a real window and the computer commands that preceded it. The rolodex concept that arose during the HIC case study (Chapter 14) had emergent properties. These concerned how people could navigate in the 'virtual' rolodex (as opposed to a real, physical one) and how the search results were presented as opposed to how they were presented following a traditional query. It is exactly these emergent properties that makes one design better than another.

For metaphors and blends to work, there must be some correspondences between the domains which come from a more generic, or abstract, space. So, for example, the metaphor 'the ship ploughs through the waves' works, but the metaphor 'the ship ran through the forest' does not. In the second of these there is not sufficient correspondence between the concepts in the two domains. Of course the generic space is itself a domain and hence may itself be using

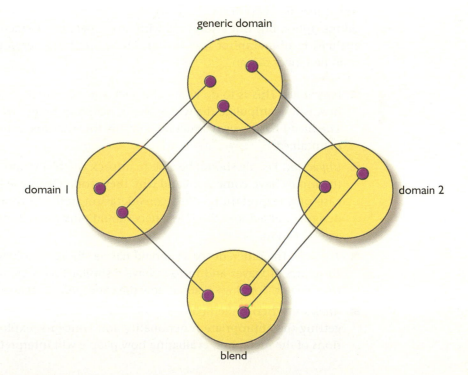

FIGURE 24-4 Illustrating the concept of a blend

metaphorical concepts. This process works its way back until we reach the fundamental image schemas that are core to our thinking. These include the container, path, link and others such as colours (red is hot, blue is cool, red is stop, green is go) and those bodily schemas that come from experience and perception (up, down, in, out, central, peripheral, etc.).

Thinking figuratively is fundamental to both the design and use of computer systems. One job of the information designer is to come up with a good metaphor that will help people in learning and using the system and in understanding the content. Metaphor design works as follows.

■ The source domain has some features (concepts and functions).
■ The target domain has some concepts and features.
■ So it is important to analyse the relationship between these.
■ Too many features in the base domain result in 'conceptual baggage' of the metaphor.
■ Too few features, or too many inappropriate features, may lead to confusion.
■ Aim for people deriving appropriate expectations.

Note that metaphor design does not imply a physical resemblance. The important thing about metaphor is to get a good *conceptual* correspondence. Sometimes it is appropriate to carry through a conceptual metaphor to a physical metaphor, but not always. As with any aspect of interactive system design, evaluation of metaphor is essential. There are, however, a few principles for good metaphor design.

■ *Integration*. This is to do with coherence and not mixing metaphors. The aim here is to manipulate the whole blend, maintaining the web of relationships. The blend has its own structure and it is this that needs to have consistency maintained.
■ *Unpacking*. People should be able to unpack the blend and understand where the inputs have come from and why they work. Of course this will often be a case of interpretation. With consideration, reflection and evaluation the designer can achieve this. Designers should only have things in the blend for a good reason.
■ *Topology*. The different spaces should have a similar topology. We saw how the structures of waves and furrows have a similar topology, whereas waves and trees do not. Topology is about how the concepts are organized and structured.
■ *Analysis*. When undertaking an analysis the designer should concentrate on getting the appropriate functionality and concepts, exploring the ramifications of the metaphor, evaluating how people will interpret it.

■ *Design.* At the design level designers should consider how to represent objects and actions. They do not have to be realistic visual representations (e.g. names of menu items are often metaphorical).

Designers cannot avoid metaphors in information design, so they need to consider them explicitly. Metaphors are really blends between two or more input spaces and have their own emergent structure. Using metaphors that exploit the fundamental domains such as bodily and perceptual schemas may help people to understand them. Designers should consider principles of good blends. Envisionment techniques, discussed in Chapter 10, can be used to help develop possible metaphors which should be evaluated against the criteria above and, of course, with potential users.

24.3 Information design for websites

'Information design' is one of the five elements of user experience advocated by Jesse James Garrett (Garrett, 2003). He conceptualizes the development of a website in terms of five elements: strategy, scope, structure, skeleton and surface (Figure 24-5).

■ The bottom layer is the 'strategy' plane concerned with understanding the overall objective of the website, the nature of the people who will be using the site and what their requirements of the site are. Strategy is concerned with business goals, the organization's brand and a market analysis.

■ The next layer is the 'scope' plane where the emphasis is on functionality (what the site will let people do) and on content (the information the site will hold). He argues that spending time on the scope plane is important so that Web designers know what they are designing and what they are not designing! The result of scoping the site is a clear, prioritized set of requirements.

■ The third layer is called the 'structure' plane. It covers information architecture (Chapter 23) but also includes specifying the interaction design. The key feature here is to establish a clear conceptual model.

■ The 'skeleton' plane is concerned with information design, navigation design and interface design.

We discuss navigation in some detail in Chapter 25

■ The final element of Garrett's scheme is the 'surface' plane concerned with the aesthetics of the site and with ensuring that good design guidelines are followed. For example, links should look like links and things that are not links should not!

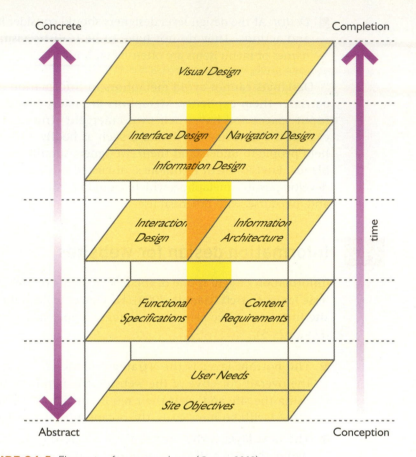

FIGURE 24-5 Elements of user experience (*Garrett, 2003*)

Garrett advocates using a simple graphical 'language' to map out the information architecture of a website. The key elements of the language are a representation of pages, files, and stacks of pages and files. These are structured into site maps, showing direction of links if appropriate. Garrett also employs other symbols to represent decisions (a diamond shape), forbidden routes (a cross bar) and other key concepts. A full explanation can be found at http://www.jjg.net/ia/visvocab/. An example of his site map is shown in Figure 24-6.

The skeleton plane of Garrett's scheme is concerned with information design, navigation design and interface design. A key technique for bringing all these elements together is the 'wireframe'. Wireframes aim to capture a skeleton of a general page layout. They are on the border between information architecture and information design as the various components of a page are assembled into the standard structures described by wireframes. Rosenfeld and Morville (2002) make the point that wireframes are a useful design technique in general, not restricted to Web pages. To construct a wireframe, designers need to identify the

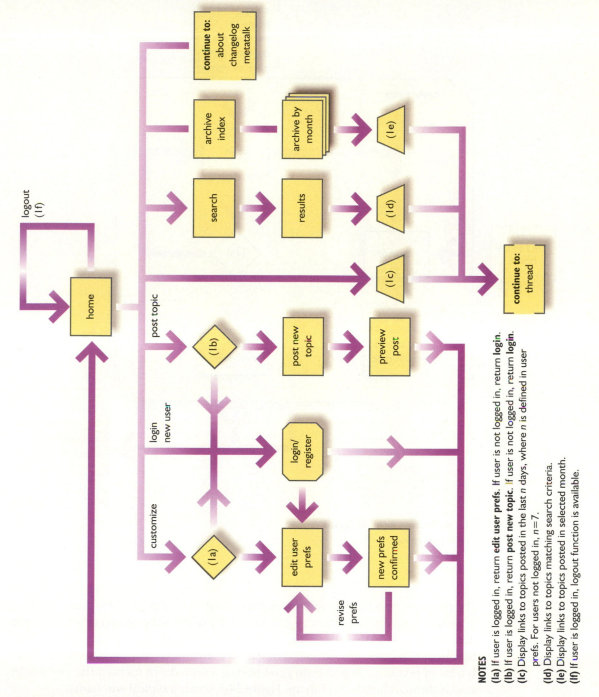

FIGURE 24-6 Site map design (continued on pages 602–603)

(*source: after site map from http://www.jjg.net/ia/visvocab/ Courtesy of Jesse James Garrett*)

NOTES

(1a) If user is logged in, return **edit user prefs**. If user is not logged in, return **login**.
(1b) If user is logged in, return **post new topic**. If user is not logged in, return **login**.
(1c) Display links to topics posted in the last *n* days, where *n* is defined in user prefs. For users not logged in, *n*=7.
(1d) Display links to topics matching search criteria.
(1e) Display links to topics posted in selected month.
(1f) If user is logged in, logout function is available.

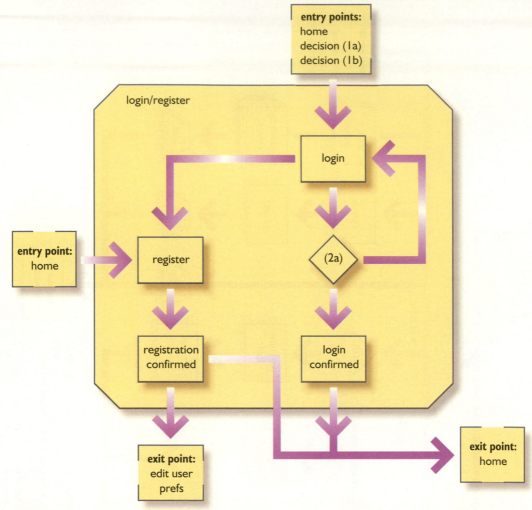

NOTES

(2a) If login info is valid, return **login confirmed**.
If login info is invalid, return **login**.

FIGURE 24-6 Continued

key components of the design for each different type of page, then place them on a layout. It is very important to consider not just the type of object – navigation bar, search box, banner headline, advert, text box, and so on – but what content that item can have. It is no use having a very small text box, for example, if there is a lot of text to go in it. It is no good having a drop-down menu if the user has to search through hundreds of items. Figure 24-7 shows a typical wireframe.

Visual design is at the top of Garrett's five elements. Consistency and appropriateness of the presentation are critical here. An effective way of achieving this

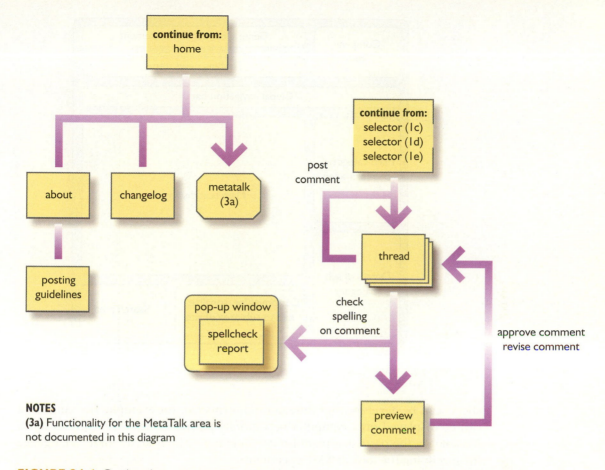

continue from:
home

about

changelog

metatalk
(3a)

posting
guidelines

continue from:
selector (1c)
selector (1d)
selector (1e)

post
comment

thread

pop-up window

spellcheck
report

check
spelling
on comment

approve comment
revise comment

preview
comment

NOTES
(3a) Functionality for the MetaTalk area is
not documented in this diagram

FIGURE 24-6 Continued

Challenge 24-2
Go to the British Airways flight selection website at http://www.britishairways.com/
travel/home/public/en_gb. Try to produce a wireframe for this site. Go to another
airline's site and do the same. Compare them.

consistency is through the use of style sheets. Style sheets describe how Web
documents are displayed, the colours that are used and other formatting issues
that will make for a clear and logical layout. Just as the wireframe specifies the
structure, so the style sheet specifies the visual language used. The World Wide
Web Consortium, W3C, has promoted the use of style sheets on the Web since
the Consortium was founded in 1994. W3C is responsible for developing the
CSS ('cascading style sheets') language, a mark-up language for specifying over
100 different style features including layouts, colours and sounds. Different style

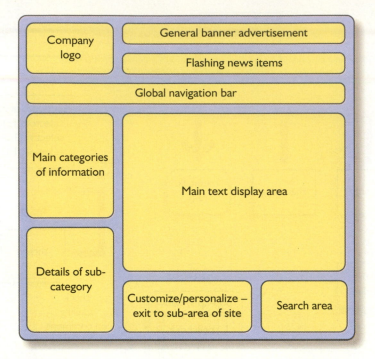

FIGURE 24-7 Wireframe

sheets can be developed for different platforms (so, for example, the same data can be displayed on a computer or a mobile phone) so that the content looks sensible on the particular platform it is aimed at. XSL is an alternative language for specifying the look of XML documents.

Box 24-2 Notions and flow systems

In contrast to many of the established views on website design, John Lenker does not like the ideas of architecture and rigid structures. He advocates the development of flowpaths and of intelligent flowpath management systems. He argues that we need to invest in understanding and composing 'notions' that effectively communicate our ideas. This more design-centred approach to Web development is laid out in his attractive and engaging book *Train of Thoughts* (Lenker, 2002).

Interactive visualizations

The other key feature of information design that the modern information architect or designer might get involved with is the interactive visualization. With the vast amounts of data that are available, novel ways of presenting and interacting with this are necessary. Card, Mackinlay and Shneiderman (1999) is an excellent set of readings covering many of the pioneering systems. Spence

(2001) provides a good introduction to the area. Interactive visualizations are concerned with harnessing the power of novel interactive techniques with novel presentations of large quantities of data.

The design principle for developing visualizations is summed up with Ben Shneiderman's 'mantra':

Overview first, zoom and filter, then details on demand

The aim of the designer is to provide the user with a good overview of the extent of the whole dataset, to allow zooming in to focus on details when required, and to provide dynamic queries that filter out the data that is not required. Card (2003) includes retrieval by example as another key feature. So rather than having to specify what is required in abstract terms, the user requests items similar to one they are viewing. Ahlberg and Shneiderman's (1994) Film Finder is an excellent example of this (Figure 24-8). In the first display we see hundreds of films represented as coloured dots and organized spatially in terms of year of release (horizontal axis) and rating (vertical axis). By adjusting the sliders on the right-hand side, the display zooms in on a selected

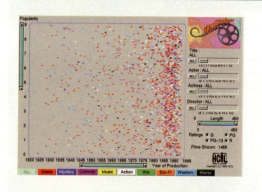
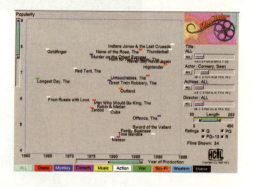

FIGURE 24-8 Film Finder

(source: Ahlberg, C. and Shneiderman, B. (1994) Visual information seeking: tight coupling of dynamic query filters and starfield displays, Proceedings of CHI' 94 Conference, Boston, MA, 24–28 April, pp. 313–17, Color plates 1, 2, 3 and 4. © 1994 ACM, Inc. Reprinted by permission)

part of the first display, allowing names to be revealed. Effectively the sliders provide dynamic queries on the data, allowing the user to focus in on the part that is of interest. Clicking on a film brings up the details of a film, allowing this to be used for retrieval-by-example style further searches.

Another classic example of a visualization is ConeTree (Figure 24-9) (VRML ConeTree Generator, 1999). If this is displayed in a VRML (virtual reality mark-up language) viewer, various facilities are available that allow the user to 'fly' around the display, identifying and picking out items of interest. Once again the interactive visualization allows for overview first, zoom and filter and details on demand. The key thing with visualizations is to facilitate 'drilling down' into the data.

Figure 24-10 shows the display of the stock market at SmartMoney.com. This display is known as a 'tree map'. The map is colour coded from red through black to green indicating a fall in value, through no change to a rise in value. The brightness of colour indicates the amount of change. Companies are represented

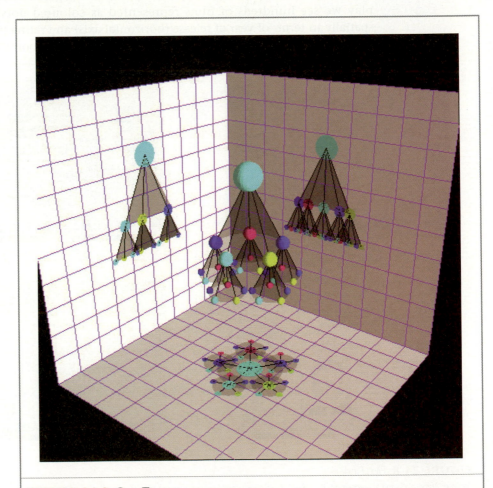

FIGURE 24-9 ConeTree

FIGURE 24-10 SmartMoney.com

(source: www.smartmoney.com. © SmartMoney 2004. All rights reserved. Used with permission. SmartMoney is a joint venture of Dow Jones & Company, Inc. and Hearst Communications, Inc.)

by blocks, the size of the block representing the size of the company. Mousing over the block brings up the name and clicking on it reveals the details.

Figure 24-11 shows a different type of display where connections are shown by connecting lines. It is an on-line thesaurus that demonstrates the 'fish-eye' capability which again allows for the focus and context feature required by visualizations.

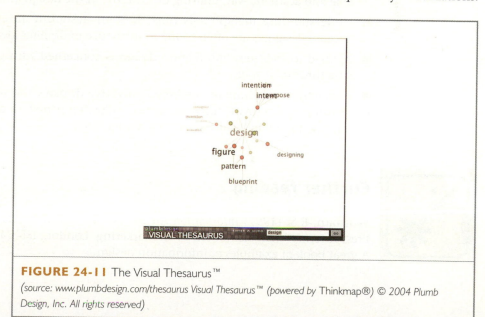

FIGURE 24-11 The Visual Thesaurus™

(source: www.plumbdesign.com/thesaurus Visual Thesaurus™ (powered by Thinkmap®) © 2004 Plumb Design, Inc. All rights reserved)

This allows users to see what is nearby and related to the thing that they are focusing on. There are many more, exciting and stimulating visualizations built for specific applications. Card (2003) lists many and Card *et al.* (1999) discuss specific designs and their rationale.

Chapter 16 discusses hearing and haptics (including earcons and tangible interaction

Card (2003) argues that the key decision in any visualization is to decide which attributes of an object are to be used to spatially organize the data. In Film Finder it is rating and year. In SmartMoney.com it is the market sector. Once this has been decided, there are relatively few visual distinctions that can be made. The designer can use points, lines, areas or volumes to mark different types of data. Objects can be connected with lines or enclosed inside containers. Objects can be distinguished in terms of colour, shape, texture, position, size and orientation. Other visual features that can be used to distinguish items include resolution, transparency, arrangements, the hue and saturation of colours, lighting and motion. Of course there are other senses, but little effective use has been made of these except for earcons and their tangible equivalent, tactons.

Summary and key points

In this chapter we have looked at how information is presented. Of course this is critically intermingled with the information architecture that has been chosen (Chapter 23). Information design is concerned with developing a visual language, through colour, layout and other perceptual methods for expressing the information architecture.

- Information design is concerned with presenting content in an understandable and aesthetic way, drawing on patterns in the design and interaction.
- Understanding metaphor is important in designing interactive systems because designers are often trying to introduce unfamiliar ideas.
- Applied to websites, information design is concerned with getting the right structure and layout.
- Interactive visualizations combine innovative displays and novel interaction techniques to provide focus in context, allowing people to obtain overviews but also to obtain details when they are required.

Further reading

Wurman, R.S. (1997) *Information Architects*. Printed in China through Palace Press International, distributed by Hi Marketing, London, ISBN 1-888001-38-0. A great book of examples of information design.

Jacobson, R. (ed.) (2000) *Information Design*. MIT Press, Cambridge, MA.
A good introduction to the area of information design by a variety of influential writers.

Card, S. (2003) Information visualization. In Jacko, J.A. and Sears, A. (eds), *The Human–Computer Interaction Handbook*. Lawrence Erlbaum Associates, Mahwah, NJ.

Going forward

Lakoff, G. and Johnson, M. (1981) *Metaphors We Live By*. Chicago University Press, Chicago, IL.

Lakoff, G. and Johnson, M. (1999) *Philosophy of the Flesh*. Basic Books, New York.

Lenker, J.C. (2002) *Train of Thoughts: Designing the Effective Web Experience*. New Riders, Indianapolis, IN.

Spence, R. (2001) *Information Visualization*. ACM Press/Addison-Wesley, New York.

Tufte, E.R. (1983) *The Visual Display of Quantitative Information*. Graphics Press, Cheshire, CT.

Tufte, E.R. (1990) *Envisioning Information*. Graphics Press, Cheshire, CT.

Tufte, E.R. (1997) *Visual Explanations*. Graphics Press, Cheshire, CT.

http://www.visualthesaurus.com/online/index.html

Comments on challenges

Challenge 24-1
The window is one of the components of the original 'desktop metaphor' that has led to the current operating systems Windows XP and Mac OS X. The window allows you to look in on something. 'Cut and paste' comes from journalism where paragraphs of stories were cut up and pasted (with glue) onto paper in a different order. A bootstrap was attached to riding boots so that people would pull themselves up. Most people are familiar with manila folders kept in a filing cabinet that needs to be opened up to see what is inside. Interestingly, since a folder contains many files, a computer folder is more like a drawer in a filing cabinet and a computer file is more like a real folder.

▶

Challenge 24-2
Figure 24-12 shows our version of the BA site.

| Global navigation bar | Country |

| Key links | Welcome banner | Log in |

Key Function

Key Function

Book a flight

Special offers

Key Function

Key Function

Site highlights links

Membership

FIGURE 24-12 BA site

Exercises

1. In computer-supported cooperative work (CSCW) systems, it is necessary to know whether people are available for discussions, or are working and do not wish to be disturbed (for an example of such a system look at Babble in Section 25.4). In some systems an open door has been used as a metaphor for 'being available' and a closed door for 'unavailable'. Discuss this metaphor, how it might be implemented, how it might be extended and how or why it might be effective.

2. Take a look at SmartMoney.com and discuss how it meets the criteria of 'overview first, zoom and filter, then details on demand'.

25

Navigation of information space

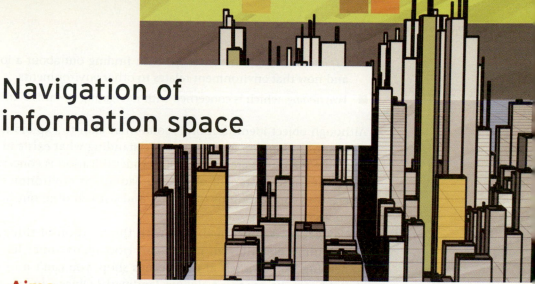

Aims

Information spaces are many and various – from paper documents, to websites, to personal organizers, to DVDs, to the complex combination of objects, information artefacts, designs and people that provide the information in large geographical spaces such as airports.

Information spaces allow people to plan, manage and control their activities. Rarely, though, is all the information that someone needs for some activity in one place. Accordingly people have to gather information from a variety of sources; they move through the information space to gather all the information that is required. This is what we call 'navigation of information space'. In this chapter we explore the ideas of navigation in information spaces. After studying this chapter you should be able to:

- Define and describe the key aspects of navigation
- Define guidelines for the design of information spaces to support navigation
- Discuss the ideas of navigation in websites
- Understand the idea of social navigation.

25.1 Navigation

Navigation is concerned with finding out about, and moving through, an environment. It includes three different but related activities:

- *Object identification*, which is concerned with understanding and classifying the objects in an environment

■ *Exploration*, which is concerned with finding out about a local environment and how that environment relates to other environments

■ *Wayfinding*, which is concerned with navigating towards a known destination.

Although object identification is somewhat akin to exploration, its purpose is different. Exploration focuses on understanding what exists in an environment and how the things are related. Object identification is concerned with finding categories and clusters of objects spread across environments, with finding interesting configurations of objects and with finding out information about the objects.

Navigation is concerned both with the location of things and with what those things mean for an individual. How many times have you been told something like 'turn left at the grocer's shop, you can't miss it', only to drive straight past the supposed obvious landmark? Objects in an environment have different meanings for different people. In this book we are primarily concerned with how people find their way through the information spaces that we create, but most work on navigation has come from navigation in geographical spaces. There are many similarities – and since we are all familiar with navigation in geographical spaces, we will look at these aspects, then look at some features unique to electronic spaces before bringing these ideas back to information spaces.

Navigation in geographical spaces

Chapter 20, Section 20.5 briefly discusses cognitive maps

Chapter 7 discusses these ideas in more detail

A lot of work in psychology has been done on how people learn about environments and with the development of 'cognitive maps', the mental representations which people are assumed to have of their environment. These representations are rarely wholly complete or static. Ecological considerations are concerned with the cues that people draw from the immediate environment as they interact with it. People develop knowledge of the space over time and through the experience of interacting with and within a space. There is still much debate about how much knowledge is 'in the head' and how much is 'in the world'. Hutchins (1995) considers a very different view in developing his ideas on distributed cognition when he looks at Polynesian navigators and the different perceptions and methods that they appear to have for navigation. Suchman's criticism of plans (Suchman, 1987) is also related.

Wayfinding is concerned with how people work out how to reach their destination. For Downs and Stea (1973) and Passini (1994) the process involves four steps: orienting oneself in the environment, choosing the correct route, monitoring this route, and recognizing that the destination has been reached. To do this people use a variety of aids such as signposts, maps and guides. They exploit landmarks in order to have something to aim for. They use 'dead reckoning' at sea or elsewhere when there are no landmarks. With dead reckoning you calculate your position by noting the direction you have headed in, the speed of travel and the time that has passed. This is usually correlated with a landmark whenever possible.

Learning to find one's way in a new space is another aspect of navigation considered by psychologists (Kuipers, 1982; Gärling *et al.*, 1982). First, we learn a linked list of items. Then we get to know some landmarks and can start relating our position with regards to these landmarks. We learn the relative position of landmarks and start building mental maps of parts of the space between these landmarks. These maps are not all complete. Some of the 'pages' are detailed, others are not, and more importantly, the relations between the pages are not perfect. Some may be distorted with respect to one another.

In the 1960s the psychologist Kevin Lynch identified five key aspects of the environment: nodes, landmarks, paths, districts and edges (Lynch, 1961). Figure 25-1 shows an example of one of his maps.

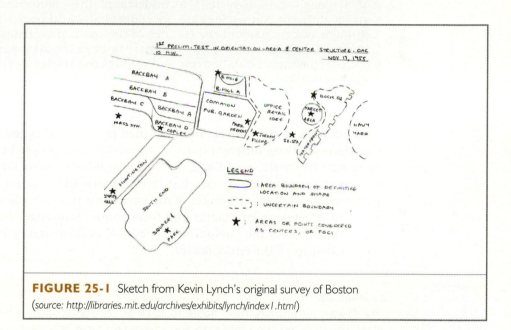

FIGURE 25-1 Sketch from Kevin Lynch's original survey of Boston (*source: http://libraries.mit.edu/archives/exhibits/lynch/index1.html*)

Districts are identifiable parts of an environment which are defined by their edges. Nodes are smaller points within the environment; those with particular significance may be seen as landmarks. Paths connect nodes. These concepts have endured, though not without criticism. The main issue is to what extent are features of the environment objectively identified. Other writers (e.g. Barthes, 1986) have pointed out that the identification of these features is much more subjective. It is also important to consider the significance and meanings that are attached to spaces by people. Different people see things differently at different times. Shoppers see shopping malls in a different way than skateboarders do. A street corner might feel very different in the middle of the day than it does at night. There are different conceptions of landmarks, districts, etc., depending on cultural differences such as race, gender or social group. The ship's captain can see many more different landmarks in the ebb and flow of a river than the novice. Navigation in a wilderness is a wholly different activity from navigation in a museum.

Further thoughts: Space syntax

An interesting approach to architectural understanding is provided by the space syntax theory of Hillier (1996). This theory looks at the connectivity of nodes in a space: how closely connected one node is to another through the paths that link them. Hillier uses the theory to explore issues of legibility of a space – how easy it is to understand the connections and how visible different connections are. By concentrating on people's movement through spaces, many of the features of the space are revealed. Using the theory, social phenomena such as burglary rates and house prices can be predicted. Chalmers (2003) adapts and applies the theory to the design of information spaces.

In addition to the five features identified by Lynch, it is generally assumed that there are three different types of knowledge that people have of an environment: landmark, route and survey knowledge (Downs and Stea, 1973). Landmark knowledge is the simplest sort of spatial knowledge in which people just recognize important features of the environment. Gradually they will fill in the details between landmarks and form route knowledge. As they become more familiar with the environment they will develop survey knowledge, the 'cognitive map' of the environment.

Challenge 25-1
Write down your journey from home to work or college. Identify where you have a clear and detailed cognitive map and where you have only sketchy knowledge. Identify the main landmarks on your route and distinguish where you have just route knowledge against where you have survey knowledge. Give examples of where ecological decisions are made (i.e. where you rely on knowledge in the world). List the nodes, paths, edges and districts on your route. Discuss this with a colleague and identify areas of agreement/disagreement.

Visual perception is covered in Chapter 5. Audio and touch are covered in Chapter 16

Navigation in electronic spaces

In electronic spaces, the physics are different. Indeed some people would consider navigation of information and electronic spaces to be quite different from navigation in geographical spaces as there is no body to be moved. However, we treat them as essentially similar activities, with the main difference being that the navigators in electronic space have to move without the full range of sensory inputs of a physical body.

By electronic spaces we include the whole range of software systems, including the 'two and a half D' (2.5D) of desktop virtual reality systems that provide apparent three-dimensional (3D) images. These are the province of many computer games where the feeling of moving through an environment is quite strong. We also include full immersive virtual reality where the person is immersed in a scene, either physically in a 'CAVE' (the person is inside a six-sided box with images displayed on all six sides) or using a head-mounted display (HMD). One of the key features of navigation in such environments is that people can jump from one part of the space to another. They can travel through virtual walls and leap over virtual buildings. Visualizations (Chapter 24) are another type of electronic space where novel techniques can be provided to give the user different views of a real or virtual landscape. For example, a fish-eye view focuses attention on one area but provides a wide angle to the overall view. Three-dimensional 'fly-overs' of virtual spaces are made possible with software technology. People navigate through these spaces using a variety of cursors and other devices. Driving games, for example, may provide the user with a steering wheel; a snowboarding game might provide the user with a snowboard that they can stand on to really feel that they are navigating through the use of their body.

FIGURE 25-2 Electronic books

Another example of an electronic space is the electronic book (Figure 25-2). Electronic books share many of the features of any hypertext space such as a CD-ROM encyclopedia. Navigation is primarily by clicking on links in such systems. The advantage that an electronic book gives is a special-purpose reader with controls as part of the hardware as well as software controls. This enables scrolling, 'page turns' and other navigational functions. The iPod (Chapter 1) is another device designed specifically to assist navigation through the space of music files.

Navigation in information spaces

As we stated in Chapter 23, 'information spaces' include both interactive and non-interactive devices and systems. Information design (Chapter 24) is central to making such spaces intelligible. The topology of the space and the distance from one object to another affect the navigability of the space, as do the other characteristics: the size and volatility of the space, the different media of the space, the conceptual and physical objects in the space, the extent to which the space has been designed, and whether it includes other agents.

In information spaces people face similar problems and undertake similar activities to those they face in geographical spaces. They may be engaged in wayfinding – searching for a known piece of information. They may be engaged in exploration of the space or in object identification. They will move rapidly between these activities and will pick up new information from the local environment. Indeed, often they will rely on designers putting information in an environment to remind them of different functions and options that are available. Information spaces have different districts, with nodes and paths linking the sections together. Landmarks will help people to recognize where they are in a space and hopefully help them to plan and monitor a route to where they want to go. People will have simple route knowledge of some information spaces and survey knowledge of others.

For example, consider writing a document using Microsoft Word. To start, the user must open a new file which involves knowing about the existence of the Open command on the File menu and finding their way to it. The existence of some physical object such as a mouse or track pad enables them to manoeuvre the perceptual cursor object to the landmark 'File' in the top left-hand corner, clicking on a mouse button, holding it down and moving down the menu to reach the Open command and releasing. A new document opens up. The user types some text and now decides to format it as italics. Once again the person is wayfinding. They have enough survey knowledge to know that they can put the text into italics and hence they plan a route to go to their destination via the Format Font command. When they arrive at their destination they find a whole district, a dialogue box of options. Exploring this, they might come across a new option, Emboss or Engrave, which they were unaware of (see Figure 25-3).

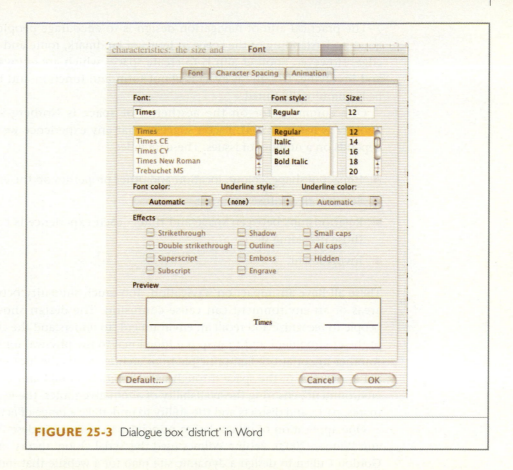

FIGURE 25-3 Dialogue box 'district' in Word

Challenge 25-2
Find a piece of software that you use in this way and undertake a similar analysis.

25.2 Designing for navigation

The essential thing about designing for navigation is to keep in mind the different activities that people undertake in a space – object identification, wayfinding and exploration – and the different purposes and meanings that people will bring to the space. Of course, designing for navigation has been the concern of architecture, interior design and urban planning for years and many useful principles have been developed that can be applied to the design of information spaces.

The practical aim of navigation design is to encourage people to develop a good understanding of the space in terms of landmark, route and survey knowledge. However, another aim is to create spaces which are enjoyable, engaging and involving. Design (as ever) is about form and function and how these can be harmoniously united.

One commentator on the aesthetics of space is Norberg-Schulz (1971), another is Bacon (1974). Bacon suggests that any experience we have of space depends on a number of issues. These include:

- Impact of shape, colour, location and other properties on the environment
- Features that infuse character
- Relationships between space and time – each experience is based partly on those preceding it
- Involvement.

These all have an impact on navigation. Too much similarity between different areas of an environment can cause confusion. The design should encourage people to recognize and recall an environment, to understand the context and use of the environment and to map the functional to the physical form of the space. Another important design principle from architecture is the idea of gaining gradual knowledge of the space through use. Designers should aim for a 'responsive environment', ensuring the availability of alternative routes, the legibility of landmarks, paths and districts and the ability to undertake a range of activities.

One application of urban design principles to websites is described in Benyon and Wilmes (2003). Bettina Wilmes used the 'serial vision' theory of town planner Gordon Cullen to design a dynamic site map for a website that indicated the distance and direction of the other pages on a site from the current position of the visitor. Cullen's theory was based on the gradually unfolding nature of vistas as one walked through an environment (see Gosling, 1996). Figure 25-4 illustrates this.

Signage

Good, clear signposting of spaces is critical in the design of spaces. There are three primary types of sign that designers can use:

- *Informational* signs provide information on objects, people and activities and hence aid object identification and classification.
- *Directional* signs provide route and survey information. They do this often through sign hierarchies, with one type of sign providing general directions being followed by another that provides local directions.
- *Warning and reassurance* signs provide feedback or information on actual or potential actions within the environment.

CASEBOOK: SERIAL VISION

To walk from one end of the plan to another, at a uniform pace, will provide a sequence of revelations which are suggested in the serial drawings opposite, reading from left to right. Each arrow on the plan represents a drawing. The even progress of travel is illuminated by a series of sudden contrasts and so an impact is made on the eye, bringing the plan to life (like nudging a man who is going to sleep in church). My drawings bear no relation to the place itself; I chose it because it seemed an evocative plan. Note that the slightest deviation in alignment and quite small variations in projections or setbacks on plan have a disproportionally powerful effect in the third dimension.

FIGURE 25-4 Gordon Cullen's serial vision *(source: Cullen, 1961)*

Of course, any particular sign may serve more than one purpose, and an effective signage system will not only help people in getting to their desired destination but also make them aware of alternative options. Signage needs to integrate aesthetically with the environment in which it is situated, so that it will help both good and poor navigators. Consistency of signage is important, but so is being able to distinguish different types of sign.

FIGURE 25-5 Signage in London (*source: Dorling Kindersley*)

Maps and guides

Maps can be used to provide navigational information. Supplemented with additional detail about the objects in the environment, they become guides. There are many different sorts of map, from the very detailed and realistic to the highly abstract schematic. We have already seen examples of schematic maps such as the map of the London Underground (Figure 24-2). We have also seen site maps in websites that show the structure of the information and how it is classified and categorized.

Maps are social things – they are there to give information and help people explore, understand and find their way through spaces. They should be designed to fit in with the signage system. Like signs there will often be a need for maps at different levels of abstraction. A global map which shows the whole extent of the environment will need to be supplemented by local maps showing the details of what is nearby. Figure 25-6 shows some different sorts of map.

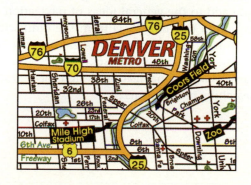

FIGURE 25-6 Maps

(sources: London Underground Map. Registered User No. 04/E/1424. Reproduced by kind permission of London's Transport Museum; http://worldatlas.com; http://graphicmaps.com; Pearson Education)

Social navigation

A well-designed environment with good signage and well-designed navigational aids such as maps will be conducive to good navigation, but even in the best-designed environment people will often turn to other people for information on navigation rather than use more formalized information artefacts. When navigating cities people tend to ask other people for advice rather than study maps. Information from other people is usually personalized and adapted to suit the individual's needs. Even when we are not directly looking for information we use a wide range of cues, both from features of the environment and from the behaviour of other people, to manage our activities. We might be influenced to pick up a book because it appears well thumbed, we walk into a sunny courtyard because it looks attractive, or we might decide to see a film because our friends enjoyed it. We find our way through spaces by talking to or following the trails of others. The whole myriad of uses that people make of other people, whether directly or indirectly, is called *social navigation*. In Section 25.4 we deal in detail with social navigation of information space.

25.3 Navigation design for websites

The concepts of navigation outlined above are common to all information spaces. A graphical user interface to a database needs good navigation support, clear signage and so on. The menu headers are your landmarks, or major routes – do you know what lies behind each item on a menu or are there sketchy areas of the application? As we saw above, navigational principles apply to electronic and information spaces. But it is perhaps with websites that the principles can be more clearly seen. The Web as a space in which we use Internet *Explorer* or Netscape *Navigator* to seek out information is a very powerful analogy.

The design of navigation mechanisms is the second main pillar of information architecture. Brinck *et al.* (2002) add to the general ideas of navigation by identifying seven types of user navigation (see Box 25-1) from the omniscient user ('they benefit from short, efficient paths') to rote memorization ('use distinctive landmarks and orientation cues'). Along with Rosenfeld and Morville (2002) they identify three key features of a good navigation design for websites: labelling, navigation support and searching mechanisms.

Box 25-1 How people navigate

- *Omniscience*: Users have perfect knowledge and make no mistakes – provide short, efficient paths.
- *Optimal rationality*: Users reason perfectly, but only know what they have seen – make sure links provide adequate cues to the content they lead to.
- *Satisficing*: Users avoid remembering and planning and make decisions on what is immediately perceptible – organize the page to make the most important content and links available immediately.
- *Mental maps*: Users actively use the cues available to try to infer the structure of a website – organize the site simply so that users can easily conceptualize it. Design the navigation bar and site maps to reinforce this mental map.
- *Rote memorization*: When users find a path that works, they tend to remember and repeat it – make sure the most obvious solution is also efficient. Use distinctive landmarks and orientation cues to help people recognize where they have been before.
- *Information foraging*: Users try to get as much as possible at one location – enable spontaneous discovery by providing context, structure and related topics.
- *Information costs*: Users have limited knowledge and reasoning ability – minimize the mental costs of sense making, decision making, remembering and planning.

Source: Brinck *et al.* (2002), pp. 126-127

Box 25-2 Information foraging theory

Peter Pirolli from Xerox PARC has developed a theory of information navigation based on evolutionary theory. He sees people as 'infovores' eagerly seeking out information much as we used to forage for food. Information foragers use perceptual and cognitive mechanisms that carry over from the evolution of food-foraging adaptations. People use proximal cues in the environment to help them search out information: 'information scent'. They seek to maximize their information-seeking activities, to yield more useful information per unit cost.

Whilst admitting that the theory has been developed for certain well-defined information-seeking problems, Pirolli and his colleagues argue that it has led to some interesting and useful designs. In particular, they make predictions about how people will navigate websites based on the closeness of the match between the labels used for links and the information that are seeking.

Whether or not you really believe in the theory, the ideas of information scent are the same as those that we have described as ecological aspects of navigation.

Labelling

Icons are discussed in Chapter 15, Section 15.6

Labels are used for internal and external links, headings and sub-headings, titles and related areas. Not all labels are text and iconic labels can be very useful if the context and design is clear. Paying attention to good, consistent, relevant labels is a critical part of information architecture. Information architects must develop a clear and unambiguous preferred vocabulary (see also Section 23.3).

There is nothing more confusing for people than a website changing its own vocabulary, for example referring to 'products' one minute and 'items' the next. The same labels should be used on searching mechanisms as on the main pages, in the names of the pages and in the link names. Figure 25-7 shows the front page of the 'Web Pages That Suck' site. This is a great site full of bad designs. However, I found it quite difficult to find what was on the site, because the labelling is not very clear. What is 'Mystery Meat Navigation'?

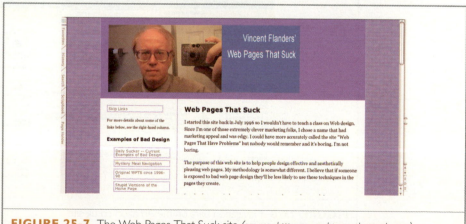

FIGURE 25-7 The Web Pages That Suck site (*source: http:www.webpagesthatsuck.com*)

Navigation support

Of course, many of the signs and labels on a website are deliberately placed in order to support navigation. It is common to have a navigation bar across the top of a site which points to the main, top-level categories. This is often called the global navigation bar. Within each of these there will be sub-categories. These might be placed down the left-hand side of the site or may drop down when the main category is selected. These are known as local navigation. It is a good design principle to have the global, top-level navigation bar the same on every page so that people can easily jump back to the home page, to a 'frequently asked questions' page or to one of the other main categories.

An essential feature of the navigation features of any website is to provide a 'you are here' sign. This is often presented by a description showing where people are in the hierarchy of the site. Other devices such as indexes and glossaries are helpful in assisting people find exactly what they are searching for. A site map should be made available that can be called up when needed. The map displays the structure and content headers of the various categories. Figure 25-8 shows the Amazon.co.uk site where several different types of navigation are used.

Global navigation is provided by the tabbed bar across the top and covers the whole site – DVD, books, videos, etc. It is supplemented by a navigation bar that shows the same key site features. An alphabetic navigation bar is shown on the left-hand side. In figure 26-5(a) and (b) (page 647) you can see a 'breadcrumbs' display. (Breadcrumbs comes from the story of Hansel and Gretel who left a trail of breadcrumbs so they could find their way back when they were taken into the forest.) Using breadcrumbs is a common way of showing people where they are. In Figure 26-5(a) the breadcrumbs tell us that we are at 'Your Recommendations', 'Improve Your Recommendations', 'Select Your Favourite Areas'.

FIGURE 25-8 Navigation bars on the Amazon.co.uk site

Navigation bars – both local and global – are essentially signposts and land-marks, leaving the site visitor to pick their way through the site structure. Site maps and good feedback on where people are in the structure will also help. Another alternative is to provide a clear path through a part of the site. This is particularly important when a number of activities or pages have to be visited in sequence. A site 'wizard' can help here that guides people and explains what each activity is for. Often this is simply a succession of pages, such as when buying a ticket or booking a flight (Figure 25-9).

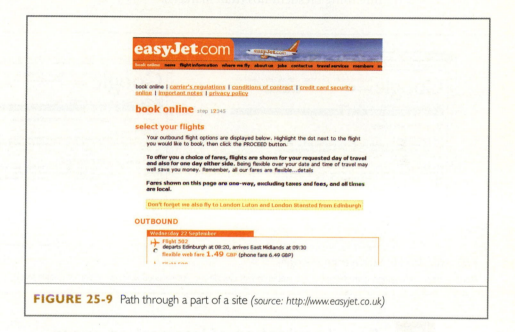

FIGURE 25-9 Path through a part of a site *(source: http://www.easyjet.co.uk)*

Searching

One of the significant features of the Web as an information space is that many sites support searching. Search engines can be bought; the better ones are quite expensive but are also effective. Once again the preferred vocabulary (Chapter 23) should form the basis of searching, and where the synonyms have been defined they too can be used in defining search terms and in helping people to refine their search.

There are two main problems with searching a website. The first is knowing exactly what sort of documents the search engine is searching. The second is how to express combinations of search criteria. A frequent failing of websites is not to make clear which items are included in the search. Is the content of different documents searched, or is it just the Web pages themselves? Does it include PDF files, or Word files, and in the latter case is it the whole content or just some tagged keywords? Sites should indicate what is searched and provide options to search different types of content.

How to express a search is another key issue. In natural language if I say I am interested in cats and dogs, I usually mean I am interested in cats, or dogs, or cats *and* dogs. In search engine language 'cats and dogs' means only 'cats and dogs'. This is because search engines are based on Boolean logic. So to find information about cats and dogs, I need to put in that I am looking for information on cats or dogs. Figure 25-10 shows the search engine Google. Notice how it can make use of a controlled vocabulary to offer alternatives to possibly misspelt words. Also notice how in the second shot it shows the positioning of the structure using breadcrumbs (trail markers).

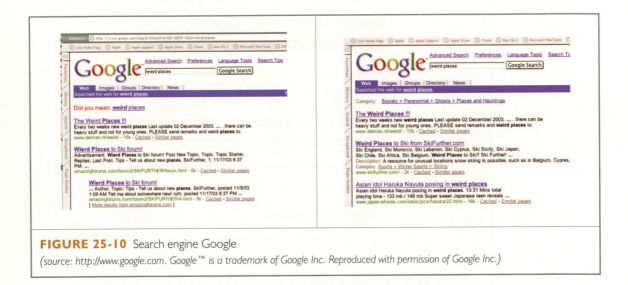

FIGURE 25-10 Search engine Google

(source: http://www.google.com. Google™ is a trademark of Google Inc. Reproduced with permission of Google Inc.)

25.4 Social navigation of information space

In the introduction to their book, Höök, Benyon and Munro (2003) illustrate the ideas of social navigation with an example of a grocery store:

'Consider the design of an on-line grocery store from the perspective of social navigation. First of all, we would assume that other people would "be around" in the store. Instead of imagining a "dead" information space, we now see before us a lively space where (in some way) the user can see other shoppers moving about, can consult or instruct specialist agents and "talk to" the personnel of the grocery store. These are examples of direct social navigation. We also see the possibility of providing information pointing to what groceries one might buy based on what other people have bought, e.g. if we want to help allergic users to find groceries and recipes that work for them, we could use the ideas of recommender systems; pointing people to products that, based on the preferences of other people, the system believes would be suitable. Sometimes we just like to peek into another's basket, or just take the most popular brand of some product. These are examples of indirect social navigation.'

(Höök *et al.*, 2003, pp. 5–6)

Social navigation of information space encompasses a whole collection of techniques and designs that make people aware of others and of what others have done. Some designs such as on-line communities exist solely for the purpose of enabling people to maintain and build links with other people. Other systems are more concerned with making people aware of what others are doing, and yet others with making aggregate knowledge of others available.

Direct social navigation

Direct social navigation is concerned with putting people in touch with other people, or with artificial agents (see Chapter 26). When we talk to someone else, the information we get back is often personalized to our needs, and the advisor may offer information that changes what we want to do or how we might approach it, making us aware of other possibilities. People can judge to what extent the information given can be trusted, depending upon the credibility of the information provider. Even if the information cannot be trusted, it may still be of value as people know where it has come from. In information spaces, using person-to-person communication is an important part of the information architecture that is often overlooked.

Direct social navigation comes in many forms. At its most prosaic it consists of a link such as 'mail info@website.com' or mail 'webmaster'. At least these impersonal connections suggest that there is a real person at the end of the line. Having individuals identified by name adds another level of personalization (but creates difficulties if that person is not answering their mail for a few days). From such beginnings rich webs of direct social navigation support can be developed. There may be an instant messaging facility, video-conferencing and so on.

→

Part VII where systems that support communication and collaboration are discussed

Systems supporting direct social navigation can soon turn into fully fledged on-line communities where the whole basis of the information space is to support communication and exchange of information around a particular theme. On-line communities are springing up devoted to all manner of social and recreational questions. They combine e-mail lists, threaded conferences, chat rooms, message boards, diaries ('weblogs' or 'blogs') into a coherent structure to support some domain (Rheingold, 2000).

GeoNotes (Persson *et al.*, 2003) is a system for augmenting the geographical world with virtual 'Post-it' notes. Thanks to the advances in positioning technologies, an electronic message can be left associated with a particular place. When another person (suitably technologically equipped) arrives at the place, the system alerts him or her to the message. As Persson *et al.* point out, such attachments of information spaces to geographical spaces go back to cave paintings and people continue to annotate places with graffiti, Post-its and fridge magnets. GeoNotes offers a technologically enhanced version, putting people in contact with other people (Figure 25-11).

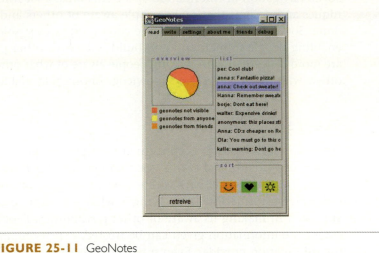

FIGURE 25-11 GeoNotes
(*source: http://www.sics.se/~espinoza/documents/Geonotes_ubicomp_final.htm, Fig. 2*)

Recommender and filtering systems

If other people are not around to provide help and advice then there are a number of systems that try to filter out uninteresting information and point people to things that they will find relevant (see, e.g., Konstan and Riedl, 2003). Just as a newspaper editor filters news into a form that readers of that newspaper like, so filtering systems aim to tailor information to people. (Conversely the newspaper or TV channel that we choose is selected because we like the way that news is filtered and presented.)

In content-based filtering the information is scanned for specific articles that match some criteria. Based on a statistical analysis the system rates the relevance of the information to the user. Usually keyword-matching techniques are used to filter the information. The user supplies a preference file to the system with keywords that the system should look for in documents. For example, an agent scans a newsgroup for documents that contain the keywords on a regular basis. This is the basis of systems such as MyYahoo! (Figure 25-12).

Recommender systems make suggestions to people for information based on what other people with similar tastes like or dislike. All users of the system are connected to a server that keeps track of every user – users can be anonymous – by storing each user's personal profile. Personal profiles are matched and the system creates clusters of users with similar tastes. Book recommendations from the Amazon.co.uk site is probably the best example of a mature recommender system. People who subscribe to Amazon.co.uk can have the system recommend books based on those that they have bought previously and on those that they rank (Figure 25-13).

Another method of providing social navigation is to provide a tag so that whenever a user comes upon a new piece of information she can see what other

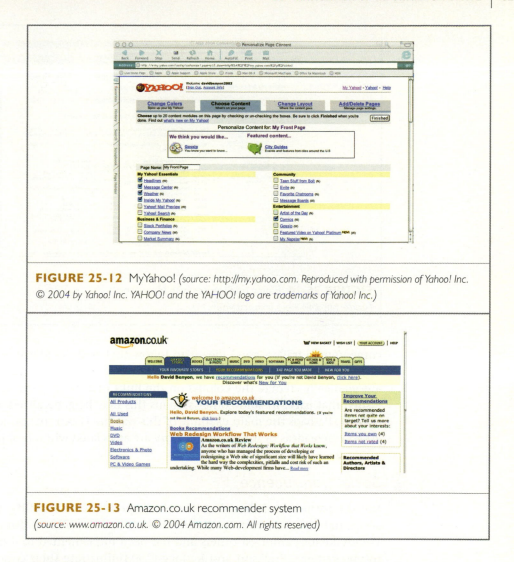

FIGURE 25-12 MyYahoo! *(source: http://my.yahoo.com. Reproduced with permission of Yahoo! Inc. © 2004 by Yahoo! Inc. YAHOO! and the YAHOO! logo are trademarks of Yahoo! Inc.)*

FIGURE 25-13 Amazon.co.uk recommender system
(source: www.amazon.co.uk. © 2004 Amazon.com. All rights reserved)

people with similar interests to hers think of that particular piece of information. Some sort of rating of the information pieces has to be done by the users of the system so that the system can create and cluster personal profiles. The more people who rate items, the more accurately the system can group users. Ratings can be done explicitly and/or implicitly: implicit ratings are, for example, time spent reading an article; explicit ratings let users score information sources. Filtering needs some sort of input to work with, and explicit rating of information is not all that simple. How do we judge ratings from a user who has created the information? Explicitly rating information is also an additional burden on people, so sometimes they will not bother.

History-enriched environments, or 'readware', is another technique for social navigation. What other people have done in the past can tell us something about how to navigate the information space. If we get lost in the woods and

FIGURE 25-14 Rating preferences with Movielens
(source: http://movielens.umn.edu/login)

come upon a trail, a good idea is to follow that trail. Similarly, people take certain paths through information space. Another familiar technique is to automatically change the colours on the links in a webpage when a person has visited that page. In some other systems this may be generalized based on usage of links. Perhaps the main example of this was the Footprints project (Wexelblat, 2003) where ideas of interaction history are associated with an object.

Social translucence

Social translucence is based on three core principles – visibility, awareness and accountability. The concept has been developed at IBM by Tom Erickson and Wendy Kellogg amongst others and has been implemented in a number of prototype systems. Erickson and Kellogg (2003) illustrate their concept by telling the tale of a wooden door that opened outwards in their office. If opened too quickly the door would smash into anyone who was walking down the corridor. The design solution to this problem was to put a glass panel in the door. This enabled the three principles of social translucence:

1. *Visibility*. People outside were now visible to those inside who were going to open the door. Of course the transparency of the window meant that people inside the office were also visible!

2. *Awareness*. Now people could see what others were doing and could take appropriate action – opening the door carefully, perhaps.

3. *Accountability*. This is an important principle. Not only are people aware of others but now they are aware that they are aware of others. If the person

inside the office opens the door and smashes into someone in the corridor, the person in the corridor knows that the office person knew this. Hence he or she has to be socially accountable for the action.

These principles have resulted in a number of 'social proxies': software systems that capture these principles. The best known of these is Babble – a social proxy for meetings, chat and e-mail. People are represented by 'marbles' and the space of discussion by the large circle in the centre of the system (see Figure 25-15). The more active people are, the nearer the centre they are, and the marbles gradually move towards the periphery if they do not participate in the chat for some length of time. Other details of the people can be seen in the panes around the edge of the system.

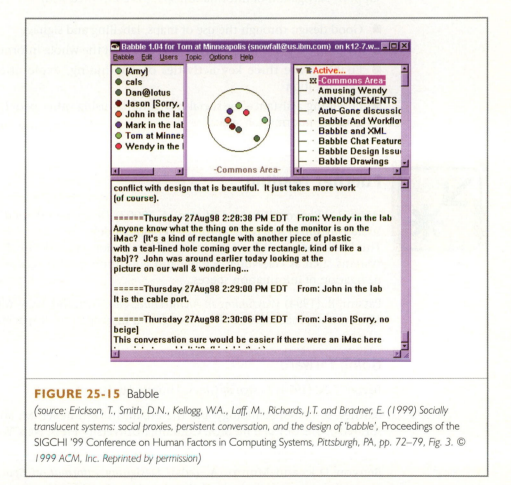

FIGURE 25-15 Babble

(*source: Erickson, T., Smith, D.N., Kellogg, W.A., Laff, M., Richards, J.T. and Bradner, E. (1999) Socially translucent systems: social proxies, persistent conversation, and the design of 'babble', Proceedings of the SIGCHI '99 Conference on Human Factors in Computing Systems, Pittsburgh, PA, pp. 72–79, Fig. 3. © 1999 ACM, Inc. Reprinted by permission*)

Summary and key points

Navigation in information spaces is a key activity that people undertake. We can learn much from studying navigation in geographical spaces and indeed apply design principles from urban planning and architecture. The principles of how we find our way in information spaces are the same as those in geographical spaces. The differences are that we have far fewer sensory cues in information spaces and the physics are different – we can jump to different parts of the space, fly over data landscapes and move through virtual walls. In information spaces, design is even more important. Also important is social navigation and there are a number of applications that seek to provide some form of navigation support. Navigation of information space is concerned with

- Good design through the use of maps, labelling and signage
- Helping people obtain a survey knowledge of the whole information space
- Enabling the three key activities of wayfinding, exploration and object identification
- Providing assistance for social navigation – using other people to help navigate the information space.

Further reading

Höök, K., Benyon D.R. and Munro, A. (2003) *Designing Information Spaces: The Social Navigation Approach*. Springer-Verlag, London.
This book contains 17 articles on social navigation, from detailed descriptions of systems such as GeoNotes, Babble and Footprints to theoretical discussions of navigation of information spaces.

Passini, R. (1994) *Wayfinding in Architecture*. Van Nostrand, New York.
The most approachable book on navigation in geographical spaces.

Going forward

Bacon, E.N. (1974) *Design of Cities*. Thomas Hudson, London.

Barthes, R. (1986) Semiology and the urban. In Gottdiener, M. and Lagopoulos, A.P. (eds), *The City and the Sign*. Columbia University Press, New York.

Chalmers, M. (2003) Informatics, architecture and language. In Höök, K., Benyon D.R. and Munro, A. (eds), *Designing Information Spaces: The Social Navigation Approach*. Springer-Verlag, London, pp. 315–342.

Cullen, G. (1971) (reprinted 2000) *The Concise Townscape*. Architectural Press, Oxford.

Downs, R. and Stea, D. (1973) Cognitive representations. In Downs, R. and Stea, D. (eds), *Image and Environment*. Aldine, Chicago, pp. 79–86.

Hillier, B. (1996) *Space is the Machine*. Cambridge University Press, Cambridge.

Lynch, K. (1961) *The Image of the City*. MIT Press, Cambridge, MA.

Norberg-Schulz, C. (1971) *Existence, Space, Architecture*. Studio Vista, London.

Comments on challenges

Challenge 25-1
There is not much that can be said in general here about what you know about where you live and work! There are some interesting points about knowledge in the world, however. When we reflect for an exercise such as this, we 'run a mental model'; that is, we visualize the journey in our 'mind's eye'. This may mean that we attend to more detail than we would do when we are really navigating the route when our minds might be on something else. In such cases we may rely much more on ecological issues than we think we do.

Challenge 25-2
I use a drawing program called Omnigraffle. In most respects this is a very good piece of software, but I constantly have trouble changing the thickness of the lines. I am in a drawing environment, so I can expect to find standard drawing features such as filling in different colours, changing lines, drawing arrows and boxes and so on.

When I come to find my way to where I can do this, however, I often get lost. Under the Format menu there are Font, Text, Grid, Align and Size but no 'Line'. Under Tools there is a walkthrough menu 'Info Panes' under which there is an entry for 'Line', but it only lets you change the shape and arrowheads, etc. In the past I have given up at this point, but if you are willing to persevere and explore other menus, the facility eventually turns up at Tools > Info Panes > Style. I bet I will forget this by the next time I come to need this function.

See Chapter 20 on structural knowledge

Exercises

1. Take a small electronic space such as a mobile (cell) phone, a PDA, or even a car radio/cassette/CD player. Look at the signs, maps and other items that are there to help you find your way through the space. Consider the design in terms of landmarks, nodes, districts, etc. How well designed is it? Do you always know 'where you are' and how to get to where you want to go?

2. Find a large website such as the Amazon.co.uk site in Figure 25-8. Write down the various navigational features that have been included in terms of local and global navigation, searching and labelling. Critique the information design of the site (perhaps reverse engineer the wire frames for different pages).

3. Consider the quotation about an on-line grocery store at the beginning of Section 25.4. Perhaps have a look at some commercial on-line stores. Now design social navigational features that could help enliven the space and help people find ways through the space.

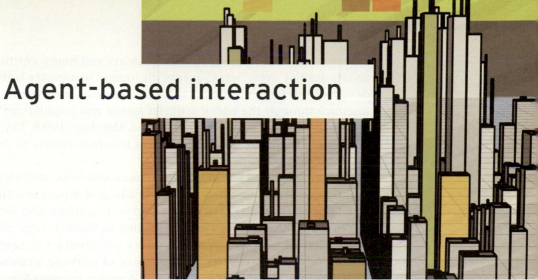

26 Agent-based interaction

Aims

Agents are autonomous, active computer processes that possess some ability to communicate with people and/or other agents and to adapt their behaviour. In short, agents are small artificial intelligence (AI) computer programs. The ones that interest us have some impact on the interaction of people with interactive systems. Agent-based interaction has long been seen as a solution to many usability problems, but so far it has not delivered as much as was hoped, something that it shares with all applications of AI. However, there have been some notable successes and many of the systems described in Section 25.3 such as recommender systems employ some form of agent or agency in the interaction.

After studying this chapter you should be able to:

- Describe the key features of interface agents
- Understand the conceptual model of agents
- Understand the key idea of user modelling
- Describe some agent-based systems.

26.1 Agents

Agents are autonomous, active computer processes that possess some ability to communicate with people and/or other agents and to adapt their behaviour. In some work in artificial intelligence, there is a 'strong view' of agents; they have beliefs, desires and intentions (and maybe emotions) and can plan, learn, adapt and communicate. Much of this work is not concerned with interface issues, but rather with activities such as planning, scheduling and controlling computer networks. In HCI circles there is the 'weaker view' presented above. There is also a large amount of hype surrounding agents and many entities proclaimed as agents are not even 'weak' agents. In human–computer interaction and the design of interactive systems, the move towards utilizing intelligence at the interface through the use of artificial agents was popularized in the 1990s by people such as Brenda Laurel (1990b) and Alan Kay (1990). Kay talked about the move away from direct manipulation of interface objects to the 'indirect management' of interface agents.

Kay's vision was of a world in which more and more activities are delegated to agents. Agents would act as 'talking heads' and attend meetings for us. They could organize our diaries in cooperation with agents acting for members of our work group. Other agents would be guiding us through large information spaces in a variety of personas, acting as tutors and mentors in teaching systems or explaining the complexities of a new piece of software, drawing on our experience with previous similar applications. However, progress towards this situation has been relatively slow. The fundamental difficulty is that computers have access to a very limited view of what people are doing. They can detect mouse movements, typing, the selection of menu items and that is just about all. Making sensible inferences about what people are trying to do from such limited data is very difficult.

Agents can be seen in a number of different ways:

- As guides they would explain the structure and features of an information space.
- As reminder agents they would help us keep appointments and keep us up to date with new developments.
- As monitors they would watch over mailing lists and announcements for relevant information.
- As collaborators they would work with us on problems.
- As surrogates they would stand in for us at meetings.

Generally there are two main types of agent:

- 'Userbots' act on behalf of and know about an individual person. This, then, allows for personalization and adapting systems to an individual's preferences, habits and knowledge.
- 'Taskbots' know about particular types of work such as indexing, scheduling, spell-checking and so on. They have more domain knowledge, but less knowledge of individuals. Predictive technologies such as the T3 text system and the systems on Web browsers that try to anticipate long URLs are examples of 'taskbots'.

Of course, robots are examples of agent-based interaction and soon we will be discussing human–robot interaction. Figure 26-1 shows a robot vacuum cleaner.

FIGURE 26-1 Robot vacuum cleaner (*source: courtesy of iRobot Corporation*)

When thinking about what agents can do it is useful to consider metaphors from real-life agents (see Box 26-1). Some agents can learn about behaviours over time; others can be programmed by the end-users (end-user programming). All are based, however, on some important principles of adaptive systems. We briefly review the concept of an adaptive system before developing an architecture of agents and looking at some examples.

BOX 26-1 Metaphors for thinking about agents

- Travel agents – the user specifies some fairly high-level goal that they have and some broad constraints. The agent tries to come up with an option that satisfies.
- Real-estate agents work independently on behalf of their clients, scanning the available options for real estate and picking likely-looking properties.
- The secret agent goes out to find out what is going on, working with and against others to discover important information.
- The agent as friend suggests someone who gets to know your likes and dislikes and who shares your interests – someone who can pick out interesting things when they see them.
- The film star's or basketball player's agent is someone who works on their behalf negotiating the best deals, or the best scripts or teams.
- The slave does the jobs for you that you do not want to do.

Challenge 26-1
Instructing agents on what you want them to do can be quite difficult. Anyone who has bought a house or rented a flat will know that estate agents seem to send houses that are completely at odds with what the buyer wanted. Try writing down some instructions that would describe which news stories you would like to know about. Exchange the descriptions with a friend and see whether you can find exceptions or whether they would be able to follow your instructions.

26.2 Adaptive systems

Agents are adaptive systems. A system is a more or less complex object which is recognized, from a particular perspective, to have a relatively stable, coherent structure (Checkland, 1981). Checkland stresses the need to declare explicitly, as part of the system definition, the perspective (or *Weltanschauung*, as he calls it) from which the phenomenon is being considered as a system and the aspects of the system which are considered to be stable and coherent. Systems contain sub-systems and are contained within super-systems (or environments). Systems interact with other systems. Systems interact with their environments, with their subsystems and with other systems at the same level of abstraction. A seed interacts with the earth and so obtains necessary nutrients for its growth. A traveller listens to an announcement at Munich airport. A hammer interacts with a nail and drives the nail into a piece of wood.

In order to interact with another system at all, every system requires some representation, or model, of the other system. So a seed embodies a representation of its environment and if this model is inaccurate or inappropriate the seed will not germinate; it will not succeed in its interaction. The interaction of the traveller and the airport announcement can be described at the following levels:

- Physical (the announcement must be clear and loud enough for the traveller to hear it)
- Conceptual (the traveller must be able to interpret what is heard in terms of airports, travel and the German language)
- Intentional (the announcement will relate more or less to some purpose of the traveller).

The hammer has been carefully designed in order to achieve its purpose of banging nails into wood; its physical model must capture the conceptual level (that it is strong enough) which must be suitable for its purpose.

In each case, the systems in question have a 'model' of the interaction which in turn is dependent on two other representations: the model which a system has of itself and the model which it has of the systems with which it can interact – those that it is adapted to. In most natural systems, these models equate with the entirety of the system, but in designed systems the system's model of itself reflects the designer's view.

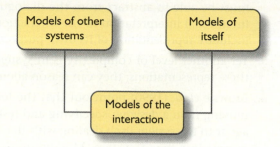

FIGURE 26-2 Basic architecture of interacting systems

We may represent the overall structure of the representations possessed by a system as shown in Figure 26-2. A system has one or more models of the other system(s) with which it is interacting. A system also includes some representations of itself.

The complexity of the various models defines a number of levels and types of adaptation. Browne, Totterdell and Norman (1990) identify a number of types of adaptive system in their consideration of adaptivity in natural and computer-based systems.

1. At the simplest level, some agents are characterized by their ability to produce a change in output in response to a change in input. These systems must have some receptor and transmitter functions (so that they can interact with other systems) and some rudimentary, rule-based adaptive mechanism. They have a generally limited variety of behaviour because the adaptive mechanism is 'hard wired'. These are the stimulus–response systems such as a thermostat: the temperature rises so the thermostat turns the heating off; the temperature falls so it turns the heating on.

2. The simple agent can be enhanced if it maintains a record of the interaction which allows it to respond to sequences of inputs rather than just individual signals. This can be further developed if it keeps a history of the interaction. Predictive text systems fall into this category.

3. A more complex system will monitor the effects of the adaptation on the subsequent interaction and evaluate this through trial and error. This evaluation mechanism then selects from a range of possible outputs for any given input. Many game-playing programs (e.g. chess games, tic-tac-toe games, etc.) use this form of adaptation.

4. Type 3 agents have to wait to observe the outcome of any adaptation on the resultant dialogue. In the case of game-playing agents, this might mean that they lose the game. More sophisticated systems monitor the effect on a *model* of the interaction. Thus possible adaptations can be tried out in theory before being put into practice. These systems now require a model of the other system with which they are interacting (in order to estimate the change of behaviour which will result from the system's own adaptive change). Moreover, these systems now require inference mechanisms and

must be able to abstract from the dialogue record and capture a design or intentional interpretation of the interaction. Similarly the system must now include a representation of its own 'purpose' in its domain model.

5. Yet another level of complexity is in systems which are capable of changing these representations; they can reason about the interaction.

6. Browne *et al.* (1990) point out that the levels reflect a change of intention moving from a designer specifying and testing the mechanisms in a (simple) agent to the system itself dealing with the design and evaluation of its mechanisms in a type 5 system. Moving up the levels also incurs an increasing cost which may not be justified. There is little to be gained by having a highly sophisticated capability if the context of the interaction is never going to change.

Dietrich *et al.* (1993) consider the interaction between two systems and various stages at which adaptations can be suggested and implemented and which system has control at the different stages. In any system–system interaction we can consider

- *Initiative*: which system starts the process off
- *Proposal*: which system make the proposal for a particular adaptation
- *Decision*: which system decides whether to go ahead with the adaptation
- *Execution*: which system is responsible for carrying out the adaptation
- *Evaluation*: which system evaluates the success of the change.

As a very simple example of a human–agent interaction, consider the spellchecker on a word processor. It is up to the user to decide whether to take the initiative (turn on the spellchecker), the system makes proposals for incorrectly spelled words, the person decides whether to accept the proposal, the system usually executes the change (but sometimes the person may type in a particular word) and it is the person who evaluates the effects.

Adaptive systems are characterized by the representations that they have of other systems, of themselves, and of the interaction. These models will only ever be partial representations of everything that goes on. Designers need to consider what is feasible (what data can be obtained about an interaction, for example) and what is desirable and useful.

Challenge 26-2
Cars illustrate well how more and more functions have been handed over to adaptive systems, or agents. Originally there were no synchromesh gears, the timing of the spark had to be advanced or retarded manually, there were no servo-break mechanisms and people had to remember to put their seat belts on. Using these and other examples, discuss what models the agents have. What do they know about the other systems that they interact with? What do they know about their own functioning?

26.3 An architecture for agents

The simple model of adaptive systems provides a framework or reference model for thinking about agent-based interaction. Agents are adaptive systems – systems that adapt to people. Hence they need some representation of people; the 'model of other systems' from Figure 26-2 becomes a 'user model' here (Figure 26-3). The 'model of itself' is the representation that the agent has of the domain, or application. The model of the interaction is an abstract representation of the interaction between the models of people and the models of the domain.

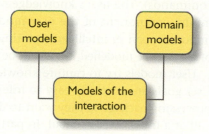

FIGURE 26-3 Basic architecture for an agent

Each of these may be further elaborated as indicated in Figure 26-4 which provides the full structural agent architecture. This architecture is elaborated and discussed below.

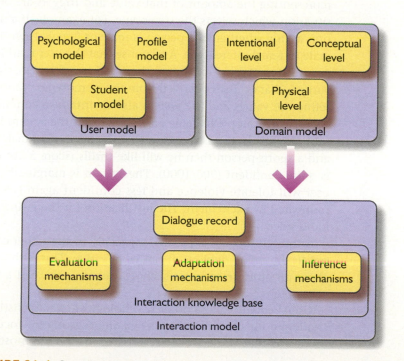

FIGURE 26-4 Overall architecture for an agent

User model

The user model describes what the system 'knows' about the user. We like to distinguish psychological data from user profile data because psychological data is more resistant to change (van der Veer *et al.*, 1985). Some systems concentrate on developing models of user habits, inferred by monitoring user–system interactions over time (i.e. by keeping a dialogue record). Other user profile data can often be most easily obtained by asking the user. Other systems try to infer user goals, although it is very difficult to infer what a user is trying to do from the data typically available to a computer system (mouse clicks and a sequence of commands). The user's knowledge of the domain is represented in the student model component of the user model. The student model is typically a very important part of intelligent tutoring systems. If there are several different types of users to be modelled, there will be several user models.

User models try to capture knowledge of users at a variety of different levels. User goals are relatively easy to infer at a high level (they have selected a word processing package so they want to do some word processing), but are very difficult at a lower level of detail. In particular it is very difficult to infer what a user is trying to do from a sequence of commands.

The pioneering approach to user models comes from Elaine Rich and her system called GRUNDY (Rich, 1989). This work introduced the ideas of stereotypes – sets of characteristics shared by many users. In GRUNDY the system is recommending books to people. A simple set of characteristics is given a value representing the amount of that value and triggers are objects associated with a situation which selects the stereotype. For example, if a user responds to a question asking whether that person is male or female then the answer will trigger a male or female stereotype. A response that the user is athletic will trigger a sports-person stereotype. The system then makes inferences concerning the values of various characteristics derived from the stereotypes. Various methods are used to refine the values and the system also maintains a confidence rating in its inferences. The example in Table 26-1 shows that the system has a confidence of 900 (out of 1000) in the assumption that the person is a male. If the person is a male and a sports-person then he will like thrills (score 5 out of 5). Again the system is quite confident (900/1000). The system is marginally less confident that the user will tolerate violence and less confident again (760/1000) that he will be motivated by excitement. The justification for the ratings is shown on the right-hand side.

Although such an approach, especially in the rather crude example shown, is politically rather dubious, it can be effective. This is the sort of data that is kept about all of us on websites such as Amazon.com. Not a very sophisticated view of people!

Users' cognitive and other psychological characteristics represent a different challenge for user models. One of the reasons for focusing on psychological models is that these are characteristics which are most resistant to change in

TABLE 26-1 An example of stereotype modelling from GRUNDY

Facet	Value	Rating	Justification
Gender	Male	900	Male Name
Thrill	5	900	Man Sports-Person
Tolerate violence	5	866	Man Sports-Person
Motivations	Excitement	760	Man Sports-Person
Character strengths	Perseverance Courage Physical strength	600 700 950	Sports-Person Man Man
Interests	Sport	800	Sports-Person

Source: Rich (1989), p. 41, Fig. 4

people (van der Veer *et al.*, 1985). If you have a lower spatial ability, you will have more trouble using a virtual reality system than someone who has a higher spatial ability. Kristina Höök, for example, showed that individuals differ considerably in their ability to navigate information spaces. She developed a hypertext system that adapted to different users by automatically hiding some information for people who would not be interested in a particular node (Höök, 2000). Whereas people can learn domain knowledge and may be tolerant to different learning styles, they are less likely to be able to change fundamental psychological characteristics such as spatial ability. Where a high level of such an ability is demanded by an application, many users will be excluded from a successful interaction.

Most user models in practice are just simple pragmatic representations of a very few characteristics of people. Of course, there are important privacy issues to be considered and ethical considerations as to what people should be told about what data is kept on them. User models can quickly become out of date and need maintaining.

Domain model

The domain model describes the agent's representation of the domain. It may do so at all or any of three levels of description (see over). Physical characteristics of the domain would include things such as colours of a display, and whether data was displayed as a menu or as a list of radio buttons. The physical characteristics are to do with the 'skins' of a system. Conceptually a domain is described in terms of the objects and attributes of the things in that domain.

The intentional description is to do with purpose. For example, an e-mail filtering agent might have a domain model which describes e-mails in terms of the main concepts – header, subject, who it is from, and so on. A physical description of the domain may include font and colour options. An intentional description may have a rule that says 'if the message is classified as "urgent" then display an alarm to the user'.

Further thoughts: Levels of description

These three levels of description are apparent in Rasmussen's consideration of mental models and HCI (Rasmussen, 1986, 1987) and in the philosophical arguments of Pylyshyn (1984) and Dennett (1989). Pylyshyn argues that what 'might be called *the basic assumption of cognitive science* ... [is] that there are at least three distinct, independent levels at which we can find explanatory principles ... biological, functional and intentional' (Pylyshyn, 1984, p. 131, Pylyshyn's italics). The levels are distinguishable from each other and necessary because they reveal generalizations which would otherwise not be apparent. A functional description is necessary because different functions may be realized through the same physical states. For example, the physical action of pressing ^D will result in the application performing different functions depending on the system. The intentional level is needed because we interpret behaviours of systems not only through function, but also through relating function to purpose – by relating the representations of the system to external entities. The purely functional view of someone dialling 911 in the USA (or 999 in the UK) does not reveal that that person is seeking help. It is this level – of intentions on behalf of the user of a system – that also needs describing.

Dennett also recognizes three levels of description. We can understand the behaviour of complex systems by taking a physical view, a design view or an intentional view. The physical view (also called the physical stance or physical strategy) argues that in order to predict behaviour of a system you simply determine its physical constitution and the physical nature of any inputs and then predict the outcome based on the laws of physics. However, sometimes it is more effective to switch to a design stance. With this strategy, you predict how the system will behave by believing that it will behave as it was designed to behave. However, only designed behaviour is predictable from the design stance. If a different sort of predictive power is required then you may adopt the intentional stance which involves inferring what an agent will do based upon what it ought to do if it is a rational agent.

Domain models are needed so that the system can make inferences, can adapt, and can evaluate their adaptations. Systems can only adapt, and make inferences about what they 'know' about the application domain – the domain model. A system for filtering e-mail, for example, will probably not know anything about the content of the messages. Its representation of e-mail will be confined to knowing that a message has a header, a 'from' field, a 'to' field, etc. A system providing recommendations about films will only know about a title, director, and one or two actors. This is quite different from what it means for a human to know about a film. The domain model defines the extent of the system's knowledge.

For example, there are a number of programs available that filter out supposedly unwanted e-mail messages. These typically work by using simple 'IF–THEN' rules to make inferences (see also Interaction model below). IF the message contains <unacceptable word> THEN delete message. Of course, it is the content of the place holder <unacceptable word> that is key. At our workplace one of the 'unacceptable words' was 'XXX' and any message containing an XXX was simply deleted with no notification to either the sender or the user. Since there is a relatively common e-mail convention to say things such as 'Find the files XXX, YYY, ZZZ, etc.' many legitimate messages were simply disappearing. The domain model in this case (that XXX is an unacceptable word) was far too crude.

Interaction model

The third component of the framework is the interaction model. This consists of two main parts: an abstraction of the interaction (called the dialogue record) and a knowledge base that performs the 'intelligence'. The knowledge base consists of mechanisms for making inferences from the other models, for specifying adaptations and, possibly, for evaluating the effectiveness of the system's performance. This knowledge base consists of 'IF–THEN' rules, statistical models, genetic algorithms or any of a host of other mechanisms.

The interaction model as expressed through the adaptive, inference and evaluation mechanisms may be extremely complex, embodying theories of language, pedagogy or explanation. A tutoring model, for example, represents a particular approach to teaching concerned with the interaction between the student (the user) and the course content (the domain model). A tutoring model component of an intelligent tutoring system would be described through the inference and adaptation mechanisms in the interaction model.

An interaction is a person (or other agent) making use of the system at a level which can be monitored. From the data thus gathered:

- The system can make inferences about the user's beliefs, plans and/or goals, long-term characteristics, such as cognitive traits, or profile data, such as previous experience.
- The system may tailor its behaviour to the needs of a particular interaction.
- Given suitably 'reflective' mechanisms, the system may evaluate its inferences and adaptations and adjust aspects of its own organization or behaviour.

The dialogue record is simply a trace of the interaction at a given level of abstraction. It is kept for as long as is required according to the needs of the adaptive system and is then deleted. The dialogue record may contain details such as:

- Sequence of keystrokes made
- Mouse clicks and mouse movements
- Timing information such as the time between commands or the total time to complete a task
- System messages and other system behaviour
- Command names used.

The dialogue record is an abstraction of the interaction insofar as it does not capture everything which takes place. Facial expressions and other gestures are not yet part of the dialogue record, nor is it possible to record any non-interactive activities (such as reading a book) which people may undertake during the interaction. However, as the variety of input devices continues to increase with the introduction of video recordings of interactions, tracking of eye movements, etc., so the dialogue record may become more subtle.

The user model and domain model define what *can* be inferred. The interaction knowledge base actually does the inferencing by combining the various domain model concepts to infer user characteristics or by combining user model concepts to adapt the system. The interaction knowledge base represents the relationship between domain and user characteristics. It provides the interpretation of the dialogue record. An important design decision which the developer of agent-based systems has to make is the level of abstraction which is required for the dialogue record, the individual user data and the interaction knowledge base.

Challenge 26-3
The Amazon.co.uk website contains an agent that welcomes returning customers, gives them recommendations for books to purchase and explains its reasoning. Figure 26-5 shows a dialogue with the Amazon.co.uk agent. Speculate about the representations of people, the domain and the interaction that this agent has. Discuss with a colleague and justify your assumptions.

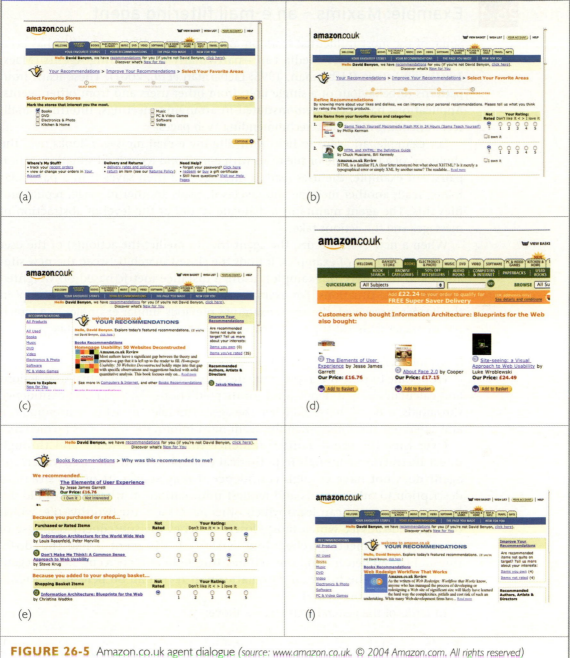

26.4   Example: Maxims – an e-mail filtering agent

Some of the most influential work on agents from an HCI perspective has been undertaken at the MIT Media Lab – particularly the Learning Agents (Maes, 1994) and Letizia (Lieberman, 1995; Lieberman *et al.*, 2001). These learn from patterns of behaviour of a single user, from other users and from other agents. Applications have been demonstrated in arranging meetings, filtering e-mail, recommending music and recommending Web pages.

For example, an agent to help with filtering e-mail messages 'looks over the shoulder' of a user as he or she deals with e-mail and records all situation–action pairs. For example, the user reads a message and then saves it in a particular folder, reads another message and deletes it, reads another message, replies and files this. The agent maintains a dialogue record at the level of abstraction of messages and the actions taken.

When a new event occurs, the agent tries to predict the action(s) of the user based on its library of examples. It finds the closest match between the new situation and its library of examples, using a distance metric based on weighted features of the situations. For example, if a message with the words 'ski-trip' in the header is received, the agent examines previous similar examples (e.g. previous messages with 'ski-trip' in the header) and sees what action was taken. If, for example, every previous message with 'ski-trip' in the header was deleted, then it is quite likely that this will be deleted too.

From time to time the agent compares its predictions with actual user actions and calculates a confidence level for its predictions. The user sets confidence thresholds: a 'do-it' threshold when the agent can take the action autonomously and a 'tell-me' threshold when the agent must inform the user of its prediction.

Over time the agent gains confidence through experience and through direct instruction (through hypothetical examples) from the user. When the agent does not have enough confidence it may send part of the situation description to other agents and request information on what they would do. From this the agent can learn which other agents are 'trustworthy' (i.e. which ones provide advice which most closely matches the subsequent response of the user). In a meeting scheduling version of this agent it had the 'do-it' threshold at 80 percent and the 'tell-me' threshold at 30 percent, i.e. the agent would perform the function automatically if it had an 80 percent or higher confidence in its prediction.

In terms of the general architecture above:

■ The agent has a user model (profile) of user preferences (read mail, delete/save, etc.).

■ The domain model consists of e-mail conceptual attributes such as keywords in the subject, the 'cc' list, the 'from' line, etc., and the possible actions: read or not read, delete, save, etc.

■ The dialogue record consists of the object details and actions.

- The inference mechanisms are a weighted closeness of fit to previous situations.
- The adaptation mechanisms are the actions taken.
- The evaluation mechanisms are expressed in the agent's ability to reflect, review confidence, etc.

It is also interesting to note the distribution of control at the various stages of the interaction. The existence of the user-defined thresholds allows the person to keep control over critical actions.

26.5 Other applications of agent-based interaction

The field of agent-based interaction, user modelling and user-adapted interaction is large and is continuing to grow. Personalization is a key aspect of interactive systems design and automatic personalization is particularly sought after. In this section we point to a few of the main areas.

Natural language processing

Natural language processing – in terms of speech input and speech output, but also in terms of typed input – has been the dream of computing since it was invented. Natural language systems adapt by generating text appropriate to the particular query and characteristics of individual users or by recognizing natural language statements. To do this they have to infer the user's needs and focus of attention from the (ambiguous) use of natural language. Anaphoric references (the use of words such as 'it', 'that', etc.) and ellipsis (where information is missing from a statement) offer difficult syntactic problems, but inferring the semantics of an utterance and the intention which the user had in making that utterance are even more intractable problems which have generated a wealth of research studies in both AI and Computational Linguistics. Even in the most restricted of systems – phone-based, flight or cinema ticketing systems – the systems are far from 100 percent accurate. In these systems the domain is quite restricted, so it can be assumed that the user is saying something relevant to the domain. In other domains which may be much more open and where background noise can easily reduce the recognition of the words to less than 40 percent, let alone a sensible interpretation of them, the technology is not yet acceptable.

Intelligent Tutoring Systems (ITS)

The rationale of computer-based teaching systems is that, for given students and topics, a computer system can alleviate the variance of human-based teaching skills and can determine the best manner in which to present individually targeted instruction in a constrained subject domain. In order to minimize the discrepancy between a student's knowledge state and the representation of an identified expert's knowledge (a 'goal state') the ITS must be able to distinguish between domain-specific expertise and tutorial strategy. ITS need to be able to recognize errors and misconceptions, to monitor and intervene when necessary at different levels of explanation, and to generate problems on a given set of instructional guidelines (Kay, 2001).

A 'student model' of the user of an ITS system stores information on how much the student 'knows' about concepts and relationships which are to be learnt and about the student's level and achievements. These student models use a method whereby the student's assumed level of knowledge is laid over the expert's; mismatches can then be revealed. An ITS often contains a history of task performance and some detailed representation of the state of an individual's knowledge in a specified subject area. Some of this may be held in the form of a user profile and can have other uses in management and score-keeping.

Critics and active help

Another popular application of intelligent interface systems is in the provision of context-dependent 'active' help (Fischer, 2001). On-line help systems track the user's context and incorporate assistant strategies and a set of action plans in order to intervene when most appropriate or when the user appears to be having difficulty. Intelligent help systems share some characteristics with ITS, since a diagnostic strategy is required to provide the most appropriate help for that user in that particular situation. However, they also have to be able to infer the user's high-level goal from the low-level data available in the form of command usage. Intelligent help has further developed into 'critiquing systems' (Fischer, 1989), where users must be competent in the subject domain being critiqued, rather than being tutees or learners.

Adaptive hypermedia

With the Web as its laboratory, adaptive hypermedia research has blossomed over recent years. Originally based around CD-ROM, educational hypermedia is one area, adaptive information retrieval is another. Brusilovsky (2001) provides an excellent review. Figure 26-6 shows his schematic of the different adaptive hypermedia systems. Adaptations in hypermedia systems are divided between adaptive presentation and adaptive navigation support. The systems can add links, change links, add annotations and so on, depending on what nodes people have visited previously and what they did there. One interesting application is in adaptive museum commentaries where the content of the description of an item is adapted to suit the inferred interests of the viewers.

Conversational agents

A significant research effort is currently being directed towards conversational agents, or embodied conversational agents (e.g. Cassell, 2000). This pulls together much of the work that we have presented in this chapter, but includes a represen-

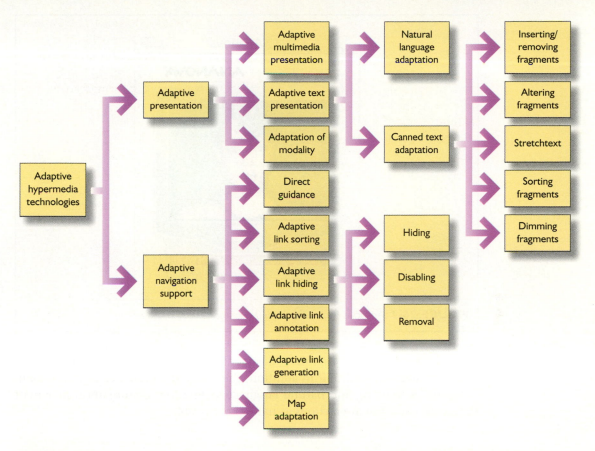

FIGURE 26-6 The updated taxonomy of adaptive hypermedia technologies *(source: after Brusilovsky, 2001, p. 100, Fig. 1)*

Chapter 17
covers emotion

tation of the agent and behaviours deliberately designed to make the agent more lifelike and more engaging. Researchers in the area of conversational agents argue that providing a 'talking head' or embodied agent is much more than a cosmetic exercise and fundamentally changes the nature of the interaction. People believe these agents more. They trust the agent more and they have an emotional engagement with the agent. A popular conversational agent that can be used by developers is Microsoft Agent (http://www.microsoft.com/msagent/default.asp).

Another conversational agent is Ananova (Figure 26-7). This character reads news stories. There is no adaptation to individual viewers but the text to speech facility is quite engaging. The synchronization of lips to speech is quite good, but there are still the tell-tale inflections that do not sound correct. No doubt this technology is set to develop in the next few years.

Some of the best work is happening at MIT where they are developing the real estate agent, Rea (Figure 26-8). Rea tries to handle all the conversational issues such as turn taking, inflection and ensuring that the conversation is as natural as possible. Conversational agents will still need to build models of the users and they will still have models of the domains in which they operate. Their adapta-

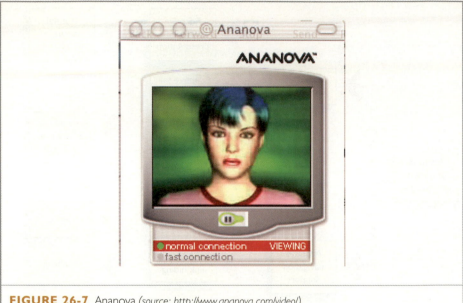

FIGURE 26-7 Ananova *(source: http://www.ananova.com/video/)*

tions and the inferences that they make will only be as good as the mechanisms that have been devised. But in addition, they have the problems of natural language understanding and natural language generation, gesture and movement that go to make the interactions as natural as possible.

Box 26-2 The Loebner Prize

The Loebner Prize Contest in Artificial Intelligence was established in 1990 by Hugh Loebner and was first held at the Boston Computer Museum in 1991. The Loebner Prize Medal and cash award is awarded annually to the designer of the computer system that best succeeds in passing a variant of the Turing Test. In accordance with the requirements of the donor (as published in the June 1994 *Communications of the ACM*) the winner of the $100,000 Gold Prize must be prepared to deal with audio visual input, and appropriate competitions will be held once competitors have reached Turing's 50:50 likelihood level of being mistaken for a human. An intermediate Silver Prize of $25,000 will be offered for reaching this level in a text-only test. There is also an annual Bronze Prize, currently $2000, which is awarded to the designer of the 'most human computer' as rated by a panel of judges.

Sources: http://www.loebner.net/Prizef/loebner-prize.html, http://www.surrey.ac.uk/dwrc/loebner/contest.html

FIGURE 26-8 Rea – a real-estate agent. Rea's domain of expertise is real estate; she has access to a database of available condominiums and houses for sale in Boston. She can display pictures of these properties and their various rooms and point out and discuss their salient features *(source: http://www.media.mit.edu/groups/gn/projects/humanoid/)*

Summary and key points

Agent-based interaction sits right on the border between human–computer interaction and artificial intelligence. This makes it a particularly difficult area to understand as work has taken place from different disciplines, with the researchers employing different techniques and specialized language to explain their concepts. What we have attempted in this chapter is to provide a unifying framework for thinking about agents. All applications of agent-based interaction share an underlying architecture.

- All are adaptive systems in that they automatically alter aspects of the system to suit the requirements of individual users or groups of users – or more generally to suit the needs of other agents in the system.
- Some systems try to infer characteristics of users and agents from the interaction. Others require users to input characteristics explicitly.
- Based on these inferences and other user and domain characteristics, they may adapt the displays or data of a system.
- Currently, few agent-based systems do an evaluation of their adaptations.
- Conversational agents have the additional difficulty of interacting naturally with a human interlocutor.

Further reading

User Modeling and User Adapted Interaction (2001) Tenth Anniversary Issue, volume 11, nos 1 & 2, pp. 1–194.
This is a good up-to-date collection of issues, mainly from the AI point of view, with details of the inference mechanisms that many systems use. The articles by Fischer (User modelling in human–computer interaction, pp. 65–86), Brusilovsky (Adaptive hypermedia, pp. 87–110) and Kay (Learner control, pp. 111–127) are particularly appropriate to this work.

Maes, P. (1994) Agents that reduce work and information overload. *Communications of the ACM*, **37**(7), 30–41.
An accessible description of her early work.

Benyon, D.R. and Murray, D.M. (1993) Adaptive systems; from intelligent tutoring to autonomous agents. *Knowledge-based Systems*, **6**(4), 197–219.
This provides a more detailed discussion of the agent architecture presented here.

Going forward

Jameson, A. (2003) Adaptive interfaces and agents. In Jacko, J.A. and Sears, A. (eds) *The Human–Computer Interaction Handbook*. Lawrence Erlbaum Associates, Mahwah, NJ.
A good up-to-date review.

Kobsa, A. and Wahlster, A. (1993) *User Models in Dialog Systems*. Springer-Verlag, Berlin.
A heavy treatment of many of the theoretical issues.

Comments on challenges

Challenge 26-1

This is one for you to try out. Only by discussing with someone else will you find just how hard it is to describe exactly what you want so that you do not exclude possibilities. Indeed a good agent – real estate, travel agent, etc. – will *interpret* any brief you give them, something artificial agents are a long way from being able to do.

Challenge 26-2

Most of the features that have been taken over by adaptive systems (or agents) in cars rely on an accurate model of the other system. Anti-lock brakes, for example, have a model of the road surface that focuses on how wet and slippery it is. They are then able to adapt the braking in the light of this representation. I need no idea what the actual representation looks like, and do not need to have; it is sufficient to understand what features are modelled. Controlling the 'spark' similarly involves a model of the fuel–air mixture, the position of the cylinder and so on. In all these, the car only has to capture a representation of some physical aspects of the interaction. Interacting with people is more difficult because the system needs to capture an intentional description.

Challenge 26-3

The dialogue shows how the recommender agent improves its suggestions. The user is asked to rate some books in (b), then in (c) we can see on the right-hand side that the user has rated 35 books. The recommender agent now knows the sort of books I like as described in its own architecture by keywords. As I continue shopping, the recommender uses its dialogue record of what other people have done to recommend related books. The domain model contains links between books that have been bought together and no doubt the strength of such links is reinforced whenever these books are bought together. In shot (e) we can see that the recommender can explain its inferences – making the relationship between me, the user model, and the domain model explicit. In (f) the system knows that I have bought some books which will be weighted more heavily than if I had just rated them.

Exercises

1. A group of research workers in a telecommunications laboratory want to make it easier to share Web pages they have visited with their colleagues. Design a Web browsing agent to help them. Describe it in terms of the agent architecture.

2. One of the social navigation features you might have thought of in considering Exercise 3 in Chapter 25 is an agent that recommends recipes based on the shopping you are doing. Discuss the design of this agent.

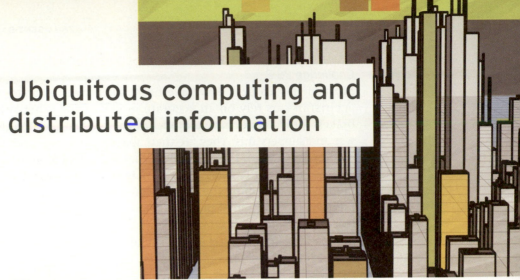

27 Ubiquitous computing and distributed information

Aims

Information and communication devices are becoming so common and so small that they can truly be said to be becoming 'ubiquitous' – they are everywhere. They may be embedded in walls, ceilings, furniture and ornaments. They are worn as jewellery or woven into clothing. They are carried. Norman (1999) reminds us of other technologies such as electric motors that used to be fixed in one place. Electric motors are now truly ubiquitous, embedded in all manner of devices. The same is happening to computers – except that they also communicate with each other.

After studying this chapter you should be able to:

- Understand the ideas of distributed information spaces and ubiquitous computing
- Describe and sketch distributed information spaces in terms of the agents, information artefacts and devices that populate them
- Develop ERMIA models of distributed spaces and the resources that are available
- Apply the ideas to future homes.

27.1 Ubiquitous computing

Ubiquitous computing (also called **ubicomp** or pervasive computing) is concerned with 'breaking the box'; it anticipates the days when computing and communication technologies disappear into the fabric of the world. This might be literally the fabrics we wear, the fabric of buildings and of objects that are carried or worn as jewellery, say. There may be a mobile phone in your tooth and

Chapter 16 deals with wearable computing

you might communicate with your distant partner by rubbing your earring. At the other end of the scale we might have wall-sized flat display technologies or augment physical environments with graphical objects.

The term ubiquitous computing is attributed to Mark Weiser (e.g. Weiser, 1993), chief scientist at Xerox Palo Alto Research Center (PARC). His vision was of technologies that effectively disappeared: 'our computers should be like our childhood – an invisible foundation that is quickly forgotten but always with us and effortlessly used through our lives' (Weiser, 1994). William Mitchell is another good source of vision for the future of the invisible computer (Mitchell, 1998).

With appliances embedded in walls, jewellery and so on, human–computer interaction becomes very different. We will input through gestures – perhaps stroking an object, perhaps waving. Output will be through haptics and other non-visual forms. The applications of this technology are many and visions include new forms of learning in the classroom of the future, augmenting the countryside with objects and placing devices in airports, university campuses and other community projects. One of the results of this development is that we enter a world of distributed information spaces.

27.2 Distributed information spaces

In Chapter 23 we introduced the concept of an information artefact and in Chapter 26 we discussed the concept of an agent. In the world of interactive systems there is one other type of object that it is useful to distinguish: devices. Devices are systems that can only receive, transform and transmit data. They do not deal in information. Things like buttons, switches and wires are devices. Information artefacts (IAs) are systems that allow information to be stored, transformed and retrieved. Agents are systems that actively seek to achieve some goal. Devices are the things that input, transmit and output data.

An information space is some combination of agents, devices and IAs along with the characteristics of the media and other features discussed in Chapter 23. People make use of and contribute to information spaces as they pursue their daily activities. Information spaces allow people to plan, manage and control their activities. Information spaces provide opportunities for action. Sometimes information spaces are designed specifically to support a well-defined activity, but often activities make use of general-purpose information spaces and information spaces have to serve multiple purposes.

For example, consider the signage system that might be employed in an airport. This is an information space that could consist of TV monitors showing the times of departures and arrivals, announcements made over a system of loudspeakers, signs showing gate numbers, directional signs, information signs and people staffing an information desk. This information space has to support all the activities that go on at an airport such as catching planes, finding the right gate, meeting with people who have landed, finding lost luggage, and so on (Figure 27-1).

FIGURE 27-1 Airport information space (*source: Dorling Kindersley*)

Another example of an information space is a website. Here there are various IAs and devices such as the Web browser, the type of computer and operating system, connection method and other programs that are available on a particular computer. There is the design of the site itself with the labels, menu structure, organizational structure, and so on. This information space has to support people browsing through the site, or going to specific parts of the site. Information design and information architecture are concerned with the design of information spaces.

We conceptualize the situation as in Figure 27-2. This shows a configuration of agents, devices and information artefacts and a number of activities. The information space covers several different activities and no activity is supported by a single information artefact. This is the nature of distributed information spaces, and is the case for almost all activities.

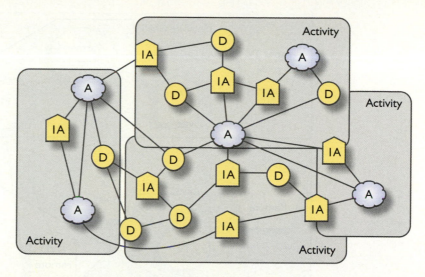

FIGURE 27-2 An information space consisting of agents (A), information artefacts (IA) and devices (D). Communication is through signs sent along the communication media (illustrated with lines)

The key feature is that people have to move from one IA to another; they have to access devices and perhaps other agents. They have to navigate through the information space (Chapter 25). In the case of a website people may navigate within the site. In the case of an airport, or other distributed information space, people need to navigate between the different objects: the agents, information artefacts and devices that constitute that space.

Sketches of information space can be used to show how the information is distributed through the components of a space. Activities are rarely correlated one-to-one with an information artefact. People will need to access various sources of information in order to complete some activity. Importantly, some of that information may be in the heads of other people and so sketches of information space should show whether this is the case. People can be treated as 'information artefacts' if we are looking at them from the perspective of the information they can provide.

Figure 27-3 illustrates some of the information space for watching TV in my house. Developing the sketch helps the analyst/designer think about issues and explore design problems. Notice the overlap of the various activities – deciding what to watch, recording TV programmes, watching TV and watching DVDs.

The space includes the agents (me and my partner), various devices such as the TV, the VCR, the DVD buttons on the remote controls and so on, and various information artefacts such as the paper TV guide, the VCR, DVD and TV displays and the various remote control units. There are a lot of relationships to be understood in this space. For example, the VCR is connected to the TV aerial so that it can record broadcast TV. The remote control units only communicate with their own device, so I need three remotes. The TV has to be on the appropriate channel to view the DVD, the VCR or the various TV channels.

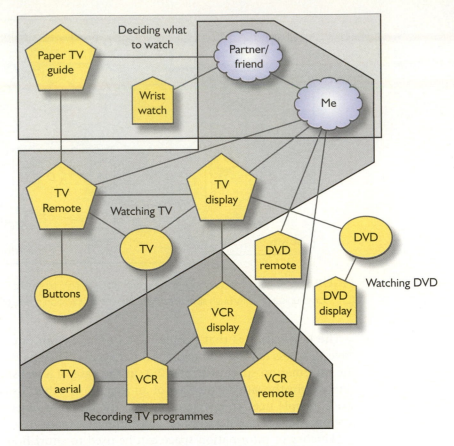

FIGURE 27-3 Some of the information space of watching TV

Looking at the activities, we can see how we move through the space in order to complete them. Choices of programme are discussed with my partner. We will need to check the time using her wristwatch, look at the TV guide and consult until a decision is made. Finally a channel is decided upon. To watch TV, I turn the TV on by pressing a button on the TV; the TV display then shows a green light. Then the channel number has to be pressed on the remote control (though in my case the button labels have become unreadable, so there is an additional process of remembering and counting to locate the required button). Indeed, if I want to record a TV programme later while I watch a DVD, then it is wiser to select the VCR channel at this point, then use the VCR remote to select the channel on the VCR. When the programme I want to record starts I can press 'rec' on the VCR remote. Then I select another channel to watch the DVD. I need to press 'menu' on the DVD remote and am then in another information space which is the DVD itself, which has its own menu structure and information architecture. Phew!

Increasingly designers are concerned with developing information spaces that surround people. In the distributed information spaces that arise from ubiquitous computing, people will move in and out of spaces that have various capabilities. We are already familiar with this through the use of mobile phones and the some-

Challenge 27-1
Sketch the information space of buying some items at a supermarket. Include all the various information artefacts, devices and agents that there are.

times desperate attempts to get a signal. As the number of devices and the number of communication methods expands, so there will be new usability and design issues concerned with how spaces can reveal what capabilities they have. The sketching method is useful and we have used it in the redesign of a radio station's information space, lighting control in a theatre and navigation facilities on a yacht. Sometimes, however, we need to be more formal.

27.3 Formal models of distributed spaces

Information spaces (Chapter 23) and the concepts of information architecture

In the TV watching example, the TV guide is organized by day and time. This means we need to know what day and (roughly) what time it is before we can make use of the guide. If I had an on-screen programme guide, I would not need to know this as the guide will have a facility to list just what is on from the current time onwards. This makes finding out what is on next much easier (but makes finding out what you have just missed more difficult). All information artefacts have to physically store the instances of the conceptual information entities in some sequence and provide interfaces onto that store depending on the characteristics of the medium that the display utilizes. A paper TV guide stores and displays the instances of the information entities (the TV programmes) in day and time order. Such is the nature of paper as a display medium. Electronic displays can be much more flexible.

In Chapter 20 we introduced ERMIA models. ERMIA stands for entity–relationship modelling of information artefacts. It is a simple technique for mapping out the main information artefacts in an information space – both the conceptual and perceptual parts. ERMIA can be used at various degrees of formality. Figure 27-3 is effectively an ERMIA model. We just replaced the more abstract idea of a general concept with more specific devices and used different-shaped boxes to distinguish agents, information artefacts and devices. ERMIA models use the notation shown in Figure 27-4 to show the things (entities) and the relationships between them. It can be useful to describe relationships in terms of the ways in

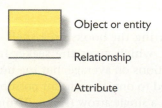

FIGURE 27-4 ERMIA notation

which instances of the objects can be related, as this may lead to useful insights into the designs (see Chapter 20). Attributes are characteristics of entities.

ERMIA models can be drawn of the way in which information is structured in a space and the way in which different information artefacts store the instances of the entities. Often the whole purpose of an information artefact is to enable people to locate one particular instance of the class: one TV programme, one address in an address book, and so on. The internal structure of the entity class may give the user more or less assistance in that. We distinguish five types. Each has its own characteristics of time taken to locate a specific item and memory requirements when it forms part of a search for information.

To illustrate the different types of entity store in concrete form we shall consider what can be done with a very familiar information artefact, namely a collection of books. The aim is to locate a specific book. The principal entity here is obviously Book, an entity store standing for all the individual books.

Pile

We can start with the case where the books are haphazardly strewn across a table, so that the entity Book contains no internal structure whatsoever. We call this kind of entity-store a *pile* and mark it in the diagram with a phi, φ (Figure 27-5).

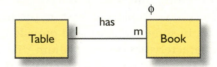

FIGURE 27-5 ERMIA model for books heaped on the table in a pile structure

If there are N books, then on average it will take $N/2$ inspections of books to find a specified book. And as the books are piled haphazardly on the table, we shall need to remember which books have been examined already (or, equivalently, which positions have been examined already); that entails remembering $N/2$ items. In the worst case, someone else is also examining the books and putting them down in different places, so that we cannot even rely on remembering the places we have looked; we have to remember each individual book.

Chain

By putting the books on a shelf – even if unsorted – more structure is introduced, which gives the seeker far more help. He or she will still need $N/2$ inspections on average, but the number of positions to be remembered has been reduced to one, the current position. We call this structure a *chain*, and represent it with a single arrow (Figure 27-6).

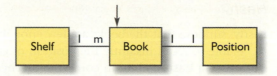

FIGURE 27-6 ERMIA model of books at random on the shelf, forming a chain structure

Sorted list

If the books are arranged in alphabetical order by title, the search can be still faster. The seeker can make a guess whether to start in the middle of the shelf or at one end, depending on whether the title sought starts with an early letter or a late letter. He or she might even adopt a 'binary chop' algorithm – start in the middle, then move halfway to one end, then move a quarter of the distance, and so on. This type of entity store is called a *sorted list*, represented as in Figure 27-7. (Notice that it is the occurrences of the Book entity which are ordered by title as indicated. If shelves are ordered by subject, say, a similar symbol and annotation is appended to the Shelf entity.)

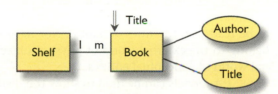

FIGURE 27-7 ERMIA model of books on the shelf in alphabetical order by title

Unsearchable

Now let us suppose that an unsympathetic library system has control of all the books, and that they are all locked away in stacks to which we are denied access. To get a book, we have to find the details and give them to the librarian, who will fetch the book. From the librarian's point of view, the books may be arranged in any of the structures above; from our point of view, however, they are *unsearchable*. They can only be accessed via some further repository such as a catalogue. An unsearchable entity store is marked with a cross, X (Figure 27-8).

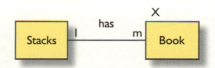

FIGURE 27-8 ERMIA model of books locked in the stacks, from the user's point of view

Hash

Lastly, suppose that the books are few enough and familiar enough for the user to be able to recall instantly the position of each book. This corresponds to the notion of a hash-coding in computer science, where an address is computed directly from the content, allowing the item to be retrieved with zero search. For this structure, which we shall not encounter frequently, we use the obvious hash symbol, # (Figure 27-9).

FIGURE 27-9 Notation for hashed organization of books

Perceptual attributes and conceptual entities

Our examples so far have ignored important differences. Attributes that differ through perceptual aspects, such as shape or colour, can be recognized or discriminated faster than attributes differing in their symbolic labels, which have to be read (e.g. the titles of books). Nor have we so far indicated which entities belong to the external world of physical objects and which belong to the internal world of conceptual entities.

ERMIA models can be used to show the distinction between entities with perceptually coded attributes and entities without, by a thick line around the attribute oval. A search process can be much faster if a perceptually coded attribute can be used ('It was a red book').

Lastly, ERMIA introduces a distinction between entities that are directly represented by some part of the information display and entities that are not, for example the plot of a book. These conceptual entities are represented by dotted lines (Figure 27-10). There is nothing to prevent conceptual or perceptually coded entities from taking part in the usual relationships: for instance, genres could be colour coded, making it easier to find a book with a given plot type.

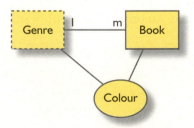

FIGURE 27-10 ERMIA including conceptual entity

Smart telephones are a simple example of a distributed information space that illustrates many of the features of ERMIA models. Smart phones contain a list of short-cut codes, so that when some code sequence like #1 is keyed, the phone actually dials a full-length number. As a rule, they do *not* contain the information about who that number calls. It is the user's responsibility to record the relationship between names and dialling code sequences. Since surprisingly many designs have no provision for externalizing that information, we have shown it in the model as located in the user's head. In practice, designers do now include a piece of paper in the handset for this. The ERMIA model (Figure 27-11) makes explicit the problem of how to store and access this information.

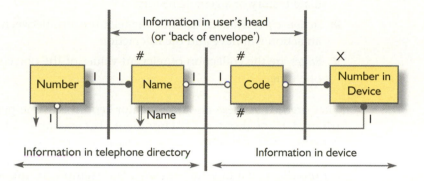

FIGURE 27-11 ERMIA model of smart phone

The model includes a further ERMIA feature which allows us to express whether an entity must participate in a certain relationship (filled dot) or whether participation in that relationship is optional (unfilled dot). Figure 27-11 may be interpreted as follows. Every Name must be associated with a (real, full length) Number. Similarly every number must have a name associated with it (otherwise we are not interested in it). Only some Names have Codes (i.e. the short-cut codes). Only some Codes are allocated to a Name. The numbers held in the smart phone (Number in Device) all correspond to real numbers, but of course not every real number is stored in the device. Nor does every Code have to be assigned to a Number in the device.

The organization of the instances of the entities is as follows. Numbers in the telephone directory are a chain, but names are in alphabetical order. In the person's head, names are hashed and we do not remember numbers. Similarly, codes are hashed both in the person's head and in the device. The numbers stored in the device are unsearchable (unlike modern mobile phones, these smart phones do not have a display).

So, what happens when you need to get a new phone? Just remember not to throw away the telephone directory. What happens when you forget the relationships between Name and Code? What happens if you put a wrong number into Number in Device?

Distributed resources

Wright, Fields and Harrison (2000) present a model of distributed information spaces called the Resources Model in which they focus on information structures and interaction strategies. They propose that there are six types of resource that are utilized when undertaking an activity:

- *Goals* describe the required state of the world.
- *Plans* are sequences of actions that could be carried out.
- *Possibilities* describe the set of possible next actions.
- *History* is the actual interaction history that has occurred – either the immediate history or a generic history.
- *Action–effect relations* describe the relationships between the effect that taking an action will have and the interaction.
- *States* are the collection of relevant values of the objects in the system at any one time.

They argue that these resources are not kept in any one place, but rather are distributed throughout an environment. For example, plans can be a mental construct of people or they might appear as an operating manual. Possibilities are often represented externally such as in (restaurant, or other) menus, as are action–effect relations and histories. For example, in the watching TV example, where the goal (distributed across my partner and me) is to be watching an enjoyable TV programme, the paper TV guide and my partner both provide possibilities. The state of the system is presented by the TV itself and by our sense of enjoyment. Knowing action–effect relations and the history (e.g. pressing button 3 now on the remote control will select channel 3) allows us to achieve the goal.

Wright *et al*. (2000) identify four interaction strategies that may be used:

- *Plan following* involves the user coordinating a pre-computed plan, bearing in mind the history so far.
- *Plan construction* involves examining possibilities and deciding on a course of action (resulting in plan following).
- *Goal matching* involves identifying the action–effect relations needed to take the current state to a goal state.
- *History-based methods* rely on knowledge of what has previously been selected or rejected in order to formulate an interaction strategy.

Chapter 7, Section 7.5 discusses distributed cognition

Wright *et al*. (2000) provide a number of examples of distributed information and how different strategies are useful at different times. They argue that action is informed by configurations of resources – 'a collection of information structures that find expression as representations internally and externally'. Clearly in any distributed space these are exactly the issues that we were considering in navigation of information space (Chapter 25). There are also strong resonances with distributed cognition.

27.4 Home environments

The home is increasingly becoming an archetypal ubiquitous computing environment. There are all sorts of novel devices to assist with activities such as looking after babies, keeping in touch with families, shopping, cooking and leisure pursuits such as reading, listening to music and watching TV. The home is ideal for short-distance wireless network connectivity and for taking advantage of broadband connection to the rest of the Internet.

The history of studying homes and technologies is well established – going back to the early impact of infrastructure technologies such as electrification and plumbing. Since the 'information age' came upon us, homes have been invaded by information and communication technologies of various sorts and the impact of these has been examined from various perspectives. Indeed it may be better to think in terms of a 'living space' rather than a physical house, since technologies enable us to bring work and community into the home and to take the home out with us. Our understanding of technologies and people needs to be expanded from the work-based tradition that has informed most methods of analysis and design to include the people-centred issues such as personalization, experience, engagement, purpose, reliability, fun, respect and identity (to name but a few) that are key to these emerging technologies.

Households are fundamentally social spaces and there are a number of key social theories that can be used. Stewart (2003) describes how theories of consumption, domestication and appropriation can be used.

- *Consumption* is concerned with the reasons why people use certain products or participate in activities. There are practical, functional reasons, experiential reasons which are more to do with having fun and enjoying an experience, and reasons of identity – both self-identity and the sense of belonging to a group.

- *Appropriation* is concerned with why people adopt certain things and why others are rejected. The household is often a mix of different ages, tastes and interests that all have to live side by side.

- *Domestication* focuses on the cultural integration of products into the home and the ways in which objects are incorporated and fit into the existing arrangement.

Alladi Venkatesh and his group (e.g. Venkatesh *et al.*, 2003) have been investigating technologies in the home over many years. He proposes a framework based around three spaces.

- The physical space of the household is very important and differs widely between cultures and between groups within a culture. Of course, wealth plays a huge role in the physical spaces that people have to operate in. The technologies that are adopted, and how they fit in, both shape and are shaped by the physical space.

■ The technological space is defined as the total configuration of technologies in the home. This is expanding rapidly as more and more gadgets are introduced that can be controlled by more and more controllers. The ideas of 'smart homes' (see below) are important here.

■ The social space concerns both the spatial and temporal relationships between members of a household. The living space may have to turn into a work space at different times. In other households there may be resistance to work intruding on the relaxing space.

It is also useful to distinguish home automation from the various information-seeking and leisure activities that go on. Climate control, lighting, heating, air conditioning and security systems are all important. There are also automatic controls for activities such as watering the garden, remote control of heating and so on. X10 technology has been popular, particularly in the USA, but it is likely that this will be overtaken by connectivity through wireless communications.

Lynne Baillie (Baillie, 2002) developed a method for looking at households in which she mapped out the different spaces in a household and the technologies that were used. Figure 27-12 is an example.

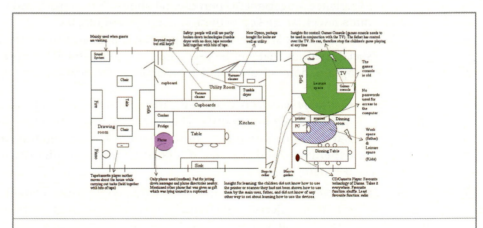

FIGURE 27-12 A map of the house showing different spaces
(source: Baillie (2002), p. 109, Figure 5.8. Reproduced by permission of Lynne Baillie)

Smart homes

Eggen *et al.* (2003) derived a number of general design principles for the home of the future from conducting focus groups with families. Their conclusions were as follows.

■ Home is about experiences (e.g., coming/leaving home, waking up, doing things together, etc.). Users are much less concerned with 'doing tasks'. This indicates the importance of the context of use in which applications or services have to run: they should fit into the rhythms, patterns and cycles of life.

- People want to create their own preferred home experience.

- People want technology to move into the background (become part of the environment), user interfaces to become transparent, and focus to shift from functions to experiences.

- Interaction with the home should become easier and more natural.

- The home should respect the preferences of the user.

- The home should adapt to the physical and social situation at hand. For example, a preference profile can be very different in a social family setting (e.g., watching TV with other family members) compared to a situation where no other persons are present.

- The home should anticipate user needs and desires as far as possible without conscious mediation.

- The home should be trustworthy. Applications should, for example, adequately take consideration of privacy issues.

- People stress that they should always be in control.

This is an interesting list. Ambience is important; the fabric of the house should contain the technologies so that they are unobtrusive. The house needs to be trustworthy and should anticipate needs. This is going to be very difficult to achieve because of the inherent problems of agent-based interaction (Chapter 26). We might also expect that people will be wearing much more technology (Chapter 16) and the interaction between what is worn, carried and embedded in the fabric of buildings will bring wholly new challenges. Essentially these are the challenges of ubiquitous computing.

Eggen *et al.* describe the 'wake-up experience' which was one concept to arise from their work. This would be a personalizable, multi-sensing experience that should be easier to create and change. It should be possible to create an experience of smelling freshly brewed coffee, listening to gentle music or the sounds of waves lapping on a beach. The only limitation would be your imagination! Unfortunately people are not very good at programming, nor are they very interested in it. Also devices have to be designed for the elderly and the young and those in between. In this case the concept was implemented by allowing people to 'paint' a scene – selecting items from a palette and positioning them on a timeline to indicate when various activities should occur (Figure 27-13).

Supportive homes

Smart homes are not just the preserve of the wealthy. They offer great promise for people to have increased independence into their old age. With increasing age comes decreasing ability to undertake activities that once were straightforward, such as opening curtains and doors. But technologies can help. In supportive homes controllers and electric motors can be added into the physical environment to ease the way on some of these once routine activities. The prob-

FIGURE 27-13 Concept for the wake-up experience *(source: Eggen et al., 2003, p. 50, Fig. 3)*

lem that arises then is how to control them – and how to know what controls what. If I have three remote controls just to watch television, we can imagine the proliferation of devices that might occur in a smart home. If physical devices do not proliferate then the functionality available on just one device will cause just as many usability problems.

Designers can sketch the information spaces, including any and as much of the information that we have discussed. It may be that designers need to identify where particular resources should be placed in an environment. It may be that ERMIA models can be developed to discuss and specify how entity stores should be structured and how access to the instances should be managed.

In Figure 27-14 we can see a specification for part of a smart home that a designer is working on. The door can be opened from the inside by the resident (who is in a wheelchair) either by moving over a mat or by using a remote control to send an RF signal; perhaps there would be a purpose-made remote with buttons labelled 'door', 'curtains', etc. The remote would also operate the TV using infra-red signals as usual. (Infra-red signals cannot go through obstacles such as walls, whereas radio frequency, RF, can.) A visitor would press a button on the video entry phone. When she hears a ring, the resident can select the video channel on the TV to see who is at the front door and then open it using the remote control. The door has an auto-close facility.

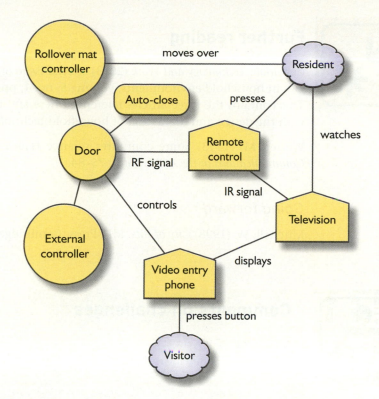

FIGURE 27-14 Information space sketch of the door system in a supportive home

Summary and key points

Computing and communication devices are becoming increasingly ubiquitous. They are carried, worn and embedded in all manner of devices. A difficulty that this brings is how to know what different devices can do and which other devices they can communicate with. The real challenge of ubiquitous computing is in designing for these distributed information spaces. Home environments are increasingly becoming archetypal ubiquitous computing environments.

■ In these environments, people navigate from one information artefact to another.

■ Designers need to think about how they can develop information spaces that indicate different uses and possibilities for action.

■ Designers can use a variety of methods for sketching information spaces and where the distributed information should reside.

Further reading

Cognition, Technology and Work (2003) Special issue on interacting with technologies in household environments, volume 5, no. 1, pp. 2–66.
This contains the three articles referenced here and three others on issues to do with the design and evaluation of household technologies.

Weiser, M. (1993) Some computer science issues in ubiquitous computing. *Communications of the ACM*, **36**(7), 75–84.

Going forward

Mitchell, W. (1998) *City of Bits*. MIT Press, Cambridge, MA.

Comments on challenges

Challenge 27-1
Here are just a few ideas (Figure 27-15).

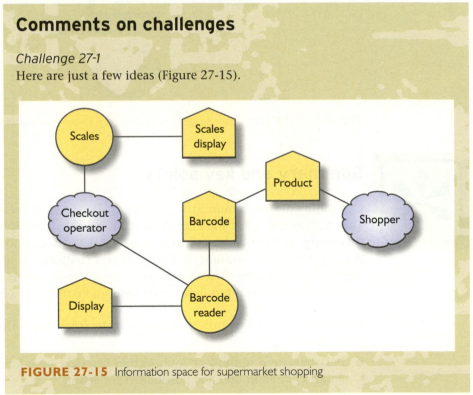

FIGURE 27-15 Information space for supermarket shopping

Exercises

1. A friend of yours wants to look at an article that you wrote four or five years ago on the future of the mobile phone. Whilst you can remember writing it, you cannot remember what it was called, nor exactly where you saved it, nor exactly when you wrote it. Write down how you will try to find this piece on your computer. List the resources that you may utilize and list the ways you will search the various files and folders on your computer.

2. Go-Pal is your friendly mobile companion. Go-Pal moves from your alarm clock to your mobile phone to your TV. Go-Pal helps you with things such as recording your favourite TV programme, setting the security alarms on your house, remembering your shopping list and remembering special days such as birthdays. Discuss the design issues that Go-Pal raises.

Part VII:

Computer-supported Cooperative Working

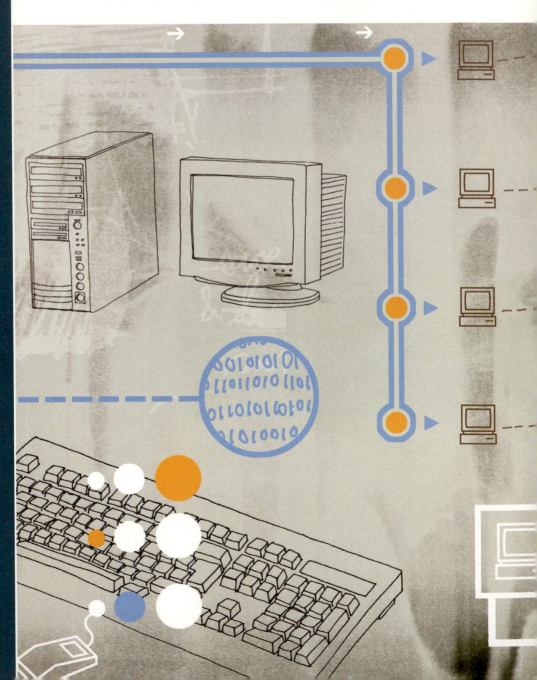

Introduction

In this final part of the book the focus is explicitly on the design of interactive systems which support people in the activities of communicating and working together. Of course, throughout the rest of this book, we have used many examples of technologies which do just that – after all, few interactive systems of any sort are exclusively single-person applications – and one of the two running case studies (DISCOVER) is a collaborative environment.

But we have not so far considered the special qualities of issues and methods in designing for people using technology together. This, broadly, is the field which is usually known as Computer Supported Cooperative Work, although the applications concerned now range beyond work *per se*.

Chapter 28 introduces computer-mediated communication. The starting point is a review of the characteristics of human face-to-face communication. This provides the context for a discussion of how the basic e-mail, messaging, texting and video-mediated mechanisms promote – or hinder – communication over distances of space and time. While technologies move on even as these chapters are finalized, the underlying issues remain constant: an understanding of these is essential for the design and appraisal of new communication tools.

In Chapter 29 we step back to consider the main conceptual foundations for the study and design of CSCW systems. The contents consider the role of the 'social' in human–computer interaction. We discuss the importance of designing for cooperation and, more particularly, cooperative working. In doing this we see how studies of small group behaviour from social psychology can inform the design of collaborative systems and identify key issues to consider. Finally, we examine the rise of workplace studies as a means of understanding collaborative behaviour and the contribution of ethnography.

The contents of Chapter 30 review technologies specifically designed for CSCW. The material builds on the consideration of communications technologies and theoretical approaches in the previous two chapters. We see how technologies can be categorized using a space–time matrix and consider how applications have developed to support both synchronous and asynchronous working. To illustrate the underlying issues in more depth, we choose two exemplar topics in this vast field: the scope and application of collaborative virtual environments (CVEs) and the considerations in designing for awareness and communication.

These chapters contain sufficient material to support a specialist module or part-module on CSCW for students who already have a good understanding of interactive systems design. Their content is therefore most appropriate for final-year undergraduates or master's level students, although extracts could also be tailored to add a CSCW or 'social' dimension to other courses. Chapter 30 in particular will also be helpful for practitioners new to the field who are introducing collaborative technologies to the workplace.

28 CSCW 1: Supporting communication

Aims

This chapter is an introduction to CMC – computer-mediated communication. The starting point is a description of human communication and from there we discuss e-mail, messaging, texting and video-mediated communication. After studying this chapter you should be able to:

- Describe the main characteristics of human communication which are relevant for the design of technologies
- Understand how communication can be supported – or restricted – by
  - E-mail
  - Messaging and texting
  - Video-mediated Communication.
- Use this understanding to reason about the impact of other technologies on human communication.

28.1 Understanding human communication

This discussion of technology to support and facilitate communication begins with an examination of human communication itself. This can be phrased as three distinct but overlapping questions:

1. Which aspects of human communication are necessary for effective communications? This, of course, begs the question what is meant by 'effective'.
2. What is lost (or what can be dispensed with) in CMC?
3. As CMC is necessarily more impoverished than face-to-face communication, what are the consequences of this reduction in 'bandwidth'?

If we can understand the default communication situation enjoyed by most people, namely face-to-face communication, we should be better able to design interactive systems to support it. Firstly, there are two key components in communication, namely a linguistic element (i.e. what is said) and a non-verbal element. The non-verbal element of communication is more popularly known as 'body language' or non-verbal communication (NVC). NVC also includes **paralinguistics**, that is, how things are said, for example tone, manner, use of humour or sarcasm. A very important component of NVC is our range of **facial expressions** – indeed, significant proportions of the brain are thought to be involved in understanding each other's expressions. Making and understanding facial expressions are vitally important in forming relationships. The psychologist Paul Ekman and his colleagues (1972, 1978) have identified six main facial expressions: (a) happiness, (b) surprise, (c) fear, (d) sadness, (e) anger, and (f) disgust, which are, generally speaking, recognized by all humans irrespective of background and culture.

Ekman's basic expressions in relation to emotion are discussed in Chapter 17

Gesture

Another key aspect of NVC for many people is the role of **gesture**. When we speak we move our hands, head and body. This is often used to display the structure of the utterance by enumerating elements or showing how they are grouped, pointing at people or objects for emphasis, a disambiguating gesture, and to give an illustration of shapes, sizes or movements. Gestures are not limited to hand movements: whole body movements are sometimes used to clarify the target of a speech reference – as in the case of someone turning towards a whiteboard when discussing its contents.

Challenge 28-1
Find someone else to do this with. First, take turns to explain to each other (1) directions to the exit from the building, and (2) the plot of a film (preferably with lots of action) that you have enjoyed recently. You should do this in a standing position and must not use gesture. Secondly, note approximately how far apart you have chosen to stand.

The role of the body in communication

Bodily posture itself is also revealing of our attitude and emotional state. Confident people are erect and square with shoulders back. A positive attitude to others is expressed by leaning forward towards them, together with smiling and looking. Bodily contact for most people is confined to shaking hands, patting each other on the back (found frequently among politicians and senior academics), and kissing; it is governed by strict rules – some of these are legally binding, others are a matter of good taste. Social anthropologists often classify cultures into contact and non-contact cultures. The term *proxemics* was coined by Edward Hall in 1963 to describe the study of our use of space and how various differences in that use can make us feel more relaxed or anxious. Proxemics applies to two main contexts: (a) physical territory, such as why desks face the front of a classroom rather than towards a centre aisle, and (b) personal territory, which may be thought of as a 'bubble' of space which we maintain between ourselves and others. Physical distances between people indicate intimacy and friendship. There are major cross-cultural differences in spatial behaviour; for example, Arabs and Latin Americans prefer to get up close while the Swedes and the Scots require a good deal more personal space. But how far apart do we stand? Proxemics tells us that the intimate distance for embracing or whispering is perhaps 15–50 cm (and occasionally even closer), the personal distance for conversations among good friends is 50–150 cm, the social distance for conversations among acquaintances is 1–3 metres, and the public distance used for public speaking is 3+ metres. If these spatial norms are violated, we may do one or more of the following:

- Shift position
- Decrease eye contact
- Change orientation (turn away from the other person)
- Decrease duration of responses
- Give fewer 'affiliative' responses.

However, there is some contrary evidence that if we spend more time in such situations, then we perceive the other person as warmer and more persuasive. In a rare experiment manipulating small-scale interpersonal distances mediated by technology – as contrasted with the greater virtual distances discussed in the next section – Grayson and Coventry (1998) experimented with video-mediated financial advice, varying the apparent distance between customer and advisor from apparently very close – the advisor's face filled the screen – to rather more distant – head, shoulders and some background were visible. The advisor was *perceived* as more persuasive in the close condition, although in fact their advice was not heeded more often. Otherwise the results were inconclusive. The explanation is probably that proxemic cues are not simply visual and/or manipulation of the video display did not produce a convincing impression of proximity.

28.2 Distance matters

'If, as it is said to be not unlikely in the near future, the principle of sight is applied to the telephone as well as that of sound, earth will be in truth a paradise, and distance will lose its enchantment by being abolished altogether.'

Arthur Mee, 1898

The question to be considered here is: 'Does distance matter or is communication technology sufficient (sufficiently what?) to overcome the problems of people being physically separated?'. A study of synchronous, co-located work (that is, working together at the same time in the same place) conducted by Gary and Judith Olson and reported in 2000 involved observing the work of people in nine corporate sites. The Olsons found that the people they observed all normally share office space. Table 28-1 summarizes their findings and is reproduced from Olson and Olson (2000). If we look at the fifth row down, *Shared local context*, people sharing a common space are all aware of the time of day (nearly lunchtime, working late) and the consequences of this knowledge – it is the end of the week, it is payday, the next working day is a week away because of the local holiday, the alarm they can hear is the 0900 Wednesday test

TABLE 28-1 Strengths and advantages of sharing the same space synchronously

Characteristic	Description	Implications
Rapid feedback	As interaction flows, feedback is rapid	Quick corrections possible
Multiple channels	Information from voice, facial expression, gesture, body posture, etc., flows among participants	There are many ways to convey a subtle or complex message (provides redundancy)
Personal information	The identity of the contributors to conversation is usually known	The characteristics of the person can help the interpretation of meaning
Nuanced information	The kind of information that flows is often analogue (continuous) with many subtle dimensions (e.g. gesture)	Very small differences in meaning can be conveyed; information can easily be modulated
Shared local context	Participants have a similar situation (time of day, local events)	Allows for easy socializing as well as mutual understanding about what is on each other's mind
Information 'Hall' time before and after	Impromptu interactions take place among participants upon arrival and departure	Opportunistic information exchanges and social bonding
Co-reference	Ease of joint reference to objects	Gaze and gesture can easily identify the referent deictic terms
Individual control	Each participant can freely choose what to attend to	Rich, flexible monitoring of how the participants are reacting
Implicit cues	A variety of cues as to what is going on are available in the periphery contextual information	Natural operations of human attention provide access to important
Spatiality of reference	People and work objects are located in space	Both people and ideas can be referred to spatiality: 'air boards'

Source: Olson and Olson (2000), p. 149, Fig. 3

Chapter 29 discusses ethnography

of the fire alarm. All of this is quite unremarkable until thought is given to supplying this background, contextual information by means of technology to people who are not present.

Moving from what might be described as an ethnographic study of nine corporate sites, the Olsons turned their attention to the adequacy of existing technology to support the creation of the common ground which the above co-workers enjoy. Table 28-2 summarizes these reflections.

TABLE 28-2 Achieving common ground

	Co-presence	Visibility	Audibility	Co-temporality	Simultaneity	Sequentiality	Reviewability	Revisability
Face-to-face	✓	✓	✓	✓	✓	✓		
Telephone			✓	✓	✓	✓		
Video-conferencing		✓	✓	✓	✓	✓		
Two-way chat				✓	✓	✓	✓	✓
Answering machine			✓				✓	
E-mail							✓	✓
Letter							✓	✓

Source: after Olson and Olson (2000), p. 160, Fig. 8

These characteristics are defined by the Olsons as follows. **Co-presence** implies access to the same artefacts to support the conversation. Co-presence also implies shared reference and shared context. **Co-temporality** leads to understanding of the same 'circadian' context (the participants know whether or not it is morning, lunchtime, evening or just much too late). **Visibility** and **audibility** provide 'rich clues' to the situation. **Simultaneity** and **sequentiality** 'relieve the person of having to remember the context of the previous utterance when receiving the current one'. **Reviewability** and **revisability** are the means by which people can review and revise carefully what they mean and have opportunities to make sense of what is being communicated to them.

Challenge 28-2
Physical distance can make a difference to how we perceive other people and interact with them in situations involving trust, persuasion and cooperation. What do you think the effects might be? When you have answered this, read the Bradner and Mark experiment below.

How does (perceived) physical distance affect interaction using CMC?

Physical distance – how far away the other person is – makes a noticeable difference to how we interact with other people. This has been well established in ordinary circumstances by social psychologists studying cooperation, deception and persuasion, but what happens when technology bridges the distance?

A study by Bradner and Mark (2002) set out to investigate this. The findings show just how influential even the illusion of distance can be. The researchers had students work in pairs with a 'confederate' (someone working for the researchers who pretended to be just an ordinary participant). The details of the experimental set-up were as follows:

- Each pair undertook tasks designed to investigate deceptive, persuasive and cooperative behaviour.
- The pairs communicated either by instant messaging or by video-conferencing (only one medium per pair).
- Some of the participants were told their co-worker was in the same city, others that they were 3000 miles away – in reality, the confederate was just in the next room.
- The researchers checked the participants' perceptions of the confederate's location by having them sketch their relative locations – two examples are shown in Figure 28-1.

Those who were told their colleague was in a distant city were more likely to deceive, were less persuaded by their colleague, and initially cooperated less with them, than those who believed that they were in the same city. The different media made no difference to the effect. Why should this have been so?

Bradner and Mark suggest that *social impact* theory may be the main explanation for the results. Essentially, people are more likely to be influenced by, and less likely to deceive, others who are located nearby. The study also reinforces other findings (discussed later in this chapter) that adding video does not make much difference to interpersonal interaction. They conclude that designers of technology need to be concerned with 'bridging social distance, as well as geographic distance'.

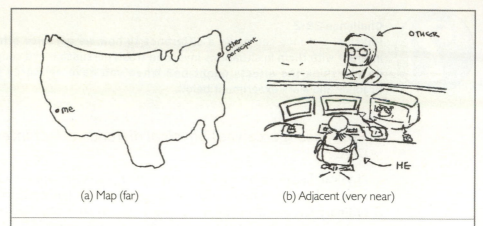

(a) Map (far)   (b) Adjacent (very near)

FIGURE 28-1 Participants' sketches of the location of self and other *(source: Bradner, E. and Mark, G. (2002) Why distance matters: effects on cooperation, persuasion and deception,* Proceedings of CSCW '02 Conference, *New Orleans, LA, 16–20 November, pp. 226–35. © ACM, Inc. Reprinted by permission)*

28.3 Voice-based communication

Prior to the invention of the telephone, voice-based communication was limited to how far one could shout, excepting perhaps for the Swiss and the Basques who independently invented yodelling. While most people are familiar with Swiss yodelling, the Basque equivalent, the *irrintzina*, has been described by the linguist Larry Trask as 'an ululation characterized by a rising pitch and concluding with a kind of demented laugh'. The *irrintzina* is used by shepherds to communicate across mountains. However, it should be noted that the use of telephony is a good deal simpler. The telephone was invented by Alexander Graham Bell in 1876. The first telephone call witnessed the words 'Mr Watson, come here, I want you!'. Bell's electric speech machine is illustrated in Figure 28-2.

Figure 28-3 is an image of a series 200 telephone which was among the first to have an integrated ear and mouthpiece, a significant ergonomic innovation. The circular disc (called the dial) on the front of the telephone is an analogue input device for entering the number to be called. The emergency numbers 999 (in the UK) and 911 (in the USA) were chosen to reflect the organization of the dial. The idea was that in a smoke-filled (or otherwise darkened) room the caller could feel the position of the numbers.

So, from the earliest telephone, which looked more like a chemistry experiment rather than the beginnings of telecommunications, what can we expect next? Well, no idea is the honest answer. However, what is currently happening is technological convergence. A picture 'phone is a mobile with picture messaging, while an up-to-date personal digital assistant is a palmtop computer with video capabilities and wireless communications. The laptop I am using to write this is equipped with wireless networking, e-mail, Internet access, chat and clients. This blurring of technology seems set to continue.

FIGURE 28-2 Bell's electric speech machine
(*source: Smithsonian Institution Neg#89-21085*)

FIGURE 28-3 A series 200 telephone
(*source: courtesy of Gavin Payne*)

FIGURE 28-4 The Nokia 9500
Communicator comes complete with a full
set of business critical applications, e.g.
e-mail, PIM and office tools, Web browser,
camera, picture messaging, and flexible and
fast network connections (*source: Nokia 9500
Communicator. Courtesy of Nokia*)

FIGURE 28-5 The Motorola A835 is a 3G
multi-media videophone with BlueTooth
wireless technology (*source: courtesy of Motorola*)

28.4 Text-based communication

The text-based communication system *par excellence* is, of course, e-mail (also written email and standing for electronic mail). E-mail is often described as by far the most common and successful groupware (see Chapter 30) application. E-mail has been in use for more than 20 years and has become widely accepted and used. Originally a simple technology to pass text messages between two people, it has been enhanced over the last 10 or so years to include attaching one or more files to a message, the use of address books, and indications of priority (e.g. urgent, normal, of low importance). Figure 28-6 is a screenshot of an e-mail message with an attachment.

FIGURE 28-6 Attaching a file to an e-mail

Chapter 30 discusses workflow

As can also be seen from the screenshot, modern e-mail supports a range of standard fonts and colours. Figure 28-7 is a image of a dialogue used to create an e-mail rule. These rules can, for example, automatically sort, process and even delete messages. Rules can be used for the automatic routing of e-mail in support of workflow.

FIGURE 28-7 Automatically routing an e-mail from one person to another

An e-mail
filtering agent
is described in
Chapter 26,
Section 26.4

The rule being created in Figure 28-7 has the descriptive label 'forward message from Susan to David' and the rule itself is

IF
    The FROM field of the email contains the name <SUSAN>
THEN
    Forward the message to <David Benyon>

Using combinations of simple IF–THEN rules, it is possible to create such things as automated mail lists and filters to weed out unwanted 'spam' (unsolicited e-mail).

Another important development in e-mail has been the move from command line systems to full graphical user interfaces. Figure 28-8 is a screenshot from a UNIX e-mail system. The command *mail –v* checks for e-mail; the *–v* flag instructs mail to be verbose (wordy), hence the wordy *'No mail for philturner'*.

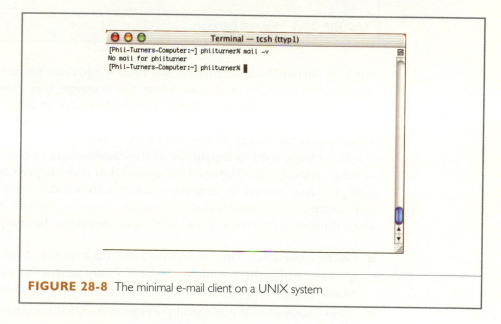

FIGURE 28-8 The minimal e-mail client on a UNIX system

Figure 28-9 is a screenshot from a state-of-the-art e-mail client. Microsoft Entourage is an integrated e-mail, address book, calendar, task list and note-taking system. This design serves to underline the centrality of e-mail-based communications in day-to-day work.

Why use e-mail?

The *advantages* of e-mail are abundantly clear. E-mail message delivery is very fast, even compared with the telephone. It also works even when the recipient is absent. E-mail can be found everywhere and is available free of charge from a number of sources. Every e-mail provides a wealth of contextual information

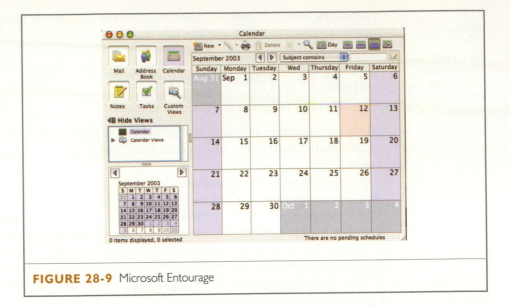

FIGURE 28-9 Microsoft Entourage

which is included automatically: the header provides sender and recipient details, and the time and date when the message was created and sent. Furthermore, messages are not ephemeral; they can be saved and archived. Finally, e-mail is a *push* technology, like radio and television, in that information is delivered to the user so all they have to do is receive it.

It is, perhaps, hard to imagine what the *disadvantages* of e-mail are – beyond sending very large files down a slow connection and the problem of too much mail. However, beyond its recreational use, e-mail is widely used in the business and academic communities and in these more serious contexts its use does present a number of problems. These overlapping issues can be grouped as follows.

■ *Crossing boundaries*: Often established organizational and cultural norms are ignored; while the president of the US may be contacted at president@whitehouse.gov, it may be that such e-mail is routinely handled by an official.

■ *Status information*: While e-mail provides contextual information, it does not provide status cues: e-mail does not automatically convey the status of the sender. Is the sender who he or she claims to be, or is the e-mail merely spam (unsolicited e-mail)? And who exactly is king_powrie@yahoo.com and do we really want to correspond with him or her?

■ *Humour and affect*: A third major problem with e-mail is its isolation from its audience. It does not provide many human cues. Humour and irony are difficult to convey in e-mail and are a frequent source of misunderstandings: not a problem between friends but a significant issue between businesses working across continents. The 'human' element is often limited to the use of *smileys* (see Box 28-1).

Box 28-1 Smileys and emoticons

Smileys and emoticons are sequences of characters used to communicate emotion, irony and amusement. They are best viewed by tilting one's head to the left. Smileys originally depicted variations of smiling, whereas emoticons convey all sorts of other expressions, but the terms are often used interchangeably. A few examples are below.

:-)	the basic smiley
@>--;--	a rose
O:-)	an angel
@:-§	Russian Folk Dancer

■ *Time for reflection*: A fourth problem is that e-mail is, perhaps, too easy to use and provides too little time to reflect on whether one should be e-mailing (*cf.* the use of recall). It provides no regulatory feedback and as we have seen may present problems with communicating the intended tone of the message.

■ *Gone in 60 seconds*: The immediacy of e-mail is a great strength for the sender but potentially a major problem for the recipient – indeed a large employer in the UK has just (September 2003) banned its employees from reading their e-mail at work. In an internal survey they had found that a typical employee was spending more than three hours every day reading, sending and following up their e-mail.

28.5 Instant messaging and text messaging

As we have seen, e-mail is a familiar communication medium and despite being 'modern' is still remarkably structured and formal. Despite the fact that we forgive spelling mistakes, the irregular use of upper and lowercase letters and frequent abbreviations (e.g. FYI) in an e-mail message, they are still very similar to traditional letters. Instant messaging (IM) and text messaging (texting) are not. IM and texting refer to text-based communication. IM is found on computers while texting utilizes the Short Message Service (SMS) capability of the *Groupe Spéciale Mobile* (GSM) wireless standard. IM can be traced back to ICQ – a program which allowed people to send short messages to each other. The technology was subsequently adopted by Internet providers such as Yahoo! and AOL who created their own (mutually incompatible) IM systems. At present there are something of the order of 100 million IM users worldwide. The success of text messaging has surprised most people. The messages are limited to 160 characters and while they can be sent from any mobile phone to any other phone on the GSM wireless network they have to be entered on a keyboard which looks as though it was designed to prevent text-based communication. Despite this, in the UK (and Germany and Finland amongst others), teenagers have made texting very much their own and it has proved to be the much sought-after 'killer application' for mobile phones.

Further thoughts: Conventions in messaging

Messaging is much more like a conversation: it is fragmented and partial and may be conducted synchronously (at the same time) or asynchronously (at different times). Voida, Newstetter and Mynatt (2002) have compared a number of the common conventions in both spoken (verbal) and written communication. This side-by-side comparison may be found in Table 28-3 which has been edited from the work of Voida *et al*.

TABLE 28-3 Comparison between the general conventions of verbal and written communication

General conventions of verbal communication	General conventions of written communication
No persistent record of communication	Persistent record of communication
Hesitations and thinking on the spot without being considered inarticulate illiterate	Crafted carefully and edited so as not to be perceived as inarticulate or
Synchronous	Asynchronous
Turn-taking by establishing 'overt cohesive links within the text of the preceding speaker'	Turn-taking explicitly granted through exchange of communicative artefact
Requires continuous attention	Attended to as circumstances allow
Situational context through shared audio or shared space	No situational context unless explicitly communicated in text
Availability communicated primarily through body language; the power in initiating communication lies with the initiator	Availability is not an issue as communication is dealt with when opportune; the power in initiating communication lies with the receiver

Source: adapted from Voida, A., Newstetter, W.C. and Mynatt, E.D. (2002) When conventions collide: the tensions of instant messaging attributed, Proceedings of CHI '02 Conference, Minneapolis, MN, 20–25 April, pp. 187–94, Table 1. © 2002 ACM, Inc. Reprinted by permission

From this we can see that messaging is indeed very similar to speech while e-mail is more like traditional written communication. Voida went on to identify what she calls *tensions* in the use of IM using this framework and an analysis of instant messaging texts. A tension is a dynamic relationship, where emphasizing one side requires a reduction on the other (so a service might be cheap or reliable but not both). The tensions identified by Voida and her colleagues are:

- Persistence and articulateness
- Synchronicity

- Turn-taking and syntax
- Attention and context
- Availability and context.

These tensions are seen to be design challenges for text-based systems such as messaging.

Box 28-2 The language of text messaging

The shortened words used in text messages sent from mobile phones are largely a consequence of the cramped keypad. To enter a favourite teenage refrain *bored* requires the user to enter the sequence of keys 22666777333. To reproduce one of Shakespeare's shorter sonnets would take weeks. A solution which has arisen to this problem is the use of partially abbreviated terms. We are all familiar with ASAP ('as soon as possible') and BTW ('by the way'); FYI ('for your information') and BYKT ('but you knew that') have also become commonplace. However, to understand intuitively expressions such as *CntTkMyiisOFfaU* ('can't take my eyes off you') and *gr8* ('great') one must be under the age of 16 or have an unhealthy interest in *youth culture*. Studies across Europe have reported the similar shortening of languages other than English, including German, Spanish and Finnish. SMS dictionaries have now appeared which provide a large number of shortened forms of familiar terms. Interestingly, one phone has recently appeared on the UK market which apparently reverses this trend by providing a near full-size keyboard (see Figure 28-10).

FIGURE 28-10 Nokia mobile phone with extended keyboard (advertisement, September 2003)
(*source: courtesy of Nokia*)

28.6 Video-based communication

Video-based communication allows two-way or multi-cast (one-to-many or many-to-many) calling: at its simplest it is a telephone system with an additional visual component. At first sight providing a video element to communication is surely a good thing – enhancing the human side of communication, improving remote work, helping to build trust. Unfortunately, as we shall see later in this chapter, it's not quite that simple. In this section we explore the development of video-based technologies and some issues in their design. Section 28.7 then looks in detail at four experimental investigations into the use of video-based communications and concludes that it is very difficult to predict the consequences of using video. Section 28.8 then offers a summary of a number of other investigations which help to muddy the picture even further.

Video-conferencing involves a group of people rather than just one-to-one communication and dates to before the Web had widespread availability. It was a popular high-end corporate solution to group communication. Video-conferencing was typically set up in a separate, specialist room which had to be scheduled and booked in advance. Often (well, usually) different video-conferencing systems were mutually incompatible, leaving companies able to talk amongst themselves but not to anyone else. Large corporations now have out-of-date video-conferencing suites gathering dust as desktop video-conferencing has become commonplace.

Video-conferencing systems have often been developed with additional features beyond simple communication and support the remote, cooperative use of shared applications. The resulting combination of application sharing and video is usually referred to as tele-conferencing.

Origins

Picturephone – the first video-telephone – was developed by AT&T. The first prototype dates from a surprisingly early 1956 but worked at a rate of only one frame per second, this low refresh rate meaning that the picture would have been very jerky. Unfortunately Picturephone was not liked: people found that it was too bulky, the controls were too 'unfriendly', and the picture was too small. Nonetheless, a commercial Picturephone service was demonstrated in central Pittsburgh in 1970. Figure 28-11 is a contemporary advertisement for Picturephone.

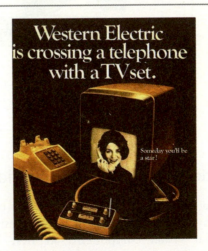

FIGURE 28-11 Picturephone *(source: property of AT&T Archives. Reprinted with permission of AT&T)*

Gaze and gesture awareness

Knowing where someone is looking has been a central concern to researchers and designers of video-based communication. We use gaze awareness in two important ways:

- To know *when* someone is looking at you – **mutual gaze**, or more commonly 'eye contact'
- To know *what* someone is looking at.

Mutual gaze helps to set up communication between people, and to pace and control the conversation – the intricacies of how this works were established by the social psychologist Michael Argyle (e.g. Argyle and Cook, 1976). This explains the difficulty often found in multi-person audio conferences which are bedevilled by long pauses and people speaking over each other. During conversations mutual gaze occurs for just under half the time (Argyle and Ingham, 1972).

Two-person video communication is typically mediated by a camera above the monitor and an on-screen video window showing the other person, sometimes with a small 'picture-in-picture' of one's own image. Under these conditions, normal mutual gaze is impossible because when looking at the video window you cannot simultaneously look directly at the camera. The effect of looking away from the other person gives a (hopefully) false impression of evasiveness.

Technologists have made numerous ingenious attempts to remedy this, generally different permutations of a 'half-silvered mirror' (the image of the other person is viewed through the mirror and the camera picks up your image from the mirror) and a 'video tunnel' (which is cowling in front of the mirror which helps to restrict gaze). By adjusting the positions of camera, mirror and video tunnel, it is possible to create mutual gaze. Much work in this area was carried out at the Rank Xerox EuroParc facility in Cambridge, UK, Buxton and Moran (1990) being one example. Incidentally, the half-silvered mirror technology is the basis of the television autocue, allowing newsreaders and politicians to gaze candidly into the eyes of their audience while reading.

However, recent work by Grayson and Monk (2003) suggests that much of this effort may not be needed, at least for two-person conversations. Their research indicates that people can identify where others are looking, even with ordinary desktop video, and so can learn when they are attempting mutual gaze. For this to be most effective, the camera needs to be directly above the image. Figure 28-12 shows one configuration of the experiment: conventional desktop video is overlaid with targets at which one participant directed their gaze while the other estimated the gaze direction. Grayson and Monk suggest that given practice, the conversational cues supplied by mutual gaze could be exploited much as usual.

Another important issue when people are working together is the need to be aware of what other people are doing with a shared work object or to see their gestures. Most video-conferencing provides only a head-and-shoulders view, thus eliminating these possibilities. ClearBoard, described below, is just one in a series of experimental applications by Hiroshi Ishii and his colleagues which are designed to improve this particular situation.

FIGURE 28-12 Desktop video configuration
(source: Grayson, D.M. and Monk, A.M. (2003) Are you looking at me? Eye contact and desktop video conferencing, ACM Transactions on Computer – Human Interaction (TOCHI), 10(3), pp. 221–43. © 2003 ACM, Inc. Reprinted by permission)

ClearBoard

ClearBoard (Ishii, Koboyashi and Grudin, 1993) was designed to integrate interpersonal space and shared workspace seamlessly, for applications such as shared design work where discussions around drawings were important. Ishii and his colleagues devised the metaphor of 'talking through and drawing on a transparent glass window'. ClearBoard allowed a pair of users to 'shift easily between interpersonal space and shared workspace using familiar everyday cues such as the partner's gestures, head movements, eye contact, and gaze direction'. The technology – a complex arrangement of half-silvered mirrors, projectors and glass work surfaces – supported real-time and remote collaboration by two users. The overall effect was of working with another person who was just the other side of a glass drawing board and drawing on their side of it, as can be seen in Figure 28-13.

Hydra

In multi-party video conferencing, the mutual gaze problem worsens. Each participant sees a small video window on their screen for each of the others. As before, this makes it difficult to establish eye-contact and to monitor visually who is attending. Moreover, since all sound output comes from a single loudspeaker, there are no audio cues as to who is speaking, nor the possibility of holding person-to-person 'side' conversations.

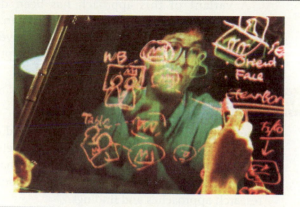

FIGURE 28-13 An image of ClearBoard (*source: Ishii and Ohkubo, 1990. Courtesy of Hiroshi Ishii*)

Hydra was a prototype four-way video-conferencing system developed in the early 1990s (Sellen *et al.*, 1992). The intention was to simulate the interpersonal interaction and physical arrangement of personal space which occurs in face-to-face meetings. Each remote participant was represented around by an individual Hydra unit arranged in front of the local participant, as shown in Figure 28-14. Each unit had its own camera, monitor and speaker, mimicking as far as possible physical co-presence around a table.

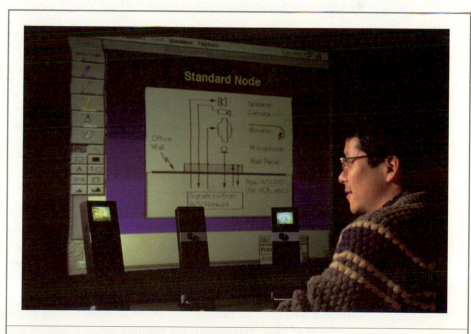

FIGURE 28-14 Hydra in use (*source: courtesy of Bill Buxton*)

A variant of this approach has been developed for the MAJIC system (Ichikawa *et al.*, 1995), where eye-contact can be made with lifesize video images of other participants and gestures and movements clearly seen. However, this again has not progressed beyond a working prototype.

28.7   Three studies of VMC

There have been numerous naturalistic and experimental studies of the use of video-telephones (audio and video) and tele-conferencing (audio, video supported with a number of tools, such as a shared whiteboard, and file transfer – see Chapter 30). We have chosen three different studies to illustrate the range of research approaches and findings.

Study 1: Audio or video or both?

Tang and Isaacs (1993) undertook a study of a distributed group of software developers working in individual offices on two different sites. The software developers had been supplied with a range of technology at the following intervals:

- Three weeks – phone, e-mail, video-conferencing rooms
- Seven weeks – desktop conferencing with video
- Four weeks – desktop conferencing without video.

Tang and Isaacs found that video encouraged more desktop conferencing and that the users liked it despite its poor picture quality, though audio quality was crucial for acceptability. The use of conferencing reduced the volume of e-mail.

Key finding

Although video may not have a direct effect on quality of end-product, it significantly enhances teamwork.

Study 2: People or tasks?

Matarazzo and Sellen (2000), in a laboratory study of the use of what they described as a Multimedia Desktop System (MDS), sought to understand the relative importance of 'person' versus 'task' space in supporting work. They defined 'person' space as the ability to see and hear remote colleagues and 'task' space as the ability to share work-based artefacts (data sharing, for short). Two different kinds of MDS were created. For the person space MDS a small 14-inch Sony monitor was used to tile four windows in which were displayed the head and shoulders of each participant. For the task space a Sun workstation with a larger 21-inch monitor was used (see Figure 28-15). A camera, a loudspeaker and a

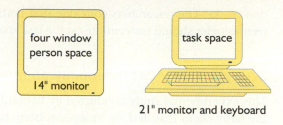

four window
person space

14" monitor

task space

21" monitor and keyboard

FIGURE 28-15 A schematic image of the Matarazzo and Sellen experiment

microphone were also provided. Matarazzo and Sellen used this set-up to investigate three important factors in the use of these MDSs:

1. The 'person' versus 'task' space
2. Video quality
3. Group size.

Video quality was limited to either narrowband or broadband. In practice narrowband was limited to 7 frames per second (fps) which resulted in a significant audio lag; in contrast broadband was able to support a refresh rate of 25 fps which ensured no audio lag. The final variable manipulated by Matarazzo and Sellen was the group size which varied between one-to-one and one-to-many. The experiment itself involved 72 female undergraduates who were largely unknown to each other.

As this was a laboratory study, the participants were given tasks to perform using the MDSs. Four 'ecologically valid' tasks were identified for the students. The first involved collaborative problem solving, the second was a negotiation, and tasks three and four comprised cooperative writing and drawing tasks respectively.

The participants were seated in separate rooms and given 30 minutes to complete each task, followed by completing a questionnaire.

Key findings

The unexpected and counter-intuitive findings of the study were as follows:

- Participants rated the poor quality video higher than the good quality!
- Participants completed the tasks more quickly with the poorer quality video than with the better quality video.

Matarazzo and Sellen offer an explanation for these results in terms of a 'distraction' effect. If the video quality is too good, it may be that people spend too much time looking at the high-quality image and are hence distracted from completing their tasks. The researchers conclude that perhaps designers of MDS and related technologies should concentrate on the task space rather than the person space.

Study 3: Can video-telephony enhance cooperation?

This experimental study conducted by Barnard, May and Salber (1996) examined the basic claim that desktop video-telephony can enhance cooperation – in short, that distance doesn't matter. In particular Barnard *et al.* considered the problem of *reference* in the use of video-telephony. Technically, this is the problem of *deixis* which means 'this one, that one'. To appreciate the difficulty of this problem we need to think about everyday face-to-face communications. Consider asking someone to hand you a particular tool from a toolbox. On being handed the wrong tool we are likely to say 'no, this one, not that one' and use a disambiguating gesture (e.g. pointing at the required tool). When using video-telephony the transmitted image is mirrored, that is, that my point of view is different from yours. And it is this which Barnard and his colleagues sought to investigate. Their experimental design investigated four sources of variation:

1. The positioning of the camera. These positions included (a) the standard face-to-face video-telephony, (b) face-to-face with the image flipped (electronically) horizontally, which reversed the mirroring effect, and (c) a novel 'over the shoulder' – this last orientation resembles a third-person perspective. Here the camera sat, so to speak, on one's shoulder.

2. As in all laboratory studies of video-telephony, the participants were give a task to perform. Here the nature of the tasks themselves varied between one with low referential ambiguity and one with high referential ambiguity.

3. The workspaces used either an explicitly flat, two-dimensional representation (Figure 28-16) or a 'three-dimensional' representation of the shared workspace (see Figure 28-17).

4. Finally, the reference was either in the workspace or a spatial reference within it.

The participants were then asked to move figures around on the drawing screen, then click OK, so, for example, 'moving a square to the right of the diamond'.

Key findings

The results of Barnard *et al.* indicate that the standard face-to-face view found on many systems does not allow gestures made towards shared areas of the screen to be understood when the verbal information is ambiguous. Barnard and his colleagues conclude that in designing systems that expect the normal use of speech, it is necessary to understand which cues are likely to resolve potential ambiguities.

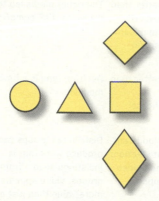

FIGURE 28-16 A (redrawn) two-dimensional representation of the shared workspace
(*source: after Barnard, May and Salber, 1996*)

FIGURE 28-17 A three-dimensional representation of the shared workspace (a garden)
(*source: after Barnard, May and Salber, 1996*)

28.8 VC experiments in summary

Authors	Communication modes	Findings	Comments
Burke *et al.* (1999)	Video-conferencing (VC), audio-conferencing (AC)	Social presence greater with VC than with AC. Communication effectiveness greater with VC than with AC. No significant differences found in performance.	Communication effectiveness and social presence improved over time. However, there were no differences between the VC and AC groups.
Chidambaram and Jones (1993)	Face-to-face (FtF), AC	Decision quality: no significant differences found. Number of alternatives discussed: no significant differences found.	Augmenting AC with GSS improves perceptions of communication effectiveness without lowering the social presence of the medium.
Galegher and Kraut (1993)	FtF, CMC, tele-conferencing, telephone	Quality: no significant differences found. Impression of quality: FtF better than CMC.	All CMC groups worked harder than the FtF groups and were less committed and satisfied.
Graetz *et al.* (1998)	FtF, CMC, tele-conferencing	Decision quality: FtF and tele-conferencing better than CMC. Decision time: CMC better than FtF and tele-conferencing.	Cognitive workloads were significantly higher in CMC groups than in FtF or tele-conferencing groups.

Authors	Communication modes	Findings	Comments
Kinney and Dennis (1994)	Audio/video, CMC	Decision time: CMC better than audio/video better than FtF. Decision quality: no significant difference. Satisfaction: no significant difference.	The richer media led to faster decisions (FtF, audio/video).
Kinney and Watson (1992)	FtF, audio, CMC	Decision time: CMC better than audio better than FtF. Satisfaction: no significant differences.	Decision time is a function of medium.
Olson et al. (1995)	Group support system, audio Group support system, video	Decision quality: no significant differences found. Satisfaction: group support system + video better than group support system + audio.	Distributed groups can produce work that is indistinguishable from FtF groups. Video appears to add more value than just audio.
Suh (1999)	CMC, audio, video, FtF	Decision quality: no significant differences found. Decision time: CMC better than video; FtF better than audio. Process satisfaction: FtF and video better than CMC and audio. Solution satisfaction: no significant differences found.	Decision quality was the same for the intellectual and negotiation task. Audio was the most efficient medium but not the most satisfying.
Valacich et al. (1994)	FtF, phone, videophone, CMC	Decision quality: no significant differences. Satisfaction: no significant differences.	The added technology (phone or video) did not add any benefit to the groups.

Source: after Turoff et al. (2002), in Carroll (ed.) Human-Computer Interaction in the New Millennium, p. 292, Table 13.4

Challenge 28-3
Many of these studies of CMC have been conducted in laboratory settings. How do you think this might have influenced the results?

28.9 Telepresence

Telepresence is a system which affords tele-immersion. Tele-immersion is

'a new telecommunications medium, which combines aspects of virtual reality with video-conferencing, aims to allow people separated by great distances to interact naturally, as though they were in the same room.'

Lanier (2001), *Scientific American*, p. 54

The telepresence system has been developed out of frustration at current video-conferencing technology which does not support the richness of human interaction, and, tele-immersion has been developed as a prototype application for Internet2. It is similar to a CVE (see Chapter 30) but the synthetic virtual environment has been replaced with a computer-generated representation of the world. A 'sea of cameras' is used to provide input to a processing system which extracts feature and depth information about the scene. The whole system is similar to a Star Trek 'holodeck'. Early versions were prone to 'confetti' problems (due to limitations of the frame rate) but the current version is reported as working well. While pointing at distant objects is greatly improved over video-conferencing, the remote manipulation of remote objects is still a dream. However, it is expected (by its inventors) to be commonplace within 10 years. Time will tell.

Summary and key points

Human communication is very rich. Computer-mediated communication is impoverished but we cope. Texting has developed as the medium of choice of the young, making e-mail look remarkably formal, grammatical and middle-aged in comparison. Despite the development of ubiquitous communications systems distance still matters, however. The sheer richness of everyday human communication cannot be replicated using technology. This richness is not merely verbal but is also reflected in our use of gesture, body posture and so on, all of which make up non-verbal communication.

Some of these difficulties have immediate relevance to the design of video-mediated communications systems. Experimental studies of video-mediated communications have revealed mixed and occasionally unexpected findings. Audio quality is probably the most important factor while too good a picture may prove to be distracting. Studies have also shown that the standard video-conferencing set-up, from the perspective of designing an interactive system, is probably the worst of all configurations. But still we cope.

Further reading

The journals *Behaviour and Information Technology*, *Human–Computer Interaction*, *Interacting with Computers* and *International Journal of Human–Computer Studies* all have regular papers on the use of computer-mediated communications.

Going forward

Finn, K.E., Sellen, A.J. and Wilbur, S.B. (eds) (1997) *Video-mediated Communication*. Lawrence Erlbaum Associates, Mahwah, NJ.
This appropriately named collection of papers is an excellent starting point for the further study of video-mediated communication.

Comments on challenges

Challenge 28-1
Most people will have found it hard to resist the urge to gesture at some point. Read the section immediately following the challenge for a commentary on social distance.

Challenge 28-2
This challenge is self-contained.

Challenge 28-3
Some factors which come to mind include the following:

- People in real situations may know each other better and find it easier to communicate even over constrained media.
- A wider range of working materials and documents may be involved.
- There will probably be a greater motivation to complete the task, etc., involved.

You will probably have thought of others. This does not mean that laboratory-based conclusions are invalid, just that we have to consider carefully what the real-life implications may be.

Exercises

1. Barnard, May and Salber (1996) suggest that one way to solve the problem of gesture and other aspects of NVC in 'head and shoulders only' video communication is to develop a new and more restricted way of talking to each other using this medium. Do you think this is practical? If not, why not? But if you do think that it is possible, what do you suppose it might look or sound like?

    It is worth remembering that astronauts have already developed their own vocabulary to ensure that there are no misunderstandings when communicating with ground control (e.g. they say *I copy that* rather than 'I understand that').

2. Imagine you are a business person. You need to agree a contract with a business partner in (say) Japan. You know little of Japanese culture, business practices or the language itself. The flight to Japan is expensive and takes more than 15 hours. Your IT department suggests that you use the

new video-conferencing system which they have just purchased instead of going to Japan yourself. So decide, and state your reasons, between video-conferencing and flying when:

(a) You have never met the Japanese partner before

(b) The contract is for 10 million (£, $ or €)

(c) The contract is one of the regular three-monthly updates

(d) You need to change the conditions of the contract to your advantage.

What do you conclude about the relevant usefulness of video-conferencing and flying in a business context?

3. Paper prototype a video-conferencing system suitable for grandparents in Australia (or anywhere distant) to wish their grandchildren 'happy birthday'. Assume that the grandparents are not very confident or familiar with Internet-based communication and/or the grandchild is very young.

   As an extended exercise, storyboard the use of the video-conferencing system from both the child's and adults' points of view.

4. We have seen the Olsons discuss the importance of being in the same place and how this affords a range of different kinds of advantages to communication as compared with being in a different place. But what exactly does it mean to be in the same place? When, exactly, do you cease to be in the same place as someone else? Are people in the back row of a large lecture theatre in the same place as those in the front row? If not, does this apply to the front and back rows of a cinema or theatre? Which of the advantages the Olsons describe disappear or are diminished first, or do they all disappear at once?

   (As a reminder the characteristics or advantages of being in the same place include co-presence, co-temporality, visibility and audibility, simultaneity, sequentiality, reviewability and revisability – these are described in Section 28.2.)

29 CSCW 2: Understanding cooperative working

Aims

This chapter introduces the role of the 'social' in human–computer interaction. The term 'social' is effectively a shorthand for the recognition that human activity is social – we work with other people, we play with other people, we learn from other people and we interact with other people using technology. Until relatively recently, this has received remarkably little attention compared with the design of single-user or personal technologies. This chapter aims to introduce the most widely researched and arguably the most widely practised aspect of this range of social interaction, namely, work. Indeed there is no escaping the scope of cooperative work. Even sitting alone at home, everything about you was created as a result of cooperative work. The supply of power, gas, light, TV and a hundred other items, tools and services are the result of cooperative work using, more often than not, computers and communication networks. After studying this chapter you should be able to describe:

- The importance of designing for cooperation and cooperative working specifically
- The role of social psychology in the design of interactive systems
- The key issues in the design of collaborative systems
- The importance of workplace studies and the role of ethnography.

29.1 Overview

This chapter considers the key issues involved in designing interactive systems which support cooperative working. This is important because, as we shall argue, (a) all work is, by its very nature, cooperative and (b) all work is mediated by an interactive system.

Is all work cooperative? Well, this depends upon how we define work and cooperative.

Challenge 29-1
Try to think of a work situation which does not involve some form of cooperation at some stage.

Is all work mediated? The question could be recast as 'Do we use tools to carry out work?' to which the answer is a resounding yes. For most people there are very few activities which are not mediated, sleep and digesting our food being two examples of unmediated activity. Cooperative work mediated by interactive (computer) systems is usually referred to as CSCW – computer supported cooperative work (or working). In essence this chapter is about CSCW.

This is hardly new, is it? Inevitably the answer is yes and no. At present there are interactive systems which can be used cooperatively, such as the word processor being used to write this chapter, though it has not been designed specifically with this in mind. Figure 29-1 is a screenshot from the MS Word for Mac which supports collaboration by way of e-mailing a Word file as an attachment to a co-worker. On searching for other means of collaborating, the Word help system suggests using shared folders (see Figure 29-2).

While either technique would undoubtedly support simple cooperative working, neither seems ideal. This should not be taken as a criticism of the software as such but as an illustration of the difficulties faced in designing for cooperative working. Surely cooperative working involves more than just sharing files by

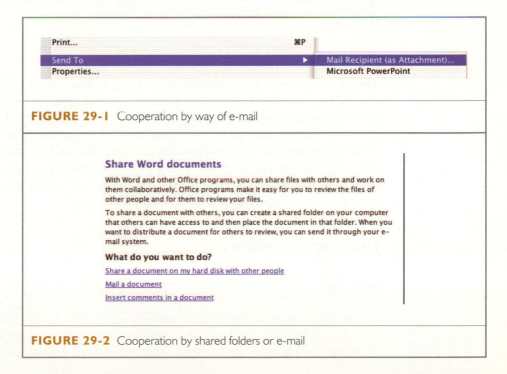

FIGURE 29-1 Cooperation by way of e-mail

Share Word documents

With Word and other Office programs, you can share files with others and work on them collaboratively. Office programs make it easy for you to review the files of other people and for them to review your files.

To share a document with others, you can create a shared folder on your computer that others can have access to and then place the document in that folder. When you want to distribute a document for others to review, you can send it through your e‑mail system.

What do you want to do?

Share a document on my hard disk with other people

Mail a document

Insert comments in a document

FIGURE 29-2 Cooperation by shared folders or e-mail

way of e-mail or shared folders. Indeed there are a number of successful applications which go beyond mere file sharing. This chapter seeks to discover how cooperative work operates in the workplace, control room or factory, while the next chapter reviews the applications designed to support cooperation. What are the psychological or sociological factors we need to recognize to understand the key challenges faced by the interactive (cooperative) system designer? To begin to answer this question, we begin by examining the key term **cooperation**.

29.2 What is cooperation?

'The behaviour towards one another of two or more persons who have convergent interests (positive interdependence). Each perceives that progress towards his own goal will be enhanced by the progress of the other person or persons as well and each expects reciprocation.'

Raven and Rubin (1976)

As you can see from this, cooperation is not an unselfish behaviour, but depends on the recognition of mutual benefits. (There is more about this important aspect of cooperation in Section 29.5.) Clearly, understanding cooperation is the core of an understanding of cooperative working. Studies of cooperation are cross- and multi-disciplinary, including anthropological and naturalistic animal studies (especially primatology), experimental and social psychology, mathematical studies, and even a few studies of cooperative working itself. We include three brief examples to show the range of findings.

A view from primatology

The idea that cooperation during hunting led to the evolution of human social and moral behaviour has received recent support. Capuchin monkeys have been observed to pay one another for the work done in getting food. US primatologists discovered that, after a collaborative hunting effort, the monkey left holding the spoils willingly shared out the food. One of the team noted: 'Tit-for-tat is essential in our economies, and even our morality emphasizes how one good turn deserves another. Our lives depend on our ability to co-operate with one another and to reciprocate for the help of others.'

Learning from history

During the First World War a British staff officer on tour of the trenches remarked:

'I was having tea with A Company when we heard a lot of shouting and went out to investigate. We found our men and the Germans standing on their respective parapets. Suddenly a salvo arrived but did no damage. Naturally

both sides got down and our men starting swearing at the Germans, when all at once a brave German stood up and shouted, "We are very sorry about that: we hope no one was hurt. It was not our fault, it is that damned Prussian artillery."'

This quotation raises the following questions. How could this live-and-let-live system have started? How was it sustained? Why was it characteristic of trench warfare in WWI and of few other wars? Axelrod (1984) offers the following analysis. Tit-for-tat is a strategy which starts with explicit cooperation and follows by doing what the other party did last:

- For WWI – you start by not shooting men.
- If the enemy shoots your men,
- you respond with tit-for-tat.
- If they stop you stop; if they continue you continue.

Axelrod has studied cooperation in the real world in many different domains, from international politics to computer chess, and has concluded that tit-for-tat is a successful model of the observed behaviour.

The Swiss at play

Swiss psychologists have been trying to work out why human beings have evolved to cooperate rather than act in a mostly selfish manner. They invented a laboratory game in which volunteers passed money to each other. The rules prevented a player from directly returning the favour to the donor – they had to give their cash to a third party. As the game developed, the researchers noticed that the most generous players actually began to accumulate the most money. The researchers conclude that doing good deeds increases the likelihood that someone else will treat you better.

Social psychological research has been somewhat neglected (and, to be honest, is unfashionable) in the study of systems to support cooperation. The next section introduces some of the most relevant findings.

29.3 The contribution of social psychology to understanding cooperation

People behave differently in groups. In its brief history, the study of cooperative working has made much of the contributions of sociology and anthropology towards understanding how we work together. We discuss this later in this chapter. Social psychology – the study of groups – has attracted rather less attention. This may be because much of the research in this field takes place in the confines of the laboratory rather than the rich, varied context of everyday life. Nonetheless the findings make a significant contribution to pinpointing issues in designing for people working together and assessing the likely impact of different design choices. A classic definition of social psychology states that it is

'... an attempt to understand and explain how the thoughts, feelings and behaviours of individuals are influenced by the actual, imagined, or implied presence of others.'

Allport (1968)

This section describes just a few of the many studies of groups which have direct application to the design of technologies.

Group formation

Groups do not just pop into existence, they need to be formed. Studies by social psychologists suggest that most groups (larger than two people – which is a special case) go through a series of predictable phases. Figure 29-3 showing these phases and their characteristics is derived from the work of Tuckerman (1965) and other authors – note that 'decay' is not always regarded as a phase in the life of a group. You might be familiar with the ideas since they are often used – and misused – by people leading group activities of various sorts.

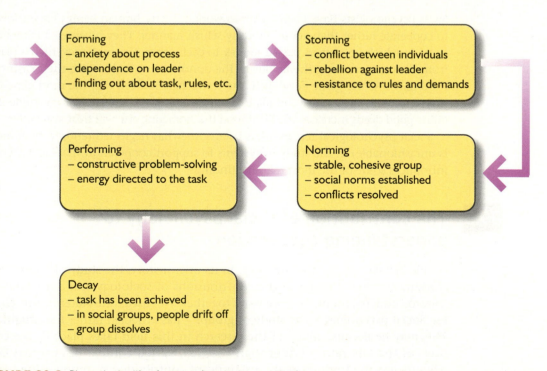

FIGURE 29-3 Phases in the life of a group (*after Tuckerman, 1965*)

Challenge 29-2
Think of groups you have been part of. At what stages in the group's life could you have used (or did you use) technologies to support the communication process?

Concepts such as these are useful for considering when and how technology might help group functioning. For example, Abel's (1990) study of an early 'video wall' linking two remote research labs found that technology helped to maintain links once people knew each other (i.e. in the norming and cooperation phases) but was not effective in supporting people as they were becoming acquainted (forming and storming). The finding has been replicated by many later studies.

29.4   Social norms, compliance and conformance

The Hawthorne effect – changing social norms

This is the classic study carried out at the Hawthorne Works of the Western Electric Company in the late 1920s and early 1930s. It is most often cited as an example of how merely taking an interest in behaviour can change that behaviour, but here we are interested in the findings about **social norms**. The original intention was to investigate how improved working conditions might improve productivity in the factory's 'Bank Wiring Room'. The variables which the researcher manipulated were the temperature, lighting, humidity and length of working day (including such things as rest periods). The workers were placed in a separate experimental room where each of these factors was varied one by one. It was found that each change increased productivity. As a final test all of the improvements were removed, yet productivity remained at the same high level. Much thought has been given as to why this should be. One popular conclusion was that the workers in the experimental room felt that because their supervisor had been replaced by an observer they were freer to talk to each other and were more cheerful. Alongside this, social norms – what is considered acceptable behaviour – changed: absenteeism had fallen, morale had increased, hard work was the norm.

There are two lessons for CSCW here: firstly the way in which changes in technology and working practice can change behaviour in unpredictable ways, and secondly, the similarly unpredictable consequences of observation in a work setting.

← Chapter 22 discusses observational techniques in the study of CSCW

Compliance

Haney *et al*. (1973) were interested in how we adopt roles in a group. If we are assigned a role, to what extent do we comply with the demands of the role itself, regardless of how arbitrary or unreasonable they may seem? (Note: this is more usually known as the Zimbardo study, after one of the most well-known of the researchers.)

Eighteen male undergraduates from Stanford University were selected from a group of volunteers. The 18 were tested to ensure they were 'normal' using interviews and questionnaires (i.e. they had no serious emotional problems). Then a coin was flipped to divide the group into nine guards and nine prisoners. Each student had previously said that they would prefer to be a prisoner.

■ *Day 1*: With the cooperation of the local police (and as a surprise) the prisoners were arrested, cuffed, stripped, de-loused and given a smock to wear. They were then herded into 6' × 9' cells. The guards were given khaki uniforms, mirrored shades, a club and a whistle. They were told not to use physical violence.

■ *After 2–3 days*: Everyone had adopted their roles. The guards denied prisoners bathing and sleep, and made them do push-ups. The prisoners became compliant and passive, and began to call each other by number rather than by name. See http://www.prisonexp.org/slide-12.htm.

■ *After 6 days (of 14)*: The prisoners began to show signs of significant emotional stress – bouts of crying, rashes and depression. At this point the experiment was terminated.

What had happened to the participants? Haney and colleagues concluded that they had ceased to behave as individuals and had complied with group norms, which in turn were being reinforced by others' compliant behaviour.

A modified version of the experiment was recently staged by BBC television in the UK. In the later stages, prisoners and guards rebelled against their imposed roles and briefly collaborated with each other as a 'commune'. However, the structure and organization imposed by the designers of the experiment did not allow sufficient autonomy for the commune to function effectively. After a short time, the group polarized again, the guards proposing an even more severe regime for the prisoners. As in Haney's original version, the experiment was terminated before its planned end-date.

The risky-shift effect and group polarization

This is best described by way of a demonstration. *Stop reading here and carry out Exercise 1 at the end of this chapter.*

Comments on the exercise

It is probable that the groups have accepted a higher degree of risk than individuals: this has been found in many experimental studies, of which Stoner (1961) was the first. (The demonstration works best when a large number of people are involved – this minimizes the impact of exceptionally timid or reckless people.) Evidence of the effect can be found in many everyday occurrences, but usually only comes to light in cases of disaster or near disaster. The astronauts of Apollo XI, for example, are reported to have accepted a risk of 50:50 that they would not make it back from the Moon. Explanations for this effect include the theory that people who lead or dominate groups tend to be risk-takers and that the group brings with it a diffusion of personal responsibility. Later research has seen risky-shift as part of a bigger effect: group polarization. According to this view, groups adopt more extreme views than individuals – views which may be highly risky *or* highly cautious. Sometimes this has been termed 'Groupthink', a term coined by the psychologist Janis. Groupthink has been much blamed in the Challenger space shuttle disaster when a team-based decision was taken to launch with potentially vulnerable 'O' ring seals.

Conformity

Early, classic work by Asch (1951, 1956) and later studies investigated different dimensions of conformity and cross-cultural comparisons. In the classic study Asch asked participants to decide which of three comparison lines of different lengths matched a standard line. To summarize briefly, participants almost always made the right decision when tested on their own. When placed in groups with people who had been coached to give the wrong answer, 32 percent of individuals agreed with the majority – although there were wide individual differences and some people never conformed. Reasons given included:

- Didn't want to upset the experiment by disagreeing.
- Thought their eyesight might be faulty.
- Not aware of giving the wrong answer.
- Didn't want to 'appear different'.

The number of people who could be induced to conform varied according to group size and the degree of unanimity, task difficulty and whether answers were given in private.

Many later studies have found conflicting results, and among the reasons for this cultural factors are significant. A high proportion of the studies were carried out with students (easy to find, easy to persuade away from other tasks) and in the years of campus revolts lower conformity rates were observed. As well as cultural changes over time, there are well-established differences between ethnic and national cultures. To take a couple of extreme examples, the Japanese and Americans are among the most conformist nations and the French and Portuguese among the least (according to the evidence from conformity studies, which do have their limitations).

Groups and technology

These findings may be diverting insights into our own behaviour, but how might the theory help us to understand the effects of computer technologies on groups working together? One area of research has focused on the claim that group decision support systems (GDSS) help to remedy undesirable aspects of group decision making such as the effects of conformity. More specifically, researchers have investigated whether the 'social distance' and anonymity enforced by interacting through technology as disembodied entities overcomes these effects.

In a typical study, Sumner and Hostetler (2000) compared students using computer conferencing (e-mail) with those holding face-to-face meetings to complete a systems analysis project. Those in the computer condition made better decisions: more group members participated, a wider range of opinions were generated, and more rigorous analysis was carried out. They also felt at a greater psychological distance from each other and took longer to arrive at a decision. However, the effect of anonymity is less clear-cut. Postmes and Lea (2000) conducted a meta-analysis of 12 independent studies. The only reliable effect of anonymity was to lead to more contributions, especially critical ones. They argue that performance in decision-making is influenced by the strength of group identity and social norms as well as by system characteristics such as anonymity. It is suggested that this is because anonymity affects two rather different social processes – depersonalization and accountability.

Group productivity and social loafing

It is well established (e.g. Harkins and Szymanski, 1987; Geen, 1991) that people tend to under-exert themselves in groups. Typically, for example, the output of brainstorming groups tends to be less than that of the same number of individuals working in isolation. This effect has been named **social loafing** and tends to occur more frequently when it is hard for individual effort to be identified, or when there is weak group identity, or when the group is not very cohesive. However, some individuals may work harder – **social compensation** – to make up for their lazier colleagues if the group is important to them. Another phenomenon that can decrease group productivity is **production blocking** – where one person's contribution simply gets in the way of another's, principally by causing the second person to forget what they were about to say. It has been suggested that communicating via computers may help to avoid social loafing and production blocking. McKinlay, Proctor and Dunnett (1999) investigated this in their laboratory study of undergraduates. We report this in a reasonable amount of detail so you can appreciate how this type of experiment is carried out.

The groups carried out brainstorming and decision making tasks, working in groups of three. One set of groups worked under normal face-to-face conditions and a second set used computer-conferencing software. The remaining groups were 'nominal groups' only – that is they worked individually, but their outputs were aggregated to provide a comparison with that of the true groups. Two main hypotheses (or ideas) were tested:

■ Hypothesis 1. *The nominal groups would produce more ideas*. This was what previous research had suggested. The relative output from the groups' brainstorming confirmed this. (The groups had to come up with lists of the advantages and disadvantages of an extra thumb.) But it did not seem that production blocking accounted for the difference, since both the computer-mediated and face-to-face groups could 'jot down' ideas as they occurred to them.

■ Hypothesis 2. *There would be less social compensation in the computer-mediated group than in the face-to-face group.* This was based on the theory that the computer group would be less socially cohesive. These groups worked with a scenario about surviving an accident in the Arctic or the desert and had to prioritize a list of items of equipment according to their survival value. The discussion took place either around a table or by text-conferencing. A degree of social loafing was deliberately introduced by including a confederate (someone acting under instructions without the knowledge of the others) as one of the three people. Each confederate either contributed constructively or 'loafed'. It was found that when a social loafer was present, people spoke *more* in face-to-face groups, but *less* in computer-mediated groups.

What did the researchers conclude from these results? Firstly, they wondered whether the computer-mediated groups were really less cohesive or whether it was simply more difficult to identify that someone was apparently being lazy. Examining the transcripts of the sessions suggested that the computer group worked more individually, so this suggests that the loafers may have escaped undetected. The text-conferencing medium in real life may be sufficiently social to allow loafing to happen, but not to foster compensatory behaviour. It is suggested that the computer technology may need to be supplemented by activities which enhance group identity if groups are to work together effectively in such media.

In summary: the social psychology of groups

To summarize the evidence we have discussed in this section:

■ People behave differently in groups.
■ Social psychology tells us much about the change in behaviour from individuals to groups.
■ Technology has the potential to mitigate or enhance some of these effects.
■ Predicting social effects in computer-mediated groups requires careful thought to identify the real issues.

Finally, there are individual differences to take into account. We have not strayed into this area so as to keep this material to a manageable length, but you should be aware that factors such as personality, gender and so forth will also affect how individuals work in groups.

29.5   What is CSCW?

CSCW – Computer Supported Cooperative Work (or Working) – is a clumsy but accurate description of most modern work. It has largely replaced the term **groupware** which was popular for a time in the 1990s. Groupware is software specifically designed to support group working, though few software vendors cared to define what was meant by a group. Do 20 people constitute a group, and/or 100, 500, 100 000? Could one piece of software really scale from use by two or three people to the population of a large corporation? In a word, no.

A biased summary of CSCW findings

Mark Ackerman, a leading researcher in CSCW, has created what he describes as a biased, though useful, overview of CSCW for the non-CSCW literate (Ackerman, 2000). This section should be read in conjunction with Section 29.6. Ackerman writes that CSCW researchers tend to assume:

- Social activity is fluid and nuanced which makes the construction of systems to support work technically difficult.
- Members of organizations usually have differing and multiple goals, and conflicts and their resolutions may actually be an important part of cooperative working.
- Exceptional situations are a commonplace part of normal working. Job roles are often informal and fluid and this fluidity is a key means of resolving such exceptions.
- People like to know who else is in shared workspaces. People use this awareness to guide their own work.
- People learn to cooperate by observing and participating in communication and information exchange.
- How CSCW is used is a result of negotiation within the users themselves.
- CSCW relies on a critical mass of people (see Grudin's second challenge in Section 29.7). The telephone was invented as a pair of instruments – the critical mass was two.
- Co-evolution is an important factor in CSCW. We learn to adapt to the configuration of a technical system and we adapt the system to suit our needs.
- Incentives are centrally important. In a study of information sharing in a large corporate setting, Wanda Orlikowski (1992) found that people would not share important information (such as a list of clients) unless there was something in it for them (think, knowledge is power).

This is indeed a biased summary of many of the key findings and assumptions within CSCW and provides an excellent snapshot of what has been called the *indiscipline* of CSCW.

29.6 The 'turn to the social' – the birth of CSCW

However relevant social psychology may be to CSCW – and we argue that it is highly relevant – it has not been a widely acknowledged contribution to the development of the field. The history of CSCW usually starts with the mid to late 1980s, which witnessed a remarkable conjunction of complementary research work. Technological developments were complemented by fresh perspectives on human activities from researchers with their roots in anthropology and sociology. Since both these fields emphasize the collective and socially based nature of human activities and culture, a 'turn to the social' away from the emphasis on the isolated single user was not surprising. (The phrase 'turn to the social' was coined by the ethno-methodologist Graham Button in 1993.)

Paul Cashman and Irene Grief coined the term CSCW to describe the theme of a workshop they had organized to which they invited a group of people who were interested in how people work cooperatively and in the technology to support that work. Since then CSCW has become the focus of a considerable number of research projects, two international conferences (CSCW in America and ECSCW in Europe) and a highly respected international journal. In addition to this academic interest, designing for co-working or collaboration or cooperation (the terms vary with authors) is a source of interest to a number of major software vendors, the most conspicuous of which was the Lotus Corporation. Add to this the widespread interest in computer-mediated communication (CMC) which includes video-conferencing, video-telephony, CHAT and mobile phone-based *txting* (the use of SMS-based text messaging). The early accounts of CSCW as portrayed by Grudin (1988), Grudin and Poltrock (1997) and Bannon and Schmidt (1991) indicate that CSCW was very much of this time. Following the famous inaugural workshop came Lucy Suchman's *Plans and Situated Actions* in 1987. This was her critique of the underlying planning model employed by much of Artificial Intelligence (AI) research at the time, and it sparked a now famous debate in the journal *Cognitive Science* (*vide* Vera and Simon, 1993). Suchman's work effectively opened the doors to the sociological practice of ethnomethodology (see Section 29.8) which has become the tool of choice in CSCW research. Then Jonathan Grudin (1988) set out a series of design challenges for software applications to meet if they are to support cooperative working. This widely quoted set of eight challenges have largely stood the test of time and are as relevant today as they were at the time.

29.7 Grudin's eight challenges for CSCW developers

These notes have been edited down from Jonathan Grudin's paper 'Groupware and social dynamics: eight challenges for developers'. Although this now classic paper was published in 1994, the challenges are still highly applicable to designing technology for cooperative working. Jonathan Grudin has been a 'guru' figure in CSCW since at least 1988, working at first as an academic researcher and currently in Microsoft's Adaptive Systems and Interaction group.

Challenge 1. The disparity between who does the work and who gets the benefit

Almost always, different work roles and individuals in CSCW receive different benefits. Generally, some people have to contribute additional effort or change their work habits.

The practical example often quoted here is that of a shared diary (calendar) system. Everyone is expected to be disciplined and to put their appointments, etc., in the system, often in addition to their own paper-based diaries. Some people find it an additional annoyance to have their engagements and free-time available for all to see, even if they can hide behind vague labels such as 'personal engagement'. But for people who need to arrange meetings, the system makes life much easier. Grudin suggests that remedies may be to promote clearly the collective benefits of the system and provide some sort of advantage for everyone. This may have to be realized outside the system itself. In our shared diary example, Grudin proposes a commitment by meeting organizers to act on participants' ideas. Another might be an agreed limit of no more than a certain number of meeting hours per person per week – something that would be easy to calculate from the shared diary.

Challenge 2. Critical mass and prisoner's dilemma problems

CSCW needs a critical mass of people to participate. The shared diary we considered above is worse than useless if one or two people have to be chased up in person. This is critical when the application is first introduced, since early adopters may give up before enough people participate to make use worthwhile. Grudin's proposed tactics here are similar to those indicated in the previous challenge, but he also notes that sometimes the removal of alternatives may be the best solution. This would be unlikely to succeed in the diary case.

Recently, instances of the reverse difficulty have appeared – too many people using a CSCW technology for too many purposes, resulting in a huge overload of information. E-mail is the best example of this. Originally a quick, unobtrusive means of coordinating work, it is now the default means of communication about everything in many workplaces. Simply because it is so easy, people are copied into messages without much real thought as to whether they really need to share the information. Similarly, you might not bother to walk upstairs to ask a colleague about a trivial problem but deal with the matter yourself instead. But e-mail only takes a few seconds to send, and at the very least puts off thinking about the problem.

Challenge 3. Social, political and motivational factors

Work is not a just a rational activity, but a socially constructed practice, with all the shifting, conflicting motivations and politicking that this implies. We navigate through this environment using our knowledge of other people, guided by

Box 29-1 **Council bans e-mails to get staff to talk**

The following is the text of an article by David Ward in *The Guardian* newspaper, 10 July 2002:
'A city council will ban the use of internal e-mails today in an attempt to persuade staff to start talking to each other. But to ensure that withdrawal symptoms are not too extreme, Liverpool council's chief executive, David Henshaw, has decreed that the ban will only apply one day a week – Wednesdays.

He insists that the ban, described as an experiment, is designed to make council business flow more efficiently. It is not intended to put the brakes on the free exchange of scandal, gossip and mucky jokes, nor to stop Brian in council tax from making a date with Fiona from environmental health. All staff will still be able to communicate electronically with the outside world. But not with each other.

A council spokesman estimated that email now accounted for 95% of internal communications. "We want people to pick up their phones or even get up from their desks, go down the corridor and talk to someone face to face", he said. "This kind of personal contact is infinitely preferable, not least because there can be room for misunderstanding in the written word sometimes."

The main issue appears to be a concern about whether email is the most efficient way to communicate. "Without doing anything else, one can just become sucked into the technology – we want people to solve problems rather than bat them off into bureaucratic cyberspace", said the spokesman. "They might find they have been given a useful reminder about what human contact is all about."'

Source: David Ward, *The Guardian*, 10 July 2002

social conventions. Computers on the whole cannot do this, but rely on concrete information and predictable cause–effect relationships. Returning to our shared diary, acceptance will be influenced social conventions, for example that one's personal diary is not normally available for inspection. Video-mediated 'shared offices' and similar technologies attempt to support privacy conventions by such devices as alerting users when a video 'glance' is intruding into their space, but still manage to embarrass people from time to time. New group-working technologies may shift delicate power-balances through the increased availability of information.

All this means that acceptance of CSCW and its organizational consequences are unpredictable. Grudin suggests a recognition of the social complexity of work as a necessary foundation for design, coupled with involvement of end-users from the target organization.

Challenge 4. Exception handling in workgroups

Just as work is social, so it is supported by informal procedures as well as formal ones. Many work procedures have a specified set of steps, sometimes explicitly documented on paper or on-line. But sometimes it is necessary to bend the rules to get things done. A workgroup diary which would not book a meeting until all invitees had replied – in accordance with some official procedure – would keep everyone in a state of uncertainty if one person was away. Much better to have an override mechanism to deal with the situation. Human beings are good at improvising to make things work, computers are not. Disasters tend to happen when co-working technologies enforce standard procedures regardless of exceptional circumstances. Designers need to appreciate how work is actually done and design around this.

Challenge 5. Designing for infrequently used features

Of course, day-to-day tasks do not require constant communication or collaboration, even if the underlying activity is essentially cooperative. Most people at work switch fluidly between individual and co-working modes and technology should help them do this. Most shared diary designs allow users to work on their own task lists (for example) as well to reference the group's collective to-do list. Unfortunately, CSCW tools – particularly early applications – tended to emphasize cooperation at the expense of support for individual working. Grudin recommends that the design of co-working features should enhance existing single-user applications rather than enforce a switch to CSCW mode.

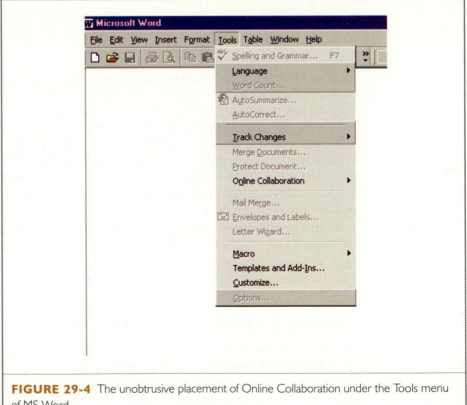

FIGURE 29-4 The unobtrusive placement of Online Collaboration under the Tools menu of MS Word

Challenge 6. The underestimated difficulty of evaluating groupware

Group applications are inevitably more difficult to evaluate. Users in different roles will have differing experiences of the tool, new co-working practices take time to become established and laboratory evaluation cannot hope to capture the nuances of organizational life. A later publication of Grudin and Palen (1995) notes how an initially unpopular shared diary became highly appreciated over a longer period.

We describe approaches to CSCW evaluation in Chapter 22

Challenge 7. The breakdown of intuitive decision-making

This difficulty is perhaps less apparent than at the time of Grudin's original publication. Grudin contrasts CSCW systems with single-user applications where intuitive decisions could be made with a reasonable degree of success. This worked because – historically – early applications were designed by programmers for programmers, and also because single-user tasks were relatively understandable. More recently, as we have stressed elsewhere, designers have recognized the complexity of even single-user activities as technologies move out from the workplace. However, it does remain true that intuitive decisions in CSCW design are rarely well-founded. This difficulty strengthens the case for user involvement. Grudin also notes that if the limitations of intuition were recognized from the start, fewer but more useful projects might result.

Challenge 8. Managing acceptance: a new challenge for product developers

User acceptance is an issue for many new technologies, but in the case of single-user applications the whole system does not become pointless if not everyone uses it – look back at the shared diary example in Challenge 2. Traditional application developers and designers are relatively insulated from acceptance issues, but they are crucial for CSCW design. Here it is suggested that add-ons to successful single-user products may foster acceptance, as will a good understanding of the work environment.

29.8   Workplace studies: understanding collaboration in context

Workplace studies have become the most widely practised information gathering method in CSCW. By studying work as it actually happens in its real-world setting, researchers and practitioners aim to overcome many of the difficulties in Grudin's list. Another factor in their popularity has been the high proportion of CSCW researchers who come with backgrounds in sociology and anthropology, where **ethnography** – the key approach in workplace studies – has long been practised. (Strictly speaking, an 'ethnography' is the output of observational fieldwork rather than the fieldwork itself.)

Further thoughts: Ethnomethodology and other theoretical difficulties

Following the work of Suchman (1987), most ethnography for technology design adopts a particular flavour of sociology termed *ethnomethodology*. In short ethnomethodologists hold that social rules, norms and practices are not imposed externally on everyday life, but that social order is continuously and dynamically constructed from the interactions of individuals. As a corollary of this it is philosophically unsound to generalize beyond the setting where the ethnomethodological ethnography has been undertaken, or to analyse the findings from a theoretical standpoint.

Ethnographic work in user-centred design projects is not always the preserve of specialist 'ethnographers'. As the approach has gained popularity, technologists and HCI practitioners frequently 'do some ethnography' for themselves. Their sometimes casual adoption of the techniques has attracted some adverse comment from those trained in the field (Forsythe, 1999), and more cautious practitioners often refer to their work as 'ethnographically informed'.

In the early twentieth century, pioneering ethnographic anthropologists endeavoured to understand an unfamiliar way of life through what has become known as **participant observation** – learning about language, activities and culture through spending months or years living in the community under study. The anthropologists talked to people, observed day-to-day life in detail, and collected not just physical artefacts but stories, myths and so on. Eventually, the resulting personal experience and field data were analysed and recorded as an ethnography. Sociologists, notably those from the University of Chicago in the 1930s, employed similar techniques in the study of societies and groups closer to home. In both domains, the basic approach continues to be used, including the core principle that the ethnographer should not interpose his own theoretical or cultural frameworks or expectations between the field data and the resulting ethnography.

Challenge 29-3
Why is it important that an ethnographer conducts his work without preconceptions? What practical difficulties might this cause in using the information from ethnography for design?

What are workplace studies and what can we learn from them?

Workplace studies consist of ethnographies and field studies of the workplace. These workplaces have included control rooms in the London Underground, the Paris Metro, air traffic control rooms, and financial institutions, to name but a few. The aim of these studies is to describe in fine detail (often called *richly descriptive*) the day-to-day work of these workplaces. Workplace ethnographies commonly aim to raise awareness of issues rather than to answer specific questions or define requirements. Typical of many such studies are those carried out in projects by the cross-disciplinary teams of sociologists and computer scientists at Lancaster University in the 1990s into such contexts as air traffic control, conference organization and banking. Hughes *et al.* (1994) and Rouncefield *et al.* (1994) are representative examples among many. However, there has been some argument as to how useful workplace studies actually are. Plowman, Rogers and Ramage (1995) reviewed 75 papers reporting workplace studies. They found 'a paucity of papers detailing specific design guidelines'. The problem lies with the lack of findings which have been progressed to prototyping, largely because of a wide gulf between the rich information generated by the studies and practical guidelines for developers.

However, many ethnographically informed workplace studies – particularly more recent examples – have attempted to bring ethnographies closer to design. Sometimes the ethnographer is a member of the design team, and will be involved in the early conceptual stage, and later with evaluation, as well as in generating requirements. Pycock and Bowers (1996) and Lewis *et al.* (1996), working with fashion designers and in film production respectively, are typical instances. The objectives for the ethnographer are very much determined by those of the design project in hand. They often focus on elucidating the role and high-level requirements for a proposed new technology through a deep understanding of work in practice. For instance, Pycock and Bowers found that ambitious proposals for virtual reality to support fashion design had ignored the mundane but essential work which in fact occupied much of the designers' time. In other projects, the ethnographer's 'added value' is in the definition of usage scenarios, the identification of practical issues for implementation and as a focus for a higher degree of user involvement (although in some instances, the ethnographers themselves have acted as proxy users). The discussion in the final chapter of Heath and Luff (2000) is a particularly clear account of moving from ethnography to requirements using video-based studies of medical consultations. These contributed to requirements definition for a patient records system. In explicitly requirements-oriented work, a set of guiding questions can be useful, such as those shown in Box 29-2.

A guide to practising workplace ethnography

Resource limitations in many CSCW projects can support only a limited amount of ethnographic work. There are also 'political' issues that are raised by the very nature of an ethnographic intervention. With these considerations in mind, Simonsen and Kensing (1997) suggest four preconditions for the use of ethnography in commercial projects:

- Both analysts and user organization must have a positive attitude to investing significant resources.
- Users must be content with the overall purpose of the new system. Ethnographic approaches, with their emphasis on close work with users, are unlikely to succeed if there are aims to de-skill or replace users.

Box 29-2 Rogers and Bellotti's 'reflective framework' for ethnographic studies

- Why is an observation about a work practice or other activity striking?
- What are the pros and cons of the existing ways technologies are used in the setting?
- How have 'workarounds' evolved and how effective are they?
- Why do certain old-fashioned practices, using seemingly antiquated technologies, persist, despite there being available more advanced technologies in the setting?

Envisioning future settings

- What would be gained and lost through changing current ways of working or carrying out an activity by introducing new kinds of technological support?
- What might be the knock-on effects (contingencies arising) for other practices and activities through introducing new technologies?
- How might other settings be enhanced and disrupted through deploying the same kinds of future technologies?

Source: Rogers and Bellotti (1997), p. 62

- ■ Analysts must be prepared to handle the 'political' issues which can arise from such an intervention.

- ■ Areas of focus must be identified (ideally, after an initial period of more opportunistic immersion in the environment).

So, how can resources best be organized to maximize the potential of the ethnographically informed work? A review of workplace studies and our own experience suggest the following:

- ■ Most can be gained in the early stages when the main design issues are unclear; later work can be focused by data from interviews and other techniques.

- ■ Most information is obtained where people collaborate in some observable way, and share information artefacts in real time.

- ■ Multiple analysts can be valuable both in observing different activities and in combining perspectives on the same activity.

- ■ Video and audio recording is valuable in capturing data, but field notes remain a vital resource.

The key to (relatively) economical ethnographic work is to recognize when enough data has been collected. One indication of 'enough' may be that no new details are emerging. Another is being able to identify what has *not* been observed, but will not happen within the span of the current work.

Of course, time is required not just to acquire the data but to analyse it. Videotape is intensely time-consuming to analyse – at least three times the length of the raw sequence and frequently more, depending on the level of detail required. The process can be streamlined by having an observer take notes of significant points in the 'live' action, which notes then act as pointers into the video recording. Software tools such as Atlas/ti and Ethnograph help in analysing pages of text notes (not just of observations, but also transcripts of interviews and group sessions) and, in some cases, audio and video data. For large projects, material can be organized into a multimedia database or Web-based repository.

Communicating ethnographic results can be challenging. One approach is to encapsulate the findings in 'vignettes' – short descriptions of typical scenes. (A vignette is rather like the text of a scene in a play script, complete with stage directions.) The vignettes are usually accompanied by a transcript of the accompanying dialogue. Vignettes are often supplemented by video extracts and sample artefacts. Box 29-3 shows a vignette from the DISCOVER CVE based training project. It is taken from a session observing a role-playing emergency exercise for ships' officers. (The DISCOVER project is introduced in Chapter 9.) The vignette here shows the need for different communication modes (phone, public address), the reference to shared artefacts (the blueprint) and the way the trainer intervenes to steer the action.

These are examples of 'user stories' that are discussed in Chapter 8, Section 8.2

Box 29-3 A vignette from a team training study

The cadet, first mate and captain are all in the simulated 'bridge' area together with the trainer, who observes their activity closely. A one-hour simulated emergency exercise is in progress. They are surrounded by alarm panels on the walls and blueprints of the ship's layout on a desk.

Cadet: Chief says he's got errm, a lot of heating problems just above the engine room ... (*Pointing to area in blueprint, others watch*) Well, if you're not sure (*to Captain*) what can you do?

Captain: Ring him. (*Pause whilst he tries to make contact by phone*) Hiya chief, bridge here. Can you just check [what deck?] (*pause*). Yeah, which deck, second deck, upper deck? (*pause*) Upper deck then, OK. (*pause*) OK (PA announcement starts. CPT puts down phone and listens.)

Captain: Can you give me a situation report please?

Mate: ... we're withdrawing the BA team now from the bottom stairwell and we're going to send another team down there. (*pause*)

Tutor: OK, can you confirm that you still have one casualty missing, er and you'll be putting the other team back in to fight the fire, is this right? (*pause*) Remember we've had no report back about the ventilation, you sent them to check.

Another possibility is for the ethnographer to act as an evaluator of early concepts or prototype designs, before the requirements are finalized and while the design is too immature to benefit from user feedback. (Variants on this type of involvement are discussed in detail in Hughes *et al.*, 1994.) Figure 29-5 illustrates the process.

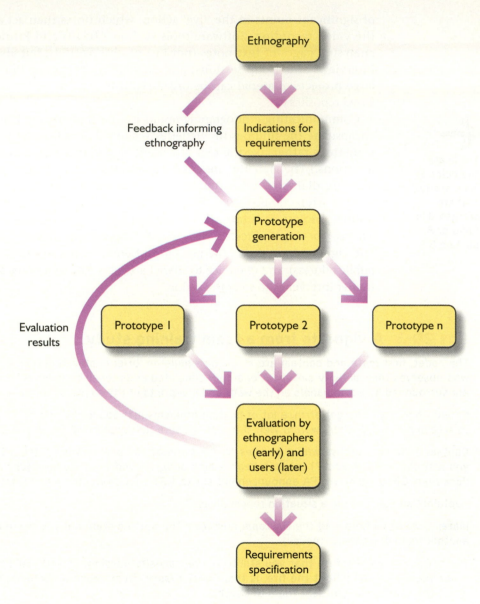

FIGURE 29-5 Ethnography, early requirements and evaluation
(source: adapted from Randall and Bentley, 1994)

From workplace studies to software design via UML and patterns

A still closer link between workplace studies and system design has been attempted by the COHERENCE project (Viller and Sommerville, 1998). This takes the output from the study and expresses its findings in the UML notation (UML is the Unified Modeling Language). Figure 29-6 is a UML use case diagram derived from an ethnographic study of a group of air traffic controllers.

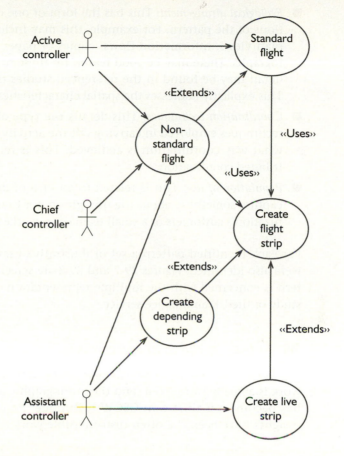

FIGURE 29-6 A use case diagram created from ethnographic data
(source: after Viller and Sommerville, 2000, p. 188, Fig. 5)

By contrast, Heath and Luff (2000) and Dourish (2001) argue that the purpose of workplace ethnography is to construct a reservoir of experience that allows designers to uncover how people make sense of technology in use, and so to design tools which support the improvised, situated and continually reconstructed nature of real-world activity. Recent work at Lancaster University (Martin *et al.*, 2001) develops this idea further by proposing patterns of cooperative interaction as a means of moving from ethnographic data to the requirements/design process. The identified fields within the agreed pattern language are:

We discussed interaction patterns in Chapter 13, Section 13.4

- *Cooperative arrangement*: The cooperative arrangement details in very basic terms the actors and resources that are constituent of the pattern of interaction: the people, the number and type of computers and artefacts, the communication medium(s) employed and the basic activity.

- *Representation of activity*: This describes how the activity is represented, for example in technology or as a plan, and may address the relationship between the activity and the representation. This is related to plans and procedures.

Alexander's patterns are discussed in Chapter 13, Section 13.4

■ *Ecological arrangement*: This has the form of one or more pictorial representations of the pattern. For example, this may include abstract representations, plan views, information flows, copies of paper forms, screenshots or photographs. There may be good reason for these to be fairly abstract as the real detail may be found in the referenced studies themselves if this is desired. This explicitly addresses the spatial characteristics.

■ *Coordination techniques*: This details the type of practices, procedures and techniques employed in carrying out the activity/interaction and how and in what way coordination is achieved. This is related to awareness and distributed coordination.

■ *Population of use*: This is related to an idea of domain, but instead seeks to capture something about the user group, for example whether it is the organization's customers or a small team of co-workers in a control room.

For each identified pattern a set of illustrative examples drawn from the field were also identified. Figures 29-7 and 29-8 are screenshots of a pattern. This pattern is concerned with the multiple representation of information taken from a study of the UK ambulance service.

Workplace studies: in conclusion

Workplace studies have afforded rich information about the way cooperative work is actually carried out, and the ethnographic approach frequently adopted has become a mainstream CSCW technique. Perhaps the most often-quoted insights have been the often near-invisible work that goes on to maintain the

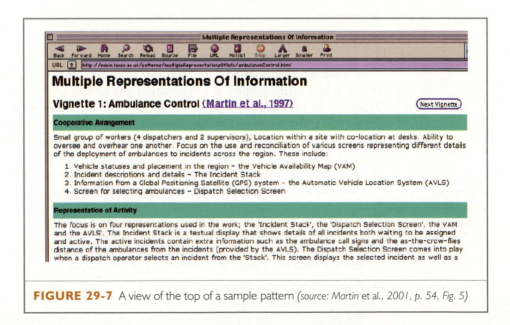

FIGURE 29-7 A view of the top of a sample pattern (*source: Martin et al., 2001, p. 54, Fig. 5*)

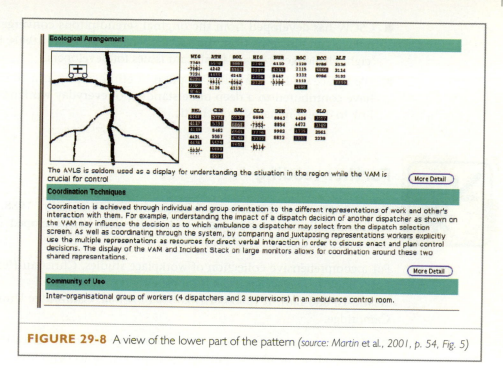

FIGURE 29-8 A view of the lower part of the pattern (*source: Martin et al., 2001, p. 54, Fig. 5*)

smooth running of work, and the importance of unobstrusive **awareness** of other people's activities – something that has stimulated developers to design technologies which support **articulation work** (the work to make the system work) and awareness. These are discussed further in the next chapter.

However, research continues into mapping the results of workplace studies more directly to CSCW design.

Summary and key points

This chapter has argued that the most significant aspect of the 'turn to the social' has been the growing interest in studying groups of people – particularly people at work – and the design of CSCW systems to support work activity. More specifically, we have seen that:

- Social psychology has made a significant – though often underestimated – contribution to our understanding of cooperation.

- People behave differently in groups, often becoming more extreme in their behaviour, conforming to the behaviour of others, and relying on their own lack of contribution going unnoticed.

- It has been suggested that computing and communication technologies can help avoid such undesirable phenomena, but the results of experimental studies do not always support this hope.

- CSCW has developed from the original serendipitous convergence of technologies and insights from the social sciences in the late 1980s, but Grudin's 'eight challenges' remain significant issues for developers.
- Workplace studies – and the adoption of ethnography as a core technique – have contributed to a deep understanding of everyday working life, but the link to design remains problematic.

Further reading

Grudin's two classic papers on challenges for CSCW (Grudin, 1988, 1994) repay reading in full as an encapsulation of how the field has developed and the main difficulties for CSCW.

For a comprehensive collection of workplace studies, Christian Heath and Paul Luff's book *Technology in Action* is thoroughly recommended:
Heath, C. and Luff, P. (2000) *Technology in Action*. Cambridge University Press, Cambridge.

For further work on patterns see the following website at Lancaster University:
www.comp.lancs.ac.uk/computing/research/cseg/projects/pointer/patterns.html
This contains a growing collection of patterns distilled from workplace studies.

Going forward

Martin, D., Rodden, T., Rouncefield, R., Sommerville, I. and Viller, S. (2001) Finding patterns in the fieldwork. *Proceedings of ECSCW '01 Conference*, Bonn, Germany, 16–20 Sept. Kluwer, Dordrecht, pp. 39–58.

Viller, S. and Sommerville, I. (2000) Ethnographically informed analysis for software engineers. *International Journal of Human–Computer Studies*, 53(1), 169–196.

Comments on challenges

Challenge 29-1
This is quite difficult to do, if you include all forms of interaction with others. However, Sections 29.1 and 29.2 will help you to think about what we mean by cooperation in this context.

Challenge 29-2
See comments below the challenge. It is likely that this situation will change as various forms of technologically mediated communication become commonplace and familiar.

Challenge 29-3
Preconceptions are likely to bias the collection of data to what the observer expects to see rather than what is actually happening. The design difficulty is making sense of the mass of information that results. The section following the challenge discusses some approaches to bridging the gap.

Exercises

1. This is best done with some people in small groups and others working as individuals. Each group or individual should consider the following scenario.

   Imagine you have a serious illness. The dynamic, brilliant and chronically undervalued Dr Susan Turner has invented a new, potentially life-saving but potentially dangerous (risky) cure. If it works, your life as a world-acclaimed concert pianist is restored, but there is a risk of death. Consider the lowest survival rate you would accept from the treatment:

   (a) a 1 in 10 chance that you will die
   (b) a 1 in 50 chance
   (c) a 1 in 5 000 000 chance.

   Decide what survival rate you would be prepared to accept. Write down the number of your choice. When everyone has finished, work out the mean choice score for groups and individuals.

2. You are an interactive systems designer working in an organization which develops innovative products for cooperative work. At present, your organization's strategy for user-centred design is limited to market research (focus groups) and questionnaire-based evaluation. Write a short report (maximum 1000 words) making the case for undertaking some ethnographic field investigation. You should include a *brief* review of how ethnography has been used in practical design situations and its benefits.

3. What are the main findings from experimental studies of group behaviour which can help inform the design of technologies to support group working? Give concrete examples.

CSCW 3: Technology to support cooperation

Aims

This chapter introduces the main features of, and underlying issues in, interactive systems which have been created to support the various forms of cooperative working. These technologies are sometimes termed 'groupware', but the term has rather fallen from favour recently because of its somewhat limited implied scope.

We start by considering one of the traditional ways of classifying such technologies, the space–time matrix. We then move on to the applications which are (for the most part) in everyday use in supporting cooperative work, before considering two of the current research topics in technology design: collaborative virtual environments and supporting awareness.

After studying this chapter you should be able to describe and understand issues in the design of

■ Technology to support synchronous and asynchronous working

■ Coordination tools.

You should also be able to appreciate current research issues relating to technology, namely

■ The scope and application of collaborative virtual environments (CVEs):

'Collaborative virtual environments are online digital places and spaces where we can be in touch, play together and work together even when we are, geographically speaking, worlds apart.'

Churchill *et al.* (2001)

■ Designing for awareness.

30.1 The space-time matrix

A number of different ways of characterizing technology to support cooperative working have been discussed since CSCW's inception in the mid-1980s. DeSanctis and Gallupe (1987) proposed the space (or place)–time matrix which sounds a good deal more interesting than it actually is. Their original formulation simply recognized that the two key variables were space and time. This very simply means that people might be co-present while they work or may be located elsewhere, and equally, they may be working together at the same time (*synchronous*) or at different times (*asynchronous*). Since the original version, various suggestions have been for additional dimensions, of which predictability is perhaps the most important. Table 30-1 maps a selection of old and new technologies (and working practice) against the space–time matrix.

TABLE 30-1 The space–time matrix

		Time	
		Same	**Different**
Place	**Same**	Face-to-face meetings and meeting support tools	Post-it messages E-mail, shared information spaces such as Lotus Notes Project management and version control software
	Different	Tele-conferencing Video-conferencing Collaborative text and drawing editors Instant messaging	Traditional letters E-mail, shared information spaces such as Lotus Notes Workflow Threaded discussion databases

A word or two of warning – while the table is a useful heuristic it can be seen that some technologies can be placed in more than one category. Many of us will have experienced the use of e-mail in an almost synchronous fashion, when we have effectively conducted a *conversation* with it. Similarly, there is no reason why workflow cannot be used between shifts of people working in the same place.

Challenge 30-1
Extending the matrix to *n* dimensions (which would of course make it difficult to draw), what other dimensions do you think might be relevant?

30.2 Technologies to support synchronous working

These technologies typically comprise a suite of related software components and may also have audio- and video-conferencing too (for a discussion of audio- and video-conferencing see Chapter 28). A representative example is Microsoft's NetMeeting (Figure 30-1) which comprises support for video- and audio-conferencing, application sharing and 'chat'. As we shall see, there are also tools which aim to support co-located synchronous working.

Chat

Chat systems permit many people to engage in text conferencing, that is, writing text messages in real time to one or more correspondents. As each person types in a message it appears at the bottom of a scrolling window (or a particular section of a screen). Chat sessions can be one-to-one, one-to-many or many-to-many and may be organized by chat rooms which are identified by name, location, number of people, topic of discussion and so forth.

FIGURE 30-1 NetMeeting in action
(source: screen shot reprinted by permission from Microsoft Corporation)

Shared whiteboards and workspaces

Shared whiteboards allow people in different places to view and draw on a shared computer-based drawing surface – think of them as multi-user graphical editors. The surface of the 'whiteboard' may simply be a window on each individual computer desktop or on a large common display in each location, typically touch-sensitive. The implementation of the parallel with physical whiteboards varies from product to product but users are normally represented as tele-pointers which are colour-coded or labelled. Input is typically by touch or stylus in the case of the large shared display, or by any normal input device for individual workstations. The backdrop of the whiteboard may be blank, as in its physical counterpart, or the contents of another software application. Since the early 1990s large shared whiteboards such as LiveBoard (Elrod *et al.*, 1992) have moved from research labs to commercial products. Their use is now commonplace in business settings, and increasingly in other domains such as education.

From the beginnings of CSCW, much research effort has been devoted to investigating the optimal features to support co-working through whiteboards or other shared workspaces such as text editors. Commune, an early example of a shared drawing space, is described in Minneman and Bly (1991). Commune raises a recurring issue in the design of shared workspaces: ownership violation. Later applications provided some means of dealing with these issues such as the provision of 'personal' and 'public' drawing tools. The series of versions of DOLPHIN, for example (e.g. Streitz *et al.*, 1997), were originally based on observational studies of newspaper editorial boards. DOLPHIN was a meeting support system which in later versions incorporated both public and private workspaces. Results indicated that work was most productive when a combination of the two was available.

Shared workspaces have been tailored for specific purposes. Instances include numerous real-time shared text-editing systems, e.g. ShrEdit (Olson *et al.*, 1992), the 'Electronic Cocktail Napkin' described by Gross *et al.* (1998) which facilitates shared freehand sketching for architectural design using handheld computers, and the page layout design application described by Gutwin *et al.* (1996). This last is one of a continuing series of studies of awareness issues in integrated group and individual workspaces: one among many examples can be found in Gutwin and Greenberg (1998). Awareness and the work of Greenberg's team at the University of Calgary are discussed further in later sections of this chapter. The most ambitious shared workspaces support the illusion of collaborating in three-dimensional space with haptic feedback from the manipulation of shared physical objects. Examples of such applications include the work of Hiroshi Ishii, most recently *Illuminating Clay* – allowing the manipulation of a 3D landscape – which is discussed in Chapter 16.

Chapter 16,
Illuminating
Clay

Video-augmented shared workspaces combine a shared information space with a video image of other participants. It has generally been shown (e.g. Tang and Isaacs, 1993; Newlands *et al.*,1996) that although task performance itself is not enhanced, the availability of visual cues improves coordination and creates a greater sense of teamwork. A number of researchers have developed more integrated combinations of shared space and video, such that other participants' gestures and/or faces may be seen in the same visual space as the shared workspace. Applications have been targeted at design tasks, with the aim of supporting the interplay of drawing and gesture observed in many studies of designers at work. Scrivener's LookingGlass system (Scrivener *et al.*, 1994) provided each of a pair of designers with a video image of the other person's face under the shared drawing surface, while the series of ClearBoard and TeamWorkStation implementations, developed by Ishii and colleagues (Ishii and Ohkubo, 1990; Ishii *et al.*,1993), integrated images of co-workers with views of the desktop or drawing surface. (ClearBoard is described in more detail in the video-based communication section of Chapter 28.)

Chapter 28,
ClearBoard

The underlying intent of this stream of innovations has been pursued more recently in the context of collaborative virtual environments, which we discuss in Section 30.5.

Application sharing

Application sharing enables people to share a normal single-user application. The application sharing software transmits the contents of the host's windows to the other participants in a real-time tele-conference. NetMeeting has such a facility, as does Fujitsu's DTC (DeskTop Conference). DTC, among other similar applications, originally required the host to establish a real-time meeting with one or more individuals. Such meetings were either *chaired* or *shared* by the host. In the first instance the host retained executive control over the subsequent application sharing (i.e. only she was able to work with the application being shared, the others being mere observers). In a *shared* meeting, a participant could request the chair, at which time control passed to that person.

A number of other application-sharing products have been created, flowered briefly and been lost to history. Despite the apparent appeal of application sharing it is not widely used. A rare practical example comes from British Telecom, who have used it to help its support staff help with customer enquiries. For example, the remote staff can request to take control of an application and then guide the customer through, say, the setting of a given software application which is giving them trouble.

Challenge 30-2
Imagine you are application sharing with a group of people and someone presses Undo. What should the Undo undo? The last action, that person's last action? And what if that person's last action has been changed by someone else in the conference?

File transfer

Last but not least in the suite of software applications which make up tele-conferencing is a file transfer utility, allowing the transfer of files between servers. This is usually simply **ftp** (file transfer protocol – a widely used software application) with a graphical wrapper to hide the users from the relative obscurity of ftp's commands. Figure 30-2 is a screenshot of a typical graphical user interface to an FTP client. As can be seen, a certain level of technical knowledge

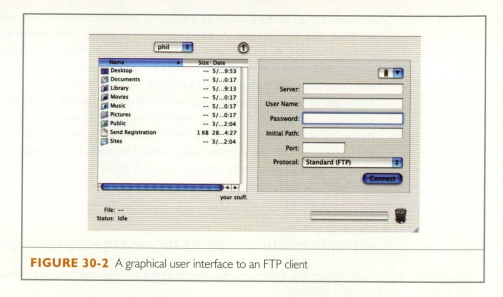

FIGURE 30-2 A graphical user interface to an FTP client

is required (for example, to select the server and port) compared to that entailed in sending an e-mail attachment.

Electronic meeting systems (EMSs)

← See Chapter 29 for a discussion of the role of anonymity and group support systems in group decision making

These are technologies which are designed to support group meetings with tools to improve group process, by enhancing communication, individual thought and decision making. There are a number of parallel terms in use for very similar types of technologies; the main variants include GSS (group support systems), GDSS (group decision support systems) and meetingware.

EMSs are largely targeted at face-to-face groups, but some can be used by distributed participants as well. Generally participants interact through their own computers, either desktop or laptop, and the results are displayed on large shared displays and/or individual screens. Typical components include tools for capturing and categorizing ideas, voting and building documentation in real time. Anonymity is often built in, on the assumption that this promotes contributions and the unbiased critique of ideas.

More recently, wireless handheld devices have been used successfully to link with large interactive displays. Ganoe (2002) describes one such application. Another approach, pioneered by Norbert Streitz and his team at the Fraunhofer IPSI Institute, is Roomware, where collaborative media are integrated in furniture, doors and walls.

The evidence about the effectiveness of meeting support systems is contradictory. Some researchers (e.g. Antunes and Costa, 2003) claim that they have been relatively unsuccessful, for reasons such as the need for skilled meeting facilitators, negative effects on meeting process, cost and usability problems. Other reviews, notably Fjermestad and Hiltz (2000), have found the technology to improve group performance as measured by effectiveness, efficiency, consensus, usability and satisfaction. As these authors propose, one reason for the apparent differences may be that many studies have used short-lived groups in artificial experimental settings. The technology is more likely to bring positive benefits in real organizational settings where task success is of genuine importance and teams are better motivated to succeed as well as generally having a history of co-working. This does not entirely explain matters, however, since Munkvold and Anson (2001) report on a long-term real-world study of meeting technology which did not win widespread adoption. The authors suggest that the main factors for enhancing uptake are permanent meeting rooms, a dedicated support team and more facilitators.

Box 30-1 Electronic meeting support for emergency management

This short case study shows the effective use of relatively simple meeting room tools to support the management of emergencies.

STATOIL is the Norwegian State Oil company and is thus responsible for many oil platforms in the North Sea. Oil platforms are dangerous places: consequently the company has a legal requirement to hold emergency exercises regularly. These generally take the form of simulated emergencies. We had the opportunity to witness one of these as part of the background work for the DISCOVER project. (DISCOVER – a training application – is introduced in Chapter 9.)

The exercise, which lasted some 90 minutes, was focused around a simulated emergency on board an actual platform, and involved the participation of platform personnel, helicopter pilots, the emergency services and numerous staff in the HQ control room. Only HQ staff and the 'on-scene commander' on the platform were aware of the simulated nature of the emergency until debriefed after the exercise. The aim of such exercises is both to provide practice and to assess the state of emergency readiness. In almost all respects, the action in the control room progresses just as it would in the real situation.

Our observation took place in the control room. This was staffed by personnel with specialist roles, each with a computer workstation, communications kit and orientated around a set of shared information displays – whiteboards, projected large screen displays and maps.

The setting for this particular exercise was a platform 100 km off the Norwegian coast. The reported situation was that a fire had been detected on the platform; one man was known to be injured but there were possibly more casualties. The nearby airport was contacted (for real) and helicopters assembled. The hospital was also contacted and switched to its emergency plan. Neither hospital nor airport knew that the 'emergency' was an exercise.

In the control room action was orchestrated by the control room leader, who prioritized issues and made the major decisions. As information came in from the platform, control room staff worked in small focused teams to deal with issues such as checking who was on the platform, notification of next of kin, liaising with hospitals and the press, helicopter and ship management and pollution control. Frequent timeouts for whole group sessions to review the situation were called. The media used included the following:

- A private (physical) whiteboard reserved for the use of the controller
- Multiple (physical) whiteboards for the teams to record the current state of information and progress

● A rolling history of events and decisions in Lotus Notes, constructed by staff using individual workstations and displayed on the large screen display
● Individual workstations for checking records, etc.
● The telephone, for external communications.

Whiteboards and the large display were located around the perimeter of the room and so visible to everyone. All could also overhear telephone conversations and so pick up relevant information. The whole set-up is an excellent example of a combination of technologies used to display the current state of affairs directly and allow people to maintain peripheral awareness of aspects outside the responsibilities of their immediate team. The effect to an observer was a combination of ballet and opera – a great deal of almost choreographed physical movement, and an orchestrated hubbub of voices, sometimes silenced as the controller took the floor as a soloist.

Groupware toolkits

The need to prototype different CSCW configurations to investigate such issues as awareness (see Section 30.6) and the management of collaborative work sessions (e.g., among very many others, Gutwin and Greenberg, 1998) led to the development of groupware toolkits, of which the best known is GroupKit. This was developed over some five years in the 1990s by Saul Greenberg's team at the University of Calgary. It is a Tcl/Tk (a UNIX-based GUI toolkit) library which supports the creation of real-time collaborative applications, such as multi-user drawing tools, text editors and meeting tools. GroupKit was and is widely used in the CSCW research community.

More recently, Gutwin (Hill and Gutwin, 2003) has developed MAUI, a Java-based toolkit with standard GUI widgets and group-specific elements such as telepointers. The toolkit is said to be 'the first ever set of UI widgets that are truly collaboration-aware'.

30.3 Technologies to support asynchronous working

Part VI deals with the general concept of information space

The use of common or shared *information* spaces (as distinct from workspaces to support synchronous work) is central to CSCW and to supporting asynchronous working (co-working across different times). While these shared information spaces vary in terms of complexity, functionality and ease of use, they do have a number of invariant features. The first of these is the underlying database itself: these potentially vary between simple flat databases through to full-blown relational databases and also include simple shared folders or directories. Next there is always some form of access control, ranging again from simple read/write access rights to the Lotus Notes multi-layer security model complete with password protection and encryption. Shared information spaces have been the subject of considerable research effort in terms of not only innovative implementations but their use in workplace studies. We now move to a brief description of a representative sample of these findings about experiences of them in use.

Bulletin boards

Bulletin boards together with threaded discussions, news groups and public/shared folders are a family of related technologies which support asynchronous working by way of access to shared information. Very simply, the option to permit shared folders is checked and then a set of permissions established with those who wish to access the folder. Sharing is usually facilitated by way of a local area network. This is an old technology and has largely been superseded by the Web.

See also the discussion on social navigation in Chapter 25, Section 25.4

Shared information spaces 1 – Lotus Notes

In its time Lotus Notes was *the* application to support cooperative working. Originally sold as 'corporate-ware' for a staggering amount of money, it consists of shared databases of documents, integrated e-mail and in later versions instant messaging, a calendar and a to-do list. A key feature is *replication*, whereby the contents of shared databases are synchronized at user-determined intervals when Notes clients are connected to the network. More recent versions of Notes are mediated over the Web, and marketed as a complete environment for both individual and collaborative work. Figure 30-3 is an example of a document from a database. As we can see from the image, the document is very similar to a structured e-mail message. It provides status information such as author, time and date of composition, subject and an attachment (a Word document).

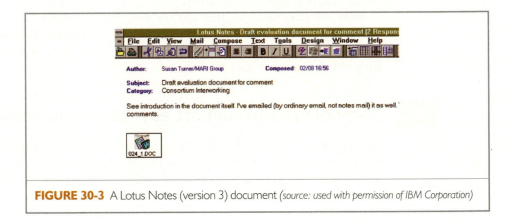

FIGURE 30-3 A Lotus Notes (version 3) document *(source: used with permission of IBM Corporation)*

Figure 30-4 is a different view of a Lotus Notes database. Here we can see the system's support for threaded conversations. A *main topic* is composed – the subject of the discussion – to which people can respond. Branching into subject topics is also supported by means of responding to a response (the * to the left of the date indicates that the documents have not been read).

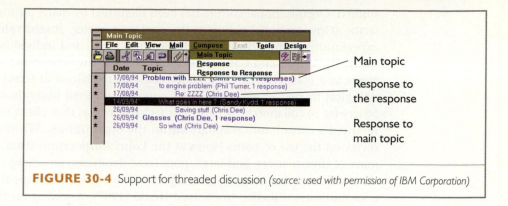

FIGURE 30-4 Support for threaded discussion *(source: used with permission of IBM Corporation)*

Shared information spaces 2 – BSCW

Figure 30-5 is a screenshot from BSCW – basic support for cooperative work. BSCW is a very successful product from a European-funded research project (of the same name) and is available (free of charge for non-commercial users) from bscw.gmd.de. It also forms the basis of commercially marketed applications.

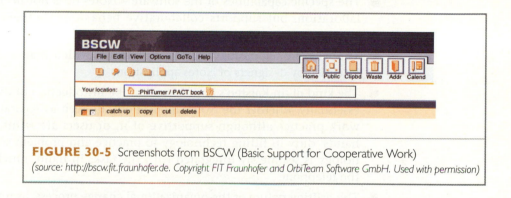

FIGURE 30-5 Screenshots from BSCW (Basic Support for Cooperative Work)
(source: http://bscw.fit.fraunhofer.de. Copyright FIT Fraunhofer and OrbiTeam Software GmbH. Used with permission)

The BSCW system, in the words of Hoschka (1998), 'offers the functionality of a comfortable and easy to use shared workspace and may be used with all major Web browsers and servers'. While BSCW was originally intended for research communities, its hosts at the Fraunhofer Institute for Applied Information Technology (FIT) state that it is used in a wide range of other domains. Essentially, the system allows teams access to working documents, images, links, threaded discussions, etc., in shared workspaces. The coordination of group working is supported by a raft of version management, access control and notification tools.

Shared information spaces in use

The adoption and use of Lotus Notes (and similar corporate information spaces) and the consequential effects on collaborative behaviour have been much studied. Organizational culture has been identified by many authors as a primary factor. (Organizational culture is the working practice, shared values, norms and expectations of the organization itself, work teams and individuals.) In a classic study, Orlikowski and Gash (1994) reported that the differential uptake of Lotus Notes in a management consultancy could be explained in terms of users' 'technological frames' or expectations of purpose and their individual willingness or otherwise to collaborate. A particular factor here was that client information represented a consultant's 'capital' within the organization. Whittaker (1996) has reviewed the use of Lotus Notes at the Lotus Corporation itself. Here a critical mass of diverse users, and large, populated databases, encouraged participation. He also found that usage in part depended on extent of competition from other communications media. In contrast Hepsø (1997), reporting on the use of Lotus Notes at the Norwegian oil corporation STATOIL, found strong and committed management support to be a key factor in the success of the project. In this instance Notes was used to share work process information for an oil installation.

In a comprehensive review of the (then) reported material on Notes installations published in 1999, Karsten summarizes the phenomena which influence the relationship between Notes and collaborative behaviour as follows:

- The specific capabilities of the software – Notes does not in itself create collaboration, but supports collaborative behaviour by making visible the activities of others
- The way the technology is used in practice, which may or may not be as intended by designers of Notes applications
- The kind of (in Karsten's terms) 'care' in the introduction of the technology – essentially, whether the Notes applications are seen as separate from normal work practice although supportive of it, or users are willing to 'get their hands' dirty in fitting technology to practice and problem solving, or technology is seamlessly integrated with the tasks in hand, much as the use of the telephone
- The drifting nature of the organizational change process, as unexpected practices and technological adaptations emerge – these can be positive or negative in terms of enhancing collaboration
- The reflective role of the technology – the characteristics of the technology itself can stimulate its users to reconsider and modify collaborative working practice
- The extent to which local work practices in the teams using Notes changes overall organizational practice
- The way in which all these aspects are intertwined.

Box 30-2 A cautionary tale

This short case study shows some of the ways in which information-sharing applications such as Lotus Notes can be adapted to particular domains. It also amply demonstrates issues in the adoption of such technologies. (Turner and Turner (1996) describes the case study in more detail.)

In our own CSCW work we introduced an early version of Lotus Notes to part of a large, geographically distributed engineering company. The project selected was engaged in the preparation of a detailed proposal for the design of a new submarine. The team at its largest comprised some 240 people who were distributed between three sites at Barrow (in the north of England, where the main project office was located), Glasgow (in Scotland), and Portsmouth (on the south coast of England). Two sub-teams were to be supported by the pilot technology:

- Engineers working on the main propulsion machinery. The design problem involved fitting a substantial bulk of machinery within fixed hull dimensions. About 20 staff worked together in this team, some in Barrow, some in Glasgow. The two sites were just over 180 miles apart, the only practical transport between the two being a drive of at least 3 hours.
- A team of human factors engineers (about 10 in total) who were concerned with the ergonomics of the submarine. They were almost all based in Glasgow but spent several days per week at other sites. The manager for this part of the work was located at Barrow.

At this stage, best practice would have been to refine the requirements gained from earlier work by working closely with people who would actually be using the technology. Technology could then have been tailored to a close match with working practice, and user confidence fostered. However, the extreme pressure of work on the SUB2 team – including its manager – and the secure conditions under which that work was carried out made this impossible. The immediate consequence of this was that insufficient information was available to model the technical system, nor could wider issues surface around the introduction of new technology. It should be said here that this set of circumstances is not unusual.

Lotus Notes (version 3) supported asynchronous working by providing a structured, shared information space, e-mail and file transfer. A number of purpose-built Notes applications were provided, described below.

- A discussion database supported asynchronous discussions of project issues.
- A requirements tracking database managed requirements for the design of the submarine. A requirement would be entered by the project manager and posted to one or more people to deal with. Their contribution would be linked to the original requirements document and progress monitored.
- A review database managed the document review process from submission of a document, through its posting to internal reviewers, receiving comments and keeping track of progress.
- A project archive would store all final versions of reviewed material. Documents from the review database were automatically transferred to the archive.
- A library was to be used for shared documents such as contract and standards information.
- A project diary was to be used to display deadlines and allow all group members to keep track of the project timetable.

While these applications matched general organizational working practice, because of the constraints noted above, they did not match closely everyday work within the teams, and hence were little used. A further factor was the amount of time required to learn the (then) rather obscure Notes interface, despite extensive user support. The one application to be intensively used was the Notes e-mail facility – e-mail or file transfer had not previously been available and its use saved thousands of miles of driving to and fro with floppy disks. All in all, it was a convincing illustration of the non-technical challenges to the adoption of CSCW technologies, as discussed at some length in Chapter 29.

30.4 Coordination technologies

Coordination technologies keep collaborative work structured and organized, however the participants are distributed in time and space. Coordination is the management of interdependencies between activities. This can be divided into

- Specification behaviours (e.g. creating shared goals)
- Planning behaviours (e.g. agreeing the set and order of tasks)
- Scheduling behaviours (e.g. assigning tasks to individuals or groups).

The main coordination tools in everyday use are **workflow** and **shared calendars**.

Designing for coordination

Early implementations of coordination mechanisms were not encouraging as they were too rigid, the underlying protocol being either inaccessible or not configurable. The best known early example is the Coordinator published by Action Technologies of Alameda, California, which indeed is still being sold, though with greatly extended functionality. The Coordinator was based on a *linguistic* model (Winograd and Flores, 1986). The original software was a structured e-mail (or workflow) system which required its users to categorize the nature of their communication, e.g. request/promise, offer/acceptance, report/acknowledge – that is, the following message is an *offer of help,* or a *request for information.* In practice this was not well received and anecdotally it was said that users of the system merely labelled each message with the first available message category on the list. Other examples include Information Lens (Malone *et al.,* 1986), Object Lens (Lai and Malone, 1988) and Conversation Builder (Kaplan *et al.,* 1991) which was a more flexible version of the Coordinator.

A different approach was adopted by OVAL, developed by Malone and his colleagues (Malone *et al.,* 1992). OVAL – **O**bjects, **V**iews, **A**gents and **L**inks – offered more of a building block approach (think software Lego) to end-user configuration (Box 30-3). Their approach was truly user participatory design – 'If you don't like the coordination software, build your own' – from objects, views, agents and links. Malone and his colleagues were able to demonstrate the power of OVAL by constructing some of the core functionality of three other collaborative systems, namely, gIBIS (a system for recording design rationale), Lotus Notes and The Coordinator.

Coordination in the real world

Researchers have spent much time attempting to understand how real-world coordination works, much of the work consisting of ethnographic, and therefore naturalistic, studies. The case study which follows, from Heath and Luff (2000), is a representative instance. We should say here that coordination is intimately related to awareness, discussed in Section 30.6, so this case study and its awareness counterpart are relevant to both topics.

Box 30-3 Objects, Views, Agents and Links

OVAL (Malone et al., 1992) showed how semi-structured documents could organize cooperative working. OVAL was a powerful tool/language for building CSCW systems. The end-user programming was very powerful and flexible but required an expert user. OVAL employed agents which are rule-based entities, triggered by events, that can run autonomously. The rules specify actions by agents on entities when certain events occur. The actions include such things as create, move, e-mail, delete, save and so forth. The entities include such things as messages and hyperlinks. Users are able to share objects, databases and files, and agents communicate through these shared entities.

Agents are discussed in Chapter 27

The setting is Reuters which provides a news service to organizations (newspapers, TV and commerce – dealers and traders). The Reuters' desks receive news stories from across the world. The desks are topic specific and subdivided; for example, the Financial News Section desk is divided into four desks, namely money and capital, equities, oil minerals and commodities. Journalists are expected to identify news of interest and tailor it to the specific needs of their clients. The technology at Reuters to support this work was based upon workstations with small (14-inch) monitors, with the consequence that others were unable to read the displayed text. At peak time four or five messages were received every minute, leaving the desk staff highly pressured.

Thus there was support for asynchronous working (information passed on to clients) but not synchronous working (e.g. with co-workers). However, all staff, while being responsible for their own clients, were required to pass on interesting and valuable pieces of news to their colleagues. But how? This is best seen by means of an example. Heath and Luff describe the behaviour of 'Peter'. Things are quiet in the newsroom. Peter is working on a story on a fall in Israeli interest rates and begins to make a joke about it in a pronounced accent to the room as a whole.

(Sample verbal protocol)

Peter: Bank of Israel interest rate drops.

Peter: Down, down, down.

Peter: Didn't it do this last week.

He continues working and then 12 seconds later, Alex, who is 6 feet away, turns to Peter and then back again. Peter then utters 'er', pauses and then ... not as a joke but as a précis,

Peter: er ...

Peter: Bank of Israel er. Cuts its er daily, the rate on its daily money tender to commercial banks.

Alex: Yeah. Got that now. Thanks Peter.

Peter: Okay.

The use of ethnography in CSCW is discussed in Chapter 29

Key points to note from this example are the reading aloud of text as the main mediating element and the level of detail in a typical ethnographic study.

Workflow defined

'Workflow technology is "any technology designed to (in some way) give order to or record the unfolding of work activities over time by, for example, providing tools and information to users at appropriate moments or enabling them to overview the work process they are part of or to design work processes for themselves or others or whatever".'

Bowers *et al.* (1995)

Workflow systems allow documents to be routed systematically for processing from person to person and from department to department through an organization. A workflow system manages the order in which tasks are executed and the flow of information. Workflow tends to be limited to routinized, rule-governed processes found in places such as government agencies, banks and insurance companies. In these domains workflow has been enthusiastically adopted, often as part of the fashion for **Business Process Re-engineering** (BPR) in the early to mid-1990s. Workflow systems provide features such as routing of information and tasks, the development of forms, monitoring of progress and support for differing jobs, roles and privileges. Such systems are often supported by scanning and imaging software, so that information which arrives on paper – such as an insurance claim form – is readily available on-line. All this requires detailed **process modelling** – a representation of how the job is done in minute detail. Not only is the process modelled, but the workflow system may also hold information about the skills and experience of its users, so that tasks can be allocated appropriately on an individual basis. Advocates of workflow claim the following (edited from Plesums, 2002):

- Work cannot be misplaced or stalled.

- Managers can focus on issues, such as individual performance, optimal procedures, and special cases, rather than the routine assignment and tracking of tasks.

- Procedures are formally documented and followed exactly, ensuring that the work is performed in the way planned by management, meeting all business and regulatory requirements.

- The best person (or machine) is assigned to each case, and the most important cases are assigned first. Users don't waste time choosing what to work on, perhaps procrastinating on important but difficult cases.

- Parallel processing is far more practical than in a traditional, manual workflow.

Thus costs are lowered and customer service improved. Despite the reductionist and Taylorist feel of workflow, it is claimed that users of workflow enjoy being able to complete well-defined tasks where all the information needed is ready to hand. (Taylor's 'scientific management' approach in the early twentieth century brought similar automation to many manual manufacturing processes, a change which was later held to be the source of much dissatisfaction in working life and was eventually superseded in some companies by a reverse move to jobs which could be completed by one person or at least within a small team.)

Box 30-4 Workflow benefits the Benefits Department

The 1998 Viewstar implementation for the Revenue and Benefits Department of Lewisham Borough Council in London had the following impacts on their operations in the first full year:

- £5 million additional revenues
- Fraud investigations saved an additional £1.7 million through speedier processes and cross-checking capability
- £0.5 million savings on operational costs.

Source: Allen (2001)

Although we have included workflow with our consideration of *cooperative* work, it should be noted that many workflow systems automate and atomize tasks to the extent that little active cooperation is required.

Further thoughts: Different flavours of workflow

Despite the drive for standardization and routinization, it is recognized that no single approach to workflow can fit every type of work. Different products address different types of workflow, and some workflow products – even within the same organization – can be used in different ways. The main categories are usually defined as set out below, although increasingly systems add features which cross boundaries.

- *Production workflow*: This is for managing large volumes of similar, repetitious tasks by automating as many as possible. Human input is only required for rare exceptions. The production workflow system can be

  - *Autonomous*: running without any integrated additional software except for database and messaging management systems. Other linked applications are invoked (automatically) at run time and thus interfaces must be defined.

  - *Embedded*: only functional within a larger application such as an Enterprise Resource Planning (ERP) system.

- *Administrative workflow*: The flow is predefined, such as the steps in authorizing a payment, but may be reviewed and altered. Generally handle smaller volumes of tasks than production systems.

- *Ad-hoc workflow*: As the name suggests, this is very flexible. New processes can be created and others modified as necessary. Used when volume processing, control and security are not major concerns.

There are also different underlying technical implementations of workflow.

- *Mail-based model*: Forms (embodying a task) are routed from one person to the next via mail.

- *Shared database model*: The form is routed, but many people have access to it (e.g. Lotus Notes).

- *Client–server database model*: Workflow rules are kept on the server, not in a database or document (e.g. Microsoft Exchange).

Creating a workflow system

Figure 30-6 shows a typical workflow system, in this case for processing a loan application form completed by the would-be customer on a website. A couple of points may require some explanation: the 'clone' and 'merge' operations allow the customer data to be used by several processes simultaneously, and the CIS (Customer Information System) files are stored externally to the workflow system itself.

Designing such a system requires a substantial amount of time, effort and negotiation from information systems staff, legal and accounting personnel and managers to define what the business processes should be. It is essential that all concerned should agree the new process. Existing manual processes are very likely not to be replicated exactly: they may have acquired redundant elements over the years, for example. (For those who have studied the Contextual Design chapters – 18 and 19 – this is *in principle* the equivalent to the work modelling and visioning stages. Parallels also exist, naturally, with dataflow diagrams and other structured system design representations.)

Shared calendars and meeting scheduling

Group (shared) calendars, such as those in Microsoft Outlook, are designed to support scheduling and coordination among many people. The Microsoft Outlook *Meeting Wizard* relies on being able to consult the e-mail address book and shared calendar. After the time and location have been set, each person invited to (or required at) the meeting will be informed by e-mail.

Grudin's design challenges are discussed in Chapter 29

This for some people is one of the problems with such systems – being required to attend. Where is the sense of choice, negotiation and privacy? Add to this the need to keep an up-to-date shared calendar to avoid schedule conflicts. It is also worth reflecting that shared diaries, meeting scheduling and calendaring system fit squarely in several of Grudin's design challenges.

Firstly, they rely on a critical mass of people to use them; secondly, they disrupt social norms (i.e. an office junior is empowered to book a meeting with the managing director); and, third, they reflect a disparity between work and benefit (*you* must maintain your diary so that someone else can book *you* into a meeting). Grudin and Palen (1995), in a long-term study of shared calendar use in large organizations, found that these problems could be overcome provided sufficient added value accrued to the individual. Peer pressure was also a significant factor in encouraging use.

Challenge 30-3
What collaboration technologies do you use in working with others? List the reasons for your choices. How far do your reasons match the issues raised in the previous material in this chapter? What can you conclude about the fit between the state of design knowledge and real-world conditions?

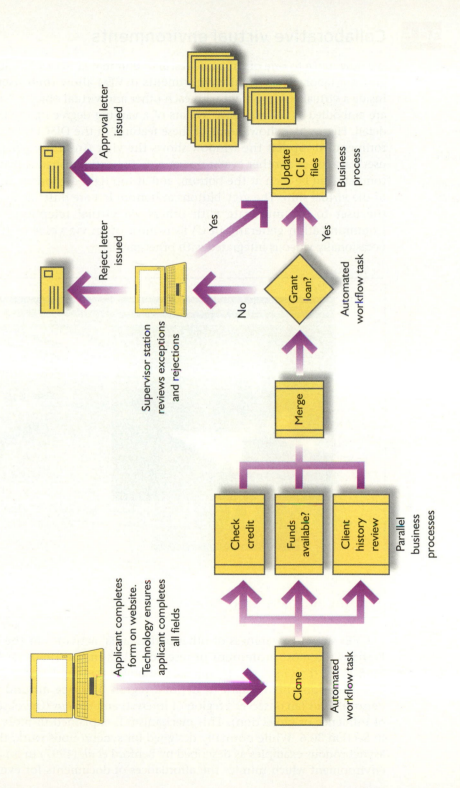

FIGURE 30-6 Workflow for processing a loan application (*source: after Allen, 2001, p. 18. Reproduced with permission from Workflow Management Coalition (wfmc.org)*)

30.5 Collaborative virtual environments

We now move to one of the more research-dominated topics in CSCW technologies. Collaborative virtual environments (CVEs) allow their users to interact inside a virtual environment with each other and virtual objects. Normally, users are embodied as 3D graphical avatars of a varying degree of sophistication and detail. Figure 30-7 shows some of these features in the DISCOVER training environment. At top left the window shows the view (from the perspective of the user's avatar) of another avatar operating a fire extinguisher. A plan of the environment can be seen at the bottom, and at top right a window on another part of the virtual ship. The grey buttons at bottom left are difficult to see, but allow the user to communicate with others via virtual telephone or intercom. Communication generally in CVEs is most often via voice or text, although occasionally video is integrated with other media.

DISCOVER was introduced in Chapter 9

FIGURE 30-7 Extinguishing a fire in the DISCOVER CVE

CVEs support awareness of other participants' activities in the shared space. Perhaps the most prominent of research CVEs in the 1990s, MASSIVE-1 and MASSIVE-2 (Bowers *et al.*, 1996), had a sophisticated model of spatial awareness based on concepts of *aura* (a defined region of space around an object or person), *focus* (an observer's region of interest) and *nimbus* (the observed's region of influence or projection). This mechanism is explained in more detail below, in Section 30.6. While normally designed for synchronous work, there are some asynchronous examples as described by Benford *et al.* (1997) in an account of an environment which mimics the affordances of documents for everyday coordination in an office setting – for example, indicating whether work has started through the position of a virtual document on a virtual desktop.

Many CVEs remain as research tools, but the technology is migrating slowly towards practical applications for collaborative work. Training applications are prominent, allowing users to practise teamwork in situations that may be inaccessible or dangerous, or to enable distributed teams and tutors to train together. Figure 30-8 is a screenshot from a CVE designed to allow tutors and trainees to interact in training to replace ATM switches. It is taken from www.discover. uottawa.ca/~mojtaba/Newbridge.html (note that the 'discover' part of this URL is a coincidence and is not related to our DISCOVER project). An interesting point here is the video window at the left of the screen which illustrates the correct procedure. The creation of the CVE was motivated by the wide geographical dispersion of trainees and tutors and the fragility and cost of the ATM equipment involved.

Issues in the training arena, aside from the usability of some technologies, relate to the following:

■ How far training in the virtual world can transfer to the real

■ The validity of training teams to interact with the rather different (but smaller) range of awareness cues available in CVEs – for example, it is often difficult to detect where a fellow avatar is looking

■ The inflexibility of even the most sophisticated virtual environments compared to the infinite possibilities of imaginary scenarios in face-to-face training exercises

■ Overcoming the perception of employers that CVEs are a just a species of game (although game-like features not surprisingly enhance participants' experience).

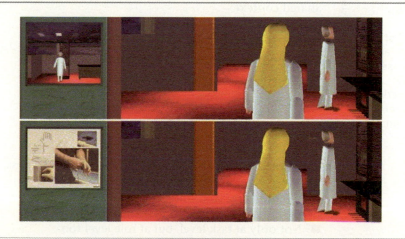

FIGURE 30-8 An application learning to replace ATM switches
(source: www.discover.uottawa.ca/~mojtaba/Newbridge.html)

Educational CVEs are also becoming commonplace. Among many recent examples are an application related to museum exhibits which allows users to play an ancient Egyptian game (Economou *et al.*, 2000) and a CVE for fostering social awareness in educational settings (Prasolova-Førland and Divitini, 2003). Among diverse other applications are collaborative information search and visualization, for example the virtual pond filled with data masquerading as aquatic creatures described by Ståhl *et al.* (2002), commercial dispute negotiation, representing evidence as virtual objects in video streams, and public entertainment (Dew *et al.*, 2002). Several ventures in this last domain are summarized by Benford *et al.* (2002). Finally, of course, very many games can be regarded as a species of CVE.

CVE research issues

There continues to be a large body of research centred on CVEs, both into the design of the technology itself and using CVEs to explore other issues in collaboration and communication. The following list of issues is summarized from Churchill *et al.* (2001). The authors identify the following topics – certainly current in 2001 and largely remaining so at the time of this book:

- CVE engines themselves
- System challenges – bandwidth, database design, system architectures
- Bodies, presence and interaction
- Sharing context in CVEs – the 'I know what I see, but what do you see?' problem
- Applications of CVE technology.

Shared context:

Many of these issues are discussed as 'social navigation' in Chapter 25, Section 25.4

- Shared knowledge of other's current activities
- Shared knowledge of other's past activities
- Shared artefacts
- Shared environment.

Awareness of others:

- Particularly the importance of peripheral awareness.

Negotiation and communication:

- Not only at task level, but at role level too
- Loss of nuance, subtle 'back channels', gesturing.

Flexible and multiple viewpoints:

■ Not only within the environment but at document and interaction level too.

30.6 Designing for awareness

Awareness has perhaps been *the* central research issue in CSCW. The term *awareness* in CSCW is often used in an everyday sense of the word – having knowledge or perception of others or events. Definitions of awareness tend to be intuitive, for example:

> 'Studies ... highlight the extent to which information sharing, knowledge of group and individual activity and coordination are central to successful collaboration. Information relating to these factors contributes to what we refer to as awareness. '... 'Awareness is an understanding of the activities of others, which provides a context for your own activity.'

Dourish and Bellotti (1992), p. 107

And, underlining the importance of awareness:

> 'There is a crucial design principle for any technology that is environmental in the sense that it surrounds people and pervasively impinges on them. Most computer interfaces are designed for people to pay attention to them. But people deal with complex situations by not attending to most of it, most of the time. It is important not to saturate people with things they cannot ignore ... On the other hand, people are very aware of what goes on in their environment; without such awareness they would feel very isolated. The environment needs to be rich with many things (including other people) that could be attended to. The environment needs to signal the availability of these things by tapping other people's ability to peripherally process the non-attended parts of the environment so that they can redirect their attention when appropriate.'

Moran and Anderson (1990), p. 386

Clearly we need to be aware of what other people are doing when we are working cooperatively and, more generally, the state of the work at any particular time. Thus in defining awareness we are establishing the conditions for coordinating work. In practice it is difficult to separate definitions of awareness and coordination (coordination has already been discussed in Section 30.4). Awareness has been researched in two distinct and related ways. What might be called the *experimental* route has involved developing novel applications; this has been in contrast to the *naturalistic* route which has studied awareness issues in the workplace, control room and aircraft cockpit – to name but a few.

Awareness issues

Awareness is ubiquitous in all collaborative applications. All successful CSCW applications embody an awareness mechanism, as do all successful cooperative working situations. Table 30-2 lists some of the information of which we need to be aware in working life. The material which follows then looks briefly at a representative selection of the tools designed to support awareness.

TABLE 30-2 Awareness issues

Category	Element	Questions
Who?	Presence	Is anyone in the workplace?
	Identity	Who is participating?
	Authorship	Who is that? Who is doing that?
What?	Action	What are they doing?
	Intention	What goal is that action part of?
	Artefact	What objects are they working on?
Where?	Location	Where are they working?
	Gaze	Where are they looking?
	View	Where can they see?
	Reach	Where can they reach?

Source: Gutwin, C. and Greenberg, S. (1999) The effects of workspace awareness support on the usability of real-time distributed groupware, ACM Transactions on Computer–Human Interaction (TOCHI), 6(3), pp. 243–81. © 1999 ACM, Inc. Reprinted by permission

Portholes – an early but classic awareness application

The Portholes system was an early example of awareness technology. It is, however, a highly representative example of CSCW research in this area, focusing as it does on the reactions of a group of workers to novel technologies under naturalistic conditions. The work was originally reported by Dourish and Bly (1992) but there have been several later implementations and related studies.

Portholes' main functionality was to provide its users with a set of small video snapshots of other areas in the workplace, both other people's offices and common areas. These were updated only every few minutes, but were enough to give people a sense of who was around and what they were doing. The original studies were conducted at Rank Xerox research labs in the US and UK. Users mostly enjoyed the opportunities for casual contact. Examples reported include the following:

- A participant at PARC (the US lab) who was spending many late nights working in his office; his presence was not only noted by EuroPARC (UK) participants but also led them to be quite aware of his dissertation progress.

- Another late-night worker at PARC was pleased to tell his local colleagues that he had watched the sun rise in England.

FIGURE 30-9 Screenshots from the Portholes system *(source: courtesy of Bill Buxton)*

- Enjoying a colleague's message when he sang Happy Birthday to himself.
- Being able to check unobtrusively that someone was in the office before going to speak to them.
- The sense of whether people were around and seeing friends.
- Feeling a connection to people at the other site.

Disadvantages included the consumption of screen real-estate and the potential for privacy violations. Later versions incorporated the sound of a door opening as a cue that a video snapshot was about to be taken. Portholes raises two of the fundamental trade-offs in designing for awareness:

- Privacy versus awareness
- Awareness versus disruption.

In normal everyday life we have unobtrusive, socially accepted ways of maintaining mutual awareness while respecting privacy. Examples include checking for a colleague's car in the car park or noticing that someone is in the office because their jacket is over the back of a chair even if they are not actually present at the time. In computer-mediated collaboration, many of these cues have to be reinvented, and the consequences of their new incarnations are often unclear until tried out in real life. Experiments have included shadowy video figures, muffled audio, and a variety of mechanisms to alert people that they are being (or about to be) captured on video or audio.

Challenge 30-4
What other simple (non-technological) cues do you use in everyday life in maintaining awareness of others?

Active badges

Wearable computing appliances are described in Chapters 16 and 17

Active badges are small wearables which identify people and transmit signals providing location information through a network of sensors. Early uses included the obvious one of locating someone within a building and being able to have one's own set-up and files instantly available from the nearest PC. The growth of wireless technologies has led to wide-ranging and more sophisticated applications such as making tourist information available as locations come into view, navigation information for the visually handicapped and making people with shared interests aware of each other at conferences.

This is well illustrated in Harper's study (Harper, 1992) of the adoption of active badges (a product called the Locator) in research laboratories, again using two communities of researchers at Rank Xerox as participants. This choice was not simply a matter of convenience: Harper (a sociologist) wished to explore the social and organizational nature of the research lab through studying technology in use. Again, this is characteristic of CSCW research, as much directed at understanding groups of people working together as an aim in itself as delineating the impact of technology. In this case, Harper concluded that the way people used the badges – reluctantly or with commitment and enthusiasm – 'is determined by what they do, their formal position, and their state of relations – meant here in the broadest sense – with others in the labs. From this view, wearing a badge, viewing the Locator as acceptable or not as the case may be, symbolically represents one's job, one's status, one's location within the moral order.' (Harper, 1992, p. 335). Among many interesting nuggets in the report, the contrast between reactions of receptionists and researchers is (yet again) an example of Grudin's 'challenge' of differential costs and benefits. Receptionists are already in a known, fixed location for most of a regular working day: using a badge to track their whereabouts changes very little. Researchers, by custom and practice, have freedom to work irregular hours, at home, in the office, or walking around thinking through an idea. Tracking their location can be perceived as significantly impinging on this liberty, but makes the receptionist's job considerably easier.

Grudin's challenges are listed in Chapter 29

Simple awareness mechanisms

As well as what we might term social awareness, there are many single-user applications which support more simple awareness mechanisms. Figure 30-10 is the so-called *tray* element of a MS Window (Windows NT) from the status bar. At a glance we can see the time, that a new e-mail message has arrived, that virus

FIGURE 30-10 A simple awareness mechanism

prevention software is running (the soldier next to the cannon) and that applications to adjust sound, screen resolution and mouse settings are to hand.

Figure 30-11 is an example of an awareness mechanism which is used to inform others of one's status. Anyone mailing Turner, Phil will be greeted with an Out of Office AutoReply from MS Outlook. The *Out of Office Assistant* facility works using simple rules which are applied to incoming e-mail. At its simplest, the assistant will send an autoreply such as 'Go away I am busy'.

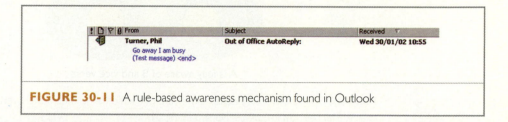

FIGURE 30-11 A rule-based awareness mechanism found in Outlook

Figure 30-12 is an example of an awareness mechanism which also supports coordination. The alert has been sent automatically from Outlook's calendaring system to remind members of TMT that their fortnightly meeting is due in 5 minutes. Here the alert is a means of both awareness and coordination.

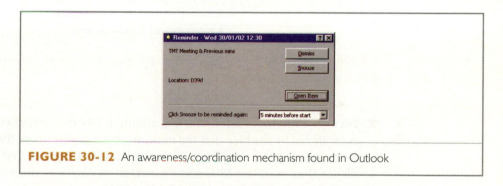

FIGURE 30-12 An awareness/coordination mechanism found in Outlook

There are a large number of simple awareness cues or indicators implemented in collaborative applications. These include such things as being aware of the cursor position in a shared application, or which menu items are being accessed, or the permission settings of files and directories.

Modelling awareness: a spatial model of interaction

This was an explicit attempt to design for interaction and awareness (Benford and Fahlén, 1993) with particular reference to virtual environments. The approach was based on a spatial model and defined the following key abstractions:

■ **Medium**: Any interaction between objects occurs through some medium. Media include audio, visual, textual, virtual or a special-purpose interface.

■ **Aura** is a subspace bounding the presence of an object in a medium. An aura accompanies an object which may have a different aura (for example audio and visual). When two auras coincide, interaction in the medium becomes possible. Once auras have agreed to interact, it is down to the objects to manage that interaction via **Focus** and **Nimbus**. See Figures 30-13 and 30-14.

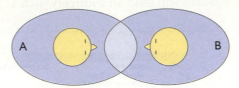

A is fully aware of B and vice versa

FIGURE 30-13 Two individuals, fully aware of each other as their auras overlap
(source: after Benford and Fahlén, 1993, p. 118, Fig. 3)

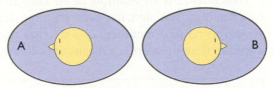

A is unaware of B and vice versa

FIGURE 30-14 The same couple, perhaps after they have argued – no overlapping auras
(source: after Benford and Fahlén, 1993, p. 118, Fig. 3)

■ **Focus** is a mechanism for directing attention (shorten, lengthen), and **Nimbus** is explained by the idea that the more an object is within another's nimbus, the more aware it is of the object. Thus the level of awareness that object A has of object B on medium M is some function of A's focus on B in M and of B's nimbus on A in M (Benford and Fahlén, 1993, p. 112). Implementations of this model include the DIVE virtual environment, its successor MASSIVE (Figure 30-15) and the CyCO text conferencing systems respectively.

An ethnographic study of awareness

In this section we conclude our consideration of awareness by briefly describing a typical example of one of the many ethnographic studies in this area, the conclusions drawn and the design challenges identified. This is the now classic study of a London Underground control room by Christian Heath and Paul Luff, as reported in Heath and Luff (2000). Our summary of the work will focus on the awareness issues, but the original report covers far more than this and would repay reading in full.

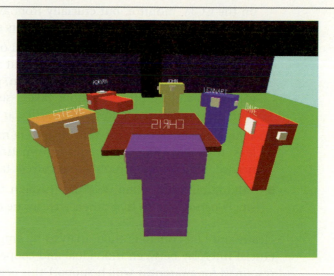

FIGURE 30-15 A screenshot from the MASSIVE 2 tele-conferencing system
(*source: http://crg.cs.nott.ac.uk/research/systems/MASSIVE/screenshots/chi1.gif*)

The team of researchers from University College London studied the operation of the Bakerloo Line control room on a day-to-day basis. The Bakerloo Line is a busy line serving the London Underground network.

The control room (CR) had been recently upgraded, replacing manual signalling with a computerized system. The CR housed the line controller responsible for the coordination of the day-to-day running of the line, the divisional information assistant (DIA) responsible for providing passenger information via a public address system (PA) and communicating with stations, and two signal assistants who supervised a busy section of track. The controller and the DIA sat together in a semicircular console facing a fixed real-time display of the traffic on the line. Lights on this display indicated the location of trains. The console was equipped with a radio telephone, touchscreen telephones, a PA system, a closed-circuit TV control system and monitors displaying line information and traffic and a number of other control systems. The London Underground system as a whole was coordinated by way of a paper timetable which details the number of trains, crew information and a dozen other items of relevance to the controller. The control room staff aimed overall to support the running of a service which matched the timetable as closely as possible.

While the control room staff have different formal responsibilities, the job was achieved in practice by a cooperative interweaving of tasks requiring close coordination, which in turn depended on a high degree of awareness. Some of the many instances were:

- In the case of service announcements delivered over the PA, information was drawn from the fixed line diagram and tailored to the arrival of trains visible on the CCTV monitor, but crucially from awareness of the activities of colleagues and their conversations with drivers about the state of train traffic.

■ Instructions to drivers similarly depended on being aware of colleagues. All staff maintained this level of awareness, but at a level which intruded neither on their colleagues' work nor on their own, picking up on key words in conversations and significant actions taken, such as instructing trains to turn round, or even glancing towards a particular information resource.

■ Temporary changes to the timetable were made using erasable acetate overlays, thus providing the change information to all concerned when it was needed, rather than intruding into current tasks.

■ Talking out loud when working through timetable changes, nominally a single-person job, so that others were aware of what was about to happen.

Heath and Luff conclude their analysis by emphasizing the fluid, informal yet crucial interplay between individual and cooperative work and the unobtrusive resources for awareness which support this achievement. A similar instance of fluid teamworking can be seen in our report of the STATOIL emergency exercise in Section 30.2, and in many of the large body of ethnographic studies of work, particular the many studies of air-traffic control. The point for designers is that any attempt to design technology which can be used only in *either* strictly individual *or* strictly collaborative modes, still less to define formal teamworking procedures to be mediated by technology, is likely to fail.

Summary and key points

This chapter has covered a wide variety of technologies, from simple awareness mechanisms such as e-mail alerts, to corporate information spaces such as Lotus Notes and the research-led domain of collaborative virtual environments. We have seen how the match of these technologies to the way in which people actually work together, and to the social conventions that govern co-working, should be a hugely significant factor in good design for cooperation. Key points to consider in the choice and design of such technologies are

■ The match of features to the way in which cooperation is spread over space and time

■ Respecting social norms about privacy in particular and working practice in general

■ Support for the flexible, dynamic mixing of individual and cooperative work

■ Provision of sufficient awareness information to coordinate co-working, but not so much as to disrupt individual work.

Further reading

As for all the chapters in Part VII, the series of CSCW and GROUP conference proceedings (accessible from the ACM digital library at www.acm.org/dl) together with the ECSCW series published by Kluwer are the best source of the latest material. More considered accounts of theory and practice can be found in the CSCW journal.

Going forward

www.wfmc.org has a good deal of publicly available information about workflow.

The CVE series of conferences, again available through the ACM, cover the latest developments in that field.

Churchill, E.F., Snowdon, D. and Munro, A. (2001) *Collaborative Virtual Environments: Digital Places and Spaces for Interaction.* Springer-Verlag, London.
This has a useful coverage of CVE research issues.

Heath, C. and Luff, P. (2000) *Technology in Action.* Cambridge University Press, Cambridge.
This contains a set of ethnographic studies, together with considered reflections on the place of ethnography in technology design. Despite the depth of detail, much of this is fascinating material.

Comments on challenges

Challenge 30-1
Some possibilities include

- Focus on interpersonal communication vs. focus on the shared work
- Text and speech only vs. mixed modalities (e.g. video, shared graphics workspaces)
- Structured vs. unstructured.

Consideration of these and other variations can be found throughout the material in the rest of this chapter.

Challenge 30-2
There is no easy answer to this and actual implementations vary. What is most important is that everyone understands the way it works.

Challenge 30-3
You may find no surprises here, but if you find some new issues, they will illustrate the context and cultural dependencies in the use of collaborative tools.

Challenge 30-4
Here are just two examples. For my part, I can hear when my colleague in the next-door office is talking – not enough to overhear the words themselves, but enough to stop me from interrupting unless it's really urgent. Similarly, when someone has headphones on while sitting at their desk it generally means they're busy. These cues are so undemanding of my attention that I normally don't think about them – unlike having a video window sitting on my screen.

Exercises

1. Test the effects of technology on group performance for yourself. Set up two groups each of three people. Each of the groups should know each other reasonably well. One group should work with a paper flipchart and individual notepads, the other with instant messaging, a shared workspace and individual (paper) notepads. Make sure that everyone in the second group has practised using the technology. Have each group brainstorm ideas for the uses for dogs which could talk to human beings. They must record their ideas on the flipchart/shared whiteboard. Count the ideas generated by each group.

2. One reason why we need to have awareness of others in the workplace is to engage with them – to speak to them, consult them, in short to interrupt them. Figure 30-16 is a collection of six pictures of an office worker in a range of typical situations. This is a re-creation of a study by Johnson and Greenberg (1999) who simply asked people to rate the availability (or interruptability) of the woman in the picture. Try this yourself – rate (put in order) when it would be most convenient for the woman in the pictures to be interrupted.

1. Entering her office

2. Leaving the office

3. Thinking / staring into space

4. Talking on the phone

5. Eating and drinking

6. Working at a computer

FIGURE 30-16 In the office

References and bibliography

Abed, M., Tabary, D. and Kolski, C. (2004) Using formal specification techniques for the modeling of tasks and the generation of human–computer user interface specifications. In Diaper, D. and Stanton, N. (eds), *The Handbook of Task Analysis for Human–Computer Interaction*. Lawrence Erlbaum Associates, Mahwah, NJ.

Abel, M. (1990) Experiences in an exploratory distributed organization. In Galegher, J., Kraut, R.E. and Egido, C. (eds), *Intellectual Teamwork: Social Foundations of Cooperative Work*. Lawrence Erlbaum Associates, Hillsdale, NJ, pp. 489–510.

Ackerman, M. (2000) The intellectual challenge of CSCW: the gap between social requirements and technical feasibility. *Human–Computer Interaction*, **15**(2–3), 181–205.

ACM SIGCHI (1992) Curriculum for human–computer interaction. ACM Special Interest Group on Computer–Human Interaction, Curriculum Development Group, New York. http://www.acm.org/sigchi/cdg/cdg1.html

Ahlberg, C. and Shneiderman, B. (1994) Visual information seeking: tight coupling of dynamic query filters with starfield displays. *Proceedings of CHI '94 Conference*, Boston, MA, 24–28 April. ACM Press, New York, pp. 313–317.

Alexander, C. (1979) *The Timeless Way of Building*. Oxford University Press, New York.

Allen, R. (2001) Workflow: an introduction. In *The Workflow Handbook 2001*, pdf file available from www.wfmc.org.

Allport, G.W. (1968) *The Person in Psychology: Selected Essays*. Beacon Press, Boston, MA.

Anderson, J.R. and Reder, L. (1979) An elaborate processing explanation for depth of processing. In Cermak, L.S. and Craik, F.I.M. (eds), *Levels of Processing in Human Memory*. Lawrence Erlbaum Associates, Hillsdale, NJ.

Anderson, R. (1997) Work, ethnography and system design. In Kent, A. and Williams, J.G. (eds), *The Encyclopaedia of Microcomputers*, vol. 20. Marcel Dekker, New York, pp. 159–183. Also available as Technical Report EPC-1996-103 from Rank Xerox Research Centre, Cambridge, UK.

Andriessen, J.H.E. (2002) *Working with Groupware. Understanding and Evaluating Collaboration Technology*. Springer-Verlag, London.

Annett, J. (2004) Hierarchical task analysis. In Diaper, D. and Stanton, N. (eds), *The Handbook of Task Analysis for Human–Computer Interaction*. Lawrence Erlbaum Associates, Mahwah, NJ.

Antikainen, A., Kälviäinen, M. and Miller, H. (2003) User information for designers: a visual research package. *Proceedings of DPPI '03 Conference*, Pittsburgh, PA, 23–26 June. ACM Press, New York, pp. 1–5.

Antunes, P. and Costa, C.J. (2003) From genre analysis to the design of meetingware. *Proceedings of Group '03 Conference*, Sanibel Island, FL, 9–12 Dec. ACM Press, New York, pp. 302–310.

Argyle, M. and Cook, M. (1976) *Gaze and Mutual Gaze*. Cambridge University Press, Cambridge.

Argyle, M. and Ingham, R. (1972) Mutual gaze and proximity. *Semiotica*, **6**, 32–49.

Asch, S.E. (1951) Effects of group pressure upon the modification and distortion of judgement. In Guetzkow, H. (ed.), *Groups, Leadership and Men*. Carnegie Press, Pittsburgh, PA.

Asch, S.E. (1956) Studies of independence and conformity: A minority of one against a unanimous majority. *Psychological Monographs*, **70** (whole no. 416).

Atkinson, R.C. and Shiffrin, R.M. (1968) Human memory: a proposed system and its control processes. In Spence, K.W. and Spence, J.T. (eds), *The Psychology of Learning and Motivation*, vol. 2. Academic Press, London.

Axelrod, R. (1984) *The Evolution of Cooperation*. Basic Books, New York.

Bacon, E.N. (1974) *Design of Cities*. Thomas Hudson, London.

Baddeley, A. (1997) *Human Memory: Theory and Practice*. Psychology Press, Hove, Sussex.

Baddeley, A.D. and Hitch, G. (1974) Working memory. In Bower, G.H. (ed.), *Recent Advances in Learning and Motivation*, vol. 8. Academic Press, New York.

Badre, A.N. (2002) *Shaping Web Usability: Interaction Design in Context*. Addison-Wesley, Boston, MA.

Bahrick, H.P. (1984) Semantic memory content in the permastore: fifty years of memory for Spanish learned in school. *Journal of Experimental Psychology: General*, **104**, 54–75.

Baillie, L. (2002) *The Home Workshop: a method for investigating the home*. PhD Thesis, School of Computing, Napier University, Edinburgh.

Baillie, L. (2003) The Home Workshop. *Home-Orientated Informatics and Telematics International Working Conference*, California, 5–10 May.

Baillie, L., Benyon, D., MacAulay, C. and Petersen, M (2003) Investigating design issues in household environments. *Cognition Technology and Work*, 5(1), 33–44.

Baker, K., Greenberg, S. and Gutwin, C. (2002) Empirical development of a heuristic evaluation methodology for shared workspace groupware. *Proceedings of CSCW '02 Conference*, New Orleans, LA, 16–20 Nov. ACM Press, New York, pp. 96–105.

Balakrishnan, R., Baudel, T., Kurtenbach, G. and Fitzmaurice, G. (1997) The Rockin'Mouse: integral 3D manipulation on a plane. *Proceedings of CHI '97 Conference*, Atlanta, GA, 22–27 March. ACM Press, New York, pp. 311–318.

Balbo, S., Ozkan, N. and Paris, C. (2004) Choosing the right task modeling notation: a taxonomy. In Diaper, D. and Stanton, N. (eds), *The Handbook of Task Analysis for Human–Computer Interaction*. Lawrence Erlbaum Associates, Mahwah, NJ.

Bannon, L.J. (1991) From human factors to human actors: the role of psychology and human–computer interaction studies in system design. In Greenbaum, J. and Kyng, M. (eds), *Design at Work: Cooperative Design of Computer Systems*. Lawrence Erlbaum Associates, Hillsdale, NJ, pp. 25–44.

Bannon, L.J. and Schmidt, K. (1991) CSCW: four characters in search of context. In Bowers, J.M. and Benford, S.D. (eds), *Studies in Computer Supported Collaborative Work*. Elsevier North-Holland, Amsterdam.

Bardram, J.E. (1998) Designing for the dynamics of cooperative work activities. *Proceedings of CSCW '98 Conference*, Seattle, WA, 14–18 Nov. ACM Press, New York, pp. 89–98.

Barnard, P.J. (1985) Interacting cognitive subsystems: a psycholinguistic approach to short term memory. In Ellis, A. (ed.), *Progress in the Psychology of Language*, vol. 2. Lawrence Erlbaum Associates, London, pp. 197–258.

Barnard, P.J., May, J. and Salber, D. (1996) Deixis and points of view in media spaces: an empirical gesture. *Behaviour and Information Technology*, **15**, 37–50.

Barthes, R. (1986) Semiology and the urban. In Gottdiener, M. and Lagopoulos, A.P. (eds), *The City and the Sign*. Columbia University Press, New York.

Bartlett, M.S., Hager, J.C., Ekman, P. and Sejnowski, T.J. (1999) Measuring facial expressions by computer image analysis. *Psychophysiology*, **36**, 253–263.

Bauersfeld, K. and Halgren, S. (1996) 'You've got three days!' Case studies in field techniques for the time-challenged. In Wixon, D. and Ramey, J. (eds), *Field Methods Casebook for Software Design*. Wiley, New York, pp. 177–195.

Beaudouin-Lafon, M. and Mackay, W. (2003) Prototyping tools and techniques. In Jacko, J.A. and Sears, A. (eds), *The Human–Computer Interaction Handbook*. Lawrence Erlbaum Associates, Mahwah, NJ.

Benda, P. and Sanderson, P. (1999) New technology and work practice: modelling change with cognitive work analysis. In Sasse, M. and Johnson, C. (eds), *Proceedings of INTERACT '99*. IOS Press, Amsterdam, pp. 566–573.

Benford, S.D. and Fahlén, L.E. (1993) A spatial model of interaction in large virtual environments. *Proceedings of ECSCW '93 Conference*, Milan, Italy, 13–17 Sept. De Michelis *et al.* (eds) Kluwer, Dordrecht, pp. 109–124.

Benford, S., Snowdon, D., Colebourne, A., O'Brien, J. and Rodden, T. (1997) Informing the design of collaborative virtual environments. *Proceedings of Group '97 Conference*, Phoenix, AZ, 16–19 Nov. ACM Press, New York, pp. 71–80.

Benford, S., Fraser, M., Reynard, G., Koleva, B. and Drozd, A. (2002) Staging and evaluating public performances as an approach to CVE research. *Proceedings of CVE '02 Conference*, Bonn, Germany, 30 Sept.–2 Oct. ACM Press, New York, pp. 80–87.

Benyon, D.R. and Murray, D.M. (1993) Adaptive systems; from intelligent tutoring to autonomous agents. *Knowledge-based Systems*, 6(4), 197–219.

Benyon, D.R. and Skidmore, S. (eds) (1988) *Automating Systems Development*. Plenum, New York.

Benyon, D.R. and Wilmes, B. (2003) The application of urban design principles to navigation of web sites. In O'Neill, E., Palanque, P. and Johnson, P. (eds), *People and Computers XVII – Proceedings of HCI 2003 Conference*, Bath, UK, 8–12 Sept.

Benyon, D.R., Green, T.R.G. and Bental, D. (1999) *Conceptual Modelling for Human–Computer Interaction, Using ERMIA*. Springer-Verlag, London.

Benyon, D.R., Crerar, A. and Wilkinson, S. (2001) Individual differences and inclusive design. In Stephanidis, C. (ed.), *User Interfaces for All: Concepts, Methods and Tools*. Lawrence Erlbaum Associates, Mahwah, NJ.

Bertin, J. (1981) *Graphics and Graphic Information Processing*. Walter de Gruyter, Berlin.

Beyer, H. and Holtzblatt, K. (1998) *Contextual Design*. Morgan Kaufmann, San Francisco.

Bickmore, T. (2003) *Relational agents: Effecting change through human–computer relationships*. PhD thesis, MIT Media Arts and Science.

Blackler, F. (1993) Knowledge and the theory of organizations: organizations as activity systems and the reframing of management. *Journal of Management Studies*, 30(6), 863–884.

Blackler, F. (1995) Activity theory, CSCW and organizations. In Monk, A.F. and Gilbert, N. (eds), *Perspectives on HCI – Diverse Approaches*. Academic Press, London.

Blackmon, M.H., Polson, P.G., Kitajima, M. and Lewis, L. (2002) Cognitive walkthrough for the web. *Proceedings of CHI '02 Conference*, Minneapolis, MN, 20–25 April. ACM Press, New York, pp. 463–470.

Blackwell, A. and Green, T. (2003) Notational systems – the cognitive dimensions of notations framework. In Carroll, J.M. (ed.), *HCI Models, Theories and Frameworks*. Morgan Kaufmann, San Francisco.

Blakemore, C. (1988) *The Mind Machine*. BBC Publications, London.

Blattner, M., Sumikawa, D. and Greenberg, R. (1989) Earcons and icons: their structure and common design principles. *Human–Computer Interaction*, 4(1), 11–44.

Blauert, J. (1997) *Spatial Hearing*. MIT Press, Cambridge, MA.

Bødker, S. and Christiansen, E. (1997) Scenarios as springboards in CSCW design. In Bowker, G.C., Star, S.L., Turner, W. and Gasser, L. (eds), *Social Science, Technical Systems and Cooperative Work: Beyond the Great Divide*. Lawrence Erlbaum Associates, Mahwah, NJ, pp. 217–234.

Bødker, S., Ehn, P., Kammersgaard, J., Kyng, M. and Sundblad, Y. (1987) A UTOPIAN experience: on design of powerful computer-based tools for skilled graphical workers. In Bjerknes, G., Ehn, P. and Kyng, M. (eds), *Computers and Democracy – A Scandinavian Challenge*. Avebury, Aldershot, pp. 251–278.

Bødker, S., Gronbaek, K. and Kyng, M. (1993) Cooperative design: techniques and experiences from the Scandinavian scene. In Schuler, D. and Namioka, A. (eds), *Participatory Design: Principles and Practices*. Lawrence Erlbaum Associates, Hillsdale, NJ, pp. 157–175.

Bowers, J., Button, G. and Sharrock, W. (1995) Workflow from within and without: technology and cooperative work on the print industry shopfloor. *Proceedings of ECSCW '95 Conference*, Stockholm, Sweden, 11–15 Sept. Kluwer, Dordrecht, pp. 51–66.

Bowers, J., Pycock, J. and O'Brien, J. (1996) Talk and embodiment in collaborative virtual environments. *Proceedings of CHI '96 Conference*, Vancouver, 13–18 April. ACM Press, New York, pp. 58–65.

Bradner, E. and Mark, G. (2002) Why distance matters: effects on cooperation, persuasion and deception. *Proceedings of CSCW '02 Conference*, New Orleans, LA, 16–20 Nov. ACM Press, New York, pp. 226–235.

Bransford, J.R., Barclay, J.R. and Franks, J.J. (1972) Sentence memory: a constructive versus interpretative approach. *Cognitive Psychology*, 3, 193–209.

Brems, D.J. and Whitten, W.B. (1987) Learning and preference for icon-based interface. *Proceedings of the Human Factors Society 31st Annual Meeting*, pp. 125–129.

Brewster, S. (1998) Using non-speech sounds to provide navigation cues. *ACM Transactions on Computer–Human Interaction (TOCHI)*, 5(3), 224–259.

Brewster, S. (2003) Non-speech auditory output. In Jacko, J.A. and Sears, A. (eds), *The Human–Computer Interaction Handbook*. Lawrence Erlbaum Associates, Mahwah, NJ.

Brewster, S.A., Wright, P.C. and Edwards, A.D.N. (1993) An evaluation of earcons for use in auditory human–computer interfaces. *Proceedings of INTERCHI '93*. ACM Press, New York, pp. 222–227.

Brinck, T., Gergle, D. and Wood, S.D. (2002) *Designing Web Sites that Work: Usability for the Web*. Morgan Kaufmann, San Francisco.

Broadbent, D.E. (1958) *Perception and Communication*. Pergamon, Oxford.

Brown, D.S. (1996) The challenges of user-based design in a medical equipment market. In Wixon, D. and Ramey, J. (eds), *Field Methods Casebook for Software Design*. Wiley, New York, pp. 157–176.

Brown, R. and McNeill, D. (1966) The 'tip-of-the-tongue' phenomenon. *Journal of Verbal Learning and Verbal Behaviour*, 5, 325–327.

Browne, D.P., Totterdell, P.A. and Norman, M.A. (1990) *Adaptive User Interfaces*. Academic Press, London.

Browne, G.J. and Rogich, M.B. (2001) An empirical investigation of user requirements elicitation: comparing the effectiveness of prompting techniques. *Journal of Management Information Systems*, 17(4), 223–249.

Bruner, J. and Postman, L. (1949) On the perception of incongruity: a paradigm. *Journal of Personality*, 18, 206–223.

Brusilovsky, P. (2001) Adaptive hypermedia. *User Modeling and User Adapted Interaction*, 11(1–2), 87–110.

Bucciarelli, L.L. (1994) *Designing Engineers*. MIT Press, Cambridge, MA.

Buckingham Shum, S., MacLean, A., Bellotti, V. and Hammond, N. (1997) Graphical argumentation and design cognition. *Human–Computer Interaction*, 12, 267–300.

Burke, K., Aytes, K., Chidambaram, L. and Johnson, J. (1999) A study of partially distributed work groups: the impact of media, location and time on perceptions and performance. *Small Group Research*, 30(4), 452–490.

Button, G. (ed.) (1993) *Technology in Working Order*. Routledge & Kegan Paul, London.

Buxton, W. and Moran, T. (1990) EuroPARC's integrated interactive intermedia facility (IIIF): early experiences. *Proceedings of the IFIP WG8.4 Conference on Multi-user Interfaces and Applications*. Elsevier, pp. 11–34.

Card, S. (2003) Information visualization. In Jacko, J.A. and Sears, A. (eds), *The Human–Computer Interaction Handbook*. Lawrence Erlbaum Associates, Mahwah, NJ.

Card, S.K., Moran, T.P. and Newell, A. (1983) The *Psychology of Human–Computer Interaction*. Lawrence Erlbaum Associates, Hillsdale, NJ.

Card, S.K., Robertson, G.G. and York, W. (1996) The WebBook and the Web Forager: an information workspace for the World-Wide Web. *Proceedings of CHI '96 Conference*, Vancouver, 13–18 April. ACM Press, New York, pp. 111–117.

Card, S., Mackinlay, S. and Shneiderman, B. (1999) *Information Visualization: Using Vision to Think*. Morgan Kaufmann, San Francisco.

Carlsson, C. and Hagsand, O. (1993) DIVE: a platform for multi-user virtual environments. *Computers and Graphics*, **17**(6), 663–669.

Carroll, J.M. (1990) *The Nurnberg Funnel: Designing Minimalist Instructions for Practical Computer Skill*. MIT Press, Cambridge, MA.

Carroll, J.M. (1994) Making use: a design representation. *Communications of the ACM*, **37**(12), pp. 29–35.

Carroll, J.M. (ed.) (1995) *Scenario-based Design*. Wiley, New York.

Carroll, J.M. (2000) *Making Use: Scenario-based Design of Human–Computer Interactions*. MIT Press, Cambridge, MA.

Carroll, J.M. (ed.) (2003) *HCI Models, Theories and Frameworks*. Morgan Kaufmann, San Francisco.

Cassell, J. (2000) Embodied conversational interface agents. *Communications of the ACM*, **43**(4), 70–78.

Chalmers, M. (2003) Informatics, architecture and language. In Höök, K., Benyon, D.R. and Munro, A. (eds), *Designing Information Spaces: The Social Navigation Approach*. Springer-Verlag, London, pp. 315–342.

Chao, D. (2001) Doom as an interface for process management. *Proceedings of CHI '01 Conference*, Seattle, WA, 31 March–5 April. ACM Press, New York, pp. 152–158.

Checkland, P. (1981) *Systems Thinking, Systems Practice*. Wiley, Chichester.

Checkland, P. and Scholes, J. (1999) *Soft Systems Methodology in Action* (paperback edn). Wiley, Chichester.

Cherry, E.C. (1953) Some experiments on the experiments on the recognition of speech with one and two ears. *Journal of the Acoustical Society of America*, **26**, 554–559.

Chidambaram, L. and Jones, B. (1993) Impact of communication medium and computer support on group perceptions and performance: a comparison of face-to-face and dispersed meetings. *MIS Quarterly*, **17**(4), 465–488.

Christiansen, E. (1996) Tamed by a rose. In Nardi, B.A. (ed.), *Context and Consciousness: Activity Theory and Human–Computer Interaction*. MIT Press, Cambridge, MA, pp. 175–198.

Churchill, E.F., Snowdon, D. and Munro, A. (2001) *Collaborative Virtual Environments: Digital Places and Spaces for Interaction*. Springer-Verlag, London.

Clarke, A.C. (1968) *2001: A Space Odyssey*. New American Library, New York.

Cleary, T. (1999) Communicating customer information at Cabletron Systems, Inc. *Interactions*, **6**(1), 44–49.

Coble, J.M., Maffitt, J.S., Orland, M.J. and Kahn, M.G. (1996) Using contextual inquiry to discover physicians' true needs. In Wixon, D. and Ramey, J. (eds), *Field Methods Casebook for Software Design*. Wiley, New York, pp. 229–248.

Cockton, G. and Woolrych, A. (2002) Sale must end: should discount methods be cleared off HCI's shelves? *Interactions*, **9**(5), 13–18.

Cohen, N.J. and Squire, L.R. (1980) Preserved learning and retention of pattern-analysing skills in amnesia: dissociation of knowing how from knowing that. *Science*, **210**, 207–210.

Cole, M. (1996) *Cultural Psychology*. Harvard University Press, Cambridge, MA.

Connell, J.B., Mendelsohn, G.A., Robins, R.W. and Canny, J. (2001) Effects of communication medium on interpersonal perceptions. *Proceedings of Group '01 Conference*, Boulder, CO, 30 Sept.–3 Oct. ACM Press, New York, pp. 117–124.

Constantine, L.L. and Lockwood, L.A.D. (2001) Structure and style in use cases for user interface design. In van Harmelen, M. (ed.), *Object Modeling and User Interface Design: Designing Interactive Systems*. Addison-Wesley, Boston, MA.

Cooper, A. (1999) *The Inmates are Running the Asylum*. SAMS, Macmillan Computer Publishing, Indianapolis, IN.

Cowan, N. (2002) The magical number four in short-term memory: a reconsideration of mental storage capacity. *Behavioural and Brain Sciences*, **24**(1), 87–114.

Craik, F.I.M. and Lockhart, R. (1972) Levels of processing. *Journal of Verbal Learning and Verbal Behaviour*, **12**, 599–607.

Crampton Smith, G. and Tabor, P. (1996) The role of the artist designer. In Winograd, T. (ed.), *Bringing Design to Software*. ACM Press, New York.

Cullen, G. (1961) (reprinted 2000) *The Concise Townscape*. Architectural Press, Oxford.

Denley, I. and Long, J. (2001) Multidisciplinary practice in requirements engineering: problems and criteria for support. In Blandford, A., Vanderdonckt, J. and Gray, P. (eds), *People and Computers XV – Proceedings of HCI-IHM 2001*, Springer-Verlag, London, pp. 125–134.

Dennett, D. (1989) *The Intentional Stance*. MIT Press, Cambridge, MA.

DeSanctis, G. and Gallupe, B. (1987) A foundation for the study of group decision support systems. *Management Science*, **33**(5), 589–609.

Desmet, P. and Dijkhuis, E. (2003) A wheelchair can be fun: a case of emotion-driven design. *Proceedings of DPPI '03 Conference*, Pittsburgh, PA, 23–26 June. ACM Press, New York, pp. 22–27.

Deutsch, J.A. and Deutsch, D. (1963) Attention: some theoretical considerations. *Psychological Review*, **70**, 80–90.

Dew, P., Galata, A., Maxfield, J. and Romano, D. (2002) Virtual artefacts to support negotiation within an augmented collaborative environment for alternate dispute resolution. *Proceedings of CVE '02 Conference*, Bonn, Germany, 30 Sept.–2 Oct. ACM Press, New York, pp. 10–16.

Diaper, D. (2004) Understanding task analysis for human–computer interaction. In Diaper, D. and Stanton, N. (eds), *The Handbook of Task Analysis for Human–Computer Interaction*. Lawrence Erlbaum Associates, Mahwah, NJ.

Diaper, D. and Stanton, N. (eds) (2004a) *The Handbook of Task Analysis for Human–Computer Interaction*. Lawrence Erlbaum Associates, Mahwah, NJ.

Diaper, D. and Stanton, N. (2004b) Wishing on a star: the future of task analysis. In Diaper, D. and Stanton, N. (eds), *The Handbook of Task Analysis for Human–Computer Interaction*. Lawrence Erlbaum Associates, Mahwah, NJ.

Dick, P.K. (1968) *Do Androids Dream of Electric Sheep?* Doubleday, New York.

Dietrich, H., Malinowski, U., Kühme, T. and Schneider-Hufschmidt, M. (1993) State of the art in adaptive user interfaces. In Schneider-Hufschmidt, M., Kühme, T. and Malinowski, U. (eds), *Adaptive User Interfaces*. North-Holland, Amsterdam.

Dix, A. (2003) Network-based interaction. In Jacko, J.A. and Sears, A. (eds), *The Human–Computer Interaction Handbook*. Lawrence Erlbaum Associates, Mahwah, NJ.

Doubleday, A., Ryan, M., Springett, M. and Sutcliffe, A. (1997) A comparison of usability techniques for evaluating design. *Proceedings of DIS '97 Conference*, Amsterdam, Netherlands. ACM Press, New York, pp. 101–110.

Dourish, P. (2001) *Where the Action Is: The Foundations of Embodied Interaction*. MIT Press, Cambridge, MA.

Dourish, P. and Bellotti, V. (1992) Awareness and coordination in shared workspaces. *Proceedings of CSCW '92 Conference*, Toronto, 1–4 Nov. ACM Press, New York, pp. 107–114.

Dourish, P. and Bly, S. (1992) Portholes: supporting awareness in a distributed work group. *Proceedings of CHI '92 Conference*, Monterey, CA, 3–7 May. ACM Press, New York, pp. 541–547.

Dowell, J. and Long, J. (1998) A conception of human–computer interaction. *Ergonomics*, **41**(2), 174–178.

Downs, R. and Stea, D. (1973) Cognitive representations. In Downs, R. and Stea, D. (eds), *Image and Environment*. Aldine, Chicago, pp. 79–86.

Dye, K. (2001) As easy to use as a banking machine. In Blandford, A., Vanderdonckt, J. and Gray, P. (eds), *People and Computers XV – Proceedings of HCI-IHM 2001*, Springer-Verlag, London, pp. 3–16.

Eason, K.D. (1988) *Information Technology and Organisational Change*. Taylor & Francis, London.

Eason, K.D. and Olphert, W. (1996) Early evaluation of the organisational implications of CSCW systems. In Thomas, P. (ed.), *CSCW Requirements and Evaluation*. Springer-Verlag, London, pp. 75–89.

Eason, K.D., Harker, S.D. and Olphert, C.W. (1996) Representing socio-technical systems options in the development of new forms of work organization. *European Journal of Work and Organizational Psychology*, **5**(3), 399–420.

Economou, D., Mitchell, L.W., Pettifer, R.S. and West, J.A. (2000) CVE technology development based on real world application and user needs. *Proceedings of WET ICE '00 Conference*, Gaithersburg, MD, 14–16 June. IEEE Computer Society Press, pp. 12–20.

Edwards, A.D.N. (1989) Soundtrack: an auditory interface for blind users. *Human–Computer Interaction*, **4**(1), 45–66.

e-gadgets (2003) www.extrovert-gadgets.net, accessed 7 November 2003.

Eggen, B., Hollemans, G. and van de Sluis, R. (2003) Exploring and enhancing the home experience. *Cognition Technology and Work*, **5**(1), 44–54.

Ehn, P. and Kyng, M. (eds) (1987) *Computers and Democracy – a Scandinavian Challenge*. Avebury, Aldershot, pp. 251–278.

Ekman, P. and Friesen, W.V. (1978) *The Facial Action Coding System*. Consulting Psychologists' Press, Palo Alto, CA.

Ekman, P., Friesen, W.V. and Ellsworth, P. (1972) *Emotion in the Human Face*. Pergamon, New York.

Elrod, S., Bruce, R., Gold, R., Goldberg, D., Halasz, F., Janssen, W., Lee, D., McCall, K., Pederson, E., Pier, K., Tang, J. and Welch, B. (1992) Liveboard: a large interactive display supporting group meetings, presentations and remote collaboration. *Proceedings of CHI '92 Conference*, Monterey, CA, 3–7 May. ACM Press, New York, pp. 599–607.

Engeström, Y. (1987) *Learning by Expanding: an Activity-Theoretical Approach to Developmental Research*. Orienta-Konsultit, Helsinki.

Engeström, Y. (1995) Objects, contradictions and collaboration in medical cognition: an activity-theoretical perspective. *Artificial Intelligence in Medicine*, **7**, 395–412.

Engeström, Y. (1999) Activity theory and individual and social transformation. In Engeström, Y., Miettinen, R. and Punamaki, R.-L. (eds), *Perspectives on Activity Theory*. Cambridge University Press, Cambridge, pp. 19–38.

Engeström, Y., Miettinen, R. and Punamaki, R.-L. (1999) *Perspectives on Activity Theory*. Cambridge University Press, Cambridge.

Erickson, T. (2003) http://www.pliant.org/personal/Tom_Erickson/InteractionPatterns.html, accessed 5 January 2004.

Erickson, T. and Kellogg, W.A. (2003) Social translucence: using minimalist visualisations of social activity to support collective interaction. In Höök, K., Benyon, D.R. and Munro, A. (eds), *Designing Information Spaces: The Social Navigation Approach*. Springer-Verlag, London, pp. 17–42.

Ericsson, K.A. and Simon, H.A. (1985) *Protocol Analysis: Verbal Reports as Data*. MIT Press, Cambridge, MA.

Ericsson, K.A. and Smith, J. (eds) (1991) *Towards a General Theory of Expertise*. Cambridge University Press, Cambridge.

Fauconnier, G. and Turner, M. (2002) *The Way We Think: Conceptual Blending and the Mind's Hidden Complexities*. Basic Books, New York.

Finn, K.E., Sellen, A.J. and Wilbur, S.B. (eds) (1997) *Video-mediated Communication*. Lawrence Erlbaum Associates, Mahwah, NJ.

Fischer, G. (1989) Human–computer interaction software: lessons learned, challenges ahead. *IEEE Software*, 6(1), 44–52.

Fischer, G. (2001) User modelling in human–computer interaction. *User Modeling and User Adapted Interaction*, 11(1–2), 65–86.

Fischer, G., Lemke, A.C., McCall, R. and Morch, A.I. (1991) Making argumentations serve design. *Human–Computer Interaction*, 6, 393–419.

Fitzmaurice, G.W., Ishii, H. and Buxton, W.A.S. (1995) Bricks: laying the foundations for graspable user interfaces. *Proceedings of CHI '95 Conference*, Denver, CO, 7–11 May. ACM Press, New York, pp. 442–449.

Fjermestad, J. and Hiltz, S.R. (2000) Case and field studies of group support systems: an empirical asssessment. *Proceedings of HICSS '00 Conference*, Maui, Hawaii, 4–7 January. IEEE Computer Society Press.

Flach, J. (1995) The ecology of human–machine systems: a personal history. In Flach, J., Hancock, P., Caird, J. and Vicente, K. (eds), *Global Perspectives on the Ecology of Human–Machine Systems*. Lawrence Erlbaum Associates, Hillsdale, NJ, pp. 1–13.

Forsythe, D.E. (1999) It's just a matter of common sense: ethnography as invisible work. *Computer Supported Cooperative Work (CSCW)*, 8(1/2), 127–145.

Galegher, J. and Kraut, R.E. (1994) Computer-mediated communication for intellectual teamwork: an experiment in group writing. *Information Systems Research*, 5(2), 110–136.

Ganoe, C. (2002) Supporting the collaborative meeting place. *CHI '02 Conference Extended Abstracts*, Minneapolis, MN, 20–25 April. ACM Press, New York, pp. 546–547.

Gärling, T., Böök, A. and Ergesen, N. (1982) Memory for the spatial layout of the everyday physical environment: different rates of acquisition of different types of information. *Scandinavian Journal of Psychology*, 23, 23–35.

Garrett, J.J. (2003) *The Elements of User Experience*. New Riders, Indianapolis, IN.

Gaver, W., Dunne, T. and Pacenti, E. (1999) Cultural probes. *Interactions*, 6(1), 21–29.

Geen, R. (1991) Social motivation. *Annual Review of Psychology*, 42, 377–399.

Gibson, J.J. (1950) *The Perception of the Visual World*. Houghton Mifflin, Boston, MA.

Gibson, J.J. (1966) *The Senses Considered as Perceptual Systems*. Houghton Mifflin, Boston, MA.

Gibson, J.J. (1977) The theory of affordances. In Shaw, R. and Bransford, J. (eds), *Perceiving, Acting and Knowing*. Wiley, New York, pp. 67–82.

Gibson, J.J. (1979) *The Ecological Approach to Human Perception*. Houghton Mifflin, Boston, MA.

Gibson, J.J. (1986) *The Ecological Approach to Visual Perception*. Lawrence Erlbaum Associates, Hillsdale, NJ.

Gilkey, R.H. and Anderson, T.R. (eds) (1997) *Binaural and Spatial Hearing in Real and Virtual Environments*. Lawrence Erlbaum Associates, Mahwah, NJ.

Goguen, J.A. (1997) Toward a social, ethical theory of information. In Bowker, G.C., Star, S.L., Turner, W. and Gasser, L. (eds), *Social Science, Technical Systems and Cooperative Work: Beyond the Great Divide*. Lawrence Erlbaum Associates, Mahwah, NJ, pp. 27–56.

Gosling, D. (1996) *Gordon Cullen: Visions of Urban Design*. Academy Editions, London.

Gould, J.D., Boies, S.J., Levy, S., Richards, J.T. and Schoonard, J. (1987) The 1984 Olympic Message System: a test of behavioral principles of system design. *Communications of the ACM*, 30(9), 758–769.

Graetz, K.A., Boyle, E.S., Kimble, C.E., Thompson, P. and Garloch, J.E. (1998) Information sharing in face-to-face, teleconferencing and electronic groups. *Small Group Research*, 29(6), 714–743.

Graham, I. (2003) *A Pattern Language for Web Usability*. Addison-Wesley, Harlow.

Grayson, D. and Coventry, L. (1998) The effects of visual proxemic information in video mediated communication. *ACM SIGCHI Bulletin*, 30(3), 30–39.

Grayson, D.M. and Monk, A.M. (2003) Are you looking at me? Eye contact and desktop video conferencing. *ACM Transactions on Computer–Human Interaction (TOCHI)*, 10(3), 221–243.

Green, T.R.G. and Benyon, D.R. (1996) The skull beneath the skin: entity–relationship modelling of information artefacts. *International Journal of Human–Computer Studies*, 44(6), 801–828.

Greenbaum, J. and Kyng, M. (eds) (1991) *Design at Work: Cooperative Design of Computer Systems*. Lawrence Erlbaum Associates, Hillsdale, NJ.

Greenhalgh, C. and Benford, S. (1995) MASSIVE: a virtual reality system for teleconferencing. *ACM Transactions on Computer–Human Interaction (TOCHI)*, **2**(3), 239–261.

Gregory, R.L. (1973) *Eye and Brain* (2nd edn). World Universities Library, New York.

Gross, M.D., Do, E.Y.L., McCall, R.J., Citrin, W.V., Hamill, P., Warmack, A. and Kuczun, K.S. (1998) Collaboration and coordination in architectural design: approaches to computer-mediated teamwork. *Automation in Construction*, **7**(6), 465–473.

Gross, R. (2001) *Psychology: the Science of Mind and Behaviour*. Hodder Arnold, London.

Grudin, J. (1988) Why CSCW applications fail: problems in the design and evaluation of organization interfaces. *Proceedings of CSCW '88 Conference*, Portland, OR, 26–28 Sept. ACM Press, New York, pp. 85–93.

Grudin, J. (1994) Groupware and social dynamics: eight challenges for developers. *Communications of the ACM*, **37**, 93–105.

Grudin, J. and Palen, L. (1995) Why groupware succeeds: discretion or mandate? *Proceedings of ECSCW '95 Conference*, Stockholm, Sweden, 11–15 Sept. Kluwer, Dordrecht, pp. 263–278.

Grudin, J. and Poltrock, S.E. (1997) Computer-supported cooperative work and groupware. In Zelkowitz, M.V. (ed.), *Advances in Computing*. Academic Press, New York, pp. 269–320.

Gutwin, C. and Greenberg, S. (1998) Design for individuals, design for groups: tradeoffs between power and workspace awareness. *Proceedings of CSCW '98 Conference*, Seattle, WA, 14–18 Nov. ACM Press, New York, pp. 207–216.

Gutwin, C. and Greenberg, S. (1999) The effects of workspace awareness support on the usability of real-time distributed groupware. *ACM Transactions on Computer–Human Interaction (TOCHI)*, **6**(3), 243–281.

Gutwin, C., Roseman, M. and Greenberg, S. (1996) A usability study of awareness widgets in a shared workspace groupware system. *Proceedings of CSCW '96 Conference*, Boston, MA, 16–20 Nov. ACM Press, New York, pp. 258–267.

Haney, C., Banks, W.C. and Zimbardo, P.G. (1973) Interpersonal dynamics in a simulated prison. *International Journal of Penology and Criminology*, **1**, 69–97.

Harkins, S. and Szymanski, K. (1987) Social loafing and social facilitation: new wine in old bottles. In Hendrick, C. (ed.), *Review of Personality and Social Psychology: Group Processes and Intergroup Relations*, vol. 9. Sage, London, pp. 167–188.

Harper, R.H.R. (1992) Looking at ourselves: an examination of the social organisation of two research laboratories. *Proceedings of CSCW '92 Conference*, Toronto, 1–4 Nov. ACM Press, New York, pp. 330–337.

Hartson, H.R. and Castillo, J.C. (1998) Remote evaluation for post-deployment usability improvement. *Proceedings of the Working Conference of Advanced Visual Interfaces (AVI '98)*, pp. 22–29.

Hasan, H., Gould, E. and Hyland, P. (eds) (1998) *Information Systems and Activity Theory: Tools in Context*. University of Wollongong Press, Wollongong, New South Wales.

Heath, C. and Luff, P. (2000) *Technology in Action*. Cambridge University Press, Cambridge.

Hebb, D.O. (1949) *The Organisation of Behaviour*. Wiley, New York.

Heeren, E. and Lewis, R. (1997) Selecting communication media for distributed communities. *Journal of Computer Assisted Learning*, **13**, 85–98.

Helander, M.G., Landauer, T.K. and Prabhu, P.V. (1997) *Handbook of Human–Computer Interaction* (2nd edn). Elsevier, Amsterdam.

Hepsø, V. (1997) CSCW – Design and implementation compromises: an example from the implementation of experience transfer in Statoil. *ACM SIGGROUP Bulletin*, **18**(3), 56–60.

Hill, J. and Gutwin, C. (2003) Awareness support in a groupware widget toolkit. *Proceedings of Group '03 Conference*, Sanibel Island, FL, 9–12 Dec. ACM Press, New York, pp. 258–267.

Hillier, B. (1996) *Space is the Machine*. Cambridge University Press, Cambridge.

Hindmarsh, J., Frazer, M., Heath, C., Benford, S. and Greenhalgh, C. (1998) Fragmented interaction: establishing mutual orientation in virtual environments. *Proceedings of CSCW '98 Conference*, Seattle, WA, 14–18 Nov. ACM Press, New York, pp. 217–226.

Hix, D. and Hartson, H.R. (1993) *Developing User Interfaces: Ensuring Usability through Product and Process*. Wiley, New York.

Hofstede, G. (1994) *Cultures and Organisations*. Harper-Collins, London.

Hollan, J., Hutchins, E. and Kirsh, D. (2000) Distributed cognition: toward a new foundation for human–computer interaction research. *ACM Transactions on Computer–Human Interaction (TOCHI)*, **7**(2), 174–196.

Holland, D., Lachicotte Jr, W.S., Skinner, D. and Cain, C. (2001) *Identity and Agency in Cultural Worlds*. Harvard University Press, Cambridge, MA.

Hollnagel, E. (1997) Building joint cognitive systems: a case of horses for courses? In *Design of Computing Systems: Social and Ergonomic Considerations, Proceedings of HCI '97 International Conference*, San Francisco, 24–29 August. Elsevier, vol. 2, pp. 39–42.

Hollnagel, E. (2003) Is affective computing an oxymoron? *International Journal of Human–Computer Studies*, **59**(1–2), 65–70.

Höök, K. (2000) Seven steps to take before intelligent user interfaces become real. *Interacting with Computers*, **12**(4), 409–426.

Höök, K., Benyon, D.R. and Munro, A. (2003) *Designing Information Spaces: The Social Navigation Approach*. Springer-Verlag, London.

Hoschka, P. (1998) CSCW research at GMD-FIT: from basic groupware to the social Web. *ACM SIGGROUP Bulletin*, **19**(2), 5–9.

Hudlicka, E. (2003) To feel or not to feel: the role of affect in human–computer interaction. *International Journal of Human–Computer Studies*, **59**, 1–32.

Hudson, W. (2001) Toward unified models in user-centred and object-oriented design. In van Harmelen, M. (ed.), *Object Modeling and User Interface Design: Designing Interactive Systems*. Addison-Wesley, Boston, MA.

Hughes, J., King, V., Rodden, T. and Andersen, H. (1994) Moving out from the control room: ethnography in system design. *Proceedings of CSCW '94 Conference*, Chapel Hill, NC, 22–26 Oct. ACM Press, New York, pp. 429–439.

Hull, A., Wilkins, A.J. and Baddeley, A. (1988) Cognitive psychology and the wiring of plugs. In Gruneberg, M.M., Morris, P.E. and Sykes, R.N. (eds), *Practical Aspects of Memory: Current Research and Issues*, vol. 1: *Memory in Everyday Life*. Wiley, Chichester, pp. 514–518.

Hutchins, E. (1995) *Cognition in the Wild*. MIT Press, Cambridge, MA.

Ichikawa, Y., Okada, K., Jeong, G., Tanaka, S. and Matushita, Y. (1995) MAJIC videoconferencing system: experiments, evaluation and improvement. *Proceedings of ECSCW '95 Conference*, Stockholm, Sweden, 11–15 Sept. Kluwer, Dordrecht, pp. 279–293.

IDEO (2003) http://www.IDEO.com/identity/introduction.htm, accessed 7 November 2003.

Insko, B.E. (2001) *Passive haptics significantly enhance virtual environments*. Doctoral Dissertation, University of North Carolina at Chapel Hill, NC.

Insko, B.E. (2003) Measuring presence: subjective, behavioral and physiological methods. In Riva, G., Davide, F. and IJsselsteijn, W.A. (eds), *Being There: Concepts, Effects and Measurement of User Presence in Synthetic Environments*. Ios Press, Amsterdam.

Ishii, H. and Ohkubo, M. (1990) Design of TeamWorkStation: a realtime shared workspace fusing desktops and computer screens. In Gibbs, S. and Verrijn-Stuart, A.A. (eds), *Multi-User Interfaces and Applications*. Elsevier North-Holland, Amsterdam.

Ishii, H. and Ullmer, B. (1997) Tangible bits: towards seamless interfaces between people, bits and atoms. *Proceedings of CHI '97 Conference*, Atlanta, GA, 22–27 March. ACM Press, New York, pp. 234–241.

Ishii, H., Kobayashi, M. and Grudin, J. (1992) Integration of inter-personal space and shared workspace: ClearBoard design and experiments. *Proceedings of CSCW '92 Conference*, Toronto, 1–4 Nov. ACM Press, New York, pp. 33–42.

Ishii, H., Kobayashi, M. and Grudin, J. (1993) Integration of inter-personal space and shared workspace: ClearBoard design and experiments. *ACM Transactions on Information Systems (TOIS)*, **11**(4), 349–375.

Jacobson, R. (ed.) (2000) *Information Design*. MIT Press, Cambridge, MA.

Jameson, A. (2003) Adaptive interfaces and agents. In Jacko, J.A. and Sears, A. (eds), *The Human–Computer Interaction Handbook*. Lawrence Erlbaum Associates, Mahwah, NJ.

John, B. (2003) Information processing and skilled behaviour. In Carroll, J.M. (ed.), *HCI Models, Theories and Frameworks*. Morgan Kaufmann, San Francisco.

Johnson, B. and Greenberg, S. (1999) Judging people's availability for interaction from video snapshots. *Proceedings of the IEEE Hawaii International Conference on System Sciences, HICSS '99*.

Johnson-Laird, P. (1983) *Mental Models*. Harvard University Press, Cambridge, MA.

Jordan, P.W. (2000) *Designing Pleasurable Products*. Taylor & Francis, London.

Kahneman, D. (1973) *Attention and Effort*. Prentice-Hall, Englewood Cliffs, NJ.

Kalawsky, R.S. (1999) VRUSE – a computerised diagnostic tool: for usability evaluation of virtual/synthetic environment systems. *Applied Ergonomics*, **30**, 11–25.

Kameas, A., Bellis, S., Mavrommati, I, Delaney, K., Colley, M. and Pounds-Cornish, A. (2003) An architecture that treats everyday objects as communicating tangible components. In *Proceedings of the First IEEE International Conference on Pervasive Computing and Communications (PerCom '03)*.

Kaplan, S.M., Carroll, A.M. and MacGregor, K.J. (1991) Supporting collaborative process with conversation builder. *ACM SIGOIS Bulletin*, **12**(2–3), 69–79.

Kapor, M. (1996) A manifesto for software design. In Winograd, T. (ed.), *Bringing Design to Software*. ACM Press, New York, pp. 1–10.

Kaptelinin, V., Nardi, B.A. and Macaulay, C. (1999) The Activity Checklist: a tool for representing the 'space' of context. *Interactions*, **6**(4), 27–39.

Karsten, H. (1999) Collaboration and collaborative information technologies: a review of the evidence. *ACM SIGMIS Database*, **30**(2), 44–65.

Kay, A. (1990) User interface: a personal view. In Laurel, B. (ed.), *The Art of Human–Computer Interface Design*. Addison Wesley, Reading, MA.

Kay, J. (2001) Learner control. *User Modeling and User Adapted Interaction*, **11**(1–2), 111–127.

Kelley, D. and Hartfield, B. (1996) The designer's stance. In Winograd, T. (ed.), *Bringing Design to Software*. ACM Press, New York.

Kellogg, W. (1989) The dimensions of consistency. In Nielsen, J. (ed.), *Coordinating User Interfaces for Consistency*. Academic Press, San Diego, CA.

Kemp, J.A.M. and van Gelderen, T. (1996) Co-discovery exploring: an informal method for iteratively designing consumer products. In Jordan, P.W., Thomas, B., Weerdmeester, B.A. and McClelland, I.L. (eds), *Usability Evaluation in Industry*. Taylor & Francis, London, pp. 139–146.

Kieras, D. (2004) GOMS models for task analysis. In Diaper, D. and Stanton, N. (eds), *The Handbook of Task Analysis for Human–Computer Interaction*. Lawrence Erlbaum Associates, Mahwah, NJ.

Kieras, D.E. and Bovair, S. (1984) The role of a mental model in learning to operate a device. *Cognitive Science*, **8**, 255–273.

Kinney, S.T. and Dennis, A.R. (1994) Re-evaluating media richness: cues, feedback, and task. *Proceedings of the 27th Hawaii International Conference on Systems Sciences, HICSS '94*, vol. 4, pp. 21–30.

Kinney, S.T. and Watson, R.T. (1992) Dyadic communication: the effect of medium and task equivocality on task-related and interactional outcomes. *Proceedings of the 13th International Conference on Information Systems*, pp. 107–117.

Kobsa, A. and Wahlster, A. (1993) *User Models in Dialog Systems*. Springer-Verlag, Berlin.

Konstan, J.A. and Riedl, J. (2003) Collaborative filtering: supporting social navigation in large, crowded infospaces. In Höök, K., Benyon, D.R. and Munro, A. (eds), *Designing Information Spaces: The Social Navigation Approach*. Springer-Verlag, London, pp. 43–82.

Kuipers, B. (1982) The 'map in the head' metaphor. *Environment and Behaviour*, **14**, 202–220.

Kuniavsky, M. (2003) *Observing the User Experience – a Practitioner's Guide to User Research*. Morgan Kaufmann, San Francisco.

Kuutti, K. (1996) Activity theory as a potential framework for human–computer interaction research. In Nardi, B. (ed.), *Context and Consciousness: Activity Theory and Human–Computer Interaction*. MIT Press, Cambridge, MA, pp. 17–44.

Lai, K.-Y. and Malone, T.W. (1988) Object lens: a 'spreadsheet' for cooperative work. *Proceedings of CSCW '88 Conference*, Portland, OR, 26–28 Sept. ACM Press, New York, pp. 115–124.

Lakoff, G. and Johnson, M. (1981) *Metaphors We Live By*. Chicago University Press, Chicago, IL.

Lakoff, G. and Johnson, M. (1999) *Philosophy of the Flesh*. Basic Books, New York.

Lanier, J. (2001) Virtually there. *Scientific American*, April, 52–61.

Lapham, L.H. (1994) Introduction to the MIT Press edition. In McLuhan, M., *Understanding Media: The Extensions of Man* (new edn). MIT Press, Cambridge, MA.

Laurel, B. (ed.) (1990a) *The Art of Human–Computer Interface Design*. Addison-Wesley, Reading, MA.

Laurel, B. (1990b) Interface agents. In Laurel, B. (ed.), *The Art of Human–Computer Interface Design*. Addison Wesley, Reading, MA.

Lazarus, R.S. (1982) Thoughts on the relations between emotion and cognition. *American Psychologist*, **37**, 1019–1024.

LeCompte, D. (1999) Seven, plus or minus two, is too much to bear: three (or fewer) is the real magic number. *Proceedings of the Human Factors and Ergonomics Society 43rd Annual Meeting*, pp. 289–292.

Lenker, J.C. (2002) *Train of Thoughts: Designing the Effective Web Experience*. New Riders, Indianapolis, IN.

Lessiter, J., Freeman, J., Keogh, E. and Davidoff, J.D. (2001) A cross-media presence questionnaire: the ITC sense of presence inventory. *Presence: Teleoperators and Virtual Environments*, **10**(3), 282–297.

Lewis, C., Polson, P., Wharton, C. and Rieman, J. (1990) Testing a walkthrough methodology for theory-based design of walk-up-and-use interfaces. *Proceedings of CHI '90 Conference*, Seattle, WA, 1–5 April. ACM Press, New York, pp. 235–242.

Lewis, S., Mateas, M., Palmiter, S. and Lynch, G. (1996) Ethnographic data for product development: a collaborative process. *Interactions*, **6**(3), 52–69.

Licklider, J.C.R. (2003) http://memex.org/licklider.html, accessed 7 November 2003.

Lieberman, H. (1995) Letizia: an agent that assists Web browsing. *Proceedings of 14th International Joint Conference on Artificial Intelligence*, Montreal, August. Morgan Kaufmann, San Francisco, pp. 924–929.

Lieberman, H., Fry, C. and Weitzman, L. (2001) Exploring the Web with reconnaissance agents. *Communications of the ACM*, **44**(8), 69–75.

Lim, K.Y. and Long, J. (1994) *The MUSE Method for Usability Engineering*. Cambridge University Press, Cambridge.

Lisetti, C., Nasoz, F., LeRouge, C., Ozyer, O. and Alvarez, K. (2003) Developing multimodal intelligent affective interfaces for tele-home health care. *International Journal of Human–Computer Studies*, **59**, 245–255.

Loomis, J. and Lederman, S. (1986) Tactual perception. In Boff, K., Kaufman, L. and Thomas, J. (eds), *Handbook of Human Perception and Performance*. Wiley, New York, pp. 1–41.

Luff, P., Hindmarsh, J. and Heath, C. (2000) *Workplace Studies: Recovering Work Practice and Informing Systems Design*. Cambridge University Press, Cambridge.

Lundberg, J., Ibrahim, A., Jönsson, D., Lindquist, S. and Qvarfordt, P. (2002) 'The Snatcher Catcher' – an interactive refrigerator. *Proceedings of 2nd Nordic*

Conference on HCI, NordiCHI '02, Aarhus, October. ACM Press, New York, pp. 209–212. Available on-line at www.acm.org/dl

Lynch, K. (1961) *The Image of the City*. MIT Press, Cambridge, MA.

MacGregor, J.N. (1987) Short-term memory capacity: limitation or optimization? *Psychological Review*, **94**(1), 107–108.

MacLean, A., Young, R., Bellotti, V. and Moran, T. (1991) Questions, options and criteria: elements of design space analysis. *Human–Computer Interaction*, **6**, 201–251.

Macleod, E. (2002) *Accessibility of online galleries*. Unpublished MSc Dissertation, Napier University, Edinburgh.

Maes, P. (1994) Agents that reduce work and information overload. *Communications of the ACM*, **37**(7), 30–41.

Malone, T.W., Grant, K.R., Lai, K.-Y., Rao, R. and Rosenblitt, D. (1986) Semi-structured messages are surprisingly useful for computer-supported coordination. *Proceedings of CSCW '86 Conference*, Austin, TX, 3–5 Dec. ACM Press, New York, pp. 102–114.

Malone, T.W., Lai, K.-Y. and Fry, C. (1992) Experiments with Oval: a radically tailorable tool for cooperative work. *Proceedings of CSCW '92 Conference*, Toronto, 1–4 Nov. ACM Press, New York, pp. 289–297.

Mandler, G. (1980) Recognising: the judgement of previous occurrence. *Psychological Review*, **87**, 252–270.

Mann, S. (1998) Wearable computing as a means for personal empowerment. *Keynote address, First International Conference on Wearable Computing, WC-98*, Fairfax, VA, 12–13 May.

Marcus, A. (1992) *Graphic Design for Electronic Documents and User Interfaces*. ACM Press, New York.

Martin, D., Rodden, T., Rouncefield, R., Sommerville, I. and Viller, S. (2001) Finding patterns in the fieldwork. *Proceedings of ECSCW '01 Conference*, Bonn, Germany, 16–20 Sept. Priaz *et al.* (eds) Kluwer, Dordrecht, pp. 39–58.

Matarazzo, G. and Sellen, A. (2000) The value of video in work at a distance: addition or distraction. *Behaviour and Information Technology*, **19**(5), 339–348.

Mayhew, D. (1999) *The Usability Engineering Lifecycle: a Practitioner's Handbook for User Interface Design*. Morgan Kaufmann, San Francisco.

McAdams, S. and Bigand, E. (1993) *Thinking in Sound*. Oxford University Press, Oxford.

McCullough, M. (2002a) *Abstracting Craft: The Practiced Digital Hand*. MIT Press, Cambridge, MA.

McCullough, M. (2002b) Digital ground: fixity, flow and engagement with context. Archis, no. 5 (special 'flow issue', Oct/Nov); also on Doors of Perception website, www.doorsofperception.com.

McKinlay, A., Proctor, R. and Dunnett, A. (1999) An investigation of social loafing and social compensation in computer-supported cooperative work. *Proceedings of Group '99 Conference*, Phoenix, AZ, 14–17 Nov. ACM Press, New York, pp. 249–257.

McLuhan, M. (1964) *Understanding Media*. McGraw-Hill, New York. Reprinted 1994, MIT Press, Cambridge, MA.

McNeese, M.D. (2003) New visions of human–computer interaction: making affect compute. *International Journal of Human–Computer Studies*, **59**, 33–53.

Meehan, M. (2001) *Physiological reaction as an objective measure of presence in virtual environments*. Doctoral Dissertation, University of North Carolina at Chapel Hill, NC.

Megaw, E.D. and Richardson, J. (1979) Target uncertainty and visual scanning strategies. *Human Factors*, **21**, 303–316.

Miller, G.A. (1956) The magical number seven, plus or minus two: some limits on our capacity for processing information. *Psychological Review*, **63**, 81–97.

Miller, S. (1984) *Experimental Design and Statistics* (2nd edn), Routledge, London.

Millersville University (1999) *VRML Conetree Generator*, http://zansiii.millersv.edu/work2/conetree/ (and other references, e.g. rw4.cs.uni-sb.de/.../seminar/ ss99/6/3-xerox/conetree.jpg).

Minneman, S.L. and Bly, S.A. (1991) Managing à trois: a study of a multi-user drawing tool in distributed design work. *Proceedings of CHI '91 Conference*, New Orleans, LA, 27 April–2 May. ACM Press, New York, pp. 217–224.

Mitchell, W. (1998) *City of Bits*. MIT Press, Cambridge, MA.

Monk, A. and Gilbert, N. (eds) (1995) *Perspectives on HCI – Diverse Approaches*. Academic Press, London.

Monk, A. and Howard, S. (1998) The rich picture: a tool for reasoning about work context. *Interactions*, **5**(2), 21–30.

Monk, A., Wright, P., Haber, J. and Davenport, L. (1993) *Improving Your Human–Computer Interface: a Practical Technique*. BCS Practitioner Series, Prentice-Hall, New York and Hemel Hempstead.

Moran, T.P. and Anderson, R.J. (1990) The workaday world as a paradigm for CSCW design. *Proceedings of CSCW '90 Conference*, Los Angeles, 7–10 Oct. ACM Press, New York, pp. 381–393.

Muller, M.J. (2001) Layered participatory analysis: new developments in the CARD technique. *Proceedings of CHI '01 Conference*, Seattle, WA, 31 March–5 April. ACM Press, New York, pp. 90–97.

Muller, M.J., Matheson, L., Page, C. and Gallup, R. (1998) Methods and tools: participatory heuristic evaluation. *Interactions*, **5**(5), 13–18.

Mullin, J., Smallwood, S., Watson, A. and Wilson, G. (2001) *New techniques for assessing audio and video quality in real-time interactive communications*. Tutorial, HCI 2001, available from http://www.cs.ucl.ac.uk/staff/g.wilson/papers.htm

Mumford, E. (1983) *Designing Human Systems*. Manchester Business School, Manchester.

Mumford, E. (1993) The participation of users in systems design: an account of the origin, evolution and use of the ETHICS method. In Schuler, D. and Namioka, A. (eds), *Participatory Design: Principles and Practices*. Lawrence Erlbaum Associates, Hillsdale, NJ, pp. 257–270.

Munkvold, B.E. and Anson, R. (2001) Organizational adoption and diffusion of electronic meeting systems: a case study. *Proceedings of Group '01 Conference*, Boulder, CO, 30 Sept.–3 Oct. ACM Press, New York, pp. 279–287.

Murrell, K.F.H. (1965) *Ergonomics – Man in his Working Environment*. Chapman & Hall, London.

Myst (2003) http://www.riven.com/home.html, accessed 7 November 2003.

Nardi, B. (ed.) (1996) *Context and Consciousness: Activity Theory and Human–Computer Interaction*. MIT Press, Cambridge, MA.

Nardi, B.A. and Miller, J.R. (1990) An Ethnographic Study of Distributed Problem Solving in Spreadsheet development. *Proceedings of CSCW '90 Conference*, Los Angeles, 7–10 Oct. ACM Press, New York, pp. 197–205.

Negroponte, N. (1995) *Being Digital*. Knopf, New York.

Newell, A. (1990) *Unified Theories of Cognition*. Harvard University Press, Cambridge, MA.

Newell, A. (1995) Extra-ordinary human–computer interaction. In Edwards, A.K. (ed.), *Extra-ordinary Human–Computer Interaction: Interfaces for Users with Disabilities*. Cambridge University Press, New York.

Newell, A. and Simon, H. (1972) *Human Problem Solving*. Prentice-Hall, Englewood Cliffs, NJ.

Newell, A., Rosenbloom, P.S. and Laird, J.E. (1989) Symbolic architectures for cognition. In Posner, M.I. (ed.), *Foundations of Cognitive Science*. Bradford Books/MIT Press, Cambridge, MA.

Newlands, A., Anderson, A.H. and Mullin, J. (1996) Dialog structure and cooperative task performance in two CSCW environments. In Connolly, J.H. and Pemberton, L. (eds), *Linguistic Concepts and Methods in CSCW*. Springer-Verlag, London, pp. 41–60.

Nielsen, J. (1993) *Usability Engineering*. Academic Press, New York.

Nielsen, J. (2000) *Designing Web Usability: The Practice of Simplicity*. New Riders, Indianapolis, IN.

Nielsen, J. and Mack, R.L. (eds) (1994) *Usability Inspection Methods*. Wiley, New York.

Norberg-Schulz, C. (1971) *Existence, Space, Architecture*. Studio Vista, London.

Norman, D. (1968) Towards a theory of memory and attention. *Psychological Review*, **75**, 522–536.

Norman, D. (1981a) The trouble with UNIX: the user interface is horrid. *Datamation*, **27**(12), 139–150.

Norman, D. (1981b) Categorisation of action slips. *Psychological Review*, **88**, 1–15.

Norman, D. (1986) Cognitive engineering. In Norman, D.A. and Draper, S. (eds), *User-centred System Design: New Perspectives on Human–Computer Interaction*. Lawrence Erlbaum Associates, Hillsdale, NJ, pp. 31–61.

Norman, D. (1988) *The Psychology of Everyday Things*. Basic Books, New York.

Norman, D. (1993) *Things That Make Us Smart*. Addison-Wesley, Reading, MA.

Norman, D. (1998) *The Design of Everyday Things*. Addison-Wesley, Reading, MA.

Norman, D. (1999) *The Invisible Computer: Why Good Products Can Fail*. MIT Press, Cambridge, MA.

Norman, D.A. (1983) Some observations on mental models. In Gentner, D. and Stevens, A.L. (eds), *Mental Models*. Lawrence Erlbaum Associates, Hillsdale, NJ, pp. 7–14.

Norman, D.A. and Draper, S. (eds) (1986) *User-centred System Design: New Perspectives on Human–Computer Interaction*. Lawrence Erlbaum Associates, Hillsdale, NJ.

Oakley, I., McGee, M.R., Brewster, S. and Gray, P. (2000) Putting the feel in 'look and feel'. *Proceedings of CHI '00 Conference*, The Hague, Netherlands, 1–6 April. ACM Press, New York, pp. 415–422.

Olson, G.M. and Olson, J.S. (2000) Distance matters. *Human–Computer Interaction*, **15**, 139–179.

Olson, J.S., Olson, G.M., Storrøsten, M. and Carter, M. (1992) How a group editor changes the character of a design meeting as well as its outcome. *Proceedings of CSCW '92 Conference*, Toronto, 1–4 Nov. ACM Press, New York, pp. 91–98.

Olson, J.S., Olson, G.M. and Meader, D.K. (1995) What mix of video and audio is useful for small groups doing remote real-time design work? *Proceedings of CHI '95 Conference*, Denver, CO, 7–11 May. ACM Press, New York, pp. 362–368.

Oppenheim, A.N. (2000) *Questionnaire Design, Interviewing and Attitude Measurement* (new edn). Continuum, London.

Orlikowski, W.J. (1992) Learning from notes: organizational issues in groupware implementation. *Proceedings of CSCW '92 Conference*, Toronto, 1–4 Nov. ACM Press, New York, pp. 362–369.

Orlikowski, W.J. and Gash, D.C. (1994) Technological frames: making sense of information technology in organisations. *ACM Transactions on Information Systems*, **12**(2), 174–207.

Orr, J. (1996) *Talking about Machines: An Ethnography of a Modern Job*. Cornell University Press, Ithaca, NY.

Page, S.R. (1996) User-centered design in a commercial software company. In Wixon, D. and Ramey, J. (eds), *Field Methods Casebook for Software Design*. Wiley, New York, pp. 197–213.

Paiva, P., Costa, M., Chaves, R., Piedade, M., Mourão, D., Sobrala, D., Höök, K., Andersson, G. and Bullock, A. (2003) SenToy: an affective sympathetic interface. *International Journal of Human–Computer Studies*, **59**, 227–235.

Palen, L. and Salzman, M. (2002) Beyond the handset: designing for wireless communications usability. *ACM Transactions on Computer–Human Interaction (TOCHI)*, **9**(2), 125–151.

Pangaro, G., Maynes-Aminzade, D. and Ishii, H. (2002) The Actuated Workbench: computer-controlled actuation in tabletop tangible interfaces. *Proc. of UIST '02*, Paris, 27–30 Oct. ACM Press, New York, pp. 181–190.

Parasuraman, R. (1986) Vigilance, monitoring, and search. In Boff, K.R., Kaufman, L. and Thomas, J.P. (eds), *Handbook of Human Performance*, vol. 2: *Cognitive Processes and Performance*. Wiley, Chichester.

Pashler, H.E. (1998) *The Psychology of Attention*. MIT Press, Cambridge, MA.

Passini, R. (1994) *Wayfinding in Architecture*. Van Nostrand, New York.

Patten, J., Ishii, H., Hines, J. and Pangaro, G. (2001) SenseTable: a wireless object tracking platform for tangible user interfaces. *Proceedings of CHI '01 Conference*, Seattle, WA, 31 March–5 April. ACM Press, New York, pp. 253–260.

Payne, S.J. (1991) A descriptive study of mental models. *Behaviour and Information Technology*, **10**, 3–21.

Payne, S.J. (1993) Memory for mental models of spatial descriptions: an episodic-construction-trace hypothesis. *Memory and Cognition*, **21**(5), 591–603.

Payne, S.J. (2003) Users' mental models: the very ideas. In Carroll, J.M. (ed.), *HCI Models, Theories and Frameworks*. Morgan Kaufmann, San Francisco.

Pender, T. (2003) *UML Bible*. John Wiley & Sons.

Persson, P., Espinoza, F., Fagerberg, P., Sandin, A. and Cöster, R. (2003) GeoNotes: a location-based information system for public spaces. In Höök, K., Benyon, D.R. and Munro, A. (eds), *Designing Information Spaces: The Social Navigation Approach*. Springer-Verlag, London, pp. 151–174.

Petersen, M., Madsen, K. and Kjaer, A. (2002) The usability of everyday technology – emerging and fading opportunities. *ACM Transactions on Computer–Human Interaction (TOCHI)*, **9**(2), 74–105.

Pew, R.W. (2003) Introduction: Evolution of human–computer interaction: from Memex to Bluetooth and beyond. In Jacko, J.A. and Sears, A. (eds), *The Human–Computer Interaction Handbook*. Lawrence Erlbaum Associates, Mahwah, NJ.

Picard, R.W. (1998) *Affective Computing*. MIT Press, Cambridge, MA.

Picard, R.W. (2003) Affective computing: challenges. *International Journal of Human–Computer Studies*, **59**(1–2), 55–64.

Picard, R.W. and Healey, J. (1997) Affective wearables. *Proceedings of First International Symposium on Wearable Computers, ISWC '97*, Cambridge, MA, 13–14 Oct. IEEE Computer Society Press, pp. 90–97.

Picard, R.W., Vyzas, E. and Healey, J. (2001) Toward machine emotional intelligence: analysis of affective physiological state. *IEEE Transactions on Pattern Analysis and Machine Intelligence*, **23**(10), 1175–1191.

Piper, B., Ratti, C. and Ishii, H. (2002) Illuminating Clay: a 3-D tangible interface for landscape analysis. *Proceedings of CHI '02 Conference*, Minneapolis, MN, 20–25 April. ACM Press, New York, pp. 355–362.

Pirhonen, A., Brewster, S. and Holguin, C. (2002) Gestural and audio metaphors as a means of control for mobile devices. *Proceedings of CHI '02 Conference*, Minneapolis, MN, 20–25 April. ACM Press, New York, pp. 291–298.

Pirolli, P. (2003) Exploring and finding information. In Carroll, J.M. (ed.), *HCI Models, Theories and Frameworks*. Morgan Kaufmann, San Francisco.

Plesums, C. (2002) An introduction to workflow. In *The Workflow Handbook 2002*, pdf file available from www.wfmc.org.

Plowman, L., Rogers, Y. and Ramage, M. (1995) What are workplace studies for? *Proceedings of ECSCW '95 Conference*, Stockholm, 11–15 Sept. Kluwer, Dordrecht, pp. 309–324.

Plutchik, R. (1980) *Emotion: A Psychobioevolutionary Synthesis*. Harper and Row, New York.

Polanyi, M. (1967) *The Tacit Dimension*. Routledge & Kegan Paul, London.

Postmes, T. and Lea, M. (2000) Social processes and group decision making: anonymity in group decision support systems. *Ergonomics*, **43**(8), 1252–1274.

Prasolova-Førland, E. and Divitini, M. (2003) Collaborative virtual environments for supporting learning communities: an experience of use. *Proceedings of Group '03 Conference*, Sanibel Island, FL, 9–12 Dec. ACM Press, New York, pp. 58–67.

Preece, J., Rogers, Y. and Sharp, H. (2002) *Interaction Design*. Wiley, New York.

Pycock, J. and Bowers, J. (1996) Getting others to get it right: an ethnography of design work in the fashion industry. *Proceedings of CSCW '96 Conference*, Boston, MA, 16–20 Nov. ACM Press, New York, pp. 219–228.

Pylyshyn, Z.W. (1984) *Computation and Cognition*. MIT Press, Cambridge, MA.

Ramage, M. (1999) *A stakeholder approach to CSCW evaluation*. PhD Thesis, University of Durham.

Randall, D. and Bentley, R. (1994) Unpublished tutorial notes on ethnography and collaborative systems development, HCI '94 Conference.

Rasmussen, J. (1986) *Information Processing and Human–Machine Interaction*. Elsevier North-Holland, Amsterdam.

Rasmussen, J. (1987) Mental models and their implications for design. *Proceedings of 6th Workshop on Informatics and Psychology*, Austrian Computer Society, June.

Raven, B.H. and Rubin, J.Z. (1976) *Social Psychology*. Wiley, New York.

Read, J.C. and MacFarlane, S.J. (2000) Measuring fun. Paper presented at Computers and Fun 3 Workshop, York, UK.

Reason, J. (1990) *Human Error*. Cambridge University Press, Cambridge.

Reason, J. (1992) Cognitive underspecification: its variety and consequence. In Baars, B.J. (ed.), *Experimental Slips and Human Error: Exploring the Architecture of Volition*. Plenum Press, New York.

Reason, J. (1997) *Managing the Risks of Organizational Accidents*. Ashgate, Brookfield, VT.

Reeves, B. and Nass, C. (1996) *The Media Equation: How People Treat Computers, Television and New Media Like Real People and Places*. Cambridge University Press, New York.

Rekimoto, J. and Sciammarella, E. (2000) ToolStone: effective use of the physical manipulation vocabularies of input devices. *Proceedings of UIST '00 Conference*, San Diego, CA, 6–8 Nov. ACM Press, New York, pp. 109–117. http://doi.acm.org/10.1145/354401.354421

Rekimoto, J., Ullmer, B. and Oba, H. (2001) DataTiles: a modular for mixed physical and graphical interactions. *Proceedings of CHI '01 Conference*, Seattle, WA, 31 March–5 April. ACM Press, New York, pp. 269–276.

Rheinfrank, J. and Evenson, S. (1996) Design languages. In Winograd, T. (ed.), *Bringing Design to Software*. ACM Press, New York.

Rheingold, H. (2000) *The Virtual Community: Homesteading on the Electronic Frontier*. MIT Press, Cambridge, MA.

Rich, E. (1989) Stereotypes and user modelling. In Kobsa, A. and Wahlster, W. (eds), *User Models in Dialog Systems*. Springer-Verlag, Berlin.

Robertson, S. and Robertson, J. (1999) *Mastering the Requirements Process*. Addison-Wesley, Harlow.

Robson, C. (1993) *Real World Research: A Resource for Social Scientists and Practitioner–Researchers*. Blackwell, Oxford.

Robson, C. (1994) *Experiment, Design and Statistics in Psychology*. Penguin, London.

Rockwell, C. (1999) Customer connection creates a winning product: building success with contextual design. *Interactions*, 6(1), 51–57.

Rogers, Y. and Bellotti, V. (1997) Grounding blue-sky research: how can ethnography help? *Interactions*, 4(3), 58–63.

Rosenfeld, L. and Morville, P. (2002) *Information Architecture for the World Wide Web*. O'Reilly, Sebastopol, CA.

Rosson, M.-B. and Carroll, J. (2002) *Usability Engineering*. Morgan Kaufmann, San Francisco.

Rouncefield, M., Hughes, J.A., Rodden, T. and Viller, S. (1994) Working with constant interruption: CSCW and the small office. *Proceedings of CSCW '94 Conference*, Chapel Hill, NC, 22–26 Oct. ACM Press, New York, pp. 275–286.

Rouse, W.B. and Morris, N.M. (1986) On looking into the black box: prospects and limits in the search for mental models. *Psychological Bulletin*, **100**(3), 349–363.

Rouse, W.B. and Rouse, S.H. (1983) Analysis and classification of human error. *IEEE Transactions on Systems, Man, and Cybernetics*, **SMC-13**, 539–549.

Rowley, D.E. and Rhoades, D.G. (1992) The cognitive jogthrough: a fast-paced user interface evaluation procedure. *Proceedings of CHI '92 Conference*, Monterey, CA, 3–7 May. ACM Press, New York, pp. 389–395.

Rudd, J., Stern, K. and Isensee, S. (1996) Low vs. high fidelity prototyping debate. *Interactions*, 3(1), 76–85.

Russell, J.A. and Fernandez-Dols, J.M. (1997) *The Psychology of Facial Expression*. Cambridge University Press, New York.

Salem, B. and Earle, N. (2000) Designing a non-verbal language for expressive avatars. *Proceedings of CVE '00 Conference*, San Francisco. ACM Press, New York, pp. 93–101.

Sawyer, P., Flanders, A. and Wixon, D. (1996) Making a difference – the impact of inspections. *Proceedings of CHI '96 Conference*, Vancouver, 13–18 April. ACM Press, New York, pp. 376–382.

Schachter, S. and Singer, J.E. (1962) Cognitive, social and physiological determinants of emotional state. *Psychological Review*, **69**, 379–399.

Schank, R. and Abelson, R. (1977) *Scripts, Plans, Goals and Understanding*. Lawrence Erlbaum Associates, Hillsdale, NJ.

Schiano, D.J., Ehrlich, S.M., Rahardja, K. and Sheridan, K. (2000) Face to InterFace: facial affect in (hu)man and machine. *Proceedings of CHI '00 Conference*, The Hague, Netherlands, 1–6 April. ACM Press, New York, pp. 193–200.

Schneider, W. and Shiffrin, R.M. (1977) Controlled and automatic human information processing: 1. Detection, search and attention. *Psychological Review*, **84**, 1–66.

Scrivener, S.A.R., Clark, S.M. and Keen, N. (1994) The LookingGlass distributed shared workspace. *Computer Supported Cooperative Work*, **2**, 137–157.

Sellen, A. and Harper, R. (2002) *The Myth of the Paperless Office*. MIT Press, Cambridge, MA.

Sellen, A., Buxton, B. and Arnott, J. (1992) Using spatial cues to improve videoconferencing. *Proceedings of CHI '92 Conference*, Monterey, CA, 3–7 May. ACM Press, New York, pp. 651–652.

Shackel, B. (1959) Ergonomics for a computer. *Design*, **120**, 36–39.

Shackel, B. (1990) Human factors and usability. In Preece, J. and Keller, L. (eds), *Human–Computer Interaction: Selected Readings*. Prentice Hall, Hemel Hempstead.

Sharpe, W.P. and Stenton, S.P. (2003) Information appliances. In Jacko, J.A. and Sears, A. (eds), *The Human–Computer Interaction Handbook*. Lawrence Erlbaum Associates, Mahwah, NJ.

Shedroff, N. (2001) *Experience Design 1*. New Riders, Indianapolis, IN.

Shneiderman, B. (1980) *Software Psychology: Human Factors in Computer and Information Systems*. Winthrop, Cambridge, MA.

Shneiderman, B. (1998) *Designing the User Interface* (3rd edn). Addison-Wesley, Reading, MA.

Simonsen, J. and Kensing, F. (1997) Using ethnography in contextual design. *Communications of the ACM*, **40**(7), 82–88.

Sinclair, M. (1997) The haptic lens. *Visual Proceedings of SIGGRAPH '97 Conference*, Los Angeles, 3–8 Aug. ACM Press, New York, p. 179. www.oip.gatech.edu/imtc/html/hapticsketch.html

Slater, M. (1999) Measuring presence: a response to the Witmer and Singer questionnaire. *Presence*, **8**(5), 560–566.

Smith, D.C., Irby, C., Kimball, R., Verplank, B. and Harslem, E. (1982) Designing the Star user interface. *BYTE*, **7**(4), 242–282.

Snelling, L. and Bruce-Smith, L. (1997) The Work Mapping technique. *Interactions*, **4**(4), 25–31.

Snyder, C. (2003) *Paper Prototyping: The Fast and Easy Way to Design and Refine User Interfaces*. Morgan Kaufmann, San Francisco.

Solso, R.L. (1995) *Cognitive Psychology* (4th edn). Allyn & Bacon, Boston, MA.

Sommerville, I. and Sawyer, P. (1997) *Requirements Engineering: a Good Practice Guide*. Wiley, Chichester.

Spence, R. (2001) *Information Visualization*. ACM Press/Addison-Wesley, New York.

Spencer, R. (2000) The streamlined cognitive walkthrough method, working around social constraints encountered in a software development company. *Proceedings of CHI '00 Conference*, The Hague, Netherlands, 1–6 April. ACM Press, New York, pp. 353–359.

Spinuzzi, C. (2002) A Scandinavian challenge, a US response: methodological assumptions in Scandinavian and US prototyping approaches. *Proceedings of SIGDOC '02 Conference*, Toronto, 20–23 Oct. ACM Press, New York, pp. 208–215.

Ståhl, O., Wallberg, A., Söderberg, J., Humble, J., Fahlén, L.E., Bullock, A. and Lundberg, J. (2002) Information exploration using The Pond. *Proceedings of CVE '02 Conference*, Bonn, Germany, 30 Sept.–2 Oct. ACM Press, New York, pp. 72–79.

Stanton, N. (2003) Human error identification in human–computer interaction. In Jacko, J.A. and Sears, A. (eds), *The Human–Computer Interaction Handbook*. Lawrence Erlbaum Associates, Mahwah, NJ.

Steed, A. and Tromp, J.G. (1998) Experiences with the evaluation of CVE applications. *Proceedings of CVE '98 Conference*, Manchester, UK, 17–19 June. ACM Press, New York, pp. 123–130.

Stephanidis, C. (ed.) (2001) *User Interfaces for All: Concepts, Methods and Tools*. Lawrence Erlbaum Associates, Mahwah, NJ.

Stewart, J. (2003) The social consumption of information and communication technologies (ICTs): insights from research on the appropriation and consumption of new ICTs in the domestic environment. *Cognition Technology and Work*, **5**(1), 4–14.

Stoner, J.A.F. (1961) *A comparison of individual and group decisions involving risk*. Unpublished Master's Thesis, MIT, Cambridge, MA.

Streitz, N.A., Rexroth, P. and Holmer, T. (1997) Does 'roomware' matter? Investigating the role of personal and public information devices and their combination in meeting room collaboration. *Proceedings of ECSCW '97 Conference*, Lancaster, UK, 7–11 Sept. Kluwer, Dordrecht, pp. 297–312.

Stroop, J.R. (1935) Studies in inference in serial verbal reactions. *Journal of Experimental Psychology*, **18**, 643–662.

Suchman, L. (1987) *Plans and Situated Actions*. Cambridge University Press, New York.

Suh, K.S. (1999) Impact of communication medium on task performance and satisfaction: an examination of media-richness theory. *Information and Management*, **35**(5), 295–312.

Sumner, M. and Hostetler, D. (2000) A comparative study of computer conferencing and face-to-face communications in systems design. *Proceedings of SIGCPR '00 Conference*, Chicago. ACM Press, New York, pp. 93–99.

Sutcliffe, A.G., Maiden, N.A.M., Minocha, S. and Manuel, D. (1998) Supporting scenario-based requirements engineering. *IEEE Transactions on Software Engineering*, **12**(12), 1072–1088.

Symon, G., Long, K. and Ellis, J. (1996) The coordination of work activities: cooperation and conflict in a hospital context. *Computer Supported Cooperative Work*, **5**, 1–21.

Tan, H.Z. (2000) Perceptual user interfaces: haptic interfaces. *Communications of the ACM*, **43**(3), 40–41.

Tang, J.C. and Isaacs, E. (1993) Why do users like video? *Computer Supported Cooperative Work*, **1**, 163–196.

Taylor, B. (1990) The HUFIT planning, analysis and specification toolset. *Proceedings of INTERACT '90 Conference*, Cambridge, UK, 27–31 August. North-Holland, Amsterdam, pp. 371–376.

Taylor, R.M. (1999) Scientific applications of force feedback: molecular simulation and microscope control. Course notes for 'Haptics: from basic principles to advanced applications', SIGGRAPH '99 (taylorr@cs.unc.edu, http://www.cs.unc.edu/~taylorr/).

Thesaurus (2003) http://www.visualthesaurus.com/online/index.html

Tiger, L. (1992) *The Pursuit of Pleasure*. Little, Brown & Co., Boston, MA.

Tollmar, K. and Persson, J. (2002) Understanding remote presence. *Proceedings of 2nd Nordic Conference on HCI, NordiCHI '02*, Aarhus, October. ACM Press, New York, pp. 41–49. Available on-line at www.acm.org/dl

Triesman, A.M. (1960) Contextual cues in selective listening. *Quarterly Journal of Experimental Psychology*, **12**, 242–248.

Tromp, J., Sandos, A.-M., Steed, A. and Thie, S. (1998) COVEN D3.5, Usage evaluation of the online applications, Part C: CVE design and inspection method. Available from www.cs.ucl.ac.uk/research/vr/Coven/#docs

Tuckerman, B.W. (1965) Development sequence in small groups. *Psychological Bulletin*, **63**, 316–328.

Tudor, L.G., Muller, M.J., Dayton, T. and Root, R.W. (1993) A participatory design technique for high-level task analysis, critique and redesign: the CARD method. *Proceedings of HFES '93*, Seattle, WA, pp. 295–299.

Tufte, E.R. (1983) *The Visual Display of Quantitative Information*. Graphics Press, Cheshire, CT.

Tufte, E.R. (1990) *Envisioning Information*. Graphics Press, Cheshire, CT.

Tufte, E.R. (1997) *Visual Explanations*. Graphics Press, Cheshire, CT.

Turner, P. and Turner, S. (2001) Describing Team Work with Activity Theory, *Cognition, Technology and Work*, **3**(3), 127–139.

Turner, P. and Turner, S. (2002) Surfacing issues using activity theory, *Journal of Applied Systems Science*, **3**(1), 134–155.

Turner, P. and Turner, S. (2002) Embedding context of use in CVE design. *Presence: tele-operators and virtual environments*, **11**(6), 665–676.

Turner, P., Milne, G., Turner, S. and Kubitscheck, M. (2003) Towards the wireless ward: evaluating a trial of networked PDAs in the National Health Service. In Chittaro, L. (ed.), *Human–Computer Interaction with Mobile Devices and Services, Proceedings of Mobile HCI 2003 Symposium*, Udine, Italy, 8–11 Sept. Lecture Notes in Computer Science Proceedings Series, Springer-Verlag, pp. 202–214.

Turner, S. and Turner, P. (1996) Expectations and experiences of CSCW in an Engineering Environment, *Collaborative Computing*, **1**(4), 237–254.

Turoff, M., Hiltz, S.R., Bieber, M., Whitworth, B. and Fjermestad, J. (2002) Computer mediated communications for group support: past and future. In Carroll, J.M. (ed.), *Human–Computer Interaction in the New Millennium*. Addison-Wesley, Reading, MA.

Ullmer, B. and Ishii, H. (2002) Emerging frameworks for tangible user interfaces. In Carroll, J.M. (ed.), *Human–Computer Interaction in the New Millennium*. ACM Press, New York.

Underkoffler, J. and Ishii, H. (1999) Urp: a luminous-tangible workbench for urban planning and design.

Proceedings of CHI '99 Conference, Pittsburgh, PA, 15–20 May. ACM Press, New York, pp. 386–393. http://doi.acm.org/10.1145/302979.303114

User Interface Engineering (UIE) (2003) http://www.uie.com/whitepaperlinks.htm

Usoh, M., Arthur, K., Whitton, M.C., Bastos, R., Steed, A., Slater, M. and Brooks, F.P. (1999) Walking > walking-in-place > flying, in virtual environments. *Proceedings of SIGGRAPH '99 Conference*. ACM Press, New York, pp. 359–364.

Usoh, M., Catena, E., Arman, S. and Slater, M. (2000) Using presence questionnaires in reality. *Presence*, **9**(5), 497–503.

Valacich, J.S., Mennecke, B.E., Wachter, R.M. and Wheeler, B.C. (1994) Extensions to media richness theory: a test of task-media fit hypothesis. *Proceedings of the 27th Hawaii International Conference on Systems Sciences, HICSS '94*, vol. 4, pp. 11–20.

Van der Veer, G.C., Tauber, M., Waern, Y. and van Muylwijk, B. (1985) On the interaction between system and user characteristics. *Behaviour and Information Technology*, **4**(4), 284–308.

van Harmelen, M. (ed.) (2001) *Object Modeling and User Interface Design: Designing Interactive Systems*. Addison-Wesley, Boston, MA.

Venkatesh, A., Kruse, E. and Chuan-Fong Shih, E. (2003) The networked home: an analysis of current developments and future trends. *Cognition Technology and Work*, **5**(1), 23–32.

Vera, A.H. and Simon, H.A. (1993) Situated action: a Symbolic interpretation. *Cognitive Science*, **17**, 7–48.

Verplank, W. (2003) http://billverplank.com/professional.html

Vicente, K.J. (1999) *Cognitive Work Analysis: Toward Safe, Productive, and Healthy Computer-based Work*. Lawrence Erlbaum Associates, Mahwah, NJ.

Vicente, K.J. and Rasmussen, J. (1992) Ecological interface design: theoretical foundations. *IEEE Transactions in Systems, Man and Cybernetics*, **22**(4), 589–605.

Viller, S. and Sommerville, I. (1998) Coherence: an approach to representing ethnographic analyses in systems design. *CSEG Technical Report*, CSEG/7/97, Lancaster University, UK, available at ftp://ftp.comp.lancs.ac.uk/pub/reports/1997/CSEG.7.9

Viller, S. and Sommerville, I. (2000) Ethnographically informed analysis for software engineers. *International Journal of Human–Computer Studies*, **53**(1), 169–196.

Voida, A., Newstetter, W.C. and Mynatt, E.D. (2002) When conventions collide: the tensions of instant messaging attributed. *Proceedings of CHI '02 Conference*, Minneapolis, MN, 20–25 April. ACM Press, New York, pp. 187–194.

Vredenburg, K., Mao, J.-Y., Smith, P.W. and Carey, T. (2002) A survey of user-centred design practice. *Proceedings of CHI '02 Conference*, Minneapolis, MN, 20–25 April. ACM Press, New York, pp. 471–478.

Vygotsky, L.S. (1978) *Mind in Society: the Development of Higher Psychological Processes* (English trans. ed. M. Cole). Harvard University Press, Cambridge, MA.

Want, R., Fishkin, K.P., Gujar, A. and Harrison, B.L. (1999) Bridging physical and virtual worlds with electronic tags. *Proceedings of CHI '99 Conference*, Pittsburgh, PA, 15–20 May. ACM Press, New York, pp. 370–377.

Ward, R., Bell, D. and Marsden, P. (2003) An exploration of facial expression tracking in affective HCI. In O'Neill, E., Palanque, P. and Johnson, P. (eds), *People and Computers XVII – Proceedings of HCI 2003 Conference*, Bath, UK, 8–12 Sept., pp. 383–399.

Weiser, M. (1993) Some computer science issues in ubiquitous computing. *Communications of the ACM*, **36**(7), 75–84.

Weiser, M. (1994) Perspective. The world is not a desktop. *Interactions*, **1**(1), 7–9.

Wellner, P. (1993) Interacting with paper on the DigitalDesk. *Communications of the ACM*, **36**(7), 86–96.

Wenger, E. (1998) *Communities of Practice: Learning Memory and Identity*. Cambridge University Press, Cambridge.

Wensveen, S., Overbeeke, K. and Djajadiningrat, T. (2000) Touch me, hit me and I know how you feel: a design approach to emotionally rich interaction. *Proceedings of DPPI '00 Conference*, Amsterdam, Netherlands. ACM Press, New York, pp. 48–52.

Wexelblat, A. (2003) Results from the Footprints project. In Höök, K., Benyon, D.R. and Munro, A. (eds), *Designing Information Spaces: The Social Navigation Approach*. Springer-Verlag, London, pp. 223–248.

Wharton, C., Bradford, J., Jeffries, R. and Franzke, M. (1992) Applying cognitive walkthroughs to more complex user interfaces: experiences, issues, and recommendations. *Proceedings of CHI '92 Conference*, Monterey, CA, 3–7 May. ACM Press, New York, pp. 381–388.

Wharton, C., Rieman, J., Lewis, C. and Polson, P. (1994) The cognitive walkthrough method: a practitioner's guide. In Nielsen, J. and Mack, R.L. (eds), *Usability Inspection Methods*. Wiley, New York.

Whittaker, S. (1996) Talking to strangers: an evaluation of the factors affecting electronic collaboration. *Proceedings of CSCW '96 Conference*, Boston, MA, 16–20 Nov. ACM Press, New York, pp. 409–418.

Whittaker, S. and O'Conaill, B. (1997) The role of vision in face-to-face and mediated communication. In Finn, K.E., Sellen, A.J. and Wilbur, S.B. (eds), *Video-mediated Communication*. Lawrence Erlbaum Associates, Mahwah, NJ, pp. 23–49.

Wickens, C.D. and Hollands, J.G. (2000) *Engineering Psychology and Human Performance* (3rd edn). Prentice-Hall, Upper Saddle River, NJ.

Wikman, A.-S., Nieminen, T. and Summala, H. (1998) Driving experience and time-sharing during in-car tasks on roads of different width. *Ergonomics*, **41**, 358–372.

Willcocks, L. and Lester, S. (1998) *Beyond the IT Productivity Paradox: Assessment Issues*. Wiley, Chichester.

Wilson, G. and Sasse, M.A. (2001) Straight from the heart: using physiological measurements in the evaluation of multimedia quality. *Proceedings of the Society for the Study of Artificial Intelligence and the Simulation of Behaviour (AISB) Convention 2001, Symposium on Emotion, Cognition and Affective Computing*, York, UK, 21–24 March, pp. 63–73. UCL Research Note RN/01/21, ISBN 1-902956-19-7. Also available from http://www.cs.ucl.ac.uk/staff/g.wilson/papers.htm

Winograd, T. (ed.) (1996) *Bringing Design to Software*. ACM Press, New York.

Winograd, T. and Flores, F. (1986) *Understanding Computers and Cognition: a New Foundation for Design*. Ablex Publishing, Norwood, NJ.

Witmer, B.G. and Singer, M.J. (1998) Measuring presence in virtual environments: a presence questionnaire. *Presence*, **7**(3), 225–240.

Wixon, D. and Ramey, J. (eds) (1996) *Field Methods Casebook for Software Design*. Wiley, New York.

Wodtke, C. (2003) *Information Architecture: Blueprints for the Web*. New Riders, Indianapolis, IN.

Wood, J. and Silver, D. (1995) *Joint Application Development*. Wiley, New York.

Woolrych, A. and Cockton, G. (2000) Assessing heuristic evaluation: mind the quality, not just percentages. In Turner, S. and Turner, P. (eds), *Proceedings of British HCI Group HCI 2000 Conference*, Sunderland, UK, 5–8 Sept. British Computer Society, London, vol. 2, pp. 35–36.

Woolrych, A. and Cockton, G. (2001) Why and when five test users aren't enough. *Proceedings of IHM-HCI 2001 Conference*, Lille, France, 10–14 Sept. Cépaduès Editions, Toulouse, vol. 2, pp. 105–108.

Wright, P.C., Fields, R.E. and Harrison, M.D. (2000) Analyzing human–computer interaction as distributed cognition: the resources model. *Human–Computer Interaction*, **15**(1), 1–42.

Wurman, R.S. (1991) *New Road Atlas: US Atlas*. Simon and Schuster, New York.

Wurman, R.S. (1997) *Information Architects*. Printed in China through Palace Press International, distributed by Hi Marketing, London, ISBN 1-888001-38-0.

Wurman, R.S. (2000) *Understanding USA*. TED Conferences, Menlo Park, CA.

Yerkes, R.M. and Dodson, J.D. (1908) The relation of the strength of stimulus to rapidity of habit formation. *Journal of Comparative Neurological Psychology*, **18**, 459–482.

Young, R.M. (1983) Surrogates and mappings: two kinds of conceptual models for interactive devices. In Gentner, D. and Stevens, A.L. (eds), *Mental Models*. Lawrence Erlbaum Associates, Hillsdale, NJ, pp. 35–52.

Zajonc, R.B. (1984) On the primacy of affect. *American Psychologist*, **39**, 117–123.

Zhang, J. and Norman, D.A. (1994) Representations in distributed cognitive tasks. *Cognition Science*, **18**, 87–122.

Index